Linux®

Bible

Ninth Edition

Linux®
BIBLE

Ninth Edition

Christopher Negus

WILEY

Linux® Bible, Ninth Edition

Published by
John Wiley & Sons, Inc.
10475 Crosspoint Boulevard
Indianapolis, IN 46256
www.wiley.com

Copyright © 2015 by John Wiley & Sons, Inc., Indianapolis, Indiana

Published simultaneously in Canada

ISBN: 978-1-118-99987-5

ISBN: 978-1-118-99989-9 (ebk)

ISBN: 978-1-118-99988-2 (ebk)

Manufactured in the United States of America

10 9 8 7 6 5 4

For general information on our other products and services please contact our Customer Care Department within the United States at (877) 762-2974, outside the United States at (317) 572-3993 or fax (317) 572-4002.

Wiley publishes in a variety of print and electronic formats and by print-on-demand. Some material included with standard print versions of this book may not be included in e-books or in print-on-demand. If this book refers to media such as a CD or DVD that is not included in the version you purchased, you may download this material at http://booksupport.wiley.com. For more information about Wiley products, visit www.wiley.com.

Library of Congress Control Number: 2015937667

Trademarks: Wiley and the Wiley logo are trademarks or registered trademarks of John Wiley & Sons, Inc. and/or its affiliates, in the United States and other countries, and may not be used without written permission. Linux is a registered trademark of Linus Torvalds. All other trademarks are the property of their respective owners. John Wiley & Sons, Inc. is not associated with any product or vendor mentioned in this book.

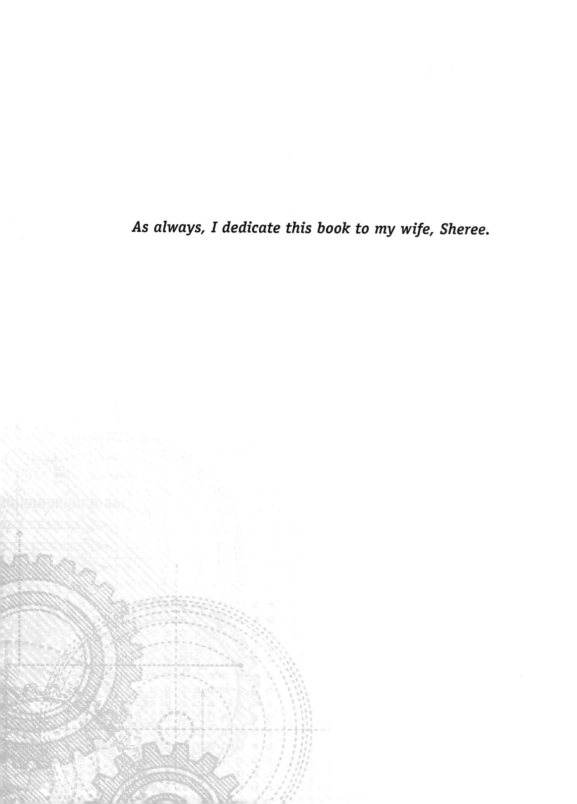

As always, I dedicate this book to my wife, Sheree.

About the Author

Chris Negus is a Red Hat Certified Instructor (RHCI), Red Hat Certified Examiner (RHCX), Red Hat Certified Architect (RHCA), and Principal Technical Writer for Red Hat Inc. In more than six years with Red Hat, Chris has taught hundreds of IT professionals aspiring to become Red Hat Certified Engineers (RHCE).

In his current position at Red Hat, Chris produces articles for the Red Hat Customer Portal. The projects he works on include Red Hat Enterprise Linux 7, Red Hat Enterprise OpenStack Platform, Red Hat Enterprise Virtualization and Linux containers in Docker format.

Besides his RHCA certification, Chris is a Red Hat Certified Virtualization Administrator (RHCVA) and Red Hat Certified Datacenter Specialist (RHCDS). He also has certificates of expertise in Deployment and Systems Management, Clustering and Storage Management, Cloud Storage, and Server Hardening.

Before joining Red Hat, Chris wrote or co-wrote dozens of books on Linux and UNIX, including *Red Hat Linux Bible* (all editions), *CentOS Bible, Fedora Bible, Linux Troubleshooting Bible, Linux Toys* and *Linux Toys II*. Chris also co-authored several books for the Linux Toolbox series for power users: *Fedora Linux Toolbox, SUSE Linux Toolbox, Ubuntu Linux Toolbox, Mac OS X Toolbox,* and *BSD UNIX Toolbox*.

For eight years Chris worked with the organization at AT&T that developed UNIX before moving to Utah to help contribute to Novell's UnixWare project in the early 1990s. When not writing about Linux, Chris enjoys playing soccer and just hanging out with his wife, Sheree, and son, Seth.

About the Technical Editor

Richard Blum, LPIC-1, has worked in the IT industry for more than 20 years as both a systems and network administrator and has published numerous Linux and open source books. He has administered UNIX, Linux, Novell, and Microsoft servers, as well as helped design and maintain a 3,500-user network utilizing Cisco switches and routers. He has used Linux servers and shell scripts to perform automated network monitoring and has written shell scripts in most of the common Linux shell environments. Rich is an online instructor for an Introduction to Linux course that is used by colleges and universities across the United States. When he isn't being a computer nerd, Rich plays electric bass in a couple of different church worship bands, and enjoys spending time with his wife, Barbara, and two daughters, Katie Jane and Jessica.

Credits

Project Editor
Martin V. Minner

Technical Editor
Richard Blum

Production Manager
Kathleen Wisor

Copy Editor
Gwenette Gaddis

**Manager of Content
Development & Assembly**
Mary Beth Wakefield

Marketing Director
David Mayhew

Marketing Manager
Carrie Sherrill

**Professional Technology & Strategy
Director**
Barry Pruett

Business Manager
Amy Knies

Associate Publisher
Jim Minatel

Project Coordinator, Cover
Brent Savage

Proofreader
Amy Schneider

Indexer
John Sleeva

Cover Designer
Wiley

Acknowledgments

Since I was hired by Red Hat Inc. more than six years ago, I have been exposed to many of the best Linux developers, testers, support professionals and instructors in the world. Since I can't thank everyone individually, I instead salute the culture of cooperation and excellence that serves to improve my own Linux skills every day.

I don't speak well of Red Hat because I work there; I work at Red Hat because it lives up to the ideals of open source software in ways that match my own beliefs. There are a few people at Red Hat I would like to acknowledge particularly. Discussions with Victor Costea, Andrew Blum, and other Red Hat instructors have helped me adapt my ways of thinking about how people learn Linux. I'm able to work across a wide range of technologies because of the great support I get from my supervisor, Adam Strong, and my senior manager, Sam Knuth, who both point me toward cool projects but never hold me back.

In this edition, particular help came from Ryan Sawhill Aroha, who helped me simplify my writing on encryption technology. For the new content I wrote in this book on Linux cloud technologies, I'd like to thank members of OpenStack, Docker, and RHEV teams, who help me learn cutting-edge cloud technology every day.

As for the people at Wiley, thanks for letting me continue to develop and improve this book over the years. Marty Minner has helped keep me on task through a demanding schedule. Mary Beth Wakefield and Ken Brown have been there to remind me at the times I forgot it was a demanding schedule. Thanks to Richard Blum for his reliably thorough job of tech editing. Thanks to Margot Maley Hutchison from Waterside Productions for contracting the book for me with Wiley and always looking out for my best interests.

Finally, thanks to my wife, Sheree, for sharing her life with me and doing such a great job raising Seth and Caleb.

Contents at a Glance

Contents

Part II: Becoming a Linux Power User   63

Contents

Part III: Becoming a Linux System Administrator   171

Chapter 8: Learning System Administration 173

Chapter 9: Installing Linux. 201

Contents

Contents

Contents

Contents

Part V: Learning Linux Security Techniques   589

Chapter 22: Understanding Basic Linux Security 591

Contents

Part VI: Extending Linux into the Cloud

727

Contents

Introduction

Y ou can't learn Linux without using it.

I've come to that conclusion over more than a decade of teaching people to learn Linux. You can't just read a book; you can't just listen to a lecture. You need someone to guide you and you need to jump in and do it.

In 1999, Wiley published my *Red Hat Linux Bible*. The book's huge success gave me the opportunity to become a full-time, independent Linux author. For about a decade, I wrote dozens of Linux books and explored the best ways to explain Linux from the quiet of my small home office.

In 2008, I hit the road. I was hired by Red Hat, Inc., as a full-time instructor, teaching Linux to professional system administrators seeking Red Hat Certified Engineer (RHCE) certification. In my three years as a Linux instructor, I honed my teaching skills in front of live people whose Linux experience ranged from none to experienced professional.

In the previous edition, I turned my teaching experience into text to take a reader from someone who has never used Linux to someone with the skills to become a Linux professional. In this edition, I set out to extend those skills into the cloud. The focus of this ninth edition of the *Linux Bible* can be summed up in these ways:

- **Beginner to certified professional:** As long as you have used a computer, mouse, and keyboard, you can start with this book. I tell you how to get Linux, begin using it, step through critical topics, and ultimately excel at administering and securing it.

- **System administrator–focused:** When you are finished with this book, you will know how to use Linux and how to modify and maintain it. All the topics needed to become a Red Hat Certified Engineer are covered in this book. That said, many software developers have also used this book to understand how to work on a Linux system as a development platform or target for their applications.

- **Emphasis on command-line tools:** Although point-and-click interfaces for managing Linux have improved greatly in recent years, many advanced features can only be utilized by typing commands and editing configuration files manually. I teach you how to become proficient with the Linux command-line shell and occasionally compare shell features with graphical tools for accomplishing the same tasks.

- **Aimed at fewer Linux distributions:** In previous editions, I described about 18 different Linux distributions. With only a few notable exceptions, most popular Linux distributions are either Red Hat–based (Red Hat Enterprise Linux, Fedora, CentOS, and so on) or Debian-based (Ubuntu, Linux Mint, KNOPPIX, and so on). Although this book most thoroughly covers Red Hat distributions, I have increased coverage of Ubuntu throughout in this edition (because that's what many of the biggest Linux fans start with).

- **Many, many demos and exercises:** Instead of just telling you what Linux does, I actually show you what it does. Then, to make sure you got it, you have the opportunity to try exercises yourself. Every procedure and exercise has been tested to work in Fedora or Red Hat Enterprise Linux. Most work in Ubuntu as well.

- **Lead into cloud technologies:** Linux is at the heart of most technological advances in cloud computing today. That means you need a solid understanding of Linux to work effectively in tomorrow's data centers. Learn Linux basics in the front of this book. Then in the last few chapters, I demonstrate how you can try out Linux systems as hypervisors, cloud controllers, and virtual machines, as well as manage virtual networks and networked storage.

How This Book Is Organized

The book is organized to enable you to start off at the very beginning with Linux and grow to become a professional Linux system administrator and power user.

Part I, "Getting Started," includes two chapters designed to help you understand what Linux is and get you started with a Linux desktop:

- Chapter 1, "Starting with Linux," covers topics such as what the Linux operating system is, where it comes from, and how to get started using it.

- Chapter 2, "Creating the Perfect Linux Desktop," provides information on how you can create a desktop system and use some of the most popular desktop features.

Part II, "Becoming a Linux Power User," provides in-depth details on how to use the Linux shell, work with filesystems, manipulate text files, manage processes, and use shell scripts:

- Chapter 3, "Using the Shell," includes information on how to access a shell, run commands, recall commands (using history), and do tab completion. The chapter also describes how to use variables, aliases, and man pages (traditional Linux command reference pages).

- Chapter 4, "Moving around the Filesystem," includes commands for listing, creating, copying, and moving files and directories. More advanced topics in this chapter include filesystem security, such as file ownership, permissions, and access control lists.

- Chapter 5, "Working with Text Files," includes everything from basic text editors to tools for finding files and searching for text within files.

- Chapter 6, "Managing Running Processes," describes how to see what processes are running on your system and change those processes. Ways of changing processes include killing, pausing, and sending other types of signals.

- Chapter 7, "Writing Simple Shell Scripts," includes shell commands and functions you can gather together into a file to run as a command itself.

In Part III, "Becoming a Linux System Administrator," you learn how to administer Linux systems:

- Chapter 8, "Learning System Administration," provides information on basic graphical tools, commands, and configuration files for administering Linux systems.

- Chapter 9, "Installing Linux," covers common installation tasks, such as disk partitioning and initial software package selection, as well as more advanced installation tools, such as installing from kickstart files.

- Chapter 10, "Getting and Managing Software," provides an understanding of how software packages work and how to get and manage software packages.

- Chapter 11, "Managing User Accounts," discusses tools for adding and deleting users and groups, as well as how to centralize user account management.

- Chapter 12, "Managing Disks and Filesystems," provides information on adding partitions, creating filesystems, and mounting filesystems, as well as working with logical volume management.

In Part IV, "Becoming a Linux Server Administrator," you learn to create powerful network servers and the tools needed to manage them:

- Chapter 13, "Understanding Server Administration," covers remote logging, monitoring tools, and the Linux boot process.

- Chapter 14, "Administering Networking," discusses how to configure networking.

- Chapter 15, "Starting and Stopping Services," provides information on starting and stopping services.

- Chapter 16, "Configuring a Print Server," describes how to configure printers to use locally on your Linux system or over the network from other computers.

- Chapter 17, "Configuring a Web Server," describes how to configure an Apache Web server.

- Chapter 18, "Configuring an FTP Server," covers procedures for setting up a vsftpd FTP server that can be used to enable others to download files from your Linux system over the network.

- Chapter 19, "Configuring a Windows File Sharing (Samba) Server," covers Windows file server configuration with Samba.

- Chapter 20, "Configuring an NFS File Server," describes how to use Network File System features to share folders of files among systems over a network.

- Chapter 21, "Troubleshooting Linux," covers popular tools for troubleshooting your Linux system.

In Part V, "Learning Linux Security Techniques," you learn how to secure your Linux systems and services:

- Chapter 22, "Understanding Basic Linux Security," covers basic security concepts and techniques.
- Chapter 23, "Understanding Advanced Linux Security," provides information on using Pluggable Authentication Modules (PAM) and cryptology tools to tighten system security and authentication.
- Chapter 24, "Enhancing Linux Security with SELinux," shows you how to enable Security Enhanced Linux (SELinux) to secure system services.
- Chapter 25, "Securing Linux on the Network," covers network security features, such as `firewalld` and `iptables` firewalls, to secure system services.

Part VI, "Extending Linux into the Cloud," takes you into cutting-edge cloud technologies:

- Chapter 26, "Using Linux for Cloud Computing," introduces concepts of cloud computing in Linux by describing how to set up hypervisors, build virtual machines, and share resources across networks.
- Chapter 27, "Deploying Linux to the Cloud," describes how to deploy Linux images to different cloud environments, including OpenStack, Amazon EC2, or a local Linux system configured for virtualization.

Part VII contains two appendixes to help you get the most from your exploration of Linux. Appendix A, "Media," provides guidance on downloading Linux distributions. Appendix B, "Exercise Answers," provides sample solutions to the exercises included in chapters 2 through 26.

Conventions Used in This Book

Throughout the book, special typography indicates code and commands. Commands and code are shown in a monospaced font:

```
This is how code looks.
```

In the event that an example includes both input and output, the monospaced font is still used, but input is presented in bold type to distinguish the two. Here's an example:

```
$ ftp ftp.handsonhistory.com
Name (home:jake): jake
Password: ******
```

As for styles in the text:

- New terms and important words appear in *italics* when introduced.
- Keyboard strokes appear like this: Ctrl+A. This means to hold the Ctrl key as you also press the letter "a" key.

- Filenames, URLs, and code within the text appear like so: `persistence.properties`.

The following items call your attention to points that are particularly important.

> **NOTE**
> A Note box provides extra information to which you need to pay special attention.

> **TIP**
> A Tip box shows a special way of performing a particular task.

> **CAUTION**
> A Caution box alerts you to take special care when executing a procedure, or damage to your computer hardware or software could result.

Jumping into Linux

If you are new to Linux, you might have vague ideas about what it is and where it came from. You may have heard something about it being free (as in cost) or free (as in freedom to use it as you please). Before you start putting your hands on Linux (which we will do soon enough), Chapter 1 seeks to answer some of your questions about the origins and features of Linux.

Take your time and work through this book to get up to speed on Linux and how you can make it work to meet your needs. This is your invitation to jump in and take the first step to becoming a Linux expert!

Visit the *Linux Bible* website

To find links to various Linux distributions, tips on gaining Linux certification, and corrections to the book as they become available, go to `http://www.wiley.com/go/linuxbible9`.

Part I

Getting Started

Starting with Linux

Linux is one of the most important technology advancements of the twenty-first century. Besides its impact on the growth of the Internet and its place as an enabling technology for a range of computer-driven devices, Linux development has been a model for how collaborative projects can surpass what single individuals and companies can do alone.

Google runs thousands upon thousands of Linux servers to power its search technology. Its Android phones are based on Linux. Likewise, when you download and run Google's Chrome OS, you get a browser that is backed by a Linux operating system.

Facebook builds and deploys its site using what is referred to as a *LAMP stack* (Linux, Apache web server, MySQL database, and PHP web scripting language)—all open source projects. In fact, Facebook itself uses an open source development model, making source code for the applications and tools that drive Facebook available to the public. This model has helped Facebook shake out bugs quickly, get contributions from around the world, and fuel Facebook's exponential growth.

Financial organizations that have trillions of dollars riding on the speed and security of their operating systems also rely heavily on Linux. These include the New York Stock Exchange, the Chicago Mercantile Exchange, and the Tokyo Stock Exchange.

As "cloud" continues to be one of the hottest buzzwords today, a part of the cloud that isn't hype is that Linux and other open source technologies are the foundation on which today's greatest cloud innovations are being built. Every software component you need to build a private or public cloud (such as hypervisors, cloud controllers, network storage, virtual networking, and authentication) is freely available for you to start using from the open source world.

The widespread adoption of Linux around the world has created huge demand for Linux expertise. This chapter starts you on a path to becoming a Linux expert by helping you understand what Linux is, where it came from, and what your opportunities are for becoming proficient in it. The rest of this book provides you with hands-on activities to help you gain that expertise. Finally, I show you how you can apply that expertise to cloud technologies.

Understanding What Linux Is

Linux is a computer operating system. An operating system consists of the software that manages your computer and lets you run applications on it. The features that make up Linux and similar computer operating systems include the following:

- **Detecting and preparing hardware**—When the Linux system boots up (when you turn on your computer), it looks at the components on your computer (CPU, hard drive, network cards, and so on) and loads the software (drivers and modules) needed to access those particular hardware devices.

- **Managing processes**—The operating system must keep track of multiple processes running at the same time and decide which have access to the CPU and when. The system also must offer ways of starting, stopping, and changing the status of processes.

- **Managing memory**—RAM and swap space (extended memory) must be allocated to applications as they need memory. The operating system decides how requests for memory are handled.

- **Providing user interfaces**—An operating system must provide ways of accessing the system. The first Linux systems were accessed from a command-line interpreter called a *shell*. Today, graphical desktop interfaces are commonly available as well.

- **Controlling filesystems**—Filesystem structures are built into the operating system (or loaded as modules). The operating system controls ownership of and access to the files and directories (folders) that the filesystems contain.

- **Providing user access and authentication**—Creating user accounts and allowing boundaries to be set between users is a basic feature of Linux. Separate user and group accounts enable users to control their own files and processes.

- **Offering administrative utilities**—In Linux, hundreds (perhaps thousands) of commands and graphical windows are available to do such things as add users, manage disks, monitor the network, install software, and generally secure and manage your computer.

- **Starting up services**—To use printers, handle log messages, and provide a variety of system and network services, processes called *daemon processes* run in the background, waiting for requests to come in. Many types of services run in Linux.

Linux provides different ways of starting and stopping these services. In other words, while Linux includes web browsers to view web pages, it can also be the computer that serves up web pages to others. Popular server features include web, mail, database, printer, file, DNS, and DHCP servers.

- **Programming tools**—A wide variety of programming utilities for creating applications and libraries for implementing specialty interfaces are available with Linux.

As someone managing Linux systems, you need to learn how to work with those features just described. While many features can be managed using graphical interfaces, an understanding of the shell command line is critical for someone administering Linux systems.

Modern Linux systems now go way beyond what the first UNIX systems (on which Linux was based) could do. Advanced features in Linux, often used in large enterprises, include the following:

- **Clustering**—Linux can be configured to work in clusters so that multiple systems can appear as one system to the outside world. Services can be configured to pass back and forth between cluster nodes, while appearing to those using the services that they are running without interruption.

- **Virtualization**—To manage computing resources more efficiently, Linux can run as a virtualization host. On that host, you could run other Linux systems, Microsoft Windows, BSD, or other operating systems as virtual guests. To the outside world, each of those virtual guests appears as a separate computer. KVM and Xen are two technologies in Linux for creating virtual hosts.

- **Cloud computing**—To manage large-scale virtualization environments, you can use full-blown cloud computing platforms based on Linux. Projects such as OpenStack and Red Hat Enterprise Virtualization can simultaneously manage many virtualization hosts, virtual networks, user and system authentication, virtual guests, and networked storage.

- **Real-time computing**—Linux can be configured for real-time computing, where high-priority processes can expect fast, predictable attention.

- **Specialized storage**—Instead of just storing data on the computer's hard disk, many specialized local and networked storage interfaces are available in Linux. Shared storage devices available in Linux include iSCSI, Fibre Channel, and Infiniband. Entire open source storage platforms include projects such as Ceph (http://ceph.com) and GlusterFS (http://gluster.org).

Some of these advanced topics are not covered in this book. However, the features covered here for using the shell, working with disks, starting and stopping services, and configuring a variety of servers should serve as a foundation for working with those advanced features.

Understanding How Linux Differs from Other Operating Systems

If you are new to Linux, chances are good that you have used a Microsoft Windows or Apple Mac OS operating system. Although Mac OS X has its roots in a free software operating system, referred to as the Berkeley Software Distribution (more on that later), operating systems from both Microsoft and Apple are considered proprietary operating systems. What that means is:

- You cannot see the code used to create the operating system.
- You, therefore, cannot change the operating system at its most basic levels if it doesn't suit your needs—and you can't use the operating system to build your own operating system from source code.
- You cannot check the code to find bugs, explore security vulnerabilities, or simply learn what that code is doing.
- You may not be able to easily plug your own software into the operating system if the creators of that system don't want to expose the programming interfaces you need to the outside world.

You might look at those statements about proprietary software and say, "What do I care? I'm not a software developer. I don't want to see or change how my operating system is built."

That may be true. But the fact that others can take free and open source software and use it as they please has driven the explosive growth of the Internet (think Google), mobile phones (think Android), special computing devices (think Tivo), and hundreds of technology companies. Free software has driven down computing costs and allowed for an explosion of innovation.

Maybe you don't want to use Linux—as Google, Facebook, and other companies have done—to build the foundation for a multi-billion-dollar company. But those and other companies who now rely on Linux to drive their computer infrastructures need more and more people with the skills to run those systems.

You may wonder how a computer system that is so powerful and flexible has come to be free as well. To understand how that could be, you need to see where Linux came from. So the next section of this chapter describes the strange and winding path of the free software movement that led to Linux.

Exploring Linux History

Some histories of Linux begin with this message posted by Linus Torvalds to the comp.os.minix newsgroup on August 25, 1991 (http://groups.google.com/group/comp.os.minix/msg/b813d52cbc5a044b?pli=1):

Linus Benedict Torvalds

Hello everybody out there using minix -

I'm doing a (free) operating system (just a hobby, won't be big and professional like gnu) for 386(486) AT clones. This has been brewing since april, and is start-ing to get ready. I'd like any feedback on things people like/dislike in minix, as my OS resembles it somewhat (same physical layout of the file-system (due to practical reasons, among other things)...Any suggestions are welcome, but I won't promise I'll implement them :-)

Linus (torvalds@kruuna.helsinki.fi)

PS. Yes — it's free of any minix code, and it has a multi-threaded fs. It is NOT protable [sic] (uses 386 task switching etc), and it probably never will support anything other than AT-harddisks, as that's all I have :-(.

Minix was a UNIX-like operating system that ran on PCs in the early 1990s. Like Minix, Linux was also a clone of the UNIX operating system. With few exceptions, such as Microsoft Windows, most modern computer systems (including Mac OS X and Linux) were derived from UNIX operating systems, created originally by AT&T.

To truly appreciate how a free operating system could have been modeled after a proprietary system from AT&T Bell Laboratories, it helps to understand the culture in which UNIX was created and the chain of events that made the essence of UNIX possible to reproduce freely.

> **NOTE**
>
> To learn more about how Linux was created, pick up the book *Just for Fun: The Story of an Accidental Revolutionary* by Linus Torvalds (HarperCollins Publishing, 2001).

Free-flowing UNIX culture at Bell Labs

From the very beginning, the UNIX operating system was created and nurtured in a communal environment. Its creation was not driven by market needs, but by a desire to overcome impediments to producing programs. AT&T, which owned the UNIX trademark originally, eventually made UNIX into a commercial product, but by that time, many of the concepts (and even much of the early code) that made UNIX special had fallen into the public domain.

If you are not old enough to remember when AT&T split up in 1984, you may not remember a time when AT&T was "the" phone company. Up until the early 1980s, AT&T didn't have to think much about competition because if you wanted a phone in the United States, you had to go to AT&T. It had the luxury of funding pure research projects. The mecca for such projects was the Bell Laboratories site in Murray Hill, New Jersey.

After a project called Multics failed in around 1969, Bell Labs employees Ken Thompson and Dennis Ritchie set off on their own to create an operating system that would offer an improved environment for developing software. Up to that time, most programs were written on punch cards that had to be fed in batches to mainframe computers. In a 1980 lecture on "The Evolution of the UNIX Time-sharing System," Dennis Ritchie summed up the spirit that started UNIX:

> What we wanted to preserve was not just a good environment in which to do programming, but a system around which a fellowship could form. We knew from experience that the essence of communal computing as supplied by remote-access, time-shared machines is not just to type programs into a terminal instead of a keypunch, but to encourage close communication.

The simplicity and power of the UNIX design began breaking down barriers that, until this point, had impeded software developers. The foundation of UNIX was set with several key elements:

- **The UNIX filesystem**—Because it included a structure that allowed levels of sub-directories (which, for today's desktop users, looks like folders inside folders), UNIX could be used to organize the files and directories in intuitive ways. Furthermore, complex methods of accessing disks, tapes, and other devices were greatly simplified by representing those devices as individual device files that you could also access as items in a directory.

- **Input/output redirection**—Early UNIX systems also included input redirection and pipes. From a command line, UNIX users could direct the output of a command to a file using a right-arrow key (>). Later, the concept of pipes (|) was added where the output of one command could be directed to the input of another command. For example, the following command line concatenates (cat) file1 and file2, sorts (sort) the lines in those files alphabetically, paginates the sorted text for printing (pr), and directs the output to the computer's default printer (lpr):

```
$ cat file1 file2 | sort | pr | lpr
```

This method of directing input and output enabled developers to create their own specialized utilities that could be joined with existing utilities. This modularity made it possible for lots of code to be developed by lots of different people. A user could just put together the pieces as needed.

- **Portability**—Simplifying the experience of using UNIX also led to it becoming extraordinarily portable to run on different computers. By having device drivers (represented by files in the filesystem tree), UNIX could present an interface to applications in such a way that the programs didn't have to know about the details of the underlying hardware. To later port UNIX to another system, developers had only to change the drivers. The application programs didn't have to change for different hardware!

To make portability a reality, however, a high-level programming language was needed to implement the software needed. To that end, Brian Kernighan and Dennis Ritchie created the C programming language. In 1973, UNIX was rewritten in C. Today, C is still the primary language used to create the UNIX (and Linux) operating system kernels.

As Ritchie went on to say in a 1979 lecture (http://cm.bell-labs.com/who/dmr/hist.html):

> Today, the only important UNIX program still written in assembler is the assembler itself; virtually all the utility programs are in C, and so are most of the application's programs, although there are sites with many in Fortran, Pascal, and Algol 68 as well. It seems certain that much of the success of UNIX follows from the readability, modifiability, and portability of its software that in turn follows from its expression in high-level languages.

If you are a Linux enthusiast and are interested in what features from the early days of Linux have survived, an interesting read is Dennis Ritchie's reprint of the first UNIX programmer's manual (dated November 3, 1971). You can find it at Dennis Ritchie's website: http://cm.bell-labs.com/cm/cs/who/dmr/1stEdman.html. The form of this documentation is UNIX man pages, which is still the primary format for documenting UNIX and Linux operating system commands and programming tools today.

What's clear as you read through the early documentation and accounts of the UNIX system is that the development was a free-flowing process, lacked ego, and was dedicated to making UNIX excellent. This process led to a sharing of code (both inside and outside Bell Labs), which allowed rapid development of a high-quality UNIX operating system. It also led to an operating system that AT&T would find difficult to reel back in later.

Commercialized UNIX

Before the AT&T divestiture in 1984, when it was split up into AT&T and seven "Baby Bell" companies, AT&T was forbidden to sell computer systems. Companies that would later become Verizon, Qwest, and Alcatel-Lucent were all part of AT&T. As a result of AT&T's monopoly of the telephone system, the U.S. government was concerned that an unrestricted AT&T might dominate the fledgling computer industry.

Because AT&T was restricted from selling computers directly to customers before its divestiture, UNIX source code was licensed to universities for a nominal fee. There was no UNIX operating system for sale from AT&T that you didn't have to compile yourself.

Berkeley Software Distribution arrives

In 1975, UNIX V6 became the first version of UNIX available for widespread use outside Bell Laboratories. From this early UNIX source code, the first major variant of UNIX was created at University of California at Berkeley. It was named the Berkeley Software Distribution (BSD).

For most of the next decade, the BSD and Bell Labs versions of UNIX headed off in separate directions. BSD continued forward in the free-flowing, share-the-code manner that was the hallmark of the early Bell Labs UNIX, whereas AT&T started steering UNIX toward commercialization. With the formation of a separate UNIX Laboratory, which moved out of Murray Hill and down the road to Summit, New Jersey, AT&T began its attempts to commercialize UNIX. By 1984, divestiture was behind AT&T and it was ready to really start selling UNIX.

UNIX Laboratory and commercialization

The UNIX Laboratory was considered a jewel that couldn't quite find a home or a way to make a profit. As it moved between Bell Laboratories and other areas of AT&T, its name changed several times. It is probably best remembered by the name it had as it began its spin-off from AT&T: UNIX System Laboratories (USL).

The UNIX source code that came out of USL, the legacy of which was sold in part to Santa Cruz Operation (SCO), was used for a time as the basis for ever-dwindling lawsuits by SCO against major Linux vendors (such as IBM and Red Hat, Inc.). Because of that, I think the efforts from USL that have contributed to the success of Linux are lost on most people.

During the 1980s, of course, many computer companies were afraid that a newly divested AT&T would pose more of a threat to controlling the computer industry than would an upstart company in Redmond, Washington. To calm the fears of IBM, Intel, Digital Equipment Corporation, and other computer companies, the UNIX Lab made the following commitments to ensure a level playing field:

- **Source code only**—Instead of producing its own boxed set of UNIX, AT&T continued to sell only source code and to make it available equally to all licensees. Each company would then port UNIX to its own equipment. It wasn't until about 1992, when the lab was spun off as a joint venture with Novell (called Univel), and then eventually sold to Novell, that a commercial boxed set of UNIX (called UnixWare) was produced directly from that source code.

- **Published interfaces**—To create an environment of fairness and community to its OEMs (original equipment manufacturers), AT&T began standardizing what different ports of UNIX had to be able to do to still be called UNIX. To that end, Portable Operating System Interface (POSIX) standards and the AT&T UNIX System V Interface Definition (SVID) were specifications UNIX vendors could use to create compliant UNIX systems. Those same documents also served as road maps for the creation of Linux.

> **NOTE**
>
> In an early email newsgroup post, Linus Torvalds made a request for a copy, preferably online, of the POSIX standard. I think that nobody from AT&T expected someone to actually be able to write his own clone of UNIX from those interfaces, without using any of its UNIX source code.

- **Technical approach**—Again, until the very end of USL, most decisions on the direction of UNIX were made based on technical considerations. Management was promoted up through the technical ranks, and to my knowledge, there was never any talk of writing software to break other companies' software or otherwise restrict the success of USL's partners.

When USL eventually started taking on marketing experts and creating a desktop UNIX product for end users, Microsoft Windows already had a firm grasp on the desktop market. Also, because the direction of UNIX had always been toward source-code licensing destined for large computing systems, USL had pricing difficulties for its products. For example, on software that it was including with UNIX, USL found itself having to pay out per-computer licensing fees that were based on $100,000 mainframes instead of $2,000 PCs. Add to that the fact that no application programs were available with UnixWare, and you can see why the endeavor failed.

Successful marketing of UNIX systems at the time, however, was happening with other computer companies. SCO had found a niche market, primarily selling PC versions of UNIX running dumb terminals in small offices. Sun Microsystems was selling lots of UNIX workstations (originally based on BSD but merged with UNIX in SVR4) for programmers and high-end technology applications (such as stock trading).

Other commercial UNIX systems were also emerging by the 1980s as well. This new ownership assertion of UNIX was beginning to take its toll on the spirit of open contributions. Lawsuits were being initiated to protect UNIX source code and trademarks. In 1984, this new, restrictive UNIX gave rise to an organization that eventually led a path to Linux: the Free Software Foundation.

GNU transitions UNIX to freedom

In 1984, Richard M. Stallman started the GNU project (http://www.gnu.org), recursively named by the phrase GNU is Not UNIX. As a project of the Free Software Foundation (FSF), GNU was intended to become a recoding of the entire UNIX operating system that could be freely distributed.

The GNU Project page (http://www.gnu.org/gnu/thegnuproject.html) tells the story of how the project came about in Stallman's own words. It also lays out the problems that proprietary software companies were imposing on those software developers who wanted to share, create, and innovate.

Although rewriting millions of lines of code might seem daunting for one or two people, spreading the effort across dozens or even hundreds of programmers made the project possible. Remember that UNIX was designed to be built in separate pieces that could be piped together. Because they were reproducing commands and utilities with well-known, published interfaces, that effort could easily be split among many developers.

It turned out that not only could the same results be gained by all new code, but in some cases, that code was better than the original UNIX versions. Because everyone could see the code being produced for the project, poorly written code could be corrected quickly or replaced over time.

If you are familiar with UNIX, try searching the thousands of GNU software packages for your favorite UNIX command from the Free Software Directory (http://directory. fsf.org/wiki/GNU). Chances are good that you will find it there, along with many, many other available software projects.

Over time, the term *free software* has been mostly replaced by the term *open source software*. The term "free software" is preferred by the Free Software Foundation, while open source software is promoted by the Open Source Initiative (http://www.opensource.org).

To accommodate both camps, some people use the term *Free and Open Source Software* (FOSS) instead. An underlying principle of FOSS, however, is that, although you are free to use the software as you like, you have some responsibility to make the improvements you make to the code available to others. In that way, everyone in the community can benefit from your work as you have benefited from the work of others.

To clearly define how open source software should be handled, the GNU software project created the GNU Public License, or GPL. Although many other software licenses cover slightly different approaches to protecting free software, the GPL is the most well known—and it's the one that covers the Linux kernel itself. Basic features of the GNU Public License include the following:

- **Author rights**—The original author retains the rights to his or her software.
- **Free distribution**—People can use the GNU software in their own software, changing and redistributing it as they please. They do, however, have to include the source code with their distribution (or make it easily available).
- **Copyright maintained**—Even if you were to repackage and resell the software, the original GNU agreement must be maintained with the software, which means all future recipients of the software have the opportunity to change the source code, just as you did.

There is no warranty on GNU software. If something goes wrong, the original developer of the software has no obligation to fix the problem. However, many organizations, big and small, offer paid support (often in subscription form) for the software when it is included in their Linux or other open source software distribution. (See the "OSI open source definition" section later in this chapter for a more detailed definition of open source software.)

Despite its success in producing thousands of UNIX utilities, the GNU project itself failed to produce one critical piece of code: the kernel. Its attempts to build an open source kernel with the GNU Hurd project (http://www.gnu.org/software/hurd) were unsuccessful at first, so it failed to become the premier open source kernel.

BSD loses some steam

The one software project that had a chance of beating out Linux to be the premier open source kernel was the venerable BSD project. By the late 1980s, BSD developers at University of California (UC) Berkeley realized that they had already rewritten most of the UNIX source code they had received a decade earlier.

In 1989, UC Berkeley distributed its own UNIX-like code as Net/1 and later (in 1991) as Net/2. Just as UC Berkeley was preparing a complete, UNIX-like operating system that was free from all AT&T code, AT&T hit them with a lawsuit in 1992. The suit claimed that the software was written using trade secrets taken from AT&T's UNIX system.

It's important to note here that BSD developers had completely rewritten the copyright-protected code from AT&T. Copyright was the primary means AT&T used to protect its rights to the UNIX code. Some believe that if AT&T had patented the concepts covered in that code, there might not be a Linux (or any UNIX clone) operating system today.

The lawsuit was dropped when Novell bought UNIX System Laboratories from AT&T in 1994. But, during that critical period, there was enough fear and doubt about the legality of the BSD code that the momentum BSD had gained to that point in the fledgling open source community was lost. Many people started looking for another open source alternative. The time was ripe for a college student from Finland who was working on his own kernel.

NOTE

Today, BSD versions are available from three major projects: FreeBSD, NetBSD, and OpenBSD. People generally characterize FreeBSD as the easiest to use, NetBSD as available on the most computer hardware platforms, and OpenBSD as fanatically secure. Many security-minded individuals still prefer BSD to Linux. Also, because of its licensing, BSD code can be used by proprietary software vendors, such as Microsoft and Apple, who don't want to share their operating system code with others. Mac OS X is built on a BSD derivative.

Linus builds the missing piece

Linus Torvalds started work on Linux in 1991, while he was a student at the University of Helsinki, Finland. He wanted to create a UNIX-like kernel so that he could use the same kind of operating system on his home PC that he used at school. At the time, Linus was using Minix, but he wanted to go beyond what the Minix standards permitted.

As noted earlier, Linus announced the first public version of the Linux kernel to the `comp .os.minix` newsgroup on August 25, 1991, although Torvalds guesses that the first version didn't actually come out until mid-September of that year.

Although Torvalds stated that Linux was written for the 386 processor and probably wasn't portable, others persisted in encouraging (and contributing to) a more portable approach in the early versions of Linux. By October 5, Linux 0.02 was released with much of the original assembly code rewritten in the C programming language, which made it possible to start porting it to other machines.

The Linux kernel was the last—and the most important—piece of code that was needed to complete a whole UNIX-like operating system under the GPL. So, when people started putting together distributions, the name Linux and not GNU is what stuck. Some distributions such as Debian, however, refer to themselves as GNU/Linux distributions. (Not including GNU in the title or subtitle of a Linux operating system is also a matter of much public grumbling by some members of the GNU project. See http://www.gnu.org.)

Today, Linux can be described as an open source UNIX-like operating system that reflects a combination of SVID, POSIX, and BSD compliance. Linux continues to aim toward compliance with POSIX as well as with standards set by the owner of the UNIX trademark, The Open Group (http://www.unix.org).

The non-profit Open Source Development Labs, renamed the Linux Foundation after merging with the Free Standards Group (http://www.linuxfoundation.org), which employs Linus Torvalds, manages the direction today of Linux development efforts. Its sponsors list is like a Who's Who of commercial Linux system and application vendors, including IBM, Red Hat, SUSE, Oracle, HP, Dell, Computer Associates, Intel, Cisco Systems, and others. The Linux Foundation's primary charter is to protect and accelerate the growth of Linux by providing legal protection and software development standards for Linux developers.

Although much of the thrust of corporate Linux efforts is on corporate, enterprise computing, huge improvements are continuing in the desktop arena as well. The KDE and GNOME desktop environments continuously improve the Linux experience for casual users. Newer lightweight desktop environments such as Xfce and LXDE now offer efficient alternatives that today bring Linux to thousands of netbook owners.

Linus Torvalds continues to maintain and improve the Linux kernel.

> **NOTE**
>
> For a more detailed history of Linux, see the book *Open Sources: Voices from the Open Source Revolution* (O'Reilly, 1999). The entire first edition is available online at http://oreilly.com/catalog/opensources/book/toc.html.

OSI open source definition

Linux provides a platform that lets software developers change the operating system as they like and get a wide range of help creating the applications they need. One of the watchdogs of the open source movement is the Open Source Initiative (OSI, http://www.opensource.org).

Although the primary goal of open source software is to make source code available, other goals of open source software are also defined by OSI in its open source definition. Most of the following rules for acceptable open source licenses serve to protect the freedom and integrity of the open source code:

- **Free distribution**—An open source license can't require a fee from anyone who resells the software.

- **Source code**—The source code must be included with the software and there can be no restrictions on redistribution.

- **Derived works**—The license must allow modification and redistribution of the code under the same terms.

- **Integrity of the author's source code**—The license may require that those who use the source code remove the original project's name or version if they change the source code.

- **No discrimination against persons or groups**—The license must allow all people to be equally eligible to use the source code.

- **No discrimination against fields of endeavor**—The license can't restrict a project from using the source code because it is commercial or because it is associated with a field of endeavor that the software provider doesn't like.

- **Distribution of license**—No additional license should be needed to use and redistribute the software.

- **License must not be specific to a product**—The license can't restrict the source code to a particular software distribution.

- **License must not restrict other software**—The license can't prevent someone from including the open source software on the same medium as non–open source software.

- **License must be technology-neutral**—The license can't restrict methods in which the source code can be redistributed.

Open source licenses used by software development projects must meet these criteria to be accepted as open source software by OSI. About 70 different licenses are accepted by OSI to be used to label software as "OSI Certified Open Source Software." In addition to the GPL, other popular OSI-approved licenses include:

- **LGPL**—The GNU Lesser General Public License (LGPL) is often used for distributing libraries that other application programs depend upon.

- **BSD**—The Berkeley Software Distribution License allows redistribution of source code, with the requirement that the source code keep the BSD copyright notice and not use the names of contributors to endorse or promote derived software without written permission. A major difference from GPL, however, is that BSD does not require people modifying the code to pass those changes on to the community.

As a result, proprietary software vendors such as Apple and Microsoft have used BSD code in their own operating systems.

- **MIT**—The MIT license is like the BSD license, except that it doesn't include the endorsement and promotion requirement.
- **Mozilla**—The Mozilla license covers the use and redistribution of source code associated with the Firefox web browser and other software related to the Mozilla project (http://www.mozilla.org). It is a much longer license than the others just mentioned because it contains more definitions of how contributors and those reusing the source code should behave. This includes submitting a file of changes when submitting modifications and that those making their own additions to the code for redistribution should be aware of patent issues or other restrictions associated with their code.

The end result of open source code is software that has more flexibility to grow and fewer boundaries in how it can be used. Many believe that the fact that numerous people look over the source code for a project results in higher-quality software for everyone. As open source advocate Eric S. Raymond says in an often-quoted line, "Given enough eyeballs, all bugs are shallow."

Understanding How Linux Distributions Emerged

Having bundles of source code floating around the Internet that could be compiled and packaged into a Linux system worked well for geeks. More casual Linux users, however, needed a simpler way to put together a Linux system. To respond to that need, some of the best geeks began building their own Linux distributions.

A Linux distribution consists of the components needed to create a working Linux system and the procedures needed to get those components installed and running. Technically, Linux is really just what is referred to as the *kernel*. Before the kernel can be useful, you must have other software such as basic commands (GNU utilities), services you want to offer (such as remote login or web servers), and possibly a desktop interface and graphical applications. Then, you must be able to gather all that together and install it on your computer's hard disk.

Slackware (http://www.slackware.com) is one of the oldest Linux distributions still being developed today. It made Linux friendly for less technical users by distributing software already compiled and grouped into packages (those packages of software components were in a format called *tarballs*). You would use basic Linux commands then to do things like format your disk, enable swap, and create user accounts.

Before long, many other Linux distributions were created. Some Linux distributions were created to meet special needs, such as KNOPPIX (a live CD Linux), Gentoo (a cool customizable Linux), and Mandrake (later called Mandriva, which was one of several desktop Linux distributions). But two major distributions rose to become the foundation for many other distributions: Red Hat Linux and Debian.

Choosing a Red Hat distribution

When Red Hat Linux appeared in the late 1990s, it quickly became the most popular Linux distribution for several reasons:

- **RPM package management**—Tarballs are fine for dropping software on your computer, but they don't work as well when you want to update, remove, or even find out about that software. Red Hat created the RPM packaging format so a software package could contain not only the files to be shared, but also information about the package version, who created it, which files were documentation or configuration files, and when it was created. By installing software packaged in RPM format, that information about each software package could be stored in a local RPM database. It became easy to find what was installed, update it, or remove it.

- **Simple installation**—The anaconda installer made it much simpler to install Linux. As a user, you could step through some simple questions, in most cases accepting defaults, to install Red Hat Linux.

- **Graphical administration**—Red Hat added simple graphical tools to configure printers, add users, set time and date, and do other basic administrative tasks. As a result, desktop users could use a Linux system without even having to run commands.

For years, Red Hat Linux was the preferred Linux distribution for both Linux professionals and enthusiasts. Red Hat, Inc., gave away the source code, as well as the compiled, ready-to-run versions of Red Hat Linux (referred to as the *binaries*). But as the needs of their Linux community users and big-ticket customers began to move further apart, Red Hat abandoned Red Hat Linux and began developing two operating systems instead: Red Hat Enterprise Linux and Fedora.

Using Red Hat Enterprise Linux

In March 2012, Red Hat, Inc., became the first open source software company to bring in more than $1 billion in yearly revenue. It achieved that goal by building a set of products around Red Hat Enterprise Linux (RHEL) that would suit the needs of the most demanding enterprise computing environments.

While other Linux distributions focused on desktop systems or small business computing, RHEL worked on those features needed to handle mission-critical applications for business and government. It built systems that could speed transactions for the world's largest financial exchanges and be deployed as clusters and virtual hosts.

Instead of just selling RHEL, Red Hat offers an ecosystem of benefits for Linux customers to draw on. To use RHEL, customers buy subscriptions that they can use to deploy any version of RHEL they desire. If they decommission a RHEL system, they can use the subscription to deploy another system.

Different levels of support are available for RHEL, depending on customer needs. Customers can be assured that, along with support, they can get hardware and third-party software that is certified to work with RHEL. They can get Red Hat consultants and engineers to help them put together the computing environments they need. They can also get training and certification exams for their employees (see the discussion of RHCE certification later in this chapter).

Red Hat has also added other products as natural extensions to Red Hat Enterprise Linux. JBoss is a middleware product for deploying Java-based applications to the Internet or company intranets. Red Hat Enterprise Virtualization is composed of the virtualization hosts, managers, and guest computers that allow you to install, run, manage, migrate, and decommission huge virtual computing environments.

In recent years, Red Hat has extended its portfolio into cloud computing. RHEL OpenStack Platform and Red Hat Enterprise Virtualization offer complete platforms for running and managing virtual machines. Red Hat Cloudforms is a cloud management platform. RHEL Atomic and Linux containers in Docker format offer ways of containerizing applications for the cloud.

There are those who have tried to clone RHEL, using the freely available RHEL source code, rebuilding and rebranding it. Oracle Linux is built from source code for RHEL but currently offers an incompatible kernel. CentOS is a community-sponsored Linux distribution that is built from RHEL source code. Recently, Red Hat took over support of the CentOS project.

I've chosen to use Red Hat Enterprise Linux for many of the examples in this book because, if you want a career working on Linux systems, there is a huge demand for those who can administer RHEL systems. If you are starting out with Linux, however, Fedora can provide an excellent entry point to the same skills you need to use and administer RHEL systems.

Using Fedora

While RHEL is the commercial, stable, supported Linux distribution, Fedora is the free, cutting-edge Linux distribution that is sponsored by Red Hat, Inc. Fedora is the Linux system Red Hat uses to engage the Linux development community and encourage those who want a free Linux for personal use and rapid development.

Fedora includes more than 16,000 software packages, many of which keep up with the latest available open source technology. As a user, you can try the latest Linux desktop, server, and administrative interfaces in Fedora for free. As a software developer, you can create and test your applications using the latest Linux kernel and development tools.

Because the focus of Fedora is on the latest technology, it focuses less on stability. So expect that you might need to do some extra work to get everything working and that not all the software will be fully baked.

However, I recommend that you use Fedora for most of the examples in this book for the following reasons:

- Fedora is used as a proving ground for Red Hat Enterprise Linux. Red Hat tests many new applications in Fedora before committing them to RHEL. By using Fedora, you will learn the skills you need to work with features as they are being developed for Red Hat Enterprise Linux.
- For learning, Fedora is more convenient than RHEL, yet still includes many of the more advanced, enterprise-ready tools that are in RHEL.
- Fedora is free, not only as in "freedom" but also as in "you don't have to pay for it."

Fedora is extremely popular with those who develop open source software. However, in the past few years, another Linux distribution has captured the attention of many people starting out with Linux: Ubuntu.

Choosing Ubuntu or another Debian distribution

Like Red Hat Linux, the Debian GNU/Linux distribution was an early Linux distribution that excelled at packaging and managing software. Debian uses deb packaging format and tools to manage all of the software packages on its systems. Debian also has a reputation for stability.

Many Linux distributions can trace their roots back to Debian. According to distrowatch (http://distrowatch.com), more than 130 active Linux distributions can be traced back to Debian. Popular Debian-based distributions include Linux Mint, elementary OS, Zorin OS, LXLE, Kali Linux, and many others. However, the Debian derivative that has achieved the most success is Ubuntu (http://www.ubuntu.com).

By relying on stable Debian software development and packaging, the Ubuntu Linux distribution was able to come along and add those features that Debian lacked. In pursuit of bringing new users to Linux, the Ubuntu project added a simple graphical installer and easy-to-use graphical tools. It also focused on full-featured desktop systems, while still offering popular server packages.

Ubuntu was also an innovator in creating new ways to run Linux. Using live CDs or live USB drives offered by Ubuntu, you could have Ubuntu up and running in just a few minutes. Often included on live CDs were open source applications, such as web browsers and word processors, that actually ran in Windows. This made the transition to Linux from Windows easier for some people.

If you are using Ubuntu, don't fear. Most of subject matter covered in this book will work as well in Ubuntu as it does in Fedora or RHEL. This edition of *Linux Bible* provides expanded coverage of Ubuntu.

Finding Professional Opportunities with Linux Today

If you want to develop an idea for a computer-related research project or technology company, where do you begin? You begin with an idea. After that, you look for the tools you need to explore and eventually create your vision. Then, you look for others to help you during that creation process.

Today, the hard costs of starting a company like Google or Facebook include just a computer, a connection to the Internet, and enough caffeinated beverage of your choice to keep you up all night writing code. If you have your own world-changing idea, Linux and thousands of software packages are available to help you build your dreams. The open source world also comes with communities of developers, administrators, and users who are available to help you.

If you want to get involved with an existing open source project, projects are always looking for people to write code, test software, or write documentation. In those projects, you will find people who use the software, work on the software, and are usually willing to share their expertise to help you as well.

But whether you seek to develop the next great open source software project or simply want to gain the skills needed to compete for the thousands of well-paying Linux administrator or development jobs, it will help you to know how to install, secure, and maintain Linux systems.

So, what are the prospects for Linux careers? "The 2014 Linux Jobs Report" from the Linux Foundation (http://www.linuxfoundation.org/publications/linux-foundation/linux-adoption-trends-end-user-report-2014) surveyed more than 1,100 hiring managers and 4,000 Linux professionals. Here is what the Linux Foundation found:

- **Linux talent is a high priority**—Hiring people with Linux expertise is a priority for 77 percent of hiring managers.
- **Career advancement with Linux**—As for career opportunities, 86 percent of Linux professionals reported that Linux knowledge increased career opportunities.
- **More Linux recruiting**—Of the hiring managers surveyed, 46 percent reported that they planned to increase recruitment of Linux talent from the previous year (up 3 percent from the previous year).

The major message to take from this survey is that Linux continues to grow and create demands for Linux expertise. Companies that have begun using Linux have continued to move forward with Linux. Those using Linux continue to expand its use and find that cost savings, security, and the flexibility it offers continue to make Linux a good investment.

Understanding how companies make money with Linux

Open source enthusiasts believe that better software can result from an open source software development model than from proprietary development models. So in theory, any company creating software for its own use can save money by adding its software contributions to those of others to gain a much better end product for themselves.

Companies that want to make money by selling software need to be more creative than they were in the old days. Although you can sell the software you create that includes GPL software, you must pass the source code of that software forward. Of course, others can then recompile that product, basically using and even reselling your product without charge. Here are a few ways that companies are dealing with that issue:

- **Software subscriptions**—Red Hat, Inc., sells its Red Hat Enterprise Linux products on a subscription basis. For a certain amount of money per year, you get binary code to run Linux (so you don't have to compile it yourself), guaranteed support, tools for tracking the hardware and software on your computer, access to the company's knowledge base, and other assets.

   Although Red Hat's Fedora project includes much of the same software and is also available in binary form, there are no guarantees associated with the software or future updates of that software. A small office or personal user might take a risk on using Fedora (which is itself an excellent operating system), but a big company that's running mission-critical applications will probably put down a few dollars for RHEL.

- **Training and certification**—With Linux system use growing in government and big business, professionals are needed to support those systems. Red Hat offers training courses and certification exams to help system administrators become proficient using Red Hat Enterprise Linux systems. In particular, the Red Hat Certified Engineer (RHCE) and Red Hat Certified System Administrator (RHCSA) certifications have become popular (http://www.redhat.com/certification). More on RHCE/RHCSA certifications later in this chapter.

   Other certification programs are offered by Linux Professional Institute (http://www.lpi.org), CompTIA (http://www.comptia.org), and Novell (https://training.novell.com/). LPI and CompTIA are professional computer industry associations. Novell centers its training and certification on its SUSE Linux products.

- **Bounties**—Software bounties are a fascinating way for open source software companies to make money. Suppose you are using XYZ software package and you need a new feature right away. By paying a software bounty to the project itself, or to other software developers, you can have your needed improvements moved to the head of the queue. The software you pay for will remain covered by its open source license, but you will have the features you need, at probably a fraction of the cost of building the project from scratch.

- **Donations**—Many open source projects accept donations from individuals or open source companies that use code from their projects. Amazingly, many open source projects support one or two developers and run exclusively on donations.
- **Boxed sets, mugs, and T-shirts**—Some open source projects have online stores where you can buy boxed sets (some people still like physical DVDs and hard copies of documentation) and a variety of mugs, T-shirts, mouse pads, and other items. If you really love a project, for goodness sake, buy a T-shirt!

This is in no way an exhaustive list, because more creative ways are being invented every day to support those who create open source software. Remember that many people have become contributors to and maintainers of open source software because they needed or wanted the software themselves. The contributions they make for free are worth the return they get from others who do the same.

Becoming Red Hat certified

Although this book is not focused on becoming certified in Linux, it touches on the activities you need to be able to master to pass popular Linux certification exams. In particular, most of what is covered in the Red Hat Certified Engineer (RHCE) and Red Hat Certified System Administrator (RHCSA) exams for Red Hat Enterprise Linux 7 is described in this book.

If you are looking for a job as a Linux IT professional, often RHCSA or RHCE certification is listed as a requirement or at least a preference for employers. The RHCSA exam (EX200) provides the basic certification, covering such topics as configuring disks and filesystems, adding users, setting up a simple web and FTP server, and adding swap space. The RHCE exam (EX300) tests for more advanced server configuration, as well an advanced knowledge of security features, such as SELinux and firewalls.

Those of us who have taught RHCE/RHCSA courses and given exams (as I did for three years) are not allowed to tell you exactly what is on the exam. However, Red Hat gives an overview of how the exams work, as well as a list of topics you can expect to see covered in the exam. You can find those exam objectives on the following sites:

- **RHCSA**—http://www.redhat.com/en/services/training/ex200-red-hat-certified-system-administrator-rhcsa-exam
- **RHCE**—http://www.redhat.com/en/services/training/ex300-red-hat-certified-engineer-rhce-exam

As the exam objectives state, the RHCSA and RHCE exams are performance-based, which means that you are given tasks to do and you must perform those tasks on an actual Red

Hat Enterprise Linux system, as you would on the job. You are graded on how well you obtained the results of those tasks.

If you plan to take the exams, check back to the exam objectives pages often, because they change from time to time. Keep in mind also that the RHCSA is a standalone certification; however, you must pass the RHCSA and the RHCE exams to get an RHCE certification. Often, the two exams are given on the same day.

You can sign up for RHCSA and RHCE training and exams at http://training.redhat. com. Training and exams are given at major cities all over the United States and around the world. The skills you need to complete these exams are described in the following sections.

RHCSA topics

As noted earlier, RHCSA exam topics cover basic system administration skills. These are the current topics listed for Red Hat Enterprise Linux 7 at the RHCSA exam objectives site (again, check the exam objectives site in case they change) and where in this book you can learn about them:

- **Understand essential tools**—You are expected to have a working knowledge of the command shell (bash), including how to use proper command syntax and do input/output redirection (< > >>). You need to know how to log in to remote and local systems. Expect to have to create, edit, move, copy, link, delete, and change permission and ownership on files. Likewise, you should know how to look up information on man pages and /usr/share/doc. Most of these topics are covered in Chapters 3 and 4 in this book. Chapter 5 describes how to edit and find files.

- **Operate running systems**—In this category, you must understand the Linux boot process, go into single-user mode, shut down, reboot, and change to different targets (previously called *runlevels*). You need to identify processes and change nice values or kill processes as requested. You must be able to start and stop virtual machines and network services, as well as find and interpret log files. Chapter 15 describes how to change targets and runlevels and manage system services. See Chapter 6 for information on managing and changing processes. Chapter 26 describes how to manage virtual machines. Logging is described in Chapter 13.

- **Configure local storage**—Setting up disk partitions includes creating physical volumes and configuring them to be used for Logical Volume Management (LVM) or encryption (LUKS). You should also be able to set up those partitions as filesystems or swap space that can be mounted or enabled at boot time. Disk partitioning and LVM are covered in Chapter 12. LUKS and other encryption topics are described in Chapter 23.

- **Create and configure filesystems**—Create and automatically mount different kinds of filesystems, including regular Linux filesystems (ext2, ext3, or ext4), LUKS-encrypted filesystems, and network filesystems (NFS and CIFS). Create collaborative directories using the set group ID bit feature and Access Control Lists (ACL).

You must also be able to use LVM to extend the size of a logical volume. Filesystem topics are covered in Chapter 12. See Chapter 19 for CIFS and Chapter 20 for NFS coverage.

- **Deploy, configure, and maintain systems**—This covers a range of topics, including configuring networking, creating `cron` tasks, setting the default runlevel, and installing RHEL systems. You must also be able to configure a simple HTTP and FTP server. For software packages, you must be able to install packages from Red Hat Network, a remote repository, or the local filesystem. Finally, you must be able to properly install a new kernel and choose that or some other kernel to boot up when the system starts. The `cron` facility is described in Chapter 13. Web server (HTTP) and FTP server setups are covered in Chapters 17 and 18, respectively.

- **Manage users and groups**—You must know how to add, delete, and change user and group accounts. Another topic you should know is password aging, using the `chage` command. You must also know how to configure a system to authenticate by connecting to an LDAP directory server. See Chapter 11 for information on configuring users and groups.

- **Manage security**—You must have a basic understanding of how to set up a firewall (`firewalld`, `system-config-firewall` or `iptables`) and how to use SELinux. You must be able to set up SSH to do key-based authentication. Learn about SELinux in Chapter 24. Firewalls are covered in Chapter 25. Chapter 13 includes a description of key-based authentication.

Most of these topics are covered in this book. Refer to Red Hat documentation (`https://access.redhat.com/documentation/`) under the Red Hat Enterprise Linux heading for descriptions of features not found in this book. In particular, the System Administrator's Guide contains descriptions of many of the RHCSA-related topics.

RHCE topics

RHCE exam topics cover more advanced server configuration, along with a variety of security features for securing those servers in Red Hat Enterprise Linux 7. Again, check the RHCE exam objectives site for the most up-to-date information on topics you should study for the exam.

System configuration and management

The system configuration and management requirement for the RHCE exam covers a range of topics, including the following:

- **Bonding**—Set up bonding to aggregate network links. Bonding is described in Chapter 14.

- **Route IP traffic**—Set up static routes to specific network addresses. Chapter 14 includes a description of how to set up custom routes.

1

- **Firewalls**—Block or allow traffic to selected ports on your system that offer services such as web, FTP, and NFS, as well as block or allow access to services based on the originator's IP address. Firewalls are covered in Chapter 25.

- **Kernel tunables**—Set kernel tunable parameters using the `/etc/sysctl.conf` file and the `sysctl` command. See Chapter 14 for a description of how to use the `/etc/sysctl.conf` file to change IP forwarding settings in `/proc/sys`.

- **Kerberos authentication**—Use Kerberos to authenticate users on a RHEL system. Chapter 11 includes a description of setting up a system to authentication to a Kerberos server.

- **Configure iSCSI**—Set up system as an iSCSI target and initiator that mounts an iSCSI target at boot time. See the Red Hat Storage Administration Guide for further information (`https://access.redhat.com/documentation/en-US/ Red_Hat_Enterprise_Linux/7/html/Storage_Administration_Guide/ ch-iscsi.html`)

- **System reports**—Use features such as `sar` to report on system use of memory, disk access, network traffic, and processor utilization. Chapter 13 describes how to use the `sar` command.

- **Shell scripting**—Create a simple shell script to take input and produce output in various ways. Shell scripting is described in Chapter 7.

- **Remote logging**—Configure the `rsyslogd` facility to gather log messages and distribute them to a remote logging server. Also, configure a remote logging server facility to gather log messages from logging clients. Chapter 13 covers remote logging with `rsyslogd`.

- **SELinux**—With Security Enhanced Linux in Enforcing mode, make sure that all server configurations described in the next section are properly secured with SELinux. SELinux is described in Chapter 24.

Installing and configuring network services

For each of the network services in the list that follows, make sure that you can go through the steps to install packages required by the service, set up SELinux to allow access to the service, set the service to start at boot time, secure the service by host or by user (using `iptables`, TCP wrappers, or features provided by the service itself), and configure it for basic operation. These are the services:

- **Web server**—Configure an Apache (HTTP/HTTPS) server. You must be able to set up a virtual host, deploy a CGI script, use private directories, and allow a particular Linux group to manage the content. Chapter 17 describes how to configure a Web server.

- **DNS server**—Set up a DNS server (bind package) to act as a caching-only name server that can forward DNS queries to another DNS server. No need to configure master or slave zones. DNS is described from the client side in

Chapter 14. For information on configuring a DNS server with Bind, see the RHEL Networking Guide (https://access.redhat.com/documentation/en-US/ Red_Hat_Enterprise_Linux/7/html-single/Networking_Guide).

- **NFS server**—Configure an NFS server to share specific directories to specific client systems so they can be used for group collaboration. Chapter 20 covers NFS.

- **Windows file sharing server**—Set up Linux (Samba) to provide SMB shares to specific hosts and users. Configure the shares for group collaboration. See Chapter 19 to learn about configuring Samba.

- **Mail server**—Configure postfix or sendmail to accept incoming mail from outside the local host. Relay mail to a smart host. Mail server configuration is not covered in this book (and should not be done lightly). See the RHEL System Administrator's Guide for information on configuring mail servers (https://access.redhat. com/documentation/en-US/Red_Hat_Enterprise_Linux/7/html-single/ System_Administrators_Guide/index.html#ch-Mail_Servers).

- **Secure Shell server**—Set up the SSH service (sshd) to allow remote login to your local system as well as key-based authentication. Otherwise, configure the sshd. conf file as needed. Chapter 13 describes how to configure the sshd service.

- **Network Time server**—Configure a Network Time Protocol server (ntpd) to synchronize time with other NTP peers. See Chapter 26 for information on configuring the ntpd service.

- **Database server**—Configure the MariaDB database and manage it in various ways. Learn how to configure MariaDB from the MariaDB.org site (https://mariadb. com/kb/en/mariadb/documentation/).

Although there are other tasks in the RHCE exam, as just noted, keep in mind that most of the tasks have you configure servers and then secure those servers using any technique you need. Those can include firewall rules (iptables), SELinux, TCP Wrappers, or any features built into configuration files for the particular service.

Summary

Linux is an operating system that is built by a community of software developers around the world and led by its creator, Linus Torvalds. It is derived originally from the UNIX operating system, but has grown beyond UNIX in popularity and power over the years.

The history of the Linux operating system can be tracked from early UNIX systems that were distributed free to colleges and improved by initiatives such as the Berkeley Software Distribution (BSD). The Free Software Foundation helped make many of the components needed to create a fully-free UNIX-like operating system. The Linux kernel itself was the last major component needed to complete the job.

Most Linux software projects are protected by one of a set of licenses that fall under the Open Source Initiative umbrella. The most prominent of these is the GNU Public License (GPL). Standards such as the Linux Standard Base and world-class Linux organizations and companies (such as Canonical Ltd. and Red Hat, Inc.) make it possible for Linux to continue to be a stable, productive operating system into the future.

Learning the basics of how to use and administer a Linux system will serve you well in any aspect of working with Linux. The remaining chapters each provide a series of exercises with which you can test your understanding. That's why, for the rest of the book, you will learn best with a Linux system in front of you so you can work through the examples in each chapter and complete the exercises successfully.

The next chapter describes how to get started with Linux by describing how to get and use a Linux desktop system.

1

Creating the Perfect Linux Desktop

U sing Linux as your everyday desktop system is becoming easier to do all the time. As with everything in Linux, you have choices. There are full-featured GNOME or KDE desktop environments or lightweight desktops such as LXDE or Xfce. There are even simpler standalone window managers.

After you have chosen a desktop, you will find that almost every major type of desktop application you have on a Windows or Mac system has equivalent applications in Linux. For applications that are not available in Linux, you can often run a Windows application in Linux using Windows compatibility software.

The goal of this chapter is to familiarize you with the concepts related to Linux desktop systems and to give you tips for working with a Linux desktop. In this chapter you:

- Step through the desktop features and technologies that are available in Linux
- Tour the major features of the GNOME desktop environment
- Learn tips and tricks for getting the most out of your GNOME desktop experience

To use the descriptions in this chapter, I recommend you have a Fedora system running in front of you. You can get Fedora in lots of ways, including these:

- **Running Fedora from a live medium**—Refer to Appendix A for information on downloading and burning Fedora Live image to a DVD or USB drive so you can boot it live to use with this chapter.

- **Installing Fedora permanently**—Install Fedora to your hard disk and boot it from there (as described in Chapter 9, "Installing Linux").

Because the current release of Fedora uses the GNOME 3 interface, most of the procedures described here work with other Linux distributions that have GNOME 3 available. If you are using an older Red Hat Enterprise Linux system (RHEL 6 uses GNOME 2, but RHEL 7 uses GNOME 3), I added descriptions of GNOME 2 that you can try as well.

> **NOTE**
>
> Ubuntu uses its own Unity desktop as its default, instead of GNOME. There is, however, an Ubuntu GNOME project. To download the medium for the latest Ubuntu version with a GNOME desktop, go to the Ubuntu GNOME download page (http://ubuntugnome.org/download/).
>
> You can add GNOME and use it as the desktop environment for Ubuntu 11.10 and later. Older Ubuntu releases use GNOME 2 by default.

Understanding Linux Desktop Technology

Modern computer desktop systems offer graphical windows, icons, and menus that are operated from a mouse and keyboard. If you are under 30 years old, you might think there's nothing special about that. But the first Linux systems did not have graphical interfaces available. Also, today, many Linux servers tuned for special tasks (for example, serving as a web server or file server) don't have desktop software installed.

Nearly every major Linux distribution that offers desktop interfaces is based on the X Window System (http://www.x.org). The X Window System provides a framework on which different types of desktop environments or simple window managers can be built.

The X Window System (sometimes simply called X) was created before Linux existed and even predates Microsoft Windows. It was built to be a lightweight, networked desktop framework.

X works in a sort of backward client/server model. The X server runs on the local system, providing an interface to your screen, mouse, and keyboard. X clients (such as word processors, music players, or image viewers) can be launched from the local system or from any system on your network, provided that the X server gives permission to do so.

X was created in a time when graphical terminals (thin clients) simply managed the keyboard, mouse, and display. Applications, disk storage, and processing power were all on larger centralized computers. So applications ran on larger machines but were displayed and managed over the network on the thin client. Later, thin clients were replaced by desktop personal computers. Most client applications on PCs ran locally, using local processing power, disk space, memory, and other hardware features, while not allowing applications that didn't start from the local system.

X itself provides a plain gray background and a simple "X" mouse cursor. There are no menus, panels, or icons on a plain X screen. If you were to launch an X client (such as a terminal window or word processor), it would appear on the X display with no border around it to move, minimize, or close the window. Those features are added by a window manager.

A window manager adds the capability to manage the windows on your desktop and often provides menus for launching applications and otherwise working with the desktop. A full-blown desktop environment includes a window manager, but also adds menus, panels, and usually an application programming interface that is used to create applications that play well together.

So how does an understanding of how desktop interfaces work in Linux help you when it comes to using Linux? Here are some ways:

- Because Linux desktop environments are not required to run a Linux system, a Linux system may have been installed without a desktop. It might offer only a plain-text, command-line interface. You can choose to add a desktop later. After it is installed, you can choose whether to start up the desktop when your computer boots or start it as needed.

- For a very lightweight Linux system, such as one meant to run on less powerful computers, you can choose an efficient, though less feature-rich, window manager (such as twm or fluxbox) or a lightweight desktop environment (such as LXDE or Xfce).

- For more robust computers, you can choose more powerful desktop environments (such as GNOME and KDE) that can do such things as watch for events to happen (such as inserting a USB flash drive) and respond to those events (such as opening a window to view the contents of the drive).

- You can have multiple desktop environments installed and you can choose which one to launch when you log in. In this way, different users on the same computer can use different desktop environments.

Many different desktop environments are available to choose from in Linux. Here are some examples:

- **GNOME**—GNOME is the default desktop environment for Fedora, Red Hat Enterprise Linux, and many others. Think of it as a professional desktop environment, focusing on stability more than fancy effects.

- **K Desktop Environment**—KDE is probably the second most popular desktop environment for Linux. It has more bells and whistles than GNOME and offers more integrated applications. KDE is also available with Fedora, RHEL, Ubuntu, and many other Linux systems.

- **Xfce**—The Xfce desktop was one of the first lightweight desktop environments. It is good to use on older or less powerful computers. It is available with RHEL, Fedora, Ubuntu, and other Linux distributions.

- **LXDE**—The Lightweight X11 Desktop Environment (LXDE) was designed to be a fast-performing, energy-saving desktop environment. Often, LXDE is used on less-expensive devices (such as netbook computers) and on live media (such as a live CD or live USB stick). It is the default desktop for the KNOPPIX live CD distribution. Although LXDE is not included with RHEL, you can try it with Fedora or Ubuntu.

GNOME was originally designed to resemble the MAC OS desktop, while KDE was meant to emulate the Windows desktop environment. Because it is the most popular desktop environment, and the one most often used in business Linux systems, most desktop procedures and exercises in this book use the GNOME desktop. Using GNOME, however, still gives you the choice of several different Linux distributions.

Starting with the Fedora GNOME Desktop Live image

A live Linux ISO image is the quickest way to get a Linux system up and running so you can start trying it out. Depending on its size, the image can be burned to a CD, DVD, or USB drive and booted on your computer. With a Linux live image, you can have Linux take over the operation of your computer temporarily, without harming the contents of your hard drive.

If you have Windows installed, Linux just ignores it and uses Linux to control your computer. When you are finished with the Linux live image, you can reboot the computer, pop out the CD or DVD, and go back to running whatever operating system was installed on the hard disk.

To try out a GNOME desktop along with the descriptions in this section, I suggest you get a Fedora Live DVD (as described in Appendix A). Because a live DVD does all its work from the DVD and in memory, it runs slower than an installed Linux system. Also, although you can change files, add software, and otherwise configure your system, by default, the work you do disappears when you reboot, unless you explicitly save that data to your hard drive or external storage.

The fact that changes you make to the live environment go away on reboot is very good for trying out Linux, but not that great if you want an ongoing desktop or server system. For that reason, I recommend that if you have a spare computer, you install Linux permanently on that computer's hard disk to use with the rest of this book (as described in Chapter 9).

After you have a live CD or DVD in hand, do the following to get started:

1. **Get a computer.** If you have a standard PC (32-bit or 64-bit) with a CD/DVD drive and at least 1GB of memory (RAM) and at least a 400-MHz processor, you are ready to start. (Just make sure the image you download matches your computer's architecture—a 64-bit medium does not run on a 32-bit computer.)

2. **Start the live CD/DVD.** Insert the live CD/DVD or USB drive into your computer and reboot your computer. Depending on the boot order set on your computer, the live image might start up directly from the BIOS (the code that controls the computer before the operating system starts).

> **NOTE**
>
> If, instead of booting the live medium, your installed operating system starts up instead, you need to perform an additional step to start the live CD/DVD. Reboot again, and when you see the BIOS screen, look for some words that say something like "Boot Order." The onscreen instructions may say to press the F12 or F1 key. Press that key immediately from the BIOS screen. Next, you should see a screen that shows available selections. Highlight an entry for CD/DVD or USB drive, and press Enter to boot the live image. If you don't see the drive there, you may need to go into BIOS setup and enable the CD/DVD or USB drive there.

3. **Start Fedora.** If the selected drive is able to boot, you see a boot screen. For Fedora, with Start Fedora highlighted, press Enter to start the live medium.

4. **Begin using the desktop.** For Fedora, the live medium lets you choose between installing Fedora or boots directly from the medium to a GNOME 3 desktop.

You can now proceed to the next section, "Using the GNOME 3 Desktop" (which includes information on using GNOME 3 in Fedora, Red Hat Enterprise Linux, and other operating systems). The section following that covers the GNOME 2 desktop.

Using the GNOME 3 Desktop

The GNOME 3 desktop offers a radical departure from its GNOME 2.x counterparts. GNOME 2.x is serviceable, but GNOME 3 is elegant. With GNOME 3, a Linux desktop now appears more like the graphical interfaces on mobile devices, with less focus on multiple mouse buttons and key combinations and more on mouse movement and one-click operations.

Instead of feeling structured and rigid, the GNOME 3 desktop seems to expand as you need it to. As a new application is run, its icon is added to the Dash. As you use the next workspace, a new one opens, ready for you to place more applications.

After the computer boots up

If you booted up a live image, when you reach the desktop, you are assigned as the Live System User for your username. For an installed system, you see the login screen, with user accounts on the system ready for you to select and enter a password. Log in with the username and password you have defined for your system.

Figure 2.1 is an example of the GNOME 3 desktop screen that appears for Fedora. Press the Windows key (or move the mouse cursor to the upper-left corner of the desktop) to toggle between a blank desktop and the Overview screen.

FIGURE 2.1

Starting with the GNOME 3 desktop in Fedora.

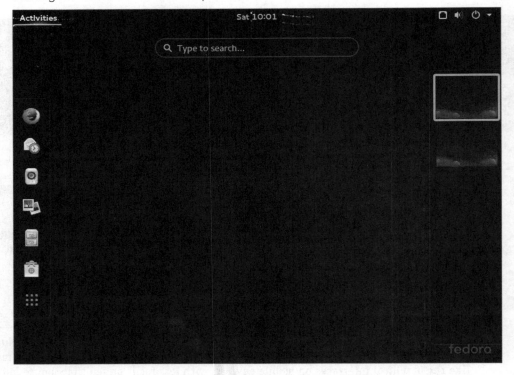

There is very little on the GNOME 3 desktop when you start out. The top bar has the word "Activities" on the left, a clock in the middle, and some icons on the right for such things as adjusting audio volume, checking your network connection, and viewing the name of the current user. The Overview screen is where you can select to open applications, active windows, or different workspaces.

Navigating with the mouse

To get started, try navigating the GNOME 3 desktop with your mouse:

1. **Toggle activities and windows.** Move your mouse cursor to the upper-left corner of the screen, near the Activities button. Each time you move there, your screen changes between showing you the windows you are actively using and a set of available Activities. (This has the same effect as pressing the Windows key.)

2. **Open windows from applications bar.** Click to open some applications from the Dash on the left (Firefox, File Manager, Shotwell, or others). Move the mouse to the upper-left corner again, and toggle between showing all active windows minimized (Overview screen) and showing them overlapping (full-sized). Figure 2.2 shows an example of the miniature windows view.

FIGURE 2.2

Show all windows on the desktop minimized.

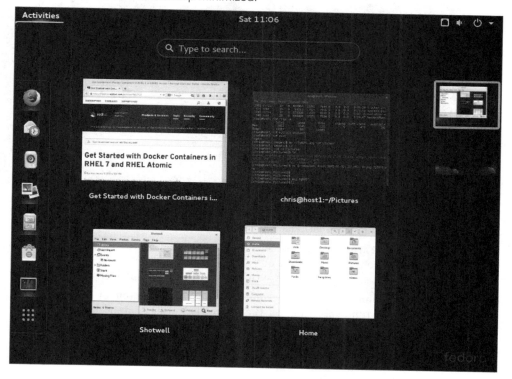

3. **Open applications from Applications list.** From the Overview screen, select the Application button from the bottom of the left column (the button has nine dots in a box). The view changes to a set of icons representing the applications installed on your system, as shown in Figure 2.3.

FIGURE 2.3

Show the list of available applications.

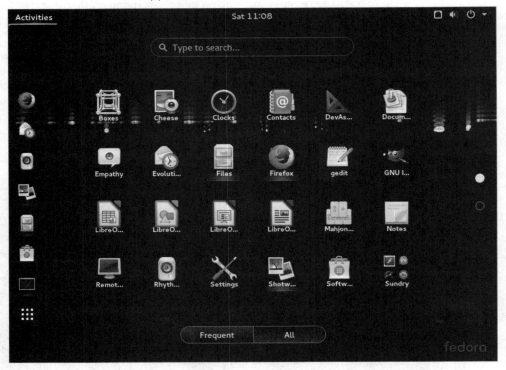

4. **View additional applications**. From the Applications screen, you can change the view of your applications in several ways, as well as launch them in different ways:

   - **Page through**—To see icons representing applications that are not onscreen, use the mouse to click dots on the right to page through applications. If you have a wheel mouse, you can use that instead to scroll the icons.

   - **Frequent**—Select the Frequent button on the bottom of the screen to see often-run applications or the All button to see all applications again.

   - **Launching an application**—To start the application you want, left-click its icon to open the application in the current workspace. Right-click to open a menu that lets you choose to open a New Window, add or remove the application from Favorites (so the application's icon appears on the Dash), or Show Details about the application. Figure 2.4 shows an example of the menu.

5. **Open additional applications**. Start up additional applications. Notice that as you open a new application, an icon representing that application appears in the Dash bar on the left. Here are other ways to start applications:

FIGURE 2.4

Click the middle mouse button to display an application's selection menu.

- **Application icon**—Click any application icon to open that application.
- **Drop Dash icons on workspace**—From the Windows view, you can drag any application icon from the Dash by pressing and holding the left mouse button on it and dragging that icon to any of the miniature workspaces on the right.

6. **Use multiple workspaces.** Move the mouse to the upper-left corner again to show a minimized view of all windows. Notice all the applications on the right jammed into a small representation of one workspace while an additional workspace is empty. Drag and drop a few of the windows to an empty desktop space. Figure 2.5 shows what the small workspaces look like. Notice that an additional empty workspace is created each time the last empty one is used. You can drag and drop the miniature windows to any workspace and then select the workspace to view it.

7. **Use the window menu.** Move the mouse to the upper-left corner of the screen to return to the active workspace (large window view). Right-click the title bar on a window to view the window menu. Try these actions from that menu:

- **Minimize**—Remove window temporarily from view.
- **Maximize**—Expand window to maximum size.
- **Move**—Change window to moving mode. Moving your mouse moves the window. Click to fix the window to a spot.
- **Resize**—Change the window to resize mode. Moving your mouse resizes the window. Click to keep the size.
- **Workspace selections**—Several selections let you use workspaces in different ways. Select Always on Top to make the current window always on top of other windows in the workspace. Select Always on Visible Workspace to always show the window on the workspace that is visible. Or select Move to Workspace Up or Move to Workspace Down to move the window to the workspace above or below, respectively.

FIGURE 2.5

As new desktops are used, additional ones appear on the right.

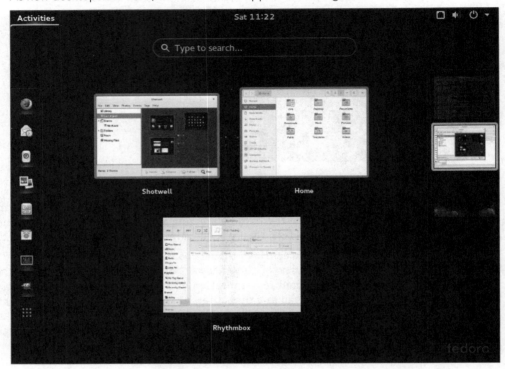

If you don't feel comfortable navigating GNOME 3 with your mouse, or if you don't have a mouse, the next section helps you navigate the desktop from the keyboard.

Navigating with the keyboard

If you prefer to keep your hands on the keyboard, you can work with the GNOME 3 desktop directly from the keyboard in a number of ways, including these:

- **Windows key**—Presses the Windows key on the keyboard. On most PC keyboards, this is the key with the Microsoft Windows logo on it next to the Alt key. This toggles the mini-window (Overview) and active-window (current workspace) views. Many people use this key often.

- **Select different views**—From the Windows or Applications view, hold Ctrl+Alt+Tab to see a menu of the different views (see Figure 2.6). Still holding the Ctrl+Alt keys, press Tab again to highlight one of the following icons from the menu and release to select it:
    - **Top bar**—Keeps the current view.

FIGURE 2.6

Press Ctrl+Alt+Tab to display additional desktop areas to select.

- **Dash**—Highlights the first application in the application bar on the left. Use arrow keys to move up and down that menu, and press Enter to open the highlighted application.

- **Windows**—Selects the Windows view.

- **Applications**—Selects the Applications view.

- **Search**—Highlights the search box. Type a few letters to show only icons for applications that contain the letters you type. When you have typed enough letters to uniquely identify the application you want, press Enter to launch the application.

- **Message tray**—Reveals the bottom message tray. This tray lets you view notifications and open removable media.

- **Select an active window**—Return to any of your workspaces (press the Windows key if you are not already on an active workspace). Press Alt+Tab to see a list of all active windows (see Figure 2.7). Continue to hold the Alt key as you press the Tab key (or right or left arrow keys) to highlight the application you want from the list of active desktop application windows. If an application has multiple windows open, press Alt+` (backtick, located above the Tab key) to choose among those sub-windows. Release the Alt key to select it.

FIGURE 2.7

Press Alt+Tab to select which running application to go to.

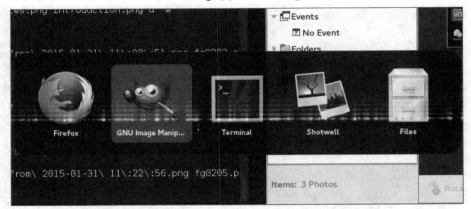

- **Launch a command or application**—From any active workspace, you can launch a Linux command or a graphical application. Here are some examples:
  - **Applications**—From the Overview screen, press Ctrl+Alt+Tab and continue to press Tab until the Applications icon is highlighted; then release Ctrl+Alt. The Applications view appears, with the first icon highlighted. Use the Tab key or arrow keys (up, down, right, and left) to highlight the application icon you want, and press Enter.
  - **Command box**—If you know the name (or part of a name) of a command you want to run, press Alt+F2 to display a command box. Type the name of the command you want to run into the box (try **gnome-calculator** to open a calculator application, for example).
  - **Search box**—From the Overview screen, press Ctrl+Alt+Tab and continue to press Tab until the magnifying glass (Search) icon is highlighted; then release Ctrl+Alt. In the search box now highlighted, type a few letters in an application's name or description (type **scr** to see what you get). Keep typing until the application you want is highlighted (in this case, Screenshot), and press Enter to launch it.
  - **Dash**—From the Overview screen, press Ctrl+Alt+Tab and continue to press Tab until the star (Dash) icon is highlighted; then release Ctrl+Alt. From the Dash, move the up and down arrows to highlight an application you want to launch, and press Enter.
- **Escape**—When you are stuck in an action you don't want to complete, try pressing the Esc key. For example, after pressing Alt+F2 (to enter a command), opening an icon from the top bar, or going to an overview page, pressing Esc returns you to the active window on the active desktop.

I hope you now feel comfortable navigating the GNOME 3 desktop. Next, you can try running some useful and fun desktop applications from GNOME 3.

Setting up the GNOME 3 desktop

Much of what you need GNOME 3 to do for you is set up automatically. However, you need to make a few tweaks to get the desktop the way you want. Most of these setup activities are available from the System Settings window (see Figure 2.8). Open the Settings icon from the Applications list.

FIGURE 2.8

Change desktop settings from the System Settings window.

Here are some suggestions for configuring a GNOME 3 desktop:

- **Configure networking**—A wired network connection is often configured automatically when you boot up your Fedora system. For wireless, you probably have to select your wireless network and add a password when prompted. An icon in the top bar lets you do any wired or wireless network configuration you need to do. Refer to Chapter 14, "Administering Networking," for further information on configuring networking.

- **Personal settings**—Tools in this group let you change your desktop background (Background), use different online accounts (Online Accounts), and set your language and date and currency format based on region (Region and Language) and screen locking (Screen). To change your background, open the System Settings window, select Background, and then select from the available Wallpapers. To add your own Background, download a wallpaper image you like to your Pictures folder, click the Wallpapers box to change it to Pictures folder, and choose the image you want.

- **Bluetooth**—If your computer has Bluetooth hardware, you can enable that device to communicate with other Bluetooth devices (such as a Bluetooth headset or printer).

- **Printers**—Instead of using the System Settings window to configure a printer, refer to Chapter 16, "Configuring a Print server," for information on setting up a printer using the CUPS service.

- **Sound**—Click the Sound settings button to adjust sound input and output devices on your system.

Extending the GNOME 3 desktop

If the GNOME 3 shell doesn't do everything you like, don't despair. You can add extensions to provide additional functionality to GNOME 3. Also, a GNOME Tweak Tool lets you change advanced settings in GNOME 3.

Using GNOME shell extensions

GNOME shell extensions are available to change the way your GNOME desktop looks and behaves. Visit the GNOME Shell Extensions site (`http://extensions.gnome.org`) from your Firefox browser on your GNOME 3 desktop. That site tells you what extensions you have installed and which ones are available for you to install (you must select to allow the site to see those extensions).

Because the extensions page knows what extensions you have and the version of GNOME 3 you are running, it can present only those extensions that are compatible with your system. Many of the extensions help you add back in features from GNOME 2, including these:

- **Applications Menu**—Adds an Applications menu to the top panel, just as it was in GNOME 2.

- **Places Status Indicator**—Adds a systems status menu, similar to the Places menu in GNOME 2, to let you quickly navigate to useful folders on your system.

- **Window list**—Adds a list of active windows to the top panel, similar to the Window list that appeared on the bottom panel in GNOME 2.

To install an extension, simply select the ON button next to the name. Or you can click the extension name from the list to see the extension's page, and click the button on that page from OFF to ON. Click Install when you are asked if you want to download and install the extension. The extension is then added to your desktop.

Figure 2.9 shows an example of the Applications Menu (the GNOME foot icon), Window List (showing several active applications icons), and Places Status Indicator (with folders displayed from a drop-down menu) extensions installed.

FIGURE 2.9

Extensions add features to the GNOME 3 desktop.

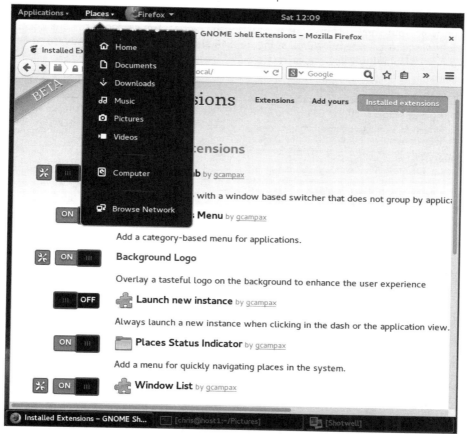

More than 100 GNOME shell extensions are available now, and more are being added all the time. Other popular extensions include Notifications Alert (which alerts you of unread messages), Presentation Mode (which prevents the screensaver from coming on when you are giving a presentation), and Music Integration (which integrates popular music players into GNOME 3 so you are alerted about songs being played).

Because the Extensions site can keep track of your extensions, you can click the Installed extensions button at the top of the page and see every extension that is installed. You can turn the extensions off and on from there and even delete them permanently.

Using the GNOME Tweak Tool

If you don't like the way some of the built-in features of GNOME 3 behave, you can change many of them with the GNOME Tweak Tool. This tool is not installed by default with the Fedora GNOME Live CD, but you can add it by installing the `gnome-tweak-tool` package. (See Chapter 10, "Getting and Managing Software," for information on how to install software packages in Fedora.)

After installation, the GNOME Tweak Tool is available by launching the Advanced Settings icon from your Applications screen. Start with the Desktop category to consider what you might want to change in GNOME 3. Figure 2.10 shows the Tweak Tool (Advanced Settings window) displaying Appearance settings.

FIGURE 2.10

Change desktop settings using the GNOME Tweak Tool (Advanced Settings).

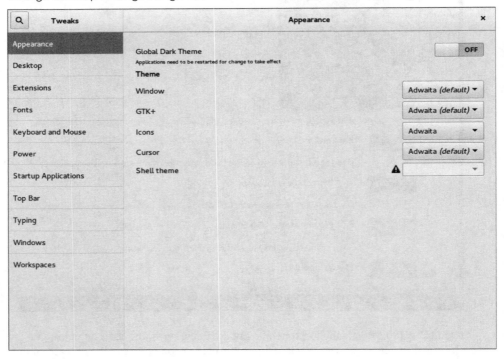

If fonts are too small for you, select the Fonts category and click the plus sign next to the Scaling Factor box to increase the font size. Or change fonts individually for documents, window titles, or monospace fonts.

Under Top Bar settings, you can change how clock information is displayed in the top bar or set whether to show the week number in the calendar. To change the look of the desktop, select the Appearance category and change the Icons theme and GTK+ theme as you like from drop-down boxes.

Starting with desktop applications

The Fedora GNOME 3 desktop live DVD comes with some cool applications you can start using immediately. To use GNOME 3 as your everyday desktop, you should install it permanently to your computer's hard disk and add the applications you need (a word processor, image editor, drawing application, and so on). If you are just getting started, the following sections list some cool applications to try out.

Managing files and folders with Nautilus

To move, copy, delete, rename, and otherwise organize files and folders in GNOME 3, you can use the Nautilus file manager. Nautilus comes with the GNOME desktop and works like other file managers you may use in Windows or Mac.

To open Nautilus, click the Files icon from the GNOME Dash or Applications list. Your user account starts with a set of folders designed to hold the most common types of content: Music, Pictures, Videos, and the like. These are all stored in what is referred to as your Home directory. Figure 2.11 shows Nautilus open to a home directory.

FIGURE 2.11

Manage files and folders from the Nautilus window.

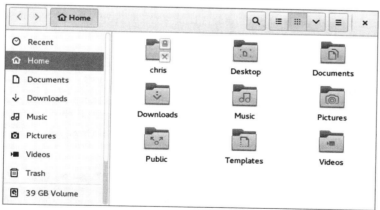

When you want to save files you downloaded from the Internet or created with a word processor, you can organize them into these folders. You can create new folders as needed, drag and drop files and folders to copy and move them, and delete them.

Because Nautilus is not much different from most file managers you have used on other computer systems, this chapter does not go into detail about how to use drag-and-drop and traverse folders to find your content. However, I do want to make a few observations that may not be obvious about how to use Nautilus:

- **Home folder**—You have complete control over the files and folders you create in your Home folder. Most other parts of the filesystem are not accessible to you as a regular user.

- **Filesystem organization**—Although it appears under the name Home, your home folder is actually located in the filesystem under the /home folder in a folder named after your username—for example, /home/liveuser or /home/chris. In the next few chapters, you learn how the filesystem is organized (especially in relation to the Linux command shell).

- **Working with files and folders**—Right-click a file or folder icon to see how you can act on it. For example, you can copy, cut, move to trash (delete), or open any file or folder icon.

- **Creating folders**—To create a new folder, right-click in a folder window and select New Folder. Type the new folder name over the highlighted Untitled Folder, and press Enter to name the folder.

- **Accessing remote content**—Nautilus can display content from remote servers as well as the local filesystem. In Nautilus, select Connect to Server from the file menu. You can connect to a remote server via SSH (secure shell), FTP with login, Public FTP, Windows share, WebDav (HTTP), or Secure WebDav (HTTPS). Add appropriate user and password information as needed, and the content of the remote server appears in the Nautilus window. Figure 2.12 shows an example of a Nautilus window displaying folders from a remote server over SSH protocol (ssh://192.168.0.138).

Installing and managing additional software

The Fedora Live Desktop comes with a web browser (Firefox), a file manager (Nautilus), and a few other common applications. However, there are many other useful applications that, because of their size, just wouldn't fit on a live CD. If you install the live Fedora Workstation to your hard disk (as described in Chapter 9), you almost certainly will want to add some more software.

> **NOTE**
>
> You can try installing software if you are running the live medium. But keep in mind that because writeable space on a live medium uses virtual memory (RAM), that space is limited and can easily run out. Also, when you reboot your system, anything you install disappears.

When Fedora is installed, it is automatically configured to connect your system to the huge Fedora software repository that is available on the Internet. As long as you have an

Internet connection, you can run the Add/Remove software tool to download and install any of thousands of Fedora packages.

FIGURE 2.12

Access remote folders using the Nautilus Connect to Server feature.

Although the entire facility for managing software in Fedora (the yum and rpm features) is described in detail in Chapter 10, "Getting and Managing Software," you can start installing some software packages without knowing much about how the feature works. Begin by going to the applications screen and opening the Software window.

With the Software window open, you can select the applications you want to install by searching (type the name into the Find box) or choosing a category. Each category offers packages sorted by subcategories and featured packages in that category. Figure 2.13 shows the results of a search for the word adventure in the description or name of a package.

You can read a description of each package that comes up in your search. When you are ready, click Install to install the package and any dependent packages needed to make it work.

By searching for and installing some common desktop applications, you should be able to start using your desktop effectively. Refer to Chapter 10 for details on how to add software repositories and use `yum` and `rpm` commands to manage software in Fedora and Red Hat Enterprise Linux.

FIGURE 2.13

Download and install software from the huge Fedora repository.

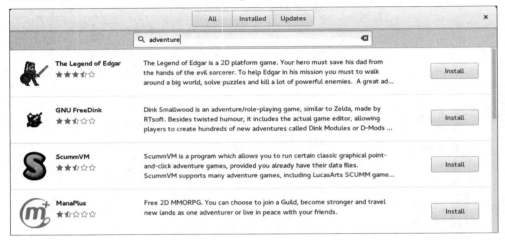

Playing music with Rhythmbox

Rhythmbox is the music player that comes on the Fedora GNOME Live Desktop. You can launch Rhythmbox from the GNOME 3 Dash and immediately play music CDs, podcasts, or Internet radio shows. You can import audio files in WAV and Ogg Vorbis formats, or add plug-ins for MP3 or other audio formats.

Figure 2.14 shows an example of the Rhythmbox window with music playing from an imported audio library.

Here are a few ways you can get started with Rhythmbox:

- **Radio**—Double-click the Radio selection under Library and choose a radio station from the list that appears to the right.
- **Podcasts**—Search for podcasts on the Internet and find the URL for one that interests you. Right-click the Podcasts entry and select New Podcast Feed. Paste or type in the URL to the podcast, and click Add. A list of podcasts from the site you selected appears to the right. Double-click the one you want to listen to.
- **Audio CDs**—Insert an audio CD, and press Play when it appears in the Rhythmbox window. Rhythmbox also lets you rip and burn audio CDs.
- **Audio files**—Rhythmbox can play WAV and Ogg Vorbis files. By adding plug-ins, you can play many other audio formats, including MP3. Because there are patent

issues related to the MP3 format, the ability to play MP3s is not included with Fedora. In Chapter 10, I describe how to get software you need that is not in the repository of your Linux distribution.

FIGURE 2.14

Play music, podcasts, and Internet radio from Rhythmbox.

Plug-ins are available for Rhythmbox to get cover art, show information about artists and songs, add support for music services (such as Last.fm and Magnatune), and fetch song lyrics.

Stopping the GNOME 3 desktop

When you are finished with your GNOME 3 session, select the down arrow button in the upper-right corner of the top bar. From there, you can choose the On/Off button, which allows you to Log Out, Suspend your session, or switch to a different user account without logging out.

Using the GNOME 2 Desktop

The GNOME 2 desktop is the default desktop interface used up through Red Hat Enterprise Linux 6. It is well-known, stable, and perhaps a bit boring.

GNOME 2 desktops provide the more standard menus, panels, icons, and workspaces. If you are using a Red Hat Enterprise Linux system up to RHEL 6 or an older Fedora or Ubuntu distribution, you are probably looking at a GNOME 2 desktop.

This section provides a tour of GNOME 2, along with some opportunities for sprucing it up a bit. Recent GNOME releases include advances in 3D effects (see "3D effects with AIGLX" later in this chapter) and improved usability features that I'll show you as well.

To use your GNOME desktop, you should become familiar with the following components:

- **Metacity (window manager)**—The default window manager for GNOME 2 is Metacity. Metacity configuration options let you control such things as themes, window borders, and controls used on your desktop.

- **Compiz (window manager)**—You can enable this window manager in GNOME to provide 3D desktop effects.

- **Nautilus (file manager/graphical shell)**—When you open a folder (by double-clicking the Home icon on your desktop, for example), the Nautilus window opens and displays the contents of the selected folder. Nautilus can also display other types of content, such as shared folders from Windows computers on the network (using SMB).

- **GNOME panels (application/task launcher)**—These panels, which line the top and bottom of your screen, are designed to make it convenient for you to launch the applications you use, manage running applications, and work with multiple virtual desktops. By default, the top panel contains menu buttons (Applications, Places, and System), desktop application launchers (Evolution email and Firefox web browser), a workspace switcher (for managing four virtual desktops), and a clock. Icons appear in the panel when you need software updates or SELinux detects a problem. The bottom panel has a Show Desktop button, window lists, a trash can, and a workspace switcher.

- **Desktop area**—The windows and icons you use are arranged on the desktop area, which supports drag-and-drop between applications, a desktop menu (right-click to see it), and icons for launching applications. A Computer icon consolidates CD drives, floppy drives, the filesystem, and shared network resources in one place.

GNOME also includes a set of Preferences windows that enable you to configure different aspects of your desktop. You can change backgrounds, colors, fonts, keyboard shortcuts, and other features related to the look and behavior of the desktop. Figure 2.15 shows how the GNOME 2 desktop environment appears the first time you log in, with a few windows added to the screen.

The desktop shown in Figure 2.15 is for Red Hat Enterprise Linux. The following sections provide details on using the GNOME 2 desktop.

Using the Metacity window manager

The Metacity window manager seems to have been chosen as the default window manager for GNOME because of its simplicity. The creator of Metacity refers to it as a "boring window manager for the adult in you" and then goes on to compare other window managers to colorful, sugary cereal, whereas Metacity is characterized as Cheerios.

> **NOTE**
>
> To use 3D effects, your best solution is to use the Compiz window manager, described later in this chapter. You can't do much with Metacity (except get your work done efficiently). You assign new themes to Metacity and change colors and window decorations through the GNOME preferences (described later). Only a few Metacity themes exist, but expect the number to grow.
>
> Basic Metacity functions that might interest you are keyboard shortcuts and the workspace switcher. Table 2.1 shows keyboard shortcuts to get around the Metacity window manager.

FIGURE 2.15

The GNOME 2 desktop environment.

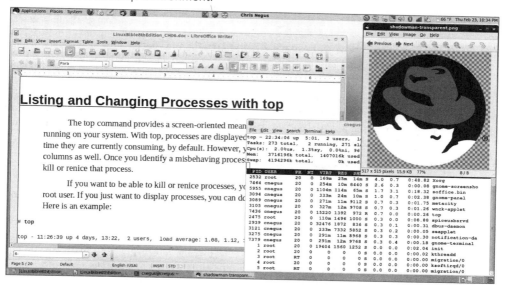

TABLE 2.1 Keyboard Shortcuts

Actions	Keystrokes
Cycle backward, without pop-up icons	Alt+Shift+Esc
Cycle backward among panels	Alt+Ctrl+Shift+Tab
Close menu	Esc

You can use other keyboard shortcuts with the window manager as well. Select System ⇨ Preferences ⇨ Keyboard Shortcuts to see a list of shortcuts, such as the following:

- **Run Dialog**—To run a command to launch an application from the desktop by command name, press Alt+F2. From the dialog box that appears, type the command and press Enter. For example, type **gedit** to run a simple graphical text editor.

- **Lock Screen**—If you want to step away from your screen and lock it, press Ctrl+Alt+L. You need to type your user password to open the screen again.

- **Show Main Menu**—To open an application from the Applications, Places, or System menu, press Alt+F1. Then use the up and down arrow keys to select from the current menu, or use the right and left arrow keys to select from other menus.

- **Print Screen**—Press the Print Screen key to take a picture of the entire desktop. Press Alt+Print Screen to take a picture of the current window.

Another Metacity feature of interest is the workspace switcher. Four virtual workspaces appear in the Workspace Switcher on the GNOME 2 panel. You can do the following with the Workspace Switcher:

- **Choose current workspace**—Four virtual workspaces appear in the Workspace Switcher. Click any of the four virtual workspaces to make it your current workspace.

- **Move windows to other workspaces**—Click any window, each represented by a tiny rectangle in a workspace, to drag and drop it to another workspace. Likewise, you can drag an application from the Window list to move that application to another workspace.

- **Add more workspaces**—Right-click the Workspace Switcher, and select Preferences. You can add workspaces (up to 32).

- **Name workspaces**—Right-click the Workspace Switcher, and select Preferences. Click in the Workspaces pane to change names of workspaces to any names you choose.

You can view and change information about Metacity controls and settings using the gconf-editor window (type gconf-editor from a Terminal window). As the window says, it is not the recommended way to change preferences, so when possible, you should change the desktop through GNOME 2 preferences. However, gconf-editor is a good way to see descriptions of each Metacity feature.

From the gconf-editor window, select apps ⇨ metacity, and choose from general, global_keybindings, keybindings_commands, window_keybindings, and workspace_names. Click each key to see its value, along with short and long descriptions of the key.

Changing GNOME's appearance

You can change the general look of your GNOME desktop by selecting System ⇨ Preferences ⇨ Appearance. From the Appearance Preferences window, select from three tabs:

- **Theme**—Entire themes are available for the GNOME 2 desktop that change the colors, icons, fonts, and other aspects of the desktop. Several different themes come with the GNOME desktop, which you can simply select from this tab to use. Or click Get more themes online to choose from a variety of available themes.

- **Background**—To change your desktop background, select from a list of backgrounds on this tab to have the one you choose immediately take effect. To add a different background, put the background you want on your system (perhaps download one by selecting Get more backgrounds online and downloading it to your Pictures folder). Then click Add, and select the image from your Pictures folder.

- **Fonts**—Different fonts can be selected to use by default with your applications, documents, desktop, window title bar, and for fixed width.

Using the GNOME panels

The GNOME panels are placed on the top and bottom of the GNOME desktop. From those panels, you can start applications (from buttons or menus), see what programs are active, and monitor how your system is running. You can also change the top and bottom panels in many ways—by adding applications or monitors or by changing the placement or behavior of the panel, for example.

Right-click any open space on either panel to see the Panel menu. Figure 2.16 shows the Panel menu on the top.

FIGURE 2.16

The GNOME Panel menu.

From GNOME's Panel menu, you can choose from a variety of functions, including these:

- **Use the menus**

    - The Applications menu displays most of the applications and system tools you will use from the desktop.

    - The Places menu lets you select places to go, such as the Desktop folder, home folder, removable media, or network locations.

    - The System menu lets you change preferences and system settings, as well as get other information about GNOME.

- **Add to Panel**—Add an applet, menu, launcher, drawer, or button.
- **Properties**—Change the panel's position, size, and background properties.
- **Delete This Panel**—Delete the current panel.
- **New Panel**—Add panels to your desktop in different styles and locations.

You can also work with items on a panel. For example, you can do the following:

- **Move items**—To move an item on a panel, right-click it, select Move, and drag and drop it to a new position.
- **Resize items**—You can resize some elements, such as the Window list, by clicking an edge and dragging it to the new size.
- **Use the Window list**—Tasks running on the desktop appear in the Window list area. Click a task to minimize or maximize it.

The following sections describe some things you can do with the GNOME panel.

Using the Applications and System menus

Click Applications on the panel, and you see categories of applications and system tools that you can select. Click the application you want to launch. To add an item from a menu so that it can launch from the panel, drag and drop the item you want to the panel.

You can add items to your GNOME 2 menus. To do that, right-click any of the menu names and select Edit Menus. The window that appears lets you add or delete menus associated with the Applications and System menus. You can also add items to launch from those menus by selecting New Item and typing the name, command, and comment for the item.

Adding an applet

You can run several small applications, called *applets*, directly on the GNOME panel. These applications can show information you may want to see on an ongoing basis or may just provide some amusement. To see what applets are available and to add applets that you want to your panel, follow these steps:

1. **Right-click an open space in the panel so the Panel menu appears.**
2. **Click Add to Panel.** An Add to Panel window appears.
3. **Select from among several dozen applets, including a clock, dictionary lookup, stock ticker, and weather report.** The applet you select appears on the panel, ready for you to use.

Figure 2.17 shows (from left to right) eyes, system monitor, weather report, terminal, and Wanda the fish.

FIGURE 2.17

Placing applets on the panel makes accessing them easy.

After an applet is installed, right-click it on the panel to see what options are available. For example, select Preferences for the stock ticker, and you can add or delete stocks whose prices you want to monitor. If you don't like the applet's location, right-click it, click Move, slide the mouse until the applet is where you want it (even to another panel), and click to set its location.

If you no longer want an applet to appear on the panel, right-click it, and click Remove From Panel. The icon representing the applet disappears. If you find that you have run out of room on your panel, you can add a new panel to another part of the screen, as described in the next section.

Adding another panel

If you run out of space on the top or bottom panels, you can add more panels to your desktop. You can have several panels on your GNOME 2 desktop. You can add panels that run along the entire bottom, top, or side of the screen. To add a panel, follow these steps:

1. **Right-click an open space in the panel so the Panel menu appears.**
2. **Click New Panel.** A new panel appears on the side of the screen.
3. **Right-click an open space in the new panel, and select Properties.**
4. **From the Panel Properties, select where you want the panel from the Orientation box (Top, Bottom, Left, or Right).**

After you've added a panel, you can add applets or application launchers to it as you did to the default panel. To remove a panel, right-click it and select Delete This Panel.

Adding an application launcher

Icons on your panel represent a web browser and several office productivity applications. You can add your own icons to launch applications from the panel as well. To add a new application launcher to the panel, follow these steps:

1. **Right-click in an open space on the panel.**
2. **Click Add to Panel ⇨ Application Launcher from the menu.** All application categories from your Applications and System menus appear.
3. **Select the arrow next to the category of application you want, and then select Add.** An icon representing the application appears on the panel.

To launch the application you just added, simply click the icon on the panel.

If the application you want to launch is not on one of your menus, you can build a launcher yourself as follows:

1. **Right-click in an open space on the panel.**
2. **Click Add to Panel ⇨ Custom Application Launcher ⇨ Add.** The Create Launcher window appears.
3. **Provide the following information for the application you want to add:**
   - **Type**—Select Application (to launch a regular GUI application) or Application in Terminal. Use Application in Terminal if the application is a character-based or ncurses application. (Applications written using the ncurses library run in a Terminal window but offer screen-oriented mouse and keyboard controls.)
   - **Name**—Choose a name to identify the application (this appears in the tooltip when your mouse is over the icon).
   - **Command**—This identifies the command line that is run when the application is launched. Use the full pathname, plus any required options.
   - **Comment**—Enter a comment describing the application. It also appears when you later move your mouse over the launcher.
4. **Click the Icon box (it might say No Icon), select one of the icons shown, and click OK.** Alternatively, you can browse your filesystem to choose an icon.
5. **Click OK.**

The application should now appear in the panel. Click it to start the application.

> **NOTE**
> Icons available to represent your application are contained in the `/usr/share/pixmaps` directory. These icons are in either `.png` or `.xpm` formats. If there isn't an icon in the directory you want to use, create your own (in one of those two formats) and assign it to the application.

Adding a drawer

A drawer is an icon that you can click to display other icons representing menus, applets, and launchers; it behaves just like a panel. Essentially, any item you can add to a panel you can add to a drawer. By adding a drawer to your GNOME panel, you can include several applets and launchers that together take up the space of only one icon. Click the drawer to show the applets and launchers as if they were being pulled out of a drawer icon on the panel.

To add a drawer to your panel, right-click the panel and select Add to Panel ⇨ Drawer. A drawer appears on the panel. Right-click it, and add applets or launchers to it as you would to a panel. Click the icon again to retract the drawer.

Figure 2.18 shows a portion of the panel with an open drawer that includes an icon for launching a weather report, sticky notes, and a stock monitor.

FIGURE 2.18

Add launchers or applets to a drawer on your GNOME 2 panel.

Changing panel properties

You can change the orientation, size, hiding policy, and background properties of your desktop panels. To open the Panel Properties window that applies to a specific panel, right-click an open space on the panel and choose Properties. The Panel Properties window that appears includes the following values:

- **Orientation**—Move the panel to a different location on the screen by clicking a new position.

- **Size**—Select the size of your panel by choosing its height in pixels (48 pixels by default).

- **Expand**—Select this check box to have the panel expand to fill the entire side, or clear the check box to make the panel only as wide as the applets it contains.

- **AutoHide**—Select whether a panel is automatically hidden (appearing only when the mouse pointer is in the area).

- **Show Hide buttons**—Choose whether the Hide/Unhide buttons (with pixmap arrows on them) appear on the edges of the panel.

- **Arrows on hide buttons**—If you select Show Hide Buttons, you can choose to have arrows on those buttons.

- **Background**—From the Background tab, you can assign a color to the background of the panel, assign a pixmap image, or just leave the default (which is based on the current system theme). Click the Background Image check box if you want to select an Image for the background, and then select an image, such as a tile from /usr/share/backgrounds/tiles or another directory.

> **TIP**
>
> I usually turn on the AutoHide feature and turn off the Hide buttons. Using AutoHide gives you more desktop space to work with. When you move your mouse to the edge where the panel is, the panel pops up—so you don't need Hide buttons.

Adding 3D effects with AIGLX

Several initiatives have made strides in recent years to bring 3D desktop effects to Linux. Ubuntu, openSUSE, and Fedora used AIGLX (http://http://fedoraproject.org/wiki/RenderingProject/aiglx).

The goal of the Accelerated Indirect GLX project (AIGLX) is to add 3D effects to everyday desktop systems. It does this by implementing OpenGL (http://opengl.org) accelerated effects using the Mesa (http://www.mesa3d.org) open source OpenGL implementation.

Currently, AIGLX supports a limited set of video cards and implements only a few 3D effects, but it does offer some insight into the eye candy that is in the works.

If your video card was properly detected and configured, you may be able to simply turn on the Desktop Effects feature to see the effects that have been implemented so far. To turn on Desktop Effects, select System ⇨ Preferences ⇨ Desktop Effects. When the Desktop Effects window appears, select Compiz. (If the selection is not available, install the compiz package.)

Enabling Compiz does the following:

- **Starts Compiz**—Stops the current window manager and starts the Compiz window manager.
- **Enables the Windows Wobble When Moved effect**—With this effect on, when you grab the title bar of the window to move it, the window wobbles as it moves. Menus and other items that open on the desktop also wobble.
- **Enables the Workspaces on a Cube effect**—Drag a window from the desktop to the right or the left, and the desktop rotates like a cube, with each of your desktop workspaces appearing as a side of that cube. Drop the window on the workspace where you want it to go. You can also click the Workspace Switcher applet in the bottom panel to rotate the cube to display different workspaces.

Other nice desktop effects result from using the Alt+Tab keys to tab among different running windows. As you press Alt+Tab, a thumbnail of each window scrolls across the screen as the window it represents is highlighted.

Figure 2.19 shows an example of a Compiz desktop with AIGLX enabled. The figure illustrates a web browser window being moved from one workspace to another as those workspaces rotate on a cube.

The following are some interesting effects you can get with your 3D AIGLX desktop:

FIGURE 2.19

Rotate workspaces on a cube with AIGLX desktop effects enabled.

- **Spin cube**—Hold Ctrl+Alt keys, and press the right and left arrow keys. The desktop cube spins to each successive workspace (forward or back).

- **Slowly rotate cube**—Hold the Ctrl+Alt keys, press and hold the left mouse button, and move the mouse around on the screen. The cube moves slowly with the mouse among the workspaces.

- **Scale and separate windows**—If your desktop is cluttered, hold Ctrl+Alt and press the up arrow key. Windows shrink down and separate on the desktop. Still holding Ctrl+Alt, use your arrow keys to highlight the window you want and release the keys to have that window come to the surface.

- **Tab through windows**—Hold the Alt key, and press the Tab key. You see reduced versions of all your windows in a strip in the middle of your screen, with the current window highlighted in the middle. Still holding the Alt key, press Tab or Shift+Tab to move forward or backward through the windows. Release the keys when the one you want is highlighted.

- **Scale and separate workspaces**—Hold Ctrl+Alt, and press the down arrow key to see reduced images of the workspace shown on a strip. Still holding Ctrl+Alt, use the right and left arrow keys to move among the different workspaces. Release the keys when the workspace you want is highlighted.

- **Send current window to next workspace**—Hold Ctrl+Alt+Shift keys together, and press the left and right arrow keys. The next workspace to the left or right, respectively, appears on the current desktop.
- **Slide windows around**—Press and hold the left mouse button on the window title bar, and then press the left, right, up, or down arrow keys to slide the current window around on the screen.

If you get tired of wobbling windows and spinning cubes, you can easily turn off the AIGLX 3D effects and return to using Metacity as the window manager. Select System ⇨ Preferences ⇨ Desktop Effects again, and toggle off the Enable Desktop Effects button to turn off the feature.

If you have a supported video card, but find that you cannot turn on the Desktop Effects, check that your X server started properly. In particular, make sure that your /etc/X11/ xorg.conf file is properly configured. Make sure that dri and glx are loaded in the Module section. Also, add an extensions section anywhere in the file (typically at the end of the file) that appears as follows:

```
Section "extensions"
 Option "Composite"
EndSection
```

Another option is to add the following line to the /etc/X11/xorg.conf file in the Device section:

```
Option "XAANoOffscreenPixmaps"
```

The XAANoOffscreenPixmaps option improves performance. Check your /var/log/ Xorg.log file to make sure that DRI and AIGLX features were started correctly. The messages in that file can help you debug other problems as well.

Summary

The GNOME desktop environment has become the default desktop environment for many Linux systems, including Fedora and RHEL. The GNOME 3 desktop (now used in Fedora and Red Hat Enterprise Linux 7) is a modern, elegant desktop, designed to match the types of interfaces available on many of today's mobile devices. The GNOME 2 desktop (used through RHEL 6) provides a more traditional desktop experience.

Besides GNOME desktops, you can try out other popular and useful desktop environments. The K Desktop Environment (KDE) offers many more bells and whistles than GNOME and is used by default in several Linux distributions. Netbooks and live CD distributions sometimes use the LXDE or Xfce desktops.

Now that you have a grasp of how to get and use a Linux desktop, it's time to start digging into the more professional administrative interfaces. Chapter 3 introduces you to the Linux command-line shell interface.

Exercises

Use these exercises to test your skill in using a GNOME desktop. You can use either a GNOME 2.*x* (Red Hat Enterprise Linux up until RHEL 6.*x*) or GNOME 3.*x* (Fedora 16 or later or Ubuntu up to 11.10, or later using the Ubuntu GNOME project) desktop. If you are stuck, solutions to the tasks for both the GNOME 2 and GNOME 3 desktops are shown in Appendix B.

1. Obtain a Linux system with either a GNOME 2 or GNOME 3 desktop available. Start the system, and log in to a GNOME desktop.

2. Launch the Firefox web browser, and go to the GNOME home page (`http://gnome.org`).

3. Pick a background you like from the GNOME art site (`http://gnome-look.org/`), download it to your Pictures folder, and select it as your current background.

4. Start a Nautilus File Manager window, and move it to the second workspace on your desktop.

5. Find the image you downloaded to use as your desktop background, and open it in any image viewer.

6. Move back and forth between the workspace with Firefox on it and the one with the Nautilus file manager.

7. Open a list of applications installed on your system, and select an image viewer to open from that list. Use as few clicks or keystrokes as possible.

8. Change the view of the windows on your current workspace to smaller views of those windows you can step through. Select any window you like to make it your current window.

9. From your desktop, using only the keyboard, launch a music player.

10. Take a picture of your desktop, using only keystrokes.

Part II

Becoming a Linux Power User

Using the Shell

IN THIS CHAPTER

Understanding the Linux shell

Using the shell from consoles or terminals

Using commands

Using command history and tab completion

Connecting and expanding commands

Understanding variables and aliases

Making shell settings permanent

Using man pages and other documentation

Before icons and windows took over computer screens, you typed commands to interact with most computers. On UNIX systems, from which Linux was derived, the program used to interpret and manage commands was referred to as the *shell*.

No matter which Linux distribution you are using, you can always count on the fact that the shell is available to you. It provides a way to create executable script files, run programs, work with filesystems, compile computer code, and manage the computer. Although the shell is less intuitive than common graphic user interfaces (GUIs), most Linux experts consider the shell to be much more powerful than GUIs. Shells have been around a long time, and many advanced features that aren't available from the desktop can be accessed by running shell commands.

The Linux shell illustrated in this chapter is called the *bash shell,* which stands for Bourne Again Shell. The name is derived from the fact that bash is compatible with the one of the earliest UNIX shells: the Bourne shell (named after its creator Stephen Bourne, and represented by the sh command).

Although bash is included with most distributions, and considered a standard, other shells are available, including the C shell (csh), which is popular among BSD UNIX users, and the Korn shell (ksh), which is popular among UNIX System V users. Ubuntu uses the dash shell, by default, which is designed to perform faster than the bash shell. Linux also has a tcsh shell (an improved C shell) and an ash shell (another Bourne shell look-alike).

The odds are strong that the Linux distribution you are using has more than one shell installed by default and available for your use. This chapter, however, focuses primarily on the bash shell. That is because the Linux distributions featured in this book, Fedora and Red Hat Enterprise Linux, both use the bash shell by default. The bash shell can also easily be added to Ubuntu.

The following are a few major reasons to learn how to use the shell:

- You will know how to get around any Linux or other UNIX-like system. For example, I can log in to my Red Hat Enterprise Linux web server, my home multi-media server, my home router, or my wife's Mac and explore and use any of those computer systems from a shell. I can even log in and run commands on my Android phone. They all run Linux or similar systems on the inside.

- Special shell features enable you to gather data input and direct data output between commands and the Linux filesystem. To save typing, you can find, edit, and repeat commands from your shell history. Many power users hardly touch a graphical interface, doing most of their work from a shell.

- You can gather commands into a file using programming constructs such as conditional tests, loops, and case statements to quickly do complex operations that would be difficult to retype over and over. Programs consisting of commands that are stored and run from a file are referred to as shell scripts. Most Linux system administrators use shell scripts to automate tasks such as backing up data, monitoring log files, or checking system health.

The shell is a command language interpreter. If you have used Microsoft operating systems, you'll see that using a shell in Linux is similar to—but generally much more powerful than—the interpreter used to run commands in DOS or in the CMD command interface. You can happily use Linux from a graphical desktop interface, but as you grow into Linux you will surely need to use the shell at some point to track down a problem or administer some features.

How to use the shell isn't obvious at first, but with the right help you can quickly learn many of the most important shell features. This chapter is your guide to working with the Linux system commands, processes, and filesystem from the shell. It describes the shell environment and helps you tailor it to your needs.

About Shells and Terminal Windows

There are several ways to get to a shell interface in Linux. Three of the most common are the shell prompt, Terminal window, and virtual console, which you learn more about in the following sections.

To start using this section, boot up your Linux system. On your screen, you should either see a plain-text login prompt similar to the following:

```
Red Hat Enterprise Linux Server release 7.0 (Maipo)
Kernel 3.10.0-121.el7.x86_64 on an X86
joe login:
```

Or you will see a graphical login screen.

In either case, you should log in with a regular user account. If you have a plain-text login prompt, continue to the "Using the shell prompt" section. If you log in through a graphical screen, go to the "Using a terminal window" section to see how to access a shell from the desktop. In either case, you can access more shells as described in the "Using virtual consoles" section.

Using the shell prompt

If your Linux system has no graphical user interface (or one that isn't working at the moment), you will most likely see a shell prompt after you log in. Typing commands from the shell will probably be your primary means of using the Linux system.

The default prompt for a regular user is simply a dollar sign:

```
$
```

The default prompt for the root user is a pound sign (also called a *hash mark*):

```
#
```

In most Linux systems, the $ and # prompts are preceded by your username, system name, and current directory name. For example, a login prompt for the user named jake on a computer named pine with /usr/share/ as the current working directory would appear as

```
[jake@pine share]$
```

You can change the prompt to display any characters you like and even read in pieces of information about your system—for example, you can use the current working directory, the date, the local computer name, or any string of characters as your prompt. To configure your prompt, see the section "Setting your prompt" later in this chapter.

Although a tremendous number of features are available with the shell, it's easy to begin by just typing a few commands. Try some of the commands shown in the remainder of this section to become familiar with your current shell environment.

In the examples that follow, the dollar ($) and pound (#) symbols indicate a prompt. A $ indicates that the command can be run by any user, but a # typically means you should run the command as the root user—many administrative tools require root permission to be able to run them. The prompt is followed by the command that you type (and then press Enter). The lines that follow show the output resulting from the command.

Using a terminal window

With the desktop GUI running, you can open a terminal emulator program (sometimes referred to as a Terminal window) to start a shell. Most Linux distributions make it easy for you to get to a shell from the GUI. Here are two common ways to launch a Terminal window from a Linux desktop:

- **Right-click the desktop.** In the context menu that appears, if you see Open in Terminal, Shells, New Terminal, Terminal Window, Xterm, or some similar item, select it to start a Terminal window. (Some distributions have disabled this feature.)
- **Click the panel menu.** Many Linux desktops include a panel at the top or bottom of the screen from which you can launch applications. For example, in some systems that use the GNOME 2 desktop, you can select Applications ⇨ System Tools ⇨ Terminal to open a Terminal window. In GNOME 3, go to the activities screen, type **Terminal**, and press Enter.

In all cases, you should be able to type a command as you would from a shell with no GUI. Different terminal emulators are available with Linux. In Fedora, Red Hat Enterprise Linux (RHEL), and other Linux distributions that use the GNOME desktop, the default Terminal emulator window is the GNOME Terminal (represented by the gnome-terminal command).

GNOME Terminal supports many features beyond the basic shell. For example, you can cut and paste text to or from a GNOME Terminal window, change fonts, set a title, choose colors or images to use as background, and set how much text to save when text scrolls off the screen.

To try some GNOME Terminal features, start up a Fedora or RHEL system and log in to the desktop. Then follow this procedure:

1. **Select Applications ⇨ Utilities ⇨ Terminal (or go the the Activities screen and type Terminal).** A Terminal window should open on your desktop.
2. **Select Edit ⇨ Profile Preferences.**
3. **On the General tab, uncheck the "Use the system fixed width font" box.**
4. From the Font field, try a different font and select OK. The new font appears in the Terminal window.
5. **Re-select the "Use system fixed width font" box.** This takes you back to the original font.
6. **On the Colors tab, clear the "Use colors from system theme" check box.** From here, you can try some different font and background colors.
7. **Re-select the "Use colors from system theme" box to go back to the default colors.**
8. **Go to the Profile window.** There are other features you may want to experiment with, such as setting how much scrolled data is kept.
9. **Close the Profile window when you are finished.** You are now ready to use your Terminal window.

If you are using Linux from a graphical desktop, you will probably most often access the shell from a Terminal window.

Using virtual consoles

Most Linux systems that include a desktop interface start multiple virtual consoles running on the computer. Virtual consoles are a way to have multiple shell sessions open at once in addition to the graphical interface you are using.

You can switch between virtual consoles by holding the Ctrl and Alt keys and pressing a function key between F1 and F6. For example, in Fedora, press Ctrl+Alt+F1 (or F2, F3, F4, and so on up to F6 on most Linux systems) to display one of seven virtual consoles. The first virtual workspace in Fedora is where the GUI is and the next six virtual consoles are text-based virtual consoles. You can return to the GUI (if one is running) by pressing Ctrl+Alt+F1. (On some systems the GUI runs on the virtual console 5 or 6. So you'd return to the GUI by pressing Ctrl+Alt+F5 or Ctrl+Alt+F6.)

Try it right now. Hold down the Ctrl+Alt keys, and press F3. You should see a plain-text login prompt. Log in using your username and password. Try a few commands. When you are finished, type **exit** to exit the shell. Then press Ctrl+Alt+F1 to return to your graphical desktop interface. You can go back and forth between these graphical consoles as much as you like.

Choosing Your Shell

In most Linux systems, your default shell is the bash shell. To find out what your default login shell is, type the following commands:

```
$ who am i
chris     pts/0          2014-10-21 22:45 (:0.0)
$ grep chris /etc/passwd
chris:x:13597:13597:Chris Negus:/home/chris:/bin/bash
```

The who am i command shows your username, and the grep command (replacing chris with your name) shows the definition of your user account in the /etc/password file. The last field in that entry shows that the bash shell (/bin/bash) is your default shell (the one that starts up when you log in or open a Terminal window).

It's possible, although not likely, that you might have a different default shell set. To try a different shell, simply type the name of that shell (examples include ksh, tcsh, csh, sh, dash, and others, assuming they are installed). You can try a few commands in that shell and type **exit** when you are finished to return to the bash shell.

You might choose to use different shells for the following reasons:

- You are used to using UNIX System V systems (often ksh by default) or Sun Microsystems and other Berkeley UNIX-based distributions (frequently csh by default), and you are more comfortable using default shells from those environments.

- You want to run shell scripts that were created for a particular shell environment, and you need to run the shell for which they were made so you can test or use those scripts from your current shell.

- You simply prefer features in one shell over those in another. For example, a member of my Linux Users Group prefers ksh over bash because he doesn't like the way aliases are used with bash.

Although most Linux users have a preference for one shell or another, when you know how to use one shell, you can quickly learn any of the others by occasionally referring to the shell's man page (for example, type **man bash**). The man pages (described later in the "Getting Information about Commands" section) provide documentation for commands, file formats, and other components in Linux. Most people use bash just because they don't have a particular reason for using a different shell. The rest of this section describes the bash shell.

Bash includes features originally developed for sh and ksh shells in early UNIX systems, as well as some csh features. Expect bash to be the default login shell in most Linux systems you are using, with the exception of some specialized Linux systems (such as some that run on embedded devices) that may require a smaller shell that needs less memory and requires fewer features. Most of the examples in this chapter are based on the bash shell.

> **TIP**
>
> The bash shell is worth knowing not only because it is the default in most installations, but because it is the one you will use with most Linux certification exams.

Running Commands

The simplest way to run a command is to type the name of the command from a shell. From your desktop, open a Terminal window. Then type the following command:

```
$ date
Sat Oct 19 08:04:00 EST 2014
```

Typing the date command, with no options or arguments, causes the current day, month, date, time, time zone, and year to be displayed as just shown. Here are a few other commands you can try:

```
$ pwd
/home/chris
$ hostname
mydesktop
```

```
$ ls
Desktop     Downloads   Pictures   Templates
Documents   Music       Public     Videos
```

The pwd command shows your current working directory. Typing hostname shows your computer's hostname. The ls command lists the files and directories in your current directory. Although many commands can be run by just typing command names, it's more common to type **more** after the command to modify its behavior. The characters and words you can type after a command are called options and arguments.

Understanding command syntax

Most commands have one or more *options* you can add to change the command's behavior. Options typically consist of a single letter, preceded by a hyphen. However, you can group single-letter options together or precede each with a hyphen, to use more than one option at a time. For example, the following two uses of options for the ls command are the same:

```
$ ls -l -a -t
$ ls -lat
```

In both cases, the ls command is run with the -l (long listing), -a (show hidden dot files), and -t options (list by time).

Some commands include options that are represented by a whole word. To tell a command to use a whole word as an option, you typically precede it with a double hyphen (--). For example, to use the help option on many commands, you enter --help on the command line. Without the double hyphen, the letters h, e, l, and p would be interpreted as separate options. (There are some commands that don't follow the double hyphen convention, using a single hyphen before a word, but most commands use double hyphens for word options.)

3

> **NOTE**
>
> You can use the --help option with most commands to see the options and arguments that they support: for example, try typing hostname --help.

Many commands also accept arguments after certain options are entered or at the end of the entire command line. An *argument* is an extra piece of information, such as a filename, directory, username, device, or other item that tells the command what to act on. For example, cat /etc/passwd displays the contents of the /etc/passwd file on your screen. In this case, /etc/passwd is the argument. Usually, you can have as many arguments as you want on the command line, limited only by the total number of characters allowed on a command line.

Sometimes, an argument is associated with an option. In that case, the argument must immediately follow the option. With single-letter options, the argument typically follows after a space. For full-word options, the argument often follows an equal sign (=). Here are some examples:

```
$ ls --hide=Desktop
Documents  Music     Public     Videos
Downloads  Pictures  Templates
```

In the previous example, the `--hide` option tells the `ls` command to not display the file or directory named `Desktop` when listing the contents of the directory. Notice that the equal sign immediately follows the option (no space) and then the argument (again, no space).

Here's an example of a single-letter option that is followed by an argument:

```
$ tar -cvf backup.tar /home/chris
```

In the `tar` example just shown, the options say to create (c) a file (f) named `backup.tar` that includes all the contents of the `/home/chris` directory and its subdirectories and show verbose messages as the backup is created (v). Because `backup.tar` is an argument to the `f` option, `backup.tar` must immediately follow the option.

Here are a few commands you can try out. See how they behave differently with different options:

```
$ ls
Desktop  Documents  Downloads  Music  Pictures  Public  Templates
   Videos
$ ls -a
.                Desktop      .gnome2_private  .lesshst      Public
..               Documents    .gnote           .local        Templates
.bash_history    Downloads    .gnupg           .mozilla      Videos
.bash_logout     .emacs       .gstreamer-0.10  Music
   .xsession-errors
.bash_profile    .esd_auth    .gtk-bookmarks   Pictures      .zshrc
.bashrc          .fsync.log   .gvfs            Pictures
$ uname
Linux
$ uname -a
Linux unused 3.10.0-121.el7.x86_64 #1 SMP Tue Oct 21 10:48:19
   EDT 2014 x86_64 x86_64 x86_64 GNU/Linux
$ date
Tue Oct 21 09:08:38 EST 2014
$ date +'%d/%m/%y'
10/21/14
$ date +'%A, %B %d, %Y'
Tuesday, October 21, 2014
```

The `ls` command, by itself, shows all regular files and directories in the current directory. By adding the `-a`, you can also see the hidden files in the directory (those beginning with a dot). The uname command shows the type of system you are running (Linux). When you add `-a`, you also can see the hostname, kernel release, and kernel version.

The date command has some special types of options. By itself, date simply prints the current day, date, and time as shown above. But the date command supports a special +

format option, which lets you display the date in different formats. Type **date --help** to see different format indicators you can use.

Try the id and who commands to get a feel for your current Linux environment, as described in the following paragraphs.

When you log in to a Linux system, Linux views you as having a particular identity, which includes your username, group name, user ID, and group ID. Linux also keeps track of your login session: It knows when you logged in, how long you have been idle, and where you logged in from.

To find out information about your identity, use the id command as follows:

```
$ id
uid=501(chris) gid=501(chris) groups=105(sales), 7(lp)
```

In this example, the username is chris, which is represented by the numeric user ID (uid) 501. The primary group for chris also is called chris, which has a group ID (gid) of 501. It is normal for Fedora and Red Hat Enterprise Linux users to have the same primary group name as their username. The user chris also belongs to other groups called sales (gid 105) and lp (gid 7). These names and numbers represent the permissions that chris has to access computer resources.

> **NOTE**
>
> Linux distributions that have Security Enhanced Linux (SELinux) enabled, such as Fedora and RHEL, show additional information at the end of the id output. That output might look something like the following:
>
> ```
> context=unconfined_u:unconfined_r:unconfined_t:s0-s0:c0.c1023
> ```
>
> SELinux provides a means of tightly locking down the security of a Linux system. See Chapter 24, "Enhancing Linux Security with SELinux," if you want to learn about SELinux.

You can see information about your current login session by using the who command. In the following example, the -u option says to add information about idle time and the process ID and -H asks that a header be printed:

```
$ who -uH
NAME        LINE    TIME            IDLE    PID    COMMENT
chris       tty1    Jan 13 20:57    .       2013
```

The output from this who command shows that the user chris is logged in on tty1 (which is the first virtual console on the monitor connected to the computer), and his login session began at 20:57 on January 13. The IDLE time shows how long the shell has been open without any command being typed (the dot indicates that it is currently active). PID shows the process ID of the user's login shell. COMMENT would show the name of the remote computer the user had logged in from, if that user had logged in from another computer on the network, or the name of the local X display if that user were using a Terminal window (such as :0.0).

Locating commands

Now that you have typed a few commands, you may wonder where those commands are located and how the shell finds the commands you type. To find commands you type, the shell looks in what is referred to as your path. For commands that are not in your path, you can type the complete identity of the location of the command.

If you know the directory that contains the command you want to run, one way to run it is to type the full, or absolute, path to that command. For example, you run the date command from the /bin directory by typing

```
$ /bin/date
```

Of course, this can be inconvenient, especially if the command resides in a directory with a long pathname. The better way is to have commands stored in well-known directories and then add those directories to your shell's PATH environment variable. The path consists of a list of directories that are checked sequentially for the commands you enter. To see your current path, type the following:

```
$ echo $PATH
/usr/local/bin:/usr/bin:/bin:/usr/local/sbin:/usr/sbin:/sbin:⏎
/home/chris/bin
```

The results show a common default path for a regular Linux user. Directories in the path list are separated by colons. Most user commands that come with Linux are stored in the /bin, /usr/bin, or /usr/local/bin directories. The /sbin and /usr/sbin directories contain administrative commands (some Linux systems don't put those directories in regular users' paths). The last directory shown is the bin directory in the user's home directory (/home/chris/bin).

> **TIP**
>
> If you want to add your own commands or shell scripts, place them in the bin directory in your home directory (such as /home/chris/bin for the user named chris). This directory is automatically added to your path in some Linux systems, although you may need to create that directory or add it to your PATH on other Linux systems. So, as long as you add the command to your bin with execute permission, you can begin using it by simply typing the command name at your shell prompt. To make commands available to all users, add them to /usr/local/bin.

Unlike some other operating systems, Linux does not, by default, check the current directory for an executable before searching the path. It immediately begins searching the path, and executables in the current directory are run only if they are in the PATH variable or you give their absolute (such as /home/chris/scriptx.sh) or relative (for example, ./scriptx.sh) address.

The path directory order is important. Directories are checked from left to right. So, in this example, if there is a command called foo located in both the /bin and /usr/bin directories, the one in /bin is executed. To have the other foo command run, you either type the full path to the command or change your PATH variable. (Changing your PATH and adding directories to it are described later in this chapter.)

Not all the commands you run are located in directories in your PATH variable. Some commands are built into the shell. Other commands can be overridden by creating aliases that define any commands and options that you want the command to run. There are also ways of defining a function that consists of a stored series of commands. Here is the order in which the shell checks for the commands you type:

1. **Aliases.** Names set by the alias command that represent a particular command and a set of options. Type **alias** to see what aliases are set. Often, aliases enable you to define a short name for a long, complicated command. (I describe how to create your own aliases later in this chapter.)

2. **Shell reserved word.** Words reserved by the shell for special use. Many of these are words that you would use in programming-type functions, such as do, while, case, and else. (I cover some of these reserved words in Chapter 7, "Writing Simple Shell Scripts.")

3. **Function.** This is a set of commands that are executed together within the current shell.

4. **Built-in command.** This is a command built into the shell. As a result, there is no representation of the command in the filesystem. Some of the most common commands you will use are shell built-in commands, such as cd (to change directories), echo (to output text to the screen), exit (to exit from a shell), fg (to bring a command running in the background to the foreground), history (to see a list of commands that were previously run), pwd (to list the present working directory), set (to set shell options), and type (to show the location of a command).

5. **Filesystem command.** This command is stored in and executed from the computer's filesystem. (These are the commands that are indicated by the value of the PATH variable.)

To find out where a particular command is taken from, you can use the type command. (If you are using a shell other than bash, use the which command instead.) For example, to find out where the bash shell command is located, type the following:

```
$ type bash
bash is /bin/bash
```

Try these few words with the type command to see other locations of commands: which, case, and return. If a command resides in several locations, you can add the -a option to have all the known locations of the command printed. For example, the command type -a ls should show an aliased and filesystem location for the ls command.

> **TIP**
>
> Sometimes, you run a command and receive an error message that the command was not found or that permission to run the command was denied. If the command was not found, check that you spelled the command correctly and that it is located in your PATH variable. If permission to run the command was denied, the command may be in the PATH variable, but may not be executable. Also remember that case is important, so typing CAT or Cat will not find the cat command.

If a command is not in your PATH variable, you can use the locate command to try to find it. Using locate, you can search any part of the system that is accessible to you (some files are only accessible to the root user). For example, if you wanted to find the location of the chage command, you could type the following:

```
$ locate chage
/usr/bin/chage
/usr/sbin/lchage
/usr/share/man/fr/man1/chage.1.gz
/usr/share/man/it/man1/chage.1.gz
/usr/share/man/ja/man1/chage.1.gz
/usr/share/man/man1/chage.1.gz
/usr/share/man/man1/lchage.1.gz
/usr/share/man/pl/man1/chage.1.gz
/usr/share/man/ru/man1/chage.1.gz
/usr/share/man/sv/man1/chage.1.gz
/usr/share/man/tr/man1/chage.1.gz
```

Notice that locate not only found the chage command, but also found the lchage command and a variety of man pages associated with chage for different languages. The locate command looks all over your filesystem, not just in directories that contain commands.

In the coming chapters, you learn to use additional commands. For now, I want you to become more familiar with how the shell itself works. So I talk next about features for recalling commands, completing commands, using variables, and creating aliases.

Recalling Commands Using Command History

Being able to repeat a command you ran earlier in a shell session can be convenient. Recalling a long and complex command line that you mistyped can save you some trouble. Fortunately, some shell features enable you to recall previous command lines, edit those lines, or complete a partially typed command line.

The *shell history* is a list of the commands that you have entered before. Using the history command in a bash shell, you can view your previous commands. Then using various shell features, you can recall individual command lines from that list and change them however you please.

The rest of this section describes how to do command-line editing, how to complete parts of command lines, and how to recall and work with the history list.

Command-line editing

If you type something wrong on a command line, the bash shell ensures that you don't have to delete the entire line and start over. Likewise, you can recall a previous command line and change the elements to make a new command.

By default, the bash shell uses command-line editing that is based on the emacs text editor. (Type **man emacs** to read about it, if you care to.) If you are familiar with emacs, you probably already know most of the keystrokes described here.

> **TIP**
>
> If you prefer the vi command for editing shell command lines, you can easily make that happen. Add the following line to the .bashrc file in your home directory:
>
> ```
> set -o vi
> ```
>
> The next time you open a shell, you can use vi commands to edit your command lines.

To do the editing, you can use a combination of control keys, meta keys, and arrow keys. For example, Ctrl+F means to hold the Ctrl key, and type f. Alt+F means to hold the Alt key, and type f. (Instead of the Alt key, your keyboard may use a Meta key or the Esc key. On a Windows keyboard, you can use the Windows key.)

To try out a bit of command-line editing, type the following:

```
$ ls /usr/bin | sort -f | less
```

This command lists the contents of the /usr/bin directory, sorts the contents in alphabetical order (regardless of case), and pipes the output to less. The less command displays the first page of output, after which you can go through the rest of the output a line (press Enter) or a page (press spacebar) at a time. Simply press **q** when you are finished. Now, suppose you want to change /usr/bin to /bin. You can use the following steps to change the command:

1. **Press the up arrow (↑) key.** This displays the most recent command from your shell history.
2. **Press Ctrl+A.** This moves the cursor to the beginning of the command line.
3. **Press Ctrl+F or the right arrow (→) key.** Repeat this command a few times to position the cursor under the first slash (/).
4. **Press Ctrl+D.** Type this command four times to delete /usr from the line.
5. **Press Enter.** This executes the command line.

As you edit a command line, at any point you can type regular characters to add those characters to the command line. The characters appear at the location of your text cursor. You can use right → and left ← arrows to move the cursor from one end to the other on the command line. You can also press the up ↑ and down ↓ arrow keys to step through previous commands in the history list to select a command line for editing. (See the "Command-line recall" section for details on how to recall commands from the history list.)

You can use many keystrokes to edit your command lines. Table 3.1 lists the keystrokes that you can use to move around the command line.

TABLE 3.1 **Keystrokes for Navigating Command Lines**

Keystroke	Full Name	Meaning
Ctrl+F	Character forward	Go forward one character.
Ctrl+B	Character backward	Go backward one character.
Alt+F	Word forward	Go forward one word.
Alt+B	Word backward	Go backward one word.
Ctrl+A	Beginning of line	Go to the beginning of the current line.
Ctrl+E	End of line	Go to the end of the line.
Ctrl+L	Clear screen	Clear screen and leave line at the top of the screen.

The keystrokes in Table 3.2 can be used to edit command lines.

TABLE 3.2 **Keystrokes for Editing Command Lines**

Keystroke	Full Name	Meaning
Ctrl+D	Delete current	Delete the current character.
Backspace	Delete previous	Delete the previous character.
Ctrl+T	Transpose character	Switch positions of current and previous characters.
Alt+T	Transpose words	Switch positions of current and previous words.
Alt+U	Uppercase word	Change the current word to uppercase.
Alt+L	Lowercase word	Change the current word to lowercase.
Alt+C	Capitalize word	Change the current word to an initial capital.
Ctrl+V	Insert special character	Add a special character. For example, to add a Tab character, press Ctrl+V+Tab.

Use the keystrokes in Table 3.3 to cut and paste text on a command line.

TABLE 3.3 Keystrokes for Cutting and Pasting Text from within Command Lines

Keystroke	Full Name	Meaning
Ctrl+K	Cut end of line	Cut text to the end of the line.
Ctrl+U	Cut beginning of line	Cut text to the beginning of the line.
Ctrl+W	Cut previous word	Cut the word located behind the cursor.
Alt+D	Cut next word	Cut the word following the cursor.
Ctrl+Y	Paste recent text	Paste most recently cut text.
Alt+Y	Paste earlier text	Rotate back to previously cut text and paste it.
Ctrl+C	Delete whole line	Delete the entire line.

Command-line completion

To save you a few keystrokes, the bash shell offers several different ways of completing partially typed values. To attempt to complete a value, type the first few characters and press Tab. Here are some of the values you can type partially from a bash shell:

- **Command, alias, or function**—If the text you type begins with regular characters, the shell tries to complete the text with a command, alias, or function name.

- **Variable**—If the text you type begins with a dollar sign ($), the shell completes the text with a variable from the current shell.

- **Username**—If the text you type begins with a tilde (~), the shell completes the text with a username. As a result, ~*username* indicates the home directory of the named user.

- **Hostname**—If the text you type begins with the at symbol (@), the shell completes the text with a hostname taken from the /etc/hosts file.

> **TIP**
>
> To add hostnames from an additional file, you can set the HOSTFILE variable to the name of that file. The file must be in the same format as /etc/hosts.

Here are a few examples of command completion. (When you see *<Tab>*, it means to press the Tab key on your keyboard.) Type the following:

```
$ echo $OS<Tab>
$ cd ~ro<Tab>
$ fing<Tab>
```

The first example causes $OS to expand to the $OSTYPE variable. In the next example, ~ro expands to the root user's home directory (~root/). Next, fing expands to the finger command.

Pressing Tab twice offers some wonderful possibilities. Sometimes, several possible completions for the string of characters you have entered are available. In those cases, you can check the possible ways text can be expanded by pressing Tab twice at the point where you want to do completion.

The following shows the result you would get if you checked for possible completions on $P:

```
$ echo $P<Tab><Tab>
$PATH $PPID $PS1 $PS2 $PS4 $PWD
$ echo $P
```

In this case, there are six possible variables that begin with $P. After possibilities are displayed, the original command line returns, ready for you to complete it as you choose. For example, if you typed another P and pressed Tab again, the command line would be completed with $PPID (the only unique possibility).

Command-line recall

After you type a command line, the entire command line is saved in your shell's history list. The list is stored in the current shell until you exit the shell. After that, it is written to a history file, from which any command can be recalled to run again at your next session. After a command is recalled, you can modify the command line, as described earlier.

To view your history list, use the history command. Type the command without options or followed by a number to list that many of the most recent commands. For example:

```
$ history 8
 382 date
 383 ls /usr/bin | sort -a | more
 384 man sort
 385 cd /usr/local/bin
 386 man more
 387 useradd -m /home/chris -u 101 chris
 388 passwd chris
 389 history 8
```

A number precedes each command line in the list. You can recall one of those commands using an exclamation point (!). Keep in mind that when using an exclamation point, the command runs blind, without presenting an opportunity to confirm the command you're referencing. There are several ways to run a command immediately from this list, including the following:

- !*n*—Run command number. Replace the n with the number of the command line and that line is run. For example, here's how to repeat the `date` command shown as command number 382 in the preceding history listing:

```
$ !382
dateWed Oct 29 21:30:06 PDT 2014
```

- !!—Run previous command. Runs the previous command line. Here's how you would immediately run that same `date` command:

```
$ !!
dateWed Oct 29 21:30:39 PDT 2014
```

- !?*string?*—Run command containing string. This runs the most recent command that contains a particular string of characters. For example, you can run the `date` command again by just searching for part of that command line as follows:

```
$ !?dat?
dateWed Oct 29 21:32:41 PDT 2014
```

Instead of just running a `history` command line immediately, you can recall a particular line and edit it. You can use the following keys or key combinations to do that, as shown in Table 3.4.

TABLE 3.4 Key Strokes for Using Command History

Key(s)	Function Name	Description
Arrow keys (↑ and ↓)	Step	Press the up and down arrow keys to step through each command line in your history list to arrive at the one you want. (Ctrl+P and Ctrl+N do the same functions, respectively.)
Ctrl+R	Reverse incremental search	After you press these keys, you enter a search string to do a reverse search. As you type the string, a matching command line appears that you can run or edit.
Ctrl+S	Forward incremental search	This is the same as the preceding function but for forward search. (It may not work in all instances.)
Alt+P	Reverse search	After you press these keys, you enter a string to do a reverse search. Type a string and press Enter to see the most recent command line that includes that string.
Alt+N	Forward search	This is the same as the preceding function but for forward search. (It may not work in all instances.)

Another way to work with your history list is to use the `fc` command. Type **fc** followed by a history line number, and that command line is opened in a text editor (vi by default; type **:wq** to save and exit or **:q!** to just exit if you are stuck in vi). Make the changes that you want. When you exit the editor, the command runs. You can also give a range of line numbers (for example, `fc 100 105`). All the commands open in your text editor, and then run one after the other when you exit the editor.

After you close your shell, the history list is stored in the `.bash_history` file in your home directory. Up to 1,000 history commands are stored for you by default.

> **NOTE**
>
> Some people disable the history feature for the root user by setting the `HISTFILE` to `/dev/null` or simply leaving `HISTSIZE` blank. This prevents information about the root user's activities from potentially being exploited. If you are an administrative user with root privileges, you may want to consider emptying your file upon exiting as well for the same reasons. Also, because shell history is stored permanently when the shell exits properly, you can prevent storing a shell's history by killing a shell. For example, to kill a shell with process ID 1234, type `kill -9 1234` from any shell.

Connecting and Expanding Commands

A truly powerful feature of the shell is the capability to redirect the input and output of commands to and from other commands and files. To allow commands to be strung together, the shell uses metacharacters. A *metacharacter* is a typed character that has special meaning to the shell for connecting commands or requesting expansion.

Metacharacters include the pipe character (|), ampersand (&), semicolon (;), right parenthesis ( )), left parenthesis (( ), less than sign (<), and greater than sign (>). The next sections describe how to use metacharacters on the command line to change how commands behave.

Piping between commands

The pipe (|) metacharacter connects the output from one command to the input of another command. This lets you have one command work on some data and then have the next command deal with the results. Here is an example of a command line that includes pipes:

```
$ cat /etc/passwd | sort | less
```

This command lists the contents of the /etc/passwd file and pipes the output to the sort command. The sort command takes the usernames that begin each line of the /etc/passwd file, sorts them alphabetically, and pipes the output to the less command (to page through the output).

Pipes are an excellent illustration of how UNIX, the predecessor of Linux, was created as an operating system made up of building blocks. A standard practice in UNIX was to connect utilities in different ways to get different jobs done. For example, before the days of graphical word processors, users created plain-text files that included macros to indicate formatting. To see how the document really appeared, they would use a command such as the following:

```
$ gunzip < /usr/share/man/man1/grep.1.gz | nroff -c -man | less
```

In this example, the contents of the grep man page (grep.1.gz) are directed to the gunzip command to be unzipped. The output from gunzip is piped to the nroff command to format the man page using the manual macro (-man). The output is piped to the less command to display the output. Because the file being displayed is in plain text, you could have substituted any number of options to work with the text before displaying it. You could sort the contents, change or delete some of the content, or bring in text from other documents. The key is that, instead of all those features being in one program, you get results from piping and redirecting input and output between multiple commands.

Sequential commands

Sometimes, you may want a sequence of commands to run, with one command completing before the next command begins. You can do this by typing several commands on the same command line and separating them with semicolons (;):

```
$ date ; troff -me verylargedocument | lpr ; date
```

In this example, I was formatting a huge document and wanted to know how long it would take. The first command (date) showed the date and time before the formatting started. The troff command formatted the document and then piped the output to the printer. When the formatting was finished, the date and time were printed again (so I knew how long the troff command took to complete).

Another useful command to add to the end of a long command line is mail. You could add the following to the end of a command line.

```
; mail -s "Finished the long command" chris@example.com
```

Then, for example, a mail message is sent to the user you choose after the command completes.

Background commands

Some commands can take a while to complete. Sometimes, you may not want to tie up your shell waiting for a command to finish. In those cases, you can have the commands run in the background by using the ampersand (&).

Text formatting commands (such as nroff and troff, described earlier) are examples of commands that are often run in the background to format a large document. You also might want to create your own shell scripts that run in the background to check continuously for certain events to occur, such as the hard disk filling up or particular users logging in.

3

The following is an example of a command being run in the background:

```
$ troff -me verylargedocument | lpr &
```

Don't close the shell until the process is completed, or that kills the process. Other ways to manage background and foreground processes are described in Chapter 6, "Managing Running Processes."

Expanding commands

With command substitution, you can have the output of a command interpreted by the shell instead of by the command itself. In this way, you can have the standard output of a command become an argument for another command. The two forms of command substitution are $(command) and `command` (backticks, not single quotes).

The command in this case can include options, metacharacters, and arguments. The following is an example of using command substitution:

```
$ vi $(find /home | grep xyzzy)
```

In this example, the command substitution is done before the vi command is run. First, the find command starts at the /home directory and prints out all files and directories below that point in the filesystem. The output is piped to the grep command, which filters out all files except for those that include the string xyzzy in the filename. Finally, the vi command opens all filenames for editing (one at a time) that include xyzzy. (If you run this and are not familiar with vi, you can type :q! to exit the file.)

This particular example is useful if you want to edit a file for which you know the name but not the location. As long as the string is uncommon, you can find and open every instance of a filename existing beneath a point you choose in the filesystem. (In other words, don't use grep from the root filesystem or you'll match and try to edit several thousand files.)

Expanding arithmetic expressions

Sometimes, you want to pass arithmetic results to a command. There are two forms you can use to expand an arithmetic expression and pass it to the shell: $[expression] or $(expression). The following is an example:

```
$ echo "I am $[2015 - 1957] years old."
I am 58 years old.
```

The shell interprets the arithmetic expression first (2015 - 1957) and then passes that information to the echo command. The echo command displays the text, with the results of the arithmetic (58) inserted.

Here's an example of the other form:

```
$ echo "There are $(ls | wc -w) files in this directory."
There are 14 files in this directory.
```

This lists the contents of the current directory (ls) and runs the word count command to count the number of files found (wc -w). The resulting number (14, in this case) is echoed back with the rest of the sentence shown.

Expanding variables

Variables that store information within the shell can be expanded using the dollar sign ($) metacharacter. When you expand an environment variable on a command line, the value of the variable is printed instead of the variable name itself, as follows:

```
$ ls -l $BASH
-rwxr-xr-x 1 root   root   1012808 Oct  8 08:53 /bin/bash
```

Using $BASH as an argument to ls -l causes a long listing of the bash command to be printed.

Using Shell Variables

The shell itself stores information that may be useful to the user's shell session in what are called *variables*. Examples of variables include $SHELL (which identifies the shell you are using), $PS1 (which defines your shell prompt), and $MAIL (which identifies the location of your mailbox).

You can see all variables set for your current shell by typing the set command. A subset of your local variables are referred to as *environment variables*. Environment variables are variables that are exported to any new shells opened from the current shell. Type **env** to see environment variables.

You can type **echo $*VALUE*,** where *VALUE* is replaced by the name of a particular environment variable you want to list. And because there are always multiple ways to do anything in Linux, you can also type **declare** to get a list of the current environment variables and their values along with a list of shell functions.

Besides those that you set yourself, system files set variables that store things such as locations of configuration files, mailboxes, and path directories. They can also store values for your shell prompts, the size of your history list, and type of operating system. You can refer to the value of any of those variables by preceding it with a dollar sign ($) and placing it anywhere on a command line. For example:

```
$ echo $USER
chris
```

This command prints the value of the USER variable, which holds your username (chris). Substitute any other value for USER to print its value instead.

When you start a shell (by logging in via a virtual console or opening a Terminal window), many environment variables are already set. Table 3.5 shows some variables that either are set when you use a bash shell or can be set by you to use with different features.

TABLE 3.5 Common Shell Environment Variables

Variable	Description
BASH	This contains the full pathname of the bash command. This is usually /bin/bash.
BASH_VERSION	This is a number representing the current version of the bash command.
EUID	This is the effective user ID number of the current user. It is assigned when the shell starts, based on the user's entry in the /etc/passwd file.
FCEDIT	If set, this variable indicates the text editor used by the fc command to edit history commands. If this variable isn't set, the vi command is used.
HISTFILE	This is the location of your history file. It is typically located at $HOME/.bash_history.
HISTFILESIZE	This is the number of history entries that can be stored. After this number is reached, the oldest commands are discarded. The default value is 1000.
HISTCMD	This returns the number of the current command in the history list.
HOME	This is your home directory. It is your current working directory each time you log in or type the cd command with any options.
HOSTTYPE	This is a value that describes the computer architecture on which the Linux system is running. For Intel-compatible PCs, the value is i386, i486, i586, i686, or something like i386-linux. For AMD 64-bit machines, the value is x86_64.
MAIL	This is the location of your mailbox file. The file is typically your username in the /var/spool/mail directory.
OLDPWD	This is the directory that was the working directory before you changed to the current working directory.
OSTYPE	This name identifies the current operating system. For Fedora Linux, the OSTYPE value is either linux or linux-gnu, depending on the type of shell you are using. (Bash can run on other operating systems as well.)
PATH	This is the colon-separated list of directories used to find commands that you type. The default value for regular users varies for different distributions, but typically includes the following: /bin:/usr/bin:/usr/local/bin:/usr/bin/X11:/usr/X11R6/bin:~/bin. You need to type the full path or a relative path to a command you want to run that is not in your PATH. For the root user, the value also includes /sbin, /usr/sbin, and /usr/local/sbin.
PPID	This is the process ID of the command that started the current shell (for example, the Terminal window containing the shell).

Variable	Description
PROMPT_ COMMAND	This can be set to a command name that is run each time before your shell prompt is displayed. Setting PROMPT_COMMAND=date lists the current date/time before the prompt appears.
PS1	This sets the value of your shell prompt. There are many items that you can read into your prompt (date, time, username, hostname, and so on). Sometimes a command requires additional prompts, which you can set with the variables PS2, PS3, and so on.
PWD	This is the directory that is assigned as your current directory. This value changes each time you change directories using the cd command.
RANDOM	Accessing this variable causes a random number to be generated. The number is between 0 and 99999.
SECONDS	This is the number of seconds since the time the shell was started.
SHLVL	This is the number of shell levels associated with the current shell session. When you log in to the shell, the SHLVL is 1. Each time you start a new bash command (by, for example, using su to become a new user, or by simply typing bash), this number is incremented.
TMOUT	This can be set to a number representing the number of seconds the shell can be idle without receiving input. After the number of seconds is reached, the shell exits. This security feature makes it less likely for unattended shells to be accessed by unauthorized people. (This must be set in the login shell for it to actually cause the shell to log out the user.)

Creating and using aliases

Using the alias command, you can effectively create a shortcut to any command and options you want to run later. You can add and list aliases with the alias command. Consider the following examples of using alias from a bash shell:

```
$ alias p='pwd ; ls -CF'
$ alias rm='rm -i'
```

In the first example, the letter p is assigned to run the command pwd, and then to run ls -CF to print the current working directory and list its contents in column form. The second example runs the rm command with the -i option each time you type rm. (This is an alias that is often set automatically for the root user. Instead of just removing files, you are prompted for each individual file removal. This prevents you from automatically removing all the files in a directory by mistakenly typing something such as rm *.)

While you are in the shell, you can check which aliases are set by typing the alias command. If you want to remove an alias, type **unalias**. (Remember that if the alias is set in a configuration file, it will be set again when you open another shell.)

Exiting the shell

To exit the shell when you are finished, type **exit** or press Ctrl+D. If you go to the shell from a Terminal window and you are using the original shell from that window, exiting causes the Terminal window to close. If you are at a virtual console, the shell exits and returns you to a login prompt.

If you have multiple shells open from the same shell session, exiting a shell simply returns you to the shell that launched the current shell. For example, the su command opens a shell as a new user. Exiting from that shell simply returns you to the original shell.

Creating Your Shell Environment

You can tune your shell to help you work more efficiently. You can set aliases to create shortcuts to your favorite command lines and environment variables to store bits of information. By adding those settings to shell configuration files, you can have the settings available every time you open a shell.

Configuring your shell

Several configuration files support how your shell behaves. Some of the files are executed for every user and every shell, whereas others are specific to the user who creates the configuration file. Table 3.6 shows the files that are of interest to anyone using the bash shell in Linux. (Notice the use of ~ in the filenames to indicate that the file is located in each user's home directory.)

TABLE 3.6 **Bash Configuration Files**

File	Description
/etc/profile	This sets up user environment information for every user. It is executed when you first log in. This file provides values for your path, in addition to setting environment variables for such things as the location of your mailbox and the size of your history files. Finally, /etc/profile gathers shell settings from configuration files in the /etc/profile.d directory.
/etc/bashrc	This executes for every user who runs the bash shell, each time a bash shell is opened. It sets the default prompt and may add one or more aliases. Values in this file can be overridden by information in each user's ~/.bashrc file.
~/.bash_profile	This is used by each user to enter information that is specific to his or her use of the shell. It is executed only once, when the user logs in. By default, it sets a few environment variables and executes the user's .bashrc file. This is a good place to add environment variables because, once set, they are inherited by future shells.

File	Description
~/.bashrc	This contains the information that is specific to your bash shells. It is read when you log in and also each time you open a new bash shell. This is the best location to add aliases so that your shell picks them up.
~/.bash_logout	This executes each time you log out (exit the last bash shell). By default, it simply clears your screen.

To change the /etc/profile or /etc/bashrc files, you must be the root user. Users can change the information in the $HOME/.bash_profile, $HOME/.bashrc, and $HOME/.bash_logout files in their own home directories.

Until you learn to use the vi editor, described in Chapter 5, "Working with Text Files," you can use a simple editor called nano to edit plain-text files. For example, type the following to edit and add stuff to your $HOME/.bashrc file:

```
$ nano $HOME/.bashrc
```

With the file open in nano, move the cursor down to the bottom of the file (using the down arrow key). Type the line you want (for example, you could type **alias d='date +%D'**). To save the file, press Ctrl+O (the letter O); to quit, press Ctrl+X. The next time you log in or open a new shell, you can use the new alias (in this case, just type **d**). To have the new information you just added to the file available from the current shell, type the following:

```
$ source $HOME/.bashrc
```

The following sections provide ideas about items to add to your shell configuration files. In most cases, you add these values to the .bashrc file in your home directory. However, if you administer a system, you may want to set some of these values as defaults for all your Linux system's users.

Setting your prompt

Your prompt consists of a set of characters that appear each time the shell is ready to accept a command. The PS1 environment variable sets what the prompt contains and is what you interact with most of the time. If your shell requires additional input, it uses the values of PS2, PS3, and PS4.

When your Linux system is installed, often a prompt is set to contain more than just a dollar sign or pound sign. For example, in Fedora or Red Hat Enterprise Linux, your prompt is set to include the following information: your username, your hostname, and the base name of your current working directory. That information is surrounded by brackets and followed by a dollar sign (for regular users) or a pound sign (for the root user). The following is an example of that prompt:

```
[chris@myhost bin]$
```

If you change directories, the bin name would change to the name of the new directory. Likewise, if you were to log in as a different user or to a different host, that information would change.

You can use several special characters (indicated by adding a backslash to a variety of letters) to include different information in your prompt. Special characters can be used to output your terminal number, the date, and the time, as well as other pieces of information. Table 3.7 provides some examples (you can find more on the bash man page).

> **TIP**
>
> If you are setting your prompt temporarily by typing at the shell, you should put the value of PS1 in quotes. For example, you could type `export PS1="[\t \w]\$ "` to see a prompt that looks like this: `[20:26:32 /var/spool]$`.

TABLE 3.7 Characters to Add Information to bash Prompt

Special Character	Description
\\!	This shows the current command history number. This includes all previous commands stored for your username.
\\#	This shows the command number of the current command. This includes only the commands for the active shell.
\\$	This shows the user prompt ($) or root prompt (#), depending on which user you are.
\\W	This shows only the current working directory base name. For example, if the current working directory was /var/spool/mail, this value simply appears as mail.
\\[	This precedes a sequence of nonprinting characters. This can be used to add a terminal control sequence into the prompt for such things as changing colors, adding blink effects, or making characters bold. (Your terminal determines the exact sequences available.)
\\]	This follows a sequence of nonprinting characters.
\\\\	This shows a backslash.
\\d	This displays the day name, month, and day number of the current date—for example, Sat Jan 23.
\\h	This shows the hostname of the computer running the shell.
\\n	This causes a newline to occur.
\\nnn	This shows the character that relates to the octal number replacing nnn.
\\s	This displays the current shell name. For the bash shell, the value would be bash.
\\t	This prints the current time in hours, minutes, and seconds—for example, 10:14:39.
\\u	This prints your current username.
\\w	This displays the full path to the current working directory.

To make a change to your prompt permanent, add the value of PS1 to your .bashrc file in your home directory (assuming that you are using the bash shell). There may already be a PS1 value in that file that you can modify. Refer to the Bash Prompt HOWTO (http://www.tldp.org/HOWTO/Bash-Prompt-HOWTO) for information on changing colors, commands, and other features of your bash shell prompt.

Adding environment variables

You might want to consider adding a few environment variables to your .bashrc file. These can help make working with the shell more efficient and effective:

- TMOUT—This sets how long the shell can be inactive before bash automatically exits. The value is the number of seconds for which the shell has not received input. This can be a nice security feature, in case you leave your desk while you are still logged in to Linux. To prevent being logged off while you are working, you may want to set the value to something like TMOUT=1800 (to allow 30 minutes of idle time). You can use any terminal session to close the current shell after a set number of seconds—for example, TMOUT=30.

- PATH—As described earlier, the PATH variable sets the directories that are searched for commands you use. If you often use directories of commands that are not in your path, you can permanently add them. To do this, add a PATH variable to your .bashrc file. For example, to add a directory called /getstuff/bin, add the following:

```
PATH=$PATH:/getstuff/bin ; export PATH
```

This example first reads all the current path directories into the new PATH ($PATH), adds the /getstuff/bin directory, and then exports the new PATH.

> **CAUTION**
>
> Some people add the current directory to their PATH by adding a directory identified simply as a dot (.) as follows:
>
> ```
> PATH=.:$PATH ; export PATH
> ```
>
> This enables you to run commands in your current directory before evaluating any other command in the path (which people may be used to if they have used DOS). However, the security risk with this procedure is that you could be in a directory that contains a command that you don't intend to run from that directory. For example, a malicious person could put an ls command in a directory that, instead of listing the content of your directory, does something devious. Because of this, the practice of adding the dot to your path is highly discouraged.

- WHATEVER—You can create your own environment variables to provide shortcuts in your work. Choose any name that is not being used and assign a useful value to it. For example, if you do lots of work with files in the /work/time/files/info/memos directory, you could set the following variable:

```
M=/work/time/files/info/memos ; export M
```

You could make that your current directory by typing cd $M. You could run a program from that directory called hotdog by typing **$M/hotdog**. You could edit a file from there called bun by typing **vi $M/bun**.

Getting Information about Commands

When you first start using the shell, it can be intimidating. All you see is a prompt. How do you know which commands are available, which options they use, or how to use advanced features? Fortunately, lots of help is available. Here are some places you can look to supplement what you learn in this chapter:

- **Check the PATH.** Type echo **$PATH**. You see a list of the directories containing commands that are immediately accessible to you. Listing the contents of those directories displays most standard Linux commands. For example:

```
$ ls /bin
```

arch	dd	fusermount	loadkeys	mv	rnano
awk	df	gawk	login	nano	rpm
basename	dmesg	gettext	ls	netstat	rvi
bash	dnsdomainname	grep	lsblk	nice	rview
cat	domainname	gtar	lscgroup	nisdomainname	sed
chgrp	echo	gunzip	lssubsys	ping	setfont
chmod	ed	gzip	mail	ping6	setserial
chown	egrep	hostname	mailx	Ops	sh
cp	env	ipcalc	mkdir	pwd	sleep
cpio	ex	kbd_mode	mknod	readlink	sort
csh	false	keyctl	mktemp	red	stty
cut	fgrep	kill	more	redhat_lsb_init	su
dash	find	link	mount	rm	sync
date	findmnt	ln	mountpoint	rmdir	tar

- **Use the help command.** Some commands are built into the shell, so they do not appear in a directory. The help command lists those commands and shows options available with each of them. (Type **help | less** to page through the list.) For help with a particular built-in command, type **help *command***, replacing *command* with the name that interests you. The help command works with the bash shell only.

- **Use --help with the command.** Many commands include a --help option that you can use to get information about how the command is used. For example, if you type **date --help | less**, the output shows not only options, but also time formats you can use with the date command. Other commands simply use a –h option, like fdisk -h.

- **Use the info command.** The info command is another tool for displaying information about commands from the shell. The info command can move among a hierarchy of nodes to find information about commands and other items. Not all commands have information available in the info database, but sometimes more information can be found there than on a man page.

- **Use the man command.** To learn more about a particular command, type **man *command***. (Replace *command* with the command name you want.) A description of the command and its options appears on the screen.

Man pages are the most common means of getting information about commands, as well as other basic components of a Linux system. Each man page falls into one of the categories listed in Table 3.8. As a regular user, you will be most interested in man pages in section 1. As a system administrator, you will also be interested in sections 5 and 8, and occasionally section 4. Programmers will be interested in section 2 and 3 man pages.

3

TABLE 3.8 Manual Page Sections

Section Number	Section Name	Description
1	User Commands	Commands that can be run from the shell by a regular user (typically no administrative privilege is needed)
2	System Calls	Programming functions used within an application to make calls to the kernel
3	C Library Functions	Programming functions that provide interfaces to specific programming libraries (such as those for certain graphical interfaces or other libraries that operate in user space)
4	Devices and Special Files	Filesystem nodes that represent hardware devices (such as terminals or CD drives) or software devices (such as random number generators)
5	File Formats and Conventions	Types of files (such as a graphics or word processing file) or specific configuration files (such as the passwd or group file)

Continues

TABLE 3.8 *(continued)*

Section Number	Section Name	Description
6	Games	Games available on the system
7	Miscellaneous	Overviews of topics such as protocols, filesystems, character set standards, and so on
8	System Administration Tools and Daemons	Commands that require root or other administrative privileges to use

Options to the man command enable you to search the man page database or display man pages on the screen. Here are some examples of man commands and options:

```
$ man -k passwd
...
passwd                    (1)  - update user's authentication tokens
passwd                    (5)  - password file
$ man passwd
$ man 5 passwd
```

Using the -k option, you can search the name and summary sections of all man pages installed on the system. About a dozen man pages include "passwd" in the name or description of a command. Let's say that the two man pages I am interested in are the passwd command (in section 1 of the man pages) and the passwd file (in section 5) man pages. Because just typing **man passwd** displays the section 1 page, I need to explicitly request the section 5 man page if I want to see that instead (**man 5 passwd**).

While you are displaying a man page, you can view different parts of the file using Page Down and Page Up keys (to move a page at a time). Use the Enter key or up and down arrows to move a line at a time. Press the forward slash (/) and type a term to search the document for that term. Press **n** to repeat the search forward or **N** to repeat the search backward. To quit the man page, type **q**.

Summary

To become an expert Linux user, you must be able to use the shell to type commands. This chapter focuses on the bash shell, which is the one that is most commonly used with Linux systems. In this chapter, you learned how commands are structured and how many special features, such as variables, command completion, and aliases are used.

The next chapter describes how to move around the Linux filesystem from the shell command line.

Exercises

Use these exercises to test your knowledge of using the shell. These tasks assume you are running a Fedora or Red Hat Enterprise Linux system (although some tasks work on other Linux systems as well). If you are stuck, solutions to the tasks are shown in Appendix B (although in Linux, there are often multiple ways to complete a task).

1. From your Desktop, switch to the second virtual console and log in to your user account. Run a few commands. Then exit the shell, and return to the desktop.

2. Open a Terminal window, and change the font color to red and the background to yellow.

3. Find the location of the `mount` command and the `tracepath` man page.

4. Type the following three commands, and then recall and change those commands as described:

```
$ cat /etc/passwd
$ ls $HOME
$ date
```

   - Use the command-line recall feature to recall the `cat` command and change /etc/passwd to /etc/group.
   - Recall the `ls` command, determine how to list files by time (using the man page), and add that option to the `ls $HOME` command line.
   - Add format indicators to the `date` command to display the date output as *month/day/year*.

5. Run the following command, typing as few characters as possible (using tab completion):

```
basename /usr/share/doc/.
```

6. Use the `cat` command to list the contents of the /etc/services file and pipe those contents to the `less` command so you can page through it (press **q** to quit when you are finished).

7. Run the `date` command in such a way that the output from that command produces the current day, month, date, and year. Have that read into another command line, resulting in text that appears like the following (your date, of course, will be different): Today is Thursday, December 10, 2015.

8. Using variables, find out what your hostname, username, shell, and home directories are currently set to.

9. Create an alias called `mypass` that displays the contents of the /etc/passwd file on your screen in such a way that it is available every time you log in or open a new shell from your user account.

10. Display the man page for the `mount` system call.

Moving around the Filesystem

The Linux filesystem is the structure in which all the information on your computer is stored. In fact, one of the defining properties of the UNIX systems on which Linux is based is that nearly everything you need to identify on your system (data, commands, symbolic links, devices, and directories) is represented by items in the filesystems. Knowing where things are and understanding how to get around the filesystem from the shell are critical skills in Linux.

In Linux, files are organized within a hierarchy of directories. Each directory can contain files, as well as other directories. You can refer to any file or directory using either a full path (for example, /home/joe/myfile.txt) or a relative path (for example, if /home/joe were your current directory, you could simply refer to the file as myfile.txt).

If you were to map out the files and directories in Linux, it would look like an upside-down tree. At the top is the *root* directory (not to be confused with the root user), which is represented by a single slash (/). Below that is a set of common directories in the Linux system, such as bin, dev, home, lib, and tmp, to name a few. Each of those directories, as well as directories added to the root directory, can contain subdirectories.

Figure 4.1 illustrates how the Linux filesystem is organized as a hierarchy. To demonstrate how directories are connected, the figure shows a /home directory that contains a subdirectory for the user joe. Within the joe directory are the Desktop, Documents, and other subdirectories. To refer to a file called memo1.doc in the memos directory, you can type the full path of /home/joe/Documents/memos/memo1.doc. If your current directory is /home/joe/Documents/memos, refer to the file as simply memo1.doc.

FIGURE 4.1

The Linux filesystem is organized as a hierarchy of directories.

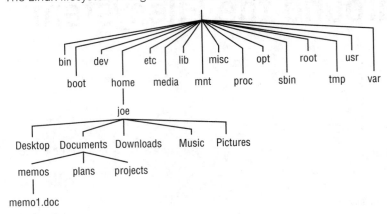

Some of these Linux directories may interest you:

- /bin—Contains common Linux user commands, such as ls, sort, date, and chmod.
- /boot—Has the bootable Linux kernel and boot loader configuration files (GRUB).
- /dev—Contains files representing access points to devices on your systems. These include terminal devices (tty*), floppy disks (fd*), hard disks (hd* or sd*), RAM (ram*), and CD-ROM (cd*). Users can access these devices directly through these device files; however, applications often hide the actual device names from end users.
- /etc—Contains administrative configuration files. Most of these files are plaintext files that can be edited with any text editor if the user has proper permission.
- /home—Contains directories assigned to each regular user with a login account. (The root user is an exception, using /root as his or her home directory.)
- /media—Provides a standard location for automounting devices (removable media in particular). If the medium has a volume name, that name is typically used as the mount point. For example, a USB drive with a volume name of myusb would be mounted on /media/myusb.
- /lib—Contains shared libraries needed by applications in /bin and /sbin to boot the system.
- /mnt—A common mount point for many devices before it was supplanted by the standard /media directory. Some bootable Linux systems still use this directory to mount hard disk partitions and remote filesystems. Many people still use this directory to temporarily mount local or remote filesystems that are not mounted permanently.
- /misc—A directory sometimes used to automount filesystems upon request.
- /opt—Directory structure available to store add-on application software.

- `/proc`—Contains information about system resources.
- `/root`—Represents the root user's home directory. The home directory for root does not reside beneath `/home` for security reasons.
- `/sbin`—Contains administrative commands and daemon processes.
- `/tmp`—Contains temporary files used by applications.
- `/usr`—Contains user documentation, games, graphical files (`X11`), libraries (`lib`), and a variety of other commands and files that are not needed during the boot process. The `/usr` directory is meant for files that don't change after installation (in theory, `/usr` could be mounted read-only).
- `/var`—Contains directories of data used by various applications. In particular, this is where you would place files that you share as an FTP server (`/var/ftp`) or a web server (`/var/www`). It also contains all system log files (`/var/log`) and spool files in `/var/spool` (such as `mail`, `cups`, and `news`). The `/var` directory contains directories and files that are meant to change often. On server computers, it is common to create the `/var` directory as a separate filesystem, using a filesystem type that can be easily expanded.

The filesystems in the DOS and Microsoft Windows operating systems differ from Linux's file structure, as the sidebar "Linux Filesystems versus Windows-Based Filesystems" explains.

Linux Filesystems versus Windows-Based Filesystems

Although similar in many ways, the Linux filesystem has some striking differences from filesystems used in MS-DOS and Windows operating systems. Here are a few:

- In MS-DOS and Windows filesystems, drive letters represent different storage devices (for example, `A:` is a floppy drive and `C:` is a hard disk). In Linux, all storage devices are connected to the filesystem hierarchy. So the fact that all of /usr may be on a separate hard disk or that `/mnt/remote1` is a filesystem from another computer is invisible to the user.
- Slashes, rather than backslashes, are used to separate directory names in Linux. So `C:\home\joe` in a Microsoft system is `/home/joe` in a Linux system.
- Filenames almost always have suffixes in DOS (such as `.txt` for text files or `.doc` for word-processing files). Although at times you can use that convention in Linux, three-character suffixes have no required meaning in Linux. They can be useful for identifying a file type. Many Linux applications and desktop environments use file suffixes to determine the contents of a file. In Linux, however, DOS command extensions such as `.com`, `.exe`, and `.bat` don't necessarily signify an executable. (Permission flags make Linux files executable.)
- Every file and directory in a Linux system has permissions and ownership associated with it. Security varies among Microsoft systems. Because DOS and Microsoft Windows began as single-user systems, file ownership was not built into those systems when they were designed. Later releases added features such as file and folder attributes to address this problem.

4

Using Basic Filesystem Commands

I want to introduce you to a few simple commands for getting around the filesystem to start out. If you want to follow along, log in and open a shell. When you log in to a Linux system and open a shell, you are placed in your home directory. In Linux, most of the files you save and work with will probably be in that directory or subdirectories that you create. Table 4.1 shows commands to create and use files and directories.

TABLE 4.1 **Commands to Create and Use Files**

Command	Result
cd	Changes to another directory
pwd	Prints the name of the current (or present) working directory
mkdir	Creates a directory
chmod	Changes the permission on a file or directory
ls	Lists the contents of a directory

One of the most basic commands you use from the shell is cd. The cd command can be used with no options (to take you to your home directory) or with full or relative paths. Consider the following commands:

```
$ cd /usr/share/
$ pwd
/usr/share
$ cd doc
/usr/share/doc
$ cd
$ pwd
/home/chris
```

The /usr/share option represents the *absolute path* to a directory on the system. Because it begins with a slash (/), this path tells the shell to start at the root of the filesystem and take you to the share directory that exists in the usr directory. The doc option to the cd command said to look for a directory called doc that is relative to the current directory. So that made /usr/share/doc your current directory.

After that, by typing cd alone, you are returned to your home directory. If you ever wonder where you are in the filesystem, the pwd command can help you. Here are a few other interesting cd command options:

```
$ cd ~
$ pwd
/home/chris
$ cd ~/Music
```

```
$ pwd
/home/chris/Music
$ cd ../../../usr
$ pwd
/usr
```

The tilde (~) represents your home directory. So cd ~ takes you there. You can use the tilde to refer to directories relative to your home directory as well, such as /home/chris/Music with ~/Music. Typing a name as an option takes you to a directory below the current directory, but you can use two dots (. .) to go to a directory above the current directory. The example shown takes you up three directory levels (to /), and then takes you into the /usr directory.

The following steps lead you through the process of creating directories within your home directory and moving among your directories, with a mention of setting appropriate file permissions:

1. **Go to your home directory.** To do this, simply type **cd** in a shell and press Enter. (For other ways of referring to your home directory, see the "Identifying Directories" sidebar.)

2. **To make sure that you're in your home directory, type** pwd. When I do this, I get the following response (yours will reflect your home directory):

   ```
   $ pwd
   /home/joe
   ```

3. **Create a new directory called test in your home directory, as follows:**

   ```
   $ mkdir test
   ```

4. **Check the permissions of the directory:**

   ```
   $ ls -ld test
   drwxr-xr-x 2 joe sales 1024 Jan 24 12:17 test
   ```

   This listing shows that test is a directory (d). The d is followed by the permissions (rwxr-xr-x), which are explained later in the "Understanding File Permissions and Ownership" section. The rest of the information indicates the owner (joe), the group (sales), and the date that the files in the directory were most recently modified (Jan 24 at 12:17 p.m.).

NOTE

In Fedora and Red Hat Enterprise Linux, when you add a new user, the user is assigned to a group of the same name by default. For example, in the preceding text, the user joe would be assigned to the group joe. This approach to assigning groups is referred to as the user private group scheme.

For now, type the following:

```
$ chmod 700 test
```

4

This step changes the permissions of the directory to give you complete access and everyone else no access at all. (The new permissions should read rwx------.)

5. **Make the test directory your current directory as follows:**

```
$ cd test
$ pwd
/home/joe/test
```

If you followed along, at this point a subdirectory of your home directory called test is your current working directory. You can create files and directories in the test directory along with the descriptions in the rest of this chapter.

Using Metacharacters and Operators

Whether you are listing, moving, copying, removing, or otherwise acting on files in your Linux system, certain special characters, referred to as metacharacters and operators, help you to work with files more efficiently. Metacharacters can help you match one or more files without completely typing each file name. Operators enable you to direct information from one command or file to another command or file.

Using file-matching metacharacters

To save you some keystrokes and to enable you to refer easily to a group of files, the bash shell lets you use metacharacters. Any time you need to refer to a file or directory, such as to list it, open it, or remove it, you can use metacharacters to match the files you want. Here are some useful metacharacters for matching filenames:

- *—Matches any number of characters.
- ?—Matches any one character.
- [...]—Matches any one of the characters between the brackets, which can include a hyphen-separated range of letters or numbers.

Try out some of these file-matching metacharacters by first going to an empty directory (such as the test directory described in the previous section) and creating some empty files:

```
$ touch apple banana grape grapefruit watermelon
```

The touch command creates empty files. The commands that follow show you how to use shell metacharacters with the ls command to match filenames. Try the following commands to see whether you get the same responses:

```
$ ls a*
apple
$ ls g*
grape grapefruit
$ ls g*t
grapefruit
```

```
$ ls *e*
apple grape grapefruit watermelon
$ ls *n*
banana watermelon
```

The first example matches any file that begins with a (apple). The next example matches any files that begin with g (grape, grapefruit). Next, files beginning with g and ending in t are matched (grapefruit). Next, any file that contains e in the name is matched (apple, grape, grapefruit, watermelon). Finally, any file that contains n is matched (banana, watermelon).

Here are a few examples of pattern matching with the question mark (?):

```
$ ls ????e
apple grape
$ ls g???e*
grape grapefruit
```

The first example matches any five-character file that ends in e (apple, grape). The second matches any file that begins with g and has e as its fifth character (grape, grapefruit).

The following examples use braces to do pattern matching:

```
$ ls [abw]*
apple banana watermelon
$ ls [agw]*[ne]
apple grape watermelon
```

In the first example, any file beginning with a, b, or w is matched. In the second, any file that begins with a, g, or w and also ends with either n or e is matched. You can also include ranges within brackets. For example:

```
$ ls [a-g]*
apple banana grape grapefruit
```

Here, any filenames beginning with a letter from a through g are matched.

Using file-redirection metacharacters

Commands receive data from standard input and send it to standard output. Using pipes (described earlier), you can direct standard output from one command to the standard input of another. With files, you can use less than (<) and greater than (>) signs to direct data to and from files. Here are the file-redirection characters:

- <—Directs the contents of a file to the command. In most cases, this is the default action expected by the command and the use of the character is optional; using less bigfile is the same as less < bigfile.

- >—Directs the standard output of a command to a file. If the file exists, the content of that file is overwritten.

4

- `2>`—Directs standard error (error messages) to the file.
- `&>`—Directs both standard output and standard error to the file.
- `>>`—Directs the output of a command to a file, adding the output to the end of the existing file.

The following are some examples of command lines where information is directed to and from files:

```
$ mail root < ~/.bashrc
$ man chmod | col -b > /tmp/chmod
$ echo "I finished the project on $(date)" >> ~/projects
```

In the first example, the content of the `.bashrc` file in the home directory is sent in a mail message to the computer's root user. The second command line formats the `chmod` man page (using the `man` command), removes extra back spaces (`col -b`), and sends the output to the file `/tmp/chmod` (erasing the previous `/tmp/chmod` file, if it exists). The final command results in the following text being added to the user's project file:

```
I finished the project on Sat Sep 6 13:46:49 EDT 2015
```

Another type of redirection, referred to as *here text* (also called a *here document*), enables you to type text that can be used as standard input for a command. Here documents involve entering two less-than characters (`<<`) after a command, followed by a word. All typing following that word is taken as user input until the word is repeated on a line by itself. Here is an example:

```
$ mail root cnegus rjones bdecker <<thetext
> I want to tell everyone that there will be a 10 a.m.
> meeting in conference room B. Everyone should attend.
>
> -- James
> thetext
$
```

This example sends a mail message to root, cnegus, rjones, and bdecker usernames. The text entered between `<<thetext` and `thetext` becomes the content of the message. A common use of here text is to use it with a text editor to create or add to a file from within a script:

```
/bin/ed /etc/resolv.conf <<resendit
a
nameserver 100.100.100.100
.
w
q
resendit
```

With these lines added to a script run by the root user, the `ed` text editor adds the IP address of a DNS server to the `/etc/resolv.conf` file.

Using brace expansion characters

By using curly braces ({ }), you can expand out a set of characters across filenames, directory names, or other arguments you give commands. For example, if you want to create a set of files such as memo1 through memo5, you can do that as follows:

```
$ touch memo{1,2,3,4,5}
$ ls
memo1 memo2 memo3 memo4 memo5
```

The items that are expanded don't have to be numbers or even single digits. For example, you could use ranges of numbers or digits. You could also use any string of characters, as long as you separate them with commas. Here are some examples:

```
$ touch {John,Bill,Sally}-{Breakfast,Lunch,Dinner}
$ ls
Bill-Breakfast Bill-Lunch John-Dinner Sally-Breakfast Sally-Lunch
Bill-Dinner John-Breakfast John-Lunch Sally-Dinner
$ rm -f {John,Bill,Sally}-{Breakfast,Lunch,Dinner}
$ touch {a..f}{1..5}
$ ls
a1 a3 a5 b2 b4 c1 c3 c5 d2 d4 e1 e3 e5 f2 f4
a2 a4 b1 b3 b5 c2 c4 d1 d3 d5 e2 e4 f1 f3 f5
```

In the first example, the use of two sets of braces means John, Bill, and Sally each have filenames associated with Breakfast, Lunch, and Dinner. If I had made a mistake, I could easily recall the command and change touch to rm -f to delete all the files. In the next example, the use of two dots between letters a and f and numbers 1 and 5 specifies the ranges to be used. Notice the files that were created from those few characters.

Listing Files and Directories

The ls command is the most common command used to list information about files and directories. Many options available with the ls command allow you to gather different sets of files and directories, as well as to view different kinds of information about them.

By default, when you type the ls command, the output shows you all non-hidden files and directories contained in the current directory. When you type ls, however, many Linux systems (including Fedora and RHEL) assign an alias ls to add options. To see if ls is aliased, type the following:

```
$ alias ls
alias ls='ls --color=auto'
```

The --color=auto option causes different types of files and directories to be displayed in different colors. So, returning to the $HOME/test directory created earlier in the chapter, add a couple of different types of files, and then see what they look like with the ls command.

```
$ cd $HOME/test
$ touch scriptx.sh apple
$ chmod 755 scriptx.sh
$ mkdir Stuff
$ ln -s apple pointer_to_apple
$ ls
apple pointer_to_apple scriptx.sh Stuff
```

Although you can't see it in the preceding code example, the directory docs shows up in blue, pointer_to_apple (a symbolic link) appears as aqua, and scriptx.sh (which is an executable file) appears in green. All other regular files show up in black. Typing ls -l to see a long listing of those files can make these different types of files clearer still:

```
$ ls -l
total 4
-rw-rw-r--. 1 joe joe    0 Dec 18 13:38 apple
lrwxrwxrwx. 1 joe joe    5 Dec 18 13:46 pointer_to_apple -> apple
-rwxr-xr-x. 1 joe joe    0 Dec 18 13:37 scriptx.sh
drwxrwxr-x. 2 joe joe 4096 Dec 18 13:38 Stuff
```

As you look at the long listing, notice that the first character of each line shows the type of file. A hyphen (-) indicates a regular file, d indicates a directory, and l (lowercase L) indicates a symbolic link. An executable file (a script or binary file that runs as a command) has execute bits turned on (x). See more on execute bits in the upcoming "Understanding File Permissions and Ownership" section.

You should become familiar with the contents of your home directory next. Use the -l and -a options to ls.

```
$ ls -la /home/joe
total 158
drwxrwxrwx 2   joe    sales    4096 May 12 13:55 .
drwxr-xr-x 3   root   root     4096 May 10 01:49 ..
-rw------- 1   joe    sales    2204 May 18 21:30 .bash_history
-rw-r--r-- 1   joe    sales      24 May 10 01:50 .bash_logout
-rw-r--r-- 1   joe    sales     230 May 10 01:50 .bash_profile
-rw-r--r-- 1   joe    sales     124 May 10 01:50 .bashrc
drw-r--r-- 1   joe    sales    4096 May 10 01:50 .kde
-rw-rw-r-- 1   joe    sales  149872 May 11 22:49 letter

            ^       ^     ^      ^    ^     ^              ^
          col 1   col 2 col 3 col 4 col 5 col 6        col 7
```

Displaying a long list (-l option) of the contents of your home directory shows you more about file sizes and directories. The total line shows the total amount of disk space used by the files in the list (158 kilobytes in this example). Directories such as the current directory (.) and the parent directory (. .)—the directory above the current directory—are noted as directories by the letter d at the beginning of each entry. Each directory begins with a d and each file begins with a dash (-).

The file and directory names are shown in column 7. In this example, a dot (.) represents /home/joe and two dots (..) represent /home—the parent directory of /joe. Most of the files in this example are dot (.) files that are used to store GUI properties (.kde directory) or shell properties (.bash files). The only non-dot file in this list is the one named letter. Column 3 shows the directory or file owner. The /home directory is owned by root, and everything else is owned by the user joe, who belongs to the sales group (groups are listed in column 4).

In addition to the d or -, column 1 on each line contains the permissions set for that file or directory. Other information in the listing includes the number of hard links to the item (column 2), the size of each file in bytes (column 5), and the date and time each file was most recently modified (column 6).

Here are a few other facts about file and directory listings:

- The number of characters shown for a directory (4096 bytes in these examples) reflects the size of the file containing information about the directory. Although this number can grow above 4096 bytes for a directory that contains lots of files, this number doesn't reflect the size of files contained in that directory.

- The format of the time and date column can vary. Instead of displaying "May 12," the date might be displayed as "2011-05-12," depending upon the distribution and the language setting (LANG variable).

- On occasion, instead of seeing the execute bit (x) set on an executable file, you may see an s in that spot instead. With an s appearing within either the owner (-rwsr-xr-x) or group (-rwxr-sr-x) permissions, or both (-rwsr-sr-x), the application can be run by any user, but ownership of the running process is assigned to the application's user/group instead of that of the user launching the command. This is referred to as a *set UID* or *set GID* program, respectively. For example, the mount command has permissions set as -rwsr-xr-x. This allows any user to run mount to list mounted filesystems (although you still have to be root to use mount to actually mount filesystems from the command line, in most cases).

- If a t appears at the end of a directory, it indicates that the *sticky bit* is set for that directory (for example, drwxrwxr-t). By setting the sticky bit on a directory, the directory's owner can allow other users and groups to add files to the directory, but prevent users from deleting each other's files in that directory. With a set GID assigned to a directory, any files created in that directory are assigned the same group as the directory's group. (If you see a capital S or T instead of the execute bits on a directory, it means that the set GID or stick bit permission, respectively, was set, but for some reason the execute bit was not also turned on.)

- If you see a plus sign at the end of the permission bits (for example, -rw-rw-r--+), it means that extended attributes, such as Access Control Lists (ACLs) or SELinux, are set on the file.

4

Identifying Directories

When you need to identify your home directory on a shell command line, you can use the following:

- $HOME—This environment variable stores your home directory name.
- ~—The tilde (~) represents your home directory on the command line.

  You can also use the tilde to identify someone else's home directory. For example, ~joe would be expanded to the joe home directory (probably /home/joe). So, if I wanted to go to the directory /home/joe/test, I could type cd ~joe/test to get there.

Other special ways of identifying directories in the shell include the following:

- .—A single dot (.) refers to the current directory.
- ..—Two dots (..) refer to a directory directly above the current directory.
- $PWD—This environment variable refers to the current working directory.
- $OLDPWD—This environment variable refers to the previous working directory before you changed to the current one. (Typing cd – returns you to the directory represented by $OLDPWD.)

As I mentioned earlier, there are many useful options for the ls command. Return to the $HOME/test directory you've been working in. Here are some examples of ls options. Don't worry if the output doesn't exactly match what is in your directory at this point.

Any file or directory beginning with a dot (.) is considered a hidden file and is not displayed by default with ls. These dot files are typically configuration files or directories that need to be in your home directory, but don't need to be seen in your daily work. The -a lets you see those files.

The -t option displays files in the order in which they were most recently modified. With the -F option, a backslash (/) appears at the end of directory names, an asterisk (*) is added to executable files, and an at sign (@) is shown next to symbolic links.

To show hidden and non-hidden files:

```
$ ls -a
. apple    docs  grapefruit pointer_to_apple .stuff  watermelon
.. banana grape .hiddendir script.sh          .tmpfile
```

To list all files by time most recently modified:

```
$ ls -at
.tmpfile .hiddendir ..            docs    watermelon banana script.sh
.        .stuff     pointer_to_apple grapefruit apple     grape
```

To list files and append file-type indicators:

```
$ ls -F
apple banana docs/ grape grapefruit pointer_to_apple@ script.sh*
    watermelon
```

To avoid displaying certain files or directories when you use `ls`, use the `--hide=` option. In the next set of examples, any file beginning with `g` does not appear in the output. Using a `-d` option on a directory shows information about that directory instead of showing the files and directories the directory contains. The `-R` option lists all files in the current directory as well as any files or directories that are associated with the original directory. The `-S` option lists files by size.

To not include any files beginning with the letter `g` in the list:

```
$ ls --hide=g*
apple banana docs pointer_to_apple script.sh watermelon
```

To list info about a directory instead of the files it contains:

```
$ ls -ld $HOME/test/
drwxrwxr-x. 4 joe joe 4096 Dec 18 22:00 /home/joe/test/
```

To create multiple directory layers (`-p` is needed):

```
$ mkdir -p $HOME/test/documents/memos/
```

To list all files and directories recursively from current directory down:

```
$ ls -R
...
```

To list files by size:

```
$ ls -S
...
```

Understanding File Permissions and Ownership

After you've worked with Linux for a while, you are almost sure to get a `Permission denied` message. Permissions associated with files and directories in Linux were designed to keep users from accessing other users' private files and to protect important system files.

The nine bits assigned to each file for permissions define the access that you and others have to your file. Permission bits for a regular file appear as `-rwxrwxrwx`. Those bits are used to define who can read, write, or execute the file.

NOTE

For a regular file, a dash appears in front of the nine-bit permissions indicator. Instead of a dash, you might see a d (for a directory), l (for a symbolic link), b (for a block device), c (for a character device), s (for a socket), or p (for a named pipe).

Of the nine-bit permissions, the first three bits apply to the owner's permission, the next three apply to the group assigned to the file, and the last three apply to all others. The r stands for read, the w stands for write, and the x stands for execute permissions. If a dash appears instead of the letter, it means that permission is turned off for that associated read, write, or execute bit.

Because files and directories are different types of elements, read, write, and execute permissions on files and directories mean different things. Table 4.2 explains what you can do with each of them.

TABLE 4.2   Setting Read, Write, and Execute Permissions

Permission	File	Directory
Read	View what's in the file.	See what files and subdirectories it contains.
Write	Change the file's content, rename it, or delete it.	Add files or subdirectories to the directory. Remove files or directories from the directory.
Execute	Run the file as a program.	Change to the directory as the current directory, search through the directory, or execute a program from the directory. Access file metadata (file size, time stamps, and so on) of files in that directory.

As noted earlier, you can see the permission for any file or directory by typing the ls -ld command. The named file or directory appears as those shown in this example:

```
$ ls -ld ch3 test
-rw-rw-r-- 1 joe sales 4983 Jan 18 22:13 ch3
drwxr-xr-x 2 joe sales 1024 Jan 24 13:47 test
```

The first line shows that the ch3 file has read and write permission for the owner and the group. All other users have read permission, which means they can view the file but cannot change its contents or remove it. The second line shows the test directory (indicated by the letter d before the permission bits). The owner has read, write, and execute permissions while the group and other users have only read and execute permissions. As a result, the owner can add, change, or delete files in that directory, and everyone else can only read the contents, change to that directory, and list the contents of the directory. (If you had not used the -d options to ls, you would have listed files in the test directory instead of permissions of that directory.)

Changing permissions with chmod (numbers)

If you own a file, you can use the chmod command to change the permission on it as you please. In one method of doing this, each permission (read, write, and execute) is assigned a number—r=4, w=2, and x=1—and you use each set's total number to establish the permission. For example, to make permissions wide open for yourself as owner, you would set the first number to 7 (4+2+1), and then you would give the group and others read-only permission by setting both the second and third numbers to 4 (4+0+0), so that the final number is 744. Any combination of permissions can result from 0 (no permission) through 7 (full permission).

Here are some examples of how to change permission on a file (named file) and what the resulting permission would be:

The following chmod command results in this permission: rwxrwxrwx

```
# chmod 777 file
```

The following chmod command results in this permission: rwxr-xr-x

```
# chmod 755 file
```

The following chmod command results in this permission: rw-r--r--

```
# chmod 644 file rw-r--r-
```

The following chmod command results in this permission: - - - - - - - - -

```
# chmod 000 file
```

The chmod command also can be used recursively. For example, suppose you wanted to give an entire directory structure 755 permission (rwxr-xr-x), starting at the $HOME/myapps directory. To do that, you could use the -R option, as follows:

```
$ chmod -R 755 $HOME/myapps
```

All files and directories below, and including, the myapps directory in your home directory will have 755 permissions set. Because the numbers approach to setting permission changes all permission bits at once, it's more common to use letters to recursively change permission bits over a large set of files.

Changing permissions with chmod (letters)

You can also turn file permissions on and off using plus (+) and minus (−) signs, respectively, along with letters to indicate what changes and for whom. Using letters, for each file you can change permission for the user (u), group (g), other (o), and all users (a). What you would change includes the read (r), write (w), and execute (x) bits. For example, start with a file that has all permissions open (rwxrwxrwx). Run the following chmod commands using minus sign options. The resulting permissions are shown to the right of each command:

The following chmod command results in this permission: r-xr-xr-x

```
$ chmod a-w file
```

The following chmod command results in this permission: rwxrwxrw-

```
$ chmod o-x file
```

The following chmod command results in this permission: rwx------

```
$ chmod go-rwx file
```

Likewise, the following examples start with all permissions closed (---------). The plus sign is used with chmod to turn permissions on:

The following chmod command results in this permission: rw-------

```
$ chmod u+rw files
```

The following chmod command results in this permission: --x--x--x

```
$ chmod a+x files
```

The following chmod command results in this permission: r-xr-x---

```
$ chmod ug+rx files
```

Using letters to change permission recursively with chmod generally works better than using numbers because you can change bits selectively, instead of changing all permission bits at once. For example, suppose that you want to remove write permission for "other" without changing any other permission bits on a set of files and directories. You could do the following:

```
$ chmod -R o-w $HOME/myapps
```

This example recursively removes write permissions for "other" on any files and directories below the myapps directory. If you had used numbers such as 644, execute permission would be turned off for directories; using 755, execute permission would be turned on for regular files. Using o-w, only one bit is turned off and all other bits are left alone.

Setting default file permission with umask

When you create a file as a regular user, it's given permission rw-rw-r-- by default. A directory is given the permission rwxrwxr-x. For the root user, file and directory permission are rw-r--r-- and rwxr-xr-x, respectively. These default values are determined by the value of umask. Type **umask** to see what your umask value is. For example:

```
$ umask
0002
```

If you ignore the leading zero for the moment, the umask value masks what is considered to be fully opened permissions for a file 666 or a directory 777. The umask value of 002 results in permission for a directory of 775 (rwxrwxr-x). That same umask results in a file permission of 644 (rw-rw-r--). (Execute permissions are off by default for regular files.)

To temporarily change your umask value, run the umask command. Then try creating some files and directories to see how the umask value affects how permissions are set. For example:

```
$ umask 777 ; touch file01 ; mkdir dir01 ; ls -ld file01 dir01
d---------. 2 joe joe 6 Dec 19 11:03 dir01
----------. 1 joe joe 0 Dec 19 11:02 file01
$ umask 000 ; touch file02 ; mkdir dir02 ; ls -ld file02 dir02
drwxrwxrwx. 2 joe joe 6 Dec 19 11:00 dir02/
-rw-rw-rw-. 1 joe joe 0 Dec 19 10:59 file02
$ umask 022 ; touch file03 ; mkdir dir03 ; ls -ld file03 dir03
drwxr-xr-x. 2 joe joe 6 Dec 19 11:07 dir03
-rw-r--r--. 1 joe joe 0 Dec 19 11:07 file03
```

If you want to permanently change your umask value, add a umask command to the .bashrc file in your home directory (near the end of that file). The next time you open a shell, your umask is set to whatever value you chose.

Changing file ownership

As a regular user, you cannot change ownership of files or directories to have them belong to another user. You *can* change ownership as the root user. For example, suppose you created a file called memo.txt, while you were root user, in the user joe's home directory. Here's how you could change it to be owned by joe:

```
# chown joe /home/joe/memo.txt
# ls -l /home/joe/memo.txt
-rw-r--r--. 1 joe root 0 Dec 19 11:23 /home/joe/memo.txt
```

Notice that the chown command changed the user to joe but left the group as root. To change both user and group to joe, you could type the following instead:

```
# chown joe:joe /home/joe/memo.txt
# ls -l /home/joe/memo.txt
-rw-r--r--. 1 joe joe 0 Dec 19 11:23 /home/joe/memo.txt
```

The chown command can be use recursively as well. Using the recursive option (-R) is helpful if you need to change a whole directory structure to ownership by a particular user. For example, if you inserted a USB drive, which is mounted on the /media/myusb directory, and wanted to give full ownership of the contents of that drive to the user joe, you could type the following:

```
# chown -R joe:joe /media/myusb
```

4

Moving, Copying, and Removing Files

Commands for moving, copying, and deleting files are fairly straightforward. To change the location of a file, use the mv command. To copy a file from one location to another, use the cp command. To remove a file, use the rm command. These commands can be used to act on individual files and directories or recursively to act on many files and directories at once. Here are some examples:

```
$ mv abc def
$ mv abc ~
$ mv /home/joe/mymemos/ /home/joe/Documents/
```

The first mv command moves the file abc to the file def in the same directory (essentially renaming it), whereas the second moves the file abc to your home directory (~). The next command moves the mymemos directory (and all its contents) to the /home/joe/Documents directory.

By default, the mv command overwrites any existing files if the file you are moving to exists. However, many Linux systems alias the mv command so that it uses the -i option (which causes mv to prompt you before overwriting existing files). Here's how to check if that is true on your system:

```
$ alias mv
alias mv='mv -i'
```

Here are some examples of using the cp command to copy files from one location to another:

```
$ cp abc def
$ cp abc ~
$ cp -r /usr/share/doc/bash-completion* /tmp/a/
$ cp -ra /usr/share/doc/bash-completion* /tmp/b/
```

The first copy command (cp) copies abc to the new name def in the same directory, whereas the second copies abc to your home directory (~), keeping the name abc. The two recursive (-r) copies copy the bash-completion directory, and all files it contains, first to new /tmp/a/ and /tmp/b/ directories. If you run ls -l on those two directories, you see that for the cp command run with the archive (-a) option, the date/time stamps and permissions are maintained by the copy. Without the -a, current date/time stamps are used and permissions are determined by your unmask.

The cp command typically also is aliased with the -i option, to prevent you from inadvertently overwriting files.

As with the cp and mv commands, rm is also usually aliased to include the -i option. This can prevent the damage that can come from an inadvertent recursive remove (-r) option. Here are some examples of the rm command:

```
$ rm abc
$ rm *
```

The first remove command deletes the abc file; the second removes all the files in the current directory (except that it doesn't remove directories or any files that start with a dot). If you want to remove a directory, you need to use the recursive (-r) option to rm or, for an empty directory, you can use the rmdir command. Consider the following examples:

```
$ rmdir /home/joe/nothing/
$ rm -r /home/joe/bigdir/
$ rm -rf /home/joe/hugedir/
```

The rmdir command in the preceding code only removes the directory (nothing) if it is empty. The rm -r example removes the directory bigdir and all its contents (files and multiple levels of subdirectories) but prompts you before each is removed. By adding the force option (-f), the hugedir directory and all its contents are immediately removed, without prompting.

> ### Caution
>
> When you override the -i option on the mv, cp, and rm commands, you risk removing some (or lots of) files by mistake. Using wildcards (such as *) and no -i makes mistakes even more likely. That said, sometimes you don't want to be bothered to step through each file you delete. You have other options:
>
> - As noted with the -f option, you can force rm to delete without prompting. An alternative is to run rm, cp, or mv with a backslash in front of it (\rm bigdir). The backslash causes any command to run unaliased.
> - Another alternative with mv is to use the -b option. With -b, if a file of the same name exists at the destination, a backup copy of the old file is made before the new file is moved there.

Summary

Commands for moving around the filesystem, copying files, moving files, and removing files are among the most basic commands you need to work from the shell. This chapter covers lots of commands for moving around and manipulating files, as well as commands for changing ownership and permission.

The next chapter describes commands for editing and searching for files. These commands include the vim/vi text editors, the find command and the grep command.

Exercises

Use these exercises to test your knowledge of efficient ways to move around the filesystem and work with files and directories. When possible, try to use shortcuts to type as little as possible to get the desired results. These tasks assume you are running a Fedora or Red Hat Enterprise Linux system (although some tasks work on other Linux systems as well).

If you are stuck, solutions to the tasks are shown in Appendix B (although in Linux, there are often multiple ways to complete a task).

1. Create a directory in your home directory called `projects`. In the `projects` directory, create nine empty files that are named `house1`, `house2`, `house3`, and so on to `house9`. Assuming there are lots of other files in that directory, come up with a single argument to `ls` that would list just those nine files.

2. Make the `$HOME/projects/houses/doors/` directory path. Create the following empty files within this directory path (try using absolute and relative paths from your home directory):

   ```
   $HOME/projects/houses/bungalow.txt
   $HOME/projects/houses/doors/bifold.txt
   $HOME/projects/outdoors/vegetation/landscape.txt
   ```

3. Copy the files `house1` and `house5` to the `$HOME/projects/houses/` directory.

4. Recursively copy the `/usr/share/doc/initscripts*` directory to the `$HOME/projects/` directory. Maintain the current date/time stamps and permissions.

5. Recursively list the contents of the `$HOME/projects/` directory. Pipe the output to the `less` command so you can page through the output.

6. Remove the files `house6`, `house7`, and `house8` without being prompted.

7. Move `house3` and `house4` to the `$HOME/projects/houses/doors` directory.

8. Remove the `$HOME/projects/houses/doors` directory and its contents.

9. Change the permissions on the `$HOME/projects/house2` file so it can be read and written by the user who owns the file, only read by the group, and have no permission for others.

10. Recursively change permissions of the `$HOME/projects/` directory so nobody has write permission to any files or directory beneath that point in the filesystem.

Working with Text Files

IN THIS CHAPTER

Using `vim` and `vi` to edit text files

Searching for files

Searching in files

When the UNIX system, on which Linux was based, was created, most information was managed on the system in plain-text files. Thus, it was critical for users to know how to use tools for searching for and within plain-text files and to be able to change and configure those files.

Today, most configurations of Linux systems can still be done by editing plain-text files. Even when a graphical tool is available for working with a configuration file, the graphical tool rarely provides a way to do everything you might want to do in that file. As a result, you may find a need to use a text editor to configure a file manually. Likewise, some document file types, such as HTML and XML, are also plain-text files that can be edited manually.

Before you can become a full-fledged system administrator, you need to be able to use a plain-text editor. The fact that most professional Linux servers don't even have a graphical interface available makes the need for editing of plain-text configuration files with a non-graphical text editor necessary.

After you know how to edit text files, you still might find it tough to figure out where the files are located that you need to edit. With commands such as `find`, you can search for files based on various attributes (filename, size, modification date, and ownership, to name a few). With the `grep` command, you can search inside text files to find specific search terms.

Editing Files with vim and vi

It's almost impossible to use Linux for any period of time and not need a text editor because, as noted earlier, most Linux configuration files are plain-text files that you will almost certainly need to change manually at some point.

If you are using a GNOME desktop, you can run `gedit` (type `gedit` into the Search box and press Enter, or select Applications ⇨ Accessories ⇨ gedit), which is fairly intuitive for editing text.

You can also run a simple text editor called nano from the shell. However, most Linux shell users use either the vi or emacs command to edit text files.

The advantage of vi or emacs over a graphical editor is that you can use the command from any shell, character terminal, or character-based connection over a network (using telnet or ssh, for example)—no graphical interface is required. They also each contain tons of features, so you can continue to grow with them.

This section provides a brief tutorial on the vi text editor, which you can use to manually edit a text file from any shell. It also describes the improved versions of vi called vim. (If vi doesn't suit you, see the sidebar "Exploring Other Text Editors" for other options.)

The vi editor is difficult to learn at first, but after you know it, you never have to use a mouse or a function key—you can edit and move around quickly and efficiently within files just by using the keyboard.

Exploring Other Text Editors

Dozens of text editors are available for use with Linux. Some alternatives might be in your Linux distribution. You can try them out if you find vi to be too taxing. Here are some of the options:

- nano—This popular, streamlined text editor is used with many bootable Linux systems and other limited-space Linux environments. For example, nano is available to edit text files during a Gentoo Linux install process.

- gedit—The GNOME text editor runs on the desktop.

- jed—This screen-oriented editor was made for programmers. Using colors, jed can highlight code you create so you can easily read the code and spot syntax errors. Use the Alt key to select menus to manipulate your text.

- joe—The joe editor is similar to many PC text editors. Use control and arrow keys to move around. Press Ctrl+C to exit with no save or Ctrl+X to save and exit.

- kate—This nice-looking editor comes in the kdebase package. It has lots of bells and whistles, such as highlighting for different types of programming languages and controls for managing word wrap.

- kedit—This GUI-based text editor comes with the KDE desktop.

- mcedit—In this editor, function keys help you get around, save, copy, move, and delete text. Like jed and joe, mcedit is screen-oriented. It comes in the mc package in RHEL and Fedora.

- nedit—This is an excellent programmer's editor. You need to install the optional nedit package to get this editor.

If you use ssh to log in to other Linux computers on your network, you can use any available text editor to edit files. If you use ssh -X to connect to the remote system, a GUI-based editor pops up on your local screen. When no GUI is available, you need a text editor that runs in the shell, such as vi, jed, or joe.

Starting with vi

Most often, you start `vi` to open a particular file. For example, to open a file called `/tmp/test`, type the following command:

```
$ vi /tmp/test
```

If this is a new file, you should see something similar to the following:

```
❏
~
~
~
~
~
~
"/tmp/test" [New File]
```

A blinking box at the top represents where your cursor is. The bottom line keeps you informed about what is going on with your editing (here, you just opened a new file). In between, there are tildes (~) as filler because there is no text in the file yet. Now, here's the intimidating part: There are no hints, menus, or icons to tell you what to do. To make it worse, you can't just start typing. If you do, the computer is likely to beep at you. (And some people complain that Linux isn't friendly.)

First, you need to know the two main operating modes: command and input. The `vi` editor always starts in command mode. Before you can add or change text in the file, you have to type a command (one or two letters, sometime preceded by an optional number) to tell `vi` what you want to do. Case is important, so use uppercase and lowercase exactly as shown in the examples!

> **NOTE**
>
> On Red Hat Enterprise Linux, Fedora, and other Linux distributions, for regular users the `vi` command is aliased to run `vim`. If you type `alias vi`, you should see `alias vi='vim'`. The first obvious difference between `vi` and `vim` is that any known text file type, such as HTML, C code, or a common configuration file, appears in color. The colors indicate the structure of the file. Other features of `vim` that are not in `vi` include features such as visual highlighting and split-screen mode. By default, the root user doesn't have `vi` aliased to `vim`.

Adding text

To get into input mode, type an input command letter. To begin, type any of the following letters. When you are finished inputting text, press the Esc key (sometimes twice) to return to command mode. Remember the Esc key!

- a—The add command. With this command, you can input text that starts to the *right* of the cursor.
- A—The add at end command. With this command, you can input text starting at the end of the current line.

- i—The insert command. With this command, you can input text that starts to the *left* of the cursor.
- I—The insert at beginning command. With this command, you can input text that starts at the beginning of the current line.
- o—The open below command. This command opens a line below the current line and puts you in insert mode.
- O—The open above command. This command opens a line above the current line and puts you in insert mode.

> **TIP**
>
> When you are in insert mode, `-- INSERT --` appears at the bottom of the screen.

Type a few words, and press Enter. Repeat that a few times until you have a few lines of text. When you're finished typing, press Esc to return to command mode. Now that you have a file with some text in it, try moving around in your text with the keys or letters described in the next section.

> **TIP**
>
> Remember the Esc key! It always places you back into command mode. Remember that sometimes you must press Esc twice. For example, if you type a colon (:) to go into ex mode, you must press Esc twice to return to command mode.

Moving around in the text

To move around in the text, you can use the up, down, right, and left arrows. However, many of the keys for moving around are right under your fingertips when they are in typing position:

- **Arrow keys**—Move the cursor up, down, left, or right in the file one character at a time. To move left and right, you can also use Backspace and the spacebar, respectively. If you prefer to keep your fingers on the keyboard, move the cursor with h (left), l (right), j (down), or k (up).
- **w**—Moves the cursor to the beginning of the next word (delimited by spaces, tabs, or punctuation).
- **W**—Moves the cursor to the beginning of the next word (delimited by spaces or tabs).
- **b**—Moves the cursor to the beginning of the previous word (delimited by spaces, tabs, or punctuation).
- **B**—Moves the cursor to the beginning of the previous word (delimited by spaces or tabs).
- **0 (zero)**—Moves the cursor to the beginning of the current line.
- **$**—Moves the cursor to the end of the current line.

- **H**—Moves the cursor to the upper-left corner of the screen (first line on the screen).
- **M**—Moves the cursor to the first character of the middle line on the screen.
- **L**—Moves the cursor to the lower-left corner of the screen (last line on the screen).

Deleting, copying, and changing text

The only other editing you need to know is how to delete, copy, or change text. The x, d, y, and c commands can be used to delete and change text. These can be used along with movement keys (arrows, PgUp, PgDn, letters, and special keys) and numbers to indicate exactly what you are deleting, copying, or changing. Consider the following examples:

- **x**—Deletes the character under the cursor.
- **X**—Deletes the character directly before the cursor.
- *d<?>*—Deletes some text.
- *c<?>*—Changes some text.
- *y<?>*—Yanks (copies) some text.

The <?> after each letter in the preceding list identifies the place where you can use a movement command to choose what you are deleting, changing, or yanking. For example:

- **dw**—Deletes (d) a word (w) after the current cursor position.
- **db**—Deletes (d) a word (b) before the current cursor position.
- **dd**—Deletes (d) the entire current line (d).
- **c$**—Changes (c) the characters (actually erases them) from the current character to the end of the current line ($) and goes into input mode.
- **c0**—Changes (c) (again, erases characters) from the previous character to the beginning of the current line (0) and goes into input mode.
- **cl**—Erases (c) the current letter (l) and goes into input mode.
- **cc**—Erases (c) the line (c) and goes into input mode.
- **yy**—Copies (y) the current line (y) into the buffer.
- **y)**—Copies (y) the current sentence ( )), to the right of the cursor, into the buffer.
- **y}**—Copies (y) the current paragraph (}), to the right of the cursor, into the buffer.

Any of the commands just shown can be further modified using numbers, as you can see in the following examples:

- **3dd**—Deletes (d) three (3) lines (d), beginning at the current line.
- **3dw**—Deletes (d) the next three (3) words (w).
- **5cl**—Changes (c) the next five (5) letters (l) (that is, removes the letters and enters input mode).

5

- `12j`—Moves down (j) 12 lines (12).
- `5cw`—Erases (c) the next five (5) words (w) and goes into input mode.
- `4y)`—Copies (y) the next four (4) sentences ( )).

Pasting (putting) text

After text has been copied to the buffer (by deleting, changing, or yanking it), you can place that text back in your file using the letter p or P. With both commands, the text most recently stored in the buffer is put into the file in different ways.

- `P`—Puts the copied text to the left of the cursor if the text consists of letters or words; puts the copied text above the current line if the copied text contains lines of text.
- `p`—Puts the buffered text to the right of the cursor if the text consists of letters or words; puts the buffered text below the current line if the buffered text contains lines of text.

Repeating commands

After you delete, change, or paste text, you can repeat that action by typing a period (.). For example, with the cursor on the beginning of the name Joe, you type cw and type Jim to change Joe to Jim. You search for the next occurrence of Joe in the file, position the cursor at the beginning of that name, and press a period. The word changes to Jim, and you can search for the next occurrence. You can go through a file this way, pressing n to go to the next occurrence and period (.) to change the word.

Exiting vi

To wrap things up, use the following commands to save or quit the file:

- `ZZ`—Saves the current changes to the file and exits from vi.
- `:w`—Saves the current file but doesn't exit from vi.
- `:wq`—Works the same as ZZ.
- `:q`—Quits the current file. This works only if you don't have any unsaved changes.
- `:q!`—Quits the current file and *doesn't* save the changes you just made to the file.

> **TIP**
>
> If you've really trashed the file by mistake, the :q! command is the best way to exit and abandon your changes. The file reverts to the most recently changed version. So, if you just saved with :w, you are stuck with the changes up to that point. However, despite having saved the file, you can type u to back out of changes (all the way back to the beginning of the editing session if you like) and then save again.

You have learned a few vi editing commands. I describe more commands in the following sections. First, however, consider the following tips to smooth out your first trials with vi:

- **Esc**—Remember that Esc gets you back to command mode. (I've watched people press every key on the keyboard trying to get out of a file.) Esc followed by ZZ gets you out of command mode, saves the file, and exits.

- **u**—Press u to undo the previous change you made. Continue to press u to undo the change before that and the one before that.

- **Ctrl+R**—If you decide you didn't want to undo the previous undo command, use Ctrl+R for Redo. Essentially, this command undoes your undo.

- **Caps Lock**—Beware of hitting Caps Lock by mistake. Everything you type in vi has a different meaning when the letters are capitalized. You don't get a warning that you are typing capitals; things just start acting weird.

- **:!command**—You can run a shell command while you are in vi using :! followed by a shell command name. For example, type :!date to see the current date and time, type :!pwd to see what your current directory is, or type :!jobs to see whether you have any jobs running in the background. When the command completes, press Enter and you are back to editing the file. You could even use this technique to launch a shell (:!bash) from vi, run a few commands from that shell, and then type exit to return to vi. (I recommend doing a save before escaping to the shell, just in case you forget to go back to vi.)

- **Ctrl+G**—If you forget what you are editing, pressing these keys displays the name of the file that you are editing and the current line that you are on at the bottom of the screen. It also displays the total number of lines in the file, the percentage of how far you are through the file, and the column number the cursor is on. This just helps you get your bearings after you've stopped for a cup of coffee at 3 a.m.

Skipping around in the file

Besides the few movement commands described earlier, there are other ways of moving around a vi file. To try these out, open a large file that you can't do much damage to. (Try copying /etc/services to /tmp and opening it in vi.) Here are some movement commands you can use:

- **Ctrl+f**—Pages ahead, one page at a time.
- **Ctrl+b**—Pages back, one page at a time.
- **Ctrl+d**—Pages ahead one-half page at a time.
- **Ctrl+u**—Pages back one-half page at a time.
- **G**—Goes to the last line of the file.
- **1G**—Goes to the first line of the file.
- **35G**—Goes to any line number (35, in this case).

5

Searching for text

To search for the next or previous occurrence of text in the file, use either the slash (/) or the question mark (?) character. Follow the slash or question mark with a pattern (string of text) to search forward or backward, respectively, for that pattern. Within the search, you can also use metacharacters. Here are some examples:

- **/hello**—Searches forward for the word hello.
- **?goodbye**—Searches backward for the word goodbye.
- **/The.*foot**—Searches forward for a line that has the word The in it and also, after that at some point, the word foot.
- **?[pP]rint**—Searches backward for either print or Print. Remember that case matters in Linux, so make use of brackets to search for words that could have different capitalization.

After you have entered a search term, simply type **n** or **N** to search again in the same direction (n) or the opposite direction (N) for the term.

Using ex mode

The vi editor was originally based on the ex editor, which didn't let you work in full-screen mode. However, it did enable you to run commands that let you find and change text on one or more lines at a time. When you type a colon and the cursor goes to the bottom of the screen, you are essentially in ex mode. The following are examples of some of those ex commands for searching for and changing text. (I chose the words Local and Remote to search for, but you can use any appropriate words.)

- **:g/Local**—Searches for the word Local, and prints every occurrence of that line from the file. (If there is more than a screenful, the output is piped to the more command.)
- **:s/Local/Remote**—Substitutes Remote for the first occurrence of the word Local on the current line.
- **:g/Local/s//Remote**—Substitutes the first occurrence of the word Local on every line of the file with the word Remote.
- **:g/Local/s//Remote/g**—Substitutes every occurrence of the word Local with the word Remote in the entire file.
- **:g/Local/s//Remote/gp**—Substitutes every occurrence of the word Local with the word Remote in the entire file, and then prints each line so you can see the changes (piping it through less if output fills more than one page).

Learning more about vi and vim

To learn more about the vi editor, try typing vimtutor. The vimtutor command opens a tutorial in the vim editor that steps you through common commands and features you can use in vim.

Finding Files

Even a basic Linux installation can have thousands of files installed on it. To help you find files on your system, you can use commands such as `locate` (to find commands by name), `find` (to find files based on lots of different attributes), and `grep` (to search within text files to find lines in files that contain search text).

Using locate to find files by name

On most Linux systems (Fedora and RHEL included), the `updatedb` command runs once per day to gather the names of files throughout your Linux system into a database. By running the `locate` command, you can search that database to find the location of files stored in that database.

Here are a few things you should know about searching for files using the `locate` command:

- There are advantages and disadvantages to using `locate` to find filenames instead of the `find` command. A `locate` command finds files faster because it searches a database instead of having to search the whole filesystem live. A disadvantage is that the `locate` command cannot find any files added to the system since the previous time the database was created. Not every file in your filesystem is stored in the database. The contents of the `/etc/updatedb.conf` file limit which filenames are collected by pruning out select mount types, filesystem types, file types, and mount points. For example, filenames are not gathered from remotely mounted filesystems (`cifs`, `nfs`, and so on) or locally mounted CDs or DVDs (`iso9660`). Paths containing temporary files (`/tmp`) and spool files (`/var/spool/cups`) are also pruned. You can add items to prune (or remove some items that you don't want pruned) the locate database to your needs. In RHEL 7, the `updatedb.conf` file contains the following:

  ```
  PRUNE_BIND_MOUNTS = "yes"

  PRUNEFS = "9p afs anon_inodefs auto autofs bdev binfmt_misc cgroup
  cifs coda configfs cpuset debugfs devpts ecryptfs exofs fuse fuse.
  sshfs fusectl gfs gfs2 hugetlbfs inotifyfs iso9660 jffs2 lustre
  mqueue ncpfs nfs nfs4 nfsd pipefs proc ramfs rootfs rpc_pipefs
  securityfs selinuxfs sfs sockfs sysfs tmpfs ubifs udf usbfs"

  PRUNENAMES = ".git .hg .svn"

  PRUNEPATHS = "/afs /media /mnt /net /sfs /tmp /udev /var/cache/
  ccache /var/lib/yum/yumdb /var/spool/cups /var/spool/squid /
  var/tmp"
  ```

- As a regular user, you can't see any files from the locate database that you can't see in the filesystem normally. For example, if you can't type `ls` to view files in the `/root` directory, you can't locate files stored in that directory.

5

- When you search for a string, the string can appear anywhere in a file's path. For example, if you search for passwd, you could turn up /etc/passwd, /usr/bin/passwd, /home/chris/passwd/pwdfiles.txt, and many other files with passwd in the path.
- If you add files to your system after updatedb runs, you can't locate those files until updatedb runs again (probably that night). To get the database to contain all files up to the current moment, you can simply run updatedb from the shell as root.

Here are some examples of using the locate command to search for files:

```
$ locate .bashrc
/etc/skel/.bashrc
/home/cnegus/.bashrc
# locate .bashrc
/etc/skel/.bashrc
/home/bill/.bashrc
/home/joe/.bashrc
/root/.bashrc
```

When run as a regular user, locate only finds .bashrc in /etc/skel and the user's own home directory. Run as root, the same command locates .bashrc files in everyone's home directory.

```
$ locate muttrc
/usr/share/doc/mutt-1.5.20/sample.muttrc
. . .
$ locate -i muttrc
/etc/Muttrc
/etc/Muttrc.local
/usr/share/doc/mutt-1.5.20/sample.muttrc
. . .
```

Using locate -i, filenames are found regardless of case. In the previous example, Muttrc and Muttrc.local were found with -i whereas they weren't found without that option.

```
$ locate services
/etc/services
/usr/share/services/bmp.kmgio
/usr/share/services/data.kmgio
```

Unlike the find command, which uses the -name option to find filenames, the locate command locates the string you enter if it exists in any part of the file's path. For example, if you search for services using the locate command, you find files and directories that contain the "services" string of text.

Searching for files with find

The `find` command is the best command for searching your filesystem for files, based on a variety of attributes. After files are found, you can act on those files as well (using the `-exec` or `-okay` options) by running any commands you want on them.

When you run `find`, it searches your filesystem live, which causes it to run slower than `locate`, but gives you an up-to-the-moment view of the files on your Linux system. However, you can also tell `find` to start at a particular point in the filesystem, so the search can go faster by limiting the area of the filesystem being searched.

Nearly any file attribute you can think of can be used as a search option. You can search for filenames, ownership, permission, size, modification times, and other attributes. You can even use combinations of attributes. Here are some basic examples of using the `find` command:

```
$ find
$ find /etc
# find /etc
$ find $HOME -ls
```

Run on a line by itself, the `find` command finds all files and directories below the current directory. If you want to search from a particular point in the directory tree, just add the name of the directory you want to search (such as `/etc`). If you run `find` as a regular user, you do not have special permission to find files that are readable only by the root user. So `find` produces a bunch of error messages. If you run `find` as the root user, `find /etc` finds all files under `/etc`.

A special option to the `find` command is `-ls`. A long listing (ownership, permission, size, and so on) is printed with each file when you add `-ls` to the `find` command (similar to output of the `ls -l` command). This option helps you in later examples when you want to verify that you have found files that contain the ownership, size, modification times, or other attributes you are trying to find.

> **NOTE**
>
> If, as a regular user, you are searching an area of the filesystem where you don't have full permission to access all files it contains (such as the `/etc` directory), you might receive lots of error messages when you search with `find`. To get rid of those messages, direct standard errors to `/dev/null`. To do that, add the following to the end of the command line: `2> /dev/null`. The `2>` redirects standard error (STDERR) to the next option (in this case `/dev/null`, where the output is discarded).

Finding files by name

To find files by name, you can use the `-name` and `-iname` options. The search is done by base name of the file; the directory names are not searched by default. To make the search

5

more flexible, you can use file-matching characters, such as asterisks (*) and question marks (?), as in the following examples:

```
# find /etc -name passwd
/etc/pam.d/passwd
/etc/passwd
# find /etc -iname '*passwd*'
/etc/pam.d/passwd
/etc/passwd-
/etc/passwd.OLD
/etc/passwd
/etc/MYPASSWD
/etc/security/opasswd
```

Using the -name option and no asterisks, the first example above lists any files in the /etc directory that are named passwd exactly. By using -iname instead, you can match any combination of upper and lower case. Using asterisks, you can match any filename that includes the word passwd.

Finding files by size

If your disk is filling up and you want to find out where your biggest files are, you can search your system by file size. The -size option enables you to search for files that are exactly, smaller than, or larger than a selected size, as you can see in the following examples:

```
$ find /usr/share/ -size +10M
$ find /mostlybig -size -1M
$ find /bigdata -size +500M -size -5G -exec du -sh {} \;
4.1G    /bigdata/images/rhel6.img
606M    /bigdata/Fedora-16-i686-Live-Desktop.iso
560M    /bigdata/dance2.avi
```

The first example in the preceding code finds files larger than 10MB. The second finds files less than 1MB. In the third example, I'm searching for ISO images and video files that are between 500MB and 5GB. This includes an example of the -exec option (which I describe later) to run the du command on each file to see its size.

Finding files by user

You can search for a particular owner (-user) or group (-group) when you try to find files. By using -not and -or, you can refine your search for files associated with specific users and groups, as you can see in the following examples:

```
$ find /home -user chris -ls
131077    4 -rw-r--r--    1 chris   chris 379 Jun 29  2014 ./.bashrc
# find /home -user chris -or -user joe -ls
131077    4 -rw-r--r--    1 chris   chris 379 Jun 29  2014 ./.bashrc
181022    4 -rw-r--r--    1 joe     joe   379 Jun 15  2014 ./.bashrc
# find /etc -group ntp -ls
131438    4 drwxrwsr-x    3 root    ntp  4096 Mar  9 22:16 /etc/ntp
# find /var/spool -not -user root -ls
262100 0 -rw-rw---- 1 rpc   mail 0 Jan 27 2014 /var/spool/mail/rpc
278504 0 -rw-rw---- 1 joe   mail 0 Apr 3 2014  /var/spool/mail/joe
261230 0 -rw-rw---- 1 bill  mail 0 Dec 18 2014 /var/spool/mail/bill
277373 0 -rw-rw---- 1 chris mail 0 Mar 15 2014 /var/spool/mail/chris
```

The first example outputs a long listing of all files under the /home directory that are owned by the user chris. The next lists files owned by chris or joe. The find command of /etc turns up all files that have ntp as their primary group assignment. The last example shows all files under /var/spool that are not owned by root. You can see files owned by other users in the sample output.

Finding files by permission

Searching for files by permission is an excellent way to turn up security issues on your system or uncover access issues. Just as you changed permissions on files using numbers or letters (with the chmod command), you can likewise find files based on number or letter permissions along with the -perm options. (Refer to Chapter 4, "Moving around the Filesystem," to see how to use numbers and letters with chmod to reflect file permissions.)

If you use numbers for permission, as I do below, remember that the three numbers represent permissions for the user, group, and other. Each of those three numbers varies from no permission (0) to full read/write/execute permission (7), by adding read (4), write (2), and execute (1) bits together. With a hyphen (-) in front of the number, all three of the bits indicated must match; with a plus (+) in front of it, any of the numbers can match for the search to find a file. The full, exact numbers must match if neither a hyphen or plus is used.

Consider the following examples:

```
$ find /bin -perm 755 -ls
788884 28 -rwxr-xr-x 1 root root 28176 Mar 10 2014 /bin/echo

$ find /home/chris/ -perm -222 -type d -ls
144503 4 drwxrwxrwx 8 chris chris 4096 June 23 2014 /home/chris
```

By searching for -perm 755, any files or directories with exactly rwxr-xr-x permission are matched. By using -perm -222, only files that have write permission for user, group, and other are matched. Notice that, in this case, the -type d is added to match only directories.

```
$ find /myreadonly -perm +222 -type f
685035 0 -rw-rw-r-- 1 chris chris 0 Dec 30 2014 /tmp/write/abc

$ find . -perm -002 -type f -ls
266230 0 -rw-rw-rw- 1 chris chris 0 Dec 20 2014 ./LINUX_BIBLE/a
```

Using -perm +222, you can find any file (-type f) that has write permission turned on for the user, group, or other. You might do that to make sure that all files are read-only in a particular part of the filesystem (in this case, beneath the /myreadonly directory). The last example, -perm +002, is very useful for finding files that have open write permission for "other," regardless of how the other permission bits are set.

Finding files by date and time

Date and time stamps are stored for each file when it is created, when it is accessed, when its content is modified, or when its metadata is changed. Metadata includes owner, group, time stamp, file size, permissions, and other information stored in the file's inode. You might want to search for file data or metadata changes for any of the following reasons:

- You just changed the contents of a configuration file, and you can't remember which one. So you search /etc to see what has changed in the past 10 minutes:

  ```
  $ find /etc/ -mmin -10
  ```

- You suspect that someone hacked your system three days ago. So you search the system to see if any commands have had their ownership or permissions changed in the past three days:

  ```
  $ find /bin /usr/bin /sbin /usr/sbin -ctime -3
  ```

- You want to find files in your FTP server (/var/ftp) and web server (/var/www) that have not been accessed in more than 300 days, so you can see if any need to be deleted:

  ```
  $ find /var/ftp /var/www -atime +300
  ```

As you can glean from the examples, you can search for content or metadata changes over a certain number of days or minutes. The time options (-atime, -ctime, and -mtime) enable you to search based on the number of days since each file was accessed, was changed, or had its metadata changed. The min options (-amin, -cmin, and -mmin) do the same in minutes.

Numbers that you give as arguments to the min and time options are preceded by a hyphen (to indicate a time from the current time to that number of minutes or days ago) or a plus (to indicate time from the number of minutes or days ago and older). With no hyphen or plus, the exact number is matched.

Using 'not' and 'or' when finding files

With the -not and -or options, you can further refine your searches. There may be times when you want to find files owned by a particular user, but not assigned to a particular group. You may want files larger than a certain size, but smaller than another size. Or you might want to find files owned by any of several users. The -not and -or options can help you do that. Consider the following examples:

- There is a shared directory called /var/all. This command line enables you to find files that are owned by either joe or chris.

```
$ find /var/all \( -user joe -o -user chris \) -ls
679967 0 -rw-r--r-- 1 chris chris 0    Dec 31 2014 /var/all/cn
679977 0 -rw-r--r-- 1 joe   joe   4379 Dec 31 2014 /var/all/jj
679972 0 -rw-r--r-- 1 joe   sales 0    Dec 31 2014 /var/all/js
```

- This command line searches for files owned by the user joe, but only those that are not assigned to the group joe:

```
$ find /var/all/ -user joe -not -group joe -ls
679972 0 -rw-r--r-- 1 joe   sales 0    Dec 31 2014 /var/all/js
```

- You can also add multiple requirements on your searches. Here, a file must be owned by the user joe and must also be more than 1MB in size:

```
$ find /var/all/ -user joe -and -size +1M -ls
679977 0 -rw-r--r-- 1 joe   joe   4379 Dec 31 2014 /var/all/jj
```

Finding files and executing commands

One of the most powerful features of the find command is the capability to execute commands on any files you find. With the -exec option, the command you use is executed on every file found, without stopping to ask if that's okay. The -ok option stops at each matched file and asks whether you want to run the command on it.

The advantage of using -ok is that, if you are doing something destructive, you can make sure that you okay each file individually before the command is run on it. The syntax for using -exec and -ok is the same:

```
$ find [options] -exec command {} \;
$ find [options] -ok command {} \;
```

With -exec or -ok, you run find with any options you like to find the files you are looking for. Then enter the -exec or -ok option, followed by the command you want to run on each file. The set of curly braces indicates where on the command line to read in each file that is found. Each file can be included in the command line multiple times,

5

if you like. To end the line, you need to add a backslash and semicolon (\;). Here are some examples:

- This command finds any file named iptables under the /etc directory and includes that name in the output of an echo command:

```
$ find /etc -iname iptables -exec echo "I found {}" \;
I found /etc/bash_completion.d/iptables
I found /etc/sysconfig/iptables
```

- This command finds every file under the /usr/share directory that is more than 5MB in size. Then it lists the size of each file with the du command. The output of find is then sorted by size, from largest to smallest. With -exec entered, all entries found are processed, without prompting:

```
$ find /usr/share -size +5M -exec du {} \; | sort -nr
116932    /usr/share/icons/HighContrast/icon-theme.cache
69048     /usr/share/icons/gnome/icon-theme.cache
20564     /usr/share/fonts/cjkuni-uming/uming.ttc
```

- The -ok option enables you to choose, one at a time, whether each file found is acted upon by the command you enter. For example, you want to find all files that belong to joe in the /var/allusers directory (and its subdirectories) and move them to the /tmp/joe directory:

```
# find /var/allusers/ -user joe -ok mv {} /tmp/joe/ \;
< mv ... /var/allusers/dict.dat > ? y
< mv ... /var/allusers/five > ? y
```

Notice in the preceding code that you are prompted for each file that is found before it is moved to the /tmp/joe directory. You would simply type y and press Enter at each line to move the file, or just press Enter to skip it.

For more information on the find command, type **man find**.

Searching in files with grep

If you want to search for files that contain a certain search term, you can use the grep command. With grep, you can search a single file or search a whole directory structure of files recursively.

When you search, you can have every line containing the term printed on your screen (standard output) or just list the names of the files that contain the search term. By default, grep searches text in a case-sensitive way, although you can do case-insensitive searches as well.

Instead of just searching files, you can also use grep to search standard output. So, if a command turns out lots of text and you want to find only lines that contain certain text, you can use grep to filter just want you want.

Here are some examples of grep command lines, used to find text strings in one or more files:

```
$ grep desktop /etc/services
desktop-dna 2763/tcp  # Desktop DNA
desktop-dna 2763/udp  # Desktop DNA

$ grep -i desktop /etc/services
sco-dtmgr    617/tcp   # SCO Desktop Administration Server
sco-dtmgr    617/udp   # SCO Desktop Administration Server
airsync      2175/tcp  # Microsoft Desktop AirSync Protocol
...
```

In the first example, a grep for the word desktop in the /etc/services file turned up two lines. Searching again, using the -i to be case-insensitive (as in the second example), there were 29 lines of text produced.

To search for lines that don't contain a selected text string, use the -v option. In the following example, all lines from the /etc/services file are displayed except those containing the text tcp (case-insensitive):

```
$ grep -vi tcp /etc/services
```

To do recursive searches, use the -r option and a directory as an argument. The following example includes the -l option, which just lists files that include the search text, without showing the actual lines of text. That search turns up files that contain the text peerdns (case-insensitive).

```
$ grep -rli peerdns /usr/share/doc/
/usr/share/doc/dnsmasq-2.66/setup.html
/usr/share/doc/initscripts-9.49.17/sysconfig.txt
...
```

The next example recursively searches the /etc/sysconfig directory for the term root. It lists every line in every file beneath the directory that contains that text. To make it easier to have the term root stand out on each line, the --color option is added. By default, the matched term appears in red.

```
$ grep -ri --color root /etc/sysconfig/
```

To search the output of a command for a term, you can pipe the output to the grep command. In this example, I know that IP addresses are listed on output lines from the ip command that include the string inet. So, I use grep to just display those lines:

```
$ ip addr show | grep inet
inet 127.0.0.1/8 scope host lo
inet 192.168.1.231/24 brd 192.168.1.255 scope global wlan0
```

5

Summary

Being able to work with plain-text files is a critical skill for using Linux. Because so many configuration files and document files are in plain-text format, you need to become proficient with a text editor to effectively use Linux. Finding filenames and content in files are also critical skills. In this chapter, you learned to use the locate and find commands for finding files and grep for searching files.

The next chapter covers a variety of ways to work with processes. There, you learn how to see what processes are running, run processes in the foreground and background, and change processes (send signals).

Exercises

Use these exercises to test your knowledge of using the vi (or vim) text editor, commands for finding files (locate and find), and commands for searching files (grep). These tasks assume you are running a Fedora or Red Hat Enterprise Linux system (although some tasks work on other Linux systems as well). If you are stuck, solutions to the tasks are shown in Appendix B (although in Linux, there are often multiple ways to complete a task).

1. Copy the /etc/services file to the /tmp directory. Open the /tmp/services file in vim, and search for the term WorldWideWeb. Change that to read World Wide Web.

2. Find the following paragraph in your /tmp/services file (if it is not there, choose a different paragraph) , and move it to the end of that file.

   ```
   # Note that it is presently the policy of IANA to assign a single
       well-known
   # port number for both TCP and UDP; hence, most entries here have two
       entries
   # even if the protocol doesn't support UDP operations.
   # Updated from RFC 1700, "Assigned Numbers" (October 1994). Not all
       ports
   # are included, only the more common ones.
   ```

3. Using ex mode, search for every occurrence of the term tcp (case-sensitive) in your /tmp/services file and change it to WHATEVER.

4. As a regular user, search the /etc directory for every file named passwd. Redirect error messages from your search to /dev/null.

5. Create a directory in your home directory called TEST. Create files in that directory named one, two, and three that have full read/write/execute permissions on for everyone (user, group, and other). Construct a find command to find those files and any other files that have write permission open to "others" from your home directory and below.

6. Find files under the `/usr/share/doc` directory that have not been modified in more than 300 days.

7. Create a `/tmp/FILES` directory. Find all files under the `/usr/share` directory that are more than 5MB and less than 10MB and copy them to the `/tmp/FILES` directory.

8. Find every file in the `/tmp/FILES` directory, and make a backup copy of each file in the same directory. Use each file's existing name, and just append `.mybackup` to create each backup file.

9. Install the `kernel-doc` package in Fedora or Red Hat Enterprise Linux. Using `grep`, search inside the files contained in the `/usr/share/doc/kernel-doc*` directory for the term `e1000` (case-insensitive) and list the names of the files that contain that term.

10. Search for the `e1000` term again in the same location, but this time list every line that contains the term and highlight the term in color.

Managing Running Processes

IN THIS CHAPTER

Displaying processes

Running processes in the foreground and background

Killing and renicing processes

I n addition to being a multiuser operating system, Linux is also a multitasking system. *Multitasking* means that many programs can be running at the same time. An instance of a running program is referred to as a *process*. Linux provides tools for listing running processes, monitoring system usage, and stopping (or killing) processes when necessary.

From a shell, you can launch processes, and then pause, stop, or kill them. You can also put them in the background and bring them to the foreground. This chapter describes tools such as ps, top, kill, jobs, and other commands for listing and managing processes.

Understanding Processes

A process is a running instance of a command. For example, there may be one vi command on the system. But if vi is currently being run by 15 different users, that command is represented by 15 different running processes.

A process is identified on the system by what is referred to as a *process ID*. That process ID is unique for the current system. In other words, no other process can use that number as its process ID while that first process is still running. However, after a process is ended, another process can reuse that number.

Along with a process ID number, other attributes are associated with a process. Each process, when it is run, is associated with a particular user account and group account. That account information helps determine what system resources the process can access. For example, processes run as the root user have much more access to system files and resources than a process running as a regular user.

The ability to manage processes on your system is critical for a Linux system administrator. Sometimes, runaway processes may be killing your system's performance. Finding and dealing with processes, based on attributes such as memory and CPU usage, are covered in this chapter.

> **NOTE**
>
> Commands that display information about running processes get most of that information from raw data stored in the /proc file system. Each process stores its information in a subdirectory of /proc, named after the process ID of that process. You can view some of that raw data by displaying the contents of files in one of those directories (using cat or less commands).

Listing Processes

From the command line, the ps command is the oldest and most common command for listing processes currently running on your system. The top command provides a more screen-oriented approach to listing processes and can also be used to change the status of processes. If you are using the GNOME desktop, you can use gnome-system-monitor to provide a graphical means of working with processes. These commands are described in the following sections.

Listing processes with ps

The most common utility for checking running processes is the ps command. Use it to see which programs are running, the resources they are using, and who is running them. The following is an example of the ps command:

```
$ ps u
USER    PID  %CPU %MEM  VSZ    RSS  TTY   STAT  START  TIME  COMMAND
jake    2147 0.0  0.7  1836   1020  tty1  S+    14:50  0:00  -bash
jake    2310 0.0  0.7  2592    912  tty1  R+    18:22  0:00  ps u
```

In this example, the u option asks that usernames be shown, as well as other information such as the time the process started and memory and CPU usage for processes associated with the current user. The processes shown are associated with the current terminal (tty1). The concept of a terminal comes from the old days, when people worked exclusively from character terminals, so a terminal typically represented a single person at a single screen. Now, you can have many "terminals" on one screen by opening multiple virtual terminals or Terminal windows on the desktop.

In this shell session, not much is happening. The first process shows that the user named jake opened a bash shell after logging in. The next process shows that jake has run the ps u command. The terminal device tty1 is being used for the login session. The STAT column represents the state of the process, with R indicating a currently running process and S representing a sleeping process.

> **NOTE**
>
> Several other values can appear under the STAT column. For example, a plus sign (+) indicates that the process is associated with the foreground operations.

The USER column shows the name of the user who started the process. Each process is represented by a unique ID number referred to as a process ID (PID). You can use the PID if you ever need to kill a runaway process or send another kind of signal to a process. The %CPU and %MEM columns show the percentages of the processor and random access memory, respectively, that the process is consuming.

VSZ (virtual set size) shows the size of the image process (in kilobytes), and RSS (resident set size) shows the size of the program in memory. The VSZ and RSS sizes may be different because VSZ is the amount of memory allocated for the process, whereas RSS is the amount that is actually being used. RSS memory represents physical memory that cannot be swapped.

START shows the time the process began running, and TIME shows the cumulative system time used. (Many commands consume very little CPU time, as reflected by 0:00 for processes that haven't even used a whole second of CPU time.)

Many processes running on a computer are not associated with a terminal. A normal Linux system has many processes running in the background. Background system processes perform such tasks as logging system activity or listening for data coming in from the network. They are often started when Linux boots up and run continuously until the system shuts down. Likewise, logging into a Linux desktop causes many background processes to kick off, such as processes for managing audio, desktop panels, authentication, and other desktop features.

To page through all the processes running on your Linux system for the current user, add the pipe (|) and the less command to ps ux:

```
$ ps ux | less
```

To page through all processes running for all users on your system, use the ps aux command as follows:

```
$ ps aux | less
```

A pipe (located above the backslash character on the keyboard) enables you to direct the output of one command to be the input of the next command. In this example, the output of the ps command (a list of processes) is directed to the less command, which enables you to page through that information. Use the spacebar to page through and type q to end the list. You can also use the arrow keys to move one line at a time through the output.

The ps command can be customized to display selected columns of information and to sort information by one of those columns. Using the -o option, you can use keywords to indicate the columns you want to list with ps. For example, the next example lists every running process (-e) and then follows the -o option with every column of information I want to display, including:

The process ID (pid), username (user), user ID (uid), group name (group), group ID (gid), virtual memory allocated (vsz), resident memory used (rss), and the full command line that was run (comm). By default, output is sorted by process ID number.

```
$ ps -eo pid,user,uid,group,gid,vsz,rss,comm | less
  PID USER       GROUP      GID     VSZ    RSS COMMAND
    1 root       root         0   19324   1320 init
    2 root       root         0       0      0 kthreadd
```

If you want to sort by a specific column, you can use the sort= option. For example, to see which processes are using the most memory, I sort by the rss field. That sorts from lowest memory use to highest. Because I want to see the highest ones first, I put a hyphen in front of that option to sort (sort=-rss).

```
$ ps -eo pid,user,group,gid,vsz,rss,comm --sort=-rss | less
  PID USER       GROUP      GID     VSZ    RSS COMMAND
12005 cnegus     cnegus   13597 1271008 522192 firefox
 5412 cnegus     cnegus   13597  949584 157268 thunderbird-bin
25870 cnegus     cnegus   13597 1332492 112952 swriter.bin
```

Refer to the ps man page for information on other columns of information you can display and sort by.

Listing and changing processes with top

The top command provides a screen-oriented means of displaying processes running on your system. With top, the default is to display processes based on how much CPU time they are currently consuming. However, you can sort by other columns as well. After you identify a misbehaving process, you can also use top to kill (completely end) or renice (reprioritize) that process.

If you want to be able to kill or renice processes, you need to run top as the root user. If you just want to display processes, and possibly kill or change your own processes, you can do that as a regular user. Figure 6.1 shows an example of the top window:

General information about your system appears at the top of the top output, followed by information about each running process (or at least as many as will fit on your screen). At the top, you can see how long the system has been up, how many users are currently logged in to the system, and how much demand there has been on the system for the past 1, 5, and 10 minutes.

Other general information includes how many processes (tasks) are currently running, how much CPU is being used, and how much RAM and swap are available and being used. Following the general information are listings of each process, sorted by what percent of the CPU is being used by each process. All this information is redisplayed every 5 seconds, by default.

6

FIGURE 6.1

Displaying running processes with top.

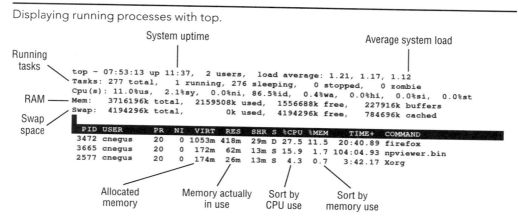

The following list includes actions you can do with top to display information in different ways and modify running processes:

- Press **h** to see help options, and then press any key to return to the top display.
- Press **M** to sort by memory usage instead of CPU, and then press **P** to return to sorting by CPU.
- Press the number **1** to toggle showing CPU usage of all your CPUs, if you have more than one CPU on your system.
- Press **R** to reverse sort your output.
- Press **u** and enter a username to display processes only for a particular user.

A common practice is to use top to find processes that are consuming too much memory or processing power and then act on those processes in some way. A process consuming too much CPU can be reniced to give it less priority to the processors. A process consuming too much memory can be killed. With top running, here's how to renice or kill a process:

- **Renicing a process:** Note the process ID of the process you want to renice and press **r**. When the PID to renice: message appears, type the process ID of the process you want to renice. When prompted to Renice PID to value: type in a number from −19 to 20. (See "Setting processor priority with nice and renice" later in this chapter for information on the meanings of different renice values.)
- **Killing a process:** Note the process ID of the process you want to kill and press **k**. Type **15** to terminate cleanly or **9** to just kill the process outright. (See "Killing processes with kill and killall" later in this chapter for more information on using different signals you can send to processes.)

Listing processes with System Monitor

If you have GNOME desktop available on your Linux system, System Monitor (gnome-system-monitor) is available to provide a more graphical way of displaying processes on your system. You sort processes by clicking columns. You can right-click processes to stop, kill, or renice them.

To start System Monitor from the GNOME 2 desktop, select Applications ⇨ System Tools ⇨ System Monitor. Or in GNOME 3, press the Windows key, then type System Monitor and press Enter. Then select the Processes tab. Figure 6.2 shows an example of the System Monitor window.

FIGURE 6.2

Use the System Monitor window to view and change running processes.

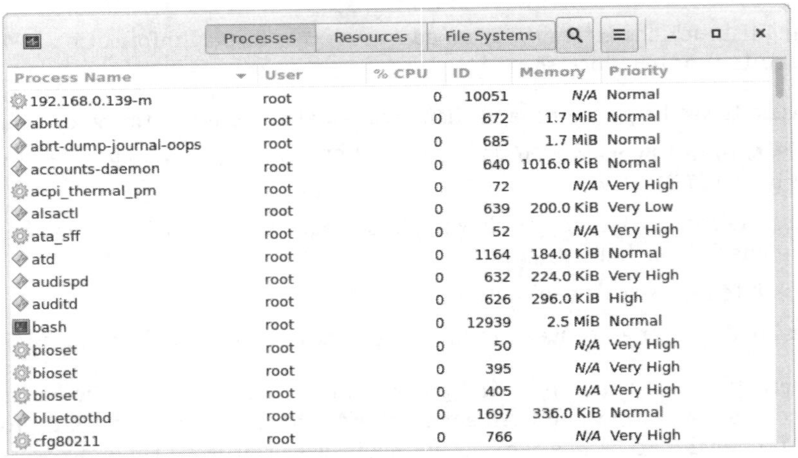

Process Name	User	% CPU	ID	Memory	Priority
192.168.0.139-m	root	0	10051	N/A	Normal
abrtd	root	0	672	1.7 MiB	Normal
abrt-dump-journal-oops	root	0	685	1.7 MiB	Normal
accounts-daemon	root	0	640	1016.0 KiB	Normal
acpi_thermal_pm	root	0	72	N/A	Very High
alsactl	root	0	639	200.0 KiB	Very Low
ata_sff	root	0	52	N/A	Very High
atd	root	0	1164	184.0 KiB	Normal
audispd	root	0	632	224.0 KiB	Very High
auditd	root	0	626	296.0 KiB	High
bash	root	0	12939	2.5 MiB	Normal
bioset	root	0	50	N/A	Very High
bioset	root	0	395	N/A	Very High
bioset	root	0	405	N/A	Very High
bluetoothd	root	0	1697	336.0 KiB	Normal
cfg80211	root	0	766	N/A	Very High

By default, only running processes associated with your user account are displayed. Those processes are listed alphabetically at first. You can re-sort the processes by clicking any of the field headings (forward and reverse). For example, click the %CPU heading to see which processes are consuming the most processing power. Click the Memory heading to see which processes consume the most memory.

You can change your processes in various ways by right-clicking a process name and selecting from the menu that appears (see Figure 6.3 for an example).

Here are some of the things you can do to a process from the menu you clicked:

- **Stop**—Pauses the process, so no processing occurs until you select Continue Process. (This is the same as pressing Ctrl+Z on a process from the shell.)

- **Continue**—Continues running a paused process.

- **End**—Sends a Terminate signal (15) to a process. In most cases, this terminates the process cleanly.

- **Kill**—Sends a Kill signal (9) to a process. This should kill a process immediately, regardless of whether it can be done cleanly.

- **Change**—Presents a slider bar from which you can renice a process. Normal priority is 0. To get better processor priority, use a negative number from –1 to –20. To have a lower processor priority, use a positive number (0 to 19). Only the root user can assign negative priorities, so you need to provide the root password, when prompted, to set a negative nice value.

- **Memory Maps**—Lets you view the system memory map to see which libraries and other components are being held in memory for the process.

- **Open Files**—Lets you view which files are currently being held open by the process.

- **Properties**—Lets you see other settings associated with the process (such as security context, memory usage, and CPU use percentages).

FIGURE 6.3

Renice, kill, or pause a process from the System Monitor window.

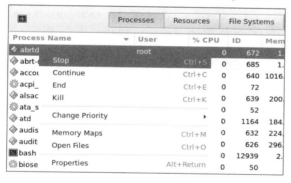

You can display running processes associated with users other than yourself. To do that, highlight any process in the display (just click it). Then, from the menu button (button with three bars on it), select All Processes. You can modify processes you don't own only if you are the root user or if you can provide the root password when prompted after you try to change a process.

Sometimes, you don't have the luxury of working with a graphical interface. To change processes without a graphical interface, you can use a set of commands and keystrokes to change, pause, or kill running processes. Some of those are described next.

Managing Background and Foreground Processes

If you are using Linux over a network or from a *dumb terminal* (a monitor that allows only text input with no GUI support), your shell may be all that you have. You may be used to a graphical environment in which you have lots of programs active at the same time so you can switch among them as needed. This shell thing can seem pretty limited.

Although the bash shell doesn't include a GUI for running many programs at once, it does let you move active programs between the background and foreground. In this way, you can have lots of stuff running and selectively choose the one you want to deal with at the moment.

You can place an active program in the background in several ways. One is to add an ampersand (&) to the end of a command line when you first run the command. You can also use the at command to run commands in such a way that they are not connected to the shell.

To stop a running command and put it in the background, press Ctrl+Z. After the command is stopped, you can either bring it back into the foreground to run (the fg command) or start it running in the background (the bg command). Keep in mind that any command running in the background might spew output during commands that you run subsequently from that shell. For example, if output appears from a command running in the background during a vi session, simply press Ctrl+L to redraw the screen to get rid of the output.

> **TIP**
>
> To avoid having the output appear, you should have any process running in the background send its output to a file or to null (add 2> /dev/null to the end of the command line).

Starting background processes

If you have programs that you want to run while you continue to work in the shell, you can place the programs in the background. To place a program in the background at the time you run the program, type an ampersand (&) at the end of the command line, like this:

```
$ find /usr > /tmp/allusrfiles &
[3] 15971
```

This example command finds all files on your Linux system (starting from /usr), prints those filenames, and puts those names in the file /tmp/allusrfiles. The ampersand (&) runs that command line in the background. Notice that the job number, [3], and process ID number, 15971, are displayed when the command is launched. To check which commands you have running in the background, use the jobs command, as follows:

```
$ jobs
[1]   Stopped (tty output)  vi /tmp/myfile
[2]   Running               find /usr -print > /tmp/allusrfiles &
[3]   Running               nroff -man /usr/man2/* >/tmp/man2 &
[4]- Running                nroff -man /usr/man3/* >/tmp/man3 &
[5]+ Stopped                nroff -man /usr/man4/* >/tmp/man4
```

The first job shows a text-editing command (vi) that I placed in the background and stopped by pressing Ctrl+Z while I was editing. Job 2 shows the find command I just ran. Jobs 3 and 4 show nroff commands currently running in the background. Job 5 had been running in the shell (foreground) until I decided too many processes were running and pressed Ctrl+Z to stop job 5 until a few processes had completed.

The plus sign (+) next to number 5 shows that it was most recently placed in the background. The minus sign (-) next to number 4 shows that it was placed in the background just before the most recent background job. Because job 1 requires terminal input, it cannot run in the background. As a result, it is Stopped until it is brought to the foreground again.

TIP

To see the process ID for the background job, add a -l (the lowercase letter L) option to the jobs command. If you type ps, you can use the process ID to figure out which command is for a particular background job.

Using foreground and background commands

Continuing with the example, you can bring any of the commands on the jobs list to the foreground. For example, to edit myfile again, type:

```
$ fg %1
```

As a result, the vi command opens again. All text is as it was when you stopped the vi job.

CAUTION

Before you put a text processor, word processor, or similar program in the background, make sure you save your file. It's easy to forget you have a program in the background, and you will lose your data if you log out or the computer reboots.

To refer to a background job (to cancel or bring it to the foreground), use a percent sign (%) followed by the job number. You can also use the following to refer to a background job:

- %—Refers to the most recent command put into the background (indicated by the plus sign when you type the jobs command). This action brings the command to the foreground.

- %*string*—Refers to a job where the command begins with a particular *string* of characters. The *string* must be unambiguous. (In other words, typing %vi when there are two vi commands in the background results in an error message.)

- %?*string*—Refers to a job where the command line contains a *string* at any point. The string must be unambiguous or the match fails.
- %---—Refers to the previous job stopped before the one most recently stopped.

If a command is stopped, you can start it running again in the background using the bg command. For example, take job 5 from the jobs list in the previous example:

```
[5]+ Stopped nroff -man man4/* >/tmp/man4
```

Type the following:

```
$ bg %5
```

After that, the job runs in the background. Its jobs entry appears as follows:

```
[5] Running nroff -man man4/* >/tmp/man4 &
```

Killing and Renicing Processes

Just as you can change the behavior of a process using graphical tools such as System Monitor (described earlier in this chapter), you can also use command-line tools to kill a process or change its CPU priority. The kill command can send a kill signal to any process to end it, assuming you have permission to do so. It can also send different signals to a process to otherwise change its behavior. The nice and renice commands can be used to set or change the processor priority of a process.

Killing processes with kill and killall

Although usually used for ending a running process, the kill and killall commands can actually be used to send any valid signal to a running process. Besides telling a process to end, a signal might tell a process to reread configuration files, pause (stop), or continue after being paused, to name a few possibilities.

Signals are represented by both numbers and names. Signals that you might send most commonly from a command include SIGKILL (9), SIGTERM (15), and SIGHUP (1). The default signal is SIGTERM, which tries to terminate a process cleanly. To kill a process immediately, you can use SIGKILL. The SIGHUP signal tells a process to reread its configuration files. SIGSTOP pauses a process, while SIGCONT continues a stopped process.

Different processes respond to different signals. Processes cannot block SIGKILL and SIGSTOP signals, however. Table 6.1 shows examples of some signals (type **man 7 signal** to read about other available signals):

TABLE 6.1 **Signals Available in Linux**

Signal	Number	Description
SIGHUP	1	Hang-up detected on controlling terminal or death of controlling process.
SIGINT	2	Interrupt from keyboard.
SIGQUIT	3	Quit from keyboard.
SIGABRT	6	Abort signal from abort(3).
SIGKILL	9	Kill signal.
SIGTERM	15	Termination signal.
SIGCONT	19,18,25	Continue if stopped.
SIGSTOP	17,19,23	Stop process.

Notice that there are multiple possible signal numbers for SIGCONT and SIGSTOP because different numbers are used in different computer architectures. For most x86 and power PC architectures, use the middle value. The first value usually works for Alpha and Sparc, while the last one is for MIPS architecture.

Using kill to signal processes by PID

Using commands such as ps and top, you can find processes you want to send a signal to. Then you can use the process ID of that process as an option to the kill command, along with the signal you want to send.

For example, you run the top command and see that the bigcommand process is consuming most of your processing power:

```
  PID USER     PR  NI  VIRT  RES  SHR S %CPU %MEM    TIME+  COMMAND
10432 chris    20   0  471m 121m  18m S 99.9  3.2  77:01.76 bigcommand
```

Here, the bigcommand process is consuming 99.9 percent of the CPU. You decide you want to kill it so that other processes have a shot at the CPU. If you use the process ID of the running bigcommand process, here are some examples of the kill command you can use to kill that process:

```
$ kill 10432
$ kill -15 10432
$ kill -SIGKILL 10432
```

The default signal sent by kill is 15 (SIGTERM), so the first two examples have exactly the same results. On occasion, a SIGTERM doesn't kill a process, so you may need a SIGKILL to kill it. Instead of SIGKILL, you can use −9.

Another useful signal is SIGHUP. Some server processes, such as the httpd process, which provides web services, respond to a SIGHUP (1) signal by rereading its configuration files. In fact, the command service httpd reload (in RHEL 6) or systemctl reload httpd (RHEL 7) actually sends SIGHUP to httpd processes running on your system to tell them that configuration files need to be read again. If the httpd process had a PID of 1833, you could use either of these commands to have it read configuration files again:

```
# kill -1 1833
# systemctl reload httpd
```

Using killall to signal processes by name

With the killall command, you can signal processes by name instead of by process ID. The advantage is that you don't have to look up the process ID of the process you want to kill. The potential downside is that you can kill more processes than you mean to if you are not careful. (For example, typing killall bash may kill a bunch of shells that you don't mean to kill.)

Like the kill command, killall uses SIGTERM (signal 15) if you don't explicitly enter a signal number. Also as with kill, you can send any signal you like to the process you name with killall. For example, if you see a process called testme running on your system and you want to kill it, you can simply type the following:

```
$ killall -9 testme
```

The killall command can be particularly useful if you want to kill a bunch of commands of the same name.

Setting processor priority with nice and renice

When the Linux kernel tries to decide which running processes get access to the CPUs on your system, one of the things it takes into account is the nice value set on the process. Every process running on your system has a nice value between –20 and 19. By default, the nice value is set to 0. Here are a few facts about nice values:

- The lower the nice value, the more access to the CPUs the process has. In other words, the nicer a process is, the less CPU attention it gets. So, a –20 nice value gets more attention than a process with a 19 nice value.

- A regular user can set nice values only from 0 to 19. No negative values are allowed. So a regular user can't ask for a value that gives a process more attention than most processes get by default.

- A regular user can set the nice value higher, not lower. So, for example, if a user sets the nice value on a process to 10, and then later wants to set it back to 5, that action will fail. Likewise, any attempt to set a negative value will fail.

- A regular user can set the nice value only on the user's own processes.

- The root user can set the nice value on any process to any valid value, up or down.

You can use the `nice` command to run a command with a particular nice value. When a process is running, you can change the nice value using the `renice` command, along with the process ID of the process, as in the example that follows:

```
# nice +5 updatedb &
```

The `updatedb` command is used to generate the locate database manually by gathering names of files throughout the file system. In this case, I just wanted `updatedb` to run in the background (&) and not interrupt work being done by other processes on the system. I ran the `top` command to make sure that the nice value was set properly:

```
PID USER         PR  NI  VIRT  RES  SHR S %CPU %MEM   TIME+  COMMAND
20284 root        25   5 98.7m  932  644 D  2.7  0.0  0:00.96 updatedb
```

Notice that under the NI column, the nice value is set to 5. Because the command was run as the root user, the root user can lower the nice value later by using the `renice` command. (Remember that a regular user can't reduce the nice value or ever set it to a negative number.) Here's how you would change the nice value for the `updatedb` command just run to −5:

```
# renice -n -5 20284
```

If you ran the `top` command again, you might notice that the `updatedb` command is now at or near the top of the list of processes consuming CPU time because you gave it priority to get more CPU attention.

Limiting Processes with cgroups

You can use a feature like "nice" to give a single process more or less access to CPU time. Setting the nice value for one process, however, doesn't apply to child processes that a process might start up or any other related processes that are part of a larger service. In other words, "nice" doesn't limit the total amount of resources a particular user or application can consume from a Linux system.

As cloud computing takes hold, many Linux systems will be used more as hypervisors than as general-purpose computers. Their memory, processing power, and access to storage will become commodities to be shared by many users. In that model, more needs to be done to control the amount of system resources to which a particular user, application, container, or virtual machine running on a Linux system has access.

That's where *cgroups* come in.

Cgroups can be used to identify a process as a *task*, belonging to a particular *control group*. Tasks can be set up in a hierarchy where, for example, there may be a task called daemons that sets default limitations for all daemon server processes, then subtasks that may set specific limits on a web server daemon (`httpd`) or FTP service daemon (`vsftpd`).

As a task launches a process, other processes the initial process launches (called *child processes*) inherit the limitations set for the parent process. Those limitations might say that all the processes in a control group have access only to particular processors and certain sets of RAM. Or they may allow access only to up to 30 percent of the total processing power of a machine.

The types of resources that can be limited by cgroups include the following:

- `Storage (blkio)`—Limits total input and output access to storage devices (such as hard disks, USB drives, and so on).
- `Processor scheduling (cpu)`—Assigns the amount of access a cgroup has to be scheduled for processing power.
- `Process accounting (cpuacct)`—Reports on CPU usage. This information can be leveraged to charge clients for the amount of processing power they use.
- `CPU assignment (cpuset)`—On systems with multiple CPU cores, assigns a task to a particular set of processors and associated memory.
- `Device access (devices)`—Allows tasks in a cgroup to open or create (`mknod`) selected device types.
- `Suspend/resume (freezer)`—Suspends and resumes cgroup tasks.
- `Memory usage (memory)`—Limits memory usage by task. It also creates reports on memory resources used.
- `Network bandwidth (net_cls)`—Limits network access to selected cgroup tasks. This is done by tagging network packets to identify the cgroup task that originated the packet and having the Linux traffic controller monitor and restrict packets coming from each cgroup.
- `Network traffic (net_prio)`—Sets priorities of network traffic coming from selected cgroups and lets administrators change these priorities on the fly.
- `Name spaces (ns)`—Separates cgroups into namespaces, so processes in one cgroup can only see the namespaces associated with the cgroup. Namespaces can include separate process tables, mount tables, and network interfaces.

Creating and managing cgroups, at its most basic level, is generally not a job for new Linux system administrators. It can involve editing configuration files to create your own cgroups (`/etc/cgconfig.conf`) or limit particular users or groups (`/etc/cgrules.conf`). Or you can use the `cgreate` command to create cgroups, which results in those groups being added to the `/sys/fs/cgroup` hierarchy. Setting up cgroups can be tricky and, if done improperly, can make your system unbootable.

The reason I introduce cgroups here is to help you understand some of the underlying features in Linux that you can use to limit and monitor resource usage. In the future, you will probably run into these features from controllers that manage your cloud infrastructure. You will be able to set rules like: "Allow the marketing department's virtual machines to consume up to 40 percent of the available memory" or "Pin the database application to a particular CPU and memory set."

Knowing how Linux can limit and contain the resource usage by the set of processes assigned to a task will ultimately help you manage your computing resources better. If you are interested in learning more about cgroups, you can refer to the following:

- **Red Hat Enterprise Linux Resource Management and Linux Containers Guide**—`https://access.redhat.com/documentation/en-US/Red_Hat_Enterprise_Linux/7/html-single/Resource_Management_and_Linux_Containers_Guide/index.html`

- **Kernel documentation on cgroups**—Refer to files in the `/usr/share/doc/kernel-doc-*/Documentation/cgroups` directory after installing the kernel-doc package.

Summary

Even on a Linux system where there isn't much activity, typically dozens or even hundreds of processes are running in the background. Using the tools described in this chapter, you can view and manage the processes running on your system.

Managing processes includes viewing processes in different ways, running them in the foreground or background, and killing or renicing them. More advanced features for limiting resource usage by selected processes are available using the cgroups feature.

In the next chapter, you learn how to combine commands and programming functions into files that can be run as shell scripts.

Exercises

Use these exercises to test your knowledge of viewing running processes and then changing them later by killing them or changing processor priority (nice value). These tasks assume you are running a Fedora or Red Hat Enterprise Linux system (although some tasks work on other Linux systems as well). If you are stuck, solutions to the tasks are shown in Appendix B (although in Linux, you can often use multiple ways to complete a task).

1. List all processes running on your system, showing a full set of columns. Pipe that output to the `less` command so you can page through the list of processes.

2. List all processes running on the system, and sort those processes by the name of the user running each process.

3. List all processes running on the system, and display the following columns of information: process ID, user name, group name, virtual memory size, resident memory size, and the command.

4. Run the `top` command to view processes running on your system. Go back and forth between sorting by CPU usage and memory consumption.

5. Start the `gedit` process from your desktop. Make sure you run it as the user you are logged in as. Use the System Monitor window to kill that process.

6. Run the `gedit` process again. This time, using the kill command, send a signal to the `gedit` process that causes it to pause (stop). Try typing some text into the `gedit` window and make sure that no text appears yet.

7. Use the `killall` command to tell the `gedit` command you paused in the previous exercise to continue working. Make sure the text you type in after `gedit` was paused now appears on the window.

8. Install the `xeyes` command (in Red Hat Enterprise Linux, it is in the `xorg-x11-apps` package). Run the `xeyes` command about 20 times in the background so that 20 `xeyes` windows appear on the screen. Move the mouse around and watch the eyes watch your mouse pointer. When you have had enough fun, kill all `xeyes` processes in one command using `killall`.

9. As a regular user, run the `gedit` command so it starts with a nice value of 5.

10. Using the `renice` command, change the nice value of the `gedit` command you just started to 7. Use any command you like to verify that the current nice value for the `gedit` command is now set to 7.

Writing Simple Shell Scripts

IN THIS CHAPTER

Working with shell scripts

Doing arithmetic in shell scripts

Running loops and cases in shell scripts

Creating simple shell scripts

Y ou'd never get any work done if you typed every command that needs to be run on your Linux system when it starts. Likewise, you could work more efficiently if you grouped together sets of commands that you run all the time. Shell scripts can handle these tasks.

A *shell script* is a group of commands, functions, variables, or just about anything else you can use from a shell. These items are typed into a plain text file. That file can then be run as a command. Linux systems have traditionally used system initialization shell scripts during system startup to run commands needed to get services going. You can create your own shell scripts to automate the tasks you need to do regularly.

This chapter provides a rudimentary overview of the inner workings of shell scripts and how they can be used. You learn how simple scripts can be harnessed to a scheduling facility (such as `cron` or `at`) to simplify administrative tasks or just run on demand as they are needed.

Understanding Shell Scripts

Have you ever had a task that you needed to do over and over that took lots of typing on the command line? Do you ever think to yourself, "Wow, I wish I could just type one command to do all this"? Maybe a shell script is what you're after.

Shell scripts are the equivalent of batch files in MS-DOS and can contain long lists of commands, complex flow control, arithmetic evaluations, user-defined variables, user-defined functions, and sophisticated condition testing. Shell scripts are capable of handling everything from simple one-line commands to something as complex as starting up your Linux system. Although dozens of different shells are available in Linux, the default shell for most Linux systems is called bash, the Bourne Again Shell.

Executing and debugging shell scripts

One of the primary advantages of shell scripts is that they can be opened in any text editor to see what they do. A big disadvantage is that large or complex shell scripts often execute more slowly than compiled programs. You can execute a shell script in two basic ways:

- The filename is used as an argument to the shell (as in `bash myscript`). In this method, the file does not need to be executable; it just contains a list of shell commands. The shell specified on the command line is used to interpret the commands in the script file. This is most common for quick, simple tasks.

- The shell script may also have the name of the interpreter placed in the first line of the script preceded by `#!` (as in `#!/bin/bash`) and have the execute bit of the file containing the script set (using `chmod +x filename`). You can then run your script just like any other program in your path simply by typing the name of the script on the command line.

When scripts are executed in either manner, options for the program may be specified on the command line. Anything following the name of the script is referred to as a *command-line argument*.

As with writing any software, there is no substitute for clear and thoughtful design and lots of comments. The pound sign (#) prefaces comments and can take up an entire line or exist on the same line after script code. It is best to implement more complex shell scripts in stages, making sure the logic is sound at each step before continuing. Here are a few good, concise tips to make sure things are working as expected during testing:

- In some cases, you can place an `echo` statement at the beginning of lines within the body of a loop and surround the command with quotes. That way, rather than executing the code, you can see what will be executed without making any permanent changes.

- To achieve the same goal, you can place dummy `echo` statements throughout the code. If these lines get printed, you know the correct logic branch is being taken.

- You can use `set -x` near the beginning of the script to display each command that is executed or launch your scripts using

  ```
  $ bash -x myscript
  ```

- Because useful scripts have a tendency to grow over time, keeping your code readable as you go along is extremely important. Do what you can to keep the logic of your code clean and easy to follow.

Understanding shell variables

Often within a shell script, you want to reuse certain items of information. During the course of processing the shell script, the name or number representing this information may change. To store information used by a shell script in such a way that it can be easily reused, you can set variables. Variable names within shell scripts are case-sensitive and can be defined in the following manner:

```
NAME=value
```

The first part of a variable is the variable name, and the second part is the value set for that name. Be sure that the NAME and value touch the equal sign, without any spaces. Variables can be assigned from constants, such as text, numbers, and underscores. This is useful for initializing values or saving lots of typing for long constants. The following examples show variables set to a string of characters (CITY) and a numeric value (PI):

```
CITY="Springfield"
PI=3.14159265
```

Variables can contain the output of a command or command sequence. You can accomplish this by preceding the command with a dollar sign and open parenthesis, and following it with a closing parenthesis. For example, MYDATE=$(date) assigns the output from the date command to the MYDATE variable. Enclosing the command in backticks (`) can have the same effect. In this case, the date command is run when the variable is set and not each time the variable is read.

7

Escaping Special Shell Characters

Keep in mind that characters such as dollar sign ($), backtick (`), asterisk (*), exclamation point (!), and others have special meaning to the shell, which you will see as you proceed through this chapter. On some occasions, you want the shell to use these characters' special meaning and other times you don't. For example, if you typed echo $HOME, the shell would think you meant to display the name of your home directory (stored in the $HOME variable) to the screen (such as /home/chris) because a $ indicates a variable name follows that character.

If you wanted to literally show $HOME, you would need to escape the $. Typing echo '$HOME' or echo \$HOME would literally show $HOME on the screen. So, if you want to have the shell interpret a single character literally, precede it with a backslash (\). To have a whole set of characters interpreted literally, surround those characters with single quotes (').

Using double quotes is a bit trickier. Surround a set of text with double quotes if you want all but a few characters used literally. For example, with text surrounded with double quotes, dollar signs ($), backticks (`), and exclamation points (!) are interpreted specially, but other characters (such as an asterisk) are not. Type these two lines to see the different output (shown on the right):

```
echo '$HOME *** `date`'    $HOME *** `date`
echo "$HOME *** `date`"    /home/chris file1 file2 Tue Jan 20 16:56:52 EDT 2015
```

Using variables is a great way to get information that can change from computer to computer or from day to day. The following example sets the output of the uname -n command to the MACHINE variable. Then I use parentheses to set NUM_FILES to the number of files in the current directory by piping (|) the output of the ls command to the word count command (wc -l).

```
MACHINE=`uname -n`
NUM_FILES=$(/bin/ls | wc -l)
```

Variables can also contain the value of other variables. This is useful when you have to preserve a value that will change so you can use it later in the script. Here, BALANCE is set to the value of the CurBalance variable:

```
BALANCE="$CurBalance"
```

> **NOTE**
>
> When assigning variables, use only the variable name (for example, BALANCE). When you reference a variable, meaning you want the value of the variable, precede it with a dollar sign (as in $CurBalance). The result of the latter is that you get the value of the variable, not the variable name itself.

Special shell positional parameters

There are special variables that the shell assigns for you. One set of commonly used variables is called *positional parameters* or *command line arguments* and is referenced as $0, $1, $2, $3...$n. $0 is special and is assigned the name used to invoke your script; the others are assigned the values of the parameters passed on the command line, in the order they appeared. For example, let's say you had a shell script named myscript that contained the following:

```
#!/bin/bash
# Script to echo out command-line arguments
echo "The first argument is $1, the second is $2."
echo "The command itself is called $0."
```

Assuming the script is executable and located in a directory in your $PATH, the following shows what would happen if you ran that command with foo and bar as arguments:

```
$ chmod 755 /home/chris/bin/myscript
$ myscript foo bar
The first argument is foo, the second is bar.
The command itself is called /home/chris/bin/myscript.
```

As you can see, the positional parameter $0 is the full path or relative path to myscript, $1 is foo, and $2 is bar.

Another variable, $#, tells you how many parameters your script was given. In the example, $# would be 2. The $@ variable holds all the arguments entered at the command line. Another particularly useful special shell variable is $?, which receives the exit status of the last command executed. Typically, a value of zero means the command exited successfully, and anything other than zero indicates an error of some kind. For a complete list of special shell variables, refer to the bash man page.

Reading in parameters

Using the read command, you can prompt the user for information, and store that information to use later in your script. Here's an example of a script that uses the read command:

```
#!/bin/bash
read -p "Type in an adjective, noun and verb (past tense): " a1 n1 v1
echo "He sighed and $v1 to the elixir. Then he ate the $a1 $n1."
```

In this script, after prompting for an adjective, noun, and verb, the user is expected to enter words that are then assigned to the adj1, noun1, and verb1 variables. Those three variables are then included in a silly sentence, which is displayed on the screen. If the script were called sillyscript, here's an example of how it might run:

```
$ chmod 755 /home/chris/bin/sillyscript
$ sillyscript
Type in an adjective, noun and verb (past tense): hairy football
danced
He sighed and danced to the elixir. Then he ate the hairy
football.
```

Parameter expansion in bash

As mentioned earlier, if you want the value of a variable, you precede it with a $ (for example, $CITY). This is really just shorthand for the notation ${CITY}; curly braces are used when the value of the parameter needs to be placed next to other text without a space. Bash has special rules that allow you to expand the value of a variable in different ways. Going into all the rules is probably overkill for a quick introduction to shell scripts, but the following list presents some common constructs you're likely to see in bash scripts you find on your Linux system.

- ${var:-value}—If variable is unset or empty, expand this to *value*.
- ${var#pattern}—Chop the shortest match for *pattern* from the front of *var*'s value.
- ${var##pattern}—Chop the longest match for *pattern* from the front of *var*'s value.
- ${var%pattern}—Chop the shortest match for *pattern* from the end of *var*'s value.
- ${var%%pattern}—Chop the longest match for *pattern* from the end of *var*'s value.

Try typing the following commands from a shell to test how parameter expansion works:

```
$ THIS="Example"
$ THIS=${THIS:-"Not Set"}
$ THAT=${THAT:-"Not Set"}
$ echo $THIS
Example
$ echo $THAT
Not Set
```

In the examples here, the THIS variable is initially set to the word Example. In the next two lines, the THIS and THAT variables are set to their current values or to Not Set, if they are not currently set. Notice that because I just set THIS to the string Example, when I echo the value of THIS it appears as Example. However, because THAT was not set, it appears as Not Set.

> **NOTE**
>
> For the rest of this section, I show how variables and commands may appear in a shell script. To try out any of those examples, however, you can simply type them into a shell, as shown in the previous example.

In the following example, MYFILENAME is set to /home/digby/myfile.txt. Next, the FILE variable is set to myfile.txt and DIR is set to /home/digby. In the NAME variable, the filename is cut down to simply myfile; then, in the EXTENSION variable, the file extension is set to txt. (To try these out, you can type them at a shell prompt as in the previous example and echo the value of each variable to see how it is set.) Type the code on the left. The material on the right side describes the action.

MYFILENAME=/home/digby/myfile.txt—Sets the value of MYFILENAME

FILE=${MYFILENAME##*/}—FILE becomes myfile.txt

DIR=${MYFILENAME%/*}—DIR becomes /home/digby

NAME=${FILE%.*}—NAME becomes myfile

EXTENSION=${FILE##*.}—EXTENSION becomes txt

Performing arithmetic in shell scripts

Bash uses *untyped variables,* meaning it normally treats variables as strings or text, but can change them on the fly if you want it to. Unless you tell it otherwise with declare, your variables are just a bunch of letters to bash. But when you start trying to do arithmetic with them, bash converts them to integers if it can. This makes it possible to do some fairly complex arithmetic in bash.

Integer arithmetic can be performed using the built-in let command or through the external expr or bc commands. After setting the variable BIGNUM value to 1024, the three commands that follow would all store the value 64 in the RESULT variable. The bc command is a calculator application that is available in most Linux distributions. The last command gets a random number between 0 and 10 and echoes the results back to you.

```
BIGNUM=1024
let RESULT=$BIGNUM/16
RESULT=`expr $BIGNUM / 16`
RESULT=`echo "$BIGNUM / 16" | bc`
let foo=$RANDOM; echo $foo
```

Another way to incrementally grow a variable is to use $(()) notation with ++I added to increment the value of I. Try typing the following:

```
$ I=0
$ echo The value of I after increment is $((++I))
The value of I after increment is 1

$ echo The value of I before and after increment is $((I++)) and $I
The value of I before and after increment is 1 and 2
```

Repeat either of those commands to continue to increment the value of $I.

> **NOTE**
>
> Although most elements of shell scripts are relatively freeform (where whitespace, such as spaces or tabs, is insignificant), both let and expr are particular about spacing. The let command insists on no spaces between each operand and the mathematical operator, whereas the syntax of the expr command requires whitespace between each operand and its operator. In contrast to those, bc isn't picky about spaces, but can be trickier to use because it does floating-point arithmetic.

To see a complete list of the kinds of arithmetic you can perform using the let command, type **help let** at the bash prompt.

Using programming constructs in shell scripts

One of the features that makes shell scripts so powerful is that their implementation of looping and conditional execution constructs is similar to those found in more complex scripting and programming languages. You can use several different types of loops, depending on your needs.

The "if...then" statements

The most commonly used programming construct is conditional execution, or the if statement. It is used to perform actions only under certain conditions. There are several variations of if statements for testing various types of conditions.

The first if...then example tests if VARIABLE is set to the number 1. If it is, then the echo command is used to say that it is set to 1. The fi statement then indicates that the if statement is complete and processing can continue.

```
VARIABLE=1
if [ $VARIABLE -eq 1 ] ; then
echo "The variable is 1"
fi
```

Instead of using -eq, you can use the equal sign (=), as shown in the following example. The = works best for comparing string values, while -eq is often better for comparing numbers. Using the else statement, different words can be echoed if the criterion of the if statement isn't met ($STRING = "Friday"). Keep in mind that it's good practice to put strings in double quotes.

```
STRING="Friday"
if [ $STRING = "Friday" ] ; then
echo "WhooHoo.  Friday."
else
echo "Will Friday ever get here?"
fi
```

You can also reverse tests with an exclamation mark (!). In the following example, if STRING is not Monday, then "At least it's not Monday" is echoed.

```
STRING="FRIDAY"
if [ "$STRING" != "Monday" ] ; then
    echo "At least it's not Monday"
fi
```

In the following example, elif (which stands for "else if") is used to test for an additional condition (for example, whether filename is a file or a directory).

```
filename="$HOME"
if [ -f "$filename" ] ; then
    echo "$filename is a regular file"
elif [ -d "$filename" ] ; then
    echo "$filename is a directory"
else
    echo "I have no idea what $filename is"
fi
```

As you can see from the preceding examples, the condition you are testing is placed between square brackets [ ]. When a test expression is evaluated, it returns either a value of 0, meaning that it is true, or a 1, meaning that it is false. Notice that the echo lines are indented. The indentation is optional and done only to make the script more readable.

Table 7.1 lists the conditions that are testable and is quite a handy reference. (If you're in a hurry, you can type **help test** on the command line to get the same information.)

TABLE 7.1 **Operators for Test Expressions**

Operator	What Is Being Tested?
-a *file*	Does the file exist? (same as -e)
-b *file*	Is the file a block special device?
-c *file*	Is the file character special (for example, a character device)? Used to identify serial lines and terminal devices.
-d *file*	Is the file a directory?
-e *file*	Does the file exist? (same as -a)
-f *file*	Does the file exist, and is it a regular file (for example, not a directory, socket, pipe, link, or device file)?
-g *file*	Does the file have the set-group-id (SGID) bit set?
-h *file*	Is the file a symbolic link? (same as -L)
-k *file*	Does the file have the sticky bit set?
-L *file*	Is the file a symbolic link?
-n *string*	Is the length of the string greater than 0 bytes?
-O *file*	Do you own the file?
-p *file*	Is the file a named pipe?
-r *file*	Is the file readable by you?
-s *file*	Does the file exist, and is it larger than 0 bytes?
-S *file*	Does the file exist, and is it a socket?
-t *fd*	Is the file descriptor connected to a terminal?
-u *file*	Does the file have the set-user-id (SUID) bit set?
-w *file*	Is the file writable by you?
-x *file*	Is the file executable by you?
-z *string*	Is the length of the string 0 (zero) bytes?
expr1 -a *expr2*	Are both the first expression and the second expression true?
expr1 -o *expr2*	Is either of the two expressions true?
file1 -nt *file2*	Is the first file newer than the second file (using the modification timestamp)?
file1 -ot *file2*	Is the first file older than the second file (using the modification timestamp)?
file1 -ef *file2*	Are the two files associated by a link (a hard link or a symbolic link)?
var1 = *var2*	Is the first variable equal to the second variable?
var1 -eq *var2*	Is the first variable equal to the second variable?
var1 -ge *var2*	Is the first variable greater than or equal to the second variable?
var1 -gt *var2*	Is the first variable greater than the second variable?
var1 -le *var2*	Is the first variable less than or equal to the second variable?
var1 -lt *var2*	Is the first variable less than the second variable?
var1 != *var2*	Is the first variable not equal to the second variable?
var1 -ne *var2*	Is the first variable not equal to the second variable?

7

There is also a special shorthand method of performing tests that can be useful for simple *one-command actions*. In the following example, the two pipes (||) indicate that if the directory being tested for doesn't exist (-d dirname), then make the directory (mkdir $dirname).

```
# [ test ] || action
# Perform simple single command if test is false
dirname="/tmp/testdir"
[ -d "$dirname" ] || mkdir "$dirname"
```

Instead of pipes, you can use two ampersands to test if something is true. In the following example, a command is being tested to see if it includes at least three command-line arguments.

```
# [ test ] && {action}
# Perform simple single action if test is true
[ $# -ge 3 ] && echo "There are at least 3 command line arguments."
```

You can combine the && and || operators to make a quick, one-line if-then-else statement. The following example tests that the directory represented by $dirname already exists. If it does, a message says the directory already exists. If it doesn't, the statement creates the directory:

```
# dirname=mydirectory
# [ -e $dirname ] && echo $dirname already exists || mkdir $dirname
```

The case command

Another frequently used construct is the case command. Similar to a switch statement in programming languages, this can take the place of several nested if statements. The following is the general form of the case statement:

```
case "VAR" in
    Result1)
        { body };;
    Result2)
        { body };;
    *)
        { body };;
esac
```

Among other things, you can use the case command to help with your backups. The following case statement tests for the first three letters of the current day (case 'date +%a' in). Then, depending on the day, a particular backup directory (BACKUP) and tape drive (TAPE) are set.

```
# Our VAR doesn't have to be a variable,
# it can be the output of a command as well
# Perform action based on day of week
case `date +%a` in
    "Mon")
            BACKUP=/home/myproject/data0
```

```
                TAPE=/dev/rft0
   # Note the use of the double semi-colon to end each option
          ;;
   # Note the use of the "|" to mean "or"
      "Tue" | "Thu")
             BACKUP=/home/myproject/data1
             TAPE=/dev/rft1
             ;;
      "Wed" | "Fri")
             BACKUP=/home/myproject/data2
             TAPE=/dev/rft2
             ;;
   # Don't do backups on the weekend.
      *)

   BACKUP="none"
             TAPE=/dev/null
             ;;
   esac
```

The asterisk (*) is used as a catchall, similar to the `default` keyword in the C programming language. In this example, if none of the other entries are matched on the way down the loop, the asterisk is matched, and the value of `BACKUP` becomes `none`. Note the use of `esac`, or `case` spelled backwards, to end the `case` statement.

The "for...do" loop

Loops are used to perform actions over and over again until a condition is met or until all data has been processed. One of the most commonly used loops is the `for...do` loop. It iterates through a list of values, executing the body of the loop for each element in the list. The syntax and a few examples are presented here:

```
for VAR in LIST
do
    { body }
done
```

The `for` loop assigns the values in *LIST* to *VAR* one at a time. Then for each value, the body in braces between `do` and `done` is executed. VAR can be any variable name, and LIST can be composed of pretty much any list of values or anything that generates a list.

```
for NUMBER in 0 1 2 3 4 5 6 7 8 9
do
    echo The number is $NUMBER
done

for FILE in `/bin/ls`
do
    echo $FILE
done
```

You can also write it this way, which is somewhat cleaner:

```
for NAME in John Paul Ringo George ; do
    echo $NAME is my favorite Beatle
done
```

Each element in the LIST is separated from the next by whitespace. This can cause trouble if you're not careful because some commands, such as ls -l, output multiple fields per line, each separated by whitespace. The string done ends the for statement.

If you're a die-hard C programmer, bash allows you to use C syntax to control your loops:

```
LIMIT=10
# Double parentheses, and no $ on LIMIT even though it's a variable!
for ((a=1; a <= LIMIT ; a++)) ; do
  echo  "$a"
done
```

The "while...do" and "until...do" loops

Two other possible looping constructs are the while...do loop and the until...do loop. The structure of each is presented here:

```
while condition        until condition
do                     do
    { body }               { body }
done                   done
```

The while statement executes while the condition is true. The until statement executes until the condition is true—in other words, while the condition is false.

Here is an example of a while loop that outputs the number 0123456789:

```
N=0
while [ $N -lt 10 ] ; do
    echo -n $N
    let N=$N+1
done
```

Another way to output the number 0123456789 is to use an until loop as follows:

```
N=0
until [ $N -eq 10 ] ; do
    echo -n $N
    let N=$N+1
done
```

Trying some useful text manipulation programs

Bash is great and has lots of built-in commands, but it usually needs some help to do anything really useful. Some of the most common useful programs you'll see used are grep, cut, tr, awk, and sed. As with all the best UNIX tools, most of these programs are designed to work with standard input and standard output, so you can easily use them with pipes and shell scripts.

The general regular expression parser

The name *general regular expression parser* (grep) sounds intimidating, but grep is just a way to find patterns in files or text. Think of it as a useful search tool. Gaining expertise with regular expressions is quite a challenge, but after you master it, you can accomplish many useful things with just the simplest forms.

For example, you can display a list of all regular user accounts by using grep to search for all lines that contain the text /home in the /etc/passwd file as follows:

```
$ grep /home /etc/passwd
```

Or you could find all environment variables that begin with HO using the following command:

```
$ env | grep ^HO
```

> **NOTE**
>
> The ^ in the preceding code is the actual caret character, ^, not what you'll commonly see for a backspace, ^H. Type ^, **H**, and **O** (the uppercase letter) to see what items start with the uppercase characters **HO**.

To find a list of options to use with the grep command, type **man grep**.

Remove sections of lines of text (cut)

The cut command can extract fields from a line of text or from files. It is very useful for parsing system configuration files into easy-to-digest chunks. You can specify the field separator you want to use and the fields you want, or you can break up a line based on bytes.

The following example lists all home directories of users on your system. This grep command line pipes a list of regular users from the /etc/passwd file and displays the sixth field (-f6) as delimited by a colon (-d':'). The hyphen at the end tells cut to read from standard input (from the pipe).

```
$ grep /home /etc/passwd | cut  -d':' -f6 -
```

Translate or delete characters (tr)

The tr command is a character-based translator that can be used to replace one character or set of characters with another or to remove a character from a line of text.

The following example translates all uppercase letters to lowercase letters and displays the words mixed upper and lower case as a result:

```
$ FOO="Mixed UPpEr aNd LoWeR cAsE"
$ echo $FOO | tr [A-Z] [a-z]
mixed upper and lower case
```

In the next example, the tr command is used on a list of filenames to rename any files in that list so that any tabs or spaces (as indicated by the [:blank:] option) contained in a filename are translated into underscores. Try running the following code in a test directory:

```
for file in * ; do
    f=`echo $file | tr [:blank:] [_]`
    [ "$file" = "$f" ] || mv -i -- "$file" "$f"
done
```

The stream editor (sed)

The sed command is a simple scriptable editor, so it can perform only simple edits, such as removing lines that have text matching a certain pattern, replacing one pattern of characters with another, and so on. To get a better idea of how sed scripts work, there's no substitute for the online documentation, but here are some examples of common uses.

You can use the sed command to essentially do what I did earlier with the grep example: search the /etc/passwd file for the word home. Here the sed command searches the entire /etc/passwd file, searches for the word home, and prints any line containing the word home.

```
$ sed -n '/home/p' /etc/passwd
```

In this example, sed searches the file somefile.txt and replaces every instance of the string Mac with Linux. Notice that the letter g is needed at the end of the substitution command to cause every occurrence of Mac on each line to be changed to Linux. (Otherwise, only the first instance of Mac on each line is changed.) The output is then sent to the fixed_file.txt file. The output from sed goes to stdout, so this command redirects the output to a file for safekeeping.

```
$ sed 's/Mac/Linux/g' somefile.txt > fixed_file.txt
```

You can get the same result using a pipe:

```
$ cat somefile.txt | sed 's/Mac/Linux/g' > fixed_file.txt
```

By searching for a pattern and replacing it with a null pattern, you delete the original pattern. This example searches the contents of the somefile.txt file and replaces extra blank spaces at the end of each line (s/ *$) with nothing (//). Results go to the fixed_file.txt file.

```
$ cat somefile.txt | sed 's/ *$//' > fixed_file.txt
```

Using simple shell scripts

Sometimes, the simplest of scripts can be the most useful. If you type the same sequence of commands repetitively, it makes sense to store those commands (once!) in a file. The following sections offer a couple of simple, but useful, shell scripts.

Telephone list

This idea has been handed down from generation to generation of old UNIX hacks. It's really quite simple, but it employs several of the concepts just introduced.

```
#!/bin/bash
# (@)/ph
# A very simple telephone list
# Type "ph new name number" to add to the list, or
# just type "ph name" to get a phone number

PHONELIST=~/.phonelist.txt

# If no command line parameters ($#), there
# is a problem, so ask what they're talking about.
if [ $# -lt 1 ] ; then
  echo "Whose phone number did you want? "
    exit 1
fi

# Did you want to add a new phone number?
if [ $1 = "new" ] ; then
  shift
  echo $* >> $PHONELIST
  echo $* added to database
  exit 0
fi

# Nope. But does the file have anything in it yet?
# This might be our first time using it, after all.
if [ ! -s $PHONELIST ] ; then
  echo "No names in the phone list yet! "
  exit 1
else
  grep -i -q "$*" $PHONELIST       # Quietly search the file
  if [ $? -ne 0 ] ; then           # Did we find anything?
    echo "Sorry, that name was not found in the phone list"
    exit 1
  else
    grep -i "$*" $PHONELIST
  fi
fi
exit 0
```

So, if you created the telephone list file as ph in your current directory, you could type the following from the shell to try out your ph script:

```
$ chmod 755 ph
$ ./ph new "Mary Jones" 608-555-1212
Mary Jones 608-555-1212 added to database
$ ./ph Mary
Mary Jones 608-555-1212
```

The chmod command makes the ph script executable. The ./ph command runs the ph command from the current directory with the new option. This adds Mary Jones as the name and 608-555-1212 as the phone number to the database ($HOME/.phone.txt). The next ph command searches the database for the name Mary and displays the phone entry for Mary. If the script works, add it to a directory in your path (such as $HOME/bin).

Backup script

Because nothing works forever and mistakes happen, backups are just a fact of life when dealing with computer data. This simple script backs up all the data in the home directories of all the users on your Fedora or RHEL system.

```
#!/bin/bash
# (@)/my_backup
# A very simple backup script
#

# Change the TAPE device to match your system.
# Check /var/log/messages to determine your tape device.
# You may also need to add scsi-tape support to your kernel.
TAPE=/dev/rft0

# Rewind the tape device $TAPE
mt $TAPE rew
# Get a list of home directories
HOMES=`grep /home /etc/passwd | cut -f6 -d':'`
# Back up the data in those directories
tar cvf $TAPE $HOMES
# Rewind and eject the tape.
mt $TAPE rewoffl
```

Summary

Writing shell scripts gives you the opportunity to automate many of your most common system administration tasks. This chapter covered common commands and functions you can use in scripting with the bash shell. It also provided some concrete examples of scripts for doing backups and other procedures.

In the next chapter, you transition from learning about user features into examining system administration topics. Chapter 8 covers how to become the root user, as well as how to use administrative commands, monitor log files, and work with configuration files.

Exercises

Use these exercises to test your knowledge of writing simple shell scripts. These tasks assume you are running a Fedora or Red Hat Enterprise Linux system (although some tasks work on other Linux systems as well). If you are stuck, solutions to the tasks are shown in Appendix B (although in Linux, there are often multiple ways to complete a task).

1. Create a script in your $HOME/bin directory called `myownscript`. When the script runs, it should output information that looks as follows:

   ```
   Today is Sat Dec 10 15:45:04 EST 2016.
   You are in /home/joe and your host is abc.example.com.
   ```

   Of course, you need to read in your current date/time, current working directory, and hostname. Also, include comments about what the script does and indicate that the script should run with the /bin/bash shell.

2. Create a script that reads in three positional parameters from the command line, assigns those parameters to variables named ONE, TWO, and THREE, respectively, and outputs that information in the following format:

   ```
   There are X parameters that include Y.
   The first is A, the second is B, the third is C.
   ```

   Replace X with the number of parameters and Y with all parameters entered. Then replace A with the contents of variable ONE, B with variable TWO, and C with variable THREE.

3. Create a script that prompts users for the name of the street and town where they grew up. Assign town and street to variables called `mytown` and `mystreet`, and output them with a sentence that reads as shown in the following code (of course, $mystreet and $mytown will appear with the actual town and street the user enters):

   ```
   The street I grew up on was $mystreet and the town was $mytown.
   ```

4. Create a script called `myos` that asks the user, "What is your favorite operating system?" Output an insulting sentence if the user types Windows or Mac. Respond "Great choice!" if the user types Linux. For anything else, say "Is <what is typed in> an operating system?"

5. Create a script that runs the words moose, cow, goose, and sow through a `for` loop. Have each of those words appended to the end of the line "I have a...."

Part III

Becoming a Linux System Administrator

Learning System Administration

L inux, like other UNIX-based systems, was intended for use by more than one person at a time. *Multiuser* features enable many people to have accounts on a single Linux system, with their data kept secure from others. *Multitasking* enables many people to run many programs on the computer at the same time, with each person able to run more than one program. Sophisticated networking protocols and applications make it possible for a Linux system to extend its capabilities to network users and computers around the world. The person assigned to manage all of a Linux system's resources is called the *system administrator*.

Even if you are the only person using a Linux system, system administration is still set up to be separate from other computer use. To do most administrative tasks, you need to be logged in as the *root user* (also called the *superuser*) or to temporarily get root permission (usually using the sudo command). Regular users who don't have root permission cannot change, or in some cases even see, some of the configuration information for a Linux system. In particular, security features such as stored passwords are protected from general view.

Because Linux system administration is such a huge topic, this chapter focuses on the general principles of Linux system administration. In particular, it examines some of the basic tools you need to administer a Linux system for a personal desktop or on a small server. Beyond the basics, this chapter also teaches you how to work with file systems and monitor the setup and performance of your Linux system.

Understanding System Administration

Separating the role of system administrator from that of other users has several effects. For a system that has many people using it, limiting who can manage it enables you to keep a system more secure. A separate administrative role also prevents others from casually harming your system when they are just using it to write a document or browse the Internet.

If you are the system administrator of a Linux system, you generally log in as a regular user account and then ask for administrative privileges when you need them. This is often done with one of the following:

- su **command**—Often, su is used to open a shell as root user. After it is open, the administrator can run multiple commands and then exit to return to a shell as a regular user.

- sudo **command**—With sudo, a regular user is given root privileges, but only when that user runs the sudo command to run another command. After running that one command with sudo, the user is immediately returned to a shell and acts as the regular user again. Ubuntu assigns sudo privilege to the first user account on an Ubuntu system by default. This is not done by default in Fedora and RHEL, although you can choose for your first user to have sudo privilege if you like, during Fedora or RHEL installation.

- **Graphical windows**—Many graphical administration windows, which can be launched from the System or Applications menu (GNOME 2) or Activities screen (GNOME 3), can be started by a regular user. With some tools, when root privilege is needed, you are prompted for the root password.

Tasks that can be done by only the root user tend to be those that affect the system as a whole or impact the security or health of the system. The following is a list of common features that a system administrator is expected to manage:

- **Filesystems**—When you first install Linux, the directory structure is set up to make the system usable. However, if users later want to add extra storage or change the filesystem layout outside their home directory, they need administrative privileges to do that. Also, the root user has permission to access files owned by any user. As a result, the root user can copy, move, or change any other user's files—a privilege needed to make backup copies of the filesystem for safe keeping.

- **Software installation**—Because malicious software can harm your system or make it insecure, you need root privilege to install software so it is available to all users on your system. Regular users can still install some software in their own directories and can list information about installed system software.

- **User accounts**—Only the root user can add and remove user accounts and group accounts.

- **Network interfaces**—In the past, the root user had to configure network interfaces and start and stop those interfaces. Now, many Linux desktops allow regular users to start and stop network interfaces from their desktop using Network Manager. This is particularly true for wireless network interfaces, which can come and go by location, as you move your Linux laptop or handheld device around.

- **Servers**—Configuring web servers, file servers, domain name servers, mail servers, and dozens of other servers requires root privilege, as does starting and stopping those services. Content, such as web pages, can be added to servers by non-root users if you configure your system to allow that. Services are often run as special administrative user accounts, such as apache (for the httpd service) and rpc (for the rpcbind service). So if someone cracks a service, they can't get root privilege to other services or system resources.

- **Security features**—Setting up security features, such as firewalls and user access lists, is usually done with root privilege. It's also up to the root user to monitor how the services are being used and make sure that server resources are not exhausted or abused.

The easiest way to begin system administration is to use some graphical administration tools.

Using Graphical Administration Tools

Most system administration for the first Linux systems was done from the command line. As Linux has become more popular, however, both graphical and command-line interfaces began to be offered for most common Linux administrative tasks.

Some of the first graphical system administration tools came from Red Hat. Commands for launching these GUI tools typically start with system-config-*. They can be used for doing basic administrative tasks, such as configuring a printer or setting the date, time, and time zone.

To create wider adoption of Linux in enterprise data centers, however, some of the more prominent software projects for managing cloud projects, identity management, and other services now offer browser-based interfaces. This has helped encourage adoption of Linux in organizations that had previously used Microsoft Windows systems in their data centers.

The following sections describe some of the point-and-click types of interfaces that are available for doing system administration in Linux.

Using system-config-* tools

A set of graphical tools that comes with Fedora and Red Hat Enterprise Linux systems can be launched from the Administration submenu of the System menu (GNOME 2), from the Activities screen (GNOME 3), or from the command line. Most of the Fedora and RHEL tools that launch from the command line begin with the system-config string (such as system-config-network).

These system-config tools require root permission. If you are logged in as a regular user, you must enter the root password before the Graphical User Interface (GUI) application's window opens or, in some cases, when you request to do some special activity.

The following list describes many of the graphical tools you can use to administer a Fedora or Red Hat Enterprise Linux system (some are only in Fedora and many are not installed by default). The command you can launch to get the feature is shown in parentheses (often, it is the same as the package name). The following graphical tools are available in Fedora:

- **Domain Name System** (system-config-bind)—Create and configure zones if your computer is acting as a DNS server.
- **HTTP** (system-config-httpd)—Configure your computer as an Apache web server.
- **NFS** (system-config-nfs)—Set up directories from your system to be shared with other computers on your network using the NFS service.
- **Root Password** (system-config-rootpassword)—Change the root password.
- **Samba NFS** (system-config-samba)—Configure Windows (SMB) file sharing. (To configure other Samba features, you can use the SWAT window.)

The following graphical tools are available in both Fedora and Red Hat Enterprise Linux:

- **Services** (system-config-services)—Display and change which services are running on your Fedora system at different run levels from the Service Configuration window.
- **Authentication** (authconfig-gtk)—Change how users are authenticated on your system. Typically, Shadow Passwords and MD5 Passwords are selected. However, if your network supports LDAP, Kerberos, SMB, NIS, or Hesiod authentication, you can select to use any of those authentication types.
- **Date & Time** (system-config-date)—Set the date and time or choose to have an NTP server keep system time in sync.
- **Firewall** (system-config-firewall)—Configure your firewall to allow or deny services to computers from the network.
- **Language** (system-config-language)—Select the default language used for the system.
- **Printing** (system-config-printer)—Configure local and network printers.
- **SELinux Management** (policycoreutils-gui)—Set SELinux enforcing modes and default policy.
- **Users & Groups** (system-config-users)—Add, display, and change user and group accounts for your Fedora system.

Other administrative utilities are available from the Applications menu on the top panel. Select the System Tools submenu (in GNOME 2) or go to the Activities screen (in GNOME 3) to choose some of the following tools (if they are installed):

- **Configuration Editor** (gconf-editor)—Directly edit the GNOME configuration database.
- **Disk Usage Analyzer** (gnome-utils)—Display detailed information about your hard disks and removable storage devices.

- **Disk Utility** (gnome-disks)—Manage disk partitions and add filesystems (gnome-disk-utility package).
- **Kickstart** (system-config-kickstart)—Create a kickstart configuration file that can be used to install multiple Linux systems without user interaction.

As you go through the rest of this book to configure various Linux servers, I'll describe how to use many of these tools. When you want to go beyond a point-and-click administrative interface, you need to learn how to gain root privilege from the shell, as described in the next section.

Using browser-based admin tools

To simplify the management of many enterprise-quality open source projects, those projects have begun offering browser-based graphical management tools. In most cases, these projects offer command-line tools for managing these projects as well.

For example, if you are using Red Hat Enterprise Linux, there are browser-based interfaces for managing the following projects:

- **Red Hat Enterprise Linux OpenStack Platform (RHELOSP)**—The OpenStack platform-as-a-service project lets you manage your own private, hybrid cloud through your browser. This includes the OpenStack dashboard from the OpenStack Horizon project (http://horizon.openstack.org). That interface lets you launch and manage virtual machines and all the resources around them: storage, networking, authentication, processing allocations, and so on. Refer to Chapter 27 for a description of how to use the OpenStack Dashboard.
- **Red Hat Enterprise Virtualization (RHEV)**—With RHEV, the RHEV manager provides the browser-based interface for managing virtual machines, including allocating storage and user access to resources. Many other examples of browser-based graphical administration tools are available with open source projects. If you are new to Linux, it can be easier to get started with these interfaces. However, keep in mind that often you need to use command line tools if you need to troubleshoot problems, because graphical tools are often limited in that area.

Using the root user account

Every Linux system starts out with at least one administrative user account (the root user) and possibly one or more regular user accounts (given a name that you choose, or a name assigned by your Linux distribution). In most cases, you log in as a regular user and become the root user to do an administrative task.

The root user has complete control of the operation of your Linux system. That user can open any file or run any program. The root user also installs software packages and adds accounts for other people who use the system.

8

When you first install most Linux systems (although not all systems), you add a password for the root user. You must remember and protect this password; you need it to log in as root or to obtain root permission while you are logged in as some other user.

To become familiar with the root user account, you can simply log in as the root user. I recommend trying this from a virtual console. To do so, press Ctrl+Alt+F2. When you see the login prompt, type root (press Enter) and enter the password. A login session for root opens. When you are finished, type exit, and then press Ctrl+Alt+F1 to return to the regular desktop login.

After you have logged in as root, the home directory for the root user is typically /root. The home directory and other information associated with the root user account are located in the /etc/passwd file. Here's what the root entry looks like in the /etc/passwd file:

```
root:x:0:0:root:/root:/bin/bash
```

This shows that for the user named root, the user ID is set to 0 (root user), the group ID is set to 0 (root group), the home directory is /root, and the shell for that user is /bin/bash. (Linux uses the /etc/shadow file to store encrypted password data, so the password field here contains an x.) You can change the home directory or the shell used by editing the values in this file. A better way to change these values, however, is to use the usermod command (see the section "Modifying Users with usermod" in Chapter 11 for further information).

At this point, any command you run from your shell is run with root privilege. So be careful. You have much more power to change (and damage) the system than you did as a regular user. Again, type exit when you are finished, and if you are on a virtual console and have a desktop interface running on another console, press Ctrl+Alt+F1 to return to the graphical login screen, if you are using a Linux desktop system.

Becoming root from the shell (su command)

Although you can become the superuser by logging in as root, sometimes that is not convenient.

- For example, you may be logged in to a regular user account and just want to make a quick administrative change to your system without having to log out and log back in. You may need to log in over the network to make a change to a Linux system but find that the system doesn't allow root users in from over the network (a common practice for secure Linux systems). One solution is to use the `su` command. From any Terminal window or shell, you can simply type the following:

```
$ su
Password: ******
#
```

When you are prompted, type the root user's password. The prompt for the regular user ($) changes to the superuser prompt (#). At this point, you have full permission to run any command and use any file on the system. However, one thing that the `su` command doesn't do when used this way is read in the root user's environment. As a result, you may type a command that you know is available and get the message `Command Not Found`. To fix this problem, use the `su` command with the dash (-) option instead, like this:

```
$ su -
Password: ******
#
```

You still need to type the password, but after that, everything that normally happens at login for the root user happens after the `su` command is completed. Your current directory will be root's home directory (probably `/root`), and things such as the root user's `PATH` variable are used. If you become the root user by just typing `su`, rather than `su -`, you don't change directories or the environment of the current login session.

You can also use the `su` command to become a user other than root. This is useful for troubleshooting a problem that is being experienced by a particular user, but not by others on the computer (such as an inability to print or send email). For example, to have the permissions of a user named jsmith, you'd type the following:

```
$ su - jsmith
```

Even if you were root user before you typed this command, afterward you would have only the permissions to open files and run programs that are available to jsmith. As root user, however, after you type the `su` command to become another user, you don't need a password to continue. If you type that command as a regular user, you must type the new user's password.

When you are finished using superuser permissions, return to the previous shell by exiting the current shell. Do this by pressing Ctrl+D or by typing **exit**. If you are the administrator for a computer that is accessible to multiple users, don't leave a root shell open on someone else's screen—unless you want to give that person freedom to do anything he or she wants to the computer!

8

Allowing administrative access via the GUI

As mentioned earlier, when you run GUI tools as a regular user (from Fedora, Red Hat Enterprise Linux, or some other Linux systems), you are prompted for the root password before you are able to access the tool. By entering the root password, you are given root privilege for that task.

For Linux systems using the GNOME 2 desktop, after you enter the password, a yellow badge icon appears in the top panel, indicating that root authorization is still available for other GUI tools to run from that desktop session. For GNOME 3 desktops, you must enter the root password each time you start any of the system-config tools.

Gaining administrative access with sudo

Particular users can also be given administrative permissions for particular tasks or any task by typing sudo followed by the command they want to run, without being given the root password. The sudoers facility is the most common way to provide such privilege. Using sudoers, for any users or groups on the system, you can do the following:

- Assign root privilege for any command they run with sudo.
- Assign root privilege for a select set of commands.
- Give users root privilege without telling them the root password because they only have to provide their own user password to gain root privilege.
- Allow users, if you choose, to run sudo without entering a password at all.
- Track which users have run administrative commands on your system. (Using su, all you know is that someone with the root password logged in, whereas the sudo command logs which user runs an administrative command.)

With the sudoers facility, giving full or limited root privileges to any user simply entails adding the user to /etc/sudoers and defining what privilege you want that user to have. Then the user can run any command he or she is privileged to use by preceding that command with the sudo command.

Here's an example of how to use the sudo facility to cause the user named joe to have full root privilege.

> **TIP**
>
> If you look at the sudoers file in Ubuntu, you see that the initial user on the system already has privilege, by default, for the admin group members. To give any other user the same privilege, you could simply add the additional user to the admin group when you run visudo.

1. As the root user, edit the /etc/sudoers file by running the visudo command:

   # **/usr/sbin/visudo**

   By default, the file opens in vi, unless your EDITOR variable happens to be set to some other editor acceptable to visudo (for example, export EDITOR=gedit). The reason for using visudo is that the command locks the /etc/sudoers file and does some basic sanity checking of the file to ensure it has been edited correctly.

> **NOTE**
>
> If you are stuck here, try running the vimtutor command for a quick tutorial on using vi and vim.

2. Add the following line to allow joe to have full root privileges on the computer:

   joe   ALL=(ALL)   ALL

   This line causes joe to provide a password (his own password, not the root password) in order to use administrative commands. To allow joe to have that privilege without using a password, type the following line instead:

   joe   ALL=(ALL)   NOPASSWD: ALL

3. Save the changes to the /etc/sudoers file (in vi, type Esc, and then :wq). The following is an example of a session by the user joe after he has been assigned sudo privileges:

```
[joe]$ sudo touch /mnt/testfile.txt
   We trust you have received the usual lecture
   from the local System Administrator. It usually
   boils down to these two things:
     #1) Respect the privacy of others.
     #2) Think before you type.
Password: ********
[joe]$ ls -l /mnt/testfile.txt
-rw-r--r--. 1 root root 0 Jan  7 08:42 /mnt/testfile.txt
[joe]$ rm /mnt/testfile.txt
rm: cannot remove '/mnt/testfile.txt': Permission denied
[joe]$ sudo rm /mnt/textfile.txt
[joe]$
```

In this session, the user joe runs sudo to create a file (/mnt/textfile.txt) in a directory for which he doesn't have write permission. He is given a warning and asked to provide his password (this is joe's password, *not* the root password).

Even after joe has given the password, he must still use the sudo command to run subsequent administrative commands as root (the rm fails, but the sudo rm succeeds). Notice that he is not prompted for a password for the second sudo. That's because after entering his password successfully, he can enter as many sudo commands as he wants for the next 5 minutes without having to enter it again. (You can change the timeout value from 5 minutes to any length of time you want by setting the passwd_timeout value in the /etc/sudoers file.)

8

The preceding example grants a simple all-or-nothing administrative privilege to joe. However, the /etc/sudoers file gives you an incredible amount of flexibility in permitting individual users and groups to use individual applications or groups of applications. Refer to the sudoers and sudo man pages for information about how to tune your sudo facility.

Exploring Administrative Commands, Configuration Files, and Log Files

You can expect to find many commands, configuration files, and log files in the same places in the filesystem, regardless of which Linux distribution you are using. The following sections give you some pointers on where to look for these important elements.

> **NOTE**
>
> If GUI administrative tools for Linux have become so good, why do you need to know about administrative files? For one thing, while GUI tools differ among Linux versions, many underlying configuration files are the same. So, if you learn to work with them, you can work with almost any Linux system. Also, if a feature is broken or if you need to do something that's not supported by the GUI, when you ask for help, Linux experts almost always tell you how to run commands or change the configuration file directly.

Administrative commands

Only the root user is intended to use many administrative commands. When you log in as root (or use su - from the shell to become root), your $PATH variable is set to include some directories that contain commands for the root user. In the past, these have included the following:

- /sbin—Contained commands needed to boot your system, including commands for checking filesystems (fsck) and turn on swap devices (swapon).
- /usr/sbin—Contained commands for such things as managing user accounts (such as useradd) and checking processes that are holding files open (such as lsof). Commands that run as daemon processes are also contained in this directory. Daemon processes are processes that run in the background, waiting for service requests such as those to access a printer or a web page. (Look for commands that end in d, such as sshd, pppd, and cupsd.)

The /sbin and /usr/sbin directories are still used in Ubuntu as described here. However, for RHEL 7 and the latest Fedora releases, all administrative commands from the two directories are stored in the /usr/sbin directory (which is symbolically linked to /sbin). Also, only /usr/sbin is added to the PATH of the root user, as well as the PATH of all regular users.

Some administrative commands are contained in regular user directories (such as /bin and /usr/bin). This is especially true of commands that have some options available to everyone. An example is the /bin/mount command, which anyone can use to list mounted filesystems, but only root can use to mount filesystems. (Some desktops, however, are configured to let regular users use mount to mount CDs, DVDs, or other removable media.)

> **NOTE**
>
> See the section "Mounting Filesystems" in Chapter 12 for instructions on how to mount a filesystem.

To find commands intended primarily for the system administrator, check out the section 8 manual pages (usually in /usr/share/man/man8). They contain descriptions and options for most Linux administrative commands. If you want to add commands to your system, consider adding them to directories such as /usr/local/bin or /usr/local/sbin. Some Linux distributions automatically add those directories to your PATH, usually before your standard bin and sbin directories. In that way, commands installed to those directories not only are accessible, but also can override commands of the same name in other directories. Some third-party applications that are not included with Linux distributions are sometimes placed in the /usr/local/bin, /opt/bin, or /usr/local/sbin directories.

Administrative configuration files

Configuration files are another mainstay of Linux administration. Almost everything you set up for your particular computer—user accounts, network addresses, or GUI preferences—is stored in plaintext files. This has some advantages and some disadvantages.

The advantage of plain text files is that it's easy to read and change them. Any text editor will do. The downside, however, is that as you edit configuration files, no error checking is going on. You have to run the program that reads these files (such as a network daemon or the X desktop) to find out whether you set up the files correctly.

While some configuration files use standard structures, such as XML, for storing information, many do not. So you need to learn the specific structure rules for each configuration file. A comma or a quote in the wrong place can sometimes cause an entire interface to fail.

You can check in many ways that the structure of many configuration files is correct:

- Some software packages offer a command to test the sanity of the configuration file tied to a package before you start a service. For example, the testparm command is used with Samba to check the sanity of your smb.conf file. Other times, the daemon process providing a service offers an option for checking your config file. For example, run httpd -t to check your Apache web server configuration before starting your web server.

> **NOTE**
> Some text editors, such as the `vim` command (not `vi`), understand the structure of some types of configuration files. If you open such a configuration file in `vim`, notice that different elements of the file are shown in different colors. In particular, you can see comment lines in a different color than data.

Throughout this book, you'll find descriptions of the configuration files you need to set up the different features that make up Linux systems. The two major locations of configuration files are your home directory (where your personal configuration files are kept) and the `/etc` directory (which holds system-wide configuration files).

Following are descriptions of directories (and subdirectories) that contain useful configuration files. Those descriptions are followed by some individual configuration files in `/etc` that are of particular interest. Viewing the contents of Linux configuration files can teach you a lot about administering Linux systems.

- `$HOME`—All users store information in their home directories that directs how their login accounts behave. Many configuration files are directly in each user's home directory (such as `/home/joe`) and begin with a dot (.), so they don't appear in a user's directory when you use a standard `ls` command (you need to type `ls -a` to see them). Likewise, dot files and directories won't show up in most file manager windows by default. There are dot files that define the behavior of each user's shell, the desktop look-and-feel, and options used with your text editor. There are even files such as those in each user's `$HOME/.ssh` directory that configure permissions for logging into remote systems. (To see the name of your home directory, type `echo $HOME` from a shell.)

- `/etc`—This directory contains most of the basic Linux system configuration files.

- `/etc/cron*`—Directories in this set contain files that define how the `crond` utility runs applications on a daily (`cron.daily`), hourly (`cron.hourly`), monthly (`cron.monthly`), or weekly (`cron.weekly`) schedule.

- `/etc/cups`—Contains files used to configure the CUPS printing service.

- `/etc/default`—Contains files that set default values for various utilities. For example, the file for the useradd command defines the default group number, home directory, password expiration date, shell, and skeleton directory (`/etc/skel`) that are used when creating a new user account.

- `/etc/httpd`—Contains a variety of files used to configure the behavior of your Apache web server (specifically, the `httpd` daemon process). (On Ubuntu and other Linux systems, `/etc/apache` or `/etc/apache2` is used instead.)

- `/etc/init.d`—Contains the permanent copies of System V-style run-level scripts. These scripts are often linked from the `/etc/rc?.d` directories to have each service associated with a script started or stopped for the particular run level. The

`?` is replaced by the run-level number (0 through 6). Although System V init scripts are still supported, most services are now managed by the `systemd` facility.

- `/etc/mail`—Contains files used to configure your sendmail mail transport agent.

- `/etc/pcmcia`—Contains configuration files that allow you to have a variety of PCMCIA cards configured for your computer (if the `pcmciautils` package is installed). PCMCIA slots are those openings on your laptop that enable you to have credit-card-sized cards attached to your computer. You can attach devices such as modems and external CD-ROMs. With many devices now available as USB devices, PCMCIA slots are less common than they were.

- `/etc/postfix`—Contains configuration files for the postfix mail transport agent.

- `/etc/ppp`—Contains several configuration files used to set up Point-to-Point Protocol (PPP) so you can have your computer dial out to the Internet. (PPP was more commonly used when dial-up modems were popular.)

- `/etc/rc?.d`—There is a separate `rc?.d` directory for each valid system state: `rc0.d` (shutdown state), `rc1.d` (single-user state), `rc2.d` (multiuser state), `rc3.d` (multiuser plus networking state), `rc4.d` (user-defined state), `rc5.d` (multiuser, networking, plus GUI login state), and `rc6.d` (reboot state).

- `/etc/security`—Contains files that set a variety of default security conditions for your computer, basically defining how authentication is done. These files are part of the `pam` (pluggable authentication modules) package.

- `/etc/skel`—Any files contained in this directory are automatically copied to a user's home directory when that user is added to the system. By default, most of these files are dot (.) files, such as `.kde` (a directory for setting KDE desktop defaults) and `.bashrc` (for setting default values used with the bash shell).

- `/etc/sysconfig`—Contains important system configuration files that are created and maintained by various services (including `iptables`, `samba`, and most networking services). These files are critical for Linux distributions, such as Fedora and RHEL, that use GUI administration tools but are not used on other Linux systems at all.

- `/etc/systemd`—Contains files associated with the `systemd` facility, for managing the boot process and system services. In particular, when you run `systemctl` commands to enable and disable services, files that make that happen are stored in subdirectories of the `/etc/systemd/system` directory.

- `/etc/xinetd.d`—Contains a set of files, each of which defines an on-demand network service that the `xinetd` daemon listens for on a particular port.

When the `xinetd` daemon process receives a request for a service, it uses the information in these files to determine which daemon processes to start to handle the request.

The following are some interesting configuration files in `/etc`:

- `aliases`—Can contain distribution lists used by the Linux mail services. (This file is located in `/etc/mail` in Ubuntu when you install the sendmail package.)
- `bashrc`—Sets system-wide defaults for bash shell users. (This may be called `bash.bashrc` on some Linux distributions.)
- `crontab`—Sets times for running automated tasks and variables associated with the `cron` facility (such as the SHELL and PATH associated with `cron`).
- `csh.cshrc` (or `cshrc`)—Sets system-wide defaults for `csh` (C shell) users.
- `exports`—Contains a list of local directories that are available to be shared by remote computers using the Network File System (NFS).
- `fstab`—Identifies the devices for common storage media (hard disk, floppy, CD-ROM, and so on) and locations where they are mounted in the Linux system. This is used by the `mount` command to choose which filesystems to mount when the system first boots.
- `group`—Identifies group names and group IDs (GIDs) that are defined on the system. Group permissions in Linux are defined by the second of three sets of `rwx` (read, write, execute) bits associated with each file and directory.
- `gshadow`—Contains shadow passwords for groups.
- `host.conf`—Used by older applications to set the locations in which domain names (for example, `redhat.com`) are searched for on TCP/IP networks (such as the Internet). By default, the local hosts file is searched and then any name server entries in `resolv.conf`.
- `hostname`—Contains the host name for the local system (beginning in RHEL 7 and recent Fedora and Ubuntu systems).
- `hosts`—Contains IP addresses and host names that you can reach from your computer. (Usually this file is used just to store names of computers on your LAN or small private network.)
- `hosts.allow`—Lists host computers that are allowed to use certain TCP/IP services from the local computer. (This and `hosts.deny` are part of the TCP Wrappers service.)
- `hosts.deny`—Lists host computers that are *not* allowed to use certain TCP/IP services from the local computer (although this file is used if you create it, it doesn't exist by default).

- `inittab`—On earlier Linux systems, contained information that defined which programs start and stop when Linux boots, shuts down, or goes into different states in between. This configuration file was the first one read when Linux started the init process. This file is no longer used on Linux systems that support `systemd`.

- `mtab`—Contains a list of filesystems that are currently mounted.

- `mtools.conf`—Contains settings used by DOS tools in Linux.

- `named.conf`—Contains DNS settings if you are running your own DNS server (bind or bind9 package).

- `nsswitch.conf`—Contains name service switch settings, for identifying where critical systems information (user accounts, host name-to-address mappings, and so on) comes from (local host or via network services).

- `ntp.conf`—Includes information needed to run the Network Time Protocol (NTP).

- `passwd`—Stores account information for all valid users on the local system. Also includes other information, such as the home directory and default shell. (Rarely includes the user passwords themselves, which are typically stored in the `/etc/shadow` file.)

- `printcap`—Contains definitions for the printers configured for your computer. (If the `printcap` file doesn't exist, look for printer information in the `/etc/cups` directory.)

- `profile`—Sets system-wide environment and startup programs for all users. This file is read when the user logs in.

- `protocols`—Sets protocol numbers and names for a variety of Internet services.

- `rpc`—Defines remote procedure call names and numbers.

- `services`—Defines TCP/IP and UDP service names and their port assignments.

- `shadow`—Contains encrypted passwords for users who are defined in the `passwd` file. (This is viewed as a more secure way to store passwords than the original encrypted password in the `passwd` file. The `passwd` file needs to be publicly readable, whereas the `shadow` file can be unreadable by all but the root user.)

- `shells`—Lists the shell command-line interpreters (`bash`, `sh`, `csh`, and so on) that are available on the system, as well as their locations.

- `sudoers`—Sets commands that can be run by users, who may not otherwise have permission to run the command, using the `sudo` command. In particular, this file is used to provide selected users with root permission.

- `rsyslog.conf`—Defines what logging messages are gathered by the `rsyslogd` daemon and what files they are stored in. (Typically, log messages are stored in files contained in the `/var/log` directory.)

8

- `termcap`—Lists definitions for character terminals, so character-based applications know what features are supported by a given terminal. Graphical terminals and applications have made this file obsolete to most people.
- `xinetd.conf`—Contains simple configuration information used by the `xinetd` daemon process. This file mostly points to the `/etc/xinetd.d` directory for information about individual services.

Another directory, `/etc/X11`, includes subdirectories that each contain system-wide configuration files used by X and different X window managers available for Linux. The `xorg.conf` file (configures your computer and monitor to make it usable with X) and configuration directories containing files used by `xdm` and `xinit` to start X are in here.

Directories relating to window managers contain files that include the default values that a user will get if that user starts one of these window managers on your system. Window managers that may have system-wide configuration files in these directories include twm (`twm/`) and xfce (`xdg/`).

Administrative log files and systemd journal

One of the things that Linux does well is keep track of itself. This is a good thing, when you consider how much is going on in a complex operating system.

Sometimes you are trying to get a new facility to work and it fails without giving you the foggiest reason why. Other times, you want to monitor your system to see whether people are trying to access your computer illegally. In any of those cases, you want to be able to refer to messages coming from the kernel and services running on the system.

For Linux systems that don't use the `systemd` facility, the main utility for logging error and debugging messages is the `rsyslogd` daemon. (Some older Linux systems use `syslogd` and `syslogd` daemons.) Although you can still use `rsyslogd` with `systemd` systems, `systemd` has its own method of gathering and displaying messages called the `systemd` journal (`journalctl` command).

Using journalctl to view the systemd journal

The primary command for viewing messages from the `systemd` journal is the `journalctl` command. The boot process, the kernel and all `systemd`-managed services direct their status and error messages to the `systemd` journal.

Using the `journalctl` command, you can display journal messages in many different ways. Here are some examples:

```
# journalctl
# journalctl --list-boots | head
-12 eb3d5cbdda8f4f8da7bdbc71fb94e61e Sun 2014-08-17 15:33:30 EDT...
-11 534713a5a65c41c1b5b3d056487a16db Wed 2014-08-20 06:45:15 EDT...
```

```
-10 64147da7154b4499a312a88a696c19bd Fri 2014-08-29 23:14:38 EDT...
# journalctl -b eb3d5cbdda8f4f8da7bdbc71fb94e61e
# journalctl -k
```

In these examples, the `journalctl` command with no options lets you page through all messages in the `systemd` journal. To list the boot IDs for each time the system was booted, use the `-list-boots` option. To view messages associated with a particular boot instance, use the `-b` option with one of the boot instances. To see only kernel messages, use the `-k` option. Here are some more examples:

```
# journalctl _SYSTEMD_UNIT=sshd.service
# journalctl PRIORITY=0
# journalctl -a -f
```

Use the `_SYSTEMD_UNIT=` options to show messages for specific services (here, the `sshd` service) or for any other `systemd` unit file (such as other services or mounts). To see messages associated with a particular syslog log level (from 0 to 7). In this case, only emergency (0) messages are shown. To follow messages as they come in, use the `-f` option; to show all fields, use the `-a` option.

Managing log messages with rsyslogd

The `rsyslogd` facility, and its predecessor `syslogd`, gather log messages and direct them to log files or remote log hosts. Logging is done according to information in the `/etc/rsyslog.conf` file. Messages are typically directed to log files that are usually in the `/var/log` directory, but can also be directed to log hosts for additional security. Here are a few common log files:

- `boot.log`—Contains boot messages about services as they start up.
- `messages`—Contains many general informational messages about the system.
- `secure`—Contains security-related messages, such as login activity or any other act that authenticates users.
- `XFree86.0.log` or `Xorg.0.log`—Depending on which X server you are using, contains messages about your video card, mouse, and monitor configuration.

Refer to Chapter 13, "Understanding Server Administration," for information on configuring the `rsyslogd` facility.

Using Other Administrative Accounts

You don't hear much about logging in with other administrative user accounts (besides root) on Linux systems. It was a fairly common practice in UNIX systems to have several different administrative logins that allowed administrative tasks to be split among several users. For example, people sitting near a printer could have lp permissions to move print jobs to another printer if they knew a printer wasn't working.

In any case, administrative logins are available with Linux; however, logging in directly as those users is disabled by default. The accounts are maintained primarily to provide ownership for files and processes associated with particular services. By running daemon processes under separate administrative logins, having one of those processes cracked does not give the cracker root permission and the ability to access other processes and files. Consider the following examples:

- lp—User owns such things as the /var/log/cups printing log file and various printing cache and spool files. The home directory for lp is /var/spool/lpd.

- apache—User can be used to set up content files and directories. It is primarily used to run the web server processes (httpd) in RHEL and Fedora systems, while the www-data user runs the Apache service (apache2) on Ubuntu systems.

- avahi—User runs the avahi-daemon process to provide zeroconf services on your network.

- chrony—User runs the chronyd daemon, which is used to maintain accurate computer clocks.

- postfix—User owns various mail server spool directories and files. The user runs the daemon processes used to provide the postfix service (master).

- bin—User owns many commands in /bin in traditional UNIX systems. This is not the case in some Linux systems (such as Ubuntu, Fedora and Gentoo) because root owns most executable files. The home directory of bin is /bin.

- news—User could do administration of Internet news services, depending on how you set permission for /var/spool/news and other news-related resources. The home directory for news is /etc/news.

- rpc—User runs the remote procedure calls daemon (rpcbind), which is used to receive calls for services on the host system. The NFS service uses the RPC service.

By default, the administrative logins in the preceding list are disabled. You would need to change the default shell from its current setting (usually /sbin/nologin or /bin/false) to a real shell (typically /bin/bash) to be able to log in as these users. As mentioned earlier, however, they are really not intended for interactive logins.

Checking and Configuring Hardware

In a perfect world, after installing and booting Linux, all your hardware is detected and available for access. Although Linux systems are rapidly moving closer to that world, sometimes you must take special steps to get your computer hardware working. Also, the growing use of removable USB and FireWire devices (CDs, DVDs, flash drives, digital cameras, and removable hard drives) has made it important for Linux to do the following:

- Efficiently manage hardware that comes and goes
- Look at the same piece of hardware in different ways (for example, be able to see a printer as a fax machine, scanner, and storage device, as well as a printer)

Linux kernel features added in the past few years have made it possible to change drastically the way hardware devices are detected and managed. Features in, or closely related to, the kernel include Udev (to dynamically name and create devices as hardware comes and goes) and HAL (to pass information about hardware changes to user space).

If all this sounds confusing, don't worry. It's designed to make your life as a Linux user much easier. The result of features built on the kernel is that device handling in Linux has become:

- **More automatic**—For most common hardware, when a hardware device is connected or disconnected, it is automatically detected and identified. Interfaces to access the hardware are added, so it is accessible to Linux. Then the fact that the hardware is present (or removed) is passed to the user level, where applications listening for hardware changes are ready to mount the hardware and/or launch an application (such as an image viewer or music player).
- **More flexible**—If you don't like what happens automatically when a hardware item is connected or disconnected, you can change it. For example, features built into GNOME and KDE desktops let you choose what happens when a music CD or data DVD is inserted, or when a digital camera is connected. If you prefer that a different program be launched to handle it, you can easily make that change.

This section covers several issues related to getting your hardware working properly in Linux. First, it describes how to check information about the hardware components of your system. It then covers how to configure Linux to deal with removable media. Finally, it describes how to use tools for manually loading and working with drivers for hardware that is not detected and loaded properly.

Checking your hardware

When your system boots, the kernel detects your hardware and loads drivers that allow Linux to work with that hardware. Because messages about hardware detection scroll quickly off the screen when you boot, to view potential problem messages you have to redisplay those messages after the system comes up.

There are a few ways to view kernel boot messages after Linux comes up. Any user can run the dmesg command to see what hardware was detected and which drivers were loaded by the kernel at boot time. As new messages are generated by the kernel, those messages are also made available to the dmesg command.

A second way to see boot messages on some Linux systems is by displaying the contents of the /var/log/dmesg file, if it exists. A third way is the journalctl command to show the messages associated with a particular boot instance (as shown earlier in this chapter).

> **NOTE**
>
> After your system is running, many kernel messages are sent to the /var/log/messages file. So, for example, if you want to see what happens when you plug in a USB drive, you can type tail -f /var/log/messages and watch as devices and mount points are created. Likewise, you can use the journalctl -f command to follow messages as they come into the systemd journal.

The following is an example of some output from the dmesg command that was trimmed down to show some interesting information:

```
$ dmesg | less
[    0.000000] Linux version 3.16.3-200.fc20.x86_64
        (mockbuild@bkernel02.phx2.fedoraproject.org)
        (gcc version 4.8.3 20140624 (Red Hat 4.8.3-1) (GCC) )
        #1 SMP Wed Sep 17 22:34:21 UTC 2014

[    0.000000] DMI: Dell Inc.        Precision WorkStation 490
        /0GU083, BIOS A06 08/20/2007
[    0.485293] Unpacking initramfs...

[    0.886285] Freeing initrd memory: 17284K...
[    0.056934] CPU0: Intel(R) Xeon(R) CPU E5320 @ 1.86GHz stepping 0b
[    0.272025] Brought up 4 CPUs
[    0.272029] Total of 4 processors activated (14895.38 BogoMIPS).
[    3.020618] Serial: 8250/16550 driver,4 ports,IRQ sharing enabled
[    3.041185] serial8250: ttyS0 at I/O 0x3f8 (irq = 4) is a 16550A
[    3.061880] serial8250: ttyS1 at I/O 0x2f8 (irq = 3) is a 16550A
[    3.145982] mousedev: PS/2 mouse device common for all mice
[    3.538044] scsi 6:0:0:0: CD-ROM
        TSSTcorp DVD-ROM TS-H352C DE02 PQ: 0 ANSI: 5
[    3.870128] input: ImPS/2 Generic Wheel Mouse
        as /devices/platform/i8042/serio1/input/input3
[   26.964764] e1000: Intel(R) PRO/1000 Network Driver
[   26.964767] e1000: Copyright (c) 1999-2006 Intel Corporation.
[   26.964813] e1000 0000:0c:02.0: PCI INT A -> GSI 18 (level, low)
[   27.089109] parport_pc 00:08: reported by Plug and Play ACPI
[   27.089169] parport0: PC-style at 0x378 (0x778), irq 7
[24179.176315] scsi 9:0:0:0: Direct-Access
        S31B1102 USB DISK        1100 PQ: 0 ANSI: 0 CCS
```

```
[24179.177466] sd 9:0:0:0: Attached scsi generic sg2 type 0
[24179.177854] sd 9:0:0:0: [sdb]
               8343552 512-byte logical blocks: (4.27 GB/3.97 GiB)
[24179.178593] sd 9:0:0:0: [sdb] Write Protect is off
```

From this output, you first see the Linux kernel version, followed by information about the computer (Dell Precision WorkStation), and kernel command line options. Next, you can see the type of processors (Intel Xeon) and the number of CPUs (4). After that, I trimmed down to information about hardware connected to the computer: serial ports, mouse port, CD drive, network interface card (e1000), and parallel port. The last few lines reflect a 4GB USB drive being plugged into the computer.

If something goes wrong detecting your hardware or loading drivers, you can refer to this information to see the name and model number of hardware that's not working. Then you can search Linux forums or documentation to try to solve the problem.

After your system is up and running, some other commands let you look at detailed information about your computer's hardware. The lspci command lists PCI buses on your computer and devices connected to them. Here's a snippet of output:

```
$ lspci
00:00.0 Host bridge: Intel Corporation
        5000X Chipset Memory ControllerHub
00:02.0 PCI bridge: Intel Corporation 5000 Series Chipset
        PCI Express x4 Port 2
00:1b.0 Audio device: Intel Corporation 631xESB/632xESB
        High Definition Audio Controller (rev 09)
00:1d.0 USB controller: Intel Corporation 631xESB/632xESB/3100
        Chipset UHCI USBController#1 (rev 09)
07:00.0 VGA compatible controller: nVidia Corporation NV44
0c:02.0 Ethernet controller: Intel Corporation 82541PI
        Gigabit Ethernet Controller (rev 05)
```

The host bridge connects the local bus to the other components on the PCI bridge. I cut down the output to show information about the different devices on the system that handle various features: sound (Audio device), flash drives and other USB devices (USB controller), the video display (VGA compatible controller), and wired network cards (Ethernet controller). If you are having trouble getting any of these devices to work, noting the model names and numbers gives you something to Google for.

To get more verbose output from lspci, add one or more -v options. For example, using lspci -vvv, I received information about my Ethernet controller, including latency, capabilities of the controller, and the Linux driver (e1000) being used for the device.

If you are specifically interested in USB devices, try the lsusb command. By default, lsusb lists information about the computer's USB hubs along with any USB devices connected to the computer's USB ports:

8

```
$ lsusb
Bus 001 Device 001: ID 1d6b:0002 Linux Foundation 2.0 root hub
Bus 002 Device 001: ID 1d6b:0001 Linux Foundation 1.1 root hub
Bus 003 Device 001: ID 1d6b:0001 Linux Foundation 1.1 root hub
Bus 004 Device 001: ID 1d6b:0001 Linux Foundation 1.1 root hub
Bus 005 Device 001: ID 1d6b:0001 Linux Foundation 1.1 root hub
Bus 002 Device 002: ID 413c:2105 Dell Computer Corp.
    Model L100 Keyboard
Bus 002 Device 004: ID 413c:3012 Dell Computer Corp.
    Optical Wheel Mouse
Bus 001 Device 005: ID 090c:1000 Silicon Motion, Inc. -
    Taiwan 64MB QDI U2 DISK
```

From the preceding output, you can see the model of a keyboard, mouse, and USB flash drive connected to the computer. As with lspci, you can add one or more -v options to see more details.

To see details about your processor, run the lscpu command. That command gives basic information about your computer's processors.

```
$ lscpu
Architecture:          x86_64
CPU op-mode(s):        32-bit, 64-bit
CPU(s):                4
On-line CPU(s) list:   0-3
Thread(s) per core:    1
Core(s) per socket:    4
. . .
```

From the sampling of output of lscpu, you can see that this is a 64-bit system (x86-64), it can operate in 32-bit or 64-bit modes, and there are four CPUs.

Managing removable hardware

Linux systems such as Red Hat Enterprise Linux, Fedora, and others that support full KDE and GNOME desktop environments include simple graphical tools for configuring what happens when you attach popular removable devices to the computer. So, with a KDE or GNOME desktop running, you simply plug in a USB device or insert a CD or DVD and a window may pop up to deal with that device.

Although different desktop environments share many of the same underlying mechanisms (in particular, Udev) to detect and name removable hardware, they offer different tools for configuring how they are mounted or used. Udev (using the udevd daemon) creates and removes devices (/dev directory) as hardware is added and removed from the computer. The Hardware Abstraction layer (HAL) provides the overall platform for discovering and configuring hardware. Settings that are of interest to someone using a desktop Linux system, however, can be configured with easy-to-use desktop tools.

The Nautilus file manager used with the GNOME desktop lets you define what happens when you attach removable devices or insert removable media into the computer from the File Management Preferences window. The descriptions in this section are based on GNOME 3.14 in Fedora 21.

From the GNOME 3.14 desktop, select Activities and type **Details**. Then select the Details icon. When the Details window appears, select Removable Media from the left column. Figure 8.1 shows an example of that window.

FIGURE 8.1

Change removable media settings in the Removable Media window.

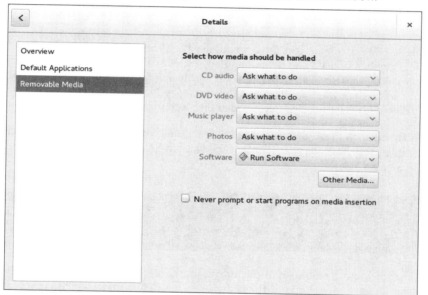

The following settings are available from the Removable Media window. These settings relate to how removable media are handled when they are inserted or plugged in. In most cases, you are prompted about how to handle a medium that is inserted or connected.

- **CD audio**—When an audio CD is inserted, you can choose to be prompted for what to do (default), do nothing, open the contents in a folder window, or select from various audio CD players to be launched to play the content. Rhythmbox (music player), Audio CD Extractor (CD burner), and Brasero (CD burner) are among the choices you have for handling an inserted audio CD.

- **DVD video**—When a commercial video DVD is inserted, you are prompted for what to do with that DVD. You can change that default to launch Totem (videos), Brasero (DVD burner) or another media player you have installed (such as MPlayer).

- **Music player**—When inserted media contains audio files, you are asked what to do. You can select to have Rhythmbox or some other music player begin playing the files by selecting that player from this box.

- **Photos**—When inserted media (such as a memory card from a digital camera) contains digital images, you are asked what to do with those images. You can select to do nothing. Or you can select to have the images opened in the Shotwell image viewer (the default application for viewing images on the GNOME desktop) or another installed photo manager.

- **Software**—When inserted media contains an autorun application, an autorun prompt opens. To change that behavior (to do nothing or open the media contents in a folder), you can select that from this box.

- **Other Media**—Select the Type box under the Other Media heading to select how less commonly used media are handled. For example, you can select what actions are taken to handle audio DVDs or blank Blu-ray discs, CDs, DVDs or HD DVD discs. You can select what applications to launch for Blu-ray video disc, ebook readers, HD DVD videos, Picture CDs, Super Video CDs, and video CDs.

Note that the settings described here are in effect only for the user who is currently logged in. If multiple users have login accounts, each can have his or her own way of handling removable media.

> **NOTE**
>
> The Totem movie player does not play movie DVDs unless you add extra software to decrypt the DVD. You should look into legal issues and other movie player options if you want to play commercial DVD movies from Linux.

The options to connect regular USB flash drives or hard drives are not listed on this window. But if you connect one of those drives to your computer, devices are created when you plug them in (named /dev/sda, /dev/sdb, and so on). Any filesystems found on those devices are automatically mounted on /run/media/*username*, and you are prompted if you want to open a Nautilus window to view files on those devices. This is done automatically, so you don't have to do any special configuration to make this happen.

When you are finished with a USB drive, right-click the device's name in the Nautilus file manager window and select Safely Remove Drive. This action unmounts the drive and removes the mount point in the /run/media/*username* directory. After that, you can safely unplug the USB drive from your computer.

Working with loadable modules

If you have added hardware to your computer that isn't properly detected, you might need to manually load a module for that hardware. Linux comes with a set of commands for loading, unloading, and getting information about hardware modules.

Kernel modules are installed in /lib/modules/ subdirectories. The name of each subdirectory is based on the release number of the kernel. For example, if the kernel were 3.17.4-301.fc21.x86_64, the /lib/modules/3.17.4-301.fc21.x86_64 directory would contain drivers for that kernel. Modules in those directories can then be loaded and unloaded as they are needed.

Commands for listing, loading, unloading, and getting information about modules are available with Linux. The following sections describe how to use those modules.

Listing loaded modules

To see which modules are currently loaded into the running kernel on your computer, use the lsmod command. Consider the following example:

```
# lsmod
Module                 Size  Used by
vfat                   17411  1
fat                    65059  1 vfat
uas                    23208  0
usb_storage            65065  2 uas
fuse                   91446  3
ipt_MASQUERADE         12880  3
xt_CHECKSUM            12549  1
nfsv3                  39043  1
rpcsec_gss_krb5        31477  0
nfsv4                 466956  0
dns_resolver           13096  1 nfsv4
nfs                   233966  3 nfsv3,nfsv4
.
.
.
i2c_algo_bit           13257  1 nouveau
drm_kms_helper         58041  1 nouveau
ttm                    80772  1 nouveau
drm                   291361  7 ttm,drm_kms_helper,nouveau
ata_generic            12923  0
pata_acpi              13053  0
e1000                 137260  0
i2c_core               55486  5 drm,i2c_i801,drm_kms_helper
```

This output shows a variety of modules that have been loaded on a Linux system, including one for a network interface card (e1000).

To find information about any of the loaded modules, use the modinfo command. For example, you can type the following:

```
# /sbin/modinfo -d e1000
Intel(R) PRO/1000 Network Driver
```

Not all modules have descriptions available and, if nothing is available, no data is returned. In this case, however, the e1000 module is described as an Intel(R) PRO/1000 Network Driver module. You can also use the -a option to see the author of the module or -n to see the object file representing the module. The author information often has the e-mail address of the driver's creator, so you can contact the author if you have problems or questions about it.

Loading modules

You can load any module (as root user) that has been compiled and installed (to a /lib/modules subdirectory) into your running kernel using the modprobe command. A common reason for loading a module is to use a feature temporarily (such as loading a module to support a special filesystem on a floppy you want to access). Another reason to load a module is to identify that module as one that will be used by a particular piece of hardware that could not be autodetected.

Here is an example of the modprobe command being used to load the parport module, which provides the core functions to share parallel ports with multiple devices:

```
# modprobe parport
```

After parport is loaded, you can load the parport_pc module to define the PC-style ports available through the interface. The parport_pc module lets you optionally define the addresses and IRQ numbers associated with each device sharing the parallel port. For example:

```
# modprobe parport_pc io=0x3bc irq=auto
```

In this example, a device is identified as having an address of 0x3bc, and the IRQ for the device is auto-detected.

The modprobe command loads modules temporarily—they disappear at the next reboot. To permanently add the module to your system, add the modprobe command line to one of the startup scripts run at boot time.

Removing modules

Use the rmmod command to remove a module from a running kernel. For example, to remove the module parport_pc from the current kernel, type the following:

```
# rmmod parport_pc
```

If it is not currently busy, the `parport_pc` module is removed from the running kernel. If it is busy, try killing any process that might be using the device. Then run `rmmod` again. Sometimes, the module you are trying to remove depends on other modules that may be loaded. For instance, the `usbcore` module cannot be unloaded while the USB printer module (`usblp`) is loaded, as shown here:

```
# rmmod usbcore

ERROR: Module usbcore is in use by wacom,usblp,ehci_hcd,ohci_hcd
```

Instead of using `rmmod` to remove modules, you could use the `modprobe -r` command. With `modprobe -r`, instead of just removing the module you request, you can also remove dependent modules that are not being used by other modules.

Summary

Many features of Linux, especially those that can potentially damage the system or impact other users, require that you gain root privilege. This chapter describes different ways of obtaining root privilege: direct login, `su` command, or `sudo` command. It also covers some of the key responsibilities of a system administrator and components (configuration files, graphical tools, and so on) that are critical to a system administrator's work.

The next chapter describes how to install a Linux system. Approaches to installing Linux that are covered in that chapter include how to install from live media and from installation media.

Exercises

Use these exercises to test your knowledge of system administration and allow you to explore information about your system hardware. These tasks assume you are running a Fedora or Red Hat Enterprise Linux system (although some tasks work on other Linux systems as well). If you are stuck, solutions to the tasks are shown in Appendix B (although in Linux, there are often multiple ways to complete a task).

1. From a GNOME desktop, open the Date and Time window. Check that your time zone is set properly.

2. Run the System Monitor to sort all processes running on your system by user name. Notice which users run which processes.

3. Find all files under the `/var/spool` directory that are owned by users other than root and display a long listing of them.

4. Become the root user using the su - command. To prove that you have root privilege, create an empty or plain text file named /mnt/test.txt. Exit the shell when you are finished. If you are using Ubuntu, you must set your root password first (sudo passwd root).

5. Log in as a regular user and become root using su -. Edit the /etc/sudoers file to allow your regular user account to have full root privilege via the sudo command.

6. As the user you just gave sudoers privilege to, use the sudo command to create a file called /mnt/test2.txt. Verify that the file is there and owned by the root user.

7. Run the journalctl -f command and plug a USB drive into a USB port on your computer. If it doesn't mount automatically, mount it on /mnt/test. In a second terminal, unmount the device and remove it, continuing to watch the output from journalctl -f.

8. Run a command to see what USB devices are connected to your computer.

9. Pretend that you added a TV card to your computer, but the module needed to use it (bttv) was not properly detected and loaded. Load the bttv module yourself, and then look to see that it was loaded. Were other modules loaded with it?

10. Remove the bttv module along with any other modules that were loaded with it. List your modules to make sure this was done.

Installing Linux

Installing Linux has become a fairly easy thing to do—if you are starting with a computer that is up to spec (hard disk, RAM, CPU, and so on) and you don't mind totally erasing your hard drive. Installation is more complex if you want to stray from a default installation. So this chapter begins with a simple installation from Live media and progresses to more complex installation topics.

To ease you into the subject of installing Linux, I cover three ways of installing Linux and step you through each process:

- **Installing from Live media**—A Linux Live media ISO is a single, read-only image that contains everything you need to start a Linux operating system. That image can be burned to a DVD or USB drive and booted from that medium. With the Live media, you can totally ignore your computer's hard disk; in fact, you can run Live media on a system with no hard disk. After you are running the Live Linux system, some Live media ISOs allow you to launch an application that permanently installs the contents of the Live medium to your hard disk. The first installation procedure in this chapter shows you how to permanently install Linux from a Fedora Live media ISO.

- **Installing from an installation DVD**—An installation DVD, available with Fedora, RHEL, Ubuntu and other Linux distributions, offers more flexible ways of installing Linux. In particular, instead of just copying the whole Live media contents to your computer, with an installation DVD you can choose exactly which software packages you want. The second installation procedure I show in this chapter steps you through an installation process from a Red Hat Enterprise Linux 7 installation DVD.

■ **Installing in the enterprise**—Sitting in front of a computer and clicking through installation questions isn't inconvenient if you are installing a single system. But what if you need to install dozens or hundreds of Linux systems? What if you want to install those systems in particular ways that need to be repeated over multiple installations? The last section of this chapter describes efficient ways of installing multiple Linux systems, using network installation features and kickstart files.

A fourth method of installation not covered in this chapter is to install Linux as a virtual machine on a virtualization host, such as Virtual Box or VMware system. Chapter 26 and 27 describe ways of installing or deploying a virtual machine on a Linux KVM host or in a cloud environment.

To try the procedures in this chapter along with me, you should have a computer in front of you that you don't mind totally erasing. As an alternative, you can use a computer that has another operating system installed (such as Windows), as long as there is enough unused disk space available outside that operating system. I describe the procedure, and risk of data loss, if you decide to set up one of these "dual boot" (Linux and Windows) arrangements.

Choosing a Computer

You can get a Linux distribution that runs on handheld devices or an old PC in your closet with as little as 24MB of RAM and a 486 processor. To have a good desktop PC experience with Linux, however, you should consider what you want to be able to do with Linux when you are choosing your computer.

Be sure to consider the basic specifications you need for a PC-type computer to run the Fedora and Red Hat Enterprise Linux distributions. Because Fedora is used as the basis for Red Hat Enterprise Linux releases, hardware requirements are similar for basic desktop and server hardware for those two distributions.

■ **Processor**—A 400 MHz Pentium processor is the minimum for a GUI installation. For most applications, a 32-bit processor is fine (x86). However, if you want to set up the system to do virtualization, you need a 64-bit processor (x86_64).

> **NOTE**
> If you have a 486 machine (at least 100 MHz), consider trying Damn Small Linux (http://www.damnsmall-linux.org) or Slackware (http://www.slackware.org). It won't have the same graphical interface, but you could do some of the shell exercises. If you have a MacBook, try a GNOME version of Ubuntu that you can get at https://help.ubuntu.com/community/MacBook.

■ **RAM**—Fedora recommends at least 1GB of RAM, but at least 2GB or 3GB would be much better. On my RHEL desktop, I'm running a web browser, word processor, and mail reader, and I'm consuming over 2GB of RAM.

- **DVD or CD drive**—You need to be able to boot up the installation process from a DVD, CD, or USB drive. In recent releases, the Fedora live media ISO has become too big to fit on a CD, so you need to burn it to a DVD or USB drive. If you can't boot from a DVD or USB drive, there are ways to start the installation from a hard disk or by using a PXE install. After the installation process is started, more software can sometimes be retrieved from different locations (over the network or from hard disk, for example).

> **NOTE**
>
> PXE (pronounced pixie) stands for Preboot eXecution Environment. You can boot a client computer from a Network Interface Card (NIC) that is PXE-enabled. If a PXE boot server is available on the network, it can provide everything a client computer needs to boot. What it boots can be an installer. So with a PXE boot, it is possible to do a complete Linux installation without a CD, DVD, or any other physical medium.

- **Network card**—You need wired or wireless networking hardware to be able to add more software or get software updates. Fedora offers free software repositories if you can connect to the Internet. For RHEL, updates are available as part of the subscription price.

- **Disk space**—Fedora recommends at least 10GB of disk space for an average desktop installation, although installations can range (depending on which packages you choose to install) from 600MB (for a minimal server with no GUI install) to 7GB (to install all packages from the installation DVD). Consider the amount of data you need to store. Although documents can consume very little space, videos can consume massive amounts of space. (By comparison, you can install the Damn Small Linux Live CD to disk with only about 200MB of disk space.)

- **Special hardware features**—Some Linux features require special hardware features. For example, to use Fedora or RHEL as a virtualization host using KVM, the computer must have a processor that supports virtualization. These include AMD-V or Intel-VT chips.

If you're not sure about your computer hardware, there are a few ways to check what you have. If you are running Windows, the System Properties window can show you the processor you have, as well as the amount of RAM that's installed. As an alternative, with the Fedora Live CD booted, open a shell and type `dmesg | less` to see a listing of hardware as it is detected on your system.

With your hardware in place, you can choose to install Linux from a Live CD or from installation media, as described in the following sections.

Installing Fedora from Live media

In Chapter 1, you learned how to get and boot up Linux Live media. This chapter steps you through an installation process of a Fedora Live DVD so it is permanently installed on your hard disk.

9

Simplicity is the main advantage of installing from Live media. Essentially, you are just copying the kernel, applications, and settings from the ISO image to the hard disk. There are fewer decisions you have to make to do this kind of installation, but you also don't get to choose exactly which software packages to install. After the installation, you can add and remove packages as you please.

The first decisions you have to make about your Live media installation include where you want to install the system and whether you want to keep existing operating systems around when your installation is done:

- **Single-boot computer**—The easiest way to install Linux is to not have to worry about other operating systems or data on the computer and have Linux replace everything. When you are done, the computer boots up directly to Fedora.

- **Multi-boot computer**—If you already have Windows installed on a computer, and you don't want to erase it, you can install Fedora along with Windows on that system. Then at boot time, you can choose which operating system to start up. To be able to install Fedora on a system with another operating system installed, you must either have extra disk space available (outside the Windows partition) or be able to shrink the Windows system to gain enough free space to install Fedora.

- **Bare metal or virtual system**—The resulting Fedora installation can be installed to boot up directly from the computer hardware or from within an existing operating system on the computer. If you have a computer that is running as a virtual host, you can install Fedora on that system as a virtual guest. Virtualization host software includes KVM, Xen, and VirtualBox (for Linux and UNIX systems, as well as Windows and the MAC), Hyper-V (for Microsoft systems), and VMWare (both Linux and Microsoft systems). You can use the Fedora Live ISO image from disk or burned to a DVD to start an installation from your chosen hypervisor host. (Chapter 16 describes how to set up a KVM virtualization host.)

The following procedure steps you through the process of installing the Fedora Live ISO described in Chapter 1 to your local computer. Because the Fedora 21 installation is very similar to the Red Hat Enterprise Linux 7 installation described later in this chapter, you can refer to that procedure if you want to go beyond the simple selections shown here (particularly in the area of storage configuration).

> **CAUTION**
>
> Before beginning the procedure, be sure to make backup copies of any data that you want to keep. Although you can choose to not erase selected disk partitions (as long as you have enough space available on other partitions), there is always a risk that data can be lost when you are manipulating disk partitions. Also, unplug any USB drives you have plugged into your computer because they could be overwritten.

1. **Get Fedora.** Choose the Fedora Live media image you want to use, download it to your local system, and burn it to a DVD, as described in Chapter 1. See Appendix A for information on how to get the Fedora Live media and burn it to a DVD or USB drive.

2. **Boot the Live image.** Insert the DVD or USB drive. When the BIOS screen appears, look for a message that tells you to press a particular function key (such as F12) to interrupt the boot process and select the boot medium. Select the DVD or USB drive, depending on which you have, and Fedora should come up and display the boot screen. When you see the boot screen, select Start Fedora Live.

3. **Start the installation.** When the Welcome to Fedora screen appears, position your mouse over the Install to Hard Drive area and select it. Figure 9.1 shows an example of the Install to Hard Drive selection on the Fedora Live media.

FIGURE 9.1

Start the installation process from Live media.

4. **Select the language.** When prompted, choose the language type that best suits you (such as U.S. English) and select Next. You should see the Installation summary screen, as shown in Figure 9.2.

5. **Select DATE & TIME.** From the DATE & TIME screen, you can select your time zone by either clicking the map or choosing the region and city from drop-down boxes. To set the date and time, if you have an Internet connection, you can select the Network Time button to turn it on. Or you can select OFF and set the date and time manually from boxes on the bottom of the screen. Select Done in the upper-right corner when you are finished.

FIGURE 9.2

Select configuration options from the Installation Summary screen.

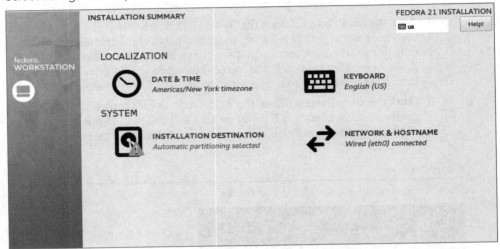

6. **Select INSTALLATION DESTINATION.** Available storage devices (such as your hard drive) are displayed, with your hard drive selected as the installation destination. If you want the installer to automatically install Fedora, just select Done in the upper-left corner. Here are your choices as this point:

   - **Automatically configure...**—If there is enough available disk space on the selected disk drive, you can continue with the installation by selecting Continue. The installer will ensure that there's enough available disk space to install Fedora.

   - **I want more space...**—If you want to get rid of some or all the space on the hard disk that is currently being used, choose this selection and click Continue. You can erase partitions that currently contain data.

   - **I want to review/modify...**—To take more control of your disk partitioning, select this option and click Continue. This lets you add and delete partitioning to divide up you disk exactly as you like.

   - **Other options**—From this screen, you can also choose your partitioning scheme (I recommend LVM because it allows you to expand your storage more easily later). You can also choose whether to encrypt the data on your disk, making your data inaccessible to anyone who tries to boot your computer without the password you set later.

   Select Done when you have configured your storage.

7. **Select KEYBOARD.** You can use the default English (U.S.) keyboard or select KEYBOARD to choose a different keyboard layout.

8. **Select NETWORK CONFIGURATION.** Choose this to be able to enable your network interface and type in a hostname for the computer. If DHCP is available on the network, you can simply set your network interfaces to pick up IP address information automatically. You can also set up IP address information manually. Select Begin Installation when you are finished, and the installation process begins.

9. **Select ROOT PASSWORD.** As Fedora installs, this selection lets you set the password for the root user. Type any password you like, and then type it again in the Confirm box. Select Done to set the password. If the password is not at least six characters long or if it is considered to be too easy (like a common word), the installer doesn't leave the password screen when you click Done. You can either change the password or click Done again to have the installer use the password anyway.

10. **Select CREATE USER.** It is good practice to have at least one regular (non-root) user on every system, because root should be used only for administrative tasks and not everyday computer use. Add the user's full name, short username, and password. To allow this user to do administrative tasks without knowing the root password, select the "Make this user administrator" box.

    By clicking the Advanced box, you can change some of the default settings. For example, with a user named chris, the default home directory would be /home/chris, and the next available user ID and group ID are assigned to the user. By selecting Advanced, you can change those settings and even assign the user to additional groups. Select Done when you are finished adding the user.

11. **Finish Configuration.** When the first part of the installation is complete, click Finish Configuration. Some final configuration happens on the system at this point. When that is finished, select Quit. At this point, the disk is repartitioned, filesystems are formatted, the Linux image is copied to hard disk, and the necessary settings are implemented.

12. **Reboot.** Select the little on/off button on the top-right corner of the screen. When prompted, click the restart button. Eject or remove the Live media. The computer should boot to your newly installed Fedora system. (You may need to actually power off the computer for it to boot back up.)

13. **Log in and begin using Fedora.** The login screen appears at this point, allowing you to log in as the user account and password you just created.

14. **Get software updates.** To keep your system secure and up to date, one of the first tasks you should do after installing Fedora is to get the latest versions of the software you just installed. If your computer has an Internet connection (plugging into a wired Ethernet network or selecting an accessible wireless network from the desktop takes care of that), you can simply open a Terminal as root and type `yum update` to download and update all your packages from the Internet. If a new kernel is installed, you can reboot your computer to have that new kernel take effect.

9

At this point, you can begin using the desktop, as described in Chapter 2. You can also use the system to perform exercises from any of the chapters in this book.

Installing Red Hat Enterprise Linux from Installation Media

In addition to offering a live DVD, most Linux distributions offer a single image or set of images that can be used to install the distribution. For this type of installation media, instead of copying the entire contents of the medium to disk, software is split up into packages that you can select to meet your exact needs. A full installation DVD, for example, can allow you to install anything from a minimal system to a full-featured desktop to a full-blown server that offers multiple services.

In this chapter, I use a Red Hat Enterprise Linux 7 server edition installation DVD as the installation medium. Review the hardware information and descriptions of dual booting in the previous section before beginning your RHEL installation.

Follow this procedure to install Red Hat Enterprise Linux from an installation DVD.

1. **Get installation media.** The process of downloading RHEL install ISO images is described on the Red Hat Enterprise Linux product page. If you are not yet a Red Hat customer, you can apply for an evaluation copy and download ISO images here: http://www.redhat.com/en/technologies/linux-platforms/ enterprise-linux.

   This requires that you create a Red Hat account. If that is not possible, you can download an installation DVD from a mirror site of the CentOS project to get a similar experience: http://wiki.centos.org/Download.

   For this example, I used the 3.4G RHEL 7 Server DVD ISO named rhel-server- 7.0-x86_64-dvd.iso. After you have the DVD ISO, you can burn it to a physical DVD as described in Appendix A.

2. **Boot the installation media.** Insert the DVD into your DVD drive, and reboot your computer. The Welcome screen appears.

3. **Select Install or Test media.** Select "Install" or "Test this media & install" to do a new installation of RHEL. The media test verifies that the DVD has not been corrupted during the copy or burning process. If you need to modify the installation process, you can add boot options by pressing the Tab key with a boot entry highlighted and typing in the options you want. See the section "Using installation boot options" later in this chapter.

4. **Select a language.** Select your language, and select Continue. The Installation Summary screen appears. From that screen, you can select to change: Date & Time, Language support, Keyboard, Installation Source, Software Selection, Installation Destination, and Network & Hostname, as shown in Figure 9.3.

5. **Date & Time.** Choose a time zone for your machine from either the map or the list shown (as described in the Fedora section). Either set the time manually with up/down arrows or select Network Time to have your system try to automatically

connect to networked time servers to sync system time. Select Done when you are finished.

FIGURE 9.3

Choose from Localization, Software, and System topics on the Installation Summary screen.

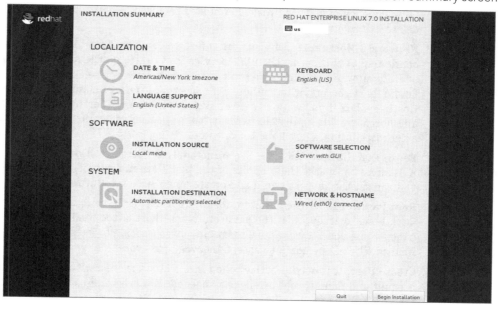

6. **Language support**. You have a chance to add support for additional languages (beyond what you set by default earlier). Select Done when you are finished.

7. **Keyboard**. Choose from different types of keyboards available with the languages you selected earlier. Type some text to see how the keys are laid out.

8. **Installation Source**. The installation DVD is used, by default, to provide the RPM packages used during installation. You have the option of selecting "On the network" and choosing a Web URL (http, https, or ftp) when a Red Hat Enterprise Linux software repository is installed. After choosing the DVD or a network location, you can add additional yum repositories to have those repositories used during installation as well. Select Done when you are finished.

9. **Software Selection**. A minimal installation is selected by default, which offers no desktop interface (shell only). If you are new to Linux and want to try out some services, the "Server with GUI" selection provides a GNOME 3 desktop system on top of a basic server install. You can select to add other services, such as a DNS, File and Storage, Identity Management, and other services. Other base environments include Infrastructure server, File and Print server, Basic Web

server, and Virtualization Host server. Select Done when you are ready to continue.

10. **Installation Destination**. The new RHEL system is installed, by default, on the local hard drive using automatic partitioning. You also have the option of attaching network storage or special storage, such as Firmware RAID. (See the section "Partitioning Hard Drives" later in this chapter for details on configuring storage.) Click Done when you are finished. You may be asked to verify that it's okay to delete existing storage.

11. **Network & Hostname**. Any network interface cards that are discovered can be configured at this point. If a DHCP service is available on the network, network address information is assigned to the interface after you select ON. Select Configure if you prefer to configure the network interface manually. Fill in the Hostname box if you want to set the system's hostname. Setting up your network and hostname during installation can make it easier to begin using your system after installation. Click Done to continue.

12. **Begin Installation**. Click the Begin Installation button to start the install process. A progress bar marks the progress of the installation. As the system is installing, you can set the root password and create a new user account for your new system.

13. **Root Password**. Set the password for the root user and verify it (type it again). Click Done to accept it. If the password is too short or too weak, you stay on the page (where you can set a new password). If you decide to keep the weak password instead, click Done again to accept the weak password.

14. **Create User**. It is good practice to log into a Linux system with a non-root user account and request root privilege as needed. You can set up a user account, including a username, full name, and password. You can select "Make this user administrator" to give that user sudo privileges (allowing the account to act as the root user as needed). Select Done when you are finished. If the password you enter is too short or otherwise weak, you must change it or click Done again if you still want to use the weak password.

15. **Complete the installation**. When installation is finished, click Reboot. Pop out the DVD when the system restarts, and Red Hat Enterprise Linux starts up from the hard disk.

16. **Run firstboot**. If you installed a desktop interface, the firstboot screen appears the first time you boot the system. Here's what you do:

   ■ **License**—Read and agree to the License Information, click Done, and click Finish Configuration.

   ■ **Kdump**—You can choose to set aside some amount of RAM for the kdump feature. If kdump is enabled, the RAM set aside can be used in the event that your kernel crashes to have a place that the kernel dump can be stored. Without kdump, there would be no way to diagnose a crashed kernel. If you enable kdump, which is done by default, you can also manually set the amount of memory to set aside for it. Click Forward when you are finished.

- **Subscription Registration**—Provided that your network is configured, you can select "Yes" to register your system now. When prompted, you can leave the default subscription management system in place (subscription.rhn.redhat.com) or enter the location of a Red Hat Satellite server to register your system. You need your Red Hat account and password to register and entitle your system for updates. In most cases, you can automatically attach an entitlement to the system. However, you can click the "Manually attach…" button if you want to choose a specific entitlement to attach to the system later when you log in to the system.

You should now be able to log in to your Red Hat Enterprise Linux system. One of the first things you should do is get software updates for the new system.

Understanding Cloud-Based Installations

When you install a Linux system on a physical computer, the installer can see the computer's hard drive, network interfaces, CPUs, and other hardware components. When you install Linux in a cloud environment, those physical components are abstracted into a pool of resources. So, to install a Linux distribution in an Amazon EC2, Google Compute Engine, or OpenStack cloud platform, you need to go about things differently.

The common way of installing Linux in a cloud is to start with a file that is an image of an installed Linux system. Typically, that image includes all the files needed by a basic, running Linux system. Metadata is added to that image from a configuration file or by filling out a form from a cloud controller that creates and launches the operating system as a virtual machine.

The kind of information added to the image might include a particular hostname, root password, and new user account. You might also want to choose to have a specific amount of disk space, particular network configuration, and a certain number of CPU processors.

Methods for installing Linux in a local cloud-like KVM environment are discussed in Chapter 26, "Using Linux for Cloud Computing." Methods for deploying cloud images are contained in Chapter 27, "Deploying Linux to the Cloud." That chapter covers how to run a Linux system as a virtual machine image on a KVM environment, Amazon EC2 cloud, or OpenStack environment.

Installing Linux in the Enterprise

If you were managing dozens, hundreds, even thousands of Linux systems in a large enterprise, it would be terribly inefficient to have to go to each computer to type and click through each installation. Fortunately, with Red Hat Enterprise Linux and other

9

distributions, you can automate installation in such a way that all you need to do is turn on a computer and boot from the computer's network interface card to get your desired Linux installation.

Although we have focused on installing Linux from a DVD or USB media, there are many other ways to launch a Linux installation and many ways to complete an installation. The following bullets step through the installation process and describe ways of changing that process along the way:

- **Launch the installation medium.** You can launch an installation from any medium you can boot from a computer: CD, DVD, USB drive, hard disk, or network interface card with PXE support. The computer goes through its boot order and looks at the master boot record on the physical medium or looks for a PXE server on the network.

- **Start the anaconda kernel.** The job of the boot loader is to point to the special kernel (and possibly an initial RAM disk) that starts the Linux installer (called anaconda). So any of the media just described simply needs to point to the location of the kernel and initial RAM disk to start the installation. If the software packages are not on the same medium, the installation process prompts you for where to get those packages.

- **Add kickstart or other boot options.** Boot options (described later in this chapter) can be passed to the anaconda kernel to configure how it starts up. One option supported by Fedora and RHEL allows you to pass the location of a kickstart file to the installer. That kickstart can contain all the information needed to complete the installation: root password, partitioning, time zone, and so on to further configure the installed system. After the installer starts, it either prompts for needed information or uses the answers provided in the kickstart file.

- **Find software packages.** Software packages don't have to be on the installation medium. This allows you to launch an installation from a boot medium that contains only a kernel and initial RAM disk. From the kickstart file or from an option you enter manually to the installer, you can identify the location of the repository holding the RPM software packages. That location can be a local CD (cdrom), website (http), FTP site (ftp), NFS share (nfs), NFS ISO (nfsiso), or local disk (hd).

- **Modify installation with kickstart scripts.** Scripts included in a kickstart can run commands you choose before or after the installation to further configure the Linux system. Those commands can add users, change permissions, create files and directories, grab files over the network, or otherwise configure the installed system exactly as you specify.

Although installing Linux in enterprise environments is beyond the scope of this book, I want you to understand the technologies that are available when you want to automate the Linux installation process. Here are some of those technologies available to use with Red Hat Enterprise Linux, along with links to where you can find more information about them:

- **Install server**—If you set up an installation server, you don't have to carry the software packages around to each machine where you install RHEL. Essentially, you copy all the software packages from the RHEL installation medium to a web server (http), FTP server (ftp), or NFS server (nfs), and then point to the location of that server when you boot the installer. The RHEL Installation Guide describes how to set up an installation server (https://access.redhat.com/documentation/ en-US/Red_Hat_Enterprise_Linux/7/html-single/Installation_Guide/ index.html#sect-making-media-sources-network).

- **PXE server**—If you have a computer with a network interface card that supports PXE booting (as most do), you can set your computer's BIOS to boot from that NIC. If you have set up a PXE server on that network, that server can present a menu to the computer containing entries to launch an installation process. The RHEL Installation Guide provides information on how to set up PXE servers for installation (https://access.redhat.com/documentation/en-US/Red_ Hat_Enterprise_Linux/7/html-single/Installation_Guide/index. html#chap-installation-server-setup).

- **Kickstart files**—To fully automate an installation, you create what is called a kickstart file. By passing a kickstart file as a boot option to a Linux installer, you can provide answers to all the installation questions you would normally have to click through.

  When you install RHEL, a kickstart file containing answers to all installation questions for the installation you just did is in the /root/anaconda-ks.cfg file. You can present that file to your next installation to repeat the installation configuration or use that file as a model for different installations.

  See the RHEL Installation Guide for information on passing a kickstart file to the anaconda installer (https://access.redhat.com/documentation/en-US/ Red_Hat_Enterprise_Linux/7/html-single/Installation_Guide/ index.html#sect-parameter-configuration-files-kickstart- s390) and creating your own kickstart files (https://access.redhat.com/ documentation/en-US/Red_Hat_Enterprise_Linux/6/html-single/ Installation_Guide/index.html#s1-kickstart2-file).

Exploring Common Installation Topics

Some of the installation topics touched upon earlier in this chapter require further explanation for you to be able to implement them fully. Read through the topics in this section to get a greater understanding of specific installation topics.

Upgrading or installing from scratch

If you have an earlier version of Linux already installed on your computer, Fedora, Ubuntu, and other Linux distributions offer an upgrade option. Red Hat Enterprise Linux offers a limited upgrade path from RHEL 6 to RHEL 7.

Upgrading lets you move a Linux system from one major release to the next. Between minor releases, you can simply update packages as needed (for example, by typing `yum update`). Here are a few general rules before performing an upgrade:

- **Remove extra packages**. If you have software packages you don't need, remove them before you do an upgrade. Upgrade processes typically upgrade only those packages that are on your system. Upgrades generally do more checking and comparing than clean installs do, so any package you can remove saves time during the upgrade process.
- **Check configuration files**. A Linux upgrade procedure often leaves copies of old configuration files. You should check that the new configuration files still work for you.

> **TIP**
>
> Installing Linux from scratch goes faster than an upgrade. It also results in a cleaner Linux system. So, if you don't need the data on your system (or if you have a backup of your data), I recommend you do a fresh installation. Then you can restore your data to a freshly installed system.

Some Linux distributions, most notably Gentoo, have taken the approach of providing ongoing updates. Instead of taking a new release every few months, you simply continuously grab updated packages as they become available and install them on your system.

Dual booting

It is possible to have multiple operating systems installed on the same computer. One way to do this is by having multiple partitions on a hard disk and/or multiple hard disks, and then installing different operating systems on different partitions. As long as the boot loader contains boot information for each of the installed operating systems, you can choose which one to run at boot time.

> **CAUTION**
>
> Although tools for resizing Windows partitions and setting up multi-boot systems have improved in recent years, there is still some risk of losing data on Windows/Linux dual-boot systems. Different operating systems often have different views of partition tables and master boot records that can cause your machine to become unbootable (at least temporarily) or lose data permanently. Always back up your data before you try to resize a Windows (NTFS or FAT) filesystem to make space for Linux.

If the computer you are using already has a Windows system on it, quite possibly the entire hard disk is devoted to Windows. Although you can run a bootable Linux, such as KNOPPIX or Damn Small Linux, without touching the hard disk, to do a more permanent installation, you'll want to find disk space outside the Windows installation. There are a few ways to do this:

- **Add a hard disk**. Instead of messing with your Windows partition, you can simply add a hard disk and devote it to Linux.

- **Resize your Windows partition**. If you have available space on a Windows partition, you can shrink that partition so free space is available on the disk to devote to Linux. Tools such as Acronis Disk Director (http://www.acronis.com) are available to resize your disk partitions and set up a workable boot manager. Some Linux distributions (particularly bootable Linuxes used as rescue CDs) include a tool called GParted (which includes software from the Linux-NTFS project for resizing Windows NTFS partitions).

> **NOTE**
>
> Type `yum install gparted` (in Fedora) or `apt-get install gparted` (in Ubuntu) to install GParted. Run `gparted` as root to start it.

Before you try to resize your Windows partition, you might need to defragment it. To defragment your disk on some Windows systems, so that all your used space is put in order on the disk, open My Computer, right-click your hard disk icon (typically C:), select Properties, click Tools, and select Defragment Now.

Defragmenting your disk can be a fairly long process. The result of defragmentation is that all the data on your disk are contiguous, creating lots of contiguous free space at the end of the partition. Sometimes, you have to complete the following special tasks to make this true:

- If the Windows swap file is not moved during defragmentation, you must remove it. Then, after you defragment your disk again and resize it, you need to restore the swap file. To remove the swap file, open the Control Panel, open the System icon, click the Performance tab, and select Virtual Memory. To disable the swap file, click Disable Virtual Memory.

- If your DOS partition has hidden files that are on the space you are trying to free up, you need to find them. In some cases, you can't delete them. In other cases, such as swap files created by a program, you can safely delete those files. This is a bit tricky because some files should not be deleted, such as DOS system files. You can use the `attrib -s -h` command from the root directory to deal with hidden files.

After your disk is defragmented, you can use commercial tools described earlier (Acronis Disk Director) to repartition your hard disk to make space for Linux. Or use the open source alternative GParted.

After you have cleared enough disk space to install Linux (see the disk space requirements described earlier in this chapter), you can install Ubuntu, Fedora, RHEL, or another Linux distribution. As you set up your boot loader during installation, you can identify Windows, Linux, and any other bootable partitions so you can select which one to boot when you start your computer.

9

Installing Linux to run virtually

Using virtualization technology, such as KVM, VMWare, VirtualBox, or Xen, you can configure your computer to run multiple operating systems simultaneously. Typically, you have a host operating system running (such as your Linux or Windows desktop), and then you configure guest operating systems to run within that environment.

If you have a Windows system, you can use commercial VMWare products to run Linux on your Windows desktop. Visit http://www.vmware.com/try-vmware to get a trial of VMWare Workstation. Then run your installed virtual guests with the free VMWare Player. With a full-blown version of VMWare Workstation, you can run multiple distributions at the same time.

Open source virtualization products that are available with Linux systems include VirtualBox (http://www.virtualbox.org), Xen (http://www.xen.org), and KVM (http://www.linux-kvm.org). VirtualBox was developed originally by Sun Microsystems. Some Linux distributions still use Xen. However, all Red Hat systems currently use KVM as the basis for Red Hat's hypervisor features in RHEL, Red Hat Enterprise Virtualization, and other cloud projects. See Chapter 26 for information on installing Linux as a virtual machine on a Linux KVM host.

Using installation boot options

When the anaconda kernel launches at boot time for RHEL or Fedora, boot options provided on the kernel command line modify the behavior of the installation process. By interrupting the boot loader before the installation kernel boots, you can add your own boot options to direct how the installation behaves.

When you see the installation boot screen, depending on the boot loader, press Tab or some other key to be able to edit the anaconda kernel command line. The line identifying the kernel might look something like the following:

```
vmlinuz initrd=initrd.img ...
```

The vmlinuz is the compressed kernel and initrd.img is the initial RAM disk (containing modules and other tools needed to start the installer). To add more options, just type them at the end of that line and press Enter.

So, for example, if you have a kickstart file available from /root/ks.cfg on a CD, your anaconda boot prompt to start the installation using the kickstart file could look like the following:

```
vmlinuz initrd=initrd.img ks=cdrom:/root/ks.cfg
```

For Red Hat Enterprise Linux 7 and the latest Fedora releases, kernel boot options used during installation are transitioning to a new naming method. With this new naming, a prefix of inst. can be placed in front of any of the boot options shown in this section that are specific to the installation process (for example, inst.xdriver or inst.repo=dvd).

For the time being, however, you can still use the options shown in the next few sections with the inst. prefix.

Boot options for disabling features

Sometimes, a Linux installation fails because the computer has some non-functioning or non-supported hardware. Often, you can get around those issues by passing options to the installer that do such things as disable selected hardware when you need to select your own driver. Table 9.1 provides some examples:

TABLE 9.1 Boot Options for Disabling Features

Installer Option	Tells System
nofirewire	Not to load support for firewire devices
nodma	Not to load DMA support for hard disks
noide	Not to load support for IDE devices
nompath	Not to enable support for multipath devices
noparport	Not to load support for parallel ports
nopcmcia	Not to load support for PCMCIA controllers
noprobe	Not to probe hardware, instead prompt user for drivers
noscsi	Not to load support for SCSI devices
nousb	Not to load support for USB devices
noipv6	Not to enable IPV6 networking
nonet	Not to probe for network devices
numa-off	To disable the Non-Uniform Memory Access (NUMA) for AMD64 architecture
acpi=off	To disable the Advanced Configuration and Power Interface (ACPI)

Boot options for video problems

If you are having trouble with your video display, you can specify video settings as noted in Table 9.2.

TABLE 9.2 Boot Options for Video Problems

Boot Option	Tells System
xdriver=vesa	Use standard vesa video driver
resolution=1024x768	Choose exact resolution to use
nofb	Don't use the VGA 16 framebuffer driver
skipddc	Don't probe DDC of the monitor (the probe can hang the installer)
graphical	Force a graphical installation

9

Boot options for special installation types

By default, installation runs in graphical mode with you sitting at the console answering questions. If you have a text-only console, or if the GUI isn't working properly, you can run an installation in plain-text mode: By typing **text**, you cause the installation to run in text mode.

If you want to start installation on one computer, but you want to answer the installation questions from another computer, you can enable a vnc (virtual network computing) installation. After you start this type of installation, you can go to another system and open a vnc viewer, giving the viewer the address of the installation machine (such as 192.168.0.99:1). Table 9.3 provides the necessary commands, along with what to tell the system to do.

TABLE 9.3   Boot Options for VNC Installations

Boot Option	Tells System
vnc	Run installation as a VNC server
vncconnect=*hostname[:port]*	Connect to VNC client hostname and optional port
vncpassword=*<password>*	Client uses password (at least 8 characters) to connect to installer

Boot options for kickstarts and remote repositories

You can boot the installation process from an installation medium that contains little more than the kernel and initial RAM disk. If that is the case, you need to identify the repository where the software packages exist. You can do that by providing a kickstart file or by identifying the location of the repositories in some way. To force the installer to prompt for the repository location (CD/DVD, hard drive, NFS, or URL), add askmethod to the installation boot options.

Using repo= options, you can identify software repository locations. The following examples show the syntax to use for creating repo= entries:

```
repo=hd:/dev/sda1:/myrepo
Repository in /myrepo on disk 1 first partition
repo=http://abc.example.com/myrepo
Repository available from /myrepo on Web server
repo=ftp://ftp.example.com/myrepo
Repository available from /myrepo on FTP server
repo=cdrom
Repository available from local CD or DVD
repo=nfs::mynfs.example.com:/myrepo/
Repository available from /myrepo on NFS share
repo=nfsiso::nfs.example.com:/mydir/rhel7.iso
Installation ISO image available from NFS server
```

Instead of identifying the repository directly, you can specify it within a kickstart file. The following are examples of some ways to identify the location of a kickstart file.

```
ks=cdrom:/stuff/ks.cfg
Get kickstart from CD/DVD.
ks=hd:sda2:/test/ks.cfg
Get kickstart from test directory on hard disk (sda2)
ks=http://www.example.com/ksfiles/ks.cfg
Get kickstart from a Web server.
ks=ftp://ftp.example.com/allks/ks.cfg
Get kickstart from a FTP server.
ks=nfs:mynfs.example.com:/someks/ks.cfg
Get kickstart from an NFS server.
```

Miscellaneous boot options

Here are a few other options you can pass to the installer that don't fit in a category.

```
rescue
Instead of installing, run the kernel to open Linux rescue mode.

mediacheck
Check the installation CD/DVD for checksum errors.
```

For further information on using the anaconda installer in rescue mode (to rescue a broken Linux system), see Chapter 21, "Troubleshooting Linux." For information on the latest boot options use in RHEL 7, refer to the RHEL 7 Installation Guide (https://access.redhat.com/documentation/en-US/Red_Hat_Enterprise_Linux/7/html-single/Installation_Guide/index.html#chap-anaconda-boot-options).

Using specialized storage

In large enterprise computing environments, it is common to store the operating system and data outside the local computer. Instead, some special storage device beyond the local hard disk is identified to the installer, and that storage device (or devices) can be used during installation.

Once identified, the storage devices you indicate during installation can be used the same way that local disks are used. You can partition them and assign a structure (filesystem, swap space, and so on) or leave them alone and simply mount them where you want the data to be available.

The following types of specialized storage devices can be selected from the Specialized Storage Devices screen when you install Red Hat Enterprise Linux, Fedora, or other Linux distributions:

9

- **Firmware RAID**—A firmware RAID device is a type of device that has hooks in the BIOS, allowing it to be used to boot the operating system, if you choose.

- **Multipath devices**—As the name implies, multipath devices provide multiple paths between the computer and its storage devices. These paths are aggregated, so these devices look like a single device to the system using them, while the underlying technology provides improved performance, redundancy, or both. Connections can be provided by iSCSI or Fibre Channel over Ethernet (FCoE) devices.

- **Other SAN devices**—Any device representing a Storage Area Network (SAN).

While configuring these specialized storage devices is beyond the scope of this book, know that if you are working in an enterprise where iSCSI and FCoE devices are available, you can configure your Linux system to use them at installation time. The types of information you need to do this include:

- **iSCSI devices**—Have your storage administrator provide you with the target IP address of the iSCSI device and the type of discovery authentication needed to use the device. The iSCSI device may require credentials.

- **Fibre Channel over Ethernet Devices (FCoE)**—For FCoE, you need to know the network interface that is connected to your FCoE switch. You can search that interface for available FCoE devices.

Partitioning hard drives

The hard disk (or disks) on your computer provide the permanent storage area for your data files, application programs, and the operating system itself. Partitioning is the act of dividing a disk into logical areas that can be worked with separately. In Windows, you typically have one partition that consumes the whole hard disk. However, with Linux there are several reasons why you may want to have multiple partitions:

- **Multiple operating systems**—If you install Linux on a PC that already has a Windows operating system, you may want to keep both operating systems on the computer. For all practical purposes, each operating system must exist on a completely separate partition. When your computer boots, you can choose which system to run.

- **Multiple partitions within an operating system**—To protect their entire operating system from running out of disk space, people often assign separate partitions to different areas of the Linux filesystem. For example, if /home and /var were assigned to separate partitions, then a gluttonous user who fills up the /home partition wouldn't prevent logging daemons from continuing to write to log files in the /var/log directory.

  Multiple partitions also make doing certain kinds of backups (such as an image backup) easier. For example, an image backup of /home would be much faster (and probably more useful) than an image backup of the root filesystem (/).

- **Different filesystem types**—Different kinds of filesystems have different structures. Filesystems of different types must be on their own partitions. Also, you might need different filesystems to have different mount options for special features (such as read-only or user quotas). In most Linux systems, you need at least one filesystem type for the root of the filesystem (/) and one for your swap area. Filesystems on CD-ROM use the iso9660 filesystem type.

> **TIP**
>
> When you create partitions for Linux, you usually assign the filesystem type as Linux native (using the ext2, ext3, ext4, or xfs type on most Linux systems). If the applications you are running require particularly long filenames, large file sizes, or many inodes (each file consumes an inode), you may want to choose a different filesystem type.
>
> For example, if you set up a news server, it can use many inodes to store small news articles. Another reason for using a different filesystem type is to copy an image backup tape from another operating system to your local disk (such as a legacy filesystem from an OS/2 or Minix operating system).

Coming from Windows

If you have only used Windows operating systems before, you probably had your whole hard disk assigned to C: and never thought about partitions. With many Linux systems, you have the opportunity to view and change the default partitioning based on how you want to use the system.

During installation, systems such as Fedora and RHEL let you partition your hard disk using graphical partitioning tools. The following sections describe how to partition your disk during a Fedora installation. See the section "Tips for creating partitions" for some ideas for creating disk partitions.

Understanding different partition types

Many Linux distributions give you the option of selecting different partition types when you partition your hard disk during installation. Partition types include:

- **Linux partitions**—Use this option to create a partition for an ext2, ext3, or ext4 filesystem type that is added directly to a partition on your hard disk (or other storage medium). The xfs filesystem type can also be used on a Linux partition.

- **LVM partitions**—Create an LVM partition if you plan to create or add to an LVM volume group. LVMs give you more flexibility in growing, shrinking, and moving partitions later than regular partitions do.

- **RAID partitions**—Create two or more RAID partitions to create a RAID array. These partitions should be on separate disks to create an effective RAID array.

9

RAID arrays can help improve performance, reliability, or both as those features relate to reading, writing, and storing your data.

- **Swap partitions**—Create a swap partition to extend the amount of virtual memory available on your system.

The following sections describe how to add regular Linux partitions, LVM, RAID, and swap partitions using the Fedora graphical installer. If you are still not sure when you should use these different partition types, refer to Chapter 12 for further information on configuring disk partitions.

Reasons for different partitioning schemes

Different opinions exist relating to how to divide up a hard disk. Here are some issues to consider:

- **Do you want to install another operating system?** If you want Windows on your computer along with Linux, you need at least one Windows (Win95, FAT16, VFAT, or NTFS type), one Linux (Linux ext4 or xfs), and usually one Linux swap partition.

- **Is it a multiuser system?** If you are using the system yourself, you probably don't need many partitions. One reason for partitioning an operating system is to keep the entire system from running out of disk space at once. That also serves to put boundaries on what an individual can use up in his or her home directory (although disk quotas provide a more refined way of limiting disk use).

- **Do you have multiple hard disks?** You need at least one partition per hard disk. If your system has two hard disks, you may assign one to / and one to /home (if you have lots of users) or /var (if the computer is a server sharing lots of data). With a separate /home partition, you can install another Linux system in the future without disturbing your home directories (and presumably all or most of your user data).

Tips for creating partitions

Changing your disk partitions to handle multiple operating systems can be very tricky, in part because each operating system has its own ideas about how partitioning information should be handled, as well as different tools for doing it. Here are some tips to help you get it right:

- If you are creating a dual-boot system, particularly for a Windows system, try to install the Windows operating system first after partitioning your disk. Otherwise, the Windows installation may make the Linux partitions inaccessible. Choosing a VFAT instead of NTFS filesystem for Windows also makes sharing files between your Windows and Linux systems easier and more reliable. (Support for NTFS partitions from Linux has improved greatly in the past few years, but not all Linux systems include NTFS support.)

- The `fdisk` man page recommends that you use partitioning tools that come with an operating system to create partitions for that operating system. For example, the DOS `fdisk` knows how to create partitions that DOS will like, and the Linux `fdisk` will happily make your Linux partitions. After your hard disk is set up for dual boot, however, you should probably not go back to Windows-only partitioning tools. Use Linux `fdisk` or a product made for multi-boot systems (such as Acronis Disk Director).

- You can have up to 63 partitions on an IDE hard disk. A SCSI hard disk can have up to 15 partitions. You typically won't need nearly that many partitions. If you need more partitions, use LVM and create as many logical volumes as you like.

If you are using Linux as a desktop system, you probably don't need lots of different partitions. However, some very good reasons exist for having multiple partitions for Linux systems that are shared by lots of users or are public web servers or file servers. Having multiple partitions within Fedora or RHEL, for example, offers the following advantages:

- **Protection from attacks**—Denial-of-service attacks sometimes take actions that try to fill up your hard disk. If public areas, such as /var, are on separate partitions, a successful attack can fill up a partition without shutting down the whole computer. Because /var is the default location for web and FTP servers, and is expected to hold lots of data, entire hard disks often are assigned to the /var filesystem alone.

- **Protection from corrupted filesystems**—If you have only one filesystem (/), its corruption can cause the whole Linux system to be damaged. Corruption of a smaller partition can be easier to fix and often allows the computer to stay in service while the correction is made.

Table 9.4 lists some directories that you may want to consider making into separate filesystem partitions.

TABLE 9.4 Assigning Partitions to Particular Directories

Directory	Explanation
/boot	Sometimes, the BIOS in older PCs can access only the first 1,024 cylinders of your hard disk. To make sure that the information in your /boot directory is accessible to the BIOS, create a separate disk partition (of about 500MB) for /boot. Even with several kernels installed, there is rarely a reason for /boot to be larger than 500MB.
/usr	This directory structure contains most of the applications and utilities available to Linux users. The original theory was that if /usr were on a separate partition, you could mount that filesystem as read-only after the operating system had been installed. This would prevent attackers from removing important system applications or replacing them with their own versions that may cause security problems. A separate /usr partition is also useful if you have diskless workstations on your local network. Using NFS, you can share /usr over the network with those workstations.

Continues

TABLE 9.4 *(continued)*

Directory	Explanation
/var	Your FTP (/var/ftp) and web server (/var/www) directories are, by default in many Linux systems, stored under /var. Having a separate /var partition can prevent an attack on those facilities from corrupting or filling up your entire hard disk.
/home	Because your user account directories are located in this directory, having a separate /home account can prevent a reckless user from filling up the entire hard disk. It also conveniently separates user data from your operating system (for easy backups or new installs). Often, /home is created as an LVM logical volume, so it can grow in size as user demands increase. It may also be assigned user quotas to limit disk use.
/tmp	Protecting /tmp from the rest of the hard disk by placing it on a separate partition can ensure that applications that need to write to temporary files in /tmp can complete their processing, even if the rest of the disk fills up.

Although people who use Linux systems casually rarely see a need for lots of partitions, those who maintain and occasionally have to recover large systems are thankful when the system they need to fix has several partitions. Multiple partitions can limit the effects of deliberate damage (such as denial-of-service attacks), problems from errant users, and accidental filesystem corruption.

Using the GRUB boot loader

A boot loader lets you choose when and how to boot the operating systems installed on your computer's hard disks. The GRand Unified Bootloader (GRUB) is the most popular boot loader used for installed Linux systems. There are two major versions of GRUB available today:

- **GRUB Legacy (version 1)**—As of this writing, this version of GRUB is used by default to boot Red Hat Enterprise Linux operating systems (at least through RHEL 6.5). It was also used with earlier versions of Fedora and Ubuntu.

- **GRUB 2**—The current versions of Red Hat Enterprise Linux, Ubuntu, and Fedora use GRUB 2 as the default boot loader.

The GRUB Legacy version is described in the following sections. After that, there is a description of GRUB 2.

> **NOTE**
> SYSLINUX is another boot loader you will encounter with Linux systems. The SYSLINUX boot loaders are not typically used for installed Linux systems. However, SYSLINUX is commonly used as the boot loader for Linux CDs and DVDs. SYSLINUX is particularly good for booting ISO9660 CD images (isolinux) and USB sticks (syslinux), and for working on older hardware or for PXE booting (pxelinux) a system over the network.

Using GRUB Legacy (version 1)

With multiple operating systems installed and several partitions set up, how does your computer know which operating system to start? To select and manage which partition is booted and how it is booted, you need a boot loader. The boot loader that is installed by default with Red Hat Enterprise Linux systems is the GRand Unified Boot loader (GRUB).

GRUB Legacy is a GNU boot loader (`http://www.gnu.org/software/grub`) that offers the following features:

- Support for multiple executable formats.
- Support for multi-boot operating systems (such as Fedora, RHEL, FreeBSD, NetBSD, OpenBSD, and other Linux systems).
- Support for non-multi-boot operating systems (such as Windows 95, Windows 98, Windows NT, Windows ME, Windows XP, Windows Vista, Windows 7, and OS/2) via a chain-loading function. Chain-loading is the act of loading another boot loader (presumably one that is specific to the proprietary operating system) from GRUB to start the selected operating system.
- Support for multiple filesystem types.
- Support for automatic decompression of boot images.
- Support for downloading boot images from a network.

At the time of this writing, GRUB version 1 is used in Red Hat Enterprise Linux 6. GRUB version 2 is used in Fedora, Ubuntu, Red Hat Enterprise Linux 7, and other Linux distributions. This section describes how to use GRUB version 1.

For more information on how GRUB works, at the command line type **man grub** or **info grub**. The `info grub` command contains more details about GRUB.

Booting with GRUB Legacy

When you install Linux, you are typically given the option to configure the information needed to boot your computer (with one or more operating systems) into the default boot loader. GRUB is very flexible to configure, so it looks different in different Linux distributions.

With the GRUB boot loader that comes with Red Hat Enterprise Linux installed in the master boot record of your hard disk, when the BIOS starts up the boot loader one of several things can happen:

- **Default**—If you do nothing, the default operating system boots automatically after five seconds. (The timeout is set by the `timeout` value, in seconds, in the `grub.conf` or `menu.lst` file.)
- **Select an operating system**—Press any key before the five seconds expires, and you see a list of titles to select from. The titles can represent one or more kernels

for the same Linux system. Or they may represent Windows, Ubuntu, or other operating systems. Use the up and down arrow keys to highlight any title, and press Enter to boot that operating system.

- **Edit the boot process**—If you want to change any of the options used during the boot process, use the arrow keys to highlight the operating system you want and type **e** to select it. Follow the next procedure to change your boot options temporarily.

If you want to change your boot options so they take effect every time you boot your computer, see the section on permanently changing boot options. Changing those options involves editing the /boot/grub/grub.conf file.

Temporarily changing boot options

From the GRUB Legacy boot screen, you can select to change or add boot options for the current boot session. On some Linux systems, the menu is hidden, so you have to press the Tab key or some other key (before a few seconds of timeout is exceeded) to see the menu. Then select the operating system you want (using the arrow keys), and type **e** (as described earlier).

Three lines in the example of the GRUB Legacy editing screen identify the boot process for the operating system you chose. Here is an example of those lines (because of the length of the kernel line, it is represented here as three lines):

```
root (hd0,0)
kernel /vmlinuz-2.6.32-131.17.1.el6.x86_64 ro
  root=/dev/mapper/vg_myhost-lv_root
 rd_NO_MD rd_NO_DM
  LANG=en_US.UTF-8 SYSFONT=latarcyrheb-sun16 KEYBOARDTYPE=pc
  KEYTABLE=us rhgb quiet crashkernel=auto
initrd /initramfs-2.6.32-131.17.1.el6.x86_64.img
```

The first line (beginning with root) shows that the entry for the GRUB boot loader is on the first partition of the first hard disk (hd0, 0). GRUB represents the hard disk as hd, regardless of whether it is a SCSI, IDE, or other type of disk. In GRUB Legacy, you just count the drive number and partition number, starting from zero (0).

The second line of the example (beginning with kernel) identifies the kernel boot image (/boot/vmlinuz-2.6.32-131.17.1.el6.x86_64) and several options. The options identify the partition as initially being loaded ro (read-only) and the location of the root filesystem on a partition with the label that begins root=/dev/mapper/vg_myhost-lv_root. The third line (starting with initrd) identifies the location of the initial RAM disk, which contains additional modules and tools needed during the boot process.

If you are going to change any of the lines related to the boot process, you will probably change only the second line to add or remove boot options. Follow these steps to do just that:

1. After interrupting the GRUB boot process and typing **e** to select the boot entry you want, position the cursor on the `kernel` line and type **e**.

2. Either add or remove options after the name of the boot image. You can use a minimal set of bash shell command-line editing features to edit the line. You can even use command completion (type part of a filename and press Tab to complete it). Here are a few options you may want to add or delete:

   - **Boot to a shell**. If you forgot your root password or if your boot process hangs, you can boot directly to a shell by adding `init=/bin/sh` to the boot line.

   - **Select a run level**. If you want to boot to a particular run level, you can add the run level you want to the end of the kernel line. For example, to have RHEL boot to run level 3 (multiuser plus networking mode), add 3 to the end of the kernel line. You can also boot to single-user mode (1), multiuser mode (2), or X GUI mode (5). Level 3 is a good choice if your GUI is temporarily broken. Level 1 is good if you have forgotten your root password.

   - **Watch boot messages**. By default, you will see a splash screen as Linux boots. If you want to see messages showing activities happening as the system boots up, you can remove the option `rhgb quiet` from the kernel line. This lets you see messages as they scroll by. Pressing Esc during boot-up gets the same result.

3. Press Enter to return to the editing screen.

4. Type **b** to boot the computer with the new options. The next time you boot your computer, the new options will not be saved. To add options so they are saved permanently, see the next section.

Permanently changing boot options

You can change the options that take effect each time you boot your computer by changing the GRUB configuration file. In RHEL and other Linux systems, GRUB configuration centers on the `/boot/grub/grub.conf` or `/boot/grub/menu.lst` file.

The `/boot/grub/grub.conf` file is created when you install Linux. Here's an example of that file for RHEL:

```
# grub.conf generated by anaconda
#
# Note you do not have to rerun grub after making changes to the file
# NOTICE:  You have a /boot partition.  This means that
#          all kernel and initrd paths are relative to /boot/, eg.
#      root (hd0,0)
#      kernel /vmlinuz-version ro root=/dev/mapper/vg_joke-lv_root
#      initrd /initrd-[generic-]version.img
#boot=/dev/sda
default=0
timeout=5
splashimage=(hd0,0)/grub/splash.xpm.gz
```

```
hiddenmenu
title Red Hat Enterprise Linux (2.6.32-131.17.1.el6.x86_64)
     root (hd0,0)
     kernel /vmlinuz-2.6.32-131.17.1.el6.x86_64 ro
          root=/dev/mapper/vg_myhost-lv_root rd_NO_MD rd_NO_DM
          LANG=en_US.UTF-8 SYSFONT=latarcyrheb-sun16 KEYBOARDTYPE=pc
          KEYTABLE=us rhgb quiet crashkernel=auto
     initrd /initramfs-2.6.32-131.17.1.el6.x86_64.img
title Windows XP
     rootnoverify (hd0,1)
     chainloader +1
```

The default=0 line indicates that the first partition in this list (in this case, Red Hat Enterprise Linux) is booted by default. The line timeout=5 causes GRUB to pause for five seconds before booting the default partition. (That's how much time you have to press **e** if you want to edit the boot line, or to press arrow keys to select a different operating system to boot.)

The splashimage line looks in the first partition on the first disk (hd0,0) for the boot partition (in this case /dev/sda1). GRUB loads splash.xpm.gz as the image on the splash screen (/boot/grub/splash.xpm.gz). The splash screen appears as the background of the boot screen.

> **NOTE**
>
> GRUB indicates disk partitions using the following notation: (hd0,0). The first number represents the disk, and the second is the partition on that disk. So (hd0,1) is the second partition (1) on the first disk (0).

The two bootable partitions in this example are Red Hat Enterprise Linux and Windows XP. The title lines for each of those partitions are followed by the name that appears on the boot screen to represent each partition.

For the RHEL system, the root line indicates the location of the boot partition as the second partition on the first disk. So, to find the bootable kernel (vmlinuz-*) and the initrd initial RAM disk boot image that is loaded (initrd-*), GRUB mounts hd0,0 as the root of the entire filesystem (represented by /dev/mapper/vg_myhost-lv_root and mounted as /). There are other options on the kernel line as well.

For the Windows XP partition, the rootnoverify line indicates that GRUB should not try to mount the partition. In this case, Windows XP is on the first partition of the first hard disk (hd0,1) or /dev/sda2. Instead of mounting the partition and passing options to the new operating system, the chainloader +1 line tells GRUB to pass the booting of the operating system to another boot loader. The +1 indicates that the first sector of the partition is used as the boot loader. (You could similarly set up to boot a Windows Vista or Windows 7 operating system.)

NOTE

Microsoft operating systems require that you use the `chainloader` to boot them from GRUB because GRUB doesn't offer native support for Windows operating systems.

If you make any changes to the /boot/grub/grub.conf file, you do *not* need to load those changes. GRUB automatically picks up those changes when you reboot your computer.

Adding a new GRUB boot image

You may have different boot images for kernels that include different features. In most cases, installing a new kernel package automatically configures grub.conf to use that new kernel. However, if you want to manually add a kernel, here is the procedure for modifying the grub.conf file in Red Hat Enterprise Linux to be able to boot that kernel:

1. Copy the new image from the directory in which it was created (such as /usr/src/kernels/linux-2.6.25-11/arch/i386/boot) to the /boot directory. Name the file something that reflects its contents, such as bz-2.6.25-11. For example:

```
# cd /usr/src/Linux-2.6.25.11/arch/i386/boot
# cp bzImage /boot/bz-2.6.25-11
```

2. Add several lines to the /boot/grub/grub.conf file so that the image can be started at boot time if it is selected. For example:

```
title Red Hat Enterprise Linux 6.3 (My own IPV6 build)
    root (hd0,4)
    kernel /bz-2.6.25-11 ro root=/dev/sda5
    initrd /initrd-2.6.25-11.img
```

3. Reboot your computer.

4. When the GRUB boot screen appears, move your cursor to the title representing the new kernel and press Enter.

The advantage to this approach, as opposed to copying the new boot image over the old one, is that if the kernel fails to boot, you can always go back and restart the old kernel. When you feel confident that the new kernel is working properly, you can use it to replace the old kernel or perhaps just make the new kernel the default boot definition.

Using GRUB 2

GRUB 2 represents a major rewrite of the GRUB Legacy project. It has been adopted as the default boot loader for Red Hat Enterprise Linux 7, Fedora, and Ubuntu. The major function of the GRUB 2 boot loader is still to find and start the operating system you want, but now much more power and flexibility is built into the tools and configuration files that get you there.

9

In GRUB 2, the configuration file is now named /boot/grub2/grub.cfg (in Fedora and other Linux systems using GRUB 2). Everything from the contents of grub.cfg to the way grub.cfg is created is different from the GRUB Legacy grub.conf file. Here are some things you should know about the grub.cfg file:

- Instead of editing grub.cfg by hand or having kernel RPM packages add to it, grub.cfg is generated from the contents of the /etc/default/grub file and the /etc/grub.d directory. You should modify or add to those files to configure GRUB 2 yourself.

- The grub.cfg file can contain scripting syntax, including such things as functions, loops, and variables.

- Device names needed to identify the location of kernels and initial RAM disks can be more reliably identified using labels or Universally Unique Identifiers (UUIDs). This prevents the possibility of a disk device such as /dev/sda being changed to /dev/sdb when you add a new disk (which would result in the kernel not being found).

Comments in the grub.cfg file indicate where the content came from. For example, information generated from the /etc/grub.d/00_header file comes right after this comment line:

```
### BEGIN /etc/grub.d/00_header ###
```

In the beginning of the 00_header section, there are some functions, such as those that load drivers to get your video display to work. After that, most of the sections in the grub.cfg file consist of menu entries. The following is an example of a menu item from the grub.cfg file that you could select to start Fedora 20 when the system boots up:

```
menuentry 'Fedora (3.16.3-200.fc20.x86_64)' --class fedora
    --class gnu-linux --class gnu --class os ...{
load_video
set gfxpayload=keep
insmod gzio
insmod part_msdos
insmod ext2
set root='(hd0,msdos1)'
search --no-floppy --fs-uuid --set=root
    eb31517f-f404-410b-937e-a6093b5a5380

linux   /vmlinuz-3.16.3-200.fc20.x86_64
    root=/dev/mapper/fedora_fedora20-root ro
    rd.lvm.lv=fedora_fedora20/swap
    vconsole.font=latarcyrheb-sun16
    rd.lvm.lv=fedora_fedora20/root rhgb quiet
    LANG=en_US.UTF-8
initrd /initramfs-3.16.3-200.fc20.x86_64.img
}
```

The menu entry for this selection appears as Fedora (`3.16.3-200.fc20.x86_64`) on the GRUB 2 boot menu. The --class entries on that line allow GRUB 2 to group the menu entries into classes (in this case, it identifies it as a fedora, gnu-linux, gnu, os type of system). The next lines load video drivers and file system drivers. After that, lines identify the location of the root file system.

The linux line shows the kernel location (`/boot/vmlinuz-3.16.3-200.fc20.x86_64`), followed by options that are passed to the kernel.

There are many, many more features of GRUB 2 you can learn about if you want to dig deeper into your system's boot loader. The best documentation for GRUB 2 is available on the Fedora system; type `info grub2` at the shell. The `info` entry for GRUB 2 provides lots of information for booting different operating systems, writing your own configuration files, working with GRUB image files, setting GRUB environment variables, and working with other GRUB features.

Summary

Although every Linux distribution includes a different installation method, you need to do many common activities, regardless of which Linux system you install. For every Linux system, you need to deal with issues of disk partitioning, boot options, and configuring boot loaders.

In this chapter, you stepped through installation procedures for Fedora (using a live media installation) and Red Hat Enterprise (from installation media). You learned how deploying Linux in cloud environments can differ from traditional installation methods by combining metadata with prebuilt base operating system image files to run on large pools of compute resources.

The chapter also covered special installation topics, including using boot options and disk partitioning. With your Linux system now installed, Chapter 10 describes how to begin managing the software on your Linux system.

Exercises

Use these exercises to test your knowledge of installing Linux. I recommend you do these exercises on a computer that has no operating system or data on it that you would fear losing (in other words, one you don't mind erasing). If you have a computer that allows you to install virtual systems, that is a safe way to do these exercises as well. These exercises were tested using a Fedora 21 Live media and an RHEL 7 Server Installation DVD.

9

1. Start installing from Fedora Live media, using as many of the default options as possible.

2. After you have completely installed Fedora, update all the packages on the system.

3. Start installing from an RHEL installation DVD, but make it so the installation runs in text mode. Complete the installation in any way you choose.

4. Start installing from an RHEL installation DVD, and set the disk partitioning as follows: a 400MB /boot, / (3GB), /var (2GB), and /home (2GB). Leave the rest as unused space.

> **CAUTION**
>
> Completing Exercise 4 ultimately deletes all content on your hard disk. If you want to use this exercise only to practice partitioning, you can reboot your computer before clicking Accept Changes at the very end of this procedure without harming your hard disk. If you go forward and partition your disk, assume that all data that you have not explicitly changed has been deleted.

Getting and Managing Software

IN THIS CHAPTER

Installing software from the desktop

Working with RPM packaging

Using yum to manage packages

Using rpm to work with packages

Installing software in the enterprise

I n Linux distributions such as Fedora and Ubuntu, you don't need to know much about how software is packaged and managed to get the software you want. Those distributions have excellent software installation tools that automatically point to huge software repositories. Just a few clicks and you're using the software in little more time than it takes to download it.

The fact that Linux software management is so easy these days is a credit to the Linux community, which has worked diligently to create packaging formats, complex installation tools, and high-quality software packages. Not only is it easy to get the software, but after it's installed, it's easy to manage, query, update, and remove it.

This chapter begins by describing how to install software in Fedora using the new Software graphical installation tool. If you are just installing a few desktop applications on your own desktop system, you may not need much more than that and occasional security updates.

To dig deeper into managing Linux software, I next describe what makes up Linux software packages (comparing deb and rpm formatted packaging), underlying software management components, and commands (yum and rpm) for managing software in Fedora and Red Hat Enterprise Linux. That's followed by a description of how to manage software packages in enterprise computing.

Managing Software on the Desktop

In Fedora 21, the Fedora Project includes the new Software application to replace the PackageKit Add/ Remove Software window. The Software window offers a more intuitive way of choosing and installing desktop applications that does not align with typical Linux installation practices. With the Software window, the smallest software you install is an application. With Linux, you install packages.

Figure 10.1 shows an example of the Software window.

FIGURE 10.1

Install and manage software packages from the Software window.

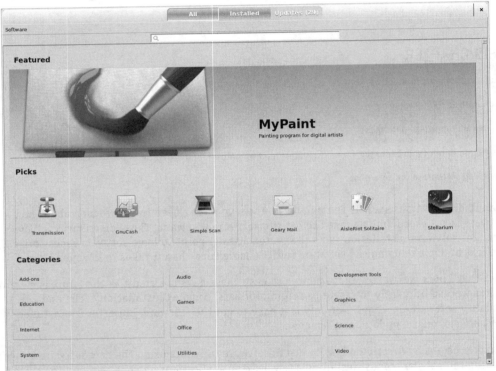

From the Software window, you can select the applications you want to install from the Picks group (a handful of popular applications), choose from categories of applications (Internet, Games, Audio, Video, and so on), or search by application name or description. Select the Install button to have the Software window download and install all the software packages needed to make the application work.

Other features of this window let you see all installed applications (Installed tab) or view a list of applications that have updated packages available for you to install (Updates tab). If you want to remove an installed application, simply click the Remove button next to the package name.

If you are using Linux purely as a desktop system, where you want to write documents, play music, and do other common desktop tasks, the Software window might be all you need to get the basic software you want. By default, your system connects to the main Fedora software repository and gives you access to hundreds of software applications.

But although the Software window lets you download and install hundreds of applications from the Fedora software repository, that repository actually contains tens of thousands of software packages. What packages can you not see from that repository, when might you want those other packages, and how can you gain access to those packages (as well as packages from other software repositories)?

Going Beyond the Software Window

If you are managing a single desktop system, you might be quite satisfied with the hundreds of packages you can find through the Software window. Open source versions of most common types of desktop applications are available to you through the Software window after you have an Internet connection from Fedora to the Internet.

However, here are some examples of why you might want to go beyond what you can do with the Software window:

- **More repositories**—Fedora and Red Hat Enterprise Linux distribute only open source, freely distributable software. You may want to install some commercial software (such as Adobe Flash Player) or non-free software (available from repositories such as rpmfusion.org).

- **Beyond desktop applications**—Tens of thousands of software packages in the Fedora repository are not available through the Software window. Most of these packages are not associated with graphical applications at all. For example, some packages contain pure command-line tools, system services, programming tools, or documentation that don't show up in the Software window.

- **Flexibility**—Although you may not know it, when you install an application through the Software window, you are actually installing multiple RPM packages. This set of packages may just be a default package set that includes documentation, extra fonts, additional software plugins, or multiple language packs that you may or may not want. With yum and rpm commands, you have more flexibility with exactly which packages related to an application or other software feature is installed on your system.

- **More complex queries**—Using commands such as yum and rpm, you can get detailed information about packages, package groups, and repositories.

- **Software validation**—Using rpm and other tools, you can check whether a signed package has been modified before you installed it or whether any of the components of a package have been tampered with since the package was installed.

- **Managing software installation**—Although the Software window works well if you are installing desktop software on a single system, it doesn't scale well for managing software on multiple systems. Other tools are built on top of the rpm facility for doing that.

10

Before I launch into some of the command-line tools for installing and managing software in Linux, the next section describes how the underlying packaging and package management systems in Linux work. In particular, I focus on RPM packaging as it is used in Fedora, Red Hat Enterprise Linux, and related distributions, as well as Deb packages, which are associated with Debian, Ubuntu, Linux Mint, and related distributions.

Understanding Linux RPM and DEB Software Packaging

On the first Linux systems, if you wanted to add software, you would grab the source code from a project that produced it, compile it into runnable binaries, and drop it onto your computer. If you were lucky, someone would have already compiled it in a form that would run on your computer.

The form of the package could be a *tarball*, containing executable files (commands), documentation, configuration files, and libraries. (A tarball is a single file in which multiple files are gathered together for convenient storage or distribution.) When you install software from a tarball, the files from that tarball might be spread across your Linux system in appropriate directories (/usr/share/man, /etc, /bin, and /lib, to name a few).

Although it is easy to create a tarball and just drop a set of software onto your Linux system, this method of installing software makes it difficult to do these things:

- **Get dependent software**—You would need to know if the software you were installing depended on other software being installed for your software to work. Then you would have to track down that software and install that too (which might itself have some dependencies).

- **List the software**—Even if you knew the name of the command, you might not know where its documentation or configuration files were located when you looked for it later.

- **Remove the software**—Unless you kept the original tarball or a list of files, you wouldn't know where all the files were when it came time to remove them. Even if you knew, you would have to remove each one individually.

- **Update the software**—Tarballs are not designed to hold metadata about the contents they contain. After the contents of a tarball are installed, you may not have a way to tell what version of the software you are using, making it difficult to track down bugs and get new versions of your software.

To deal with these problems, packages progressed from simple tarballs to more complex packaging. With only a few notable exceptions (such as Gentoo, Slackware, and a few others), the majority of Linux distributions went to one of two packaging formats—DEB and RPM:

- **DEB (.deb) packaging**—The Debian GNU/Linux project created `.deb` packaging, which is used by Debian and other distributions based on Debian (Ubuntu, Linux Mint, KNOPPIX, and so on). Using tools such as `apt-get` and `dpkg`, Linux distributions could install, manage, upgrade, and remove software.

- **RPM (.rpm) packaging**—Originally named Red Hat Package Manager but later recursively renamed RPM Package Manager, RPM is the preferred package format for SUSE, Red Hat distributions (RHEL and Fedora), and those based on Red Hat distributions (CentOS, Oracle Linux, and so on). The `rpm` command was the first tool to manage RPMs, but later `yum` was added to enhance the RPM facility.

For managing software on individual systems, there are proponents on both sides of the RPM vs. DEB debate with valid points. Although RPM is the preferred format for managing enterprise-quality software installation, updates, and maintenance, DEB is very popular among many Linux enthusiasts. This chapter covers both RPM (Fedora and Red Hat Enterprise Linux) and (to some extent) DEB packaging and software management.

Understanding DEB packaging

Debian software packages hold multiple files and metadata related to some set of software in the format of an `ar` archive file. The files can be executables (commands), configuration files, documentation, and other software items. The metadata includes such things as dependencies, licensing, package sizes, descriptions, and other information.Multiple command-line and graphical tools are available for working with DEB files in Ubuntu, Debian, and other Linux distributions. Some of these include the following:

- **Ubuntu Software Center**—Select the Ubuntu Software Center icon from the Ubuntu desktop. The window that appears lets you search for applications and packages that you want by searching for keywords or navigating categories.

- **aptitude**—The `aptitude` command is a package installation tool that provides a screen-oriented menu that runs in the shell. After you run the command, use arrow keys to highlight the selection you want and press Enter to select it. You can upgrade packages, get new packages, or view installed packages.

- **apt***—There is a set of apt commands (`apt-get`, `apt-config`, `apt-cache`, and so on) that you can use to manage package installation.

The Ubuntu Software Center is fairly intuitive for finding and installing packages. However, here are a few examples of commands that can help you install and manage packages with apt* command. In this case, I'm looking for and installing the vsftpd package:

NOTE

Notice that the `apt*` commands are preceded by the `sudo` command in these examples. That's because it is common practice for an Ubuntu administrator to run administrative commands as a regular user with sudo privilege.

10

```
$ sudo apt-get update            Get the latest package versions
$ sudo apt-search vsftpd         Find package by key word (vsftpd)
$ sudo apt-cache show vsftpd     Display information about a package
$ sudo apt-get install vsftpd    Install the vsftpd package
$ sudo apt-get upgrade           Update installed packages
$ sudo apt-cache pkgnames        List all packages that are installed
```

There are many other uses of apt* commands that you can try out. If you have an Ubuntu system installed, I recommend that you run man apt to get an understanding of what the apt and related commands can do.

Understanding RPM packaging

An RPM package is a consolidation of files needed to provide a feature, such as a word processor, a photo viewer, or a file server. Inside an RPM can be the commands, configuration files, and documentation that make up the software feature. However, an RPM file also contains metadata that stores information about the contents of that package, where the package came from, what it needs to run, and other information.

What is in an RPM?

Before you even look inside an RPM, you can tell much about it by the name of the RPM package itself. To find out the name of an RPM package currently installed on your system (such as the Firefox web browser), you could type the following from the shell in Fedora or Red Hat Enterprise Linux:

```
# rpm -q firefox
firefox-24.7.0-1.el7_0.x86_64
```

From this, you can tell that the basename of the package is firefox. The release number is 24.7 (assigned by the upstream producer of Firefox, the Mozilla Project). The version number (assigned by the packager, Red Hat, each time the package is rebuilt at the same release number) is 1. The firefox package was built for Red Hat Enterprise Linux 7.0 (el7_0) and is compiled for the x86 64-bit architecture (x86_64).

When the firefox package was installed, it was probably copied from the installation medium (such as a CD or DVD) or downloaded from a YUM repository (more on that later). If you had been given the RPM file and it was sitting in a local directory, the name would appear as firefox-24.7.0-1.el7_0.x86_64.rpm and you could install it from there. Regardless of where it came from, once installed, the name and other information about the package are stored in an RPM database on the local machine.

To find out more about what is inside an RPM package, you can use options other than the rpm command to query that local RPM database. For example:

```
# rpm -qi firefox
Name        : firefox
Version     : 24.7.0
```

```
Release      : 1.el7_0
Architecture: x86_64
Install Date: Tue 29 Jul 2014 09:39:20 AM EDT
Group        : Applications/Internet
Size         : 92377616
License      : MPLv1.1 or GPLv2+ or LGPLv2+
Signature    : RSA/SHA256, Mon 21 Jul 2014 05:09:41 PM EDT, Key ID
    199e2f91fd431d51
Source RPM   : firefox-24.7.0-1.el7_0.src.rpm
Build Date   : Fri 18 Jul 2014 07:58:58 AM EDT
Build Host   : x86-030.build.eng.bos.redhat.com
Relocations  : (not relocatable)
Packager     : Red Hat, Inc. <http://bugzilla.redhat.com/bugzilla>
Vendor       : Red Hat, Inc.
URL          : http://www.mozilla.org/projects/firefox/
Summary      : Mozilla Firefox Web browser
Description  :
Mozilla Firefox is an open-source web browser, designed for standards
compliance, performance and portability.
```

Besides the information you got from the package name itself, the `-qi` (query information) option lets you see who built the package (Red Hat, Inc.), when it was built, and when it was installed. The group the package is in (Applications/Internet), its size, and the licensing are listed. To find out more about the package, the URL points to the project page on the Internet and the Summary and Description tell you what the package is used for.

Where do RPMs come from?

The software included with Linux distributions, or built to work with those distributions, comes from thousands of open source projects all over the world. These projects, referred to as *upstream software providers*, usually make the software available to anyone who wants it, under certain licensing conditions.

A Linux distribution takes the source code and builds it into binaries. Then it gathers those binaries together with documentation, configuration files, scripts, and other components available from the upstream provider.

After gathering all those components into the RPM, the RPM package is signed (so users can test the package for validity) and placed in a repository of RPMs for the specific distribution and architecture (32-bit x86, 64-bit x86, and so on). The repository is placed on an installation CD or DVD or in a directory that is made available as an FTP, web, or NFS server.

Installing RPMs

When you initially install a Fedora or Red Hat Enterprise Linux system, many individual RPM packages make up that installation. After Linux is installed, you can add more packages using the Software window (as described earlier). Refer to Chapter 9 for information on installing Linux.

10

The first tool to be developed for installing RPM packages, however, was the rpm command. Using rpm, you can install, update, query, validate, and remove RPM packages. The command, however, has some major drawbacks:

- **Dependencies**—Most RPM packages are dependent on some other software (library, executables, and so on) being installed on the system for that package to work. When you try to install a package with rpm, if a dependent package is not installed, the package installation fails, telling you which components were needed. At that point, you have to dig around to find what package contained that component. When you go to install it, that dependent package might itself have dependencies you need to install to get it to work. This situation is lovingly referred to as "dependency hell" and is often used as an example of why DEB packages were better than RPMs. DEB packaging tools were made to automatically resolve package dependencies well before RPM-related packaging tools could do that.

- **Location of RPMs**—The rpm command expects you to provide the exact location of the RPM file when you try to install it. In other words, you would have to give firefox-24.7.0-1.el7_0.x86_64.rpm as an option if the RPM were in the current directory or http://example.com/firefox-24.7.0-1.el7_0.x86_64.rpm if it were on a server.

As Red Hat Linux and other RPM-based applications grew in popularity, it became apparent that something had to be done to make package installation more convenient. The answer was the YUM facility.

Managing RPM Packages with YUM

The Yellowdog Updater Modified (YUM) project set out to solve the headache of managing dependencies with RPM packages. Its major contribution was to stop thinking about RPM packages as individual components and think of them as parts of larger software repositories.

With repositories, the problem of dealing with dependencies fell not to the person who installed the software, but to the Linux distribution or third-party software distributor that makes the software available. So, for example, it would be up to the Fedora project to make sure that every component needed by every package in its Linux distribution could be resolved by some other package in the repository.

Repositories could also build on each other. So, for example, the rpmfusion.org repository could assume that a user already had access to the main Fedora repository. So if a package being installed from rpmfusion.org needed a library or command from the main Fedora repository, the Fedora package could be downloaded and installed at the same time you install the rpmfusion.org package.

The yum repositories could be put in a directory on a web server (http://), an FTP server (ftp://), or a local medium such as a CD, DVD, or local directory (file://). The locations of these repositories would then be stored on the user's system in the /etc/yum.conf file or, more typically, in separate configuration files in the /etc/yum.repos.d directory.

Understanding how yum works

This is the basic syntax of the yum command:

```
# yum [options] command
```

Using that syntax, you can find packages, see package information, find out about package groups, update packages, or delete packages, to name a few features. With the YUM repository and configuration in place, a user can install a package by simply typing something like this:

```
# yum install firefox
```

The user only needs to know the package name (which could be queried in different ways, as described in the section "Searching for packages" later in this chapter). The YUM facility finds the latest version of that package available from the repository, downloads it to the local system, and installs it. Figure 10.2 shows what happens when someone installs a package using the yum command.

The result of a *yum install package* command is that the package requested is copied from the yum repository to the local system. The files in the package are put in the filesystem where needed (/etc, /bin, /usr/share/man, and so on). Information about the package is stored in the local RPM database, where it can be queried.

FIGURE 10.2

Local and remote activities when installing an RPM with YUM.

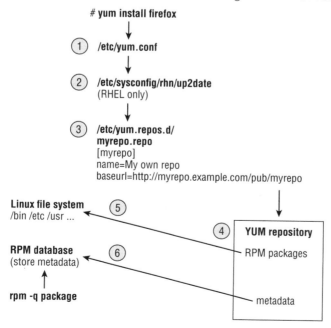

241

To gain more experience with the YUM facility, and see where there are opportunities for you to customize how YUM works on your system, follow the descriptions of each phase of the YUM install process illustrated in Figure 10.2 and defined here.

1. Checking /etc/yum.conf

When any yum command starts, it checks the file /etc/yum.conf for default settings. The /etc/yum.conf file is the basic YUM configuration file. You can also identify the location of repositories here, although the /etc/yum.repos.d directory is the more typical location for identifying repositories. Here's an example of /etc/yum.conf on a RHEL 7 system:

```
[main]
cachedir=/var/cache/yum/$basearch/$releasever
keepcache=0
debuglevel=2
logfile=/var/log/yum.log
exactarch=1

gpgcheck=1
plugins=1
```

Settings in yum.conf tell YUM where to keep cache files (/var/cache/yum) and log entries (/var/log/yum.log), and whether to keep cache files around after a package is installed (0 means no). You can raise the debuglevel value in the yum.conf file to above 2 if you want to see more details in your log files.

Next, you can see whether the exact architecture (x86, x86_64, and so on) should be matched when choosing packages to install (1 means yes) and whether to use plugins (1 means yes) to allow for things such as blacklists, whitelists, or connecting to Red Hat Network for packages.

Finally, gpgcheck says whether to validate each package against a key you receive from those who built the RPM. For packages that come with Fedora or RHEL, the key is included with the distribution to check all packages. However, if you try to install packages that are not from your distribution, you need to either import the key needed to sign those packages or turn off that feature (gpgcheck=0).

To find other features you can set in the yum.conf file, type **man yum.conf**.

2. Checking /etc/sysconfig/rhn/up2date (RHEL only)

For Red Hat Enterprise Linux systems, instead of pointing to a single public software repository (as Fedora does), you register your system with Red Hat Network and purchase entitlements to download software from different channels.

When your system is registered with Red Hat Network, information is added to the /etc/sysconfig/rhn/up2date file to tell yum where to find Red Hat Enterprise Linux packages (either from a hosted Red Hat Network or from an RHN Satellite server).

3. Checking /etc/yum.repos.d/*.repo files

Software repositories can be enabled by dropping files ending in `.repo` into the directory `/etc/yum.repos.d/` that point to the location of one or more repositories. In Fedora, even your basic Fedora repositories are enabled from `.repo` files in this directory.

Here's an example of a simple yum configuration file named `/etc/yum.repos.d/myrepo.repo`:

```
[myrepo]
name=My repository of software packages
baseurl=http://myrepo.example.com/pub/myrepo
enabled=1
gpgcheck=1
gpgkey=file:///etc/pki/rpm-gpg/MYOWNKEY
```

Each repository entry begins with the name of the repository enclosed in square brackets. The `name` line contains a human-readable description of the repository. The `baseurl` line identifies the directory containing the RPM files, which can be an `httpd://`, `ftp://`, or `file://` entry.

The `enabled` line indicates whether the entry is active. A 1 is active; 0 is inactive. If there is no `enabled` line, the entry is active. The last two lines in the preceding code indicate whether to check the signatures on packages in this repository. The `gpgkey` line shows the location of the key that is used to check the packages in this repository.

You can have as many repositories enabled as you like. However, keep in mind that when you use `yum` commands, every repository is checked and metadata about all packages is downloaded to the local system running the `yum` command. So to be more efficient, don't enable repositories you don't need.

4. Downloading RPM packages and metadata from a YUM repository

After `yum` knows the locations of the repositories, metadata from the `repodata` directory of each repository is downloaded to the local system. In fact, it is the existence of a `repodata` directory in a directory of RPMs that indicates that it is a yum repository.

Metadata information is stored on the local system in the `/var/cache/yum` directory. Any further queries about packages, package groups, or other information from the repository are gathered from the cached metadata until a timeout period is reached.

After the timeout period is reached, `yum` retrieves fresh metadata if the `yum` command is run. By default, the timeout is 90 minutes. You can change that period by setting `metadata_expire` in the `/etc/yum.conf` file. Uncomment that line, and change the number of minutes.

10

Next, yum looks at the packages you requested to install and checks if any dependent packages are needed by those packages. With the package list gathered, yum asks you if it is okay to download all those packages. If you choose yes, the packages are downloaded to the cache directories and installed.

5. RPM packages installed to Linux file system

After all the necessary packages are downloaded to the cache directories, yum runs rpm commands to install each package. If a package contains preinstall scripts (which might create a special user account or make directories), those scripts are run. The contents of the packages are copied to the filesystem (commands, config files, docs, and so on). Then any post install scripts are run. (Post install scripts run additional commands needed to configure the system after each package is installed.)

6. Store YUM repository metadata to local RPM database

The metadata contained in each RPM package that is installed is ultimately copied into the local RPM database. The RPM database is contained in files stored in the /var/lib/rpm directory.

After information about installed packages is in the local RPM database, you can do all sorts of queries of that database. You can see what packages are installed, list components of those packages, and see scripts or change logs associated with each package. You can even validate installed packages against the RPM database to see if anyone has tampered with installed components.

The rpm command (described in the section "Installing, Querying, and Verifying Software with the rpm Command" later in this chapter) is the best tool for querying the RPM database. You can run individual queries with rpm or use it in scripts to produce reports or run common queries over and over again.

Now that you understand the basic functioning of the yum command, your Fedora system should be automatically configured to connect to the main Fedora repository and the Fedora Updates repository. You can try some yum command lines to install packages right now. Or you can enable other third-party YUM repositories to draw software from.

Using YUM with third-party software repositories

The Fedora and Red Hat Enterprise Linux software repositories have been screened to contain only software that meets criteria that make it open and redistributable. In some instances, however, you may want to go beyond those repositories. Before you do, you should understand that some third-party repositories have these limitations:

- They may have less stringent requirements for redistribution and freedom from patent constraints than the Fedora and RHEL repositories have.
- They may introduce some software conflicts.

- They may include software that is not open source and, although it may be free for personal use, may not be redistributable.

- They may slow down the process of installing all your packages (because metadata is downloaded for every repository you have enabled).

For those reasons, I recommend that you either don't enable any extra software repositories, or enable only the RPM Fusion repository (http://rpmfusion.org) at first for Fedora and the EPEL repository (http://fedoraproject.org/wiki/EPEL) for Red Hat Enterprise Linux. RPM Fusion represents a fusion of several popular third-party Fedora repositories (Freshrpms, Livna.org, and Dribble). See the repository's FAQ for details (http://rpmfusion.org/FAQ). To enable the free RPM Fusion repository in Fedora, do the following:

1. **Open a Terminal window.**

2. **Type su – and enter the root password when prompted.**

3. **Type the following command on one line with no space between the slash and rpmfusion.** (I had to break the line into two because it was too long to fit in one line on the printed page, so be sure to type the entire address on one line with no space):

```
# rpm -Uvh http://download1.rpmfusion.org/free/fedora/
rpmfusion-free-release-stable.noarch.rpm
```

The RPM Fusion non-free repository contains such things as codecs needed to play many popular multimedia formats. To enable the non-free repository in Fedora, type the following (again, type the following two lines on a single line, with no space between the two):

```
# rpm -Uhv http://download1.rpmfusion.org/nonfree/fedora/
rpmfusion-nonfree-release-stable.noarch.rpm
```

Most of the other third-party repositories that might interest you contain software that is not open source. For example, if you want to install the Adobe Flash plug-in for Linux, download the YUM repository package from Adobe and you can use the yum command to install the Flash plug-in, and get updates later by running the yum update command, when updates are available.

Managing software with the YUM command

The yum command has dozens of subcommands you can use to work with RPM packages on your system. The following sections provide some examples of useful yum command lines to search for, install, query, and update packages associated with your YUM repositories. It also includes a section describing how to remove installed packages with the yum command.

10

> **NOTE**
>
> Metadata, describing the contents of YUM repositories, is downloaded from each of your enabled YUM repositories the first time you run a `yum` command. Metadata is downloaded again after the metadata_expire time is reached (90 minutes, by default). The more YUM repositories you enable and the larger they are, the longer this download can take. You can reduce this download time by increasing the expire time (in the `/etc/yum.conf` file) or by not enabling repositories you don't need.

Searching for packages

Using different searching subcommands, you can find packages based on key words, package contents, or other attributes.

Let's say you want to try out a different text editor, but you can't remember the name of the one you wanted. You could start by using the `search` subcommand to look for the term "editor" in the name or description:

```
# yum search editor
...
eclipse-veditor.noarch : Eclipse-based Verilog/VHDL plugin
ed.x86_64 : The GNU line editor
emacs.x86_64 : GNU Emacs text editor
```

The search uncovered a long list of packages containing "editor" in the name or description. The one I was looking for is named `emacs`. To get information about that package, I can use the `info` subcommand:

```
# yum info emacs
Name        : emacs
Arch        : x86_64
Epoch       : 1
Version     : 24.4
Release     : 3.fc21
Size        : 3.0 M
Repo        : updates/21/x86_64
Summary     : GNU Emacs text editor
URL         : http://www.gnu.org/software/emacs/
License     : GPLv3+ and CC0-1.0
Description : Emacs is a powerful, customizable, self-documenting,
            : modeless text editor. Emacs contains special code editing
            : features, a scripting language (elisp), and the capability
            : to read mail, news, and more without leaving the editor.
```

If you know the command, configuration file, or library name you want, but don't know what package it is in, use the `provides` subcommand to search for the package. Here you can see that the `dvdrecord` command is part of the `wodim` package:

```
# yum provides dvdrecord
wodim-1.1.11-25.fc21.x86_64 : A command line CD/DVD recording program
Repo        : fedora
Matched from:
Provides    : dvdrecord
```

The `list` subcommand can be used to list package names in different ways. Use it with a package base name to find the version and repository for a package. You can list just packages that are `available` or `installed`, or you can list `all` packages.

```
# yum list emacs
emacs.i686      1:24.4-3.fc21        updates
# yum list available
389-admin.i686                  1.1.35-2.fc21       fedora
389-admin-console.noarch        1.1.35-2.fc21       fedora
389-admin-console-doc.noarch    1.1.8-7.fc21        fedora
...
# yum list installed
Installed Packages
GConf2.x86_64           3.2.6-11.fc21       @koji-override-0/$releasever
LibRaw.x86_64           0.16.0-4.fc21       @koji-override-0/$releasever
...
# yum list all
...
```

If you find a package, but want to see what components that package is dependent on, you can use the `deplist` subcommand. With `deplist`, you can see the components (dependency) but also the package that component comes in (provider). Using `deplist` can help if no package is available to provide a dependency, but you want to know what the component is so you can search other repositories for it. Consider the following example:

```
# yum deplist emacs | less
package: emacs.x86_64 1:24.4-3.fc21
  dependency: /bin/sh
   provider: bash.x86_64 4.3.33-1.fc21
  dependency: /usr/sbin/alternatives
   provider: chkconfig.x86_64 1.3.63-1.fc21
  dependency: dejavu-sans-mono-fonts
   provider: dejavu-sans-mono-fonts.noarch 2.34-4.fc21
```

Installing and removing packages

The `install` subcommand lets you install one or more packages, along with any dependent packages needed. With `yum install`, multiple repositories can be searched to fulfill needed dependencies. Consider the following example of `yum install`:

```
# yum install emacs
...
```

10

```
Package              Arch      Version          Repository       Size
=====================================================================
Installing:
 emacs               x86_64    1:24.4-3.fc21    updates          3.0 M
Installing for dependencies:
 ImageMagick-libs    x86_64    6.8.8.10-5.fc21  fedora           2.0 M
 emacs-common        x86_64    1:24.4-3.fc21    updates          37 M
 libXaw              x86_64    1.0.12-4.fc21    fedora           190 k
 liblockfile         x86_64    1.08-16.fc21     updates          27 k
 libotf              x86_64    0.9.13-5.fc21    fedora           96 k

Transaction Summary
=====================================================================
Install  1 Package (+5 Dependent packages)

Total download size: 42 M
Installed size: 109 MIs this ok [y/N]: y
```

You can see here that emacs requires that emacs-common and several other packages be installed so all are queued up for installation. The six packages together are 26MB to download, but consume 91MB after installation. Pressing y installs them. You can put a -y on the command line (just after the yum command) to avoid having to press y to install the packages, but personally, I usually want to see all the packages about to be installed before I agree to the installation.

You can reinstall a package if you mistakenly delete components of an installed package. If you attempt a regular install, the system responds with "nothing to do." You must, instead, use the reinstall subcommand. For example, suppose you installed the zsh package and then deleted /bin/zsh by mistake. You could restore the missing components by typing the following:

```
# yum reinstall zsh
```

You can remove a single package with the erase subcommand. For example, to erase the emacs package, you could type the following:

```
# yum erase emacs
Dependencies Resolved=========================================
 Package              Arch      Version          Repository     Size
=====================================================================
Removing:
 emacs                x86_64    1:24.4-3.fc21    @updates        14 M

Transaction Summary
=====================================================================
Remove  1 Package

Installed size: 14 MIs this ok [y/N]: y
```

Notice that even though six packages were installed when emacs was installed, only the emacs package itself was removed with the erase subcommand. Although emacs required that emacs-common be installed, emacs-common did not depend on emacs and could therefore stay on the system without breaking dependencies. Running yum remove emacs-common would have removed both packages.

An alternative method to remove a set of packages you have installed is to use the history subcommand. Using history, you can see your yum activities and undo an entire transaction. In other words, all the packages you installed can be uninstalled using the undo option to the history subcommand. For example:

```
# yum history
ID   | Login user          | Date and time     | Action(s)  | Altered
-------------------------------------------------------------------------
96   | Chris Negus <cnegus> | 2016-12-10 06:25 | Install     |    2
...
# yum history info 96
Transaction ID : 96
...
Command Line    : install emacs
...
# yum history undo 96
Undoing transaction 96, from Wed Dec 14 06:25:41 2014
    Dep-Install emacs-common-1:24.4-3.fc21.x86_64   @updates
    Dep-Install libXaw-1.0.12-4.fc21.x86_64          @fedora
 ...
```

Before you undo the transaction, you can view the transaction to see exactly which packages were involved. Viewing the transaction can save you from mistakenly deleting packages you want to keep. By undoing transaction 96, you can remove all packages that were installed during that transaction. If you are trying to undo an install that included dozens or even hundreds of packages, undo can be a very useful option.

Updating packages

As new releases of a package become available, they are sometimes put in separate update repositories or simply added to the original repository. If multiple versions of a package are available (whether in the same repository or another enabled repository), yum provides the latest version when you install a package. If a new version shows up later, you can download and install the new version of the package by using the update subcommand.

The check-update subcommand can check for updates. The update subcommand can be used to update a single package or to get updates to all packages that are currently installed and have an update available. Or you can simply update a single package (such as the cups package). For example:

```
# yum check-update
...kernel.x86_64          3.10.0-123.6.3.el7      rhel-7-server-rpms
```

```
kernel-headers.x86_64   3.10.0-123.6.3.el7      rhel-7-server-rpms

# yum update
...Resolving Dependencies
--> Running transaction check
---> Package kernel.x86_64 0:3.10.0-123.6.3.el7 will be installed
---> Package kernel-headers.x86_64 0:3.10.0-123.4.4.el7 will be
   updated
...
Transaction Summary
======================================================================
Upgrade       38 Package(s)
Total download size: 50 M
Is this ok [y/N]: y
# yum update cups
```

The preceding command requested to update the cups package. If other dependent packages need to be updated to update cups, those packages would be downloaded and installed as well.

Updating groups of packages

To make it easier to manage a whole set of packages at once, YUM supports package groups. For example, you could install GNOME Desktop Environment (to get a whole desktop) or Virtualization (to get packages needed to set up the computer as a virtual host). You can start by running the grouplist subcommand to see a list of group names:

```
# yum grouplist | less
Available environment groups:
   Fedora Server
...
Installed groups:
   Administration Tools
   Design Suite
...
Available Groups:
   Authoring and Publishing
   Books and Guides
   C Development Tools and Libraries
...
```

Let's say you want to try out a different desktop environment. You see LXDE, and you want to know what is in that group. To find out, use the groupinfo subcommand:

```
# yum groupinfo LXDE
Group: LXDE
 Group-Id: lxde-desktop
```

```
Description: LXDE is a lightweight X11 desktop environment...
Mandatory Packages:
   lxde-common
   lxmenu-data
 . . .
```

In addition to showing a description of the group, groupinfo shows Mandatory Packages (those that are always installed with the group), Default Packages (those that are installed by default, but can be excluded), and Optional Packages (which are part of the group, but not installed by default). When you use some graphical tools to install package groups, you can uncheck default packages or check optional packages to change whether they are installed with the group.

If you decide you want to install a package group, use the groupinstall subcommand:

```
# yum groupinstall LXDE
```

This groupinstall resulted in 30 packages from the group being installed and 5 existing packages being updated. If you decide you don't like the group of packages, you can remove the entire group at once using the groupremove subcommand:

```
# yum groupremove LXDE
```

Maintaining your RPM package database and cache

Several subcommands to yum can help you do maintenance tasks, such as check for problems with your RPM database or clear out the cache. The YUM facility has tools for maintaining your RPM packages and keeping your system's software efficient and secure.

Clearing out the cache is something you want to do from time to time. If you decide to keep downloaded packages after they are installed (they are removed by default, based on the keepcache=0 setting in the /etc/yum.conf file), your cache directories (under /var/cache/yum) can fill up. Metadata stored in cache directories can be cleared, causing fresh metadata to be downloaded from all enabled YUM repositories the next time yum is run. Here are ways to clear that information:

```
# yum clean packages
Cleaning repos: rhel-7-server-rpms
7 package files removed
# yum clean metadata
43 metadata files removed
13 sqlite files removed
# yum clean all
Cleaning repos: rhel-7-server-rpms
Cleaning up Everything
```

Although unlikely, it's possible that the RPM database can become corrupted. This can happen if something unexpected occurs, such as pulling out the power cord when a package

10

is partially installed. You can check the RPM database to look for errors (yum check) or just rebuild the RPM database files, as follows:

```
# yum check
check all
# yum clean rpmdb
Cleaning repos: rhel-7-server-rpms
4 rpmdb files removed
```

Of the yum clean examples in the preceding three command lines, all remove cached data from the /var/cache/yum subdirectories, except for the rpmdb example. That command removed db* files from the /var/lib/rpm directory (regenerating those database files to clean up any problems).

The rpmdb option is one of the few options to yum that is used to work with the RPM database directly. In general, yum is used for manipulating yum repositories. The command best suited for working with the local RPM database is the rpm command.

Downloading RPMs from a yum repository

If you just want to examine a package without actually installing it, you can use the yumdownloader command. Running that command causes the package you name to be downloaded from the YUM repository and copied to your current directory.

For example, to download the latest version of the Firefox web browser package from the YUM repository to your current directory, type the following:

```
# yumdownloader firefox
...(1/2): firefox-35.0-3.fc21.x86_64.rpm        |  68 MB  00:00:09
(2/2): firefox-35.0-3.fc21.i686.rpm             |  68 MB  00:00:10
```

In this case, because x86_64 and i686 versions of the firefox package are available, both are downloaded to the current directory. With any downloaded RPM packages now sitting in your current directory, you can use a variety of rpm commands to query or use those packages in different ways (as described in the next section).

Installing, Querying, and Verifying Software with the rpm Command

There is a wealth of information about installed packages in the local RPM database. The rpm command contains dozens of options to enable you to find information about each package, such as the files it contains, who created it, when it was installed, how large it is, and many other attributes. Because the database contains fingerprints (md5sums) of every file in every package, it can be queried with RPM to find out if files from any package have been tampered with.

The rpm command can still do basic install and upgrade activities, although most people only use rpm in that way when there is a package sitting in the local directory, ready to be installed. So let's get one in our local directory to work with. Type the following to download the latest version of the zsh package:

```
# yumdownloader zsh
zsh-5.0.7-4.fc21.x86_64.rpm  |  2.5 MB  00:03
```

With the zsh package downloaded to your current directory, try some rpm commands on it.

Installing and removing packages with rpm

To install a package with the rpm command, type this:

```
# rpm -i zsh-5.0.7-4.fc21.x86_64.rpm
```

Notice that the entire package name is given to install with rpm, not just the package base name. If an earlier version of zsh were installed, you could upgrade the package using -U. Often, people use -h and -v options to get hash signs printed and more verbose output during the upgrade:

```
# rpm -Uhv zsh-5.0.7-4.fc21.x86_64.rpm
Preparing...              ######################### [100%]
   1:zsh                  ######################### [100%]
```

Although an install (-i) only installs a package if the package is not already installed, an upgrade (-U) installs the package even if it is already installed. A third type of install called freshen (-F) installs a package only if an existing, earlier version of a package is installed on the computer. For example:

```
# rpm -Fhv *.rpm
```

You could use the previous freshen command if you were in a directory containing thousands of RPMs but only wanted to update those that were already installed (in an earlier version) on your system and skip those that were not yet installed.You can add a few interesting options to any of your install options. The --replacepkgs option enables you to reinstall an existing version of a package (if, for example, you had mistakenly deleted some components), and the --oldpackage enables you to install an earlier version of a package.

```
# rpm -Uhv --replacepkgs emacs-common-24.4-3.fc21.x86_64.rpm
# rpm -Uhv --oldpackage zsh-4.3.10-7.el6.x86_64.rpm
```

You can remove a package with the -e option. You only need the base name of a package to remove it. For example:

```
# rpm -e emacs
```

The rpm -e emacs command would be successful because no other packages are dependent on emacs. However, it would leave behind emacs-common, which was installed as a dependency to emacs. If you had tried to remove emacs-common first, that command would fail with a "Failed dependencies" message.

10

Querying rpm information

After the package is installed, you can query for information about the package. Using the -q option, you can see information about the package, including a description (-qi), list of files (-ql), documentation (-qd), and configuration files (-qc).

```
# rpm -qi zsh
Name      : zsh
Version   : 5.0.7
Release   : 4.fc21
. . .
# rpm -ql zsh
/bin/zsh
/etc/skel/.zshrc
/etc/zlogin
/etc/zlogout
. . .
# rpm -qd zsh/usr/share/doc/zsh/BUGS
/usr/share/doc/zsh/CONTRIBUTORS
/usr/share/doc/zsh/FAQ# rpm -qc zsh
/etc/skel/.zshrc
/etc/zlogin
/etc/zlogout
```

You can use options to query any piece of information contained in an RPM. You can find what an RPM needs for it to be installed (--requires), what version of software a package provides (--provides), what scripts are run before and after an RPM is installed or removed (--scripts), and what changes have been made to an RPM (--changelog).

```
# rpm -q --requires emacs-common
/bin/sh
/sbin/install-info
/usr/bin/perl
. . .
# rpm -q --provides emacs-common
config(emacs-common) = 1:24.4-3.fc21
emacs-common = 1:24.4-3.fc21
emacs-common(x86-64) = 1:24.4-3.fc21
emacs-el = 1:24.4-3.fc21
pkgconfig(emacs) = 1:24.4
# rpm -q --scripts httpd
# Add the "apache" user
/usr/sbin/useradd -c "Apache" -u 48 \
      -s /sbin/nologin -r -d /var/www apache 2> /dev/null || :
postinstall scriptlet (using /bin/sh):
. . .
# rpm -q --changelog httpd | less*
Wed Sep 03 2014 Jan Kaluza
   <jkaluza@redhat.com> - 2.4.10-9
- fix hostname requirement and conflict with openssl-libs
. . .
```

In the previous two examples, you can see that scripts inside the httpd package add an apache user at installation time and turn on the httpd service with chkconfig. The --changelog option enables you to see why changes have been made to each version of the package. The fix # represents a fixed bug that you can look up in http://bugzilla.redhat.com.

Using a feature called --queryformat, you can query different tags of information and output them in any form you like. Run the --querytags option to be able to see all the tags that are available:

```
# rpm --querytags | less
ARCH
ARCHIVESIZE
BASENAMES
BUGURL
...
# rpm -q binutils --queryformat "The package is %{NAME} \
    and the release is %{RELEASE}\n"
The package is binutils and the release is 30.fc21
```

All the queries you have done so far have been to the local RPM database. By adding a -p to those query options, you can query an RPM file sitting in your local directory instead. The -p option is a great way to look inside a package that someone gives you to investigate what it is before you install it on your system.

If you haven't already, get the zsh package and put it in your local directory (yumdown-loader zsh). Then run some query commands on the RPM file.

```
# rpm -qip zsh-5.0.2-7.el7.x86_64.rpm    View info about the RPM file
# rpm -qlp zsh-5.0.2-7.el7.x86_64.rpm    List all files in RPM file
# rpm -qdp zsh-5.0.2-7.el7.x86_64.rpm    Show docs in the RPM file
# rpm -qcp zsh-5.0.2-7.el7.x86_64.rpm    List config files in RPM file
```

Verifying RPM packages

Using the -V option, you can check the packages installed on your system to see if the components have been changed since the packages were first installed. Although it is normal for configuration files to change over time, it is not normal for binaries (the commands in /bin, /sbin, and so on) to change after installation. Binaries that are changed are probably an indication that your system has been cracked.

In this example, I'm going to install the zsh package and mess it up. If you want to try along with the examples, be sure to remove or reinstall the package when you are finished.

```
# rpm -i zsh-5.0.7-4.fc21.x86_64.rpm
# echo hello > /bin/zsh
# rm /etc/zshrc
# rpm -V zsh
```

10

```
S.5....T.    /bin/zsh
missing    c /etc/zshrc
```

In this output, you can see that the /bin/zsh file has been tampered with and /etc/zshrc has been removed. Each time you see a letter or a number instead of a dot from the rpm -V output, it is an indication of what has changed. Letters that can replace the dots (in order) include the following:

```
S    file Size differs
M    Mode differs (includes permissions and file type)
5    MD5 sum differs
D    Device major/minor number mismatch
L    readLink(2) path mismatch
U    User ownership differs
G    Group ownership differs
T    mTime differs
P    caPabilities differ
```

Those indicators are from the Verify section of the rpm man page. In my example, you can see that the file size has changed (S), the md5sum checked against the file's fingerprint has changed (5), and the modification time (T) on the file differs.

To restore the package to its original state, use rpm with the --replacepkgs option, as shown next. (The yum reinstall zsh command would work as well). Then check it with -V again. No output from -V means that every file is back to its original state.

```
# rpm -i --replacepkgs zsh-5.0.2-7.el7.x86_64.rpm
# rpm -V zsh
```

Good practice is to back up your RPM database (from /var/lib/rpm) and copy it to some read-only medium (such as a CD). Then, when you go to verify packages that you suspect were cracked, you know you aren't checking it against a database that has also been cracked.

Managing Software in the Enterprise

At this point, you should have a good working knowledge of how to install, query, remove, and otherwise manipulate packages with graphical tools, the yum command, and the rpm command. When you start working with RPM files in a large enterprise, you need to extend that knowledge.

Features used to manage RPM packages in the enterprise with Red Hat Enterprise Linux offer a bit more complexity and much more power. Instead of having one big software repository, as Fedora does, RHEL provides deployment through Red Hat Network, which requires a paid subscription and entitlements to a variety of software channels (RHEL, Red Hat Enterprise Virtualization, Red Hat Cluster Suite, and so on).

In terms of enterprise computing, one of the great benefits of the design of RPM packages is that their management can be automated. Other Linux packaging schemes allow packages to stop and prompt you for information when they are being installed (such as asking for a directory location or a username). RPM packages install without interruption, offering some of the following advantages:

- **Kickstart files**—All the questions you answer during a manual install and all the packages you select can be added into a file called a kickstart file. When you start a Fedora or Red Hat Enterprise Linux installer, you can provide a kickstart file at the boot prompt. From that point on, the entire installation process completes on its own. Any modifications to the default package installs can be made by running pre and post scripts from the kickstart file, to do such things as add user accounts or modify configuration files.

- **PXE boot**—You can configure a PXE server to allow client computers to boot an anaconda (installer) kernel and a select kickstart file. A completely blank computer with a network interface card (NIC) that supports PXE booting can simply boot from its NIC to launch a fresh installation. In other words, turn on the computer, and if it hits the NIC in its boot order, a few minutes later you can have a freshly installed system, configured to your exact specifications without intervention.

- **Satellite server (Spacewalk)**—Red Hat Enterprise Linux systems can be deployed using what is referred to as Satellite Server (the open source project is called Spacewalk). Built into Satellite Server are the same features you have from Red Hat Network to manage and deploy new systems and updates. Without logging in directly, RHEL systems can be configured to get software updates at times set from the satellite server. Sets of packages called Errata that fix specific problems can be quickly and automatically deployed to the systems that need them.

Descriptions of how to use kickstart files, satellite servers, and other enterprise-ready installation features are beyond the scope of this book. But the understanding you have gained from learning about YUM and RPM will serve as a solid foundation for any RHEL software installation work you do in the future.

Summary

Software packaging in Fedora, Red Hat Enterprise Linux, and related systems is provided using software packages based on the RPM Package Manager (RPM) tools. Debian, Ubuntu, and related systems package software into DEB files. You can try easy-to-use graphical tools such as the Software window for finding and installing packages. The primary command-line tools include the yum and rpm commands for Red Hat-related systems and aptitude, apt*, and dkpg for Debian-related systems.

Using these software management tools, you can install, query, verify, update, and remove packages. You can also do maintenance tasks, such as clean out cache files and rebuild the

10

RPM database. This chapter describes many of the features of the Software window, as well as yum and rpm commands.

With your system installed and the software packages that you need added, it's time to further configure your Fedora, RHEL, Debian, or Ubuntu system. If you expect to have multiple people using your system, your next task could be to add and otherwise manage user accounts on your system. Chapter 11 describes user management in Fedora, RHEL, and other Linux systems.

Exercises

These exercises test your knowledge of working with RPM software packages in Fedora or Red Hat Enterprise Linux. To do the exercises, I recommend you have a Fedora system in front of you that has an Internet connection. (Most of the procedures work equally well on a registered RHEL system.)

You need to be able to reach the Fedora repositories (which should be set up automatically). If you are stuck, solutions to the tasks are shown in Appendix B (although in Linux, there are often multiple ways to complete a task).

1. Search the YUM repository for the package that provides the mogrify command.
2. Display information about the package that provides the mogrify command and determine what that package's home page (URL) is.
3. Install the package containing the mogrify command.
4. List all the documentation files contained in the package that provides the mogrify command.
5. Look through the changelog of the package that provides the mogrify command.
6. Delete the mogrify command from your system, and verify its package against the RPM database to see that the command is indeed missing.
7. Reinstall the package that provides the mogrify command, and make sure the entire package is intact again.
8. Download the package that provides the mogrify command to your current directory.
9. Display general information about the package you just downloaded by querying the package's RPM file in the current directory.
10. Remove the package containing the mogrify command from your system.

Managing User Accounts

IN THIS CHAPTER

Working with user accounts

Working with group accounts

Configuring centralized user accounts

Adding and managing users are common tasks for Linux systems administrators. *User accounts* keep boundaries between the people who use your systems and between the processes that run on your systems. *Groups* are a way of assigning rights to your system that can be assigned to multiple users at once.

This chapter describes not only how to create a new user, but also how to create predefined settings and files to configure the user's environment. Using tools such as the useradd and usermod commands, you can assign settings such as the location of a home directory, a default shell, a default group, and specific user ID and group ID values.

Creating User Accounts

Every person who uses your Linux system should have a separate user account. Having a user account provides you with an area in which to securely store files, as well as a means of tailoring your user interface (GUI, path, environment variables, and so on) to suit the way that you use the computer.

You can add user accounts to most Linux systems in several ways. Fedora and Red Hat Enterprise Linux systems have a Users window available from the Settings Window. In GNOME 3, go the the Activities screen, type Users, and press Enter. In GNOME 2, from the Applications menu, select System Tools ⇨ Settings. Then select the Users icon. Select the Unlock button, and enter the root password. Then select the plus (+) to open a window for adding a user account, as shown in Figure 11.1.

You are now ready to begin adding a new user account to your Linux system. Here are the fields you need to fill in:

- **Account Type**—Choose Standard (to create a regular user account) or Administrator (to create an account that has root permission).

FIGURE 11.1

Add user accounts from the User window.

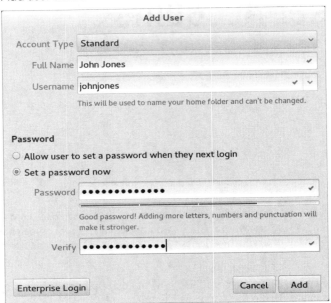

- **Full Name**—Use the user's real name, typically used with uppercase and lowercase letters as the user would write it in real life. Technically, this information is stored in the comment field of the `passwd` file but, by convention, most Linux and UNIX systems expect this field to hold each user's full name.

- **Username**—This is the name used to log in as this user. When you choose a username, don't begin with a number (for example, `26jsmith`). Also, it's best to use all lowercase letters, no control characters or spaces, and a maximum of eight characters. The `useradd` command allows up to 32 characters, but some applications can't deal with usernames that long. Tools such as `ps` display user IDs (UIDs) instead of names if names are too long. Having users named `Jsmith` and `jsmith` can cause confusion with programs (such as sendmail) that don't distinguish case.

- **Password, Verify**—Select the "Set a password now" button. Then enter the password you want the user to have in the Password and Verify fields. The password should be at least eight characters and contain a mixture of uppercase and lowercase letters, numbers, and punctuation. It should not contain real words, repeated letters, or letters in a row on the keyboard. Through this interface, you must set a password that meets the above criteria. (If you want to add a password that doesn't meet these criteria, you can use the `useradd` command, described later in this chapter.)

Select Add to add the user to the system. An entry for the new user account is added to the `/etc/passwd` file and the new group account to the `/etc/group` file. I describe those later in this chapter.

The Software window lets you modify a small set of information about a regular user after it has been created. To modify user information later, select the user account you want to change, click the Unlock button, and enter the root password. At this point, you can change the account type (Standard or Administrator), change the user's password, or allow the user account to log in automatically (without a password). This screen is shown in Figure 11.2.

FIGURE 11.2

Modify existing user accounts from the Users window.

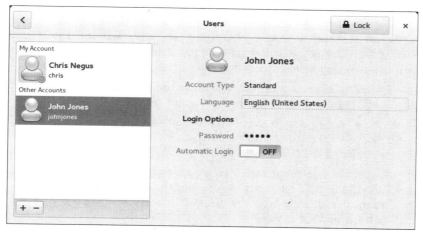

The Users window was designed to simplify the process of creating and modifying user accounts. More features associated with user accounts can be added or modified from the command line. The next part of this chapter describes how to add user accounts from the command line with `useradd` or change them with the `usermod` command.

Adding users with useradd

Sometimes, a Linux system doesn't have a desktop available to use the User Manager window. Other times, you might find it more convenient to add lots of users at once with a shell script or change user account features that are not available from the Users window. For those cases, commands are available to enable you to add and modify user accounts from the command line.

The most straightforward method for creating a new user from the shell is the useradd command. After opening a Terminal window with root permission, you simply invoke useradd at the command prompt, with details of the new account as parameters.

The only required parameter is the login name of the user, but you probably want to include some additional information ahead of it. Each item of account information is preceded by a single-letter option code with a dash in front of it. The options available with useradd include the following:

- -c *"comment here"*—Provide a description of the new user account. Typically, this is the person's full name. Replace *comment* with the name of the user account (-c Jake). Use quotes to enter multiple words (for example, -c *"Jake Jackson"*).

- -d *home_dir*—Set the home directory to use for the account. The default is to name it the same as the login name and to place it in /home. Replace *home_dir* with the directory name to use (for example, -d /mnt/homes/jake).

- -D—Rather than create a new account, save the supplied information as the new default settings for any new accounts that are created.

- -e *expire_date*—Assign the expiration date for the account in YYYY-MM-DD format. Replace *expire_date* with a date you want to use. (For example, to expire an account on May 5, 2017, use -e 2017-05-05.)

- -f -1—Set the number of days after a password expires until the account is permanently disabled. The default, -1, disables the option. Setting this to 0 disables the account immediately after the password has expired. Replace -1 (that's minus one) with the number to use.

- -g *group*—Set the primary group (it must already exist in the /etc/group file) the new user will be in. Replace *group* with the group name (for example, -g wheel). Without this option, a new group is created that is the same as the user name and is used as that user's primary group.

- -G *grouplist*—Add the new user to the supplied comma-separated list of supplementary groups (for example, -G wheel,sales,tech,lunch). (If you use -G later with usermod, be sure to use -aG and not just -G. If you don't, existing supplementary groups are removed and the groups you provide here are the only ones assigned.)

- **-k** *skel_dir*—Set the skeleton directory containing initial configuration files and login scripts that should be copied to a new user's home directory. This parameter can be used only in conjunction with the -m option. Replace *skel_dir* with the directory name to use. (Without this option, the /etc/skel directory is used.)

- **-m**—Automatically create the user's home directory and copy the files in the skeleton directory (/etc/skel) to it. (This is the default action for Fedora and RHEL, so it's not required. It is not the default for Ubuntu.)

- **-M**—Do not create the new user's home directory, even if the default behavior is set to create it.

- **-n**—Turn off the default behavior of creating a new group that matches the name and user ID of the new user. This option is available with Fedora and RHEL systems. Other Linux systems often assign a new user to the group named users instead.

- **-o**—Use with -u *uid* to create a user account that has the same UID as another username. (This effectively lets you have two different usernames with authority over the same set of files and directories.)

- **-p** *passwd*—Enter a password for the account you are adding. This must be an encrypted password. Instead of adding an encrypted password here, you can simply use the *passwd user* command later to add a password for *user*. (To generate an encrypted MD5 password, type **openssl passwd**.)

- **-s** *shell*—Specify the command shell to use for this account. Replace *shell* with the command shell (for example, -s /bin/csh).

- **-u** *user_id*—Specify the user ID number for the account (for example, -u 793). Without the -u option, the default behavior is to automatically assign the next available number. Replace **user_id** with the ID number.

Let's create an account for a new user. The user's full name is Sara Green, and her login name is sara. To begin, become root user and type the following command:

    # **useradd -c "Sara Green" sara**

Next, set the initial password for sara using the passwd command. You're prompted to type the password twice:

    # **passwd sara**
    Changing password for user sara.
    New password: *************
    Retype new password: *************

> **NOTE**
>
> Asterisks in this example represent the password you type. Nothing is actually displayed when you type the password. Also keep in mind that running passwd as root user lets you add short or blank passwords that regular users cannot add themselves.

In creating the account for Sara, the `useradd` command performs several actions:

- Reads the `/etc/login.defs` and `/etc/default/useradd` files to get default values to use when creating accounts.
- Checks command-line parameters to find out which default values to override.
- Creates a new user entry in the `/etc/passwd` and `/etc/shadow` files based on the default values and command-line parameters.
- Creates any new group entries in the `/etc/group` file. (Fedora creates a group using the new user's name.)
- Creates a home directory, based on the user's name, in the `/home` directory.
- Copies any files located within the `/etc/skel` directory to the new home directory. This usually includes login and application startup scripts.

The preceding example uses only a few of the available `useradd` options. Most account settings are assigned using default values. You can set more values explicitly, if you want to. Here's an example that uses a few more options to do so:

```
# useradd -g users -G wheel,apache -s /bin/tcsh -c "Sara Green" sara
```

In this case, `useradd` is told to make `users` the primary group sara belongs to (`-g`), add her to the wheel and apache groups, and assign `tcsh` as her primary command shell (`-s`). A home directory in `/home` under the user's name (`/home/sara`) is created by default. This command line results in a line similar to the following being added to the `/etc/passwd` file:

```
sara:x:1002:1007:Sara Green:/home/sara:/bin/tcsh
```

Each line in the `/etc/passwd` file represents a single user account record. Each field is separated from the next by a colon (`:`) character. The field's position in the sequence determines what it is. The login name is first. The password field contains an *x* because, in this example, the shadow password file is used to store encrypted password data (in `/etc/shadow`).

The user ID selected by `useradd` is 1002. The primary group ID is 1007, which corresponds to a private `sara` group in the `/etc/group` file. The comment field was correctly set to `Sara Green`, the home directory was automatically assigned as `/home/sara`, and the command shell was assigned as `/bin/tcsh`, exactly as specified with the `useradd` options.

By leaving out many of the options (as I did in the first `useradd` example), defaults are assigned in most cases. For example, by not using `-g sales` or `-G wheel,apache`, the group name `mary` was assigned to the new user. Some Linux systems (other than Fedora and RHEL) assign `users` as the group name by default. Likewise, excluding `-s /bin/tcsh` causes `/bin/bash` to be assigned as the default shell.

The `/etc/group` file holds information about the different groups on your Linux system and the users who belong to them. Groups are useful for enabling multiple users to share access to the same files while denying access to others. Here is the /etc/group entry created for sara:

```
sara:x:1007:
```

Each line in the group file contains the name of a group, a group password (usually filled with an x), the group ID number associated with it, and a list of users in that group. By default, each user is added to his or her own group, beginning with the next available GID, starting with 1000.

Setting user defaults

The useradd command determines the default values for new accounts by reading the /etc/login.defs and /etc/default/useradd files. You can modify those defaults by editing the files manually with a standard text editor. Although login.defs is different on different Linux systems, the following is an example containing many of the settings you might find in a login.defs file:

```
PASS_MAX_DAYS      99999
PASS_MIN_DAYS      0
PASS_MIN_LEN       5
PASS_WARN_AGE      7
UID_MIN                    1000
UID_MAX                   60000
GID_MIN                    1000
GID_MAX                   60000
CREATE_HOME yes
```

All uncommented lines contain keyword/value pairs. For example, the keyword PASS_MIN_LEN is followed by some white space and the value 5. This tells useradd that the user password must be at least five characters. Other lines enable you to customize the valid range of automatically assigned user ID numbers or group ID numbers. (Fedora starts at UID 1000; earlier systems started with UID 100.) A comment section that explains that keyword's purpose precedes each keyword (which I edited out here to save space). Altering a default value is as simple as editing the value associated with a keyword and saving the file before running the useradd command.

If you want to view other default settings, refer to the /etc/default/useradd file. You can also see default settings by typing the useradd command with the -D option, as follows:

```
# useradd -D
GROUP=100
HOME=/home
INACTIVE=-1
EXPIRE=
SHELL=/bin/bash
SKEL=/etc/skel
CREATE_MAIL_SPOOL=yes
```

You can also use the -D option to change defaults. When run with this flag, useradd refrains from actually creating a new user account; instead, it saves any additionally supplied options as the new default values in /etc/default/useradd. Not all useradd options can be used in conjunction with the -D option. You can use only the five options listed here.

- **-b** *default_home*—Set the default directory in which user home directories are created. Replace *default_home* with the directory name to use (for example, -b /garage). Usually, this is /home.

- **-e** *default_expire_date*—Set the default expiration date on which the user account is disabled. The *default_expire_date* value should be replaced with a date in the form YYYY-MM-DD (for example, -e 2011-10-17).

- **-f** *default_inactive*—Set the number of days after a password has expired before the account is disabled. Replace *default_inactive* with a number representing the number of days (for example, -f 7).

- **-g** *default_group*—Set the default group that new users will be placed in. Normally, useradd creates a new group with the same name and ID number as the user. Replace *default_group* with the group name to use (for example, -g bears).

- **-s** *default_shell*—Set the default shell for new users. Typically, this is /bin/bash. Replace *default_shell* with the full path to the shell that you want as the default for new users (for example, -s /usr/bin/ksh.

To set any of the defaults, give the -D option first and add the defaults you want to set. For example, to set the default home directory location to /home/everyone and the default shell to /bin/tcsh, type the following:

```
# useradd -D -b /home/everyone -s /bin/tcsh
```

In addition to setting up user defaults, an administrator can create default files that are copied to each user's home directory for use. These files can include login scripts and shell configuration files (such as .bashrc).

Other commands that are useful for working with user accounts include usermod (to modify settings for an existing account) and userdel (to delete an existing user account).

Modifying users with usermod

The usermod command provides a simple and straightforward method for changing account parameters. Many of the options available with it mirror those found in useradd. The options that can be used with this command include the following:

- **-c** *username*—Change the description associated with the user account. Replace *username* with the name of the user account (-c jake). Use quotes to enter multiple words (for example, -c "Jake Jackson").

- **-d** *home_dir*—Change the home directory to use for the account. The default is to name it the same as the login name and to place it in */home*. Replace *home_dir* with the directory name to use (for example, -d /mnt/homes/jake).

- **-e** *expire_date*—Assign a new expiration date for the account in YYYY-MM-DD format. Replace *expire_date* with a date you want to use. (For October 15, 2017, use -e 2017-10-15.)

- **-f** *-1*—Change the number of days after a password expires until the account is permanently disabled. The default, -1, disables the option. Setting this to 0 disables the account immediately after the password has expired. Replace -1 with the number to use.

- **-g** *group*—Change the primary group (as listed in the /etc/group file) the user will be in. Replace *group* with the group name (for example, -g wheel).

- **-G** *grouplist*—Set the user's secondary groups to the supplied comma-separated list of groups. If the user is already in at least one group besides the user's private group, you must add the -a option as well (-Ga). If not, the user belongs to only the new set of groups and loses membership to any previous groups.

- **-l** *login_name*—Change the login name of the account.

- **-L**—Lock the account by putting an exclamation point at the beginning of the encrypted password in /etc/shadow. This locks the account, while still allowing you to leave the password intact (the -U option unlocks it).

- **-m**—Available only when –d is used, this causes the contents of the user's home directory to be copied to the new directory.

- **-o**—Use only with -u uid to remove the restriction that UIDs must be unique.

- **-s** *shell*—Specify a different command shell to use for this account. Replace shell with the command shell (for example, -s bash).

- **-u** *user_id*—Change the user ID number for the account. Replace user_id with the ID number (for example, -u 1474).

- **-U**—Unlocks the user account (by removing the exclamation mark at the beginning of the encrypted password).

The following are examples of the usermod command:

```
# usermod -s /bin/csh chris
# usermod -Ga sales,marketing, chris
```

The first example changes the shell to the csh shell for the user named chris. In the second example, supplementary groups are added for the user chris. The -a option (-Ga) makes sure that the supplementary groups are added to any existing groups for the user chris. If the -a is not used, existing supplementary groups for chris are erased and the new list of groups includes the only supplementary groups assigned to that user.

Deleting users with userdel

Just as usermod is used to modify user settings and useradd is used to create users, userdel is used to remove users. The following command removes the user chris:

```
# userdel -r chris
```

Here, the user chris is removed from the /etc/password file. The -r option removes the user's home directory as well. If you choose not to use -r, as follows, the home directory for chris is not removed:

```
# userdel chris
```

Keep in mind that simply removing the user account does not change anything about the files that user leaves around the system (except those that are deleted when you use -r). However, ownership of files left behind appears as belonging to the previous owner's user ID number when you run ls -l on the files.

Before you delete the user, you may want to run a find command to find all files that would be left behind by the user. After you delete the user, you could search on user ID to find files left behind. Here are two find commands to do those things:

```
# find / -user chris -ls
# find / -uid 504 -ls
```

Because files that are not assigned to any username are considered to be a security risk, it is a good idea to find those files and assign them to a real user account. Here's an example of a find command that finds all files in the filesystem that are not associated with any user (the files are listed by UID):

```
# find / -nouser -ls
```

Understanding Group Accounts

Group accounts are useful if you want to share a set of files with multiple users. You can create a group and change the set of files to be associated with that group. The root user can assign users to that group so they can have access to files based on that group's permission. Consider the following file and directory:

```
$ ls -ld /var/salesdocs /var/salesdocs/file.txt
drwxrwxr-x. 2 root sales 4096 Jan 14 09:32 /var/salesstuff/
-rw-rw-r--. 1 root sales    0 Jan 14 09:32 /var/salesstuff/file.txt
```

Looking at permissions on the directory /var/salesdocs (rwxrwxr-x), you see that the second set of rwx shows that any member of the group (sales) has permission to read files in that directory (r is read), create and delete files from that directory (w is write), and change to that directory (x is execute). The file named file.txt can be read and changed by members of the sales group (based on the second rw-).

Using group accounts

Every user is assigned to a primary group. In Fedora and RHEL, by default, that group is a new group with the same name as the user. So if the user were named sara, the group assigned to her would also be sara. The primary group is indicated by the number in the third field of each entry in the /etc/passwd file, for example, the group ID 1007 here:

```
sara:x:1002:1007:Sara Green:/home/sara:/bin/tcsh
```

That entry points to an entry in the /etc/group file:

```
sara:x:1007:
```

Let's turn to the sara user and group accounts for examples. Here are a few facts about using groups:

- When sara creates a file or directory, by default, that file or directory is assigned to sara's primary group (also called sara).

- The user sara can belong to zero or more supplementary groups. If sara were a member of groups named sales and marketing, those entries could look like the following in the /etc/group file:

  ```
  sales:x:1302:joe,bill,sally,sara
  marketing:x:1303:mike,terry,sara
  ```

- The user sara can't add herself to a supplementary group. She can't even add another user to her sara group. Only someone with root privilege can assign users to groups.

- Any file assigned to the sales or marketing group is accessible to sara with group and other permissions (whichever provides the most access). If sara wants to create a file with the sales or marketing groups assigned to it, she could use the newgrp command. In this example, sara uses the newgrp command to have sales become her primary group temporarily and creates a file:

```
[sara]$ touch file1
[sara]$ newgrp sales
[sara]$ touch file2
[sara]$ ls -l file*
-rw-rw-r--. 1 sara sara  0 Jan 18 22:22 file1
-rw-rw-r--. 1 sara sales 0 Jan 18 22:23 file2
[sara]$ exit
```

It is also possible to allow users to temporarily become a member of a group with the newgrp command without actually being a member of that group. To do that, someone with root permission can use gpasswd to set a group password (such as gpasswd sales). After that, any user can type newgrp sales into a shell and temporarily use sales as their primary group by simply entering the group password when prompted.

Creating group accounts

As the root user, you can create new groups from the User Manager window or from the command line with the groupadd command. Also, as noted earlier, groups are created automatically when a user account is created.

Group ID numbers from 0 through 999 are assigned to special administrative groups. For example, the root group is associated with GID 0. Regular groups begin at 1000 for Red Hat Enterprise Linux and Fedora. On the first UNIX systems, GIDs went from 0 to 99. Other Linux systems reserve GIDs between 0 to 500 for administrative groups.

Here are some examples of creating a group account with the groupadd command:

```
# groupadd kings
# groupadd -g 1325 jokers
```

In the examples just shown, the group named kings is created with the next available group ID. After that, the group jokers is created using the 1325 group ID. Some administrators like using an undefined group number under 1000 so the group they create doesn't intrude on the group designations above 1000 (so UID and GID numbers can go along in parallel).

To change a group later, use the groupmod command. For example:

```
# groupmod -g 330 jokers
# groupmod -n jacks jokers
```

In the first example, the group ID for jokers is changed to 330. In the second, the name jokers is changed to jacks. If you wanted to then assign any of the groups as supplementary groups to a user, you can use the usermod command (as described earlier in this chapter).

Managing Users in the Enterprise

The basic Linux method of handling user and group accounts has not changed since the first UNIX systems were developed decades ago. However, as Linux systems have become used in more complex ways, features for managing users, groups, and the permissions associated with them have been added on to the basic user/group model so that it could be:

- **More flexible**—In the basic model, only one user and one group can be assigned to each file. Also, regular users have no ability to assign specific permissions to different users or groups and very little flexibility setting up collaborative files/directories. Enhancements to this model allow regular users to set up special collaborative directories (using features such as sticky bit and set GID bit directories). Using Access Control Lists (ACLs), any user can also assign specific permissions to files and directories to any users and groups they like.

■ **More centralized**—When you have only one computer, storing user information for all users in the /etc/password file is probably not a hardship. However, if you need to authenticate the same set of users across thousands of Linux systems, centralizing that information can save lots of time and heartache. Red Hat Enterprise Linux includes features that enable you to authenticate users from LDAP servers or Microsoft Active Directories servers.

The following sections describe how to use features such as Access Control Lists (ACLs) and shared directories (sticky bit and set GID bit directories) to provide powerful ways to selectively share files and directories. Next, I describe how to manage user accounts from centralized authentication servers using the Authentication Configuration window.

Setting permissions with Access Control Lists

The Access Control List (ACL) feature was created so regular users could share their files and directories selectively with other users and groups. With ACLs, a user can allow others to read, write, and execute files and directories without leaving those filesystem elements wide open or requiring the root user to change the user or group assigned to them.

Here are a few things to know about ACLs:

■ For ACLs to be used, they must be enabled on a filesystem when that filesystem is mounted.

■ In Fedora and Red Hat Enterprise Linux, ACLs are automatically enabled on any filesystem created when the system is installed.

■ If you create a filesystem after installation (such as when you add a hard disk), you need to make sure that the acl mount option is used when the filesystem is mounted (more on that later).

■ To add ACLs to a file, you use the setfacl command; to view ACLs set on a file, you use the getfacl command.

■ To set ACLs on any file or directory, you must be the actual owner (user) assigned to it. In other words, being assigned user or group permissions with setfacl does not give you permission to change ACLs on those files yourself.

■ Because multiple users and groups can be assigned to a file/directory, the actual permission a user has is based on a union of all user/group designations to which they belong. For example, if a file had read-only permission (r--) for the sales group and read/write/execute (rwx) for the market group, and mary belonged to both, mary would have rwx permission.

NOTE

If ACLs are not enabled on the filesystem you are trying to use with setfacl, see the "Enabling ACLs" section later in this chapter for information on how to mount a filesystem with ACLs enabled.

Setting ACLs with setfacl

Using the `setfacl` command, you can modify permissions (-m) or remove ACL permissions (-x). The following is an example of the syntax of the `setfacl` command:

```
setfacl -m u:username:rwx filename
```

In the example just shown, the modify option (-m) is followed by the letter u, indicating that you are setting ACL permissions for a user. After a colon (:), you indicate the username, followed by another colon and the permissions you want to assign. As with the `chmod` command, you can assign read (r), write (w), and/or execute (x) permissions to the user or group (in the example, full `rwx` permission is given). The last argument is replaced by the actual filename you are modifying.

The following are some examples of the user mary using the `setfacl` command to add permission for other users and groups on a file:

```
[mary]$ touch /tmp/memo.txt
[mary]$ ls -l /tmp/memo.txt
-rw-rw-r--. 1 mary mary 0 Jan 21 09:27 /tmp/memo.txt
[mary]$ setfacl -m u:bill:rw /tmp/memo.txt
[mary]$ setfacl -m g:sales:rw /tmp/memo.txt
```

In the preceding example, mary created a file named /tmp/memo.txt. Using the `setfacl` command, she modified (-m) permissions for the user named bill so he now has read/write (rw) permissions to that file. Then she modified permissions for the group sales so anyone belonging to that group would also have read/write permissions. Look at `ls -l` and `getfacl` output on that file now:

```
[mary]$ ls -l /tmp/memo.txt
-rw-rw-r--+ 1 mary mary 0 Jan 21 09:27 /tmp/memo.txt
[mary]$ getfacl /tmp/memo.txt
# file: tmp/memo.txt
# owner: mary
# group: mary
user::rw-
user:bill:rw-
group::rw-
group:sales:rw-
mask::rw-
other::r--
```

From the `ls -l` output, notice the plus sign (+) in the `rw-rw-r--+` output. The plus sign indicates that ACLs are set on the file, so you know to run the `getfacl` command to see how ACLs are set. The output shows mary as owner and group (same as what you see with `ls -l`), the regular user permissions (rw-), and permissions for ACL user bill (rw-). The same is true for group permissions and permissions for the group sales. Other permissions are r--.

The mask line (near the end of the previous getfacl example) requires some special discussion. As soon as you set ACLs on a file, the regular group permission on the file sets a mask of the maximum permission an ACL user or group can have on a file. So, even if you provide an individual with more ACL permissions than the group permissions allow, the individual's effective permissions do not exceed the group permissions. For example:

```
[mary]$ chmod 644 /tmp/memo.txt
[mary]$ getfacl /tmp/memo.txt
# file: tmp/memo.txt
# owner: mary
# group: mary
user::rw-
user:bill:rw-    #effective:r--
group::rw-       #effective:r--
group:sales:rw-  #effective:r--
mask::r--
other::r--
```

Notice in the preceding example that even though the user bill and group sales have rw- permissions, their effective permissions are r--. So, bill or anyone in sales would not be able to change the file unless mary were to open permissions again (for example, by typing chmod 664 /tmp/memo.txt).

Setting default ACLs

Setting default ACLs on a directory enables your ACLs to be inherited. That means that when new files and directories are created in that directory, they are assigned the same ACLs. To set a user or group ACL permission as the default, you add a d: to the user or group designation. Consider the following example:

```
[mary]$ mkdir /tmp/mary
[mary]$ setfacl -m d:g:market:rwx /tmp/mary/
[mary]$ getfacl /tmp/mary/
# file: tmp/mary/
# owner: mary
# group: mary
user::rwx
group::rwx
other::r-x
default:user::rwx
default:group::rwx
default:group:sales:rwx
default:group:market:rwx
default:mask::rwx
default:other::r-x
```

To make sure the default ACL worked, create a subdirectory. Then run getfacl again. You will see that default lines are added for user, group, mask, and other, which are inherited from the directory's ACLs.

```
[mary]$ mkdir /tmp/mary/test
[mary]$ getfacl /tmp/mary/test
# file: tmp/mary/test
# owner: mary
# group: mary
user::rwx
group::rwx
group:sales:rwx
group:market:rwx
mask::rwx
other::r-x
default:user::rwx
default:group::rwx
default:group:sales:rwx
default:group:market:rwx
default:mask::rwx
default:other::r-x
```

Notice that when you create a file in that directory, the inherited permissions are different. Because a regular file is created without execute permission, the effective permission is reduced to rw-:

```
[mary@cnegus ~]$ touch /tmp/mary/file.txt
[mary@cnegus ~]$ getfacl /tmp/mary/file.txt
# file: tmp/mary/file.txt
# owner: mary
# group: mary
user::rw-
group::rwx          #effective:rw-
group:sales:rwx     #effective:rw-
group:market:rwx    #effective:rw-
mask::rw-
other::r--
```

Enabling ACLs

Basic Linux filesystems that you create after installation have only one user and one group assigned to each file and directory and do not include ACL support by default. Linux ext filesystem types (ext2, ext3, and ext4) can add ACL support through a mount option. To add ACL support, you must add the acl mount option when you mount it. You can do that in several ways:

- Add the acl option to the fifth field in the line in the /etc/fstab file that automatically mounts the filesystem when the system boots up.

- Implant the acl line in the Default mount options field in the filesystem's super block, so the acl option is used whether the filesystem is mounted automatically or manually.

- Add the acl option to the mount command line when you mount the filesystem manually with the mount command.

Keep in mind that in Fedora and Red Hat Enterprise Linux systems, you only have to add the `acl` mount option to those filesystems you create after Linux is installed. The anaconda installer automatically adds ACL support to every filesystem it creates during install time. To check that the `acl` option has been added to a filesystem, determine the device name associated with the filesystem, and run the `tune2fs -l` command to view the implanted mount options. For example:

```
# mount | grep home
/dev/mapper/mybox-home on /home type ext4 (rw)
# tune2fs -l /dev/mapper/mybox-home | grep "mount options"
Default mount options:    user_xattr acl
```

First, I typed the `mount` command to see a list of all filesystems that are currently mounted, limiting the output by grepping for the word `home` (because I was looking for the filesystem mounted on `/home`). After I saw the filesystem's device name, I used it as an option to `tune2fs -l` to find the default mount options line. There, I could see that mount options `user_xattr` (for extended attributes such as SELinux) and `acl` were both implanted in the filesystem super block so they would be used when the filesystem was mounted.

If the Default mount options field is blank (such as when you have just created a new filesystem), you can add the `acl` mount option using the `tune2fs -o` command. For example, I created a filesystem on a removable USB drive that was assigned as the `/dev/sdc1` device. To implant the `acl` mount option and check that it is there, I ran the following commands:

```
# tune2fs -o acl /dev/sdc1
# tune2fs -l /dev/sdc1 | grep "mount options"
Default mount options:    acl
```

You can test that this worked by remounting the filesystem and trying to use the `setfacl` command on a file in that filesystem.

A second way to add `acl` support to a filesystem is to add the `acl` option to the line in the `/etc/fstab` file that automatically mounts the filesystem at boot time. The following is an example of what a line would look like that mounts the ext4 filesystem located on the `/dev/sdc1` device to the `/var/stuff` directory:

```
/dev/sdc1      /var/stuff      ext4     acl         1 2
```

Instead of the `defaults` entry in the fourth field, I added `acl`. If there were already options set in that field, add a comma after the last option and add `acl`. The next time the filesystem is mounted, ACLs are enabled. If the filesystem were already mounted, I could type the following `mount` command as root to remount the filesystem, using `acl` or any other values added to the `/etc/fstab` file:

```
# mount -o remount /dev/sdc1
```

A third way you can add ACL support to a filesystem is to mount the filesystem by hand and specifically request the `acl` mount option. So, if there is no entry for the filesystem in the /etc/fstab file, after creating the mount point (/var/stuff), type the following command to mount the filesystem and include ACL support:

```
# mount -o acl /dev/sdc1 /var/stuff
```

Keep in mind that the mount command only mounts the filesystem temporarily. When the system reboots, the filesystem is not mounted again, unless you add an entry to the /etc/fstab file.

Adding directories for users to collaborate

A special set of three permission bits are typically ignored when you use the chmod command to change permissions on the filesystem. These bits can set special permissions on commands and directories. The focus of this section is setting the bits that help you create directories to use for collaboration.

As with read, write, and execute bits for user, group, and other, these special file permission bits can be set with the chmod command. If, for example, you run chmod 775 /mnt/xyz, the implied permission is actually 0775. To change permissions, you can replace the number 0 with any combination of those three bits (4, 2, and 1), or you can use letter values instead. (Refer to Chapter 4, "Moving around the Filesystem," if you need to be reminded about how permissions work.) The letters and numbers are shown in Table 11.1.

TABLE 11.1   Commands to Create and Use Files

Name	Numeric value	Letter value
Set user ID bit	4	u+s
Set group ID bit	2	g+s
Sticky bit	1	o+t

The bits you are interested in for creating collaborative directories are the set group ID bit (2) and sticky bit (1). If you are interested in other uses of the set user ID and set group ID bits, refer to the sidebar "Using Set UID and Set GID Bit Commands."

Creating group collaboration directories (set GID bit)

By creating a set GID directory, any files created in that directory are assigned to the group assigned to the directory itself. The idea is to have a directory where all members of a group can share files but still protect them from other users. Here's a set of steps for creating a collaborative directory for all users in the group I created called sales:

1. Create a group to use for collaboration:

```
# groupadd -g 301 sales
```

2. Add some users to the group that you want to be able to share files (I used mary):

```
# usermod -aG sales mary
```

3. Create the collaborative directory:

```
# mkdir /mnt/salestools
```

Using Set UID and Set GID Bit Commands

The set UID and set GID bits are used on special executable files that allow commands set to be run differently from most. Normally, when a user runs a command, that command runs with that user's permissions. In other words, if I run the vi command as chris, that instance of the vi command would have the permissions to read and write files that the user chris could read and write.

Commands with the set UID or set GID bits set are different. It is the owner and group assigned to the command, respectively, that determines the permissions the command has to access resources on the computer. So a set UID command owned by root would run with root permissions; a set GID command owned by apache would have apache group permissions.

Examples of applications that have set UID bits turned on are the su and newgrp commands. In both of those cases, the commands must be able to act as the root user to do their jobs. However, to actually get root permissions, a user must provide a password. You can tell su is a set UID bit command because of the s where the first execute bit (x) usually goes:

```
$ ls /bin/su
-rwsr-xr-x. 1 root root  30092 Jan 30 07:11 su
```

4. Assign the group sales to the directory:

```
# chgrp sales /mnt/salestools
```

5. Change the directory permission to 2775. This turns on the set group ID bit (2), full rwx for the user (7), rwx for group (7), and r-x (5) for other:

```
# chmod 2775 /mnt/salestools
```

6. Become mary (run su - mary). As mary, create a file in the shared directory and look at the permissions. When you list permissions, you can see that the directory is a set GID directory because a lowercase s appears where the group execute permission should be (rwxrwsr-x):

```
# su - mary
[mary]$ touch /mnt/salestools/test.txt
[mary]$ ls -ld /mnt/salestools/ /mnt/salestools/test.txt
drwxrwsr-x. 2 root sales 4096 Jan 22 14:32 /mnt/salestools/
-rw-rw-r--. 1 mary sales    0 Jan 22 14:32 /mnt/salestools/test.txt
```

Typically, a file created by mary would have the group mary assigned to it. But because test.txt was created in a set group ID bit directory, the file is assigned to the sales group. Now, anyone who belongs to the sales group can read or write that file, based on group permissions.

Creating restricted deletion directories (sticky bit)

A *restricted deletion directory* is created by turning on a directory's sticky bit. What makes a restricted deletion directory different than other directories? Normally, if write permission is open to a user on a file or directory, that user can delete that file or directory. However, in a restricted deletion directory, unless you are the root user or the owner of the directory, you can never delete another user's files.

Typically, a restricted deletion directory is used as a place where lots of different users can create files. For example, the /tmp directory is a restricted deletion directory:

```
$ ls -ld /tmp
drwxrwxrwt. 116 root root 36864 Jan 22 14:18 /tmp
```

You can see the permissions are wide open, but instead of an x for the execute bit for other, the t indicates that the sticky bit is set. The following is an example of creating a restricted deletion directory with a file that is wide open for writing by anyone:

```
[mary]$ mkdir /tmp/mystuff
[mary]$ chmod 1777 /tmp/mystuff
[mary]$ cp /etc/services /tmp/mystuff/
[mary]$ chmod 666 /tmp/mystuff/services
[mary]$ ls -ld /tmp/mystuff /tmp/mystuff/services
drwxrwxrwt. 2 mary mary   4096 Jan 22 15:28 /tmp/mystuff/
-rw-rw-rw-. 1 mary mary 640999 Jan 22 15:28 /tmp/mystuff/services
```

With permissions set to 1777 on the /tmp/mystuff directory, you can see that all permissions are wide open, but a t appears instead of the last execute bit. With the /tmp/mystuff/services file open for writing, any user could open it and change its contents. However, because the file is in a sticky bit directory, only root and mary can delete that file.

Centralizing User Accounts

Although the default way of authenticating users in Linux is to check user information against the /etc/passwd file and passwords from the /etc/shadow file, you can authenticate in other ways as well. In most large enterprises, user account information is stored in a centralized authentication server, so each time you install a new Linux system, instead of adding user accounts to that system, you have the Linux system query the authentication server when someone tries to log in.

As with local passwd/shadow authentication, configuring centralized authentication requires that you provide two types of information: account information (username, user/group IDs, home directory, default shell, and so on) and authentication method (different types of encrypted passwords, smart cards, retinal scans, and so on). Linux provides ways of configuring those types of information.

Because I hope you will someday use your Linux skills to work in a large Linux installation, I want to introduce the concept of centralized authentication. For now, I just discuss how to connect to existing authentication servers (rather than set up those servers themselves) and have users of a Linux system you configure authenticate against those types of servers.

Using the Users window

If you add a new user to your system with the Users window (described earlier in this chapter), you have the option of selecting the Enterprise Login button instead of adding a password for that user. On that window, you can identify the location (Domain) of a central authentication server. When the user you add tries to log into your Linux system, the authentication Domain, and not the local /etc/passwd file, is queried to authenticate the user account.

For more complex authentication configurations than are available through the Users window, you should investigate the authconfig command. With authconfig, you can enable different types of authentication mechanisms (such as Smart Card, fingerprint readers, and Kerberos authentication).

Authentication domains that are supported via the Users window include LDAP, NIS, and Windows Active Directory. The next section describes these authentication domains.

Using the Authentication Configuration window

Earlier versions of Fedora and Red Hat Enterprise Linux use a graphical window, called the Authentication Configuration window, for configuring centralized authentication. Through that window, you can configure where your system gets account information and what type of authentication method is used to verify users. Supported centralized database types include these:

- **LDAP**—The Lightweight Directory Access Protocol is a popular protocol for providing directory services (such as phone books, addresses, and user accounts). It is an open standard that is configured in many types of computing environments.

- **NIS**—The Network Information Service was originally created by Sun Microsystems to propagate information such as user accounts, host configuration, and other types of system information across many UNIX systems. Because NIS passes information in clear text, most enterprises now use the more secure LDAP or Winbind protocols for centralized authentication.

- **Winbind**—Selecting Winbind from the Authentication Configuration window enables you to authenticate your users against a Microsoft Active Directory (AD) server. Many large companies extend their desktop authentication setup to do server configuration as well as using an AD server.

For this introduction to configuring centralized authentication servers, you will configure a Linux system to authenticate against an LDAP server, using the Authentication Configuration window in Red Hat Enterprise Linux.

To begin, you need to gather information about the LDAP service at your location. That includes information about the account database and the authentication method:

- **LDAP Search Base DN**—This is the distinguished name of the LDAP database used to identify the location of the user account records. Often, the name is constructed from the company's DNS domain name. For example, dc=example,dc=com.

- **LDAP server**—This is the host name of the LDAP server—for example, ldap://ldap.example.com.

- **Use TLS to encrypt connections**—With this selected, you must also select to identify the location of a certificate authority (CA) certificate that will be downloaded to the local system to use to validate and encrypt communications with the LDAP server. Transport Layer Security (TLS) certificates for an organization are obtained from certificate authorities such as Verisign. Or you could create self-signed certificates.

- **Authentication method**—Instead of using regular MD5 passwords, pick either LDAP password or Kerberos as the authentication method with LDAP. For Kerberos, you must also provide information about the Kerberos server, which includes the Kerberos Realm, KDCs, and Admin Servers. All this information should be provided by the administrators who manage your company's Kerberos servers.

To start the Authentication Configuration window from a Red Hat Enterprise Linux 6 desktop, select System ⇨ Administration ⇨ Authentication. For a default system that only does local (passwd/shadow) authentication, the window appears.

To add LDAP authentication, select the User Account Database box and select LDAP. Then fill in the information described in the preceding bullet points.

If the new authentication method is configured properly, you should be able to go to a shell and validate that. If you know of a user account available from the LDAP server, use the following getent command to check that the account is available:

```
# getent passwd jsmith
jsmith:x:13599:13600:John Smith:/home/jsmith:/bin/bash
```

If you see the account information, you know your system was able to retrieve it from the LDAP server. The next thing to check is that the authentication method is working as well. For that, you could try to log in as the user from the console or by using the ssh command. For example:

```
$ ssh jsmith@localhost
```

When prompted, enter the username and password. If it succeeds, you know that both the account and authentication information you entered for your LDAP server were correct.

With your authentication centralized, consider centralizing your users' home directories as well. Using the Linux automounter (autofs service), you could set up home directories that are automatically mounted when each user logs in, regardless of which machine they are logging into. (See Chapter 20, "Configuring an NFS File Server," for information on setting up an NFS server and configuring clients to automount from that server.)

Summary

Having separate user accounts is the primary method of setting secure boundaries between the people who use your Linux system. Regular users typically can control the files and directories within their own home directories, but very little outside those directories.

In this chapter, you learned how to add user and group accounts, how to modify them, and even how to extend user and group accounts beyond the boundaries of the local /etc/ password file. You also learned that authentication can be done by accessing centralized LDAP servers.

The next chapter introduces another basic topic needed by Linux system administrators: how to manage disks. In that chapter, you learn how to partition disks, add filesystems, and mount them, so the contents of the disk partitions are accessible to those using your system.

Exercises

Use these exercises to test your knowledge of adding and managing user and group accounts in Linux. These tasks assume you are running a Fedora or Red Hat Enterprise Linux system (although some tasks work on other Linux systems as well). If you are stuck, solutions to the tasks are shown in Appendix B (although in Linux, you often have multiple ways to complete a task).

1. Add a local user account to your Linux system that has a username of jbaxter and a full name of John Baxter, and uses /bin/sh as its default shell. Let the UID be assigned by default. Set the password for jbaxter to: My1N1teOut!

2. Create a group account named testing that uses group ID 315.

3. Add jbaxter to the testing group and the bin group.

4. Open a shell as jbaxter (either a new login session or using a current shell) and temporarily have the testing group be your default group so that when you type touch /home/jbaxter/file.txt, the testing group is assigned as the file's group.

5. Note what user ID has been assigned to jbaxter, and delete the user account without deleting the home directory assigned to jbaxter.

6. Find any files in the /home directory (and any subdirectories) that are assigned to the user ID that recently belonged to the user named jbaxter.

7. Copy the /etc/services file to the default skeleton directory so it shows up in the home directory of any new user. Then add a new user to the system named mjones, with a full name of Mary Jones and a home directory of /home/maryjones.

8. Find all files under the /home directory that belong to mjones. Are there any files owned by mjones that you didn't expect to see?

9. Log in as mjones, and create a file called /tmp/maryfile.txt. Using ACLs, assign the bin user read/write permission to that file. Then assign the lp group read/write permission to that file.

10. Still as mjones, create a directory named /tmp/mydir. Using ACLs, assign default permissions to that directory so the adm user has read/write/execute permission to that directory and any files or directories created in it. Create the /tmp/mydir/testing/ directory and /tmp/mydir/newfile.txt file, and make sure the adm user was also assigned full read/write/execute permissions. (Note that despite assigning rwx permission to the adm user, the effective permission on newfile.txt is only rw. What could you do to make sure adm gets execute permission as well?)

Managing Disks and Filesystems

Your operating system, applications, and data all need to be kept on some kind of permanent storage so that when you turn off your computer, it is all still there when the computer is turned on again. Traditionally, that storage has been provided by a hard disk in your computer. To organize the information on that disk, the disk is usually divided into partitions, with most partitions given a structure referred to as a *filesystem*.

This chapter describes how to work with hard disks. Hard disk tasks include partitioning, adding filesystems, and managing those filesystems in various ways. Storage devices that are attached to the systems from removable devices and network devices can be partitioned and managed in the same ways.

After covering basic partitions, I describe how logical volume management (LVM) can be used to make it easier to grow, shrink, and otherwise manage filesystems more efficiently.

Understanding Disk Storage

The basics of how data storage works are the same in most modern operating systems. When you install the operating system, the disk is divided into one or more partitions. Each partition is formatted with a filesystem. In the case of Linux, some of the partitions may be specially formatted for elements such as a swap area or LVM physical volumes. Disks are used for permanent storage; random access memory (RAM) and swap are used for temporary storage. For example, when you run a command, that command is copied from the hard disk into RAM so that your computer processor (CPU) can access it more quickly.

Your CPU can access data much faster from RAM than it can from hard disk. However, a disk is usually much larger than RAM, RAM is much more expensive, and RAM is erased when the computer reboots. Think of your office as a metaphor for RAM and disk. A disk is like a file cabinet where you store folders of information you need. RAM is like the top of your desk, where you put the folder of papers while you are using it, but you put it back in the file cabinet when you are not.

If RAM fills up, by running too many processes or a process with a memory leak, new processes fail if your system doesn't have a way to extend system memory. That's where a swap area comes in. A swap space is a hard disk swap partition or a swap file where your computer can "swap out" data from RAM that isn't being used at the moment and then "swap in" the data back to RAM when it is again needed. Although it is better to never exceed your RAM (performance takes a hit when you swap), swapping out is better than having processes just fail.

Another special partition is a logical volume management (LVM) physical volume. LVM physical volumes enable you to create pools of storage space called *volume groups*. From those volume groups, you have much more flexibility for growing and shrinking logical volumes than you have resizing disk partitions directly.

For Linux, at least one disk partition is required, assigned to the root (/) of the entire Linux filesystem. However, it is more common to have separate partitions that are assigned to particular directories, such as /home, /var, and/or /tmp. Each of the partitions is connected to the larger Linux filesystem by mounting it to a point in the filesystem where you want that partition to be used. Any file added to the mount point directory of a partition, or a subdirectory, is stored on that partition.

> **NOTE**
> The word *mount* refers to the action of connecting a filesystem from a hard disk, USB drive, or network storage device to a particular point in the filesystem. This action is done using the mount command, along with options to tell the command where the storage device is and what directory in the filesystem to connect it to.

The business of connecting disk partitions to the Linux filesystem is done automatically and invisibly to the end user. How does this happen? Each regular disk partition created when you install Linux is associated with a device name. An entry in the /etc/fstab file tells Linux each partition's device name and where to mount it (as well as other bits of information). The mounting is done when the system boots.

Most of this chapter focuses on understanding how your computer's disk is partitioned and connected to form your Linux filesystem, as well as how to partition disks, format filesystems and swap space, and have those items used when the system boots. The chapter then covers how to do partitioning and filesystem creation manually.

Coming from Windows

Filesystems are organized differently in Linux than they are in Microsoft Windows operating systems. Instead of drive letters (for example, A:, B:, C:) for each local disk, network filesystem, CD-ROM, or other type of storage medium, everything fits neatly into the Linux directory structure.

Some drives are connected (mounted) automatically into the filesystem when you insert removable media. For example, a CD might be mounted on /media/cdrom. If the drive isn't mounted automatically, it is up to an administrator to create a mount point in the filesystem and then connect the disk to that point.

Linux can understand VFAT filesystems, which are often the default format when you buy a USB flash drive. A VFAT USB flash drive provides a good way to share data between Linux and Windows systems. Linux kernel support is available for NTFS filesystems, which are usually used with Windows these days. However, NTFS often requires that you install additional kernel drivers in Linux.

VFAT file systems are often used when files need to be exchanged between different types of operating systems. Because VFAT was used in MS-DOS and early Windows operating systems, it offers a good lowest common denominator for sharing files with many types of systems (including Linux). NTFS is the file system type most commonly used with modern Microsoft Windows systems.

12

Partitioning Hard Disks

Linux provides several tools for managing your hard disk partitions. You need to know how to partition your disk if you want to add a disk to your system or change your existing disk configuration.

This section demonstrates disk partitioning using an 8GB removable USB flash drive and a fixed hard disk. To be safe, I use a USB flash drive that doesn't contain any data I want to keep to practice partitioning.

Changing partitioning can make a system unbootable!

I don't recommend using your system's primary hard disk to practice changing partitioning because a mistake can make your system unbootable. Even if you use a separate USB flash drive to practice, a bad entry in /etc/fstab can hang your system on reboot. If after changing partitions your system fails to boot, refer to Chapter 21, "Troubleshooting Linux," for information on how to fix the problem.

Understanding partition tables

PC architecture computers have traditionally used Master Boot Record (MBR) partition tables to store information about the sizes and layouts of the hard disk partitions. There are many tools for managing MBR partitions that are quite stable and well known. In the past few years, however, a new standard called Global Unique Identifiers (GUID) partition tables began being used on systems as part of the UEFI computer architecture to replace the older BIOS method of booting the system.

Some Linux partitioning tools have been updated to handle GUID partition tables. Other tools for handling GUID partition tables have been added. If you happen to have a system that uses GUID partition tables, you can use a tool called gdisk instead of the fdisk command described in this chapter.

Limitations imposed by the MBR specification brought about the need for GUID partitions. In particular, MBR partitions are limited to 2TB in size. GUID partitions can create partitions up to 9.4ZB (zettabytes). While the gdisk command lets you manage partitions that are potentially much larger the subcommands for creating, deleting, and changing disk partitions are essentially the same as those available with fdisk.

Viewing disk partitions

To view disk partitions, use the fdisk command with the -l option. The following is an example of partitioning on a 160GB fixed hard drive on a Red Hat Enterprise Linux 7 system:

```
# fdisk -l /dev/sda
Disk /dev/sda: 160.0 GB, 160000000000 bytes, 312500000 sectors
Units = sectors of 1 * 512 = 512 bytes
Sector size (logical/physical): 512 bytes / 512 bytes
I/O size (minimum/optimal): 512 bytes / 512 bytes
Disk label type: dos
Disk identifier: 0x0008870c
    Device Boot      Start         End      Blocks   Id  System
/dev/sda1   *         2048     1026047      512000   83  Linux
/dev/sda2           1026048   304281599   151627776   8e  Linux LVM
```

When a USB flash drive is inserted, it is assigned to the next available sd device. The following shows the partitioning on a USB drive from a RHEL system, where /dev/sdc is assigned as the device name (the third disk on the system). Use the -c option with fdisk to turn off DOS compatibility mode and -u to show the size in sectors instead of cylinders, because partitions may not fall on cylinder boundaries (default options changed recently, so the -c and -u options are no longer needed in the latest RHEL or Fedora releases):

```
# fdisk -cul /dev/sdc
Disk /dev/sdc: 8059 MB, 8059355136 bytes
248 heads, 62 sectors/track, 1023 cylinders, total 15740928 sectors
```

```
Units = sectors of 1 * 512 = 512 bytes
Sector size (logical/physical): 512 bytes / 512 bytes
I/O size (minimum/optimal): 512 bytes / 512 bytes
Disk identifier: 0x0007a9f4
   Device Boot    Start      End   Blocks   Id  System
/dev/sdc1    *     2048   194559    96256   83  Linux
/dev/sdc2        194560  2148351   976896   82  Linux swap / Solaris
/dev/sdc3       2150398 15738879  6794241    5  Extended
/dev/sdc5       2150400 15738879  6794240   83  Linux
```

The example just shown is for a USB drive that had a bootable Linux system installed on it. The first partition (/dev/sdc1) is a small /boot partition. The second (/dev/sdc2) is assigned as a swap area. The rest of the disk is assigned as an extended partition (/dev/sdc3), which allows any further partitions to take space from that partition. The final partition (/dev/sdc5) is assigned to the root filesystem (/) and consumes all the remaining disk space.

Your drive might be assigned to a different device name. Here are some things to look for:

- A SCSI or USB storage device, represented by an *sd?* device (such as sda, sdb, sdc, and so on), can have up to 16 minor devices (such as the main /dev/sdc device and /dev/sdc1 through /dev/sdc15). So there can be 15 partitions total.

- For x86 computers, disks can have up to four primary partitions. So, to have more than four total partitions, at least one must be an extended partition. Notice that /dev/sdc3 is an extended partition that consumes all remaining disk space not used by the first two partitions. Any partitions beyond the four primary partitions are logical partitions that use space from the extended partition.

- The id field indicates the type of partition. Notice that there is a mixture of Linux and swap partitions in both examples and Linux LVM partitions in the first example.

Your first primary hard disk usually appears as /dev/sda. With RHEL and Fedora installations, there is usually at least one LVM partition created by the installer, out of which other partitions can be assigned. So the output of fdisk might be as simple as the following:

```
# fdisk -cul /dev/sda
Disk /dev/sda: 500.1 GB, 500107862016 bytes
255 heads, 63 sectors/track, 60801 cylinders, total 976773168 sectors
Units = sectors of 1 * 512 = 512 bytes
Sector size (logical/physical): 512 bytes / 512 bytes
I/O size (minimum/optimal): 512 bytes / 512 bytes
Disk identifier: 0x000ebb20
   Device Boot     Start       End    Blocks   Id  System
/dev/sda1    *      2048    411647    204800   83  Linux
/dev/sda2         411648 976773119 488180736   8e  Linux LVM
```

The first partition is roughly 200MB and is mounted on the /boot directory. The asterisk (*) under the Boot column indicates that the partition is bootable (that's where the kernel and other components needed to boot the system are stored). The rest of the disk is consumed by the LVM partition, which is ultimately used to create logical volumes. You can find out more on LVM in the section "Using Logical Volume Management Partitions" later in this chapter.

For the moment, I recommend you leave the hard disk alone and find a USB flash drive that you do not mind erasing. You can try the commands I demonstrate on that drive.

Creating a single-partition disk

To add a new storage medium (hard disk, USB flash drive, or similar device) to your computer so that it can be used by Linux, you need to first connect the disk device to your computer and then partition the disk. Here's the general procedure:

1. Install the new hard drive or insert the new USB flash drive.
2. Partition the new disk.
3. Create the filesystems on the new disk.
4. Mount the filesystems.

The easiest way to add a disk or flash drive to Linux is to have the entire disk devoted to a single Linux partition. You can have multiple partitions, however, and assign them each to different types of filesystems and different mount points, if you like.

The following process takes you through partitioning a USB flash drive to be used for Linux that has only one partition. If you have a USB flash drive (any size) that you don't mind erasing, you can work through this procedure as you read. The section following this describes how to partition a disk with multiple partitions.

> **WARNING**
>
> If you make a mistake partitioning your disk with fdisk, just type q to exit without saving your changes. If you are stuck in the middle of an operation, such as adding a partition, just complete that operation, and then type q after you see the command prompt.

1. For a USB flash drive, just plug it into an available USB port. Going forward, I use an 8GB USB flash drive, but you can get a USB flash drive of any size.
2. Determine the device name for the USB drive. As root user from a shell, type the following tail command, and then insert the USB flash drive. Messages appear, indicating the device name of the drive you just plugged in (press Ctrl+C to exit the tail command when you are finished):

```
# tail -f /var/log/messages
kernel: usb 3-2: new high speed USB device number 69 using xhci_hcd
kernel: usb 3-2: New USB device found, idVendor=0930,
idProduct=6545
kernel: usb 3-2: New USB device strings:
     Mfr=1, Product=2, SerialNumber=3
kernel: usb 3-2: Product: USB Flash Memory
kernel: usb 3-2: Manufacturer:
kernel: usb 3-2: SerialNumber: 001D92AD6ADAB98043230329
kernel: usb 3-2: configuration #1 chosen from 1 choice
kernel: scsi8 : SCSI emulation for USB Mass Storage devices
kernel: sd 8:0:0:0: Attached scsi generic sg2 type 0
kernel: sd 8:0:0:0: [sdc] 15740928 512-byte
     logical blocks: (8.05 GB/7.50 GiB)
kernel: sd 8:0:0:0: [sdc] Write Protect is off
kernel: sd 8:0:0:0: [sdc] Assuming drive cache: write through
kernel: sd 8:0:0:0: [sdc] Assuming drive cache: write through
kernel: sdc: sdc1 sdc2 sdc3 < sdc5 >
```

3. From the output, you can see that the USB flash drive was found and assigned to /dev/sdc. (Your device name may be different!) It also contains multiple partitions: sdc1, sdc2, sdc3, and sdc5. Be sure you identify the correct disk, or you could lose all data from disks you may want to keep!

4. If the USB flash drive mounts automatically, unmount it. From a GNOME 2 desktop, right-click the 8.0GB Filesystem icon that appears and select Unmount. From a GNOME 3 desktop, move your mouse to select the bottom tray, click the removable storage icon, and click the eject button. Or, in this case, as root you could instead type **umount /dev/sdc1**.

5. Use the fdisk command to create partitions on the USB drive. For example, if you are formatting the third USB, SATA, or SCSI disk (sdc), you can type the following:

```
# fdisk /dev/sdc
Command (m for help):
```

Now you are in fdisk command mode, where you can use the fdisk single-letter command set to work with your partitions. (For RHEL 6, adding the -c and -u options enables you to select the size of each partition based on sectors instead of cylinders. Those options are not needed for RHEL 7.)

6. If you start with a new USB flash drive, it may have one partition that is entirely devoted to a Windows-compatible filesystem (such as VFAT). Use p to view all partitions and d to delete the partition. Here's what it looked like when I did that:

```
Command (m for help): p
...
   Device Boot      Start        End      Blocks   Id   System
/dev/sdc1            2048     15667199    7832576    c   W95 FAT32 (LBA)
Command (m for help): d
Selected partition 1
```

7. To create a new partition, type the letter **n**. You are prompted for the type of partition.

8. Choose an extended (e) or primary partition (p). Type the letter **p** to choose primary.

9. Type the partition number. If you are creating the first partition (or for only one partition), type the number **1**. You are prompted for the first sector to start the partition.

10. Select the first available sector number (you can just press Enter to choose it). You are prompted for the last sector.

11. Enter the size of the partition. Because you are just creating one partition to consume the whole disk, choose the last available sector. To do that you can just press Enter to accept the default.

12. Double-check that the drive is partitioned the way you want by pressing **p**. (Your output will differ, depending on the size of your drive.)

    ```
    Command (m for help): p
    . . .
       Device Boot      Start         End      Blocks   Id  System
    /dev/sdc1             2048    15667199     7832576   83  Linux
    ```

13. To make changes to the partition table permanent, type **w**. This writes the changes, tries to sync those changes with the Linux kernel, and quits `fdisk`. If you see a message like the following, don't worry; you can fix that in the next step:

    ```
    WARNING: Re-reading the partition table failed with error 16:
    Device or resource busy.
    ```

14. If `fdisk` cannot sync the partition table on the disk with the kernel, the most likely reason is that a partition from the disk is still mounted. Unmount the partition, and try running the following command to sync the disk partition table with the kernel:

    ```
    # partprobe /dev/sdc
    ```

    If `partprobe` does not work, rebooting the computer will make sure the disk and kernel are in sync.

15. Although the partitioning is done, the new partition is not yet ready to use. For that, you have to create a filesystem on the new partition. To create a filesystem on the new disk partition, use the `mkfs` command. By default, this command creates an `ext2` filesystem, which is usable by Linux. However, in most cases you want to use a journaling filesystem (such as `ext3` or `ext4`). To create an `ext4` filesystem on the first partition of the third hard disk, type the following:

    ```
    # mkfs -t ext4 /dev/sdc1
    ```

> **TIP**
>
> You can use other commands, or options to this command, to create other filesystem types. For example, use `mkfs.vfat` to create a VFAT filesystem, `mkfs.msdos` for DOS, or `mkfs.reiserfs` for the Reiser filesystem type. You may want a VFAT filesystem if you want to share files among Linux, Windows, and Mac systems.

16. To be able to use the new filesystem, you need to create a mount point and mount it to the partition. Here is an example of how to do that. You then check to make sure that the mount succeeded.

```
# mkdir /mnt/test
# mount /dev/sdc1 /mnt/test
# df -h /mnt/test
Filesystem           Size  Used Avail Use% Mounted on
/dev/sdc1            7.4G   17M  7.0G   1% /mnt/test
# mount | grep sdc1
/dev/sdc1 on /mnt/test type ext4 (rw)
```

The `df` command shows that `/dev/sdc1` is mounted on `/mnt/test` and that it offers about 7.4GB of disk space. The `mount` command shows all mounted filesystems, but here I used `grep` to show that `sdc1` is mounted and is an `ext4` filesystem type.

Any files or directories you create later in the `/mnt/test` directory and any of its subdirectories are stored on the `/dev/sdc1` device.

17. When you are finished using the drive, you can unmount it with the `umount` command, after which you can safely remove the drive (see the description of the `umount` command later if this command fails):

```
# umount /dev/sdc1
```

18. You don't usually set up a USB flash drive to mount automatically every time the system boots because it mounts automatically when you plug it in. But if you decide you want to do that, edit `/etc/fstab` and add a line describing what and where to mount. Here is an example of a line you might add:

```
/dev/sdc1    /mnt/test      ext4     defaults    0 1
```

In this example, the partition (`/dev/sdc1`) is mounted on the `/mnt/test` directory as an `ext4` filesystem. The `defaults` keyword causes the partition to be mounted at boot time. The number 0 tells the system not to back up files from this filesystem with the `dump` command (`dump` is rarely used any more, but the field is here). The 1 in the last column tells the system to check the partition for errors after a certain number of mounts.

At this point, you have a working, permanently mounted disk partition. The next section describes how to partition a disk that has multiple partitions.

Creating a multiple-partition disk

Now that you understand the basic process of partitioning a disk, adding a filesystem, and making that filesystem available (temporarily and permanently), it is time to try a more complex example. Taking that same 8GB USB flash drive, I ran the procedure described later in this section to create multiple partitions on one disk.

In this procedure, I create a partition of 500MB (sdc1 and sdc2), 300MB (sdc3), 350MB (sdc5), and 400MB (sdc6). The sdc4 device is an extended partition, which consumes all remaining disk space. Space from the sdc5 and sdc6 partitions is taken from the extended partition.

As before, insert the USB flash drive and determine the device name (in my case, /dev/sdc). Also, be sure to unmount any partitions that mount automatically when you insert the USB flash drive.

> **TIP**
>
> When you indicate the size of each partition, type the plus sign and the number of megabytes or gigabytes you want to assign to the partition. For example, +1024M to create a 1024 megabyte partition or +10G for a 10 gigabyte partition. Be sure to remember the plus sign (+) and the M or G! If you forget the M or G, fdisk thinks you mean sectors and you get unexpected results.

1. To start, open the /dev/sdc device with fdisk, delete the first (only) partition, and then add six new partitions.

```
# fdisk /dev/sdc
Command (m for help): d
Selected partition 1
Command (m for help): n
Command action
   e   extended
   p   primary partition (1-4)
p
Partition number (1-4): 1
First sector (2048-15667199, default 2048):
 <Enter>
Using default value 2048
Last sector,+sectors or +size{K,M,G}(...default 15667199):+500M
Command (m for help): n
Command action
   e   extended
   p   primary partition (1-4)
p
Partition number (1-4): 2
First sector (1026048-15667199, default 1026048):
 <Enter>
```

```
Using default value 1026048
Last sector, +sectorsor +size
{K,M,G}(default 15667199):+500M
Command (m for help): n
Command action
   e   extended
   p   primary partition (1-4)
p
Partition number (1-4): 3
First sector (2050048-15667199, default 2050048):
 <Enter>
Using default value 2050048
Last sector, +sectorsor +size {K,M,G} (...default 15667199):+300M
Command (m for help): n
Command action
   e   extended
   p   primary partition (1-4)
e
Selected partition 4
First sector (2664448-15667199, default 2664448):
<Enter>
Using default value 2664448
Last sector,+sectors or + size{K,M,G}(... default 15667199):
<Enter>
Using default value 15667199
Command (m for help): n
First sector (2666496-15667199, default 2666496):
<Enter>
Using default value 2666496
Last sector, +sectors or +size{K,M,G} (...default 15667199): +350M
Command (m for help): n
First sector (...default 3385344):
<Enter>
Using default value 3385344
Last sector, +sectors or +size {K,M,G} (...default 15667199): +400M
```

2. Check the partitioning before saving by typing **p**. Notice that there are five usable partitions (sdc1, sdc2, sdc3, sdc5, and sdc6) and that the sectors between the Start and End for sdc4 are being consumed by sdc5 and sdc6.

```
Command (m for help): p
...
    Device Boot      Start           End       Blocks   Id  System
/dev/sdc1             2048       1026047       512000   83  Linux
/dev/sdc2          1026048       2050047       512000   83  Linux
/dev/sdc3          2050048       2664447       307200   83  Linux
/dev/sdc4          2664448      15667199      6501376    5  Extended
/dev/sdc5          2666496       3383295       358400   83  Linux
/dev/sdc6          3385344       4204543       409600   83  Linux
```

3. The default partition type is Linux. I decided I want to use some of the partitions for swap space (type 82), FAT32 (type x), and Linux LVM (type 8e). To do that, I type **t** and indicate which partition type to use. Type **L** to see a list of partition types.

```
Command (m for help): t
Partition number (1-6): 2
Hex code (type L to list codes): 82
Changed system type of partition 2 to 82 (Linux swap / Solaris)
Command (m for help): t
Partition number (1-6): 5
Hex code (type L to list codes): c
Changed system type of partition 5 to c (W95 FAT32 (LBA))
Command (m for help): t
Partition number (1-6): 6
Hex code (type L to list codes): 8e
Changed system type of partition 6 to 8e (Linux LVM)
```

4. I check that the partition table is the way I want it and then write the changes:

```
Command (m for help): p
...
    Device Boot     Start       End      Blocks  Id  System
/dev/sdc1            2048    1026047     512000  83  Linux
/dev/sdc2         1026048    2050047     512000  82  Linux swap /
Solaris
/dev/sdc3         2050048    2664447     307200  83  Linux
/dev/sdc4         2664448   15667199    6501376   5  Extended
/dev/sdc5         2666496    3383295     358400   c  W95 FAT32 (LBA)
/dev/sdc6         3385344    4204543     409600  8e  Linux LVM
Command (m for help): w
The partition table has been altered!
Calling ioctl() to re-read partition table.
...
```

5. After the write is completed, check that the kernel knows about the changes to the partition table. To do that, search the /proc/partitions for sdc. If the new devices are not there, run the partprobe /dev/sdc command on the drive or reboot your computer.

```
# grep sdc /proc/partitions
   8    32    7833600 sdc
   8    33     512000 sdc1
   8    34     512000 sdc2
   8    35     307200 sdc3
   8    36          1 sdc4
   8    37     358400 sdc5
   8    38     409600 sdc6
```

6. While the partitions are now set for different types of content, other commands are needed to structure the partitions into filesystems or swap areas. Here's how to do that for the partitions just created:

- **sdc1**—To make this into a regular Linux `ext4` filesystem, type the following:

  ```
  # mkfs -t ext4 /dev/sdc1
  ```

- **sdc2**—To format this as a swap area, type the following:

  ```
  # mkswap /dev/sdc2
  ```

- **sdc3**—To make this into an `ext2` filesystem (the default) type the following:

  ```
  # mkfs /dev/sdc3
  ```

- **sdc5**—To make this into a VFAT filesystem (the default) type the following:

  ```
  # mkfs -t vfat /dev/sdc5
  ```

- **sdc6**—To make this into a LVM physical volume type the following:

  ```
  # pvcreate /dev/sdc6
  ```

These partitions are now ready to be mounted, used as a swap area, or added to an LVM volume group. See the next section, "Using Logical Volume Management Partitions," to see how LVM physical volumes are used to ultimately create LVM logical volumes from volume groups. See the section "Mounting Filesystems" for descriptions of how to mount filesystems and enable swap areas.

Using Logical Volume Management Partitions

Basic disk partitioning in Linux has its shortcomings. What happens if you run out of disk space? In the old days, a common solution was to copy data to a bigger disk, restart the system with the new disk, and hope that you didn't run out of space again any time soon. This process meant downtime and inefficiency.

Logical volume management (LVM) offers lots of flexibility and efficiency in dealing with constantly changing storage needs. With LVM, physical disk partitions are added to pools of space called *volume groups*. Logical volumes are assigned space from volume groups as needed. This gives you these abilities:

- Add more space to a logical volume from the volume group while the volume is still in use.

- Add more physical volumes to a volume group if the volume group begins to run out of space. The physical volumes can be from disks.

- Move data from one physical volume to another, so you can remove smaller disks and replace them with larger ones while the filesystems are still in use—again, without downtime.

With LVM it is also easier to shrink filesystems to reclaim disk space, although shrinking does require that you unmount the logical volume (but no reboot is needed). LVM also supports advanced features, such as mirroring and working in clusters.

Checking an existing LVM

Let's start by looking at an existing LVM example on a Red Hat Enterprise Linux system. The following command displays the partitions on my first hard disk:

```
# fdisk -l /dev/sda | grep /dev/sda
Disk /dev/sda: 160.0 GB, 160000000000 bytes
/dev/sda1    *       2048      1026047      512000   83   Linux
/dev/sda2    *    1026048    312498175   155736064   8e   Linux LVM
```

On this RHEL system, the 160GB hard drive is divided into one 500MB Linux partition (sda1) and a second (Linux LVM) partition that consumes the rest of the disk (sda2). Next, I use the pvdisplay command to see if that partition is being used in an LVM group:

```
# pvdisplay /dev/sda2
--- Physical volume ---
PV Name               /dev/sda2
VG Name               vg_abc
PV Size               148.52 GiB / not usable 2.00 MiB
Allocatable           yes (but full)
PE Size               4.00 MiB
Total PE              38021
Free PE               0
Allocated PE          38021
PV UUID               wlvuIv-UiI2-pNND-f39j-oH0X-9too-AOII7R
```

You can see that the LVM physical volume represented by /dev/sda2 has 148.52GiB of space, all of which has been totally allocated to a volume group named vg_abc. The smallest unit of storage that can be used from this physical volume is 4.0MiB, which is referred to as a Physical Extent (PE).

> **NOTE**
>
> Notice that LVM tools show disk space in MiB and GiB. One MB is 1,000,000 bytes (10^6), while a MiB is 1,048,576 bytes (2^{20}). A MiB is a more accurate way to reflect how data are stored on a computer. But marketing people tend to use MB because it makes the hard disks, CDs, and DVDs they sell look like they have more capacity than they do. Keep in mind that most tools in Linux display storage data in MiB and GiB, although some can display MB and GB as well.

Next, you want to see information about the volume group:

```
# vgdisplay vg_abc
--- Volume group ---
VG Name               vg_abc
System ID
```

```
Format                lvm2
Metadata Areas        1
Metadata Sequence No  4
VG Access             read/write
VG Status             resizable
MAX LV                0
Cur LV                3
Open LV               3
Max PV                0
Cur PV                1
Act PV                1
VG Size               148.52 GiB
PE Size               4.00 MiB
Total PE              38021
Alloc PE / Size       38021 / 148.52 GiB
Free  PE / Size       0 / 0
VG UUID               c2SGHM-KU9H-wbXM-sgca-EtBr-UXAq-UnnSTh
```

You can see that all of the 38,021 PEs have been allocated. Using lvdisplay as follows, you can see where they have been allocated (I have snipped some of the output):

```
# lvdisplay vg_abc
--- Logical volume ---
LV Name             /dev/vg_abc/lv_root
VG Name             vg_abc
LV UUID             33VeDc-jd01-hlCc-RMuB-tkcw-QvFi-cKCZqa
LV Write Access     read/write
LV Status           available
# open              1
LV Size             50.00 GiB
Current LE          12800
Segments            1
Allocation          inherit
Read ahead sectors  auto
- currently set to  256
Block device        253:0
--- Logical volume ---
LV Name             /dev/vg_abc/lv_home
VG Name             vg_abc
...
LV Size             92.64 GiB
--- Logical volume ---
LV Name             /dev/vg_abc/lv_swap
VG Name             vg_abc
...
LV Size             5.88 GiB
```

There are three logical volumes drawing space from vg_abc. Each logical volume is associated with a device name that includes the volume group name and the logical volume name: /dev/vg_abc/lv_root (50GB), /dev/vg_abc/lv_home (92.64GB), and

/dev/vg_abc/lv_swap (5.88GB). Other devices linked to these names are located in the /dev/mapper directory: vg_abc-lv_home, vg_abc-lv_root, and vg_abc-lv_swap. Either set of names can be used to refer to these logical volumes.

The root and home logical volumes are formatted as ext4 filesystems, whereas the swap logical volume is formatted as swap space. Let's look in the /etc/fstab file to see how these logical volumes are used:

```
# grep vg_ /etc/fstab
/dev/mapper/vg_abc-lv_root  /      ext4  defaults  1 1
/dev/mapper/vg_abc-lv_home  /home  ext4  defaults  1 2
/dev/mapper/vg_abc-lv_swap  swap   swap  defaults  0 0
```

Figure 12.1 illustrates how the different partitions, volume groups, and logical volumes relate to the complete Linux filesystem. The sda1 device is formatted as a filesystem and mounted on the /boot directory. The sda2 device provides space for the vg_abc volume group. Then logical volumes lv-home and lv-root are mounted on the /home and / directories, respectively.

FIGURE 12.1

LVM logical volumes can be mounted like regular partitions on a Linux filesystem.

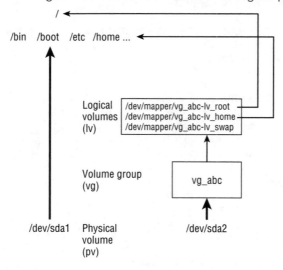

If you run out of space on any of the logical volumes, you can assign more space from the volume group. If the volume group is out of space, you can add another hard drive or network storage drive and add space from that drive to the volume group, so more is available.

Now that you know how LVM works, the next section shows you how to create LVM logical volumes from scratch.

Creating LVM logical volumes

LVM logical volumes are used from the top down, but they are created from the bottom up. As illustrated in Figure 12.1, first you create one or more physical volumes (pv), use the physical volumes to create volume groups (vg), and then create logical volumes from the volume groups (lv).

Commands for working with each LVM component begin with the letters pv, vg, and lv. For example, pvdisplay shows physical volumes, vgdisplay shows volume groups, and lvdisplay shows logical volumes.

The following procedure takes you through the steps of creating LVM volumes from scratch. To do this procedure, you could use the USB flash drive and partitions I described earlier in this chapter. Use these steps:

1. Obtain a disk with some spare space on it and create a disk partition on it of the LVM type (8e). Then use the pvcreate command to identify this partition as an LVM physical volume. The process of doing this is described in the section "Creating a multiple-partition disk" using the /dev/sdc6 device in that example.

2. To add that physical volume to a new volume group, use the vgcreate command. The following command shows you how to create a volume group called myvg0 using the /dev/sdc6 device:

   ```
   # vgcreate myvg0 /dev/sdc6
     Volume group "myvg0" successfully created
   ```

3. To see the new volume group, type the following:

   ```
   # vgdisplay myvg0
     --- Volume group ---
     VG Name                myvg0
     ...
     VG Size                396.00 MiB
     PE Size                4.00 MiB
     Total PE               99
     Alloc PE / Size        0 / 0
     Free  PE / Size        99 / 396.00 MiB
   ```

4. Of the 400MiB partition, 396MiB of space can be used in blocks of 4MiB. Here's how to create a logical volume from some of the space in that volume group and then check that the device for that logical volume exists:

   ```
   # lvcreate -n music -L 100M myvg0
     Logical volume "music" created
   # ls /dev/mapper/myvg0*
   /dev/mapper/myvg0-music
   ```

5. The procedure created a device named `/dev/mapper/myvg0-music`. That device can now be used to put a filesystem on and mount, just as you did with regular partitions in the first part of this chapter. For example:

```
# mkfs -t ext4 /dev/mapper/myvg0-music
# mkdir /mnt/mymusic
# mount /dev/mapper/myvg0-music /mnt/mymusic
# df -h /mnt/mymusic
Filesystem                Size  Used  Avail Use%  Mounted on
/dev/mapper/myvg0-music   97M   5.6M  87M   7%    /mnt/mymusic
```

6. As with regular partitions, logical volumes can be mounted permanently by adding an entry to the `/etc/fstab` file, such as:

```
/dev/mapper/myvg0-music /mnt/mymusic  ext4 defaults 1 2
```

The next time you reboot, the logical volume is automatically mounted on `/mnt/mymusic`. (Be sure to unmount the logical volume and remove this line if you want to remove the USB flash drive from your computer.)

Growing LVM logical volumes

If you run out of space on a logical volume, you can add space to it without even unmounting it. To do that, you must have space available in the volume group, grow the logical volume, and grow the filesystem to fill it. Building on the procedure in the previous section, here's how to grow a logical volume:

1. Note how much space is currently on the logical volume, and then check that space is available in the logical volume's volume group:

```
# vgdisplay myvg0
...
  VG Size               396.00 MiB
  PE Size               4.00 MiB
  Total PE              99
  Alloc PE / Size       25 / 100.00 MiB
  Free  PE / Size       74 / 296.00 MiB
# df -h /mnt/mymusic/
Filesystem                Size  Used  Avail Use% Mounted on
/dev/mapper/myvg0-music   97M   5.6M  87M   7%   /mnt/mymusic
```

2. Expand the logical volume using the `lvextend` command:

```
# lvextend -L +100M /dev/mapper/myvg0-music
  Extending logical volume music to 200.00 MiB
  Logical volume music successfully resized
```

3. Resize the filesystem to fit the new logical volume size:

```
# resize2fs -p /dev/mapper/myvg0-music
```

4. Check to see that the filesystem is now resized to include the additional disk space.

```
# df -h /mnt/mymusic/
Filesystem                 Size  Used Avail Use% Mounted on
/dev/mapper/myvg0-music    194M  5.6M  179M   3% /mnt/mymusic
```

You can see that the filesystem is now about 100MB larger.

Mounting Filesystems

Now that you have had a chance to play with disk partitioning and filesystems, I'm going to step back and talk about how filesystems are set up to connect permanently to your Linux system.

Most of the hard disk partitions created when you install Linux are mounted automatically for you when the system boots. When you install Fedora, Ubuntu, Red Hat Enterprise Linux, and other Linux systems, you have the option to let the installer automatically configure your hard disk or create partitions yourself and indicate the mount points for those partitions.

When you boot Linux, usually all the Linux partitions on your hard disk are listed in your /etc/fstab file and are mounted. For that reason, this section describes what you might expect to find in that file. It also describes how you can mount other partitions so that they become part of your Linux filesystem.

The mount command is used not only to mount local storage devices, but also to mount other kinds of filesystems on your Linux system. For example, mount can be used to mount directories (folders) over the network from NFS or Samba servers. It can be used to mount filesystems from a new hard drive or USB flash drive that is not configured to automount. It can also mount filesystem image files using loop devices.

> **NOTE**
> With the addition of automatic mounting features and changes in how removable media are identified with the Linux 2.6 kernel (using features such as Udev and Hardware Abstraction Layer), you no longer need to manually mount removable media for many Linux desktop systems. Understanding how to manually mount and unmount filesystems on a Linux server, however, can be a very useful skill if you want to mount remote filesystems or temporarily mount partitions in particular locations.

Supported filesystems

To see filesystem types that are loaded in your kernel, type cat /proc/filesystems. The list that follows shows a sample of filesystem types that are currently supported in Linux, although they may not be in use at the moment or even available on the Linux distribution you are using.

- **befs**—Filesystem used by the BeOS operating system.

- **btrfs**—A copy-on-write filesystem that implements advanced filesystem features. It offers fault tolerance and easy administration. The btrfs file system has recently grown in popularity for enterprise applications.

- **cifs**—Common Internet Filesystem (CIFS), the virtual filesystem used to access servers that comply with the SNIA CIFS specification. CIFS is an attempt to refine and standardize the SMB protocol used by Samba and Windows file sharing.

- **ext4**—Successor to the popular ext3 filesystem. It includes many improvements over ext3, such as support for volumes up to 1 exbibyte and file sizes up to 16 tebibytes. (This replaced ext3 as the default filesystem used in Fedora and RHEL. It has since been supplanted by xfs as the default for RHEL.)

- **ext3**—Ext filesystems are the most common in most Linux systems. The ext3 filesystem, also called the third extended filesystem, includes journaling features that, compared to ext2, improve a filesystem's capability to recover from crashes.

- **ext2**—The default filesystem type for earlier Linux systems. Features are the same as ext3, except that ext2 doesn't include journaling features.

- **ext**—This is the first version of ext3. It is not used very often anymore.

- **iso9660**—Evolved from the High Sierra filesystem (the original standard for CD-ROMs). Extensions to the High Sierra standard (called Rock Ridge extensions) allow iso9660 filesystems to support long filenames and UNIX-style information (such as file permissions, ownership, and links). Data CD-ROMs typically use this filesystem type.

- **kafs**—AFS client filesystem. Used in distributed computing environments to share files with Linux, Windows, and Macintosh clients.

- **minix**—Minix filesystem type, used originally with the Minix version of UNIX. It supports filenames of up to only 30 characters.

- **msdos**—An MS-DOS filesystem. You can use this type to mount floppy disks that come from Microsoft operating systems.

- **vfat**—Microsoft extended FAT (VFAT) filesystem.

- **umsdos**—An MS-DOS filesystem with extensions to allow features that are similar to UNIX (including long filenames).

- **proc**—Not a real filesystem, but rather a filesystem interface to the Linux kernel. You probably won't do anything special to set up a proc filesystem. However, the `/proc` mount point should be a proc filesystem. Many utilities rely on `/proc` to gain access to Linux kernel information.

- **reiserfs**—ReiserFS journaled filesystem. ReiserFS was once a common default filesystem type for several Linux distributions. However, ext and xfs filesystems are by far more common filesystem types used with Linux today.

- **swap**—Used for swap partitions. Swap areas are used to hold data temporarily when RAM is used up. Data is swapped to the swap area and then returned to RAM when it is needed again.

- **squashfs**—Compressed, read-only filesystem type. Squashfs is popular on live CDs, where there is limited space and a read-only medium (such as a CD or DVD).

- **nfs**—Network Filesystem (NFS) type of filesystem. NFS is used to mount filesystems on other Linux or UNIX computers.

- **hpfs**—Filesystem is used to do read-only mounts of an OS/2 HPFS filesystem.

- **ncpfs**—A filesystem used with Novell NetWare. NetWare filesystems can be mounted over a network.

- **ntfs**—Windows NT filesystem. Depending upon the distribution you have, it may be supported as a read-only filesystem (so that you can mount and copy files from it).

- **affs**—Filesystem used with Amiga computers.

- **ufs**—Filesystem popular on Sun Microsystems' operating systems (that is, Solaris and SunOS).

- **jfs**—A 64-bit journaling filesystem by IBM that is relatively lightweight for the many features it has.

- **xfs**—A high performance filesystem originally developed by Silicon Graphics that works extremely well with large files. This filesystem is the default type for RHEL 7.

- **gfs2**—A shared disk filesystem that allows multiple machines to all use the same shared disk without going through a network filesystem layer such as CIFS, NFS, and so on.

To see the list of filesystems that come with the kernel you are currently using, type `ls /lib/modules/`*kernelversion*`/kernel/fs/`. The actual modules are stored in subdirectories of that directory. Mounting a filesystem of a supported type causes the filesystem module to be loaded, if it is not already loaded.

Type `man fs` to see descriptions of Linux filesystems.

Enabling swap areas

A swap area is an area of the disk that is made available to Linux if the system runs out of memory (RAM). If your RAM is full and you try to start another application without a swap area, that application will fail.

With a swap area, Linux can temporarily swap out data from RAM to the swap area and then get it back when needed. You take a performance hit, but it is better than having processes fail.

To create a swap area from a partition or a file, use the `mkswap` command. To temporarily enable that swap area, you can use the `swapon` command. For example, here's how to check your available swap space, create a swap file, enable the swap file, and then check that the space is available on your system:

```
# free -m
          total     used     free    shared  buffers   cached
Mem:       1955      663     1291         0       42      283
-/+ buffers/cache:             337      1617
Swap:       819        0      819
# dd if=/dev/zero of=/var/tmp/myswap bs=1M count=1024
# mkswap /var/opt/myswap
# swapon /var/opt/myswap
# free -m
          total     used     free    shared  buffers     cached
Mem:       1955     1720      235         0       42       1310
-/+ buffers/cache:             367      1588
Swap:      1843        0     1843
```

The free command shows the amount of swap before and after creating, making, and enabling the swap area with the swapon command. That amount of swap is available immediately and temporarily to your system. To make that swap area permanent, you need to add it to your /etc/fstab file. Here is an example:

```
/var/opt/myswap   swap    swap    defaults   0 0
```

This entry indicates that the swap file named /var/opt/myswap should be enabled at boot time. Because there is no mount point for a swap area, the second field is just set to swap, as is the partition type. To test that the swap file works before rebooting, you can enable it immediately (swapon -a) and check that the additional swap area appears:

```
# swapon -a
```

Disabling a swap area

If at any point you want to disable a swap area, you can do so using the swapoff command. You might do this, in particular, if the swap area is no longer needed and you want to reclaim the space being consumed by a swap file or remove a USB drive that is providing a swap partition.

First, make sure that no space is being used on the swap device (using the free command), and then use swapoff to turn off the swap area so you can reuse the space. Here is an example:

```
# free -m
          total     used     free    shared  buffers     cached
Mem:       1955     1720      235         0       42       1310
-/+ buffers/cache: 367       1588
Swap:      1843        0     1843
# swapoff /var/opt/myswap
```

```
# free -m
Mem:         1955    1720       235        0        42       1310
-/+ buffers/cache:  367      1588
Swap:         819       0       819
```

Using the fstab file to define mountable file systems

The hard disk partitions on your local computer and the remote filesystems you use every day are probably set up to automatically mount when you boot Linux. The /etc/fstab file contains definitions for each partition, along with options describing how the partition is mounted. Here's an example of an /etc/fstab file:

```
# /etc/fstab
/dev/mapper/vg_abc-lv_root      /           ext4     defaults     1 1
UUID=78bdae46-9389-438d-bfee-06dd934fae28 /boot ext4   defaults  1 2
/dev/mapper/vg_abc-lv_home      /home       ext4     defaults     1 2
/dev/mapper/vg_abc-lv_swap      swap        swap     defaults     0 0
# Mount entries added later
/dev/sdb1                       /win        vfat     ro           1 2
192.168.0.27:/nfsstuff          /remote     nfs      users,_netdev 0 0
//192.168.0.28/myshare          /share      cifs     guest,_netdev 0 0
# special Linux filesystems
tmpfs                           /dev/shm    tmpfs    defaults     0 0
devpts                          /dev/pts    devpts   gid=5,mode=620 0 0
sysfs                           /sys        sysfs    defaults     0 0
proc                            /proc       proc     defaults     0 0
```

The /etc/fstab file just shown is from a default Red Hat Enterprise Linux 6 server install, with a few lines added.

For now, you can ignore the tmpfs, devpts, sysfs, and proc entries. Those are special devices associated with shared memory, terminal windows, device information, and kernel parameters, respectively.

In general, the first column of /etc/fstab shows the device or share (what is mounted), while the second column shows the mount point (where it is mounted). That is followed by the type of filesystem, any mount options (or defaults), and two numbers (used to tell commands such as dump and fsck what to do with the filesystem).

The first three entries represent the disk partitions assigned to the root of the filesystem (/), the /boot directory, and the /home directory. All three are ext4 filesystems. The fourth line is a swap device (used to store data when RAM overflows). Notice that the device names for /, /home, and swap all start with /dev/mapper. That's because they are LVM logical volumes that are assigned space from a pool of space called an LVM volume group (more on LVM in the section "Using Logical Volume Management Partitions" later in this chapter).

The /boot partition is on its own physical partition, /dev/sda1. Instead of /dev/sda1, however, a unique identifier (UUID) identifies the device. Why use a UUID instead of

/dev/sda1 to identify the device? Suppose you plugged another disk into your computer and booted up. It probably won't happen, but it is possible that the new disk might be identified as /dev/sda, causing the system to look for the contents of /boot on the first partition of that disk.

To see all the UUIDs assigned to storage devices on your system, type the blkid command, as follows:

```
# blkid
/dev/sda1:
   UUID="78bdae46-9389-438d-bfee-06dd934fae28" TYPE="ext4"
/dev/sda2:
   UUID="wlvuIv-UiI2-pNND-f39j-oH0X-9too-AOII7R" TYPE="LVM2_member"
/dev/mapper/vg_abc-lv_root:
   UUID="3e6f49a6-8fec-45e1-90a9-38431284b689" TYPE="ext4"
/dev/mapper/vg_abc-lv_swap:
   UUID="77662950-2cc2-4bd9-a860-34669535619d" TYPE="swap"
/dev/mapper/vg_abc-lv_home:
   UUID="7ffbcff3-36b9-4cbb-871d-091efb179790" TYPE="ext4"
/dev/sdb1:
   SEC_TYPE="msdos" UUID="75E0-96AA" TYPE="vfat"
```

Any of the device names can be replaced by the UUID designation in the left column of an /etc/fstab entry.

I added the next three entries in /etc/fstab to illustrate some different kinds of entries. I connected a hard drive from an old Microsoft Windows system, and I had it mounted on the /win directory. I added the ro option so it would mount read-only.

The next two entries represent remote filesystems. On the /remote directory, the /nfsstuff directory is mounted read/write (rw) from the host at address 192.168.0.27 as an NFS share. On the /share directory, the Windows share named myshare is mounted from the host at 192.168.0.28. In both cases, I added the _netdev option, which tells Linux to wait for the network to come up before trying to mount the shares. (For more information on mounting CIFS and NFS shares, refer to Chapters 19, "Configuring a Windows File Sharing (Samba) Server," and 20, "Configuring an NFS File Server," respectively.)

Coming from Windows

The section "Using the fstab file to define mountable file systems" shows mounting a hard disk partition from an old VFAT filesystem being used in Windows. Most Windows systems today use the NTFS filesystem. Support for this system, however, is not delivered with every Linux system. NTFS is available from Fedora in the ntfs-3g package.

To help you understand the contents of the `/etc/fstab` file, here is what is in each field of that file:

- **Field 1**—The name of the device representing the filesystem. This field can include the LABEL or UUID option, with which you can indicate a volume label or universally unique identifier (UUID) instead of a device name. The advantage to this approach is that because the partition is identified by volume name, you can move a volume to a different device name and not have to change the `fstab` file. (See the description of the `mkfs` command in the section "Using the mkfs Command to Create a Filesystem" for information on creating and using labels.)

- **Field 2**—The mount point in the filesystem. The filesystem contains all data from the mount point down the directory tree structure unless another filesystem is mounted at some point beneath it.

- **Field 3**—The filesystem type. Valid filesystem types are described in the section "Supported filesystems" earlier in this chapter (although you can only use filesystem types for which drivers are included for your kernel).

- **Field 4**—Use `defaults` or a comma-separated list of options (no spaces) you want to use when the entry is mounted. See the `mount` command manual page (under the `-o` option) for information on other supported options.

> **TIP**
>
> Typically, only the root user is allowed to mount a filesystem using the `mount` command. However, to allow any user to mount a filesystem (such as a filesystem on a CD), you could add the `user` option to Field 4 of `/etc/fstab`.

- **Field 5**—The number in this field indicates whether the filesystem needs to be dumped (that is, have its data backed up). A 1 means that the filesystem needs to be dumped, and a 0 means that it doesn't. (This field is no longer particularly useful because most Linux administrators use more sophisticated backup options than the `dump` command. Most often, a 0 is used.)

- **Field 6**—The number in this field indicates whether the indicated filesystem should be checked with `fsck` when the time comes for it to be checked: 1 means it needs to be checked first, 2 means to check after all those indicated by 1 have already been checked, and 0 means don't check it.

If you want to find out more about mount options as well as other features of the `/etc/fstab` file, there are several man pages you can refer to, including `man 5 nfs` and `man 8 mount`.

Using the mount command to mount file systems

Linux systems automatically run `mount -a` (mount all filesystems from the `/etc/fstab` file) each time you boot. For that reason, you generally use the `mount` command only for special situations. In particular, the average user or administrator uses mount in two ways:

- To display the disks, partitions, and remote filesystems currently mounted
- To temporarily mount a filesystem

Any user can type mount (with no options) to see what filesystems are currently mounted on the local Linux system. The following is an example of the mount command. It shows a single hard disk partition (/dev/sda1) containing the root (/) filesystem, and proc and devpts filesystem types mounted on /proc and /dev, respectively.

```
$ mount
/dev/sda3 on / type ext4 (rw)
/dev/sda2 on /boot type ext4 (rw)
/dev/sda1 on /mnt/win type vfat (rw)
/dev/proc on /proc type proc (rw)
/dev/sys on /sys type sysfs (rw)
/dev/devpts on /dev/pts type devpts (rw,gid=5,mode=620)
/dev/shm on /dev/shm type tmpfs (rw)
none on /proc/sys/fs/binfmt_misc type binfmt_misc (rw)
/dev/cdrom on /media/MyOwnDVD type iso9660 (ro,nosuid,nodev)
```

Traditionally, the most common devices to mount by hand are removable media, such as DVDs or CDs. However, depending on the type of desktop you are using, CDs and DVDs may be mounted for you automatically when you insert them. (In some cases, applications are launched as well when media is inserted. For example, a CD music player or photo editor may be launched when your inserted medium has music or digital images on it.)

Occasionally, however, you may find it useful to mount a filesystem manually. For example, you want to look at the contents of an old hard disk, so you install it as a second disk on your computer. If the partitions on the disk did not automount, you could mount partitions from that disk manually. For example, to mount read-only a disk partition sdb1 that has an older ext3 filesystem, you could type this:

```
# mkdir /mnt/temp
# mount -t ext3 -o ro /dev/sdb1 /mnt/tmp
```

Another reason to use the mount command is to remount a partition to change its mount options. Suppose you want to remount /dev/sdb1 as read/write, but you do not want to unmount it (maybe someone is using it). You could use the remount option as follows:

```
# mount -t ext3 -o remount,rw /dev/sdb1
```

Mounting a disk image in loopback

Another valuable way to use the mount command has to do with disk images. If you download a CD or floppy disk image from the Internet and you want to see what it contains, you can do so without burning it to CD or floppy. With the image on your hard disk, create a mount point and use the `-o loop` option to mount it locally. Here's an example:

```
# mkdir /mnt/mycdimage
# mount -o loop whatever-i686-disc1.iso /mnt/mycdimage
```

In this example, the `/mnt/mycdimage` directory is created, and then the disk image file (`whatever-i686-disc1.iso`) residing in the current directory is mounted on it. You can now `cd` to that directory, view the contents of it, and copy or use any of its contents. This is useful for downloaded CD images from which you want to install software without having to burn the image to CD. You could also share that mount point over NFS, so you could install the software from another computer. When you are finished, just type `umount /mnt/mycdimage` to unmount it.

Other options to `mount` are available only for specific filesystem types. See the `mount` manual page for those and other useful options.

Using the umount command

When you are finished using a temporary filesystem, or you want to unmount a permanent filesystem temporarily, use the `umount` command. This command detaches the filesystem from its mount point in your Linux filesystem. To use `umount`, you can give it either a directory name or a device name. For example:

```
# umount /mnt/test
```

This unmounts the device from the mount point `/mnt/test`. You can also unmount using this form:

```
# umount /dev/sdb1
```

In general, it's better to use the directory name (`/mnt/test`) because the `umount` command will fail if the device is mounted in more than one location. (Device names all begin with `/dev`.)

If you get the message `device is busy`, the `umount` request has failed because either an application has a file open on the device or you have a shell open with a directory on the device as a current directory. Stop the processes or change to a directory outside the device you are trying to unmount for the `umount` request to succeed.

An alternative for unmounting a busy device is the `-l` option. With `umount -l` (a lazy unmount), the unmount happens as soon as the device is no longer busy. To unmount a remote NFS filesystem that's no longer available (for example, the server went down), you can use the `umount -f` option to forcibly unmount the NFS filesystem.

> **TIP**
>
> A useful tool for discovering what's holding open a device you want to unmount is the `lsof` command. Type `lsof` with the name of the partition you want to unmount (such as `lsof /mnt/test`). The output shows you what commands are holding files open on that partition. The `fuser -v /mnt/test` command can be used in the same way.

Using the mkfs Command to Create a Filesystem

You can create a filesystem for any supported filesystem type on a disk or partition that you choose. You do so with the `mkfs` command. Although this is most useful for creating filesystems on hard-disk partitions, you can create filesystems on USB flash drives, floppy disks, or rewritable CDs as well.

Before you create a new filesystem, make sure of the following:

- You have partitioned the disk as you want (using the `fdisk` command).
- You get the device name correct, or you may end up overwriting your hard disk by mistake. For example, the first partition on the second SCSI or USB flash drive on your system is `/dev/sdb1` and the third disk is `/dev/sdc1`.
- To unmount the partition if it's mounted before creating the filesystem.

The following are two examples of using `mkfs` to create a filesystems on two partitions on a USB flash drive located as the first and second partitions on the third SCSI disk (`/dev/sdc1` and `/dev/sdc2`). The first creates an xfs partition, while the second creates an ext4 partition.

```
# mkfs -t ext4 /dev/sdc1
meta-data=/dev/sda3        isize=256     agcount=4, agsize=256825 blks
         =                 sectsz=512    attr=2, projid32bit=1
         =                 crc=0
data     =                 bsize=4096    blocks=1027300, imaxpct=25
         =                 sunit=0       swidth=0 blks
naming   =version 2        bsize=4096    ascii-ci=0 ftype=0
log      =internal log     bsize=4096    blocks=2560, version=2
         =                 sectsz=512    sunit=0 blks, lazy-count=1
realtime =none             extsz=4096    blocks=0, rtextents=0
# mkfs -t ext4 /dev/sdc2
mke2fs 1.42.9 (28-Dec-2013)
Filesystem label=
OS type: Linux
Block size=4096 (log=2)
Fragment size=4096 (log=2)
Stride=0 blocks, Stripe width=0 blocks
```

```
257024 inodes, 1027300 blocks
51365 blocks (5.00%) reserved for the super user
First data block=0
Maximum filesystem blocks=1052770304
32 block groups
32768 blocks per group, 32768 fragments per group
8032 inodes per group
Superblock backups stored on blocks:
        32768, 98304, 163840, 229376, 294912, 819200, 884736
Allocating group tables: done
Writing inode tables: done
Creating journal (16384 blocks): done
Writing superblocks and filesystem accounting information: done
```

You can see the statistics that are output with the formatting done by the mkfs command. The number of inodes and blocks created are output, as are the number of blocks per group and fragments per group. An inode, which holds metadata such as ownership and timestamps for each file, is consumed for every file and directory in the filesystem. So the number of inodes shown here limits the total number of files you can create in that filesystem.

Now mount this filesystem (mkdir /mnt/myusb ; mount /dev/sdc1 /mnt/myusb), change to /mnt/myusb as your current directory (cd /mnt/myusb), and create files on it as you please.

Summary

Managing filesystems is a critical part of administering a Linux system. Using commands such as fdisk, you can view and change disk partitions. Filesystems can be added to partitions using the mkfs command. Once created, filesystems can be mounted and unmounted using the mount and umount commands, respectively.

Logical Volume Management (LVM) offers a more powerful and flexible way of managing disk partitions. With LVM, you create pools of storage, called volumes, that can allow you to grow and shrink logical volumes, as well as extend the size of your volume groups by adding more physical volumes.

With most of the basics needed to become a system administrator covered at this point in the book, Chapter 13 introduces concepts for extending those skills to manage network servers. Topics in that chapter include information on how to install, manage, and secure servers.

Exercises

Use these exercises to test your knowledge of creating disk partitions, logical volume management, and working with filesystems. You need a USB flash drive that is at least 1GB that you can erase for these exercises.

These tasks assume you are running a Fedora or Red Hat Enterprise Linux system (although some tasks work on other Linux systems as well). If you are stuck, solutions to the tasks are shown in Appendix B (although in Linux, there are often multiple ways to complete a task).

1. Run a command as root to watch the /var/log/messages file and insert your USB flash drive. Determine the device name of the USB flash drive.

2. Run a command to list the partition table for the USB flash drive.

3. Delete all the partitions on your USB flash drive, save the changes, and make sure the changes were made both on the disk's partition table and in the Linux kernel.

4. Add three partitions to the USB flash drive: 100MB Linux partition, 200MB swap partition, and 500MB LVM partition. Save the changes.

5. Put an ext3 filesystem on the Linux partition.

6. Create a mount point called /mnt/mypart, and mount the Linux partition on it.

7. Enable the swap partition, and turn it on so additional swap space is immediately available.

8. Create a volume group called abc from the LVM partition, create a 200MB logical volume from that group called data, add a VFAT partition, and then temporarily mount the logical volume on a new directory named /mnt/test. Check that it was successfully mounted.

9. Grow the logical volume from 200MB to 300MB.

10. Do what you need to do to safely remove the USB flash drive from the computer: unmount the Linux partition, turn off the swap partition, unmount the logical volume, and delete the volume group from the USB flash drive.

Part IV

Becoming a Linux Server Administrator

Understanding Server Administration

Although some system administration tasks are needed even on a desktop system (installing software, setting up printers, and so on), many new tasks appear when you set up a Linux system to act as a server. That's especially true if the server you configure is made public to anyone on the Internet, where you can be overloaded with requests from good guys, while needing to be constantly on guard against attacks from bad guys.

Dozens of different kinds of servers are available for Linux systems. Most servers serve up data to remote clients, but others serve the local system (such as those that gather logging messages or kick off maintenance tasks at set times using the `cron` facility). Many servers are represented by processes that run continuously in the background and respond to requests that come to them. These processes are referred to as *daemon* processes.

As the name implies, servers exist to serve. The data they serve can include web pages, files, database information, e-mail, and lots of other types of content. As a server administrator, some of the additional challenges to your system administration skills include the following:

- **Remote access**—To use a desktop system, you typically sit at its console. Server systems, by contrast, tend to be housed in racks in climate-controlled environments under lock and key. More often than not, after the physical computers are in place, most administration of those machines is done using remote access tools. Often, no graphical interface is available, so you must rely on command-line tools to do such things as remote login, remote copying, and remote execution. The most common of these tools are built on the Secure Shell (SSH) facility.

- **Diligent security**—To be useful, a server must be able to accept requests for content from remote users and systems. Unlike desktop systems, which can simply close down all network ports that allow incoming requests for access, a server must make itself vulnerable by allowing some access to its ports. That's why it is important as a server administrator to open ports to services that are needed and lock down ports that are not needed. You can secure services using tools such as `iptables` and `firewalld` (firewall tools), TCP wrappers (to allow and deny service access), and Security Enhanced Linux (to limit the resources a service can access from the local system).

- **Continuous monitoring**—Although you typically turn off your laptop or desktop system when you are not using it, servers usually stay on 24x7, 365 days per year. Because you don't want to sit next to each server and continuously monitor it personally, you can configure tools to monitor each server, gather log messages, and even forward suspicious messages to an e-mail account of your choice. You can enable system activity reporters to gather data around the clock on CPU usage, memory usage, network activity, and disk access.

In this chapter, I lay out some of the basic tools and techniques you need to know to administer remote Linux servers. You learn to use SSH tools to access your server securely, transfer data back and forth, and even launch remote desktops or graphical applications and have them appear on your local system. You learn to use remote logging and system activity reports to continuously monitor system activities.

Starting with Server Administration

Whether you are installing a file server, web server, or any of the other server facilities available with Linux systems, many of the steps required for getting the server up and running are the same. Where server setup diverges is in the areas of configuration and tuning.

In later chapters, I describe specific servers and how they differ. In each of the server-related chapters that follow this chapter, you'll go through the same basic steps for getting that server started and available to be used by your clients.

Step 1: Install the server

Although most server software is not preinstalled on the typical Linux system, any general-purpose Linux system offers the software packages needed to supply every major type of server available.

Sometimes, multiple software packages associated with a particular type of server are gathered together in Package Groups (sometimes called Package Collections). Other times, you just need to install the server packages you want individually. Here are some server package categories in Fedora and some of the packages available in each category:

- **System Logging Server**—The `rsyslog` service allows the local system to gather log messages delivered from a variety of components on the system. It can also act as a remote logging server, gathering logging messages sent from other logging servers. (The `rsyslog` service is described later in this chapter.) In recent Ubuntu, Fedora, and RHEL systems, log messages are gathered in the `systemd` journal, which can be picked up and redirected by the `rsyslog` service or displayed locally by the `journalctl` command.

- **Print Server**—The Common UNIX Printing Service (`cups` package) is used most often to provide print server features on Linux systems. Packages that provide graphical administration of CUPS (`system-config-printer`) and printer drivers (`foomatic`, `hpijs`, and others) are also available when you install CUPS. (See Chapter 16, "Configuring a Print Server.")

- **Web Server**—The Apache (`httpd` package) web server is the software used most often to serve web pages (HTTP content). Related packages include modules to help serve particular types of content (Perl, Python, PHP, and SSL connections). Likewise, there are packages of related documentation (`httpd-manual`), tools for monitoring web data (`webalizer`), and tools for providing web proxy services (`squid`). (See Chapter 17, "Configuring a Web Server.")

- **FTP Server**—The Very Secure FTP daemon (`vsftpd` package) is the default FTP server used in Fedora and RHEL. Other FTP server packages include `proftpd` and `pure-ftpd`. (See Chapter 18, "Configuring an FTP Server.")

- **Windows File Server**—Samba (`samba` package) allows a Linux system to act as a Windows file and print server. (See Chapter 19, "Configuring a Windows File Sharing (Samba) Server.")

- **NFS**—Network File System (NFS) is the standard Linux and UNIX feature for providing shared directories to other systems over a network. The `nfs-utils` package provides NFS services and related commands. (See Chapter 20, "Configuring an NFS File Server.")

- **Mail Server**—These types of packages enable you to configure e-mail servers, sometimes referred to as a Mail Transport Agent (MTA) server. You have several choices of e-mail servers, including `sendmail` (default in Fedora), `postfix` (default in RHEL), and `exim`. Related packages, such as `dovecot`, allow the mail server to deliver e-mail to clients.

- **Directory Server**—Packages in this category provide remote and local authentication services. These include Kerberos (`krb5-server`), LDAP (`openldap-servers`), and NIS (`ypserv`).

- **DNS Server**—The Berkeley Internet Name Domain service (`bind`) provides the software needed to configure a server to resolve host names into IP addresses.

- **Network Time Protocol Server**—The `ntpd` package provides a service you can enable to sync up your system clock with clocks from public or private NTP servers.

13

■ **SQL Server**—The PostgreSQL (`postgresql` and `postgresql-server` packages) service is an object-relational database management system. Related packages provide PostgreSQL documentation and related tools. The MySQL (`mysql` and `mysql-server` packages) service is another popular open source SQL database server. Recently, a new community-developed branch of MySQL called MariaDB has supplanted MySQL on many Linux distributions.

Step 2: Configure the server

Most server software packages are installed with a default configuration that leans more toward security than immediate full use. Here are some things to think about when you set out to configure a server.

Using configuration files

Most Linux servers are configured using plain text files in the `/etc` directory (or subdirectories). Often, there is a primary configuration file; sometimes, there is a related configuration directory in which files ending in `.conf` can be pulled into the main configuration file.

The `httpd` package (Apache web server) is an example of a server package that has a primary configuration file and a directory where other configuration files can be dropped in and be included with the service. The main configuration file in Fedora and RHEL is `/etc/httpd/conf/httpd.conf`. The configuration directory is `/etc/httpd/conf.d/`.

After installing `httpd`, you will see files in the `/etc/httpd/conf.d/` directory that were placed there by different packages: `mod_ssl`, `mod_perl`, and so on. This is a way that add-on packages to a service can have their configuration information enabled in the `httpd` server, without the package trying to run a script to edit the main `httpd.conf` file.

The one downside to plain-text configuration files is that you don't get the kind of immediate error checking you get when you use graphical administration tools. You either have to run a test command (if the service includes one) or actually try to start the service to see if there is any problem with your configuration file.

> **TIP**
>
> Instead of using `vi` to edit configuration files, use `vim` instead. Using the `vim` command can help you catch configuration file errors as you are editing.
>
> The `vim` command knows about the formats of many configuration files (`passwd`, `httpd.conf`, `fstab`, and others). If you make a mistake and type an invalid term or option in one of those files, or break the format somehow, the color of the text changes. For example, in `/etc/fstab`, if you change the option `defaults` to `default`, the word's color changes from green to black.

Checking the default configuration

Most server software packages in Fedora and RHEL are installed with minimal configuration and lean more toward being secure than totally useful out of the box. Some Linux distributions ask you, while installing a software package, such things as the directory you want to install it in or the user account you want to manage it.

Because RPM packages are designed to be installed unattended, the person installing the package has no choice on how it is installed. The files are installed in set locations, specific user accounts are enabled to manage it, and when you start the service, it might well offer limited accessibility. You are expected to configure the software after the package is installed to make the server fully functional.

Two examples of servers that are installed with limited functionality are mail servers (sendmail or postfix packages) and DNS servers (bind package). Both of these servers are installed with default configurations and start up on reboot. However, both also only listen for requests on your localhost. So, until you configure those servers, people who are not logged in to your local server cannot send mail to that server or use your computer as a public DNS server, respectively.

Step 3: Start the server

Most services you install in Linux are configured to start up when the system boots, then run continuously, listening for requests for its service, until the system is shut down. There are two major facilities for managing services: systemd (used now by RHEL 7, Ubuntu, and Fedora) and SystemVinit scripts (used by Red Hat Enterprise Linux through RHEL 6.x).

Regardless of which facility is used on your Linux system, it is your job to do such things as set whether you want the service to come up when the system boots and to start, stop, and reload the service as needed (possibly to load new configuration files or temporarily stop access to the service). Commands for doing these tasks are described in Chapter 15, "Starting and Stopping Services."

Most, but not all, services are implemented as daemon processes. Here are a few things you should know about those processes:

- **User and group permissions**—Daemon processes often run as users and groups other than root. For example, httpd runs as apache and ntpd runs as the ntp user. The reason for this is that if someone cracks these daemons, they would not have permissions to access files beyond what that service can access.

- **Daemon configuration files**—Often, a service has a configuration file for the daemon stored in the /etc/sysconfig directory. This is different than the service configuration file in that its job is often just to pass arguments to the server process itself, rather than configure the service. For example, options you set in the /etc/sysconfig/rsyslogd file are passed to the rsyslogd daemon when it starts up. You can tell the daemon, for example, to output additional debugging information or accept remote logging messages. See the man page for the service (for example, `man rsyslogd`) to see what options are supported.

- **Port numbers**—Packets of data go to and from your system over network interfaces through ports for each supported protocol (usually UDP or TCP). Most standard services have specific port numbers that daemons listen to and clients connect to. Unless you are trying to hide the location of a service, you typically don't change the ports that a daemon process listens on. When you go to secure a service, you must make sure the port to the service is open on the firewall (see Chapter 25, "Securing Linux on a Network," for information on `iptables` and `firewalld` firewalls). Also, if you change a port the service is listening on, and SELinux is in enforcing mode, SELinux may prevent the daemon from listening on that port (see Chapter 24, "Enhancing Linux Security with SELinux," for more information on SELinux).

> **NOTE**
>
> One reason for changing port numbers on a service is "security by obscurity." For example, the `sshd` service is a well-known target for people trying to break into a system by guessing logins and passwords on TCP port 22.
>
> I have heard of people changing their Internet-facing `sshd` service to listen on some other port number (perhaps some unused, very high port number). Then they tell their friends or colleagues to log into their machine from ssh by pointing to this other port. The idea is that port scanners looking to break into a system might be less likely to scan the normally unused port.

Not all services run continuously as daemon processes. Some services run on demand using the `xinetd` super server. Other services just run once on start-up and exit. Still others run only a set number of times, being launched when the `crond` daemon sees that the service was configured to run at the particular time.

Of the services just mentioned, the on-demand services are the primary way of running always available (if not always running) services. On-demand services don't run continuously listening for requests. Instead, their services are registered with the `xinetd` daemon. When requests come to the `xinetd` daemon for a service, at that time, the `xinetd` launches the requested service and hands the request off to that service.

The advantage of the `xinetd` daemon is that you can have fewer daemon processes running and consuming memory and process slots. The `xinetd` super server (originally called `inetd` when it was created in the early days of UNIX) came about in a time when memory was very expensive, so freeing up space by only launching rarely used services on demand made sense. Because the amount of memory consumed by a daemon process is not that big a deal anymore, you may notice that most `xinetd` services are older services (such as `telnet` and `tftp`).

For more information on starting services as regular services or on-demand (`xinetd`) services, refer to Chapter 15, "Starting and Stopping Services").

Step 4: Secure the server

Opening your system to allow remote users to access it over the network is not a decision you should take lightly. There are crackers all over the world running programs to scan for vulnerable servers they can take over for their data or their processing power. Luckily, there are measures you can put in place on Linux systems to protect your servers and services from attacks and abuse.

Some common security techniques are described in the following sections. These and other topics are covered in more depth in Part V, "Learning Linux Security Techniques."

Password protection

Good passwords and password policies are the first line of defense in protecting a Linux system. If someone can log in to your server via ssh as the root user with a password of foobar, expect to be cracked. A good technique is to disallow direct login by root and require every user to log in as a regular user and then use su or sudo to become root.

You can also use the Pluggable Authentication Module (PAM) facility to adjust the number of times someone can have failed login attempts before blocking access to that person. PAM also includes other features for locking down authentication to your Linux server. For a description of PAM, see Chapter 23, "Understanding Advanced Linux Security."

Of course, you can bypass passwords altogether by requiring public key authentication. To use that type of authentication, any user you want to have access to your server must have their public key copied to the server (such as through ssh-copy-id). Then they can use ssh, scp, or related commands to access that server without typing the user's password. See the "Using key-based (passwordless) authentication" section later in this chapter for further information.

13

Firewalls

The iptables firewall service can track and respond to every packet coming from and going to network interfaces on your computer. Using iptables, you can drop or reject every packet making requests for services on your system, except for those few that you have enabled. Further, you can tell iptables to only allow service requests from certain IP addresses (good guys) or not allow requests from other addresses (bad guys).

In RHEL 7 and Fedora, the relatively new firewalld feature adds a layer of functionality to Linux firewall rules. Firewalld not only lets you insert iptables firewall rules into the kernel, it also can help organize firewall rules by dividing them up into zones and can change firewall rules on the fly to react to different events.

In each of the server chapters coming up, I describe what ports need to be open to allow access to services. Descriptions of how iptables and firewalld work are included in Chapter 25, "Securing Linux on a Network."

TCP Wrappers

Using the /etc/hosts.allow and /etc/hosts.deny files, you can allow or deny access to those services that have the TCP Wrappers features enabled (libwrap). Access can be allowed or denied based on IP address or host name. Descriptions of TCP Wrappers are contained in Chapter 25.

SELinux

Fedora, Red Hat Enterprise Linux, and other Linux distributions come with the Security Enhanced Linux (SELinux) feature included and in Enforcing mode. Although the default targeted mode doesn't have much impact on most applications you run in Linux, it has a major impact on most major services.

A major function of SELinux is to protect the contents of your Linux system from the processes running on the system. In other words, SELinux makes sure that a web server, FTP server, Samba server, or DNS server can access only a restricted set of files on the system (as defined by file contexts) and allow only a restricted set of features (as defined by Booleans and limited port access).

Details about how to use SELinux are contained in Chapter 24, "Enhancing Linux Security with SELinux."

Security settings in configuration files

Within the configuration files of most services are values you can set to further secure the service. For example, for file servers and web servers, you can restrict access to certain files or data based on username, hostname, IP address of the client, or other attributes.

Step 5: Monitor the server

Because you can't be there to monitor every service every minute, you need to put monitoring tools in place to watch your servers for you and make it easy for you to find out when something needs attention. Some of the tools you can use to monitor your servers are described in the sections that follow.

Configure logging

Using the rsyslog service (rsyslogd daemon), you can gather critical information and error conditions into log files about many different services. By default in RHEL, log messages from applications are directed into log files in the /var/log directory. For added security and convenience, log messages can also be directed to a centralized server, providing a single location to view and manage logging for a group of systems.

Several different software packages are available to work with rsyslog and manage log messages. The logwatch feature scans your log files each night and sends critical information gathered from those files to an e-mail account of your choice. The logrotate feature backs up log files into compressed archives when the logs reach a certain size or pass a set amount of time since the previous backup.

The features for configuring and managing system logging are described in the "Configuring System Logging" section later in this chapter.

Run system activity reports

The `sar` facility (which is enabled by the `sysstat` package) can be configured to watch activities on your system, such as memory usage, CPU usage, disk latency, network activities, and other resource drains. By default, the `sar` facility launches the `sadc` program every few minutes, day and night, to gather data. Viewing that data later can help you go back and figure out where and when demand is spiking on your system. The `sar` facility is described in the "Checking System Resources with sar" section later in this chapter.

Keep system software up to date

As security holes are discovered and patched, you must make sure that the updated software packages containing those patches are installed on your servers. Again, with mission-critical servers, the safest and most efficient way is to use subscribed Red Hat Enterprise Linux systems for your servers, and then deploy security-related package updates to your system as soon as they are released and tested.

To keep your personal server and desktop systems up to date, there are various graphical tools to add software and to check for updates. You can also use the `yum` command to check for and install all packages that are available for your RHEL or Fedora systems (type **yum update**).

Check the filesystem for signs of crackers

To check your filesystem for possible intrusion, you can run commands such as `rpm -V` to check if any commands, document files, or configuration files have been tampered with on your system. For more information on `rpm -V`, refer to the description of `rpm -V` in Chapter 10, "Getting and Managing Software."

Now that you have an overview of how Linux server configuration is done, the next sections of this chapter focus on the tools you need to access, secure, and maintain your Linux server systems.

Managing Remote Access with the Secure Shell Service

The Secure Shell tools are a set of client and server applications that allow you to do basic communications between client computers and your Linux server. The tools include `ssh`, `scp`, `sftp`, and many others. Because communication is encrypted between the server and the clients, these tools are more secure than similar, older tools. For example, instead of using older remote login commands such as `telnet` or `rlogin`, you could use `ssh`. The

13

ssh command can also replace older remote execution commands, such as `rsh`. Remote copy commands, such as `rcp`, can be replaced with secure commands such as `scp` and `rsync`.

With Secure Shell tools, both the authentication process and all communications that follow are encrypted. Communications from `telnet` and the older "r" commands expose passwords and all data to someone sniffing the network. Today, `telnet` and similar commands should be used only for testing access to remote ports, providing public services such as PXE booting, or doing other tasks that don't expose your private data.

> **NOTE**
> For a deeper discussion of encryption techniques, refer to Chapter 23, "Understanding Advanced Linux Security."

Most Linux systems include secure shell clients, and many include the secure shell server as well. If you are using the Fedora or RHEL distribution, for example, the client and server software packages that contain the `ssh` tools are `openssh`, `openssh-clients`, and `openssh-server` packages, as follows:

```
# yum list installed | grep ssh
...
openssh.x86_64              6.4p1-5.fc20        @updates
openssh-clients.x86_64      6.4p1-5.fc20        @updates
openssh-server.x86_64       6.4p1-5.fc20        @updates
```

On Ubuntu, only the `openssh-clients` package is installed. It includes the functionality of the `openssh` package. If you need the server installed, use the `sudo apt-get install openssh-server` command.

```
$ sudo dpkg --list | grep openssh
ii  openssh-client  1:6.6p1-2ubuntu2  amd64
    secure shell (SSH) client, for secure access to remote machines
ii  openssh-server  1:6.6p1-2ubuntu2  amd64
    secure shell (SSH) server, for secure access from remote machines
ii  openssh-sftp-server  1:6.6p1-2ubuntu2  amd64
    secure shell (SSH) sftp server module, for SFTP access
$ sudo apt-get install openssh-server
```

Starting the openssh-server service

Linux systems that come with the `openssh-server` package already installed sometimes are not configured for it to start automatically. Managing Linux services (see Chapter 15, "Starting and Stopping Services") can be very different depending on the different distributions. Table 13.1 shows the commands to use, in order to ensure the `ssh` server daemon, `sshd`, is up and running on a Linux system.

TABLE 13.1 **Commands to Determine sshd Status**

Distribution	Command to Determine sshd Status
RHEL 6	chkconfig --list sshd
Fedora and RHEL 7	systemctl status sshd.service
Ubuntu	status ssh

If sshd is not currently running, you can start it by issuing one of the commands listed in Table 13.2. These commands need root privileges in order to work.

TABLE 13.2 **Commands to Start sshd**

Distribution	Command to Start sshd
RHEL 6	service sshd start
Fedora and RHEL 7	systemctl start sshd.service
Ubuntu	service ssh start

The commands in Table 13.2 only start the ssh or sshd service. They do not configure it to start automatically at boot. To make sure the server service is set up to start automatically, you need to use one of the commands in Table 13.3 using root privileges.

TABLE 13.3 **Commands to Start sshd at Boot**

Distribution	Command to Start sshd at Boot
RHEL 6	chkconfig sshd on
Fedora and RHEL 7	systemctl enable sshd.service
Ubuntu	update-rc.d ssh defaults

When you install openssh-server on Ubuntu, the sshd daemon is configured to start automatically at boot. Therefore, you may not need to run the command in Table 13.3 for your Ubuntu server.

> **TIP**
>
> To manage services on an older Fedora distribution, use the chkconfig command both for starting the ssh service and to ensure it starts at boot.

13

Modify your `netfilter/iptables` firewall settings to allow the `openssh-client` to access port 22 (firewalls are covered in Chapter 25, "Securing Linux on a Network"). After the service is up and running and the firewall is properly configured, you should be able to use `ssh` client commands to access your system via the `ssh` server.

Any further configurations for what the `sshd` daemon is allowed to do are handled in the `/etc/ssh/sshd_config` file. At a minimum, change the `PermitRootLogin` setting from `yes` to `no`. This stops anyone from remotely logging in as root.

```
# grep PermitRootLogin /etc/ssh/sshd_config
PermitRootLogin no
```

After you have changed the `sshd_config` file, restart the `sshd` service. After that point, if you use `ssh` to log in to that system from a remote client, you must do so as a regular user, and then use `su` or `sudo` to become the root user.

Using SSH client tools

Many tools for accessing remote Linux systems have been created to make use of the SSH service. The most frequently used of those tools is the `ssh` command, which can be used for remote login, remote execution, and other tasks. Commands such as `scp` and `rsync` can copy one or more files at a time between SSH client and server systems. The `sftp` command provides an FTP-like interface for traversing a remote filesystem and getting and putting files between the systems interactively.

By default, all the SSH-related tools authenticate using standard Linux usernames and passwords, all done over encrypted connections. However, SSH also supports key-based authentication, which can be used to configure passwordless authentication between clients and SSH servers (as described in the "Using key-based (passwordless) authentication" section later in this chapter).

Using ssh for remote login

Use the `ssh` command from another Linux computer to test that you can log in to the Linux system running your `sshd` service. The `ssh` command is one you will use often to access a shell on the servers you are configuring.

Try logging in to your Linux server from another Linux system using the `ssh` command. (If you don't have another Linux system, you can simulate this by typing **localhost** instead of the IP address and logging in as a local user.) The following is an example of remotely logging in to `johndoe`'s account on `10.140.67.23`:

```
$ ssh johndoe@10.140.67.23
The authenticity of host '10.140.67.23 (10.140.67.23)'
    can't be established.
```

```
RSA key fingerprint is
    a4:28:03:85:89:6d:08:fa:99:15:ed:fb:b0:67:55:89.
Are you sure you want to continue connecting (yes/no)? yes
Warning: Permanently added '10.140.67.23' (RSA) to the
    list of known hosts.
johndoe@10.140.67.23's password: ********
```

If this is the very first time you have logged in to that remote system using the `ssh` command, the system asks you to confirm that you want to connect. Type **yes**, and press Enter. When prompted, type the user's password.

When you type **yes** to continue, you accept the remote host's public key. At that point, the remote host's public key is downloaded to the client in the client's `~/.ssh/known_hosts` file. Now, data exchanged between these two systems can be encrypted and decrypted using RSA asymmetric encryption (see Chapter 23, "Understanding Advanced Linux Security").

After you are logged in to the remote system, you can begin typing shell commands. The connection functions like a normal login. The only difference is that the data is encrypted as it travels over the network.

When you are finished, type **exit** to end the remote connection. The connection is closed, and you are returned to the command prompt on your local system. (If the local shell doesn't return after you exit the remote shell, typing ~. usually closes the connection.)

```
$ exit
logout
Connection to 10.140.67.23 closed.
```

After you have remotely connected to a system, a file in your local system subdirectory, `~.ssh/known_hosts`, will exist. This file contains the public key of the remote host along with its IP address. Your server's public and private keys are stored in the `/etc/ssh` directory.

```
$ ls .ssh
known_hosts
$ cat .ssh/known_hosts
10.140.67.23 ssh-rsa
AAAAB3NzaC1yc2EAAAABIwAAAQEAoyfJK1YwZhNmpHE4yLPZAZ9ZNEdRE7I159f3I
yGiH21IjfqsNYFR10ZlBLlYyTQi06r/9O19GwCaJ753InQ8FWHW+OOYOG5pQmghhn
/x0LD2uUb6egOu6zim1NECJwZf5DWkKdy4euCUEMSqADh/WYeuOSoZ0pp2IAVCdh6
w/PIHMF1HVR069cvdv+OTL4vD0X8llSpw0ozqRptz2UQgQBBbBjK1RakD7fY1TrWv
NQhYG/ugt gPaY4JDYeY6OBzcadpxZmf7EYUw0ucXGVQ1aNP/erIDOQ9rA0YNzCRv
y2LYCm2/9adpAxc+UYi5UsxTw4ewSBjmsXYq//Ahaw4mjw==
```

> **TIP**
>
> Any later attempts by this user to contact the server at 10.140.67.23 are authenticated using this stored key. If the server should change its key (which happens if the operating system is reinstalled), attempts to `ssh` to that system result in a refused connection and dire warnings that you may be under attack. If the key has indeed changed, to be able to `ssh` to that address again, just remove the host's key (the whole line) from your `know_hosts` file and you can copy over the new key.

Using ssh for remote execution

Besides logging into a remote shell, the `ssh` command can be used to execute a command on the remote system and have the output returned to the local system. Here is an example:

```
$ ssh johndoe@10.140.67.23 hostname
johndoe@10.140.67.23's password: **********
host01.example.com
```

In the example just shown, the `hostname` command runs as the user `johndoe` on the Linux system located at IP address `10.140.67.23`. The output of the command is the name of the remote host (in this case, `host01.example.com`), which appears on the local screen.

If you run a remote execution command with `ssh` that includes options or arguments, be sure to surround the whole remote command line in quotes. Keep in mind that if you refer to files or directories in your remote commands, relative paths are interpreted in relation to the user's home directory. For example:

```
$ ssh johndoe@10.140.67.23 "cat myfile"
johndoe@10.140.67.23's password: **********
Contents of the myfile file located in johndoe's home directory.
```

The `ssh` command just shown goes to the remote host located at 10.140.67.23 and runs the `cat myfile` command as the user johndoe. This causes the contents of the `myfile` file from that system to be displayed on the local screen.

Another type of remote execution you can do with `ssh` is X11 forwarding. If X11 forwarding is enabled on the server (`X11Forwarding yes` is set in the `/etc/sshd/sshd_config` file), you can run graphical applications from the server securely over the SSH connection using `ssh -X`. For a new server administrator, this means that if there are graphical administration tools installed on a server, you can run those tools without having to sit at the console. For example:

```
$ ssh -X johndoe@10.140.67.23 system-config-date
johndoe@10.140.67.23's password: **********
```

After running this command, you are prompted for the root password. After that, the Date/Time Properties window appears, ready for you to change the current date and time. Just close the window when you are finished, and the local prompt returns. You can do this for any graphical administration tool or just regular X applications (such as the `gedit` graphical editor, so you don't have to use `vi`).

If you want to run several X commands and don't want to have to reconnect each time, you can use X11 forwarding directly from a remote shell as well. Put them in the background and you can have several remote X applications running on your local desktop at once. For example:

```
$ ssh -X johndoe@10.140.67.23
johndoe@10.140.67.23's password: **********
$ system-config-network &
$ gedit &
$ exit
```

After you have finished using the graphical applications, close them as you would normally. Then type **exit**, as shown in the preceding code, to leave the remote shell and return to your local shell.

Copying files between systems with scp and rsync

The scp command is similar to the old UNIX rcp command for copying files to and from Linux systems, except all communications are encrypted. Files can be copied from the remote system to the local system or local to remote. You can also copy files recursively through a whole directory structure, if you choose.

The following is an example of using the scp command to copy a file called memo from the home directory of the user chris to the /tmp directory on a remote computer as the user johndoe:

```
$ scp /home/chris/memo johndoe@10.140.67.23:/tmp
johndoe@10.140.67.23's password: ***************
memo          100%|***************|   153    0:00
```

You must enter the password for johndoe. After the password is accepted, the file is copied to the remote system successfully.

You can do recursive copies with scp using the -r option. Instead of a file, pass a directory name to the scp command and all files and directories below that point in the filesystem are copied to the other system.

```
$ scp johndoe@10.140.67.23:/usr/share/man/man1/ /tmp/
johndoe@10.140.67.23's password: ***************
volname.1.gz                                    100%  543    0.5KB/s  00:00
mtools.1.gz                                     100% 6788    6.6KB/s  00:00
roqet.1.gz                                      100% 2496    2.4KB/s  00:00
...
```

As long as the user johndoe has access to the files and directories on the remote system and the local user can write to the target directory (both are true in this case), the directory structure from /usr/share/man/man1 down is copied to the local /tmp directory.

The scp command can be used to back up files and directories over a network. However, if you compare scp to the rsync command, you see that rsync (which also works over SSH connections) is a better backup tool. Try running the scp command shown previously to copy the man1 directory (you can simulate the command using localhost instead of the IP address, if you only have one accessible Linux system). Now type the following on the system you copied the files to:

```
$ ls -l /usr/share/man/man1/batch* /tmp/man1/batch*
-rw-r--r--.1 johndoe johndoe 2628 Apr 15 15:32 /tmp/man1/batch.1.gz
lrwxrwxrwx.1 root root 7 Feb 14 17:49 /usr/share/man/man1/batch.1.gz
        -> at.1.gz
```

Next, run the scp command again and list the files again:

```
$ scp johndoe@10.140.67.23:/usr/share/man/man1/ /tmp/
johndoe@10.140.67.23's password: ***************
$ ls -l /usr/share/man/man1/batch* /tmp/man1/batch*
-rw-r--r--.1 johndoe johndoe 2628 Apr 15 15:40 /tmp/man1/batch.1.gz
lrwxrwxrwx.1 root root 7 Feb 14 17:49 /usr/share/man/man1/batch.1.gz
        -> at.1.gz
```

The output of those commands tells you a few things about how scp works:

- **Attributes lost**—Permissions or date/time stamp attributes were not retained when the files were copied. If you were using scp as a backup tool, you would probably want to keep permissions and time stamps on the files if you needed to restore the files later.

- **Symbolic links lost**—The batch.1.gz file is actually a symbolic link to the at.1.gz file. Instead of copying the link, scp follows the link and actually copies the file. Again, if you were to restore this directory, batch.1.gz would be replaced by the actual at.1.gz file instead of a link to it.

- **Copy repeated unnecessarily**—If you watched the second scp output, you would notice that all files were copied again, even though the exact files being copied were already on the target. The updated modification date confirms this. By contrast, the rsync can determine that a file has already been copied and not copy the file again.

The rsync command is a better network backup tool because it can overcome some of the shortcomings of scp just listed. Try running an rsync command to do the same action scp just did, but with a few added options:

```
$ rm -rf /tmp/man1/
$ rsync -avl johndoe@10.140.67.23:/usr/share/man/man1/ /tmp/
johndoe@10.140.67.23's password: ***************
sending incremental file list
man1/
man1/HEAD.1.gz
man1/Mail.1.gz -> mailx.1.gz
...
$ rsync -avl johndoe@10.140.67.23:/usr/share/man/man1/ /tmp/
```

```
johndoe@10.140.67.23's password: **************
sending incremental file list
sent 42362 bytes  received 13 bytes  9416.67 bytes/sec
total size is 7322223  speedup is 172.80
$ ls -l /usr/share/man/man1/batch* /tmp/man1/batch*
lrwxrwxrwx.1 johndoe johndoe 7 Feb 14 17:49 /tmp/man1/batch.1.gz
      -> at.1.gz
lrwxrwxrwx.1 root root 7 Feb 14 17:49 /usr/share/man/man1/batch.1.gz
      -> at.1.gz
```

After removing the /tmp/man1 directory, you run an rsync command to copy all the files to the /tmp/man1 directory, using -a (recursive archive), -v (verbose), and -l (copy symbolic links). Then run the command immediately again and notice that nothing is copied. The rsync command knows that all the files are there already, so it doesn't copy them again. This can be a tremendous savings of network bandwidth for directories with gigabytes of files where only a few megabytes change.

Also notice from the output of ls -l that the symbolic links have been preserved on the batch.1.gz file and so has the date/time stamp on the file. If you need to restore those files later, you can put them back exactly as they were.

This use of rsync is good for backups. But what if you wanted to mirror two directories, making the contents of two directory structures exactly the same on two machines? The following commands illustrate how to create an exact mirror of the directory structure on both machines, using the directories shown with the previous rsync commands.

First, on the remote system, copy a new file into the directory being copied:

```
# cp /etc/services /usr/share/man/man1
```

Next, on the local system, run rsync to copy across any new files (in this case, just the directory and the new file, services):

```
$ rsync -avl johndoe@10.140.67.23:/usr/share/man/man1 /tmp
johndoe@10.140.67.23's password:
***************
sending incremental file list
man1/
man1/services
```

After that, go back to the remote system and remove the new file:

```
$ sudo rm /usr/share/man/man1/services
```

Now, on the local system, run rsync again and notice that nothing happens. At this point, the remote and local directories are different because the local system has the services file and the remote doesn't. That is correct behavior for a backup directory (you want to have files on the backup in case something was removed by mistake). However, if you want the remote and local directories to be mirrored, you would have to add the --delete option.

The result is that the services file is deleted on the local system, making the remote and local directory structures in sync.

```
$ rsync -avl /usr/share/man/man1 localhost:/tmp
johndoe@10.140.67.23's password: ***************
sending incremental file list
man1/
$ rsync -avl --delete johndoe@10.140.67.23:/usr/share/man/man1 /tmp
johndoe@10.140.67.23's password: ***************
sending incremental file list
deleting man1/services
```

Interactive copying with sftp

If you don't know exactly what you want to copy to or from a remote system, you can use the sftp command to create an interactive FTP-style session over the SSH service. Using sftp, you can connect to a remote system over SSH, change directories, list directory contents, and then (given proper permission) get files from and put files on the server. Keep in mind that, despite its name, sftp has nothing to do with the FTP protocol and doesn't use FTP servers. It simply uses an FTP style of interaction between a client and an sshd server.

The following example shows the user johndoe connecting to jd.example.com:

```
$ sftp johndoe@jd.example.com
Connecting to jd.example.com
johndoe@jd.example.com's password: ***************
sftp>
```

At this point, you can begin an interactive FTP session. You can use get and put commands on files as you would with any FTP client, but with the comfort of knowing you are working on an encrypted and secure connection. Because the FTP protocol passes usernames, passwords, and data in clear text, using sftp over SSH, if possible, is a much better alternative for allowing your users to interactively copy files from the system.

Using key-based (passwordless) authentication

If you are using SSH tools to connect to the same systems throughout the day, you might find it inconvenient to be typing your password over and over again. Instead of using password-based authentication, SSH allows you to set up key-based authentication to use instead. Here's how it works:

- You create a public key and a private key.

- You guard the private key, but copy the public key across to the user account on the remote host to which you want to do key-based authentication.

- With your keys copied to the proper locations, you use any SSH tools to connect to the user account on the remote host, but instead of asking you for a password, the remote SSH service compares the public key and the private key and allows you access if the two keys match.

When you create the keys, you are given the option to add a passphrase to your private key. If you decide to add a passphrase, even though you don't need to enter a password to authenticate to the remote system, you still need to enter your passphrase to unlock your private key. If you don't add a passphrase, you can communicate using your private/public key pairs in a way that is completely passwordless. However, if someone should get hold of your private key, they could act as you in any communication that required that key.

The following procedure demonstrates how a local user named chris can set up key-based authentication to a remote user named johndoe at IP address 10.140.67.23. If you don't have two Linux systems, you can simulate this by using two user accounts on your local system. I start by logging in as the local user named chris and typing the following to generate my local public/private key pair:

```
$ ssh-keygen
Generating public/private rsa key pair.
Enter file in which to save the key (/home/chris/.ssh/id_rsa): ENTER
Enter passphrase (empty for no passphrase): ENTER
Enter same passphrase again: ENTER
Your identification has been saved in /home/chris/.ssh/id_rsa.
Your public key has been saved in /home/chris/.ssh/id_rsa.pub.
The key fingerprint is:
bf:06:f8:12:7f:f4:c3:0a:3a:01:7f:df:25:71:ec:1d chris@abc.example.com
The key's randomart image is:
 ...
```

I accepted the default RSA key (DSA keys are also allowed) and pressed Enter twice to have a blank passphrase associated with the key. As a result, my private key (id_rsa) and public key (id_rsa.pub) are copied to the .ssh directory in my local home directory. The next step is to copy that key over to a remote user, so I can use key-based authentication each time I connect to that user account with ssh tools:

```
$ ssh-copy-id -i ~/.ssh/id_rsa.pub johndoe@10.140.67.23
johndoe@10.140.67.23's password:
***************
Now try logging into the machine, with "ssh 'johndoe@10.140.67.23'",
and check in:
  .ssh/authorized_keys
to make sure we haven't added extra keys that you weren't expecting.
```

When prompted, I entered johndoe's password. With that accepted, the public key belonging to chris is copied to the authorized_keys file in johndoe's .ssh directory on the remote system. Now, the next time chris tries to connect to johndoe's account, the SSH connection is authenticated using those keys. Because no passphrase is put on the private key, no passphrase is required to unlock that key when it is used.

```
[chris]$ ssh johndoe@10.140.67.23
Last login: Sun Apr 17 10:12:22 2016 from  10.140.67.22
[johndoe]$
```

With the keys in place, chris could now use ssh, scp, rsync, or any other SSH-enabled command to do key-based authentication. Using these keys, for example, an rsync command could go into a cron script and automatically back up johndoe's home directory every night.

Want to further secure your remote system? After you have the keys in place on your remote system for everyone you want to allow to log in to that system, you can set the sshd service on the remote system to not allow password authentication by changing the PasswordAuthentication setting in the /etc/ssh/sshd_config file to no so it appears as follows:

```
PasswordAuthentication no
```

Then restart the sshd service (systemctl restart sshd). After that, anyone with a valid key is still accepted. Anyone who tries to log in without a key gets the following failure message and doesn't even get a chance to enter a username and password:

```
Permission denied (publickey,gssapi-keyex,gssapi-with-mic).
```

Configuring System Logging

With the knowledge of how to access your remote server using SSH tools, you can log in to the server and set up some of the services needed to make sure it's running smoothly. System logging is one of the basic services configured for Linux to keep track of what is happening on the system.

The rsyslog service (rsyslogd daemon) provides the features to gather log messages from software running on the Linux system and direct those messages to local log files, devices, or remote logging hosts. Configuration of rsyslog is similar to the configuration of its predecessor, syslog. However, rsyslog allows you to add modules to more specifically manage and direct log messages.

In Red Hat Enterprise Linux 7 and recent Fedora releases, the rsyslog facility leverages messages that are gathered and stored in the systemd journal. To display journal log messages directly from the systemd journal, instead of viewing them from files in the /var/log directory, use the journalctl command.

Enabling system logging with rsyslog

Most of the files in the /var/log directory are populated with log messages directed to them from the rsyslog service. The rsyslogd daemon is the system logging daemon. It accepts log messages from a variety of other programs and writes them to the appropriate log files. This is better than having every program write directly to its own log file because it enables you to centrally manage how log files are handled.

Configuring rsyslogd to record varying levels of detail in the log files is possible. It can be told to ignore all but the most critical messages, or it can record every detail.

The `rsyslogd` daemon can even accept messages from other computers on your network. This remote logging feature is particularly handy because it enables you to centralize the management and review of the log files from many systems on your network. There is also a major security benefit to this practice.

With remote logging, if a system on your network is broken into, the cracker cannot delete or modify the log files because those files are stored on a separate computer. It is important to remember, however, that those log messages are not, by default, encrypted (though encryption can be enabled). Anyone tapping into your local network can eavesdrop on those messages as they pass from one machine to another. Also, although the cracker may not be able to change old log entries, he or she can affect the system such that any new log messages should not be trusted.

Running a dedicated loghost, a computer that serves no other purpose than to record log messages from other computers on the network, is not uncommon. Because this system runs no other services, it is unlikely that it will be broken into. This makes it nearly impossible for crackers to completely erase their tracks.

Understanding the rsyslog.conf file

The `/etc/rsyslog.conf` file is the primary configuration file for the `rsyslog` service. If you have used the older `syslog` facility, you will notice that the rules section is the same in both files. So the way you define which type of messages get logged and where they are logged to is exactly the same; however, the configuration files are different related to the use of modules in `rsyslog.conf`.

In the `/etc/rsyslog.conf` file, a Modules section lets you include or not include specific features in your `rsyslog` service. The following is an example of the modules section of `/etc/rsyslog.conf` in RHEL 7:

```
$ModLoad imuxsock
        # provides support for local system logging (logger command)
$ModLoad imjournal # provides access to the systemd journal
$ModLoad imklog
        # reads kernel messages (the same are read from journald)
#$ModLoad immark   # provides --MARK-- message capability
# Provides UDP syslog reception
#$ModLoad imudp
#$UDPServerRun 514
# Provides TCP syslog reception
#$ModLoad imtcp
#$InputTCPServerRun 514
```

Entries beginning with $ModLoad load the modules that follow. Modules that are currently disabled are preceded by a pound sign (#). The `imjournal` module lets `rlogind` access the `systemd` journal. The `imuxsock` module is needed to accept messages from the local system (it should not be commented out—preceded by a pound sign—unless you have a specific reason to do so). The `imklog` module logs kernel messages.

Modules not enabled by default include the `immark` module, which allows `--MARK--` messages to be logged (used to indicate that a service is alive). The `imudp` and `imtcp` modules and related port number entries are used to allow the `rsyslog` service to accept remote logging messages and are discussed in more detail in the "Setting up and using a loghost with rsyslogd" section.

Most of the work done in the `/etc/rsyslog.conf` configuration file involves modifying the RULES section. The following is an example of some of the rules in the RULES section of the `/etc/rsyslog.conf` file (note that in Ubuntu, you need to look in the `/etc/rsyslog.d` directory for this configuration information):

```
#### RULES ####
# Log all kernel messages to the console.
# Logging much else clutters up the screen.
#kern.*                                              /dev/console
# Log anything (except mail) of level info or higher.
# Don't log private authentication messages!
*.info;mail.none;authpriv.none;cron.none            /var/log/messages
# The authpriv file has restricted access.
authpriv.*                                          /var/log/secure
# Log all the mail messages in one place.
mail.*                                             -/var/log/maillog
# Log cron stuff
cron.*                                              /var/log/cron
```

Rules entries come in two columns. In the left column are designations of what messages are matched; the right column shows where matched messages go. Messages are matched based on facility (`mail`, `cron`, `kern`, and so on) and priority (starting at `debug`, `info`, `notice` and up to `crit`, `alert`, and `emerg`), separated by a dot (.). So `mail.info` matches all messages from the mail service that are info level and above.

As for where the messages go, most messages are directed to files in the `/var/log` directory. You can, however, direct messages to a device (such as `/dev/console`) or a remote log host (such as `@loghost.example.com`). The at sign (@) indicates that the name that follows is the name of the loghost.

By default, logging is done only to local files in the `/var/log` directory. However, if you uncomment the `kern.*` entry, you can easily direct kernel messages of all levels to your computer's console screen.

The first working entry in the preceding example shows that info level messages from all services (*) are matched by that rule, with the exception of messages from `mail`, `authpriv`, and `cron` services (which are excluded with the word `none`). All the matched messages are directed to the `/var/log/messages` file.

The `mail`, `authpriv` (authentication messages), and `cron` (cron facility messages) services each have their own log files, as listed in the columns to their right. To understand the format of those and other log files, the format of the `/var/log/messages` file is described next.

Understanding the messages log file

Because of the many programs and services that record information to the messages log file, understanding the format of this file is important. You can get a good early warning of problems developing on your system by examining this file. Each line in the file is a single message recorded by some program or service. Here is a snippet of an actual messages log file:

```
Feb 25 11:04:32 toys network: Bringing up loopback:  succeeded
Feb 25 11:04:35 toys network: Bringing up interface eth0:  succeeded
Feb 25 13:01:14 toys vsftpd(pam_unix)[10565]: authentication failure;
     logname= uid=0 euid=0 tty= ruser= rhost=10.0.0.5  user=chris
Feb 25 14:44:24 toys su(pam_unix)[11439]: session opened for
     user root by chris(uid=500)
```

The default message format in the /var/log/messages file is divided into five main parts. This format is determined by the following entry in the /etc/rsyslog.conf file:

```
$ActionFileDefaultTemplate RSYSLOG_TraditionalFileFormat
```

When you view messages in files from the /var/log directory, from left to right, message parts include:

- The date and time that the message was logged
- The name of the computer from which the message came
- The program or service name to which the message pertains
- The process number (enclosed in square brackets) of the program sending the message
- The actual text message

Take another look at the preceding file snippet. In the first two lines, you can see that the network was restarted. The next line shows that the user named chris tried and failed to get to the FTP server on this system from a computer at address 10.0.0.5 (he typed the wrong password and authentication failed). The last line shows chris using the su command to become root user.

By occasionally reviewing the messages and secure files, you could catch a cracking attempt before it is successful. If you see an excessive number of connection attempts for a particular service, especially if they are coming from systems on the Internet, you may be under attack.

Setting up and using a loghost with rsyslogd

To redirect your computer's log files to another computer's rsyslogd, you must make changes to both the local and remote rsyslog configuration file, /etc/rsyslog.conf. Become root using the su - command and then open the /etc/rsyslog.conf file in a text editor (such as vi).

On the client side

To send the messages to another computer (the loghost) instead of a file, start by replacing the log file name with the @ character followed by the name of the loghost. For example, to direct the output of messages that are being sent to the messages, secure, and maillog log files to a loghost as well, add the bolded lines to the messages file:

```
# Log anything (except mail) of level info or higher.
# Don't log private authentication messages!
*.info;mail.none;news.none;authpriv.none;cron.none   /var/log/messages
*.info;mail.none;news.none;authpriv.none;cron.none  @loghost
# The authpriv file has restricted access.
authpriv.*                                  /var/log/secure
authpriv.*                                  @loghost
# Log all the mail messages in one place.
mail.*                                       -/var/log/maillog
mail.*                                      @loghost
```

The messages are now sent to the rsyslogd running on the computer named loghost. The name "loghost" was not an arbitrary choice. Creating such a hostname and making it an alias to the actual system acting as the loghost is customary. That way, if you ever need to switch the loghost duties to a different machine, you need to change only the loghost alias; you do not need to re-edit the syslog.conf file on every computer.

On the loghost side

The loghost that is set to accept the messages must listen for those messages on standard ports (514 UDP, although it can be configured to accept messages on 514 TCP as well). Here is how you would configure the Linux loghost that is also running the rsyslog service:

- Edit the /etc/rsyslog.conf file on the loghost system and uncomment the lines that enable the rsyslogd daemon to listen for remote log messages. Uncomment the first two lines to enable incoming UDP log messages on port 514 (default); uncomment the two lines after that to allow messages that use TCP protocol (also port 514):

```
$ModLoad imudp.so
$UDPServerRun 514
$ModLoad imtcp.so
$InputTCPServerRun 514
```

- Open your firewall (iptables or firewalld) to allow new messages to be directed to your loghost. (See Chapter 25, "Securing Linux on a Network," for a description of how to open specific ports to allow access to your system.)

- Restart the rsyslog service (service rsyslog restart or systemctl restart rsyslog.service).

- If the service is running, you should be able to see that the service is listening on the ports you enabled (UDP and/or TCP ports 514). Run the netstat command as follows to see that the rsyslogd daemon is listening on IPv4 and IPv6 ports 514 for both UDP and TCP services:

```
# netstat -tupln | grep 514
tcp     0     0 0.0.0.0:514      0.0.0.0:*       LISTEN     25341/rsyslogd
tcp     0     0 :::514           :::*            LISTEN     25341/rsyslogd
udp     0     0 0.0.0.0:514      0.0.0.0:*                  25341/rsyslogd
udp     0     0 :::514           :::*                       25341/rsyslogd
```

Watching logs with logwatch

The logwatch service runs in most Linux systems that do system logging with rsyslog. Because logs on busy systems can become very large over time, it doesn't take long for there to be too many messages for a system administrator to watch every message in every log. To install the logwatch facility, type the following:

```
# yum install logwatch
```

What logwatch does is gather messages once each night that look like they might represent a problem, put them in an e-mail message, and send it to any e-mail address the administrator chooses. To enable logwatch all you have to do is install the logwatch package.

The logwatch service runs from a cron job (01logwatch) placed in /etc/cron.daily. The /etc/logwatch/conf/logwatch.conf file holds local settings. The default options used to gather log messages are set in the /usr/share/logwatch/default.conf/logwatch.conf file.

Some of the default settings define the location of log files (/var/log), the location of the temporary directory (/var/cache/logwatch), and the recipient of the daily logwatch e-mail (the local root user). Unless you expect to log in to the server to read logwatch messages, you probably want to change the MailTo setting in the /etc/logwatch/conf/logwatch.conf file:

```
MailTo = chris@example.com
```

Look in /usr/share/logwatch/default.conf/logwatch.conf for other settings to change (such as detail level or the time range for each report). Then make your additions to /etc/logwatch/conf/logwatch.conf as mentioned.

When the service is enabled (which it is just by installing the logwatch package), you will see a message each night in the root user's mailbox. When you are logged in as root, you can use the old mail command to view the root user's mailbox:

```
# mail
Heirloom Mail version 12.5 7/5/10.  Type ? for help.
"/var/spool/mail/root": 2 messages 2 new
>N  1 logwatch@abc.ex  Sun Feb 15 04:02 45/664    "Logwatch for abc"
    2 logwatch@abc.ex  Mon Feb 16 04:02 45/664    "Logwatch for abc"
& 1
& x
```

In mail, you should see e-mail messages from logwatch run each day (here at 4:02 a.m.). Type the number of the message you want to view and page through it with the spacebar or line by line by pressing Enter. Type **x** to exit when you are finished.

The kind of information you see includes kernel errors, installed packages, authentication failures, and malfunctioning services. Disk space usage is reported, so you can see if your storage is filling up. Just by glancing through this logwatch message, you should get an idea whether sustained attacks are under way or if some repeated failures are taking place.

Checking System Resources with sar

The System Activity Reporter (sar) is one of the oldest system monitoring facilities created for early UNIX systems—predating Linux by a few decades. The sar command itself can display system activity continuously, at set intervals (every second or two), and display it on the screen. It can also display system activity data that was gathered earlier.

The sar command is part of the sysstat package. By installing sysstat and enabling the sysstat service, your system immediately begins gathering system activity data that can be reviewed later using certain options to the sar command. The data gathering is done by a crontab configuration file (/etc/cron.d/sysstat) that is launched at regular intervals. Look at what that file contains:

```
# cat /etc/cron.d/sysstat
# Run system activity accounting tool every 10 minutes
*/10 * * * * root /usr/lib64/sa/sa1 1 1
# 0 * * * * root /usr/lib64/sa/sa1 600 6 &
# Generate a daily summary of process accounting at 23:53
53 23 * * * root /usr/lib64/sa/sa2 -A
```

The first uncommented line runs the sa1 1 1 command every 10 minutes. This sa1 command gathers a range of system activity information just once (one time after waiting 1 second) and copies it to the /var/log/sa/sa?? file, where ?? is replaced by the current day. The sa2 -A command gathers all data gathered to this point in the day (at 11:23 p.m.) and places that in the /var/log/sa/sar?? file, where ?? is replaced by the current day.

To read the data in the *sa??* and *sar??* files, you can use some of the following sar commands:

```
# sar -u | less
Linux 3.10.0-123.el7.x86_64 (rhel7-01)  4/16/2017  _x86_64_  (4 CPU)
12:00:01 AM     CPU     %user   %nice   %system %iowait %steal  %idle
12:10:01 AM     all     6.48    0.00    0.82    0.59    0.00    92.12
12:20:01 AM     all     6.50    0.00    0.78    0.82    0.00    91.91
```

The -u option shows CPU usage. By default, the output starts at midnight on the current day and then shows how much processing time is being consumed by different parts of the system. The output continues to show the activity every 10 minutes until the current time is reached.

To see disk activity output, run the `sar -d` command. Again, output comes in 10-minute intervals starting at midnight.

```
# sar -d | less
Linux 3.10.0-123.el7.x86_64 (rhel7-01) 4/16/2017 _x86_64_  (4 CPU)
12:00:01 AM     DEV    tps rd_sec/s wr_sec/s avgrq-sz avgqu-sz ...
12:10:01 AM  dev8-0   1.39    0.24    18.49    13.44     0.04  ...
12:10:01 AM dev253- 02.59    0.24    18.49     7.24     0.04  ...
```

If you want to run `sar` activity reports live, you can do that by adding counts and time intervals to the command line. For example:

```
# sar -n DEV 5 2
Linux 3.10.0-123.el7.x86_64 (rhel7-01) 4/16/2017 _x86_64_ (4 CPU)
11:19:36 PM IFACE rxpck/s txpck/s  rxkB/s  txkB/s rxcmp/s txcmp/s...
11:19:41 PM    lo    5.42    5.42    1.06    1.06    0.00    0.00...
11:19:41 PM  eth0    0.00    0.00    0.00    0.00    0.00    0.00...
11:19:41 PM wlan0    1.00    1.00    0.10    0.12    0.00    0.00...
11:19:41 PM  pan0    0.00    0.00    0.00    0.00    0.00    0.00...
11:19:41 PM  tun0    0.00    0.00    0.00    0.00    0.00    0.00...
...
Average:  IFACE rxpck/s txpck/s rxkB/s txkB/ rxcmp/s txcmp/s rxmcst/s
Average:     lo    7.21    7.21    1.42   1.42    0.00    0.00    0.00
Average:   eth0    0.00    0.00    0.00   0.00    0.00    0.00    0.00
Average:  wlan0    4.70    4.00    4.81   0.63    0.00    0.00    0.00
Average:   pan0    0.00    0.00    0.00   0.00    0.00    0.00    0.00
Average:   tun0    3.70    2.90    4.42   0.19    0.00    0.00    0.00
```

With the `-n Dev` example just shown, you can see how much activity came across the different network interfaces on your system. You can see how many packets were transmitted and received and how many KB of data were transmitted and received. In that example, samplings of data were taken every 5 seconds and repeated twice.

Refer to the `sar`, `sadc`, `sa1`, and `sa2` man pages for more information on how `sar` data can be gathered and displayed.

Checking System Space

Although `logwatch` can give you a daily snapshot of space consumption on your system disks, the `df` and `du` commands can help you immediately see how much disk space is available. The following sections show examples of those commands.

Displaying system space with df

You can display the space available in your filesystems using the df command. To see the amount of space available on all the mounted filesystems on your Linux computer, type df with no options:

```
$ df
Filesystem     1k-blocks      Used  Available  Use%  Mounted on
/dev/sda3       30645460   2958356   26130408   11%  /
/dev/sda2          46668      8340      35919   19%  /boot
. . .
```

This example output shows the space available on the hard disk partition mounted on the / (root) directory (/dev/sda1) and /boot partition (/dev/sda2). Disk space is shown in 1KB blocks. To produce output in a more human-readable form, use the -h option:

```
$ df -h
Filesystem      Size  Used  Avail  Use%  Mounted on
/dev/sda3       29G   2.9G    24G   11%  /
/dev/sda2       46M   8.2M    25M   19%  /boot
. . .
```

With the df -h option, output appears in a friendlier megabyte or gigabyte listing. Other options with df enable you to do the following:

- Print only filesystems of a particular type (-t type).
- Exclude filesystems of a particular type (-x type). For example, type df -x tmpfs -x devtmpfs to exclude temporary filesystem types (limiting output to filesystems that represent real storage areas).
- Include filesystems that have no space, such as /proc and /dev/pts (-a).
- List only available and used inodes (-i).
- Display disk space in certain block sizes (--block-size=#).

Checking disk usage with du

To find out how much space is being consumed by a particular directory (and its subdirectories), use the du command. With no options, du lists all directories below the current directory, along with the space consumed by each directory. At the end, du produces total disk space used within that directory structure.

The du command is a good way to check how much space is being used by a particular user (du /home/jake) or in a particular filesystem partition (du /var). By default, disk space is displayed in 1KB block sizes. To make the output friendlier (in kilobytes, megabytes, and gigabytes), use the -h option as follows:

```
$ du -h /home/jake
114k     /home/jake/httpd/stuff
234k     /home/jake/httpd
137k     /home/jake/uucp/data
701k     /home/jake/uucp
1.0M     /home/jake
```

The output shows the disk space used in each directory under the home directory of the user named jake (/home/jake). Disk space consumed is shown in kilobytes (k) and megabytes (M). The total space consumed by /home/jake is shown on the last line. Add the -s option to see total disk space used for a directory and its subdirectories.

Finding disk consumption with find

The find command is a great way to find file consumption of your hard disk using a variety of criteria. You can get a good idea of where disk space can be recovered by finding files that are over a certain size or were created by a particular person.

> **NOTE**
> You must be the root user to run this command effectively, unless you are just checking your personal files. If you are not the root user, there are many places in the filesystem that you do not have permission to check. Regular users can usually check their own home directories but not those of others.

In the following example, the find command searches the root filesystem (/) for any files owned by the user named jake (-user jake) and prints the filenames. The output of the find command is organized in a long listing in size order (ls -ldS). Finally, that output is sent to the file /tmp/jake. When you view the file /tmp/jake (for example, less/tmp/jake), you will find all the files that are owned by the user jake listed in size order. Here is the command line:

```
# find / -xdev -user jake -print | xargs ls -ldS > /tmp/jake
```

> **TIP**
> The -xdev option prevents filesystems other than the selected filesystem from being searched. This is a good way to cut out lots of junk that may be output from the /proc filesystem. It can also keep large remotely mounted filesystems from being searched.

Here's another example, except that instead of looking for a user's files, we're looking for files larger than 100 kilobytes (-size +100M):

```
# find / -xdev -size +100M | xargs ls -ldS > /tmp/size
```

You can save yourself lots of disk space by just removing some of the largest files that are no longer needed. In this example, you can see that large files are sorted by size in the /tmp/size file.

Managing Servers in the Enterprise

As you pat yourself on the back for mastering tools for managing Linux servers, keep in mind that these skills are just the foundation for what you need to manage hundreds or thousands of Linux systems in a large enterprise. Managing large sets of enterprise computers is different from managing just one or two systems in some of the following ways:

- **Deployment**—Rather than set up a single system manually, enterprise servers are typically preconfigured, tested, and then deployed over and over again. A single automated Linux install can be done from a PXE server using a kickstart file. However, to manage the installation and configuration of sets of computers, provisioning and configuration management tools such as Chef (www.getchef. com) and Puppet (www.puppetlabs.com) are now available. Other tools, such as Ansible (www.ansible.com) and Vagrant (www.vagrantup.com), can be used to start planning system deployments as part of developing your applications.

- **Monitoring**—Because there are too many systems for a system administrator to check individually, enterprise-level monitoring tools are required. Nagios (www. nagios.com) is perhaps the most popular facility for monitoring IT infrastructures. As cloud environments become more popular, look for monitoring tools that go with OpenStack, Red Hat Enterprise Virtualization, and other cloud platforms to improve centralized monitoring of hypervisors, virtual machines, containers, and the underlying storage, networking, and authentications services that support them.

Although in-depth coverage of enterprise deployment and monitoring tools is outside the scope of this book, refer to Chapter 26, "Using Linux for Cloud Computing," for further information on how different Linux-based cloud platforms manage these issues.

Summary

Although many different types of servers are available with Linux systems, the basic procedure for installing and configuring a server is essentially the same. The normal course of events is to install, configure, start, secure, and monitor your servers. Basic tasks that apply to all servers include using networking tools (particularly SSH tools) to log in, copy files, or execute remote commands.

Because an administrator can't be logged in watching servers all the time, tools for gathering data and reviewing the log data later are very important when administering Linux servers. The rsyslog facility can be used for local and remote logging. The sar facility gathers live data or plays back data gathered earlier at 10-minute intervals. To watch disk space, you can run df and du commands.

The skills described in this chapter are designed to help you build a foundation to do enterprise-quality system administration in the future. Although these skills are useful, to manage many Linux systems at the same time, you need to extend your skills by using automating deployment and monitoring tools such as Puppet and Nagios.

Although it is easy to set up networking to reach your servers in simple, default cases, more complex network configuration requires a knowledge of networking configuration files and related tools. The next chapter describes how to set up and administer networking in Linux.

Exercises

The exercises in this section cover some of the basic tools for connecting to and watching over your Linux servers. As usual, you can accomplish the tasks here in several ways. So don't worry if you don't go about the exercises in the same way as shown in the answers, as long as you get the same results. If you are stuck, solutions to the tasks are shown in Appendix B.

Some of the exercises assume you have a second Linux system available that you can log in to and try different commands. On that second system, you need to make sure that the sshd service is running, that the firewall is open, and that ssh is allowed for the user account you are trying to log in to (root is often blocked by sshd).

If you have only one Linux system, you can create an additional user account and simply simulate communications with another system by connecting to the name localhost instead. For example:

```
# useradd joe
# passwd joe
# ssh joe@localhost
```

1. Using the ssh command, log in to another computer (or the local computer) using any account you have access to. Enter the password when prompted.

2. Using remote execution with the ssh command, display the contents of a remote /etc/system-release file and have its contents displayed on the local system.

3. Use the ssh command to use X11 forwarding to display a gedit window on your local system; then save a file in the remote user's home directory.

4. Recursively copy all the files from the /usr/share/selinux directory on a remote system to the /tmp directory on your local system in such a way that all the modification times on the files are updated to the time on the local system when they are copied.

5. Recursively copy all the files from the /usr/share/logwatch directory on a remote system to the /tmp directory on your local system in such a way that all the modification times on the files from the remote system are maintained on the local system.

6. Create a public/private key pair to use for SSH communications (no passphrase on the key), copy the public key file to a remote user's account with `ssh-copy-id`, and use key-based authentication to log in to that user account without having to enter a password.

7. Create an entry in `/etc/rsyslog.conf` that stores all authentication messages (`authpriv`) info level and higher into a file named `/var/log/myauth`. From one terminal, watch the file as data comes into it, and in another terminal, try to ssh into your local machine as any valid user, with a bad password.

8. Use the `du` command to determine the largest directory structures under `/usr/share`, sort them from largest to smallest, and list the top ten of those directories in terms of size.

9. Use the `df` command to show the space that is used and available from all the filesystems currently attached to the local system, but exclude any `tmpfs` or `devtmpfs` filesystems.

10. Find any files in the `/usr` directory that are more than 10MB in size.

Administering Networking

C onnecting a single desktop system or laptop to a network, particularly one that connects to the Internet, has become so easy that I felt I could put off a full chapter on Linux networking until now. If you are trying to connect your Fedora, RHEL, Ubuntu, or other Linux desktop system to the Internet, here's what you can try, given an available wired or wireless network interface:

- **Wired network**—If your home or office has a wired Ethernet port that provides a path to the Internet and your computer has an Ethernet port, use an Ethernet cable to connect the two ports. After you turn on your computer, boot up Linux and log in. Clicking the NetworkManager icon on the desktop should show you that you are connected to the Internet or allow you to connect with a single click.

- **Wireless network**—For a wireless computer running Linux, log in and click the NetworkManager icon on the desktop. From the list of wireless networks that appear, select the one you want and, when prompted, enter the password required. Each time you log in from that computer from the same location, it automatically connects to that wireless network.

If either of those types of network connections works for you, and you are not otherwise curious about how networking works in Linux, that may be all you need to know. However, what if your Linux system doesn't automatically connect to the Internet? What if you want to configure your desktop to talk to a private network at work (VPN)? What if you want to lock down network settings on your server or configure your Linux system to work as a router?

In this chapter, topics related to networking are divided into networks for desktops, servers, and enterprise computing. The general approach to configuring networking in these three types of Linux systems is as follows:

- **Desktop/laptop networking**—On desktop systems, NetworkManager runs by default to manage network interfaces. With NetworkManager, you can automatically accept address and server information you need to connect to the Internet. However, you can also set address information manually. You can configure such things as proxy servers or virtual private network connections to allow your desktop to work from behind an organization's firewall or to connect through a firewall, respectively.

- **Server networking**—Although NetworkManager is an excellent service for desktop and laptop network configuration, until recently it did not work as well on servers. In Red Hat Enterprise Linux 7 and recent Fedora releases, however, features that are useful for configuring servers, such as Ethernet channel bonding and configuring aliases, can now be done in NetworkManager.

- **Enterprise networking**—Configuring networking in a large enterprise can fill several volumes itself. However, to give you a head start using Linux in an enterprise environment, I discuss basic networking technologies, such as DHCP and DNS, which make it possible for desktop systems to connect to the Internet automatically.

Configuring Networking for Desktops

Whether you connect to the Internet from Linux, Windows, a smartphone, or any other kind of network-enabled device, certain things must be in place for that connection to work. The computer must have a network interface (wired or wireless), an IP address, an assigned DNS server, and a route to the Internet (identified by a gateway device).

Before I discuss how to change your networking configuration in Linux, let's look at the general activities that occur when Linux is set to automatically connect to the Internet with NetworkManager:

- **Activate network interfaces**—NetworkManager looks to see what network interfaces (wired or wireless) are set to start. By default, external interfaces are set to start automatically using DHCP.

- **Request DHCP service**—The Linux system acts as a DHCP client to send out a request for DHCP service on each enabled interface. It uses the MAC address of the network interface to identify itself in the request.

- **Get response from DHCP server**—A DHCP server, possibly running on the DSL modem, cable modem, or other device providing a route to the Internet from your location, responds to the DHCP request. It can provide lots of different types of information to the DHCP client. That information probably contains at least the following:

    - **IP address**—The DHCP server typically has a range of Internet Protocol (IP) addresses it can hand out to any system on the network that requests an address. In more secure environments, or one in which you want to be sure that specific machines get specific addresses, the DHCP server provides a specific IP address to requests from specific MAC addresses. (MAC addresses are made to be unique among all network interface cards and are assigned by the manufacturer of each card.)

- **Subnet mask**—When the DHCP client is assigned an IP address, the accompanying subnet mask tells that client which part of the IP address identifies the subnetwork and which identifies the host. For example, an IP address of 192.168.0.100 and subnet mask of 255.255.255.0 tells the client that the network is 192.168.0 and the host part is 100.

- **Lease time**—When an IP address is dynamically allocated to the DHCP client (Linux system), that client is assigned a lease time. The client doesn't own that address, but must lease it again when the time expires and request it again when the network interface restarts. Usually, the DHCP server remembers the client and assigns the same address when the system starts up again or asks to renew the lease. The default lease time is 86,400 seconds (24 hours).

- **Domain name server**—Because computers like to think in numbers (such as IP addresses like 192.168.0.100) and people tend to think in names (such as the hostname www.example.com), computers need a way to translate hostnames into IP addresses and sometimes the opposite as well. The domain name system (DNS) was designed to handle that problem by providing a hierarchy of servers to do name-to-address mapping on the Internet. The location of one or more DNS servers (usually two or three) is usually assigned to the DHCP client from the DHCP host.

- **Default gateway**—Although the Internet has one unique namespace, it is actually organized as a series of interconnected subnetworks. In order for a network request to leave your local network, it must know what node on your network provides a route to addresses outside your local network. The DHCP server usually provides the "default gateway" IP address. By having network interfaces on both your subnetwork and the next network on the way to the ultimate destination of your communication, a gateway can route your packets to their destination.

- **Other information**—A DHCP server can be configured to provide all kinds of information to help the DHCP client. For example, it can provide the location of an NTP server (to sync time between clients), font server (to get fonts for your X display), IRC server (for online chats), or print server (to designate available printers).

- **Update local network settings**—After the settings are received from the DHCP server, they are implemented as appropriate on the local Linux system. For example, the IP address is set on the network interface, the DNS server entries are added to the local /etc/resolv.conf file (by NetworkManager), and the lease time is stored by the local system, so it knows when to request that the lease be renewed.

14

All the steps just described typically happen without your having to do anything but turn on your Linux system and log in. Suppose you want to be able to verify your network interfaces or change some of those settings. You can do that using tools described in the next sections.

Checking your network interfaces

There are both graphical and command-line tools for viewing information about your network interfaces in Linux. From the desktop, NetworkManager tools are a good place to start.

Checking your network from NetworkManager

The easiest way to check the basic setting for a network interface started by NetworkManager is to open the NetworkManager icon on your desktop. Figure 14.1 shows an example of the NetworkManager icon in the top panel of a GNOME 3 desktop in Fedora, along with the window that appears when you open the icon.

FIGURE 14.1

Checking network interfaces with NetworkManager.

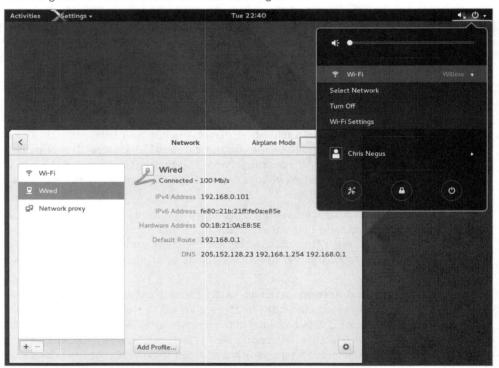

As you can see from Figure 14.1, the wired network connection is on. The network interface card has a Media Access Control (MAC) address of 00:1B:21:0A:E8:5E. The interface was assigned an IP address of 192.168.0.101 and a subnet mask of 255.255.255.0.

Any packet not destined for the local network is sent to the router located at address 192.168.0.1 (although other routes can be defined as needed). Three DNS servers are available (205.152.128.23, 192.168.1.254, and 192.168.0.1), so if one is not available, requests for DNS service can be directed to the address of the next DNS server in the list.

To see more about how your Linux system is configured, click the Add Profile button in the NetworkManager window. Figure 14.2 shows an example of the window that appears.

FIGURE 14.2

Viewing network settings with NetworkManager.

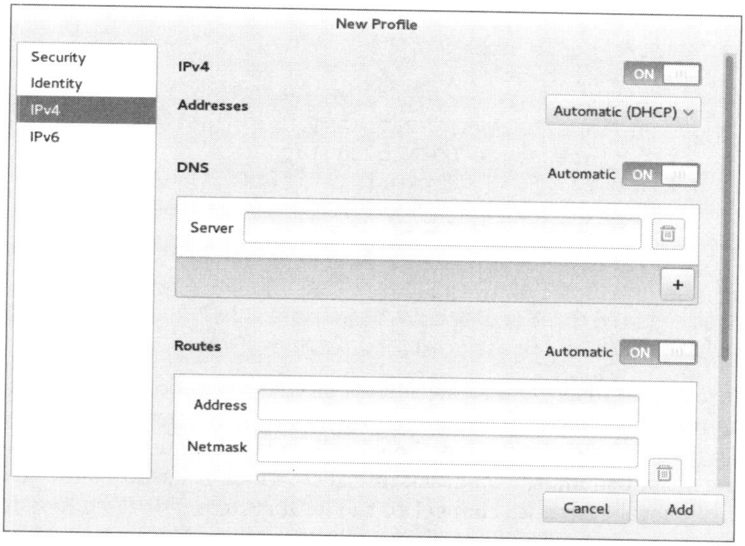

Figure 14.2 shows the IPv4 Settings tab, because that tab contains information you are most likely to want to change. The Automatic (DHCP) setting is what tells this interface to connect to DHCP at startup so you might want to change that to manually set IPv4 information. The IPv6 tab sets how connections to IPv6 networks are made from this Interface (also Automatic, by default). Later in this chapter, you learn how to manually configure IPv4 network interfaces.

The Security tab lets you set up secure connections to remote systems using 802.1x specifications from the IEEE. By default, this feature is off, but you can enable it and then identify remote hosts that you want to connect to using secure protocols. The last tab on the window is Identity. That tab lets you select the MAC address of the network interface card (NIC) you are interested in and set an aliased address for that interface.

Checking your network from the command line

To get more detailed information about your network interfaces, try running some commands. There are commands that can show you information about your network interfaces, routes, hosts, and traffic on the network.

Viewing network interfaces

To see information about each network interface on your local Linux system, type the following:

```
# ip addr show
1: lo: <LOOPBACK,UP,LOWER_UP> mtu 16436 qdisc noqueue state UNKNOWN
   link/loopback 00:00:00:00:00:00 brd 00:00:00:00:00:00
   inet 127.0.0.1/8 scope host lo
   inet6 ::1/128 scope host
      valid_lft forever preferred_lft forever
2: eth0: <NO-CARRIER,BROADCAST,MULTICAST,UP> mtu 1500
      qdisc pfifo_fast state DOWN qlen 1000
   link/ether f0:de:f1:28:46:d9 brd ff:ff:ff:ff:ff:ff
3: wlan0: <BROADCAST,MULTICAST,UP,LOWER_UP> mtu 1500
      qdisc mq state UP qlen 1000
   link/ether 00:24:d7:69:5b:2c brd ff:ff:ff:ff:ff:ff
   inet 192.168.0.105/24 brd 192.168.0.255 scope global wlan0
   inet6 fe80::224:d7ff:fe69:5b2c/64 scope link
      valid_lft forever preferred_lft forever
```

The ip addr show output displays information about your network interfaces, in this case from a laptop running RHEL 6. The names of the network interfaces are different in Fedora and RHEL 6 (more on that later), but should otherwise be similar. The lo entry in the first line of the output shows the loopback interface, which is used to allow network commands run on the local system to connect to the local system. The IP address for localhost is 127.0.0.1/8 (the /8 is CIDR notation, indicating that 127.0 is the network number and 0.1 is the host number).

In this case, the wired Ethernet interface (eth0) is down (no cable), but the wireless interface is up (wlan). The MAC address on the wireless interface (wlan0) is 00:24:d7:69:5b:2c and the Internet (IPv4) address is 192.168.0.105. An IPv6 address is also enabled.

In Fedora and RHEL 7, instead of assigning network interface names such as eth0 and wlan0, interfaces are named by their locations on the computer's bus. For example, the first port on the network card seated in the third PCI bus for a Fedora system is named p3p1. The first embedded Ethernet port would be em1. Wireless interfaces sometimes appear using the name of the wireless network as the device name.

Another popular command for seeing network interface information is the `ifconfig` command. By default, `ifconfig` shows similar information to that of `ip addr`, but `ifconfig` also shows the number of packets received (RX) and transmitted (TX), as well as the amount of data and any errors or dropped packets:

```
# ifconfig wlan0
wlan0 Link encap:Ethernet  HWaddr 00:24:D7:69:5B:2C
       inet addr:192.168.0.105 Bcast:192.168.0.255 Mask:255.255.255.0
       inet6 addr: fe80::224:d7ff:fe69:5b2c/64 Scope:Link
       UP BROADCAST RUNNING MULTICAST  MTU:1500  Metric:1
       RX packets:22482 errors:0 dropped:0 overruns:0 frame:0
          TX packets:9699 errors:0 dropped:0 overruns:0 carrier:0
          collisions:0 txqueuelen:1000
          RX bytes:9456897 (9.0 MiB)  TX bytes:1232234 (1.1 MiB)
```

Checking connectivity to remote systems

To make sure you can reach systems that are available on the network, you can use the `ping` command. As long as the computer responds to `ping` requests (not all do), you can use `ping` to send packets to that system in a way that asks them to respond. Here is an example:

```
$ ping host1
PING host1 (192.168.0.15 ) 56(84) bytes of data.
64 bytes from host1 (192.168.0.15 ): icmp_seq=1 ttl=64 time=0.062 ms
64 bytes from host1 (192.168.0.15 ): icmp_seq=2 ttl=64 time=0.044 ms
^C
--- host1 ping statistics ---
2 packets transmitted, 2 received, 0% packet loss, time 1822ms
rtt min/avg/max/mdev = 0.044/0.053/0.062/0.009 ms
```

The `ping` command shown here continuously pings the host named `host1`. After a few pings, press Ctrl+C to end the pings, and the last few lines show you how many of the `ping` requests succeeded.

You could have used the IP address (192.168.0.15, in this case) to see that you could reach the system. However, using the hostname gives you the additional advantage of knowing that your name-to-IP-address translation (being done by your DNS server or local hosts file) is working properly as well. In this case, however, host1 appeared in the local `/etc/hosts` file.

Checking routing information

Routing is the next thing you can check with respect to your network interfaces. The following shows how to use the `route` command to do that:

```
# route
Kernel IP routing table
Destination    Gateway        Genmask          Flags Metric Ref Use Iface
default        192.168.0.1    0.0.0.0          UG    0      0     0 p4p1
192.168.0.0    *              255.255.255.0    U     1      0     0 p4p1
```

The output from the kernel routing table is from a Fedora system with a single network interface card. The network interface card is on PCI slot 4, port 1 (p4p1). Any packets destined for the 192.168.0 network use the p4p1 NIC. Packets destined for any other location are forwarded to the gateway system at 192.168.0.1. That system represents my router to the Internet. Here's a more complex routing table:

```
# route
Kernel IP routing table
Destination     Gateway       Genmask         Flags Metric Ref Use Iface
vpn.example.    192.168.0.1 255.255.255.255 UGH   0      0     0 wlan0
192.168.0.0     *             255.255.255.0   U     2      0     0 wlan0
10.99.8.0       *             255.255.255.0   U     0      0     0 tun0
172.1.0.0       *             255.255.0.0     U     0      0     0 tun0
10.0.0.0        *             255.0.0.0       U     0      0     0 tun0
192.168.99.0    192.168.0.2 255.255.255.0   UG    0      0     0 wlan0
default         192.168.0.1 0.0.0.0         UG    0      0     0 wlan0
```

In the route example just shown, there is a wireless interface (wlan0), as well as an interface representing a virtual private network (VPN) tunnel. A VPN provides a way to have encrypted, private communications between a client and a remote network over an insecure network (such as the Internet). Here, the tunnel goes from the local system over the wlan0 interface to a host named vpn.example.com (some of the name is truncated).

All communication to 192.168.0.0/24 network still goes directly over the wireless LAN. However, packets destined for the 10.99.8.0/24, 172.1.0.0/16, and 10.0.0.0/8 networks are routed directly to vpn-a.example.com for communication with hosts on the other side of the VPN connection over the tunneled interface (tun0).

A special route to the 192.168.99.0/24 network is accessible via the node (presumably a router) at IP address 192.168.0.2. All other packets go to the default route via the address 192.168.0.1. As for the flags shown in the output, a U says the route is up, a G identifies the interface as a gateway, and an H says the target is a host (as is the case with the VPN connection).

So far, I have shown you the routes to leave the local system. If you want to follow the entire route to a host from beginning to end, you can use the traceroute command. For example, to trace the route a packet takes from your local system to the google.com site, type the following traceroute command:

```
# traceroute google.com
traceroute to google.com (74.125.235.136), 30 hops max, 60 byte pkts
...
 7   rrcs-70-62-95-197.midsouth.biz.rr.com (70.62.95.197)  ...
 8   ge-2-1-0.rlghncpop-rtr1.southeast.rr.com (24.93.73.62)  ...
 9   ae-3-0.cr0.dca10.tbone.rr.com (66.109.6.80) ...
10   107.14.19.133 (107.14.19.133)   13.662 ms  ...
11   74.125.49.181 (74.125.49.181)   13.912 ms ...
12   209.85.252.80 (209.85.252.80)   61.265 ms ...
13   66.249.95.149 (66.249.95.149)   18.308 ms ...
```

```
14   66.249.94.22 (66.249.94.22)  18.344 ms ...
15   72.14.239.83 (72.14.239.83)  85.342 ms ...
16   64.233.174.177 (64.233.174.177)  167.827 ms ...
17   209.85.255.35 (209.85.255.35)  169.995 ms ...
18   209.85.241.129 (209.85.241.129)  170.322 ms ...
19   nrt19s11-in-f8.1e100.net (74.125.235.136)  169.360 ms ...
```

I truncated some of the output to drop off some of the initial routes and the amount of time (in milliseconds) that the packets were taking to traverse each route. Using `traceroute`, you can see where the bottlenecks are along the way if your network communication is stalling.

Viewing the host and domain names

To see the hostname assigned to the local system, type `hostname`. To just see the domain portion of that name, use the `dnsdomainname` command.

```
# hostname
spike.example.com
# dnsdomainname
example.com
```

Configuring network interfaces

If you don't want to have your network interfaces assigned automatically from a DHCP server (or if there is no DHCP server), you can configure network interfaces manually. This can include assigning IP addresses, the locations of DNS servers and gateway machines, and routes. This basic information can be set up using NetworkManager.

Setting IP addresses manually

To change the network configuration for your wired network interface through NetworkManager, do the following:

1. Select the Settings icon from the upper-right corner of the desktop, and open the Network icon.

2. Select Wired, and click the settings button (small gear icon) next to the interface you want to change.

3. Choose IPv4, and change the box that says Automatic (DHCP) to Manual.

4. Fill in the following information (only Address and Netmask are required):

   - **Address**—The IP address you want to assign to your local network interface. For example, 192.168.0.40.

   - **Netmask**—The subnetwork mask that defines which part of the IP address represents the network and which the host. For example, a netmask of 255.255.255.0 would identify the network portion of the previous address as 192.168.0 and the host portion as 40.

14

- **Gateway**—The IP address of the computer or device on the network that acts as the default route. The default route will route packets from the local network to any address that is not available on the local network or via some other custom route.

- **DNS servers**—Fill in the IP addresses for the systems providing DNS service to your computer. Click the plus button to add a second DNS server (it's common to have two or three, in case the first is not available). Click the Automatic OFF button to override any DNS server information you might get automatically via DHCP.

5. Click the Apply button. The new information is saved, and the network is restarted using the new information. Figure 14.3 shows an example of those network settings.

FIGURE 14.3

Changing network settings with NetworkManager.

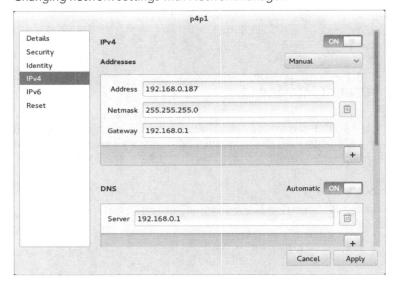

Setting IP address aliases

You can attach multiple IP addresses to a single network interface. In the same NetworkManager screen, this is done by simply clicking the plus sign (+) at the bottom of the Addresses box and adding the new IP address information. Here are a few things you should know about adding address aliases:

- A Netmask is required for each address, but a gateway is not required.

- The Apply button stays grayed out until you include valid information in the fields.

- The new address does not have to be on the same subnetwork as the original address, although it is listening for traffic on the same physical network.

After adding the address 192.168.99.1 to my wired interface, running `ip addr show p4p1` displays the following indication of the two IP addresses on the interface:

```
2: p4p1: <BROADCAST,MULTICAST,UP,LOWER_UP> mtu 1500
      qdisc pfifo_fast state UP group default qlen 1000
   link/ether 00:1b:21:0a:e8:5e brd ff:ff:ff:ff:ff:ff
   inet 192.168.0.187/24 brd 192.168.0.255 scope global p4p1
      valid_lft forever preferred_lft forever
   inet 192.168.99.1/24 brd 192.168.99.255 scope global p4p1
      valid_lft forever preferred_lft forever
```

For information on setting up aliases directly in configuration files, refer to the section "Setting alias network interfaces" later in this chapter.

Setting routes

When you request a connection to an IP address, your system looks through your routing table to determine the path on which to connect to that address. Information is sent in the form of packets. Packets are routed as follows:

- A packet intended for the local system is sent to the `lo` interface.
- A packet intended for a system on your local network is directed through your NIC directly to the intended recipient system's NIC.
- A packet intended for any other system is sent to the gateway (router) that directs the packet on to its intended address on the Internet.

Of course, what I have described here is one of the simplest cases. You may, in fact, have multiple NICs with multiple interfaces to different networks. You may also have multiple routers on your local network that provide routes to particular private networks.

For example, suppose you have a router (or other system acting as a router) on your local network; you can add a custom route to that router via NetworkManager. Using the NetworkManager example shown previously, scroll down the page to view the Routes box. Then add the following information:

- **Address**—The network address of the subnetwork you route to. For example, if the router (gateway) will provide you access to all systems on the 192.168.100 network, add the address 192.168.100.0.
- **Netmask**—Add the netmask needed to identify the subnetwork. For example, if the router provides access to the Class C address 192.168.100, you could use the netmask 255.255.255.0.
- **Gateway**—Add the IP address for the router (gateway) that provides access to the new route. For example, if the router has an IP address on your 192.168.0 network of 192.168.0.199, add that address in this field.

14

Click Apply to apply the new routing information. You may have to restart the interface for this to take effect (for example, ifup p4p1). Type route -n to make sure the new routing information has been applied.

```
# route -n
Kernel IP routing table
Destination     Gateway        Genmask          Flags Metric Ref Use Iface
0.0.0.0         192.168.0.1    0.0.0.0          UG    1024   0     0 p4p1
192.168.0.0     0.0.0.0        255.255.255.0    U     0      0     0 p4p1
192.168.99.0    0.0.0.0        255.255.255.0    U     0      0     0 p4p1
192.168.100.0   192.168.0.199  255.255.255.0    UG    1      0     0 p4p1
```

In the example just shown, the default gateway is 192.168.0.1. However, any packets destined for the 192.168.100 network are routed through the gateway host at IP address 192.168.0.199. Presumably, that host has a network interface that faces the 192.168.100 network and is set up to allow other hosts to route through it to that network.

See the section "Setting custom routes" later in this chapter for information on how to set routes directly in configuration files.

Configuring a network proxy connection

If your desktop system is running behind a corporate firewall, you might not have direct access to the Internet. Instead, you might have to reach the Internet via a proxy server. Instead of allowing you full access to the Internet, a proxy server lets you make requests only for certain services outside the local network. The proxy server then passes those requests on to the Internet or other network.

Proxy servers typically provide access to web servers (http:// and https://) and FTP servers (ftp://). However, a proxy server that supports SOCKS can provide a proxy service for different protocols outside the local network. (SOCKS is a network protocol made to allow client computers to access the Internet through a firewall.) You can identify a proxy server in NetworkManager and have communications for selected protocols go through that server (select Network proxy in the Network Settings window).

Instead of identifying a proxy server to your network interfaces (via NetworkManager), you can configure your browser to use a proxy server directly by changing your Firefox preferences to use a proxy server. Here's how to define a proxy server from the Firefox window:

1. From Firefox, select Edit Preferences. The Firefox Preferences window appears.

2. From the Firefox Preferences window, click the Advanced button.

3. Choose the Network tab, and choose the Settings button under the Connection heading. The Configure Proxies window appears.

4. You can try to auto-detect the proxy settings or, if you set the proxy in NetworkManager, you can choose to use system proxy settings. You can also select Manual Proxy Configuration, fill in the following information, and click OK.

- **HTTP Proxy**—The IP address of the computer providing the proxy service. This causes all requests for web pages (`http://` protocol) to be forwarded to the proxy server.

- **Port**—The port associated with the proxy service. By default, the port number is 3128, but it can differ.

- **Use this proxy server for all protocols**—Select this box to use the same proxy server and port associated with the HTTP proxy for all other service requests. This causes other proxy settings to be grayed out. (Instead of selecting this box, you can set those proxy services separately.)

- **No Proxy for**—By leaving localhost and the local IP address (127.0.0.1) in this box, any requests to the local system that would otherwise be directed to the proxy server go directly to the local system.

Figure 14.4 shows an example of the Configure Proxies window filled in to configure a connection to a proxy server located at IP address 10.0.100.254 for all protocols. After you click OK, all requests from the Firefox browser to locations outside the local system are directed to the proxy server, which forwards those requests on to the appropriate server.

FIGURE 14.4

Setting up Firefox to use a proxy server.

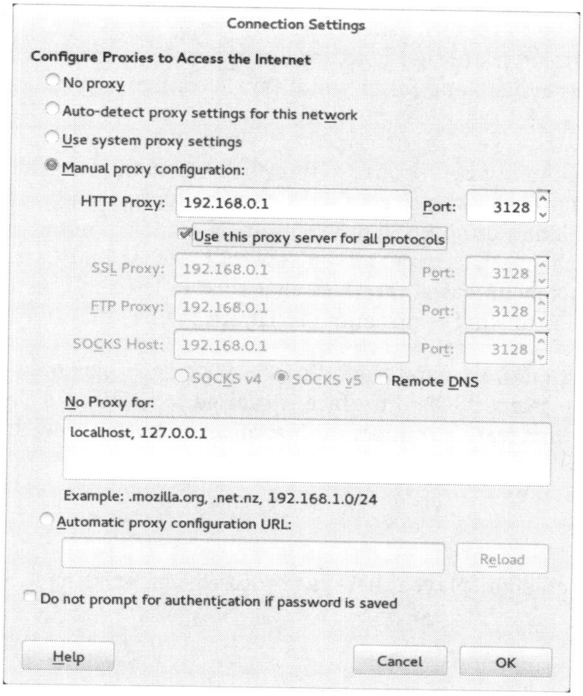

Configuring Networking from the Command Line

While NetworkManager does a great job of auto-detecting wired networks or presenting you with lists of wireless networks for your laptop to connect to, it has only recently added features for more complex networking configurations on servers. Therefore, sometimes you need to abandon the NetworkManager GUI and go directly to commands and configuration files to get the network features you want. These are some of the networking features in RHEL and Fedora described in the coming sections:

- **Basic configuration**—See how to use the nmtui or system-config-network commands to configure basic networking with a menu-based interface from a shell. These tools provide an intuitive interface for configuring networking on servers that have no graphical interface for running GUI-based tools.

- **Configuration files**—Understand configuration files associated with Linux networking and how to configure them directly.

- **Ethernet channel bonding**—Set up Ethernet channel bonding (multiple network cards listening on the same IP address).

- **Network configuration commands**—Use commands such as nmcli to configure networking from the shell.

Many servers don't have graphical interfaces available. So if you want to configure networking, you must be able to do so from the shell. One way to do that is to edit networking configuration files directly. Another is to use menu-based commands that let you press arrow and Tab keys to navigate and forms you fill in to configure your network interface.

Before NetworkManager existed, the system-config-network command launched a graphical interface that was the primary way to configure networking in earlier Fedora releases and Red Hat Enterprise Linux up to RHEL 6. The system-config-network command has been replaced by the nmtui command (or NetworkManager Text User Interface) in RHEL 7. It provides a menu-based interface that runs in the shell. As root, type **nmtui** to see a screen similar to what is presented in Figure 14.5.

Use arrow keys and the Tab key to move around the interface. With the item you want to select highlighted, press Enter to select it. The interface is limited to modifying the following kinds of information: Edit or Activate a connection (network interface cards) and Set system hostname (hostname and DNS configuration).

Editing a connection

From the NetworkManager TUI screen displayed, here is how to edit an existing connection.

FIGURE 14.5

Configuring networking with NetworkManager TUI.

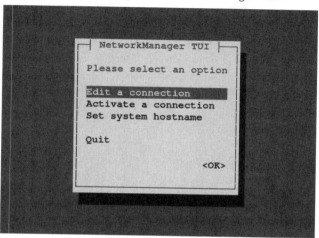

1. **Edit a connection**—With Edit a connection highlighted, press Enter. A list of network devices (usually wired or wireless Ethernet cards) is displayed, along with any wireless networks you have connected to in the past.

2. **Network devices**—Highlight one of the network devices (in my case, I chose a wired Ethernet interface enp0s25) and press Enter.

3. **IPv4 Configuration**—Move to the IPv4 Configuration show button, and press Enter. The Edit connection window that appears lets you change information relating to the selected network device.

4. **Change to Manual**—You can leave the Profile name and Device fields as they are. By default, Automatic is enabled. Automatic is what allows the network interface to come up automatically on the network if a DHCP service is available. To enter address and other information yourself, use the Tab key to highlight the Automatic field and press the spacebar; then use the arrow keys to highlight Manual, and press Enter.

5. **Addresses**—Now fill in the address information (IP address and netmask). For example, 192.168.0.150/24 (where 24 is the CIDR equivalent for the 255.255.255.0 netmask).

6. **Gateway**—Type in the IP address for the computer or router that is supplying the route to the Internet.

7. **DNS servers**—Type in the IP addresses of either one or two DNS servers, to tell the system where to go to translate hostnames you request into IP addresses.

8. **Search domains**—The Search domains entries are used when you request a host from an application without using a fully qualified domain name. For example, if you type `ping host1` with an `example.com` search path, the command would try to send ping packets to `host1.example.com`.

9. **Routing**—You can set custom routes by highlighting Edit in the Routing field and pressing Enter. Fill in the Destination/Prefix and Next Hop, and select OK to save the new custom route.

10. **Other selections**—Of the other selections on the screen, consider setting "Automatically connect" by highlighting that box and using the spacebar to add an X to the box. This ensures that the interface comes up automatically every time the system boots.

Figure 14.6 shows the screen after Manual has been selected and the address information has been filled in.

FIGURE 14.6

Set static IP addresses by selecting Manual from the Edit connections screen.

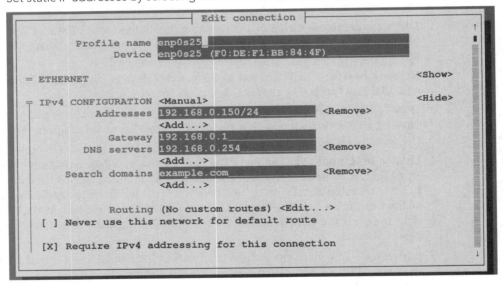

Tab to the OK button and press the spacebar. Then click Quit to exit.

Understanding networking configuration files

Whether you change your network setup using NetworkManager or `nmtui`, most of the same configuration files are updated. In Fedora and RHEL, network interfaces and custom routes are set in files in the `/etc/sysconfig/network-scripts` directory. Other network settings are stored in other files in the `/etc` directory.

Instead of using some of the tools just described, you can configure networking in Linux by directly editing configuration files. If you do edit these files directly, you should consider turning off the NetworkManager service and turning on the `network` service. The reason for doing this is that NetworkManager sometimes overwrites files you configure manually (from information gathered from DHCP or when using the NetworkManager GUI).

To turn NetworkManager off (immediately and permanently) on a RHEL 6 or older Fedora system, type the following as root (do this on a console because this procedure stops your networking if you are logged in over the network):

```
# service NetworkManager stop
# service network restart
# chkconfig NetworkManager off
# chkconfig network on
```

For RHEL 7 and newer Fedora systems that use the `systemctl` command to start, stop, enable, and disable services, you could type the following:

```
# systemctl stop NetworkManager.service
# systemctl disable NetworkManager.service
# systemctl restart network.service
# systemctl enable network.service
```

At this point, you can safely use the following sections to help you directly edit network configuration files. Find descriptions of these files in the `/usr/share/doc/initscripts*/sysconfig.txt` file.

Network interface files

Configuration files for each wired, wireless, ISDN, dialup, or other type of network interface are represented by files in the `/etc/sysconfig/network-scripts` directory that begin with `ifcfg-interface`. The *interface* is replaced by the name of the network interface.

In Red Hat Enterprise Linux 6 and older Fedora systems, network interfaces have names such as `eth0`, `eth1`, `eth2` (for each wired network interface), `wlan0` (for the first wireless interface), and `ppp0` (for the first dial-up point-to-point interface). In RHEL 6, the configuration file for the first Ethernet interface would be `ifcfg-eth0`. Here's an example of an `ifcfg-eth0` file for a wired DHCP connection:

```
DEVICE=eth0
HWADDR=F0:DE:F1:28:46:D9
TYPE=Ethernet
BOOTPROTO=dhcp
ONBOOT=yes
USERCTL=no
```

14

In this ifcfg-eth0 example, the first three lines set the device name, MAC address, and the type of interface to Ethernet. The BOOTPROTO variable is set to dhcp, which causes it to request address information from a DHCP server. With ONBOOT=yes, the interface starts automatically at system boot time. Another setting in the ifcfg-eth0 example keeps regular users from being able to start and stop the interface (USERCTL=no).

Here's what an ifcfg-eth1 file might look like for a wired Ethernet interface that uses static IP addresses:

```
DEVICE=eth1
HWADDR=00:1B:21:0A:E8:5E
TYPE=Ethernet
BOOTPROTO=none
ONBOOT=yes
USERCTL=no
IPADDR=192.168.0.140
NETMASK=255.255.255.0
GATEWAY=192.168.0.1
```

In this ifcfg-eth1 example, because this is setting address and other information statically, BOOTPROTO is set to none. Other differences are needed to set the address information that is normally gathered from a DHCP server. In this case, the IP address is set to 192.168.0.140, with a netmask of 255.255.255.0. The GATEWAY=192.168.0.1 identifies the address of the router to the Internet.

Here are a couple of other settings that might interest you:

- **PEERDNS**—Setting PEERDNS=no prevents DHCP from overwriting the /etc/resolv.conf file. This allows you to set which DNS servers your system uses without fear of that information being erased by data that is provided by the DHCP server.

- **DNS?**—If an ifcfg file is being managed by NetworkManager, it sets the address of DNS servers using DNS? entries. For example, DNS1=192.168.0.2 causes that IP address to be written to /etc/resolv.conf as the first DNS server being used on the system. You can have multiple DNS? entries (DNS2=, DNS3=, and so on).

After an ifcfg-* file is created, you can bring the interface up and down individually using the ifup and ifdown commands, instead of bringing all interfaces up or down together. For example, you can bring the localhost lo (ifcfg-lo) interface up and down using the following commands:

```
# ifdown lo
# ifconfig
# ifup lo
# ifconfig
```

The commands just shown turn off the loopback network interface (ifdown lo) and then let you see that it is not active (ifconfig). After that, you turn it back on again (ifup lo) and check again to see that it is on (ifconfig).

In addition to configuring the primary network interfaces, you can also create files in the /etc/sysconfig/network-scripts directory that can be used to set aliases (multiple IP addresses for the same interface), bonded interfaces (multiple NICs listening on the same address), and custom routes. Those are described later in this section.

Other networking files

In addition to the network interface files, there are other network configuration files that you can edit directly to configure Linux networking. Here are some of those files.

/etc/sysconfig/network file

System-wide settings associated with your local networking can be included in your /etc/sysconfig/network file. The system's hostname was commonly set in this file up to RHEL 6, but other settings can be added to this file as well. Here is an example of the contents of a /etc/sysconfig/network file:

```
GATEWAY=192.168.0.1
```

The previous example the default GATEWAY is set to 192.168.0.1. Different interfaces can use different GATEWAY addresses. For other settings that can appear in the network files, check the sysconfig.txt file in the /usr/share/doc/initscripts-* directory.

/etc/hostname file

In RHEL 7 and the latest Fedora releases, the system's hostname is stored in the /etc/hostname file. For example, if the file included the hostname host1.example.com, that hostname would be set each time the system booted up. You can check how the current hostname is set at any time by typing the hostname command.

/etc/hosts file

Before DNS was created, translating hostnames to IP addresses was done by passing around a single hosts file. While there were only a few dozen, and then a few hundred, hosts on the Internet, this approach worked pretty well. But as the Internet grew, the single hosts file became unscalable and DNS was invented.

The /etc/hosts file still exists on Linux systems. It can still be used to map IP addresses to hostnames. The /etc/hosts file is a way to set up names and addresses for a small local network or just create aliases, to make it easier to access systems you use all the time.

Here's an example of an /etc/hosts file:

```
127.0.0.1   localhost localhost.localdomain
::1         localhost localhost.localdomain
```

14

```
192.168.0.201  node1.example.com node1 joe
192.168.0.202  node2.example.com node2 sally
```

The first two lines (127.0.0.1 and ::1) set addresses for the local system. The IPv4 address for the local host is 127.0.0.1; the IPv6 address for the local host is ::1. There are also entries for two IP addresses. You could reach the first IP address (192.168.0.201) by the names node1.example.com, node1, or joe. For example, typing **ping joe** results in packets being sent to 192.168.0.201.

/etc/resolv.conf file

DNS servers and search domains are set in the /etc/resolv.conf file. If NetworkManager is enabled and running, you should not edit this file directly. Using DNS?= entries from ifcfg-* files, NetworkManager overwrites the /etc/resolv.conf file so you would lose any entries you add to that file. Here's an example of the /etc/resolv.conf file that was modified by NetworkManager.

```
# Generated by NetworkManager
nameserver 192.168.0.2
nameserver 192.168.0.3
```

Each name server entry identifies the IP address of a DNS server. The order is the order in which the DNS servers are checked. It's normal to have two or three name server entries, in case the first is not available. More than that and it can take too long for an unresolvable hostname to get checked for each server.

Another type of entry you can add to this file is a search entry. A search entry lets you indicate domains to be searched when a hostname is requested by its base name instead of its entire fully qualified domain name. You can have multiple search entries by identifying one or more domain names after the search keyword. For example:

```
search example.com example.org example.net
```

The search options are separated by spaces or tabs.

/etc/nsswitch.conf

Settings in the /etc/nsswitch.conf file determine that hostname resolution is done by first searching the local /etc/hosts file (files) and then DNS servers listed in the /etc/resolv.conf file (dns). This is how the hosts entry in the /etc/resolv.conf file appears in Red Hat Enterprise Linux:

```
hosts:        files dns
```

You can add other locations, such as Network Information Service (nis or nisplus) databases, for querying hostname to IP address resolution. You can also change the order in which the different services are queried. You can check that host-to-IP-address resolution is working properly using different commands.

If you want to check that your DNS servers are being queried properly, you can use the host or dig commands. For example:

```
$ host redhat.com
redhat.com has address 209.132.183.181
redhat.com mail is handled by 5 mx1.redhat.com.
redhat.com mail is handled by 10 mx2.redhat.com.
$ dig redhat.com
; <<>> DiG 9.9.6-RedHat-9.9.6-4.fc21 <<>> redhat.com
;; global options: +cmd
;; Got answer:
;; ->>HEADER<<- opcode: QUERY, status: NOERROR, id: 54399
;; flags: qr rd ra; QUERY: 1, ANSWER: 1, AUTHORITY: 0, ADDITIONAL: 0
;; QUESTION SECTION:
;redhat.com.                    IN      A
;; ANSWER SECTION:
redhat.com.             60      IN      A       209.132.183.181
;; Query time: 105 msec
;; SERVER: 8.8.128.23#53(8.8.128.23)
;; WHEN: Sun Apr 24 08:32:32 2016
;; MSG SIZE  rcvd: 44
```

By default, the host command produces simpler output for DNS queries. It shows the IP address for redhat.com and the names of the mail servers (MX records) that serve redhat.com. The dig command shows information similar to what appears in the files that hold DNS records. The QUESTION section of the output shows that the address section asked for the address of redhat.com and the ANSWER section showed the answer (209.132.183.181). You can also see the address of the DNS server that was queried.

The host and dig commands are only used to query DNS servers. They don't check the nsswitch.conf file to find other places to query, such as the local hosts file. For that, you would have to use the getent command. For example:

```
# getent hosts node1
192.168.0.201  node1
```

This getent example finds a host named node1 that was entered into my local /etc/hosts file. (The getent command can be used to query any information setup in the nsswitch.conf file. For example, typing getent passwd root shows the entry for the root user account in the local file, but can also query a remote LDAP database for user information if you have configured that feature, as described in Chapter 11, "Managing User Accounts.")

Setting alias network interfaces

Sometimes you might want your network interface card listening on multiple IP addresses. For example, if you were setting up a web server that was serving secure content (https) for multiple domains (example.com, example.org, and so on), each domain would

14

require a separate IP address (associated with a separate certificate). In that case, instead of adding multiple network interface cards to the computer, you could simply create multiple aliases on a single NIC.

To create an alias network interface in RHEL 6 and earlier Fedora releases, you just have to create another ifcfg- file. Following the example of an eth0 interface on a RHEL system, you could create an eth0:0 interface associated with the same network interface card. To do this, create a file in the /etc/sysconfig/network-scripts directory called ifcfg-eth0:0 that contains information such as the following:

```
DEVICE=eth0:0
ONPARENT=yes
IPADDR=192.168.0.141
NETMASK=255.255.255.0
```

The example code creates an alias for the network interface eth0 called eth0:0. Instead of ONBOOT, the ONPARENT entry says to bring up this interface if the parent (eth0) is started and listen on address 192.168.0.141. You can bring up that interface by typing ifup eth0:0. You can then check that the interface came up using the ip command:

```
$ ip addr show eth0
2: eth0: <BROADCAST,MULTICAST,UP,LOWER_UP> mtu 1500 qdisc
        pfifo_fast state UP qlen 1000
  link/ether f0:de:f1:28:46:d9 brd ff:ff:ff:ff:ff:ff
  inet 192.168.0.140/24 brd 192.168.0.255 scope global eth0
inet 192.168.0.141/24 brd 192.168.0.255 scope global secondary eth0:0
inet6 fe80::f2de:f1ff:fe28:46d9/64 scope link
    valid_lft forever preferred_lft forever
```

You can see that the network interface card represented by eth0 is listening on two addresses: 192.168.0.140 (eth0) and 192.168.0.141 (eth0:0). So this system will respond to packets destined for either of those two addresses. You could add more IP addresses to that interface by creating more ifcfg-eth0:? files (ifcfg-eth0:1, ifcfg-eth0:2, and so on).

In RHEL 7 and Fedora 21, you can create aliases directly in the primary ifcfg file for an alias. For example, a primary (192.168.0.187) and alias (192.168.99.1) address for a NIC interface named p4p1 might be represented by the following address settings in the ifcfg-p4p1 file:

```
IPADDR=192.168.0.187
PREFIX=24
IPADDR1=192.168.99.1
PREFIX1=24
```

Setting up Ethernet channel bonding

Ethernet channel bonding allows you to have more than one network interface card on a computer associated with a single IP address. There are several reasons you might want to do this:

- **High availability**—Multiple NICs on the same IP address can ensure that if one subnet goes down or one NIC breaks, the address can still be reached on a NIC connected to another subnet.

- **Performance**—If there is too much network traffic to be handled by one NIC, you can spread that traffic across multiple NICs.

In Red Hat Enterprise Linux and Fedora on a computer with multiple NICs, you can set up Ethernet channel bonding by creating a few ifcfg files and loading the necessary module. You can start with one bonding file (for example, ifcfg-bond0), and then point multiple ifcfg-eth? files at that bond interface. Then you can load the bond module.

Depending on the type of bonding you want to do, you can set your bonding interface to different modes. Using the BONDING_OPTS variable, you define the mode and other bonding options (all of which are passed to the bonding module). You can read about the bonding module by typing modinfo bonding or by installing the kernel-docs package and reading the bonding.txt file from the /usr/share/doc/kernel-doc*/ Documentation/networking/directory.

Here is an example of the file that defines a bonded interface. The file in this example is /etc/sysconfig/network-scripts/ifcfg-bond0:

```
DEVICE=bond0
ONBOOT=yes
IPADDR=192.168.0.50
NETMASK=255.255.255.0
BOOTPROTO=none
BONDING_OPTS="mode=active-backup"
```

The bond0 interface in this example uses the IP address 192.168.0.50. It starts up on boot. The BONDING_OPTS sets the bonding mode to active-backup. That means that only one NIC is active at a time and the next NIC only takes over when the previous one fails (failover). No network interface card is associated with the bond0 interface yet. For that, you must create separate ifcfg file options. For example, create an /etc/sysconfig/network-scripts/ifcfg-eth0 that looks like the following (then create eth1, eth2, eth3, and so on for each NIC you want to use in the bonding interface):

```
DEVICE=eth0
MASTER=bond0
SLAVE=yes
BOOTPROTO=none
ONBOOT=yes
```

With the eth0 interface used as part of the bond0 interface, there is no IP address assigned. That's because the eth0 interface uses the IP address from the bond0 interface by defining itself as a slave (SLAVE=yes) to bond0 (MASTER=bond0).

14

The last thing you want to do is make sure the bond0 interface is set to use the bonding module. To do that, create a /etc/modprobe.d/bonding.conf file that contains the following entry:

```
alias bond0 bonding
```

Because all the interfaces are set to ONBOOT=yes, the bond0 interface starts and all the eth? interfaces are available as they are needed.

Setting custom routes

On a simple network configuration, communications that are destined for the local network are directed to the appropriate interface on your LAN, while communications for hosts outside your LAN go to a default gateway to be sent on to remote hosts. As an alternative, you can set custom routes to provide alternative paths to specific networks.

To set a custom route in Fedora and RHEL, you create a configuration file in the /etc/sysconfig/network-scripts directory. In that route, you define:

- *GATEWAY?*—The IP address of the node on the local network that provides the route to the subnetwork represented by the static route.
- *ADDRESS?*—The IP address representing the network that can be reached by the static route.
- *NETMASK?*—The netmask that determines which part of the ADDRESS? represents the network and which represents the hosts that can be reached on that network.

The name of each custom route file is *route-interface*. So, for example, a custom route that can be reached through your eth0 interface would be named route-eth0. You could have multiple custom routes in that file, with each route entry replacing the *?* with the interface number. For example:

```
ADDRESS0=192.168.99.0
NETMASK0=255.255.255.0
GATEWAY0=192.168.0.5
```

In this example, any packet destined for a host on the 192.168.99 network would be sent through the local eth0 interface and directed to the gateway node at 192.168.0.5. Presumably, that node would provide a route to another network containing hosts in the 192.168.99 address range. This route would take effect when the eth0 network interface was restarted.

To check that the route is working after you restart the network interface, you could type the following:

```
# route
Kernel IP routing table
Destination  Gateway      Genmask            Flags Metric Ref Use Iface
```

```
default        192.168.0.1 0.0.0.0        UG    0    0    0 eth0
192.168.0.0    *           255.255.255.0  U     1    0    0 eth0
192.168.99.0 192.168.0.5 255.255.255.0    UG    0    0    0 eth0
```

The output from the `route -n` command shows that the default route (anything not destined for the local network 192.168.0 or the 192.168.99 network) is via the 192.168.0.1 address. Any packets destined for the 192.168.99 network are directed through the address 192.168.0.5.

If you wanted to add more custom routes, you could add them to this same `route-eth0` file. The next set of information would be named ADDRESS1, NETMASK1, GATEWAY1, and so on.

Configuring Networking in the Enterprise

So far, the network configuration described in this chapter has centered on setting up single systems to connect to a network. Features available in Linux can go well beyond that by providing software that supports the actual network infrastructure needed by host computers to communicate.

This section introduces you to a few of the network infrastructure types of services available in Linux. Full implementation of these features is beyond the scope of this book, but know that if you find yourself needing to manage network infrastructure features, this section will give you a sense of how those features are implemented in Linux.

Configuring Linux as a router

If you have more than one network interface on a computer (typically two or more NICs), you can configure Linux as a router. To make this happen, all that is needed is a change to one kernel parameter that allows packet forwarding. To turn on the `ip_forward` parameter immediately and temporarily, type the following as root:

```
# cat /proc/sys/net/ipv4/ip_forward
0
# echo 1 > /proc/sys/net/ipv4/ip_forward
# cat /proc/sys/net/ipv4/ip_forward
1
```

Packet forwarding (routing) is disabled by default, with the value of ip_forward set to 0. By setting it to 1, packet forwarding is immediately enabled. To make this change permanent, you must add that value to the `/etc/sysctl.conf` file, so it appears as follows:

```
net.ipv4.ip_forward = 1
```

With that file modified as shown, each time the system reboots, the value for ip_for-ward is reset to 1. (Notice that net.ipv4.ip_forward reflects the actual location of the `ip_forward` file, minus the `/proc/sys` and with dots replacing slashes. You can change any kernel parameters set in the `/proc/sys` directory structure in this way.)

When a Linux system is used as a router, it is often used as a firewall between a private network and a public network, such as the Internet, as well. If that is the case, you might also want to use that same system as a firewall that does network address translation (NAT) and provides DHCP service, so the systems on the private network can route through the Linux system using private IP addresses. (See Chapter 25, "Securing Linux on a Network," for information on working with Linux firewall rules using the `iptables` facility.)

Configuring Linux as a DHCP server

Not only can a Linux system use a DHCP server to get its IP address and other information, it can also be configured to act as a DHCP server itself. In its most basic form, a DHCP server can hand out IP addresses from a pool of addresses to any system that requests it. Usually, however, the DHCP server also distributes the locations of DNS servers and the default gateway.

Configuring a DHCP server is not something that should be done without some thought. Don't add a DHCP server on a network that is not under your control and that already has a working DHCP server. Many clients are set up to get address information from any DHCP server that will hand it out.

DHCP service is provided by the `dhcp` package in Fedora and RHEL. The service is named dhcpd in RHEL 6 and `dhcpd.service` in RHEL 7 and the latest Fedora release. The primary configuration file is `/etc/dhcp/dhcpd.conf` for IPv4 networks (there is a `dhcpd6.conf` file in the same directory to provide DHCP service for IPv6 networks). By default, the dhcpd daemon listens on UDP port 67, so remember to keep that port open on your firewall.

To configure a DHCP server, you could copy the `dhcpd.conf.sample` file from the `/usr/share/doc/dhcp-4*` directory and replace the `/etc/dhcp/dhcpd.conf` file. Then modify it as you like. Before using that file, you want to change the domain-name options to reflect your domain and IP address ranges to suit those you are using. The comments in the file will help you do this.

When you install some virtualization and cloud services on a Linux system, by default a DHCP server is set up for you within that system. For example, when you install KVM and start the `libvirtd` service in RHEL or Fedora, it automatically configures a default private network in the 192.168.122.0/24 address range. When you launch virtual machines, they are given IP addresses in that range. When you install and start the Docker service on those Linux distributions, it likewise sets up a private network and hands out IP addresses to Docker containers launched on that system.

Configuring Linux as a DNS server

In Linux, most professional Domain Name System (DNS) servers are implemented using the Berkeley Internet Name Domain (BIND) service. This is implemented in Fedora and RHEL by installing the `bind`, `bind-utils`, and `bind-libs` packages. For added security, some people install the `bind-chroot` package.

By default, `bind` is configured by editing the `/etc/named.conf` file. Hostname-to-IP address mapping is done in zone files located in the `/var/named` directory. If you install the `bind-chroot` package, `bind` configuration files are moved under the `/var/named/chroot` directory, which attempts to replicate the files from `/etc` and `/var` that are needed to configure `bind`, so that the named daemon (which provides the service) is confined to the `/etc/named/chroot` directory structure.

If you are interested in trying out `bind`, I recommend you first try it out by configuring DNS for a small home network behind a firewall as a way to make it easier for the people in your household to communicate with each other. You can lock down the IP addresses of the machines in your home by attaching MAC addresses of each computer's network interface card to specific IP addresses on a DHCP server, and then mapping those names to addresses in a DNS server.

> **CAUTION**
>
> Before you create a public DNS server, keep in mind that it is very important to secure your DNS server properly. A cracked public DNS server can be used to redirect traffic to any server the bad guys choose. So, if you are using that server, you are in danger of being presented with sites that are not the sites you think they are.

Configuring Linux as a proxy server

A proxy server provides a means of restricting network traffic from a private network to a public one, such as the Internet. Such servers provide an excellent way to lock down a computer lab at a school or restrict websites employees can visit from work.

By physically setting up Linux as a router, but configuring it as a proxy server, all the systems on your home or business network can be configured to access the Internet using only certain protocols and only after you filter the traffic.

Using the Squid Proxy Server, which comes with most Linux systems (`squid` package in Fedora and RHEL), you can enable the system to accept requests to web servers (HTTP and HTTPS), file servers (FTP), and other protocols. You can restrict which systems can use your proxy server (by hostname or IP address) and even limit which sites they can visit (by specific address, range of addresses, hostname, or domain names).

Configuring a squid proxy server can be as simple as installing the `squid` package, editing the `/etc/squid/squid.conf` file, and starting the `squid` service. The file comes with a recommended minimal configuration. However, you might want to define the hosts (based on IP address or name) you want to allow to use the service. There are blacklists available with `squid` that allow you to deny access to whole sets of sites that might be inappropriate for children to visit.

Summary

Most network connections from a Linux desktop or laptop system can be made with little or no user intervention. If you use NetworkManager over a wired or wireless Ethernet connection, address and server information needed to start up can be automatically obtained from a DHCP server.

With NetworkManager's graphical interface, you can do some network configuration, if you like. You can set static IP addresses and select the name server and gateway computers to use. To do more manual and complex network configuration, consider turning off NetworkManager and working more directly with network configuration files.

Network configuration files in Linux can be used to set up more advanced features such as Ethernet channel bonding. To use these more advanced services, you can enable the network service.

Beyond the basics of network connectivity in Linux, features are available that enable you to provide network infrastructure types of services. This chapter introduced services and features such as routing, DHCP, and DNS that you need to know when working with more advanced networking features in Linux.

With your networking configured, you can now begin configuring services to run over your networks. Chapter 15 describes the tools you need to enable, disable, start, stop, and check the status of the services that are configured for your Linux system.

Exercises

The exercises in this section help you to examine and change the network interfaces on your Linux system, as well as understand how to configure more advanced networking features. Start these exercises on a Linux system that has an active network connection, but is *not* in the middle of some critical network activity.

I recommend you do these exercises directly from your computer console (in other words, don't ssh into the computer to do them). Some of the commands you run may interrupt your network connectivity, and some of the configuration you do, if you make a mistake, can result in your computer being temporarily unavailable from the network.

There are often multiple ways to complete the tasks described in these exercises. If you are stuck, refer to the task solutions that are shown in Appendix B.

1. Use the desktop to check that NetworkManager has successfully started your network interface (wired or wireless) to the network. If it has not, then try to start your network interface.

2. Run a command to check the active network interfaces available on your computer.

3. Try to contact google.com from the command line in a way that ensures that DNS is working properly.

4. Run a command to check the routes being used to communicate outside your local network.

5. Trace the route being taken to connect to google.com.

6. Turn off and disable NetworkManager and start the network service.

7. Create a host entry that allows you to communicate with your local host system using the name myownhost.

8. Add the public Google DNS server (IP address 8.8.8.8) as the last in your list of DNS servers.

9. Create a custom route that directs traffic destined for the 192.168.99.0/255.255.255.0 network to some IP address on your local network, such as 192.168.0.5 (first ensuring that the 10.0.99 network is not being used at your location).

10. Check to see if your system has been configured to allow IPv4 packets to be routed between network interfaces on your system.

14

Starting and Stopping Services

IN THIS CHAPTER

Understanding the various Linux init services

Auditing Linux daemon-controlled services

Stopping and starting services

Changing the Linux server's default runlevel

Removing services

The primary job of a Linux server system is to offer services to local or remote users. A server can provide access to Web pages, files, database information, streaming music, or other types of content. Name servers can provide access to lists of host computer or user names. Hundreds of these and other types of services can be configured on your Linux systems.

Ongoing services offered by a Linux system, such as access to a printer service or login service, are typically implemented by what is referred to as a *daemon* process. Most Linux systems have a method of managing each daemon process as a *service* using one of several popular initialization systems (also referred to as init systems). Advantages of using init systems include the ability to do the following:

- **Identify runlevels**—Put together sets of services in what are referred to as *runlevels* or *targets*
- **Establish dependencies**—Set service dependencies so, for example, a service that requires network interfaces won't start until all network startup services have started successfully
- **Set the default runlevel**—Select which runlevel or target starts up when the system boots
- **Manage services**—Run commands that tell individual services to start, stop, pause, restart, or even reload configuration files

Several different init systems are in use with Linux systems today. The one you use depends on the Linux distribution and release you are using. In this chapter, I cover the following init systems that have been used in Fedora, Red Hat Enterprise Linux, Ubuntu, and many other Linux distributions:

- **SysVinit**—This traditional init system was created for UNIX System V systems in the early 1980s. It offers an easy-to-understand method of starting and stopping services based on runlevel. Most UNIX and Linux systems up until a few years ago used SysVinit.

- **Upstart**—Popularized in Ubuntu and used briefly in Fedora and RHEL, this init system improved handling of dependencies between services and could substantially improve system startup time. It has only recently been supplanted by systemd in Fedora and RHEL, and will soon do so in Ubuntu.

- **Systemd**—The latest versions of Fedora and RHEL use the systemd init system. It is the most complex of the init systems, but also offers much more flexibility. Systemd not only offers features for starting and working with services, but also lets you manage sockets, devices, mount points, swap areas, and other unit types.

This chapter describes these three major init systems. In the process of using the init system that matches your Linux distribution, you learn how the boot process works to start services, how you can start and stop services individually, and how you enable and disable services.

Understanding the Initialization Daemon (init or systemd)

In order to understand service management, you need to understand the initialization daemon. The initialization daemon can be thought of as the "mother of all processes." This daemon is the first process to be started by the kernel on the Linux server. For Linux distributions that use SysvInit or Upstart, the init daemon is literally named init. For systemd, the init daemon is named systemd.

The Linux kernel has a process ID (PID) of 0. Thus, the initialization process (init or systemd) daemon has a parent process ID (PPID) of 0, and a PID of 1. Once started, init is responsible for spawning (launching) processes configured to be started at the server's boot time, such as the login shell (getty or mingetty process). It is also responsible for managing services.

The Linux init daemon was based upon the UNIX System V init daemon. Thus, it is called the SysVinit daemon. However, it was not the only classic init daemon. The init daemon is not part of the Linux kernel. Therefore, it can come in different flavors, and Linux distributions can choose which flavor to use. Another classic init daemon was based on Berkeley UNIX, also called BSD. Therefore, the two original Linux init daemons were BSD init and SysVinit.

The classic init daemons worked without problems for many years. However, these daemons were created to work within a static environment. As new hardware, such as USB devices, came along, the classic init daemons had trouble dealing with these and other hot-plug devices. Computer hardware had changed from static to event-based. New init daemons were needed to deal with these fluid environments.

In addition, as new services came along, the classic init daemons had to deal with starting more and more services. Thus, the entire system initialization process was less efficient and ultimately slower.

The modern initialization daemons have tried to solve the problems of inefficient system boots and non-static environments. Two of these init daemons are the Upstart init and systemd daemons. Recently, Ubuntu, RHEL, and Fedora distributions have made the move to the newer systemd daemon while maintaining backward compatibility to the classic SysVinit, Upstart, or BSD init daemons.

Upstart, available at http://upstart.ubuntu.com, was originally developed by Canonical, the parent of the Ubuntu distribution. Earlier releases of other distributions adopted it for a short time before transitioning to systemd, including:

- RHEL version 6
- Fedora versions 9 through 14
- Ubuntu versions 6–14.10
- openSUSE versions 11.3–12.1

A new daemon, systemd, available at http://fedoraproject.org/wiki/Systemd, was written primarily by Lennart Poettering, a Red Hat developer. It is currently used by Fedora 15, Red Hat Enterprise Linux 7, OpenSUSE 12.2, and later versions and is being implemented for Ubuntu 15.04.

In order to properly manage your services, you need to know which initialization daemon your server has. Figuring that out can be a little tricky. The initialization process running on a SysVinit or Upstart is named init. For the first systemd systems, it was also called init, but is now named systemd. Running ps -e can immediately tell you if yours is a Systemd system:

```
# ps -e | head
  PID TTY          TIME CMD
    1 ?        00:04:36 systemd
    2 ?        00:00:03 kthreadd
    3 ?        00:00:15 ksoftirqd/0
```

If your initialization process is init, look through the following to help determine your Linux server's initialization system:

- Do your Linux distribution and version appear in the preceding list of Upstart adopters? If they do, your Linux init daemon is the Upstart init daemon.

15

- Try searching your Linux distribution's init daemon for clues, using the strings and the grep commands. The following code example shows the init daemon on a Linux Mint distribution being searched for systemd and Upstart init daemon references. The search for systemd yields nothing. However, the search for Upstart produces results. Thus, in the second example, the Linux Mint distribution uses the Upstart init daemon.

```
$ sudo strings /sbin/init | grep -i systemd
$ sudo strings /sbin/init | grep -i upstart
upstart-devel@lists.ubuntu.com
UPSTART_CONFDIR
UPSTART_NO_SESSIONS
...
```

On an older Fedora server, the search for Upstart yields nothing. However, you can see that the search for systemd yields the existence of the systemd daemon.

```
# strings /sbin/init | grep -i upstart
# strings /sbin/init | grep -i systemd
systemd.unit=
systemd.log_target=
systemd.log_level=
...
```

> **TIP**
>
> If you do not have the strings command on your Linux system, you can install it via the binutils package. On RHEL and Fedora, use the command yum install binutils. On Ubuntu, use the command sudo apt-get install binutils.

- If you still cannot tell what init daemon your server has, try looking on the init Wikipedia page (http://wikipedia.org/wiki/Init) under "Replacements for init?"

Keep in mind that some Linux distributions have not moved to the newer daemons. Most of those that have moved maintain backward compatibility with the SysVinit and BSD init daemons.

Understanding the classic init daemons

The classic init daemons, SysVinit and BSD init, are worth understanding, even if your Linux server has a different init daemon. Not only is backward compatibility to the classics often used in the newer init daemons, but many are based upon them. Understanding the classic init daemons will help you to understand the modern init daemons.

The classic SysVinit and BSD init daemons operate in a very similar fashion. Although in the beginning they may have been rather different, over time, very few significant differences remained. For example, the older BSD init daemon would obtain configuration information from the /etc/ttytab file. Now, like the SysVinit daemon, the BSD init daemon's configuration information is taken at boot time from the /etc/inittab file. The following is a classic SysVinit /etc/inittab file:

```
# cat /etc/inittab
# inittab  This file describes how the INIT process should set up
# Default runlevel. The runlevels used by RHS are:
#    0 - halt (Do NOT set initdefault to this)
#    1 - Single user mode
#    2 - Multiuser, no NFS (Same as 3, if you do not have networking)
#    3 - Full multiuser mode
#    4 - unused
#    5 - X11
#    6 - reboot (Do NOT set initdefault to this)
#
id:5:initdefault:

# System initialization.
si::sysinit:/etc/rc.d/rc.sysinit

l0:0:wait:/etc/rc.d/rc 0
l1:1:wait:/etc/rc.d/rc 1
l2:2:wait:/etc/rc.d/rc 2
l3:3:wait:/etc/rc.d/rc 3
l4:4:wait:/etc/rc.d/rc 4
l5:5:wait:/etc/rc.d/rc 5
l6:6:wait:/etc/rc.d/rc 6

# Trap CTRL-ALT-DELETE
ca::ctrlaltdel:/sbin/shutdown -t3 -r now
pf::powerfail:/sbin/shutdown -f -h +2
     "Power Failure; System Shutting Down"

# If power was restored before the shutdown kicked in, cancel it.
pr:12345:powerokwait:/sbin/shutdown -c
     "Power Restored; Shutdown Cancelled"

# Run gettys in standard runlevels
1:2345:respawn:/sbin/mingetty tty1
2:2345:respawn:/sbin/mingetty tty2
3:2345:respawn:/sbin/mingetty tty3
4:2345:respawn:/sbin/mingetty tty4
5:2345:respawn:/sbin/mingetty tty5
6:2345:respawn:/sbin/mingetty tty6

# Run xdm in runlevel 5
x:5:respawn:/etc/X11/prefdm -nodaemon
```

15

The `/etc/inittab` file tells the `init` daemon which runlevel is the default runlevel. A runlevel is a categorization number that determines what services are started and what services are stopped. In the preceding example, a default runlevel of 5 is set with the line `id:5:initdefault:`. Table 15.1 shows the standard seven Linux runlevels.

TABLE 15.1 **Standard Linux Runlevels**

Runlevel #	Name	Description
0	Halt	All services are shut down and the server is stopped.
1 or S	Single User Mode	The root account is automatically logged in to the server. Other users cannot log in to the server. Only the command line interface is available. Network services are not started.
2	Multiuser Mode	Users can log in to the server, but only the command line interface is available. On some systems, network interfaces and services are started; on others they are not. Originally, this runlevel was used to start dumb terminal devices so users could log in (but no network services were started).
3	Extended Multiuser Mode	Users can log in to the server, but only the command line interface is available. Network interfaces and services are started. This is a common runlevel for servers.
4	User Defined	Users can customize this `runlevel`.
5	Graphical Mode	Users can log in to the server. Command line and graphical interfaces are available. Network services are started. This is a common runlevel for desktop systems.
6	Reboot	The server is rebooted.

Linux distributions can differ slightly on the definition of each runlevel as well as which runlevels are offered. The Ubuntu distribution, for example, offers runlevels 0–6, but runlevels 2–5 start the same services as standard runlevel 5 listed in Table 15.1.

> **CAUTION**
>
> The only runlevels that should be used in the `/etc/inittab` file are 2 through 5. The other runlevels could cause problems. For example, if you put runlevel 6 in the `/etc/inittab` file as the default, when the server reboots, it would go into a loop and continue to reboot over and over again.

The runlevels are not only used as a default runlevel in the `/etc/inittab` file. They can also be called directly using the `init` daemon itself. Thus, if you want to immediately halt your server, you type **init 0** at the command line:

```
# init 0
...
System going down for system halt NOW!
```

The init command accepts any of the runlevel numbers in Table 15.1, allowing you to quickly switch your server from one runlevel category to another. For example, if you need to perform troubleshooting that requires the graphical interface to be down, you can type **init 3** at the command line:

```
# init 3
INIT: Sending processes the TERM signal
starting irqbalance:                     [ OK ]
Starting setroubleshootd:
Starting fuse:   Fuse filesystem already available.
...
Starting console mouse services:         [ OK ]
```

To see your Linux server's current runlevel, simply type in the command **runlevel**. The first item displayed is the server's previous runlevel, which in the following example is 5. The second item displayed shows the server's current runlevel, which in this example is 3.

```
$ runlevel
5 3
```

In addition to the init command, you can also use the telinit command, which is functionally the same. In the example that follows, the telinit command is used to reboot the server by taking it to runlevel 6:

```
# telinit 6
INIT: Sending processes the TERM signal
Shutting down smartd:                     [ OK ]
Shutting down Avahi daemon:               [ OK ]
Stopping dhcdbd:                          [ OK ]
Stopping HAL daemon:                      [ OK ]
...
Starting killall:
Sending all processes the TERM signal...  [ OK ]
Sending all processes the KILL signal...  [ OK ]
...
Unmounting filesystems                    [ OK ]
Please stand by while rebooting the system
...
```

On a freshly booted Linux server, the current runlevel number should be the same as the default runlevel number in the /etc/inittab file. However, notice that the previous runlevel in the example that follows is N. The N stands for "Nonexistent" and indicates the server was freshly booted to the current runlevel.

```
$ runlevel
N 5
```

How does the server know which services to stop and which ones to start when a particular runlevel is chosen? When a runlevel is chosen, the scripts located in the /etc/rc.d/rc#.d directory (where # is the chosen runlevel) are run. These scripts are run whether the runlevel is chosen via a server boot and the /etc/inittab initdefault setting, or when the

15

init or telinit command is used. For example, if runlevel 5 is chosen, then all the scripts in the /etc/rc.d/rc5.d directory are run; your list will be different, depending on what services you have installed and enabled.

```
# ls /etc/rc.d/rc5.d
K01smolt                        K88wpa_supplicant    S22messagebus
K02avahi-dnsconfd               K89dund              S25bluetooth
K02NetworkManager               K89netplugd          S25fuse
K02NetworkManagerDispatcher     K89pand              S25netfs
K05saslauthd                    K89rdisc             S25pcscd
K10dc_server                    K91capi              S26hidd
K10psacct                       S00microcode_ctl     S26udev-post
K12dc_client                    S04readahead_early   S28autofs
K15gpm                          S05kudzu             S50hplip
K15httpd                        S06cpuspeed          S55cups
K20nfs                          S08ip6tables         S55sshd
K24irda                         S08iptables          S80sendmail
K25squid                        S09isdn              S90ConsoleKit
K30spamassassin                 S10network           S90crond
K35vncserver                    S11auditd            S90xfs
K50netconsole                   S12restorecond       S95anacron
K50tux                          S12syslog            S95atd
K69rpcsvcgssd                   S13irqbalance        S96readahead_later
K73winbind                      S13mcstrans          S97dhcdbd
K73ypbind                       S13rpcbind           S97yum-updatesd
K74nscd                         S13setroubleshoot    S98avahi-daemon
K74ntpd                         S14nfslock           S98haldaemon
K84btseed                       S15mdmonitor         S99firstboot
K84bttrack                      S18rpcidmapd         S99local
K87multipathd                   S19rpcgssd           S99smartd
```

Notice that some of the scripts within the /etc/rc.d/rc5.d directory start with a K and some start with an S. The K refers to a script that will kill (stop) a process. The S refers to a script that will start a process. Also, each K and S script has a number before the name of the service or daemon they control. This allows the services to be stopped or started in a particular controlled order. You would not want your Linux server's network services to be started before the network itself was started.

An /etc/rc.d/rc#.d directory exists for all the standard Linux runlevels. Each one contains scripts to start and stop services for its particular runlevel.

```
# ls -d /etc/rc.d/rc?.d
/etc/rc.d/rc0.d   /etc/rc.d/rc2.d   /etc/rc.d/rc4.d   /etc/rc.d/rc6.d
/etc/rc.d/rc1.d   /etc/rc.d/rc3.d   /etc/rc.d/rc5.d
```

Actually, the files in the /etc/rc.d/rc#.d directories are not scripts, but instead symbolic links to scripts in the /etc/rc.d/init.d directory. Thus, there is no need to have multiple copies of particular scripts.

```
# ls -l /etc/rc.d/rc5.d/K15httpd
lrwxrwxrwx 1 root root 15 Oct 10 08:15
 /etc/rc.d/rc5.d/K15httpd -> ../init.d/httpd
# ls /etc/rc.d/init.d
anacron              functions   multipathd          rpcidmapd
atd                  fuse        netconsole          rpcsvcgssd
auditd               gpm         netfs               saslauthd
autofs               haldaemon   netplugd            sendmail
avahi-daemon         halt        network             setroubleshoot
avahi-dnsconfd       hidd        NetworkManager      single
bluetooth            hplip       NetworkManagerDispatcher smartd
btseed               hsqldb      nfs                 smolt
bttrack              httpd       nfslock             spamassassin
capi                 ip6tables   nscd                squid
ConsoleKit           iptables    ntpd                sshd
cpuspeed             irda        pand                syslog
crond                irqbalance  pcscd               tux
cups                 isdn        psacct              udev-post
cups-config-daemon   killall     rdisc               vncserver
dc_client            kudzu       readahead_early     winbind
dc_server            mcstrans    readahead_later     wpa_supplicant
dhcdbd               mdmonitor   restorecond         xfs
dund                 messagebus  rpcbind             ypbind
firstboot            microcode   rpcgssd             yum-updatesd
```

Notice that each service has a single script in /etc/rc.d/init.d. There aren't separate scripts for stopping and starting a service. These scripts will stop or start a service depending upon what parameter is passed to them by the init daemon.

Each script in /etc/rc.d/init.d takes care of all that is needed for starting or stopping a particular service on the server. The following is a partial example of the httpd script on a Linux system that uses the SysVinit daemon. It contains a case statement for handling the parameter ($1) that was passed to it, such as start, stop, status, and so on.

```
# cat /etc/rc.d/init.d/httpd
#!/bin/bash
#
# httpd          Startup script for the Apache HTTP Server
#
# chkconfig: - 85 15
# description: Apache is a World Wide Web server.
#              It is used to serve \
#              HTML files and CGI.
# processname: httpd
# config: /etc/httpd/conf/httpd.conf
# config: /etc/sysconfig/httpd
# pidfile: /var/run/httpd.pid

# Source function library.
```

```
. /etc/rc.d/init.d/functions
...
# See how we were called.
case "$1" in
  start)
        start
        ;;
  stop)
        stop
        ;;
  status)
        status $httpd
        RETVAL=$?
        ;;
  ...
  esac

  exit $RETVAL
```

After the runlevel scripts linked from the appropriate /etc/rc.d/rc#.d directory are executed, the SysVinit daemon's process spawning is complete. The final step the init process takes at this point is to do anything else indicated in the /etc/inittab file (such as spawn mingetty processes for virtual consoles and start the desktop interface, if you are in runlevel 5).

Understanding the Upstart init daemon

As mentioned earlier, many Linux distributions moved for a while from the classic init daemons to the Upstart init daemon. Included in that distribution list are the RHEL 6 and Ubuntu (prior to 15.04) distributions.

Learning Upstart init daemon basics

The primary difference between the classics and Upstart is the handling of stopping and starting services. The SysVinit daemon was created to operate in a static environment. The Upstart init daemon was created to operate in a flexible and ever-changing environment.

With SysVinit, services are stopped and started based upon runlevels. The Upstart init daemon is not concerned with runlevels but with system events. Events are what determine when services are stopped and/or started.

An *event* is a Linux server occurrence that triggers a needed system state change, which is communicated to the Upstart init daemon. The following are examples of system events:

- The server boots up.
- The init command is used.
- A USB device is plugged into the server.

The classic init daemons could handle the first two event examples, but they could not deal well with the third.

Upstart handles services through defined jobs. An Upstart *job* can be either a task or a service. A *task* performs a limited duty, completes its work, and then returns to a waiting state. A *service*, on the other hand, is a long-running program that never finishes its work or self-terminates, but instead stays in a running state. A daemon is an example of an Upstart service job.

The example that follows shows several Upstart jobs that include both task and service jobs. The task jobs are in a stop/waiting state, such as the task rc. The service jobs are in a start/running state, such as the cups daemon.

```
$ initctl list
avahi-daemon start/running, process 456
mountall-net stop/waiting
rc stop/waiting
rsyslog start/running, process 411
...
ssh start/running, process 405
udev-fallback-graphics stop/waiting
control-alt-delete stop/waiting
hwclock stop/waiting
mounted-proc stop/waiting
network-manager start/running, process 458
...
rc-sysinit stop/waiting
cups start/running, process 1066
...
tty6 start/running, process 833
ureadahead stop/waiting
```

These various jobs are defined via a jobs definition file. All the job definition files are located in the /etc/init directory as shown here:

```
$ ls /etc/init
acpid.conf                    networking.conf
alsa-restore.conf             network-interface.conf
alsa-store.conf               network-interface-security.conf
anacron.conf                  network-manager.conf
control-alt-delete.conf       procps.conf
cron.conf                     rc.conf
cups.conf                     rcS.conf
dbus.conf                     rc-sysinit.conf
dmesg.conf                    rsyslog.conf
failsafe.conf                 setvtrgb.conf
friendly-recovery.conf        ssh.conf
hostname.conf                 tty1.conf
```

15

```
hwclock.conf              tty2.conf
hwclock-save.conf         tty3.conf
irqbalance.conf           tty4.conf
lightdm.conf              tty5.conf
...
```

The Upstart init daemon depends upon events to trigger certain services to start, stop, restart, and so on. Events are either communicated to the Upstart init daemon or created by the Upstart daemon. This is called an *emitted event*. The actions taken when an event is emitted are dependent upon the settings in a job's configuration file. Consider the following Network Manager daemon's configuration file:

```
$ cat /etc/init/network-manager.conf
# network-manager - network connection manager
#
# The NetworkManager daemon manages the system's network connections
# automatically switching between the best available.

description      "network connection manager"

start on (local-filesystems and started dbus)
stop on stopping dbus

expect fork
respawn

exec NetworkManager
$
```

From the example, you can see that there are two events that must take place in order to trigger the Upstart init daemon to start the NetworkManager daemon:

- **The** local-filesystems **event**—The Upstart init daemon emits this event when all the local filesystems in the /etc/fstab configuration file have been mounted.

- **The** dbus daemon started **event**—The Upstart init daemon emits this started event when the dbus daemon has reached the start/running state.

Thus, when these two events occur, the Upstart init daemon is informed and starts the NetworkManager daemon.

Because the Upstart init daemon can handle these events and tracks the status (state) of processes, it is often referred to as a "state machine." The Upstart init daemon is also referred to as an "event engine" because it emits events itself.

Learning Upstart's backward compatibility to SysVinit

Upstart provides backward compatibility to the SysVinit daemon. This has allowed the Linux distributions time to slowly migrate to Upstart.

The /etc/inittab file is still on some distributions. RHEL 6 and the Fedora distributions still using Upstart use /etc/inittab to boot to the default runlevel listed. The example of the /etc/inittab file that follows comes from a server running a version of Fedora, which uses the Upstart init daemon.

```
$ cat /etc/inittab
# inittab is only used by upstart for the default runlevel.
#
# ADDING OTHER CONFIGURATION HERE WILL HAVE NO EFFECT ON YOUR SYSTEM.
#
...
#
id:5:initdefault:
```

As you can see from the comment lines in the /etc/inittab file, the only thing this file is used for on Linux distributions that maintain it is to change the default runlevel at server boot time.

> **TIP**
>
> To change the default runlevel on an Ubuntu distribution that uses Upstart, edit /etc/init/rc-sysinit.conf and change the line env DEFAULT_RUNLEVEL=# where # is 2 to 5. However, remember that the runlevels 2-5 on Ubuntu are equivalent to SysVinit runlevel 5. Therefore, this activity is rather pointless.

System initialization compatibility to SysVinit is maintained on some distributions, such as Ubuntu, via the /etc/init/rc-sysinit.conf configuration file. This is one of the configuration files used at system boot. In the example that follows, Upstart checks for a /etc/inittab file and also runs any scripts that may still be in the /etc/init.d/rcS directory:

```
$ cat /etc/init/rc-sysinit.conf
# rc-sysinit - System V initialisation compatibility
#
# This task runs the old System V-style system init scripts,
# and enters the default runlevel when finished.
...
start on (filesystem and static-network-up) or failsafe-boot
stop on runlevel

# Default runlevel, this may be overriden on the kernel command-line
# or by faking an old /etc/inittab entry
env DEFAULT_RUNLEVEL=2

emits runlevel
...
task
```

15

```
script
    # Check for default runlevel in /etc/inittab
    if [ -r /etc/inittab ]
    then
      eval "$(sed -nre 's/^[^#][^:]*:([0-6sS]):initdefault:
.*/DEFAULT_RUNLEVEL="\1";/p' /etc/inittab || true)"
    fi

    # Check kernel command-line for typical arguments
    for ARG in $(cat /proc/cmdline)
    do
      case "${ARG}" in
      -b|emergency)
          # Emergency shell
          [ -n "${FROM_SINGLE_USER_MODE}" ] || sulogin
          ;;
        [0123456sS])
          # Override runlevel
          DEFAULT_RUNLEVEL="${ARG}"
          ;;
      -s|single)
          # Single user mode
          [ -n "${FROM_SINGLE_USER_MODE}" ] || DEFAULT_RUNLEVEL=S
          ;;
      esac
    done

    # Run the system initialisation scripts
    [ -n "${FROM_SINGLE_USER_MODE}" ] || /etc/init.d/rcS

    # Switch into the default runlevel
    telinit "${DEFAULT_RUNLEVEL}"
end script
```

As you can see from the preceding example, the runlevel concept is maintained in the Upstart init daemon. In fact, there is even a runlevel signal that Upstart can emit.

```
# man -k "event signal"
control-alt-delete    (7) - ... console press of Control-Alt-Delete
keyboard-request      (7) - ... console press of Alt-UpArrow
power-status-changed  (7) - ... change of power status
runlevel              (7) - ... change of system runlevel
started               (7) - ... a job is running
starting              (7) - ... a job is starting
startup               (7) - ... system startup
stopped               (7) - ... a job has stopped
stopping              (7) - ... a job is stopping
```

Switching to a different runlevel is still allowed through the init or telinit commands. Any runlevel event is handled by the rc task.

```
$ initctl status rc
rc stop/waiting
```

The rc task job's configuration file is shown next. When a runlevel event is emitted, the rc configuration file calls the /etc/rc.d/rc script. When called, the /etc/rc.d/rc script runs the scripts located in the /etc/rc.d/rc#.d, where # is the chosen runlevel. This provides runlevel backward compatibility to SysVinit.

```
$ cat /etc/init/rc.conf
# rc - System V runlevel compatibility
#
# This task runs the old sysv-rc runlevel scripts.  It
# is usually started by the telinit compatibility wrapper.

start on runlevel [0123456]

stop on runlevel [!$RUNLEVEL]

task

export RUNLEVEL
console output
exec /etc/rc.d/rc $RUNLEVEL
```

If you look back at the /etc/inittab in the classic SysVinit daemon section, you will notice that /etc/inittab also handled spawning the getty or mingetty processes. The Upstart init daemon handles this via the start-ttys task.

```
# initctl status start-ttys
start-ttys stop/waiting
```

The start-ttys task job's configuration file is shown next. When a runlevel event is emitted, the start-ttys configuration file spawns the getty or mingetty process.

```
$ cat /etc/init/start-ttys.conf
# This service starts the configured number of gettys.

start on stopped rc RUNLEVEL=[2345]

env ACTIVE_CONSOLES=/dev/tty[1-6]
env X_TTY=/dev/tty1
task
script
   . /etc/sysconfig/init
   for tty in $(echo $ACTIVE_CONSOLES) ; do
     [ "$RUNLEVEL" = "5" -a "$tty" = "$X_TTY" ] && continue
     initctl start tty TTY=$tty
   done
end script
```

15

Although the Upstart `init` daemon provides backward compatibility to the classic SysVinit daemon, is a state-machine, and can handle ever-changing events on a server, it is not the only modern `init` daemon available for the Linux server. Another even more modern `init` daemon is `systemd`.

Understanding systemd initialization

The `systemd` initialization daemon is the newer replacement for the SysVinit and the Upstart `init` daemons. This modern initialization daemon currently runs on Fedora 15 and above and RHEL 7 and above, and is backward compatible with both SysVinit and Upstart. System initialization time is reduced by `systemd` because it can start services in a parallel manner.

Learning systemd basics

With the SysVinit daemon, services are stopped and started based upon runlevels. The `systemd` is also concerned with runlevels, but they are called *target units*. Although the main job of `systemd` is to start services, it can manage other types of things called *units*. A unit is a group consisting of a name, type, and configuration file and is focused on a particular service or action. There are eight `systemd` unit types:

- `automount`
- `device`
- `mount`
- `path`
- `service`
- `snapshot`
- `socket`
- `target`

The two primary `systemd` units you need to be concerned with for dealing with services are service units and target units. A *service unit* is for managing daemons on your Linux server. A *target unit* is simply a group of other units.

The example that follows shows several `systemd` service units and target units. The service units have familiar daemon names, such as `cups` and `sshd`. Note that each service unit name ends with `.service`. The target units shown have names like `sysinit`. (`sysinit` is used for starting up services at system initialization.) The target unit names end with `.target`.

```
# systemctl list-units | grep .service
...
cups.service          loaded active running CUPS Printing Service
dbus.service          loaded active running D-Bus Message Bus
```

```
...
NetworkManager.service loaded active running Network Manager
prefdm.service         loaded active running Display Manager
remount-rootfs.service loaded active exited  Remount Root FS
rsyslog.service        loaded active running System Logging
...
sshd.service           loaded active running OpenSSH server daemon
systemd-logind.service loaded active running Login Service
...
# systemctl list-units | grep .target
basic.target        loaded active active  Basic System
cryptsetup.target   loaded active active  Encrypted Volumes
getty.target        loaded active active  Login Prompts
graphical.target    loaded active active  Graphical Interface
local-fs-pre.target loaded active active  Local File Systems (Pre)
local-fs.target     loaded active active  Local File Systems
multi-user.target   loaded active active  Multi-User
network.target      loaded active active  Network
remote-fs.target    loaded active active  Remote File Systems
sockets.target      loaded active active  Sockets
sound.target        loaded active active  Sound Card
swap.target         loaded active active  Swap
sysinit.target      loaded active active  System Initialization
syslog.target       loaded active active  Syslog
```

The Linux system unit configuration files are located in the `/lib/systemd/system` and `/etc/systemd/system` directories. You could use the `ls` command to look through those directories, but the preferred method is to use an option on the `systemctl` command as follows:

```
# systemctl list-unit-files --type=service
UNIT FILE                               STATE
...
cups.service                            enabled
...
dbus.service                            static
...
NetworkManager.service                  enabled
...
poweroff.service                        static
...
sshd.service                            enabled
sssd.service                            disabled
...
134 unit files listed.
```

The unit configuration files shown in the preceding code are all associated with a service unit. Configuration files for target units can be displayed via the following method.

15

```
# systemctl list-unit-files --type=target
UNIT FILE                 STATE
anaconda.target           static
basic.target              static
bluetooth.target          static
cryptsetup.target         static
ctrl-alt-del.target       disabled
default.target            enabled
...
shutdown.target           static
sigpwr.target             static
smartcard.target          static
sockets.target            static
sound.target              static
swap.target               static
sysinit.target            static
syslog.target             static
time-sync.target          static
umount.target             static
43 unit files listed.
```

Notice that both of the configuration units' file examples shown display units with a status of either static, enabled, or disabled. The enabled status means that the unit is currently enabled. The disabled status means that the unit is currently disabled. The next status, static, is slightly confusing. It stands for "statically enabled," and it means that the unit is enabled by default and cannot be disabled, even by root.

The service unit configuration files contain lots of information, such as what other services must be started, when this service can be started, which environmental file to use, and so on. The following example shows the sshd's unit configuration file:

```
# cat /lib/systemd/system/sshd.service
[Unit]
Description=OpenSSH server daemon
After=syslog.target network.target auditd.service

[Service]
EnvironmentFile=/etc/sysconfig/sshd
ExecStartPre=/usr/sbin/sshd-keygen
ExecStart=/usr/sbin/sshd -D $OPTIONS
ExecReload=/bin/kill -HUP $MAINPID
KillMode=process
Restart=on-failure
RestartSec=42s

[Install]
WantedBy=multi-user.target
```

This basic service unit configuration file has the following options:

- `Description`—A free-form description (comment line) of the service.
- `After`—Configures ordering. In other words, it lists which units should be activated before this service is started.
- `Environment File`—The service's configuration file.
- `ExecStart`—The command used to start this service.
- `ExecReload`—The command used to reload this service.
- `WantedBy`—The target unit this service belongs to.

Notice that the target unit, `multi-user.target`, is used in the sshd service unit configuration file. The sshd service unit is wanted by the `multi-user.target`. In other words, when the `multi-user.target` unit is activated, the sshd service unit is started.

You can view the various units that a target unit will activate by using the following command:

```
# systemctl show --property "Wants" multi-user.target
Wants=multipathd.service avahi-daemon.service sshd-keygen.se
(END) q
```

Unfortunately, the `systemctl` command does not format the output for this well. It literally runs off the right edge of the screen so you cannot see the full results. And you must enter **q** to return to the command prompt. To fix this problem, pipe the output through some formatting commands to produce a nice alphabetically sorted display, as shown in the example that follows.

```
# systemctl show --property "Wants" multi-user.target \
    | fmt -10 | sed 's/Wants=//g' | sort
abrt-ccpp.service
abrtd.service
abrt-oops.service
abrt-vmcore.service
atd.service
auditd.service
avahi-daemon.service
crond.service
cups.path
dbus.service
fcoe.service
getty.target
irqbalance.service
iscsid.service
iscsi.service
livesys-late.service
livesys.service
lldpad.service
mcelog.service
```

15

```
mdmonitor.service
multipathd.service
netfs.service
NetworkManager.service
plymouth-quit.service
plymouth-quit-wait.service
remote-fs.target
rsyslog.service
sendmail.service
sm-client.service
sshd-keygen.service
sshd.service...
```

This display shows all the services and other units that will be activated (started), including sshd, when the multi-user.target unit is activated. Remember that a target unit is simply a grouping of other units, as shown in the preceding example. Also notice that the units in this group are not all service units. There are path units and other target units as well.

A target unit has both Wants and requirements, called Requires. A *Wants* means that all the units listed are triggered to activate (start). If they fail or cannot be started, no problem—the target unit continues on its merry way. The preceding example is a display of Wants only.

A Requires is much more stringent and potentially catastrophic than a Wants. A *Requires* means that all the units listed are triggered to activate (start). If they fail or cannot be started, the entire unit (group of units) is deactivated.

You can view the various units a target unit Requires (must activate or the unit will fail), using the command in the example that follows. Notice that the Requires output is much shorter than the Wants for the multi-user target. Thus, no special formatting of the output is needed.

```
# systemctl show --property "Requires" multi-user.target
Requires=basic.target
```

The target units also have configuration files, as do the service units. The following example shows the contents of the multi-user.target configuration file.

```
# cat /lib/systemd/system/multi-user.target
#  This file is part of systemd.
#
...

[Unit]
Description=Multi-User
Requires=basic.target
Conflicts=rescue.service rescue.target
```

```
After=basic.target rescue.service rescue.target
AllowIsolate=yes

[Install]
Alias=default.target
```

This basic target unit configuration file has the following options:

- Description—This is just a free-form description of the target.

- Requires—If this multi-user.target gets activated, the listed target unit is also activated. If the listed target unit is deactivated or fails, then multi-user. target is deactivated. If there are no After and Before options, then both multi-user.target and listed target unit activate simultaneously.

- Conflicts—This setting avoids conflicts in services. Starting multi-user. target stops the listed targets and services, and vice-versa.

- After—This setting configures ordering. In other words, it determines which units should be activated before starting this service.

- AllowIsolate—This option is a Boolean setting of yes or no. If set to yes, then this target unit, multi-user.target, is activated along with its dependencies and all others are deactivated.

- ExecStart—This command starts the service.

- ExecReload—This command reloads the service.

- Alias—With this command, systemd creates a symbolic link from the target unit names listed to this unit, multi-user.target.

To get more information on these configuration files and their options, enter **man systemd .service, man systemd.target**, and **man systemd.unit** at the command line.

For the Linux server using systemd, the boot process is easier to follow now that you understand systemd target units. At boot, systemd activates the default.target unit. This unit is aliased to either multi-user.target or graphical.target. Thus, depending upon the alias set, the services targeted by the target unit are started.

If you need more help understanding the systemd daemon, you can enter **man -k systemd** at the command line to get a listing of the various systemd utilities' documentation in the man pages.

Learning systemd's backward compatibility to SysVinit

The systemd daemon has maintained backward compatibility to the SysVinit daemon. This allows Linux distributions time to slowly migrate to systemd.

While runlevels are not truly part of systemd, the systemd infrastructure has been created to provide compatibility with the concept of runlevels. There are seven target unit configuration files specifically created for backward compatibility to SysVinit:

15

- runlevel0.target
- runlevel1.target
- runlevel2.target
- runlevel3.target
- runlevel4.target
- runlevel5.target
- runlevel6.target

As you probably have already figured out, there is a target unit configuration file for each of the seven classic SysVinit runlevels. These target unit configuration files are symbolically linked to target unit configuration files that most closely match the idea of the original runlevel. In the example that follows, the symbolic links are shown for runlevel target units. Notice that the runlevel target units for runlevel 2, 3, and 4 are all symbolically linked to multi-user.target. The multi-user.target unit is similar to the legacy Extended Multi-user Mode.

```
# ls -l /lib/systemd/system/runlevel*.target
lrwxrwxrwx. 1 root root 15 Mar 27 15:39
 /lib/systemd/system/runlevel0.target -> poweroff.target
lrwxrwxrwx. 1 root root 13 Mar 27 15:39
 /lib/systemd/system/runlevel1.target -> rescue.target
lrwxrwxrwx. 1 root root 17 Mar 27 15:39
 /lib/systemd/system/runlevel2.target -> multi-user.target
lrwxrwxrwx. 1 root root 17 Mar 27 15:39
 /lib/systemd/system/runlevel3.target -> multi-user.target
lrwxrwxrwx. 1 root root 17 Mar 27 15:39
 /lib/systemd/system/runlevel4.target -> multi-user.target
lrwxrwxrwx. 1 root root 16 Mar 27 15:39
 /lib/systemd/system/runlevel5.target -> graphical.target
lrwxrwxrwx. 1 root root 13 Mar 27 15:39
 /lib/systemd/system/runlevel6.target -> reboot.target
```

The /etc/inittab file still exists, but it contains only comments stating this configuration file is not used and gives some basic systemd information. The /etc/inittab file no longer has any true functional use. The following is an example of a /etc/inittab file on a Linux server that uses systemd.

```
# cat /etc/inittab
# inittab is no longer used when using systemd.
#
# ADDING CONFIGURATION HERE WILL HAVE NO EFFECT ON YOUR SYSTEM.
#
# Ctrl-Alt-Delete is handled by
# /etc/systemd/system/ctrl-alt-del.target
#
```

```
# systemd uses 'targets' instead of runlevels.
# By default, there are two main targets:
#
# multi-user.target: analogous to runlevel 3
# graphical.target: analogous to runlevel 5
#
# To set a default target, run:
#
# ln -s /lib/systemd/system/<target name>.target
# /etc/systemd/system/default.target
```

The /etc/inittab explains that if you want something similar to a classic 3 or 5 runlevel as your default runlevel, you need to create a symbolic link from the default.target unit to the runlevel target unit of your choice. To check what default.target is currently symbolically linked to (or in legacy terms, to check the default runlevel), use the command shown here. You can see that on this Linux server, the default is to start up at legacy runlevel 3.

```
# ls -l /etc/systemd/system/default.target
lrwxrwxrwx. 1 root root 36 Mar 13 17:27
 /etc/systemd/system/default.target ->
    /lib/systemd/system/runlevel3.target
```

The capability to switch runlevels using the init or telinit command is still available. When issued, either of the commands is translated into a systemd target unit activation request. Therefore, typing **init 3** at the command line really issues the command systemctl isolate multi-user.target. Also, you can still use the runlevel command to determine the current legacy runlevel, but it is strongly discouraged.

The classic SysVinit /etc/inittab handled spawning the getty or mingetty processes. The systemd init handles this via the getty.target unit. The getty.target is activated by the multi-user.target unit. You can see how these two target units are linked by the following command:

```
# systemctl show --property "WantedBy" getty.target
WantedBy=multi-user.target
```

Now that you have a basic understanding of classic and modern init daemons, it's time to do some practical server administrator actions that involve the init daemon.

Checking the Status of Services

As a Linux administrator, you need to check the status of the services being offered on your server. For security reasons, you should disable and remove any unused system services discovered through the process. Most importantly for troubleshooting purposes, you need to be able to quickly know what should and should not be running on your Linux server.

15

Of course, knowing which initialization service is being used by your Linux server is the first piece of information to obtain. How to determine this was covered in the "Understanding the Initialization Daemon" section of this chapter. The rest of this section is organized into subsections on the various initialization daemons.

Checking services for SysVinit systems

To see all the services that are being offered by a Linux server using the classic SysVinit daemon, use the chkconfig command. The example that follows shows the services available on a classic SysVinit Linux server. Note that each runlevel (0–6) is shown for each service with a status of on or off. The status denotes whether a particular service is started (on) or not (off) for that runlevel.

```
# chkconfig --list
ConsoleKit       0:off  1:off  2:off  3:on   4:on   5:on   6:off
NetworkManager   0:off  1:off  2:off  3:off  4:off  5:off  6:off
...
crond            0:off  1:off  2:on   3:on   4:on   5:on   6:off
cups             0:off  1:off  2:on   3:on   4:on   5:on   6:off
...
sshd             0:off  1:off  2:on   3:on   4:on   5:on   6:off
syslog           0:off  1:off  2:on   3:on   4:on   5:on   6:off
tux              0:off  1:off  2:off  3:off  4:off  5:off  6:off
udev-post        0:off  1:off  2:off  3:on   4:on   5:on   6:off
vncserver        0:off  1:off  2:off  3:off  4:off  5:off  6:off
winbind          0:off  1:off  2:off  3:off  4:off  5:off  6:off
wpa_supplicant   0:off  1:off  2:off  3:off  4:off  5:off  6:off
xfs              0:off  1:off  2:on   3:on   4:on   5:on   6:off
ypbind           0:off  1:off  2:off  3:off  4:off  5:off  6:off
yum-updatesd     0:off  1:off  2:off  3:on   4:on   5:on   6:off
```

Some services in the example are never started, such as vncserver. Other services, such as the cups daemon, are started on runlevels 2 through 5.

Using the chkconfig command, you cannot tell if a service is currently running. To do that, you need to use the service command. To help isolate only those services that are currently running, the service command is piped into the grep command and then sorted, as follows.

```
# service --status-all | grep running... | sort
anacron (pid 2162) is running...
atd (pid 2172) is running...
auditd (pid 1653) is running...
automount (pid 1952) is running...
console-kit-daemon (pid 2046) is running...
crond (pid 2118) is running...
cupsd (pid 1988) is running...
...
```

```
sshd (pid 2002) is running...
syslogd (pid 1681) is running...
xfs (pid 2151) is running...
yum-updatesd (pid 2205) is running...
```

You can also use both the chkconfig and the service commands to view an individual service's settings. Using both commands in the example that follows, you can view the cups daemon's settings.

```
# chkconfig --list cups
cups              0:off    1:off    2:on     3:on     4:on     5:on     6:off
# service cups status
cupsd (pid 1988) is running...
```

You can see that the cupsd daemon is set to start on every runlevel but 0, 1, and 6, and from the service command, you can see that it is currently running. Also, the process ID (PID) number is given for the daemon.

Checking services for Upstart systems

To see all the services running on a Linux server using the Upstart init daemon, use the following command:

```
# initctl list | grep start/running
tty (/dev/tty3) start/running, process 1163
...
system-setup-keyboard start/running, process 656
prefdm start/running, process 1154
```

Keep in mind that there may still be services that have not been ported to the Upstart init daemon. Therefore, you also need to use the classic SysVinit command, service, to check for any leftover SysVinit services. Note that on some distributions, you may see a few services in *both* the initctl and the service command output.

```
# service --status-all | grep running
abrtd (pid   1118) is running...
acpid (pid   996) is running...
atd (pid   1146) is running...
...
rsyslogd (pid   752) is running...
sendmail (pid   1099) is running...
...
```

TIP

Just because a service is not in a running state does not mean it is unavailable. The service could be in a stopped/wait state, awaiting an event on the system. To see all the services, no matter what their state, remove the grep portion of the preceding initctl list and service --status-all commands.

15

To show the status of a single service, use `initctl` if the service has been ported to Upstart and the `service` command if it has not been ported yet. The following example shows two service statuses—one that has been ported to Upstart and one that has not.

```
# initctl status vpnc-cleanup
vpnc-cleanup stop/waiting
# service ssh status
sshd (pid  970) is running...
```

In this example, the ssh daemon had not yet been ported to Upstart. Therefore, ssh needs the `service` command with the `status` option to be used to check its status. The vpnc-cleanup service is an Upstart service. Thus, it needed the `initctl status` command to be used. In some distributions, such as Ubuntu, you can also use the `initctl status` command for services that have not yet been migrated to Upstart.

Checking services for systemd systems

To see all the services that are being offered by a Linux server using `systemd`, use the following command:

```
# systemctl list-unit-files --type=service | grep -v disabled
UNIT FILE                                   STATE
abrt-ccpp.service                           enabled
abrt-oops.service                           enabled
abrt-vmcore.service                         enabled
abrtd.service                               enabled
alsa-restore.service                        static
alsa-store.service                          static
anaconda-shell@.service                     static
arp-ethers.service                          enabled
atd.service                                 enabled
auditd.service                              enabled
avahi-daemon.service                        enabled
bluetooth.service                           enabled
console-kit-log-system-restart.service      static
console-kit-log-system-start.service        static
console-kit-log-system-stop.service         static
crond.service                               enabled
cups.service                                enabled
...
sshd-keygen.service                         enabled
sshd.service                                enabled
system-setup-keyboard.service               enabled
...
134 unit files listed.
```

Remember that the three status possibilities for a `systemd` service are enabled, disabled, or static. There's no need to include disabled to see which services are set to be active, which is effectively accomplished by using the -v option on the grep command, as shown in the preceding example. The state of static is essentially enabled, and thus should be included.

To see if a particular service is running, use the following command:

```
# systemctl status cups.service
cups.service - CUPS Printing Service
  Loaded: loaded (/lib/systemd/system/cups.service; enabled)
  Active: active (running) since Mon, 30 Apr 12:36:31 -0400; 13h ago
  Main PID: 1315 (cupsd)
   CGroup: name=systemd:/system/cups.service
          └ 1315 /usr/sbin/cupsd -f
```

The systemctl command can be used to show the status of a single service. In the preceding example, the printing service was chosen. Notice that the name of the service is cups. service. A great deal of helpful information about the service is given here, such as the fact that it is enabled and active, its start time, and its process ID (PID) as well.

Now that you can check the status of services and determine some information about them, you need to know how to accomplish starting, stopping, and reloading the services on your Linux server.

Stopping and Starting Services

The tasks of starting, stopping, and restarting services typically refer to immediate needs—in other words, managing services without a server reboot. For example, if you want to temporarily stop a service, then you are in the right section. However, if you want to stop a service and not allow it to be restarted at server reboot, then you need to actually disable the service, which is covered in the "Enabling Persistent Services" section later in this chapter.

Stopping and starting SysVinit services

The primary command for stopping and starting SysVinit services is the service command. With the service command, the name of the service you want to control comes second in the command line. The last option is what you want to do to the service, stop, start, restart, and so on. The following example shows how to stop the cups service. Notice that an OK is given, which lets you know that cupsd has been successfully stopped.

```
# service cups status
cupsd (pid 5857) is running...
# service cups stop
Stopping cups:          [  OK  ]
# service cups status
cupsd is stopped
```

15

To start a service, you simply use a start option instead of a stop option on the end of the service command as follows.

```
# service cups start
Starting cups:            [  OK  ]
# service cups status
cupsd (pid 6860) is running...
```

To restart a SysVinit service, the restart option is used. This option stops the service and then immediately starts it again.

```
# service cups restart
Stopping cups:            [  OK  ]
Starting cups:            [  OK  ]
# service cups status
cupsd (pid 7955) is running...
```

When a service is already stopped, a restart generates a FAILED status on the attempt to stop it. However, as shown in the example that follows, the service is successfully started when a restart is attempted.

```
# service cups stop
Stopping cups:            [  OK  ]
# service cups restart
Stopping cups:            [FAILED]
Starting cups:            [  OK  ]
# service cups status
cupsd (pid 8236) is running...
```

Reloading a service is different from restarting a service. When you reload a service, the service itself is not stopped. Only the service's configuration files are loaded again. The following example shows how to reload the cups daemon.

```
# service cups status
cupsd (pid 8236) is running...
# service cups reload
Reloading cups:           [  OK  ]
# service cups status
cupsd (pid 8236) is running...
```

If a SysVinit service is stopped when you attempt to reload it, you get a FAILED status. This is shown in the following example:

```
# service cups status
cupsd is stopped
# service cups reload
Reloading cups:              [FAILED]
```

Stopping and starting Upstart services

The primary command for stopping and starting Upstart init services is the initctl command. The options are very similar to SysVinit's service command:

- **Stopping a service with Upstart**—In the following example, the status of the cups daemon is checked and then stopped using the initctl stop cups command.

```
# initctl status cups
cups start/running, process 2390
# initctl stop cups
cups stop/waiting
# initctl status cups
cups stop/waiting
```

- **Starting a service with Upstart**—In the following example, the cups daemon is started using the initctl start cups command.

```
# initctl start cups
cups start/running, process 2408
# initctl status cups
cups start/running, process 2408
```

- **Restarting a service with Upstart**—Restarting a service with Upstart stops and then starts the service. However, the configuration file is not reloaded.

```
# initctl restart cups
cups start/running, process 2430
# initctl status cups
cups start/running, process 2490
```

- **Reloading a service with Upstart**—Reloading does *not* stop and start the service. It only loads the configuration file again. This is the option to use when you have made changes to the configuration file.

  The following example illustrates how to reload the cups daemon with initctl. Notice that the process ID (PID) is still 2490, which is the same as it was in the example for restarting the cups daemon because the process was not stopped and started in the reload process.

```
# initctl reload cups
# initctl status cups
cups start/running, process 2490
```

> **NOTE**
>
> You need root privileges to stop and start services. However, you do not need root privileges to check a service's status.

15

Stopping and starting systemd services

For the `systemd` daemon, the `systemctl` command works for stopping, starting, reloading, and restarting services. The options to the `systemctl` command should look familiar.

Stopping a service with systemd

In the example that follows, the status of the `cups` daemon is checked and then stopped using the `systemctl stop cups.service` command:

```
# systemctl status cups.service
cups.service - CUPS Printing Service
    Loaded: loaded (/lib/systemd/system/cups.service; enabled)
    Active: active (running) since Mon, 30 Apr 2018 12:36:3...
  Main PID: 1315 (cupsd)
    CGroup: name=systemd:/system/cups.service
            1315 /usr/sbin/cupsd -f
# systemctl stop cups.service
# systemctl status cups.service
cups.service - CUPS Printing Service
    Loaded: loaded (/lib/systemd/system/cups.service; enabled)
    Active: inactive (dead) since Tue, 01 May 2018 04:43:4...
    Process: 1315 ExecStart=/usr/sbin/cupsd -f
  (code=exited, status=0/SUCCESS)
    CGroup: name=systemd:/system/cups.service
```

Notice that when the status is taken, after stopping the `cups` daemon, the service is inactive (dead) but still considered enabled. This means that the `cups` daemon is still started upon server boot.

Starting a service with systemd

Starting the `cups` daemon is just as easy as stopping it. The example that follows demonstrates this ease.

```
# systemctl start cups.service
# systemctl status cups.service
cups.service - CUPS Printing Service
    Loaded: loaded (/lib/systemd/system/cups.service; enabled)
    Active: active (running) since Tue, 01 May 2018 04:43:5...
  Main PID: 17003 (cupsd)
    CGroup: name=systemd:/system/cups.service
            └ 17003 /usr/sbin/cupsd -f
```

After the `cups` daemon is started, using `systemctl` with the status option shows that the service is active (running). Also, its process ID (PID) number, 17003, is shown.

Restarting a service with systemd

Restarting a service means that a service is stopped and then started again. If the service was not currently running, restarting it simply starts the service.

```
# systemctl restart cups.service
# systemctl status cups.service
cups.service - CUPS Printing Service
   Loaded: loaded (/lib/systemd/system/cups.service; enabled)
   Active: active (running) since Tue, 01 May 2018 04:45:2...
 Main PID: 17015 (cupsd)
   CGroup: name=systemd:/system/cups.service
           └ 17015 /usr/sbin/cupsd -f
```

You can also perform a conditional restart of a service using `systemctl`. A conditional restart only restarts a service if it is currently running. Any service in an inactive state is not started.

```
# systemctl status cups.service
cups.service - CUPS Printing Service
   Loaded: loaded (/lib/systemd/system/cups.service; enabled)
   Active: inactive (dead) since Tue, 01 May 2015 06:03:32...
  Process: 17108 ExecStart=/usr/sbin/cupsd -f
 (code=exited, status=0/SUCCESS)
   CGroup: name=systemd:/system/cups.service
# systemctl condrestart cups.service
# systemctl status cups.service
cups.service - CUPS Printing Service
   Loaded: loaded (/lib/systemd/system/cups.service; enabled)
   Active: inactive (dead) since Tue, 01 May 2015 06:03:32...
  Process: 17108 ExecStart=/usr/sbin/cupsd -f
 (code=exited, status=0/SUCCESS)
   CGroup: name=systemd:/system/cups.service
```

Notice in the example that the `cups` daemon was in an inactive state. When the conditional restart was issued, no error messages were generated! The `cups` daemon was not started because conditional restarts affects active services. Thus, it is always a good practice to check the status of a service, after stopping, starting, conditionally restarting, and so on.

Reloading a service with systemd

Reloading a service is different from restarting a service. When you `reload` a service, the service itself is not stopped. Only the service's configuration files are loaded again.

```
# systemctl status sshd.service
sshd.service - OpenSSH server daemon
   Loaded: loaded (/usr/lib/systemd/system/sshd.service; enabled)
```

15

```
       Active: active (running) since Fri 2018-11-24 14:06:57 EST...
     Main PID: 1675 (sshd)
       CGroup: /system.slice/sshd.service
               └─1675 /usr/sbin/sshd -D
   # systemctl reload sshd.service
   # systemctl status sshd.service
   sshd.service - OpenSSH server daemon
       Loaded: loaded (/lib/systemd/system/sshd.service; enabled)
       Active: active (running) since Fri 2018-11-24 14:06:57 EST...
      Process: 2149 ExecReload=/bin/kill -HUP $MAINPID
            (code=exited, status=0/SUCCESSd)
     Main PID: 1675 (sshd)
       CGroup: /system.slice/sshd.service
               └─1675 /usr/sbin/sshd -D
```

Doing a reload of a service, instead of a restart, prevents any pending service operations from being aborted. A reload is a better method for a busy Linux server.

Now that you know how to stop and start services for troubleshooting and emergency purposes, you can learn how to enable and disable services.

Enabling Persistent Services

You use stop and start for immediate needs, not for services that need to be persistent. A *persistent* service is one that is started at server boot time or at a particular runlevel. Services that need to be set as persistent are typically new services that the Linux server is offering.

Configuring persistent services for SysVinit

One of the nice features of the classic SysVinit daemon is that making a particular service persistent or removing its persistence is very easy to do. Consider the following example:

```
   # chkconfig --list cups
   cups            0:off  1:off  2:off  3:off  4:off  5:off  6:off
```

On this Linux server, the cups service is not started at any runlevel, as shown with the chkconfig command. You can also check and see if any start (S) symbol links are set up in each of the seven runlevel directories, /etc/rc.d/rc?.d. Remember that SysVinit keeps symbolic links here for starting and stopping various services at certain runlevels. Each directory represents a particular runlevel; for example, rc5.d is for runlevel 5. Notice that only files starting with a K are listed, so there are links for killing off the cups daemon. None are listed with S, which is consistent with chkconfig that the cups daemon does not start at any runlevel on this server.

```
# ls /etc/rc.d/rc?.d/*cups
/etc/rc.d/rc0.d/K10cups    /etc/rc.d/rc3.d/K10cups
/etc/rc.d/rc1.d/K10cups    /etc/rc.d/rc4.d/K10cups
/etc/rc.d/rc2.d/K10cups    /etc/rc.d/rc5.d/K10cups
/etc/rc.d/rc6.d/K10cups
```

To make a service persistent at a particular runlevel, the chkconfig command is used again. Instead of the --list option, the --level option is used, as shown in the following code:

```
# chkconfig --level 3 cups on
# chkconfig --list cups
cups              0:off  1:off  2:off  3:on   4:off  5:off  6:off
# ls /etc/rc.d/rc3.d/S*cups
/etc/rc.d/rc3.d/S56cups
```

The service's persistence at runlevel 3 is verified by both using the chkconfig --list command and looking at the rc3.d directory for any files starting with the letter S.

To make a service persistent on more than one runlevel, you can do the following:

```
# chkconfig --level 2345 cups on
# chkconfig --list cups
cups              0:off  1:off  2:on   3:on   4:on   5:on   6:off
# ls /etc/rc.d/rc?.d/S*cups
/etc/rc.d/rc2.d/S56cups    /etc/rc.d/rc4.d/S56cups
/etc/rc.d/rc3.d/S56cups    /etc/rc.d/rc5.d/S56cups
```

Disabling a service is just as easy as enabling one with SysVinit. You just need to change the on in the chkconfig command to off. The following example demonstrates using the chkconfig command to disable the cups service at runlevel 5.

```
# chkconfig --level 5 cups off
# chkconfig --list cups
cups              0:off  1:off  2:on   3:on   4:on   5:off  6:off
# ls /etc/rc.d/rc5.d/S*cups
ls: cannot access /etc/rc.d/rc5.d/S*cups: No such file or directory
```

As expected, there is now no symbolic link, starting with the letter S, for the cups service in the /etc/rc.d/rc5.d directory.

Configuring persistent services for Upstart

The Upstart init daemon emits the startup signal that triggers the service jobs to start. At server boot time, various jobs may themselves emit signals. These emitted signals then cause other jobs to start. Thus, the key to making a service persistent is to ensure the service's definition file is triggered by one of the signals emitted as the server boots.

15

Remember that the Upstart `init` daemon's job definition files are located in the `/etc/init` directory. Consider the following job definition file for the `ssh` daemon:

```
# cat /etc/init/ssh.conf
# ssh - OpenBSD Secure Shell server
# The OpenSSH server provides secure shell access to the system.
description    "OpenSSH server"
start on filesystem or runlevel [2345]
stop on runlevel [!2345]
respawn
```

To determine what emitted events trigger a service, look for *start on* in the configuration file. The `ssh` daemon is triggered by several possible emitted events, filesystem, runlevel 2, runlevel 3, runlevel 4, or runlevel 5. Basically, the `ssh` daemon starts upon server boot and is set as persistent. The syntax for the runlevel events, runlevel [2345], is used in many of the job files and denotes that the name "runlevel" can end in 2, 3, 4, or 5.

To make a job persistent (start at boot), you need to modify the *start on* line in its configuration file so it starts on certain events emitted at server boot. To disable a job at boot, just comment out the *start on* line with a pound sign (#). See the "Adding New or Customized Services" section for Upstart for a more thorough explanation of these configuration files.

Configuring persistent services for systemd

For the `systemd` daemon, again the `systemctl` command is used. With it, you can disable and enable services on the Linux server.

Enabling a service with systemd

Using the `enable` option on the `systemctl` command sets a service to always start at boot (be persistent). The following shows exactly how to accomplish this:

```
# systemctl status cups.service
cups.service - CUPS Printing Service
   Loaded: loaded (/lib/systemd/system/cups.service; disabled)
   Active: inactive (dead) since Tue, 01 May 2018 06:42:38 ...
 Main PID: 17172 (code=exited, status=0/SUCCESS)
   CGroup: name=systemd:/system/cups.service
# systemctl enable cups.service
ln -s '/lib/systemd/system/cups.service'
   '/etc/systemd/system/printer.target.wants/cups.service
ln -s '/lib/systemd/system/cups.socket'
   '/etc/systemd/system/sockets.target.wants/cups.socket'
ln -s '/lib/systemd/system/cups.path' '
   /etc/systemd/system/multi-user.target.wants/cups.path'
```

```
# systemctl status cups.service
cups.service - CUPS Printing Service
   Loaded: loaded (/lib/systemd/system/cups.service; enabled)
   Active: inactive (dead) since Tue, 01 May 2018 06:42:38...
 Main PID: 17172 (code=exited, status=0/SUCCESS)
   CGroup: name=systemd:/system/cups.service
```

Notice that the status of `cups.service` changes from *disabled* to *enabled* after using the `enable` option on `systemctl`. Also, notice that the `enable` option simply creates a few symbolic links. You may be tempted to create these links yourself. However, the preferred method is to use the `systemctl` command to accomplish this.

Disabling a service with systemd

You can use the `disable` option on the `systemctl` command to keep a service from starting at boot. However, it does not immediately stop the service. You need to use the `stop` option discussed in the "Stopping a service with systemd" section. The following example shows how to `disable` a currently `enabled` service.

```
# systemctl disable cups.service
rm '/etc/systemd/system/printer.target.wants/cups.service'
rm '/etc/systemd/system/sockets.target.wants/cups.socket'
rm '/etc/systemd/system/multi-user.target.wants/cups.path'
# systemctl status cups.service
cups.service - CUPS Printing Service
   Loaded: loaded (/lib/systemd/system/cups.service; disabled)
   Active: active (running) since Tue, 01 May 2018 06:06:41...
 Main PID: 17172 (cupsd)
   CGroup: name=systemd:/system/cups.service
           17172 /usr/sbin/cupsd -f
```

The `disable` option simply removes a few files via the preferred method of the `systemctl` command. Notice also in the preceding example that although the `cups` service is now disabled, the `cups` daemon is still *active* (running). With `systemd`, some services cannot be disabled. These services are static services. Consider the following service, `dbus.service`:

```
# systemctl status dbus.service
dbus.service - D-Bus System Message Bus
  Loaded: loaded (/lib/systemd/system/dbus.service; static)
  Active: active (running) since Mon, 30 Apr 2018 12:35:...
 Main PID: 707 (dbus-daemon)
...
# systemctl disable dbus.service
# systemctl status dbus.service
dbus.service - D-Bus System Message Bus
  Loaded: loaded (/lib/systemd/system/dbus.service; static)
  Active: active (running) since Mon, 30 Apr 2018 12:35:...
 Main PID: 707 (dbus-daemon)
...
```

15

When the `systemctl disable` command is issued on `dbus.service`, it is simply ignored. Remember that static means that the service is enabled by default and cannot be disabled, even by root.

Sometimes, disabling a service is not enough to make sure that it does not run. For example, you might want `network.service` to replace `NetworkManager.service` for starting network interfaces on your system. Disabling NetworkManager would keep the service from starting on its own. However, if some other service listed NetworkManager as a dependency, that service would try to start NetworkManager when it started.

To disable a service in a way that prevents it from ever running on your system, you can use the `mask` option. For example, to set the NetworkManager service so it never runs, type the following:

```
# systemctl mask NetworkManager.service
ln -s '/dev/null' '/etc/systemd/system/NetworkManager.service'
```

As the output shows, the `NetworkManager.service` file in /etc is linked to /dev/null. So even if someone tried to run that service, nothing would happen. To be able to use the service again, you could type **systemctl unmask NetworkManager.service.**

Now that you understand how to enable individual services to be persistent (and how to disable or mask individual services), you need to look at service groups as a whole. The next section covers how to start groups of services at boot time.

Configuring a Default Runlevel or Target Unit

Whereas a persistent service is one that is started at server boot time, a persistent (default) *runlevel* or *target unit* is a group of services that are started at boot time. Both classic SysVinit and Upstart define these groups of services as *runlevels*, while `systemd` calls them *target units*.

Configuring the SysVinit default runlevel

You set the persistent **runlevel** for a Linux server using SysVinit in the /etc/inittab file. A portion of this file is shown here:

```
# cat /etc/inittab
#
# inittab       This file describes how the INIT process should
#               set up the system in a certain run-level.
...
id:5:initdefault:
...
```

The initdefault line in the example shows that the current default runlevel is runlevel 5. To change this, simply edit the /etc/inittab file using your favorite editor and change the 5 to one of the following runlevels: 2, 3, or 4. Do *not* use the runlevels 0 or 6 in this file! This would cause your server to either halt or reboot when it is started up.

Configuring the default runlevel in Upstart

Some distributions still use the /etc/inittab file to set the default runlevel, whereas others use the /etc/init/rc-sysinit.conf file.

Earlier Fedora and RHEL's Upstart init daemon still uses the /etc/inittab file. Therefore, just change the default runlevel as you would on a SysVinit system.

Ubuntu's Upstart init daemon uses the /etc/init/rc-sysinit.conf file to set the default runlevel, a portion of which is shown in the code that follows. The code line to change is env DEFAULT_RUNLEVEL=. Simply edit this file and change that number to the runlevel you desire. However, remember that Ubuntu's runlevel 2 is equivalent to runlevels 3, 4, and 5.

```
$ cat /etc/init/rc-sysinit.conf
# rc-sysinit - System V initialisation compatibility
...
# Default runlevel, this may be overriden on the kernel command-line
# or by faking an old /etc/inittab entry
env DEFAULT_RUNLEVEL=2
```

Configuring the default target unit for systemd

For systemd, the term *target units* refers to groups of services to be started. The following shows the various target units you can configure to be persistent and their equivalent backward-compatible, runlevel-specific target units.

- multi-user.target =
  - runlevel2.target
  - runlevel3.target
  - runlevel4.target
- graphical.target = runlevel5.target

The persistent target unit is set via a symbolic link to the default.target unit file. Consider the following:

```
# ls -l /etc/systemd/system/default.target
lrwxrwxrwx. 1 root root 36 Mar 13 17:27
 /etc/systemd/system/default.target ->
 /lib/systemd/system/runlevel5.target
```

15

```
# ls -l /lib/systemd/system/runlevel5.target
lrwxrwxrwx. 1 root root 16 Mar 27 15:39
 /lib/systemd/system/runlevel5.target ->
 graphical.target
```

The example shows that the current persistent target unit on this server is `runlevel5.target` because `default.target` is a symbolic link to the `runlevel5.target` unit file. However, notice that `runlevel5.target` is also a symbolic link and it points to `graphical.target`. Thus, this server's current persistent target unit is `graphical.target`.

To set a different target unit to be persistent, you simply need to change the symbolic link for `default.target`. To be consistent, stick with the runlevel target units if they are used on your server.

The following example changes the server's persistent target unit from `graphical.target` to `multi-user.target` by changing the `default.target` symbolic link from `runlevel5.target` to `runlevel3.target`. The `-f` option is used on the `ls -s` command to force any current symbolic link to be broken and the new designated symbolic link to be enforced.

```
# ls -l /lib/systemd/system/runlevel3.target
lrwxrwxrwx. 1 root root 17 Mar 27 15:39
 /lib/systemd/system/runlevel3.target ->
 multi-user.target
# ln -sf /lib/systemd/system/runlevel3.target \
 /etc/systemd/system/default.target
# ls -l /etc/systemd/system/default.target
lrwxrwxrwx. 1 root root 36 May  1 10:06
 /etc/systemd/system/default.target ->
 /lib/systemd/system/runlevel3.target
```

When the server is rebooted, the `multi-user.target` is the persistent target unit. Any services in the `multi-user.target` unit are started (activated) at that time.

Adding New or Customized Services

Occasionally, you need to add a new service to your Linux server. Also, you may have to customize a particular service. When these needs arise, you must follow specific steps for your Linux server's initialization daemon to either take over the management of the service or recognize the customization of it.

Adding new services to SysVinit

When adding a new or customized service to a Linux SysVinit server, you must complete three steps in order to have the service managed by SysVinit.

1. Create a new or customized service script file.
2. Move the new or customized service script to the proper location for SysVinit management.
3. Add the service to a specific runlevel.

Step 1: Create a new or customized service script file

If you are customizing a service script, simply make a copy of the original unit file from /etc/rc.d/init.d and add any desired customizations.

If you are creating a new script, you need to make sure you handle all the various options you want the service command to accept for your service, such as start, stop, restart, and so on.

For a new script, especially if you have never created a service script before, it would be wise to make a copy of a current service script from /etc/rc.d/init.d and modify it to meet your new service's needs. Consider the following partial example of the cupsd service's script:

```
# cat /etc/rc.d/init.d/cups
#!/bin/sh
...
#    chkconfig: 2345 25 10
...
start () {
        echo -n $"Starting $prog: "
        # start daemon
        daemon $DAEMON
        RETVAL=$?
        echo
        [ $RETVAL = 0 ] && touch /var/lock/subsys/cups
        return $RETVAL
}

stop () {
        # stop daemon
        echo -n $"Stopping $prog: "
        killproc $DAEMON
        RETVAL=$?
        echo          [ $RETVAL = 0 ] && rm -f /var/lock/subsys/cups
}

restart() {
        stop
        start
}
```

15

```
case $1 in
. . .
```

The cups service script starts out by creating functions for each of the start, stop, and restart options. If you feel uncomfortable with shell script writing, review Chapter 7, "Writing Simple Shell Scripts," to improve your skills.

One line you should be sure to check and possibly modify in your new script is the chkconfig line that is commented out. For example:

```
#    chkconfig: 2345 25 10
```

When you add the service script in a later step, the chkconfig command reads that line to set runlevels at which the service starts (2, 3, 4, and 5), its run order when the script is set to start (25), and its kill order when it is set to stop (10).

Check the boot order in the default runlevel before adding your own script. For example:

```
# ls /etc/rc5.d
. . .
/etc/rc5.d/S22messagebus
/etc/rc5.d/S23NetworkManager
/etc/rc5.d/S24nfslock
/etc/rc5.d/S24openct
/etc/rc5.d/S24rpcgssd
/etc/rc5.d/S25blk-availability
/etc/rc5.d/S25cups
/etc/rc5.d/S25netfs
/etc/rc5.d/S26acpid
/etc/rc5.d/S26haldaemon
/etc/rc5.d/S26hypervkvpd
/etc/rc5.d/S26udev-post

. . .
```

In this case, the chkconfig line in the S25My_New_Service script will cause the script to be added after S25cups and before S25netfs in the boot order. You can change the chkconfig line in the service script if you want the service to start earlier (use a smaller number) or later (use a larger number) in the list of service scripts.

Step 2: Add the service script to /etc/rc.d/init.d

After you have modified or created and tested your service's script file, you can move it to the proper location: /etc/rc.d/init.d:

```
# cp My_New_Service /etc/rc.d/init.d
# ls /etc/rc.d/init.d/My_New_Service
/etc/rc.d/init.d/My_New_Service
```

Step 3: Add the service to runlevel directories

This final step sets up the service script to start and stop at different runlevels and checks that the service script works.

1. To add the script based on the chkconfig line in the service script, type the following:

```
# chkconfig --add My_New_Service
# ls /etc/rc?.d/*My_New_Service
/etc/rc0.d/K10My_New_Service    /etc/rc4.d/S25My_New_Service
/etc/rc1.d/K10My_New_Service    /etc/rc5.d/S25My_New_Service
/etc/rc2.d/S25My_New_Service    /etc/rc6.d/K10My_New_Service
/etc/rc3.d/S25My_New_Service
```

Based on the previous example (chkconfig: 2345 25 10), symbolic links to the script set the service to start in the position 25 (S25) for runlevels 2, 3, 4, and 5. Also, links are set to stop (or not start) at runlevels 0, 1, and 6.

2. After you have made the symbolic link(s), test that your new or modified service works as expected before performing a server reboot.

```
# service My_New_Service start
Starting My_New_Service:        [  OK  ]
# service My_New_Service stop
Stopping My_New_Service:        [  OK  ]
```

After everything is in place, your new or modified service starts at every runlevel you have selected on your system. Also, you can start or stop it manually using the sservice command.

Adding new services to Upstart

You need to complete only one step to add a new service or customize an existing service with Upstart. Just add a new job configuration file or modify an existing one. However, this one step can be rather complicated.

The Upstart service job configuration files are all located in the /etc/init directory. These files are plain text only. They use a special syntax for directing Upstart on how to deal with a particular service. The following example of a configuration file has some very simple syntax:

```
# cat ck-log-system-restart.conf
# Upstart event
# ck-log-system-restart - write system restart to log
start on runlevel 6
task
exec /usr/sbin/ck-log-system-restart
```

15

Any pound sign (#) denotes a comment line and is ignored by Upstart. The other lines are called stanzas and have special syntax for controlling Upstart jobs. The stanzas from the preceding file are as follows:

- start on—This stanza defines what emitted event starts the service or task. In this particular case, when the runlevel 6 event is emitted, the ck-log-system-restart starts.

- task—The stanza here defines that this particular job is a task job as opposed to a service.

- exec—This stanza defines what program runs to start the task. Instead of the exec stanza, you can embed an actual command line script to run here by using the script stanza before the actual code and end script after it.

A slightly more complicated job configuration file is shown next—for the cron daemon. There are some additional stanzas that were not in the previous example. Notice that the task stanza is missing in the file. This indicates that this particular job is a service job instead of a task job.

```
# cat cron.conf
# cron - regular background program processing daemon
# cron is a standard UNIX program that runs user-specified
# programs at periodic scheduled times
description    "regular background program processing daemon"
start on runlevel [2345]
stop on runlevel [!2345]
expect fork
respawn
exec cron
```

The additional stanzas in this example are as follows:

- description—This stanza is optional and simply describes the service.

- start on—Though the start on portion of this stanza was previously covered, the [2345] syntax was not. Using brackets means that the stanza is valid for any of those numbers. Thus, the service starts on runlevel 2, 3, 4, or 5.

- stop on—The stanza here defines what emitted events the service stops on. The [!2345] in this stanza means not runlevel 2 or 3 or 4 or 5. In other words, it stops only on runlevel 0, runlevel 1, or runlevel 6.

- expect—This particular stanza is rather important and a little tricky. The expect fork syntax allows Upstart to track this daemon and any of its child processes (forks).

- respawn—The stanza here tells Upstart to restart this service if it is ever terminated via a means outside its normal stop on.

> **TIP**
>
> To test your new or modified job configuration files, you can set the `start` on stanza to a non-standard event. In other words, you can make up your own event name. For example, use the event name `MyTest`. To test the new configuration file, you type `initctl emit MyTest` at the command line. If your configuration file works correctly, then modify the `start` on stanza to the correct Upstart event.

Every job configuration file must follow at least three rules. The job configuration file must:

- Not be empty
- Be syntactically correct
- Contain at least one legal stanza

Although there are only three rules, creating or modifying a service job configuration file correctly can be a rather difficult task. See `http://upstart.ubuntu.com/cookbook` for help on the syntax needed for these files. Also, you can find out more about events that emits by typing **man upstart-events** at the command line.

Adding new services to systemd

When adding a new or customized service to a Linux `systemd` server, you have to complete three steps in order to have the service managed by `systemd`:

1. Create a new or customized service configuration unit file for the new or customized service.
2. Move the new or customized service configuration unit file to the proper location for `systemd` management.
3. Add the service to a specific target unit's `Wants` to have the new or customized service start automatically with other services.

Step 1: Create a new or customized service configuration unit file

If you are customizing a service configuration unit file, simply make a copy of the original unit file from `/lib/systemd/system` and add any desired customizations.

For new files, obviously, you are creating a service unit configuration file from scratch. Consider the following basic service unit file template. At bare minimum, you need `Description` and `ExecStart` options for a service unit configuration file.

```
# cat My_New_Service.service
[Unit]
Description=My New Service
[Service]
ExecStart=/usr/bin/My_New_Service
```

15

For additional help on customizing or creating a new configuration unit file and the various needed options, you can use the man pages. At the command line, type **man systemd.service** to find out more about the various service unit file options.

Step 2: Move the service configuration unit file

Before you move the new or customized service configuration unit file, you need to be aware that there are two potential locations to store service configuration unit files. The one you choose determines whether the customizations take effect and if they remain persistent through software upgrades.

You can place your system service configuration unit file in one of the following two locations:

- /etc/systemd/system
    - This location is used to store customized local service configuration unit files.
    - Files in this location are not overwritten by software installations or upgrades.

Files here are used by the system *even* if there is a file of the same name in the /lib/systemd/system directory.

- /lib/systemd/system
    - This location is used to store system service configuration unit files.
    - Files in this location are overwritten by software installations and upgrades.

Files here are used by the system *only* if there is *not* a file of the same name in the /etc/systemd/system directory.

Thus, the best place to store your new or customized service configuration unit file is in /etc/systemd/system.

> **TIP**
>
> When you create a new or customized service, in order for the change to take effect without a server reboot, you need to issue a special command. At the command line, type systemctl daemon-reload.

Step 3: Add the service to the Wants directory

This final step is optional. It needs to be done only if you want your new service to start with a particular systemd target unit. For a service to be activated (started) by a particular target unit, it must be in that target unit's Wants directory.

First, add the line WantedBy=*desired.target* to the bottom of your service configuration unit file. The following example shows that the desired target unit for this new service is multi-user.target.

```
# cat /etc/systemd/system/My_New_Service.service
[Unit]
Description=My New Fake Service
[Service]
ExecStart=/usr/bin/My_New_Service
[Install]
WantedBy=multi-user.target
```

To add a new service unit to a target unit, you need to create a symbolic link. The following example shows the files located in the `multi-user.target` unit's `Wants` directory. Previously, in the "Understanding systemd init" section, the `systemctl` command was used to list `Wants`, and it is still the preferred method. Notice that in this directory, the files are symbolic links pointing to service unit configuration files in the `/lib/systemd/system` directory.

```
# ls /etc/systemd/system/multi-user.target.wants
abrt-ccpp.service        cups.path              remote-fs.target
abrtd.service            fcoe.service           rsyslog.service
abrt-oops.service        irqbalance.service     sendmail.service
abrt-vmcore.service      lldpad.service         sm-client.service
atd.service              mcelog.service         sshd-keygen.service
auditd.service           mdmonitor.service      sshd.service
...
# ls -l /etc/systemd/system/multi-user.target.wants
total 0
lrwxrwxrwx. 1 root root 37 Nov  2 22:29 abrt-ccpp.service ->
    /lib/systemd/system/abrt-ccpp.service
lrwxrwxrwx. 1 root root 33 Nov  2 22:29 abrtd.service ->
    /lib/systemd/system/abrtd.service
...
lrwxrwxrwx. 1 root root 32 Apr 26 20:05 sshd.service ->
    /lib/systemd/system/sshd.service
```

The following illustrates the process of adding a symbolic link file for `My_New_Service`:

```
# ln -s /etc/systemd/system/My_New_Service.service
  /etc/systemd/system/multi-user.target.wants/My_New_Service.service
```

A symbolic link is created in the `multi-user.target.wants` directory. Now, the new service, `My_New_Service`, is activated (started) when the `multi-user.target` unit is activated.

TIP

If you want to change the `systemd` target unit for a service, you need to change the symbol link to point to a new target `Wants` directory location. Use the `ls -sf` command to force any current symbolic link to be broken and the new designated symbolic link to be enforced.

15

Together, the three steps get your new or customized service added to a Linux `systemd` server. Remember that at this point, a new service is not running until a server reboot. To start the new service before a reboot, review the commands in the "Stopping and Starting Services" section.

Summary

How you start and stop services is dependent upon what initialization daemon is used by your Linux server: SysVinit, Upstart, or Systemd. Before you do any service management, be sure to use the examples in this chapter to help you determine your Linux server's initialization daemon.

The concepts of starting and stopping services go along with other service management concepts, such as making a service persistent, starting certain services at server boot time, reloading a service, and restarting a service. These concepts are very helpful as you learn about configuring and managing a Linux print server in the next chapter.

Exercises

Refer to the material in this chapter to complete the tasks that follow. If you are stuck, solutions to the tasks are shown in Appendix B (although in Linux, there are often multiple ways to complete a task). Try each of the exercises before referring to the answers. These tasks assume you are running a Fedora or Red Hat Enterprise Linux system (although some tasks work on other Linux systems as well).

1. Determine which initialization daemon your server is currently using.

2. What command can you use to check the status of the sshd daemon, depending on the initialization daemon in use on your Linux server?

3. Determine your server's previous and current runlevel.

4. How can you change the default runlevel or target unit on your Linux server?

5. For each initialization daemon, what commands list services running (or active) on your server?

6. List the running (or active) services on your Linux server.

7. For each initialization daemon, what commands show a particular service's current status?

8. Show the status of the cups daemon on your Linux server.

9. Attempt to restart the cups daemon on your Linux server.

10. Attempt to reload the cups daemon on your Linux server.

Configuring a Print Server

IN THIS CHAPTER

Understanding printing in Linux

Setting up printers

Using printing commands

Managing document printing

Sharing printers

Y ou can configure your Linux system to use printers that are connected directly to it (via a USB or parallel port) or that are available for printing over the network. Likewise, any printer you configure on your local system can be shared with users on other Linux, Windows, or Mac systems by opening up your printer as a print server.

You configure a printer as a native Linux printer in Fedora, RHEL, Ubuntu, and other Linux systems with the Common UNIX Printing System (CUPS). To configure a printer to work as a Microsoft Windows style of print server, you can use the Samba service in Linux.

This chapter focuses on CUPS. In particular, it shows you the graphical front end to CUPS, called the Print Settings window, which comes with Fedora, Red Hat Enterprise Linux, and other Linux distributions. Using Print Settings, you can also configure your printers as print servers so people can print to your printer from their own computers.

If you don't have a desktop or want to print from within a shell script, this chapter shows you how to use printing commands. From the command line, print commands such as lpr are available for carrying out printing. Commands also exist for querying print queues (lpq), manipulating print queues (lpc), and removing print queues (lprm).

Common UNIX Printing System

CUPS has become the standard for printing from Linux and other UNIX-like operating systems. It was designed to meet today's needs for standardized printer definitions and sharing on Internet Protocol–based networks (as most computer networks are today). Nearly every Linux distribution today comes with CUPS as its printing service. Here are some of the service's features:

- **IPP**—CUPS is based on the Internet Printing Protocol (http://www.pwg.org/ipp), a standard that was created to simplify how printers can be shared over IP networks. In the IPP model, printer servers and clients who want to print can exchange information about the model and features of a printer using HTTP (that is, web content) protocol. A server can also broadcast the availability of a printer so a printing client can easily find a list of locally available printers without configuration.

- **Drivers**—CUPS also standardized how printer drivers are created. The idea was to have a common format that could be used by printer manufacturers so that a driver could work across all different types of UNIX systems. That way, a manufacturer had to create the driver only once to work for Linux, Mac OS X, and a variety of UNIX derivatives.

- **Printer classes**—You can use printer classes to create multiple print server entries that point to the same printer or one print server entry that points to multiple printers. In the first case, multiple entries can each allow different options (such as pointing to a particular paper tray or printing with certain character sizes or margins). In the second case, you can have a pool of printers so that printing is distributed. In this instance, a malfunctioning printer or a printer that is dealing with very large documents won't bring all printing to a halt. CUPS also supports *implicit classes*, which are print classes that form by merging identical network printers automatically.

- **Printer browsing**—With printer browsing, client computers can see any CUPS printers on your local network with browsing enabled. As a result, clients can simply select the printers they want to use from the printer names broadcast on the network, without needing to know in advance what the printers are named and where they are connected. You can turn off the feature to prevent others on the local network from seeing a printer.

- **UNIX print commands**—To integrate into Linux and other UNIX environments, CUPS offers versions of standard commands for printing and managing printers that have been traditionally offered with UNIX systems.

Instead of using the Print Settings window, you can configure CUPS printing in other ways as well:

- **Configuring CUPS from a browser**—The CUPS project itself offers a web-based interface for adding and managing printers. With the cupsd service running, type **localhost:631** from a web browser on the computer running the CUPS service to manage printing. (See the section "Using web-based CUPS administration" later in this chapter.)

- **Configuring CUPS manually**—You also can configure CUPS manually (that is, edit the configuration files and start the cupsd daemon from the command line). Configuration files for CUPS are contained in the /etc/cups directory. In particular, you might be interested in the cupsd.conf file, which identifies permission, authentication, and other information for the printer daemon, and `printers.conf`, which identifies addresses and options for configured printers. Use the `classes.conf` file to define local printer classes.

Coming from Windows

You can print to CUPS from non-UNIX systems as well. For example, you can use a PostScript printer driver to print directly from a Windows system to your CUPS server. You can use CUPS without modification by configuring the Windows computer with a PostScript driver that uses `http://printserver-name:631/printers/targetPrinter` as its printing port.

You may also be able to use the native Windows printer drivers for the printer instead of the PostScript driver. If the native Windows driver does not work right out of the box on your CUPS print queue, you can create a Raw Print Queue under CUPS and use that instead. The Raw Print Queue directly passes through the data from the Windows native print driver to the printer.

To use CUPS, you must have the cups package installed in Fedora or RHEL. Most desktop Linux distributions include CUPS during the initial system install. If it is not installed in a Fedora or RHEL install, install it by typing the following:

```
# yum install cups
```

Setting Up Printers

Although using the printer administration tools specifically built for your distribution is usually best, many Linux systems simply rely on the tools that come with the CUPS software package.

This section explores how to use CUPS web-based administration tools that come with every Linux distribution and then examines the Print Settings tool `system-config-printer`, which is available with Fedora and Red Hat Enterprise Linux systems to enable you to set up printers. In some cases, no configuration is necessary, because connected printers can be automatically detected and configured. To install the Print Settings tool, as root type:

```
# yum install system-config-printer
```

Adding a printer automatically

CUPS printers can be configured to automatically broadcast their availability on the network so a client system can detect and use them without configuration. Connect a USB printer to your computer, and the printer can be automatically detected and made available. In fact, if you attach a local printer in Fedora and the print driver is not yet installed, you are prompted to install the software packages needed to use the printer.

The first time you go to print a document or view your Print Settings tool, the printers are ready to use. Further configuration can be done using the web-based CUPS administration tool or the Print Settings window.

Using web-based CUPS administration

CUPS offers its own web-based administrative tool for adding, deleting, and modifying printer configurations on your computer. The CUPS print service (using the cupsd daemon) listens on port 631 to provide access to the CUPS web-based administrative interface and share printers.

If CUPS is already running on your computer, you can immediately use CUPS web-based administration from your web browser. To see whether CUPS is running and to start setting up your printers, open a web browser on the local computer and type the following into its location box: **http://localhost:631/**.

A prompt for a valid login name and password may appear when you request functions that require it. If so, type the root login name and the root user's password, and click OK. A screen similar to the one shown in Figure 16.1 appears.

FIGURE 16.1

CUPS provides a web-based administration tool.

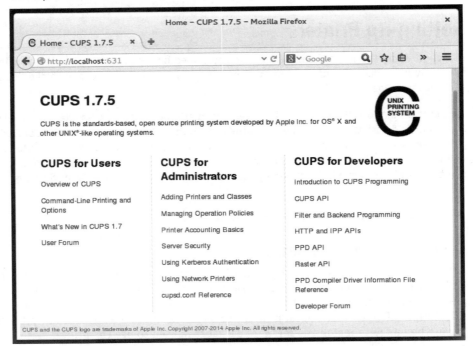

By default, web-based CUPS administration is available only from the local host. To access web-based CUPS administration from another computer, from the main CUPS page, select the Administration tab, select the check box next to Allow remote administration, and select the Change Settings button. Then, from a remote browser, you can access the CUPS Administration page by going to port 631 on the CUPS server (for example, `http://host.example.com:631`).

You may need to restart CUPs for the change to take effect: `systemctl restart cups.service`. If you are not already running the browser as the root user, you must also enter the root user name and password.

To configure a printer that is not automatically detected, you can add a printer from the Administration screen. With the Administration screen displayed, you can add a printer as follows:

1. **Click the Add Printer button.** The Add New Printer screen appears.

2. **Select the device to which the printer is connected.** The printer can be connected locally to a parallel, SCSI, serial, or USB port directly on the computer. Alternatively, you can select a network connection type for Apple printers (appSocket/HP JetDirect), Internet Printing Protocol (`http` or `ipp`), or a Windows printer (using Samba or SMB).

3. **If prompted for more information, you may need to further describe the connection to the printer.** For example, you may need to enter the baud rate and parity for a serial port, or you might be asked for the network address for an IPP or Samba printer.

4. **Type a Name, Location, and Description for the printer; select if you want to share this printer, and click Continue.**

5. **Select the make of the print driver.** If you don't see the manufacturer of your printer listed, choose PostScript for a PostScript printer or HP for a PCL printer. For the manufacturer you choose, you can select a specific model.

6. **Set options.** If you are asked to set options for your printer, you may do so. Then select Set Printer Options to continue.

7. **Your printer should be available.** If the printer is added successfully, click the name of your printer to have the new printer page appear; from the printer page, you can select Maintenance or Administration to print a test page or modify the printer configuration.

With the basic printer configuration done, you can now do further work with your printers. Here are a few examples of what you can do:

- **List print jobs.** Click Show All Jobs to see what print jobs are currently active from any of the printers configured for this server. Click Show Completed Jobs to see information about jobs that are already printed.

- **Create a printer class.** Click the Administration tab, choose Add Class, and identify a name, description, and location for a printer class. From the list of Printers (Members) configured on your server, select the ones to go into this class.

- **Cancel or move a print job.** If you print a 100-page job by mistake or if the printer is spewing out junk, the Cancel feature can be very handy. Likewise, if you sent a print job to the wrong printer, the Move Job selection can be useful. From the Administration tab, click Manage Jobs; then click Show Active Jobs to see what print jobs are currently in the queue for the printer. Select the Cancel Job button next to the print job you want to cancel, or select Move Job to move the print job to a different printer.

- **View printers.** You can click the Printers tab from the top of any of the CUPS web-based administration pages to view the printers you have configured. For each printer that appears, you can select Maintenance or Administrative tasks. Under Maintenance, click Pause Printer (to stop the printer from printing but still accept print jobs for the queue), Reject Jobs (to not accept any further print jobs for the moment), Move All Jobs (to move them to another printer), Cancel All Jobs (to delete all print jobs), or Print Test Page (to print a page). Figure 16.2 shows the information on the Printers tab for a specific printer.

FIGURE 16.2

You can do administration tasks from the Printers tab.

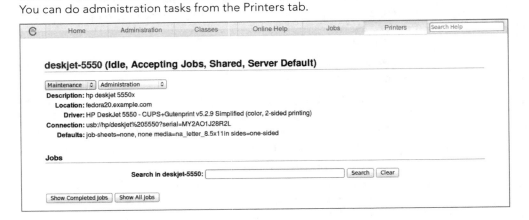

Using the Print Settings window

If you are using Fedora, RHEL, or other Red Hat–based systems, you can use the Print Settings window to set up your printers. In fact, I recommend that you use it instead of CUPS web administration because the resulting printer configuration files are tailored to work with the way the CUPS service is started on those systems.

After the package is installed (`yum install system-config-printer`), to install a printer from your GNOME desktop, start the Print Settings window by typing **Print Settings** from the Activity screen, or as root user by typing `system-config-printer`. This tool enables you to add and delete printers and edit printer properties. It also enables you to send test pages to those printers to make sure they are working properly.

The key here is that you are configuring printers that are managed by your print daemon (`cupsd` for the CUPS service). After a printer is configured, users on your local system can use it. You can refer to the section "Configuring Print Servers" to learn how to make the server available to users from other computers on your network.

The printers that you set up can be connected directly to your computer (as on a USB port) or to another computer on the network (for example, from another UNIX system or Windows system).

Configuring local printers with the Print Settings window

Add a local printer (in other words, a printer connected directly to your computer) with the Print Settings window using the procedure that follows.

Adding a local printer

To add a local printer from a GNOME desktop in Fedora 21, follow these steps:

1. **Select Print Settings from the Activities screen or type the following as root user from a Terminal window:**

   ```
   # system-config-printer &
   ```

   The Printing window appears.

2. **Click Add.** (If asked, select the button to Adjust Firewall to allow access to the printer port 631.) A New Printer window appears.

3. **If the printer you want to configure is detected, simply select it and click Forward.** If it is not detected, choose the device to which the printer is connected (LPT #1 and Serial Port #1 are the first parallel and serial ports, respectively) and click Forward. (Type **/usr/sbin/lpinfo -v | less** in a shell to see printer connection types.) You are asked to identify the printer's driver.

4. **To use an installed driver for your printer, choose Select Printer From Database, and then choose the manufacturer of your printer.** As an alternative, you could select Provide PPD File and supply your own PPD file (for example, if you have a printer that is not supported in Linux and you have a driver that was supplied with the printer). PPD stands for PostScript Printer Description. Select Forward to see a list of printer models from which you can choose.

> **TIP**
>
> If your printer doesn't appear on the list but supports PCL (HP's Printer Control Language), try selecting one of the HP printers (such as HP LaserJet). If your printer supports PostScript, select PostScript printer from the list. Selecting Raw Print Queue enables you to send documents that are already formatted for a particular printer type to a specific printer.

5. **With your printer model selected, click the driver you want to use with that printer, and then click Forward to continue.**

6. **Add the following information, and click Forward:**

   ■ **Printer Name**—Add the name you want to give to identify the printer. The name must begin with a letter, but after the initial letter, it can contain a combination of letters, numbers, dashes (-), and underscores (_). For example, an HP printer on a computer named maple could be named hp-maple.

   ■ **Description**—Add a few words describing the printer, such as its features (for example, an HP LaserJet 2100M with PCL and PS support).

   ■ **Location**—Add some words that describe the printer's location (for example, "In Room 205 under the coffeepot").

7. **When the printer is added, click No or Yes if you're prompted to print a test page.** The new printer entry appears in the Print Settings window. Double-click the printer to see the Properties window for that printer, as shown in Figure 16.3.

FIGURE 16.3

The Printer Properties window after adding a printer.

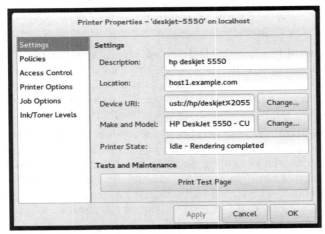

8. **If you want the printer to be your default printer, right-click the printer and select Set As Default.** As you add other printers, you can change the default printer by selecting the one you want and Set As Default again.

9. **Make sure printing is working.** Open a Terminal window and use the `lpr` command to print a file (such as `lpr /etc/hosts`). (If you want to share this printer with other computers on your network, refer to the section "Configuring Print Servers," later in this chapter.)

Editing a local printer

After double-clicking the printer you want to configure, choose from the following menu options to change its configuration:

- **Settings**—The Description, Location, Device URI, and Make and Model information you created earlier are displayed in this dialog box.

- **Policies**—Click Policies to set the following items:

  - **State**—Select check boxes to indicate whether the printer will print jobs that are in the queue (Enabled), accept new jobs for printing (Accepting Jobs), or be available to be shared with other computers that can communicate with your computer (Shared). You also must select Server Settings and click the Share Published printers connected to this system check box before the printer will accept print jobs from other computers.

  - **Policies**—In case of error, the stop-printer selection causes all printing to that printer to stop. You can also select to have the job discarded (abort-job) or retried (retry-job) in the event of an error condition.

  - **Banner**—There are no starting or ending banner pages by default for the printer. Choose starting or ending banner pages that include text such as Classified, Confidential, Secret, and so on.

- **Access Control**—If your printer is a shared printer, you can select this window to create a list that either allows users access to the printer (with all others denied) or denies users access to the printer (with all others allowed).

- **Printer Options**—Click Printer Options to set defaults for options related to the printer driver. The available options are different for different printers. Many of these options can be overridden when someone prints a document. Here are examples of a few of the options you might (or might not) have available:

  - **Watermark**—Several Watermark settings are available to enable you to add and change watermarks on your printed pages. By default, Watermark and Overlay are off (None). By selecting Watermark (behind the text) or Overlay (over the text), you can set the other Watermark settings to determine how watermarks and overlays are done. Watermarks can go on every page (All) or only the first page (First Only). Select Watermark Text to choose what words are used for the watermark or overlay (Draft, Copy, Confidential, Final, and so on). You can then select the font type, size, style, and intensity of the watermark or overlay.

- **Resolution Enhancement**—You can use the printer's current settings or choose to turn resolution enhancement on or off.
- **Page Size**—The default is U.S. letter size, but you can also ask the printer to print legal size, envelopes, ISO A4 standard, or several other page sizes.
- **Media Source**—Choose which tray to print from. Select Tray 1 to insert pages manually.
- **Levels of Gray**—Choose to use the printer's current levels of gray or have enhanced or standard gray levels turned on.
- **Resolution**—Select the default printing resolution (such as 300, 600, or 1,200 dots per inch). Higher resolutions result in better quality but take longer to print.
- **EconoMode**—Either use the printer's current setting or choose a mode where you save toner or one where you have the highest possible quality.

- **Job Options**—Click Job Options to set common default options that will be used for this printer if the application printing the job doesn't already set them. These include Common Options (number of copies, orientation, scale to fit, and pages per side), Image Options (scaling, saturation, hue, and gamma), and Text Options (characters/inch, lines/inch, and margin settings).

- **Ink/Toner Levels**—Click Ink/Toner Levels to see information on how much ink or toner your printer has left. (Not all printers report these values.)

Click Apply when you are satisfied with the changes you made to the local printer.

Configuring remote printers

To use a printer that is available on your network, you must identify that printer to your Linux system. Supported remote printer connections include Networked CUPS (IPP) printers, Networked UNIX (LPD) printers, Networked Windows (Samba) printers, and JetDirect printers. (Of course, both CUPS and UNIX print servers can be run from Linux systems as well as other UNIX systems.)

In each case, you need a network connection from your Linux system to the servers to which those printers are connected. To use a remote printer requires that someone set up that printer on the remote server computer. See the section "Configuring Print Servers" later in this chapter for information on how to do that on your Linux server.

Use the Print Settings window (`system-config-printer`) to configure each of the remote printer types. This is how it is done in Fedora 21:

1. **From the GNOME 3 Activities screen, type** Print Settings **and press Enter.**

2. **Click Add.** The New Printer window appears.

3. **Depending on the type of ports you have on your computer, select one of the following:**

- **LPT #1**—Use this for a printer connected to your parallel port.
- **Serial Port #1**—Use this for a printer connected to your serial port.
- **Network Printer**—Under this heading, you can search for network printers (by hostname or IP address) or type in the URI for several different printer types:
    - **Find Network Printer**—Instead of entering a printer URI, you can provide a hostname or IP address for the system that has the printer you want to print to. Any printers found on that host appear on the window, ready for you to add.
    - **AppleSocket/HP JetDirect**—Use this for a JetDirect printer.
    - **Internet Printing Protocol (IPP)**—Use this for a CUPS or other IPP printer. Most Linux and Mac OS X printers fall into this category.
    - **Internet Printing Protocol (HTTPS)**—Use this for a CUPS or other IPP printer being shared over a secure connection (valid certificates required).
    - **LPD/LPR Host or Printer**—Use this for a UNIX printer.
    - **Windows Printer via SAMBA**—Use this for a Windows system printer.

Continue with the steps in whichever of the following sections is appropriate.

Adding a remote CUPS printer

If you chose to add a CUPS (IPP) printer that is accessible over your local network from the Print Settings window, you must add the following information to the window that appears:

- **Host**—This is the hostname of the computer to which the printer is attached (or otherwise accessible). This can be an IP address or TCP/IP hostname for the computer. The TCP/IP name is accessible from your /etc/hosts file or through a DNS name server.
- **Queue**—This is the printer name on the remote CUPS print server. CUPS supports printer instances, which allows each printer to have several sets of options. If the remote CUPS printer is configured this way, you can choose a particular path to a printer, such as hp/300dpi or hp/1200dpi. A slash character separates the print queue name from the printer instance.

Complete the rest of the procedure as you would for a local printer (see the section "Adding a local printer" earlier in this chapter).

Adding a remote UNIX (LDP/LPR) printer

If you chose to add a UNIX printer (LPD/LPR) from the Print Settings window, you must add the following information to the window that appears:

- **Host**—This is the IP address or hostname of the computer to which the printer is attached (or otherwise accessible). The hostname is accessible from your `/etc/hosts` file or through a DNS name server. Select the Probe button to search for the host.
- **Queue**—This is the printer name on the remote UNIX computer.

Complete the rest of the procedure as you would for a local printer (see the section "Adding a local printer" earlier in this chapter).

TIP

If the print job you send to test the printer is rejected, the print server computer may not have allowed you access to the printer. Ask the remote computer's administrator to add your hostname to the `/etc/lpd.perms` file. (Type `lpq -P printer` to see the status of your print job.)

Adding a Windows (SMB) printer

Enabling your computer to access an SMB printer (the Windows printing service) involves adding an entry for the printer in the Select Connection window.

When you choose to add a Windows printer to the Print Settings window (Windows Printer via Samba), select Browse to see a list of computers on your network that have been detected as offering SMB services (file and/or printing service). You can configure the printer from this window as follows:

1. **Type the URI of the printer, excluding the leading** `smb://`. For example, you might type **/host1/myprinter** or **/mygroup/host1/myprinter**.
2. **Select either Prompt user if authentication is required or Set authentication details now.**
3. **If you chose to Set authentication details now, fill in the username and password needed to access the SMB printer; then click Verify to check that you can authenticate to the server.**
4. **Click Forward to continue.**

Alternatively, you can identify a server that does not appear on the list of servers. Type the information needed to create an SMB URI that contains the following information:

- **Workgroup**—This is the workgroup name assigned to the SMB server. Using the workgroup name isn't necessary in all cases.
- **Server**—This is the NetBIOS name or IP address for the computer, which may or may not be the same as its TCP/IP name. To translate this name into the address needed to reach the SMB host, Samba checks several places where the name may be assigned to an IP address. Samba checks the following (in the order shown) until it finds a match: the local `/etc/hosts` file, the local `/etc/lmhosts` file, a WINS

server on the network, and responses to broadcasts on each local network interface to resolve the name.

- **Share**—This is the name under which the printer is shared with the remote computer. It may be different from the name by which local users of the SMB printer know the printer.
- **User**—A username is required by the SMB server system to give you access to the SMB printer. A username is not necessary if you are authenticating the printer based on share-level rather than user-level access control. With share-level access, you can add a password for each shared printer or file system.
- **Password**—Use the password associated with the SMB username or the shared resource, depending on the kind of access control being used.

> **CAUTION**
>
> When you enter a User and Password for SMB, the information is stored unencrypted in the `/etc/cups/printers.conf` file. Be sure that the file remains readable only by root.

The following is an example of the SMB URI you could add to the SMB:// box:

```
jjones:my9passswd@FSTREET/NS1/hp
```

The URI shown here identifies the username (jjones), the user's password (my9passswd), the workgroup (FSTREET), the server (NS1), and the printer queue name (hp).

Complete the rest of the procedure as you would for a local printer (see the section "Adding a local printer" earlier in this chapter).

If everything is set up properly, you can use the standard lpr command to print the file to the printer. Using this example, employ the following form for printing:

```
$ cat file1.ps | lpr -P NS1-PS
```

> **TIP**
>
> If you are receiving failure messages, make sure the computer to which you are printing is accessible. For the Printer NS1 hp example, you can type `smbclient -L NS1 -U jjones`. Then type the password (my9passswd, in this case). The `-L` asks for information about the server; the `-U jjones` says to log in the user jjones. If you get a positive name query response after you enter a password, you should see a list of shared printers and files from that server. Check the names, and try printing again.

Working with CUPS Printing

Tools such as CUPS web-based administration and the Print Settings window effectively hide the underlying CUPS facility. Sometimes, however, you want to work directly with the tools and configuration files that come with CUPS. The following sections describe how to use some special CUPS features.

Configuring the CUPS server (cupsd.conf)

The cupsd daemon process listens for requests to your CUPS print server and responds to those requests based on settings in the /etc/cups/cupsd.conf file. The configuration variables in the cupsd.conf file are in the same form as those in the Apache configuration file (httpd.conf or apache2.conf). Type **man cupsd.conf** to see details on any of the settings.

The Print Settings window adds access information to the cupsd.conf file. For other Linux systems, or if you don't have a desktop on your server, you may need to configure the cupsd.conf file manually. You can step through the cupsd.conf file to further tune your CUPS server. Most of the settings are optional or can just be left as the default. Let's look at some of the settings that you can use in the cupsd.conf file.

No classification is set by default. With the classification set to topsecret, you can have Top Secret displayed on all pages that go through the print server:

```
Classification topsecret
```

Other classifications you can substitute for topsecret include classified, confidential, secret, and unclassified.

The ServerCertificate and ServerKey lines (not set by default) can be set up to indicate where the certificate and key are stored, respectively:

```
ServerCertificate /etc/cups/ssl/server.crt
ServerKey /etc/cups/ssl/server.key
```

Activate these two lines if you want to do encrypted connections. These files are automatically generated for your system when you first start the cupsd service. So you can just use those files, or you can generate your own certificate and key and set the path to ServerCertificate and ServerKey entries. Using a certificate and key lets you share your printer as an HTTPS IPP printer.

The term *browsing* refers to the act of broadcasting information about your printer on your local network and listening for other print servers' information. Browsing is on by default only for the local host (@LOCAL). You can allow CUPS browser information (BrowseAllow) for additional selected addresses. Browsing information is broadcast, by default, on address 255.255.255.255. Here are examples of several browsing settings:

```
Browsing On
BrowseProtocols cups
BrowseOrder Deny,Allow
BrowseAllow from @LOCAL
```

```
BrowseAddress 255.255.255.255
Listen *:631
```

To enable web-based CUPS administration and to share printers with others on the network, the cupsd daemon can be set to listen on port 631 for all network interfaces to your computer based on this entry: Listen *:631. By default, it listens on the local interface only on many Linux systems (Listen localhost:631). For Fedora, CUPS listens on all interfaces by default.

By turning on BrowseRelay (it's off by default), you can allow CUPS browse information to be passed among two or more networks. The source-address and destination-address can be individual IP addresses or can represent network numbers:

```
BrowseRelay source-address destination-address
```

This is a good way to enable users on several connected LANs to discover and use printers on other nearby LANs.

You can allow or deny access to different features of the CUPS server. An access definition for a CUPS printer (created from the Print Settings window) might appear as follows:

```
<Location /printers/ns1-hp1>
Order Deny,Allow
Deny From All
Allow From 127.0.0.1
AuthType None
</Location>
```

Here, printing to the ns1-hp1 printer is allowed only for users on the local host (127.0.0.1). No password is needed (AuthType None). To allow access to the administration tool, CUPS must be configured to prompt for a password (AuthType Basic).

Starting the CUPS server

For Linux systems that use SystemV-style startup scripts (such as earlier releases of Fedora and RHEL), starting and shutting down the CUPS print service is pretty easy. Use the chkconfig command to turn on CUPS so it starts at each reboot. Run the cups startup script to have the CUPS service start immediately. In RHEL 6.x or earlier, type the following as root user:

```
# chkconfig cups on
# service cups start
```

If the CUPS service was already running, you should use restart instead of start. Using the restart option is also a good way to reread any configuration options you may have changed in the cupsd.conf file (although, if CUPS is already running, service cups reload rereads configuration files without restarting).

In Fedora 21 and RHEL 7, you use the `systemctl` command instead of `service` to start and stop services:

```
# systemctl status cups.service
* cups.service - CUPS Printing Service
   Loaded: loaded (/usr/lib/systemd/system/cups.service; enabled)
   Active: active (running) since Sat 2016-07-23 22:41:05 EDT; 18h
     ago
 Main PID: 20483 (cupsd)
   Status: "Scheduler is running..."
   CGroup: /system.slice/cups.service
           └─20483 /usr/sbin/cupsd -f
```

You can tell the CUPS service is running because the status shows the `cupsd` daemon active with PID 20483. If that service were not running, you could start the CUPS service as follows:

```
# systemctl start cups.service
```

See Chapter 15, "Starting and Stopping Services," for more information on the `systemctl` and `service` commands for working with services.

Configuring CUPS printer options manually

If your Linux distribution doesn't have a graphical means of configuring CUPS, you can edit configuration files directly. For example, when a new printer is created from the Print Settings window, it is defined in the `/etc/cups/printers.conf` file. This is what a printer entry looks like:

```
<DefaultPrinter printer>
Info HP LaserJet 2100M
Location HP LaserJet 2100M in hall closet
DeviceURI parallel:/dev/lp0
State Idle
Accepting Yes
Shared No
JobSheets none none
QuotaPeriod 0
PageLimit 0
KLimit 0
</Printer>
```

This is an example of a local printer that serves as the default printer for the local system. The `Shared No` value is set because the printer is currently available only on the local system. The most interesting information relates to `DeviceURI`, which shows that the printer is connected to parallel port `/dev/lp0`. The state is `Idle` (ready to accept printer jobs), and the `Accepting` value is `Yes` (the printer is accepting print jobs by default).

The `DeviceURI` has several ways to identify the device name of a printer, reflecting where the printer is connected. Here are some examples listed in the `printers.conf` file:

```
DeviceURI parallel:/dev/plp
DeviceURI serial:/dev/ttyd1?baud=38400+size=8+parity=none+flow=soft
DeviceURI scsi:/dev/scsi/sc1d6l0
DeviceURI socket://hostname:port
DeviceURI tftp://hostname/path
DeviceURI ftp://hostname/path
DeviceURI http://hostname[:port]/path
DeviceURI ipp://hostname/path
DeviceURI smb://hostname/printer
```

The first three examples show the form for local printers (parallel, serial, and scsi). The other examples are for remote hosts. In each case, *hostname* can be the host's name or IP address. Port numbers or paths identify the locations of each printer on the host.

> **TIP**
>
> If you find that you cannot print because a particular printer driver is not supported in CUPS, you can set up your printer to accept jobs in raw mode. This can work well if you are printing from Windows clients that have the correct print drivers installed. To enable raw printing in CUPS, uncomment the following line in the `/etc/cups/mime.types` file in Linux:
>
> `application/octet-stream`
>
> and uncomment the following line in the `/etc/cups/mime.convs` file:
>
> `application/octet-stream application/vnd.cups-raw 0 -`
>
> After that, you can print files as raw data to your printers without using the `-oraw` option to `print` commands.

Using Printing Commands

To remain backward compatible with older UNIX and Linux printing facilities, CUPS supports many of the old commands for working with printing. Most command-line printing with CUPS can be performed with the `lpr` command. Word processing applications such as LibreOffice, OpenOffice, and AbiWord are set up to use this facility for printing.

You can use the Print Settings window to define the filters needed for each printer so that the text can be formatted properly. Options to the `lpr` command can add filters to properly process the text. Other commands for managing printed documents include `lpq` (for viewing the contents of print queues), `lprm` (for removing print jobs from the queue), and `lpc` (for controlling printers).

Printing with lpr

You can use the lpr command to print documents to both local and remote printers (provided the printers are configured locally). Document files can be either added to the end of the lpr command line or directed to the lpr command using a pipe (|). Here's an example of a simple lpr command:

```
$ lpr doc1.ps
```

When you specify just a document file with lpr, output is directed to the default printer. As an individual user, you can change the default printer by setting the value of the PRINTER variable. Typically, you add the PRINTER variable to one of your startup files, such as $HOME/.bashrc. Adding the following line to your .bashrc file, for example, sets your default printer to lp3:

```
export PRINTER=lp3
```

To override the default printer, specify a particular printer on the lpr command line. The following example uses the -P option to select a different printer:

```
$ lpr -P canyonps doc1.ps
```

The lpr command has a variety of options that enable lpr to interpret and format several different types of documents. These include -# *num*, where *num* is replaced by the number of copies to print (from 1 to 100) and -l (which causes a document to be sent in raw mode, presuming that the document has already been formatted). To learn more options to lpr, type **man lpr**.

Listing status with lpc

Use the lpc command to list the status of your printers. Here is an example:

```
$ /usr/sbin/lpc status
hp:
                printer is on device 'usb' speed -1
                queuing is enabled
                printing is disabled
                no entries
                daemon present
deskjet_5550:
                printer is on device '/dev/null' speed -1
                queuing is enabled
                printing is disabled
                no entries
                daemon present
```

This output shows two active printers. The first (hp) is connected to a local USB port. The second (deskjet_5550) is a network printer (shown as /dev/null). The hp printer is currently disabled (offline), although the queue is enabled so people can continue to send jobs to the printer.

Removing print jobs with lprm

Users can remove their own print jobs from the queue with the lprm command. Used alone on the command line, lprm removes all the user's print jobs from the default printer. To remove jobs from a specific printer, use the -P option, as follows:

```
$ lprm -P lp0
```

To remove all print jobs for the current user, type the following:

```
$ lprm -
```

The root user can remove all the print jobs for a specific user by indicating that user on the lprm command line. For example, to remove all print jobs for the user named mike, the root user types the following:

```
# lprm -U mike
```

To remove an individual print job from the queue, indicate its job number on the lprm command line. To find the job number, type the lpq command. Here's what the output of that command may look like:

```
# lpq
printer is ready and printing
Rank    Owner                  Job Files                Total Size Time
active  root                   133 /home/jake/pr1         467
2       root                   197 /home/jake/mydoc     23948
```

The output shows two printable jobs waiting in the queue. (The printer is ready and printing the job listed as active.) Under the Job column, you can see the job number associated with each document. To remove the first print job, type the following:

```
# lprm 133
```

Configuring Print Servers

You've configured a printer so that you and the other users on your computer can print to it. Now you want to share that printer with other people in your home, school, or office. Basically, that means configuring the printer as a print server.

The printers configured on your Linux system can be shared in different ways with other computers on your network. Not only can your computer act as a Linux print server (by configuring CUPS), but it can also appear as an SMB (Windows) print server to client computers. After a local printer is attached to your Linux system and your computer is connected to your local network, you can use the procedures in this section to share the printer with client computers using a Linux (UNIX) or SMB interface.

Configuring a shared CUPS printer

Making the local printer added to your Linux computer available to other computers on your network is fairly easy. If a TCP/IP network connection exists between the computers sharing the printer, you simply grant permission to all hosts, individual hosts, or users from remote hosts to access your computer's printing service.

To manually configure a printer entry in the /etc/cups/printers.conf file to accept print jobs from all other computers, make sure the Shared Yes line is set. The following example from a printers.conf entry earlier in this chapter demonstrates what the new entry would look like:

```
<DefaultPrinter printer>
Info HP LaserJet 2100M
Location HP LaserJet 2100M in hall closet
DeviceURI parallel:/dev/lp0
State Idle
Accepting Yes
Shared Yes
JobSheets none none
QuotaPeriod 0
PageLimit 0
KLimit 0
</Printer>
```

On Linux systems that use the Print Settings window described earlier in this chapter, it's best to set up your printer as a shared printer using that window. Here's how, using Fedora 21:

1. **From the Activities screen on a GNOME 3 desktop in Fedora, type Print Settings and press Enter.** The Print Settings window appears.

2. **To allow all your printers to be shared, select Server ⇨ Settings.** If you are not the root user, you are prompted for the root password. The Basic Server Settings pop-up appears.

3. **Select the check box next to Publish shared printers connected to this system, and click OK.** You may be asked to modify your firewall to open the necessary ports for remote systems to access your printers.

4. **To further allow or restrict printing for a particular printer, double-click the name of the printer you want to share.** (If the printer is not yet configured, refer to the section "Setting Up Printers" earlier in this chapter.)

5. **Choose the Policies heading, and select Shared so a check mark appears in the box.**

6. **If you want to restrict access to the printer to selected users, select the Access Control heading and choose one of the following options:**

- **Allow Printing for Everyone Except These Users**—With this selected, all users are allowed access to the printer. By typing usernames into the Users box and clicking Add, you exclude selected users.

- **Deny Printing for Everyone Except These Users**—With this selected, all users are excluded from using the printer. Type usernames into the Users box and click Add to allow access to the printer for only those names you enter.

Now you can configure other computers to use your printer, as described in the section "Setting Up Printers" in this chapter. If you try to print from another computer and it doesn't work, try these troubleshooting tips:

- **Open your firewall.** If you have a restrictive firewall, it may not permit printing. You must enable access to TCP port 631 to allow access to printing on your computer. The Printing window may prompt you at some point to open this port. (Check the /etc/sysconfig/iptables file to see if a firewall rule is set that accepts printing from TCP port 631 or, if you are running firewalld, run firewall-config and open the ipp service.)

- **Check names and addresses.** Make sure you entered your computer's name and print queue properly when you configured it on the other computer. Try using the IP address instead of the hostname. (If that works, it indicates a DNS name resolution problem.) Running a tool such as tcpdump enables you to see where the transaction fails.

- **Check which addresses cupsd is listening on.** The cupsd daemon must be listening outside the localhost for remote systems to print to it. Use the netstat command (as the root user) as follows to check this. The first example shows cupsd only listening on local host (127.0.0.1:631); the second shows cupsd listening on all network interfaces (0 0.0.0.0:631):

```
# netstat -tupln | grep 631
tcp        0      0 127.0.0.1:631    0.0.0.0:*    LISTEN    6492/cupsd
# netstat -tupln | grep 631
tcp        0      0 0.0.0.0:631      0.0.0.0:*    LISTEN    6492/cupsd
```

Access changes to your shared printer are made in the cupsd.conf and printers.conf files in your /etc/cups directory.

Configuring a shared Samba printer

Your Linux printers can be configured as shared SMB printers so they appear to be available from Windows systems. To share your printer as if it were a Samba (SMB) printer, simply configure basic Samba server settings as described in Chapter 19, "Configuring a Windows File Sharing (Samba) Server." All your printers should be shared on your local network by default. The next section shows what the resulting settings look like and how you might want to change them.

Understanding smb.conf for printing

When you configure Samba, the /etc/samba/smb.conf file is constructed to enable all your configured printers to be shared. Here are a few lines from the smb.conf file that relate to printer sharing:

```
[global]
    ...
  load printers = yes
  cups options = raw
; printcap name = /etc/printcap
; printing = cups
    ...
[printers]
        comment = All Printers
        path = /var/spool/samba
        browseable = yes
        writeable = no
        printable = yes
```

These example settings are the result of configuring Samba from the Samba Server Configuration window (system-config-samba) in Fedora. You can read the comment lines to learn more about the file's contents. Lines beginning with a semicolon (;) indicate the default setting for the option on a comment line. Remove the semicolon to change the setting.

The selected lines show that printers from /etc/printcap were loaded and that the CUPS service is being used. With cups options set to raw, Samba assumes that print files have already been formatted by the time they reach your print server. This allows the Linux or Windows clients to provide their own print drivers.

The last few lines are the actual printers' definition. By changing the browseable option from no to yes, users can print to all printers (printable = yes).

You can also store Windows native print drivers on your Samba server. When a Windows client uses your printer, the driver automatically becomes available. You do not need to download a driver from the vendor's website. To enable the printer driver share, add a Samba share called print$ that looks like the following:

```
[print$]
comment = Printer Drivers
path = /var/lib/samba/drivers
browseable = yes
guest ok = no
```

```
read only = yes
write list = chris, dduffey
```

After you have the share available, you can start copying Windows print drivers to the /var/lib/samba/drivers directory, as described in the Samba HOWTO: http://www.samba.org/samba/docs/man/Samba-HOWTO-Collection/classicalprinting.html#id2626941

Setting up SMB clients

Chances are good that if you are configuring a Samba printer on your Linux computer, you want to share it with Windows clients. If Samba is set up properly on your computer and the client computers can reach you over the network, users should have no trouble finding and using your printer.

For many Windows systems, click Start ⇨ Devices and Printers and select the printer from the list to configure it. In some older Windows systems, look for your shared Samba printer in Network Neighborhood (or My Network Places). From the Windows 9x desktop, double-click the Network Neighborhood icon. (From Windows 2000 or XP, double-click the My Network Places icon.)

With Windows Vista, you open the Network icon. The name of your host computer (the NetBIOS name, which is probably also your TCP/IP name) appears on the screen or within a workgroup folder on the screen. Open the icon that represents your computer. The window that opens shows your shared printers and folders.

> **TIP**
>
> If your computer's icon doesn't appear in Network Neighborhood or My Network Places, try using the Search window. From Windows XP, choose Start ⇨ Search ⇨ Computer or People ⇨ A Computer on the Network. Type your computer's name into the Computer Name box, and click Search. Double-click your computer in the Search window results panel. A window displaying the shared printers and folders from your computer appears.

After your shared printer appears in the window, configure a pointer to that printer by opening (double-clicking) the printer icon. A message tells you that you must set up the printer before you can use it. Click Yes to proceed to configure the printer for local use. The Add Printer Wizard appears. Answer the questions that ask you how you intend to use the printer, and add the appropriate drivers. When you are finished, the printer appears in your printer window.

Another way to configure an SMB printer from a Windows XP operating system is to go to Start ⇨ Printers and Faxes. In the Printers and Faxes window that appears, click the Add a Printer icon in the upper-left portion of the window, and select Network Printer from the first window. From there you can browse and/or configure your SMB printer.

Summary

Providing networked printing services is essential on today's business networks. With the use of a few network-attached devices, you can focus your printer spending on a few high-quality devices that multiple users can share instead of numerous lower-cost devices. In addition, a centrally located printer can make it easier to maintain the printer, while still enabling everyone to get his or her printing jobs done.

The default printing service in nearly every major Linux distribution today is the Common UNIX Printing System (CUPS). Any Linux system that includes CUPS offers the CUPS web-based administrative interface for configuring CUPS printing. It also offers configuration files in the /etc/cups directory for configuring printers and the CUPS service (cupsd daemon).

In RHEL, Fedora, Ubuntu, and other Linux systems, you can configure your printer with the printing configuration windows available in both KDE and GNOME desktops. A variety of drivers makes it possible to print to different kinds of printers, as well as to printers that are connected to computers on the network.

You can set up your computer as a Linux print server, and you can also have your computer emulate an SMB (Windows) print server. After your network is configured properly and a local printer is installed, sharing that printer over the network as a UNIX or SMB print server is not very complicated.

Exercises

Use these exercises to test your knowledge of configuring printers in Linux. These tasks assume you are running a Fedora or Red Hat Enterprise Linux system (although some tasks work on other Linux systems as well). If you are stuck, solutions to the tasks are shown in Appendix B (although in Linux, you can often complete a task in multiple ways).

1. Use the Print Settings window (system-config-printer package) to add a new printer called myprinter to your system (the printer does not have to be connected to set up a print queue for the new printer). Make it a generic PostScript printer connected to a local serial, LPT, or other port.

2. Use the lpc command to see the status of all your printers.

3. Use the lpr command to print the /etc/hosts file to that printer.

4. Check the print queue for that printer to see that the print job is there.

5. Remove the print job from the queue (cancel it).

6. Using the printing window, set the basic server setting that publishes your printers so other systems on your local network can print to your printers.

7. Allow remote administration of your system from a web browser.

8. Demonstrate that you can do remote administration of your system by opening a web browser to port 631 from another system to the Linux system running your print server.

9. Use the `netstat` command to see which addresses the `cupsd` daemon is listening on (the printing port is 631).

10. Delete the `myprinter` printer entry from your system.

16

Configuring a Web Server

IN THIS CHAPTER

Installing an Apache web server

Configuring Apache

Securing Apache with iptables and SELinux

Creating virtual hosts

Building a secure (HTTPS) website

Checking Apache for errors

Web servers are responsible for serving up the content you view on the Internet every day. By far, the most popular web server is the Apache (HTTPD) web server, which is sponsored by the Apache Software Foundation (http://apache.org). Because Apache is an open source project, it is available with every major Linux distribution, including Fedora, RHEL, and Ubuntu.

You can configure a basic web server to run in Linux in just a few minutes. However, you can configure your Apache web server in a tremendous number of ways. You can configure an Apache web server to serve content for multiple domains (virtual hosting), provide encrypted communications (HTTPS), and secure some or all of a website using different kinds of authentication.

This chapter takes you through the steps to install and configure an Apache web server. These steps include procedures for securing your server, as well as using a variety of modules so you can incorporate different authentication methods and scripting languages into your web server. Then I describe how to generate certificates to create an HTTPS Secure Sockets Layer (SSL) website.

Understanding the Apache Web Server

Apache HTTPD (also known as the Apache HTTPD Server) provides the service with which the client web browsers communicate. The daemon process (httpd) runs in the background on your server and waits for requests from web clients. Web browsers provide those connections to the HTTP daemon and send requests, which the daemon interprets, sending back the appropriate data (such as a web page or other content).

Apache HTTPD includes an interface that allows modules to tie into the process to handle specific portions of a request. Among other things, modules are available to handle the processing of scripting languages, such as Perl or PHP, within web documents and to add encryption to connections between clients and the server.

Apache began as a collection of patches and improvements from the National Center for Supercomputing Applications (NCSA), University of Illinois, Urbana-Champaign, to the HTTP daemon. The NCSA HTTP daemon was the most popular HTTP server at the time, but had started to show its age after its author, Rob McCool, left NCSA in mid-1994.

> **NOTE**
> Another project that came from NCSA is Mosaic. Most modern web browsers can trace their origins to Mosaic.

In early 1995, a group of developers formed the Apache Group and began making extensive modifications to the NCSA HTTPD code base. Apache soon replaced NCSA HTTPD as the most popular web server, a title it still holds today.

The Apache Group later formed the Apache Software Foundation (ASF) to promote the development of Apache and other free software. With the start of new projects at ASF, the Apache server became known as Apache HTTPD, although the two terms are still used interchangeably. Currently, ASF has more than 100 top-level projects, including TomCat (which includes open source Java Servlet and JavaServer Pages technologies), Hadoop (a project providing highly available, distributed computing), and SpamAssassin (an e-mail filtering program).

Getting and Installing Your Web Server

Although Apache is available with every major Linux distribution, it is often packaged in different ways. In most cases, all you need to start a simple Apache web server is the package containing the Apache daemon itself (/usr/sbin/httpd) and its related files. In Fedora, RHEL, and others, the Apache web server comes in the httpd package.

Understanding the httpd package

To examine the httpd package in Fedora or RHEL before you install it, download the package using the yumdownloader command and run a few rpm commands on it to view its contents:

```
# yumdownloader httpd
# rpm -qpi httpd-*rpm
Name      : httpd
Version   : 2.4.10
Release   : 1.fc20
```

```
Architecture: x86_64
Install Date: (not installed)
Group         : System Environment/Daemons
Size          : 3950241
License       : ASL 2.0
Signature     : RSA/SHA256, Wed 23 Jul 2014 09:23:23 AM EDT, Key
     ID 2eb161fa246110c1
Source RPM    : httpd-2.4.10-1.fc20.src.rpm
Build Date    : Wed 23 Jul 2014 06:32:07 AM EDT
Build Host    : buildvm-22.phx2.fedoraproject.org
Relocations   : (not relocatable)
Packager      : Fedora Project
Vendor        : Fedora Project
URL           : http://httpd.apache.org/
Summary       : Apache HTTP Server
Description   :
The Apache HTTP Server is a powerful, efficient, and extensible
web server.
```

The yumdownloader command downloads the latest version of the httpd package to the current directory. The rpm -qpi command queries the httpd RPM package you just downloaded for information. You can see that the package was created by the Fedora project, that it is signed, and that it is indeed the Apache HTTP Server package. Next, look inside to the package to see the configuration files:

```
# rpm -qpc httpd-*rpm
/etc/httpd/conf.d/autoindex.conf
/etc/httpd/conf.d/userdir.conf
/etc/httpd/conf.d/welcome.conf
/etc/httpd/conf.modules.d/00-base.conf
/etc/httpd/conf.modules.d/00-dav.conf
...
/etc/httpd/conf/httpd.conf
/etc/httpd/conf/magic
/etc/logrotate.d/httpd
/etc/sysconfig/htcacheclean
/etc/sysconfig/httpd
...
```

The main configuration file is /etc/httpd/conf/httpd.conf for Apache. The welcome. conf file defines the default homepage for your website, until you add some content. The magic file defines rules the server can use to figure out a file's type when the server tries to open it. Command line options used with the httpd daemon are defined in the /etc/sysconfig/httpd file.

The /etc/logrotate.d/httpd file defines how log files produced by Apache are rotated. The /etc/tmpfiles.d/httpd.conf file defines a directory that contains temporary run-time files (no need to change that file). The last configuration file entries are in the

/var/www/error directory. Files in that directory define the responses that a user sees when an error is encountered, such as a file not found or permission denied message.

Some Apache modules drop configuration files (*.conf) into the /etc/httpd/conf. modules.d/ directory. Any file in that directory that ends in .conf is pulled into the main httpd.conf file and used to configure Apache. Most module packages that come with configuration files put those configuration files in the /etc/httpd/conf.d directory. For example, the mod_ssl (for secure web servers) and mod_python (for interpreting python code) modules have related configuration files in the /etc/httpd/conf.d directory named ssl.conf and python.conf, respectively.

You can just install the httpd package to begin setting up your web server. However, you might prefer to add some other packages that are often associated with the httpd package. One way to do that is to install the entire Web Server group as follows:

```
# yum groupinstall "Web Server"
```

Here are the packages, along with the httpd package, in the Web Server group in Fedora that you get by default:

- **httpd-manual**—Fills the /var/www/manual directory with the Apache documentation manuals. After you start the httpd service (as shown in later steps), you can access this set of manuals from a web browser on the local machine by typing **http://localhost/manual** into the location box.

- Externally, instead of localhost, you could use the fully qualified domain name or IP address of the system. The Apache Documentation screen appears as shown in Figure 17.1.

- **mod_ssl**—Contains the module and configuration file needed for the web server to provide secure connections to clients using Secure Sockets Layer (SSL) and Transport Layer Security (TLS) protocols. These features are necessary if you need encrypted communications for online shopping or other data you want to keep private. The configuration file is located at /etc/httpd/conf.d/ssl.conf.

- **crypto-utils**—Contains commands for generating keys and certificates needed to do secure communications with the Apache web server.

- **mod_perl**—Contains the Perl module (mod_perl), configuration file and associated files needed to allow the Apache web server to directly execute any Perl code.

- **php**—Contains the PHP module and configuration file needed to run PHP scripts directly in Apache. Related packages include php-ldap (for running PHP code that needs to access LDAP databases) and php-mysql (to add database support to the Apache server).

- **php-ldap**—Adds support for Lightweight Directory Access Protocol (LDAP) to the PHP module, allowing directory service access over networks.

FIGURE 17.1

Access Apache documentation directly from the local Apache server.

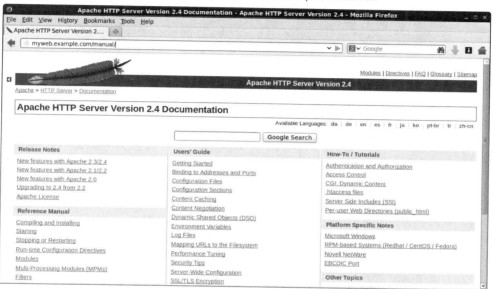

- **squid**—Provides proxy services for specific protocols (such as HTTP), as mentioned in Chapter 14, "Administering Networking." Although it doesn't provide HTTP content itself, a Squid proxy server typically forwards requests from proxy clients to the Internet or other network providing web content. This provides a means of controlling or filtering content that clients can reach from a home, school, or place of business.

- **webalizer**—Contains tools for analyzing web server data.

Optional packages in the Web Server group come from the web-server sub-group. Run `yum groupinfo web-server` to display those packages. Some of those packages offer special ways of providing content, such as wikis (`moin`), content management systems (`drupal7`), and blogs (`wordpress`). Others include tools for graphing web statistics (`awstats`) or offer lightweight web server alternatives to Apache (`lighttpd` and `cherokee`).

Installing Apache

Although you only need `httpd` to get started with an Apache web server, if you are just learning about Apache, you should install the manuals (`httpd-manual`) as well. If you are thinking of creating a secure (SSL) site and possibly generating some statistics about your website, you can just install the entire group:

```
# yum groupinstall "Web Server"
```

Assuming you have an Internet connection to the Fedora repository (or RHEL repository, if you are using RHEL), all the mandatory and default packages from that group are installed. You have all the software you need to do the procedures and exercises described in this chapter.

Starting Apache

To get the Apache web server going, you want to enable the service to start on every reboot and you want to start it immediately. In Red Hat Enterprise Linux (up to RHEL 6) and in older Fedora distributions, you could type the following as root:

```
# chkconfig httpd on
# service httpd start
Starting httpd:                    [  OK  ]
```

In recent Fedora systems and RHEL 7, you enable and start httpd using the systemctl command:

```
# systemctl enable httpd.service
# systemctl start httpd.service
# systemctl status httpd.service
httpd.service - The Apache HTTP Server
   Loaded: loaded (/usr/lib/systemd/system/httpd.service; enabled)
   Active: active (running) since Thu 2014-08-28 08:49:54 EDT; 11h
       ago
 Main PID: 14575 (/usr/sbin/httpd)
   Status: "Total requests: 17; Current requests/sec: 0; Current
       traffic:    0 B/sec"
   CGroup: /system.slice/httpd.service
           ├─14575 /usr/sbin/httpd -DFOREGROUND
           ├─14582 /usr/sbin/httpd -DFOREGROUND
           ├─14583 /usr/sbin/httpd -DFOREGROUND
           ├─14584 /usr/sbin/httpd -DFOREGROUND
    . . .
```

When the httpd service starts, six httpd daemon processes are launched by default to respond to requests for the web server. You can configure more or fewer httpd daemons to be started based on settings in the httpd.conf file (described in the section "Understanding the Apache configuration files"). To change the behavior of the httpd daemon, you can add options to the OPTIONS= variable in the /etc/sysconfig/httpd file.

Because there are different versions of httpd around, check the man page (man httpd) to see what options can be passed to the httpd daemon. For example, setting OPTIONS="-e debug" increases the log level so the maximum number of Apache messages are sent to log files. Restart the `httpd` service for the changes to take effect. Type the `ps` command to make sure the options took effect:

```
$ ps -ef | grep httpd
root    14575 1     0 08:49 ? 00:00:01 /usr/sbin/httpd -DFOREGROUND -X
apache 14582 14575 0 08:49 ? 00:00:00 /usr/sbin/httpd -DFOREGROUND -X
```

If you added a debug option (`-X`), remember to remove that option from `/etc/sysconfig/httpd` when you are done debugging Apache and restart the service. Leaving debugging on quickly fills up your log files.

Securing Apache

To secure Apache, you need to be aware of standard Linux security features (permissions, ownership, firewalls, and Security Enhanced Linux) as well as security features that are specific to Apache. The following sections describe security features that relate to Apache.

Apache file permissions and ownership

The `httpd` daemon process runs as the user `apache` and group `apache`. By default, HTML content is stored in the `/var/www/html` directory (as determined by the value of `DocumentRoot` in the `httpd.conf` file).

For the `httpd` daemon to be able to access that content, standard Linux permissions apply: If read permission is not on for "other" users, it must be on for the `apache` user or group for the files to be read and served to clients. Likewise, any directory the `httpd` daemon must traverse to get to the content must have execute permission on for the `apache` user, `apache` group, or other user.

Although you cannot log in as the `apache` user (`/sbin/nologin` is the default shell), you can create content as root and change its ownership (`chown` command) or permission (`chmod` command). Often, however, separate user or group accounts are added to create content that is readable by everyone (other) but only writable by that special user or group.

Apache and iptables

If you have locked down your `iptables` firewall in Linux, you need to open several ports for clients to be able to talk to Apache through the firewall. Standard web service (HTTP) is accessible over TCP port 80; secure web service (HTTPS) is accessible via TCP port 443. To verify which ports are being used by the `httpd` server, use the `netstat` command:

```
# netstat -tupln | grep httpd
tcp6   0     0 :::80        :::*        LISTEN      29169/httpd
tcp6   0     0 :::443       :::*        LISTEN      29169/httpd
```

The output shows that the `httpd` daemon (process ID 29169) is listening on all addresses for port 80 (`:::80`) and port 443 (`:::443`). Both ports are associated with the TCP protocol (tcp6). To open those ports in Fedora or Red Hat Enterprise Linux, you need to add some firewall rules.

On a current Fedora or RHEL 7 system, open the Firewall window (type **Firewall**, and press Enter from the Activities screen on the GNOME 3 desktop). From there, select Permanent as the Configuration. Then, with the public zone selected, click the check boxes next to the http and https service boxes. Those ports immediately become open.

For RHEL 6 or older Fedora releases, add rules to the /etc/sysconfig/iptables file (somewhere before a final DROP or REJECT) such as the following:

```
-A INPUT -m state --state NEW -m tcp -p tcp --dport 80 -j ACCEPT
-A INPUT -m state --state NEW -m tcp -p tcp --dport 443 -j ACCEPT
```

Restart iptables (service iptables restart) for the new rules to take effect.

Apache and SELinux

If Security Enhanced Linux (SELinux) is set to Enforcing (as it is by default in Fedora and Red Hat Enterprise Linux), SELinux adds another layer of security over your httpd service. In essence, SELinux actually sets out to protect the system from being damaged by someone who may have cracked the httpd daemon. SELinux does this by creating policies that do the following:

- Deny access to files that are not set to the right file contexts. For httpd in SELinux, there are different file contexts for content, configuration files, log files, scripts, and other httpd-related files. Any file that is not set to the proper context is not accessible to the httpd daemon.

- Prevent insecure features from being used, such as file uploading and clear-text authentication, by setting Booleans for such features to the off position. You can selectively turn on Booleans as they are needed, if they meet your security requirements.

- Keep the httpd daemon from accessing nonstandard features, such as a port outside the default ports the service would expect to use.

A full description of SELinux is contained in Chapter 24, "Enhancing Linux Security with SELinux." However, here are a few specifics you should know about using SELinux with the Apache httpd service:

- **Turn off SELinux.** You don't have to use SELinux. You can set SELinux to Permissive mode if you feel it is too difficult and unnecessary to create the SELinux policies needed to get your web server to work with SELinux in Enforcing mode. You can change the mode to Permissive by editing the /etc/sysconfig/selinux file so the SELINUX value is set as follows. With this set, the next time you reboot the system, it is in Permissive mode. This means that if you break SELinux policies, that event is logged, but not prevented (as it would be in Enforcing mode).

```
SELINUX=permissive
```

- **Read the httpd_selinux man page.** Type `man httpd_selinux` from the shell. This man page shows you the proper file contexts and available Booleans.

- **Use standard locations for files.** When you create new files, those files inherit the file contexts of the directories they are in. Because /etc/httpd is set to the right file context for configuration files, /var/www/html is right for content files, and so on, simply copying files to or creating new files in those locations causes the file contexts to be set properly.

- **Modify SELinux to allow nonstandard features.** You may want to serve web content from the /mystuff directory or put configuration files in the /etc/ whatever directory. Likewise, you may want to allow users of your server to upload files, run scripts, or enable other features that are disabled by SELinux by default. In those cases, you can use SELinux commands to set the file contexts and Booleans you need to get SELinux working the way you want.

Be sure to read Chapter 24 to learn more about SELinux.

Understanding the Apache configuration files

The configuration files for Apache HTTPD are incredibly flexible, meaning that you can configure the server to behave in almost any manner you want. This flexibility comes at the cost of increased complexity in the form of a large number of configuration options (called *directives*). But in practice, you need to be familiar with only a few directives in most cases.

> **NOTE**
>
> See http://httpd.apache.org/docs/current/mod/directives.html for a complete list of directives supported by Apache. If you have httpd-manual installed, you can reach descriptions of these directives and other Apache features by opening the manual from the server you have running Apache: http://localhost/manual/.

In Fedora and RHEL, the basic Apache server's primary configuration file is in /etc/httpd/conf/httpd.conf. Besides this file, any file ending in .conf in the /etc/httpd/conf.d directory is also used for Apache configuration (based on an Include line in the httpd.conf file). In Ubuntu, the Apache configuration is stored in text files read by the Apache server, beginning with /etc/apache2/apache2.conf. Configuration is read from start to finish, with most directives being processed in the order in which they are read.

Using directives

The scope of many configuration directives can be altered based on context. In other words, some parameters may be set on a global level and then changed for a specific file, directory, or virtual host. Other directives are always global in nature, such as those specifying which IP addresses the server listens on. Still others are valid only when applied to a specific location.

Locations are configured in the form of a start tag containing the location type and a resource location, followed by the configuration options for that location, and finishing with an end tag. This form is often called a *configuration block*, and it looks very similar to HTML code. A special type of configuration block, known as a *location block*, is used to limit the scope of directives to specific files or directories. These blocks take the following form:

```
<locationtag specifier>
(options specific to objects matching the specifier go within this
    block)
</locationtag>
```

Different types of location tags exist and are selected based on the type of resource location that is being specified. The specifier included in the start tag is handled based on the type of location tag. The location tags you generally use and encounter are `Directory`, `Files`, and `Location`, which limit the scope of the directives to specific directories, files, or locations, respectively.

- `Directory` tags are used to specify a path based on the location on the filesystem. For instance, `<Directory />` refers to the root directory on the computer. Directories inherit settings from directories above them, with the most specific `Directory` block overriding less-specific ones, regardless of the order in which they appear in the configuration files.

- `Files` tags are used to specify files by name. `Files` tags can be contained within `Directory` blocks to limit them to files under that directory. Settings within a `Files` block override the ones in `Directory` blocks.

- `Location` tags are used to specify the URI used to access a file or directory. This is different from `Directory` in that it relates to the address contained within the request and not to the real location of the file on the drive. `Location` tags are processed last and override the settings in `Directory` and `Files` blocks.

Match versions of these tags—`DirectoryMatch`, `FilesMatch`, and `LocationMatch`—have the same function but can contain regular expressions in the resource specification. `FilesMatch` and `LocationMatch` blocks are processed at the same time as `Files` and `Location`, respectively. `DirectoryMatch` blocks are processed after Directory blocks.

Apache can also be configured to process configuration options contained within files with the name specified in the `AccessFileName` directive (which is generally set to `.htaccess`). Directives in access configuration files are applied to all objects under the directory they contain, including subdirectories and their contents. Access configuration files are processed at the same time as `Directory` blocks, using a similar "most specific match" order.

> **NOTE**
>
> Access control files are useful for allowing users to change specific settings without having access to the server configuration files. The configuration directives permitted within an access configuration file are determined by the `AllowOverride` setting on the directory in which they are contained. Some directives do not make sense at that level and generally result in a "server internal error" message when trying to access the URI. The `AllowOverride` option is covered in detail at `http://httpd.apache.org/docs/mod/core.html#allowoverride`.

Three directives commonly found in location blocks and access control files are `DirectoryIndex`, `Options`, and `ErrorDocument`:

- `DirectoryIndex` tells Apache which file to load when the URI contains a directory but not a filename. This directive doesn't work in `Files` blocks.

- `Options` is used to adjust how Apache handles files within a directory. The `ExecCGI` option tells Apache that files in that directory can be run as CGI scripts, and the `Includes` option tells Apache that server-side includes (SSI) are permitted. Another common option is the `Indexes` option, which tells Apache to generate a list of files if one of the filenames found in the `DirectoryIndex` setting is missing. An absolute list of options can be specified, or the list of options can be modified by adding + or - in front of an option name. See `http://httpd.apache.org/docs/mod/core.html#options` for more information.

- `ErrorDocument` directives can be used to specify a file containing messages to send to web clients when a particular error occurs. The location of the file is relative to the `/var/www` directory. The directive must specify an error code and the full URI for the error document. Possible error codes include 403 (access denied), 404 (file not found), and 500 (server internal error). You can find more information about the `ErrorDocument` directive at `http://httpd.apache.org/docs/mod/core.html#errordocument`. As an example, when a client requests a URL from the server that is not found, the following ErrorDocument line causes the 404 error code to send the client an error message that is listed in the `/var/www/error/HTTP_NOT_FOUND.html.var` file.

```
ErrorDocument 404 /error/HTTP_NOT_FOUND.html.var
```

Another common use for location blocks and access control files is to limit or expand access to a resource. The `Allow` directive can be used to permit access to matching hosts, and the `Deny` directive can be used to forbid it. Both of these options can occur more than once within a block and are handled based on the `Order` setting. Setting `Order` to `Deny,Allow` permits access to any host that is not listed in a `Deny` directive. A setting of `Allow,Deny` denies access to any host not allowed in an `Allow` directive.

As with most other options, the most specific `Allow` or `Deny` option for a host is used, meaning that you can `Deny` access to a range and `Allow` access to subsets of that range. By adding the `Satisfy` option and some additional parameters, you can add password authentication. For more information on Allow or Deny, Satisfy or other directives, refer to the Apache Directive Index: http://httpd.apache.org/docs/current/mod/directives.html.

Understanding default settings

The reason you can start using your Apache web server as soon as you install it is that the httpd.conf file includes default settings that tell the server such things as where to find web content, scripts, log files, and other items the server needs to operate. It also includes settings that tell the server how many server processes to run at a time and how directory contents are displayed.

If you want to host a single website (such as for the example.com domain), you can simply add content to the /var/www/html directory and add the address of your website to a DNS server so others can browse to it. You can then change directives, such as those described in the previous section, as needed.

To help you understand the settings that come in the default httpd.conf file, I've displayed some of those settings with descriptions below. I have removed comments and rearranged some of the settings for clarity.

The following settings show locations where the httpd server is getting and putting content by default:

```
ServerRoot "/etc/httpd"
Include conf.d/*.conf
ErrorLog logs/error_log
CustomLog "logs/access_log" combined
DocumentRoot "/var/www/html"
ScriptAlias /cgi-bin/ "/var/www/cgi-bin/"
```

The ServerRoot directive identifies /etc/httpd as the location where configuration files are stored.

At the point in the file where the Include line appears, any files ending in .conf from the /etc/httpd/conf.d directory are included in the httpd.conf file. Configuration files are often associated with Apache modules (which are often included in the software package with a module) or with virtual host blocks (which you might add yourself to virtual host configurations in separate files). See the section "Adding a virtual host to Apache."

As errors are encountered and content is served, messages about those activities are placed in files indicated by the ErrorLog and CustomLog entries. In this example, those logs are stored in the /etc/httpd/logs/error_log and /etc/httpd/logs/access_log directories, respectively. Those logs are also hard linked to the /var/log/httpd directory, so you can access the same file from there as well.

The `DocumentRoot` and `ScriptAlias` directives determine where content that is served by your `httpd` server is stored. Traditionally, you would place an `index.html` file in the `DocumentRoot` directory (`/var/www/html`, by default) as the homepage and add other content as needed. The `ScriptAlias` directive tells the `httpd` daemon that any scripts requested from the `cgi-bin` directory should be found in the `/var/www/cgi-bin` directory. For example, a client could access a script located in `/var/www/cgi-bin/script.cgi` by entering a URL such as `http://example.com/cgi-bin/script.cgi`.

In addition to file locations, you can find other information in the `httpd.conf` file. Here are some examples:

```
Listen 80
User apache
Group apache
ServerAdmin root@localhost
DirectoryIndex index.html index.php
AccessFileName .htaccess
```

The `Listen 80` directive tells `httpd` to listen for incoming requests on port 80 (the default port for the HTTP web server protocol). By default, it listens on all network interfaces, although you could restrict it to selected interfaces by IP address (for example, `Listen 192.168.0.1:80`).

The `User` and `Group` directives tell `httpd` to run as `apache` for both the user and group. The value of `ServerAdmin` (`root@localhost`, by default) is published on some web pages to tell users where to email if they have problems with the server.

The `DirectoryIndex` lists files that `httpd` will serve if a directory is requested. For example, if a web browser requested *http://host/whatever/*, `httpd` would see whether `/var/www/html/whatever/index.html` existed and serve it if the file existed. If it didn't exist, in this example, `httpd` would look for `index.php`. If that file couldn't be found, the contents of the directory would be displayed.

An `AccessFileName` directive can be added to tell `httpd` to use the contents of the `.htaccess` file if it exists in a directory to read in settings that apply to access to that directory. For example, the file could be used to require password protection for the directory or to indicate that the contents of the directory should be displayed in certain ways. For this file to work, however, a `Directory` container (described next) would have to have `AllowOverride` opened. (By default, the `AllowOverride None` setting prevents the `.htaccess` file from being used for any directives.)

The following `Directory` containers define behavior when the root directory (/), `/var/www`, and `/var/www/html` directories are accessed:

```
<Directory />
    AllowOverride none
    Require all denied
```

```
    </Directory>
    <Directory "/var/www">
        AllowOverride None
        # Allow open access:
        Require all granted
    </Directory>
    <Directory "/var/www/html">
        Options Indexes FollowSymLinks
        AllowOverride None
        Require all granted
    </Directory>
```

The first `Directory` container (/) indicates that if `httpd` tries to access any files in the Linux file system, access is denied. The `AllowOverride none` directive prevents `.htaccess` files from overriding settings for that directory. Those settings apply to any subdirectories that are not defined in other `Directory` containers.

Content access is relaxed within the `/var/www` directory. Access is granted to content added under that directory, but overriding settings is not allowed.

The `/var/www/html Directory` container follows symbolic links and does not allow overrides. With `Require all granted` set, `httpd` doesn't prevent any access to the server.

If all the settings just described work for you, you can begin adding the content you want to the var/www/html and var/www/cgi-bin directories. One reason you might not be satisfied with the default setting is that you might want to serve content for multiple domains (such as example.com, example.org, and example.net). To do that, you need to configure virtual hosts. Virtual hosts, which are described in greater detail in the next section, are a convenient (and almost essential) tool for serving different content to clients based on the server address or name that a request is directed to. Most global configuration options are applied to virtual hosts but can be overridden by directives within the `VirtualHost` block.

Adding a virtual host to Apache

Apache supports the creation of separate websites within a single server to keep content separate. Individual sites are configured on the same server in what are referred to as virtual hosts.

Virtual hosts are really just a way to have the content for multiple domain names available from the same Apache server. Instead of needing to have one physical system to serve content for each domain, you can serve content for multiple domains from the same operating system.

An Apache server that is doing virtual hosting may have multiple domain names that resolve to the IP address of the server. The content that is served to a web client is based on the name used to access the server.

For example, if a client got to the server by requesting the name www.example.com, the client would be directed to a virtual host container that had its ServerName set to respond to www.example.com. The container would provide the location of the content and possibly different error logs or Directory directives from the global settings. This way, each virtual host could be managed as if it were on a separate machine.

To use name-based virtual hosting, turn on the NameVirtualHost directive. Then add as many VirtualHost containers as you like. Here's how to configure a virtual host:

> **NOTE**
>
> After you enable NameVirtualHost, your default DocumentRoot (/var/www/html) is no longer used if some-one accesses the server by IP address or some name that is not set in a VirtualHost container. Instead, the first VirtualHost container is used as the default location for the server.

17

1. **In Fedora or RHEL, create a file named /etc/httpd/conf.d/example.org. conf using this template:**

```
NameVirtualHost *:80
<VirtualHost *:80>
    ServerAdmin      webmaster@example.org
    ServerName       www.example.org
    ServerAlias      web.example.org
    DocumentRoot     /var/www/html/example.org/
DirectoryIndex  index.php index.html index.htm
</VirtualHost>
```

This example includes the following settings:

- The NameVirtualHost line tells Apache to determine which virtual host to serve documents from based on the hostname provided by the HTTP client. The *:80 means that requests to port 80 on any IP address will be treated in this manner.

- Similarly, the *:80 specification in the VirtualHost block indicates what address and port this virtual host applies to. With multiple IP addresses associated with your Linux system, the * can be replaced by a specific IP address. The port is optional for both NameVirtualHost and VirtualHost specifications but should always be used to prevent interference with SSL virtual hosts (which use port 443 by default).

- The ServerName and ServerAlias lines tell Apache which names this virtual host should be recognized as, so replace them with names appropriate to your site. You can leave out the ServerAlias line if you do not have any alternate names for the server, and you can specify more than one name per ServerAlias line or have multiple ServerAlias lines if you have several alternate names.

- The DocumentRoot specifies where the web documents (content served for this site) are stored. Although shown as a subdirectory that you create under the default DocumentRoot (/var/www/html), often sites are attached to the home directories of specific users (such as /home/chris/public_html) so that each site can be managed by a different user.

2. **With the host enabled, use apachectl to check the configuration, and then do a graceful restart:**

```
# apachectl configtest
Syntax OK
# apachectl graceful
```

Provided you have registered the system with a DNS server, a web browser should be able to access this website using either www.example.org or web.example.org. If that works, you can start adding other virtual hosts to the system as well.

Another way to extend the use of your website is to allow multiple users to share their own content on your server. You can enable users to add content they want to share via your web server in a subdirectory of their home directories, as described in the next section.

> **NOTE**
>
> Keeping individual virtual hosts in separate files is a convenient way to manage virtual hosts. However, you should be careful to keep your primary virtual host in a file that will be read before the others because the first virtual host receives requests for site names that don't match any in your configuration. In a commercial web-hosting environment, it is common to create a special default virtual host that contains an error message indicating that no site by that name has been configured.

Allowing users to publish their own web content

In situations where you do not have the ability to set up a virtual host for every user that you want to provide web space for, you can easily make use of the mod_userdir module in Apache. With this module enabled (which it is not by default), the public_html directory under every user's home directory is available to the web at http://servername/~username/.

For example, a user named wtucker on www.example.org stores web content in /home/wtucker/public_html. That content would be available from http://www.example.org/~wtucker.

Make these changes to the /etc/httpd/conf/httpd.conf file to allow users to publish web content from their own home directories. Not all versions of Apache have these blocks in their httpd.conf file, so you might have to create them from scratch:

1. **Create a `<IfModule mod_userdir.c>` block.** Change chris to any username you want to allow to create their own `public_html` directory. You can add multiple usernames.

```
<IfModule mod_userdir.c>
    UserDir enabled chris
    UserDir public_html
</IfModule>
```

2. **Create a `<Directory /home/*/public_html>` directive block and change any settings you like.** This is how the block will look:

```
</IfModule>
<Directory "/home/*/public_html">
    Options Indexes Includes FollowSymLinks
    Require all granted
</Directory>
```

3. **Have your users create their own `public_html` directories in their own home directories.**

```
$ mkdir $HOME/public_html
```

4. **Set the execute permission (as root user) to allow the `httpd` daemon to access the home directory:**

```
# chmod +x /home /home/*
```

5. **If SELinux is in Enforcing mode (which is it by default in Fedora and RHEL), set the SELinux file context properly on the content so SELinux allows the `httpd` daemon to access the content:**

```
# chcon -R --reference=/var/www/html/ /home/*/public_html
```

6. **Set the SELinux Boolean to allow users to share HTML content from their home directories:**

```
# setsebool -P httpd_enable_homedirs true
```

7. **Restart or reload the `httpd` service.**

At this point, you should be able to access content placed in a user's `public_html` directory by pointing a web browser to `http://hostname/~user`.

Securing your web traffic with SSL/TLS

Any data you share from your website using standard HTTP protocol is sent in clear text. That means that anyone who can watch the traffic on a network between your server and your client can view your unprotected data. To secure that information, you can add certificates to your site (so a client can validate who you are) and encrypt your data (so nobody can sniff your network and see your data).

Electronic commerce applications such as online shopping and banking are generally encrypted using either the Secure Sockets Layer (SSL) or Transport Layer Security (TLS) specifications. TLS is based on version 3.0 of the SSL specifications, so they are very similar in nature. Because of this similarity—and because SSL is older—the SSL acronym is often used to refer to either variety. For web connections, the SSL connection is established first, and then normal HTTP communication is "tunneled" through it.

> **NOTE**
>
> Because SSL negotiation takes place before any HTTP communication, name-based virtual hosting (which occurs at the HTTP layer) does not work easily with SSL. As a consequence, every SSL virtual host you configure should have a unique IP address. (See the Apache site for more information: `httpd.apache.org/docs/vhosts/name-based.html`.)

While you are establishing a connection between an SSL client and an SSL server, asymmetric (public key) cryptography is used to verify identities and establish the session parameters and the session key. A symmetric encryption algorithm such as DES or RC4 is then used with the negotiated key to encrypt the data that are transmitted during the session. The use of asymmetric encryption during the handshaking phase allows safe communication without the use of a preshared key, and the symmetric encryption is faster and more practical for use on the session data.

For the client to verify the identity of the server, the server must have a previously generated private key, as well as a certificate containing the public key and information about the server. This certificate must be verifiable using a public key that is known to the client.

Certificates are generally digitally signed by a third-party certificate authority (CA) that has verified the identity of the requester and the validity of the request to have the certificate signed. In most cases, the CA is a company that has made arrangements with the web browser vendor to have its own certificate installed and trusted by default client installations. The CA then charges the server operator for its services.

Commercial certificate authorities vary in price, features, and browser support, but remember that price is not always an indication of quality. Some popular CAs include InstantSSL (http://www.instantssl.com), Thawte (http://www.thawte.com), and Symantec (http://www.symantec.com/ssl-certificates#).

You also have the option of creating self-signed certificates, although these should be used only for testing or when a very small number of people will be accessing your server and you do not plan to have certificates on multiple machines. Directions for generating a self-signed certificate are included in the section "Generating an SSL key and self-signed certificate."

The last option is to run your own certificate authority. This is probably practical only if you have a small number of expected users and the means to distribute your CA certificate to them (including assisting them with installing it in their browsers). The process for creating a CA is too elaborate to cover in this book, but it is a worthwhile alternative to generating self-signed certificates.

The following sections describe how HTTPS communications are configured by default in Fedora and RHEL when you install the mod_ssl package. After that, I describe how to better configure SSL communications by generating your own SSL keys and certificates to use with the web server (running on a Fedora or RHEL system) configured in this chapter.

Understanding how SSL is configured

If you have installed the mod_ssl package in Fedora or RHEL (which is done by default if you installed the Web Server group), a self-signed certificate and private key are created when the package is installed. This allows you to immediately use HTTPS protocol to communicate with the web server.

Although the default configuration of mod_ssl allows you to have encrypted communications between your web server and clients, because the certificate is self-signed, a client accessing your site is warned that the certificate is untrusted. To begin exploring the SSL configuration for your Apache web server, make sure the mod_ssl package is installed on the server running your Apache (httpd) service:

```
# yum install mod_ssl
```

The mod_ssl package includes the module needed to implement SSL on your web server (mod_ssl.so) and a config file for your SSL hosts: /etc/httpd/conf.d/ssl.conf. There are many comments in this file, to help you understand what to change. Those lines that are not commented out define some initial settings and a default virtual host. Here are some of those lines:

```
Listen 443 https
...
<VirtualHost _default_:443>
ErrorLog logs/ssl_error_log
TransferLog logs/ssl_access_log
LogLevel warn
SSLEngine on
...
SSLCertificateFile /etc/pki/tls/certs/localhost.crt
SSLCertificateKeyFile /etc/pki/tls/private/localhost.key
...
</VirtualHost>The SSL service is set to listen on standard SSL port
    443 on all the system's network interfaces.
```

A VirtualHost block is created that causes error messages and access messages to be logged to log files that are separate from the standard logs used by the server (ssl_error_log and ssl_access_log in the /var/log/httpd/ directory). The level of log messages is set to warn and the SSLEngine is turned on.

In the preceding sample code, two entries associated with SSL Certificates in the `VirtualHost` block identify the key and certificate information. A key is generated when `mod_ssl` is installed and placed in the file `/etc/pki/tls/private/localhost.key`. A self-signed certificate, `/etc/pki/tls/certs/localhost.crt`, is created using that key. When you create your own key and certificate later, you need to replace the values of `SSLCertificateFile` and `SSLCertificateKeyFile` in this file.

After installing the `mod_ssl` package and reloading the configuration file, you can test that the default certificate is working by following these steps:

1. **Open a connection to the website from a web browser, using the HTTPS protocol.** For example, if you are running Firefox on the system where the web server is running, type `https://localhost` into the location box and press Enter. Figure 17.2 shows an example of the page that appears.

FIGURE 17.2

Accessing an SSL website with a default certificate

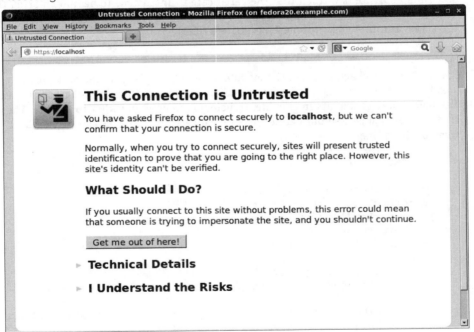

This page warns you that there is no way of verifying who created the certificate you are accepting.

2. **Because you are accessing the site via a browser on the local host, click Add Exception to allow connections to this site.** You are warned that you are overriding Firefox to accept this certificate.

3. **Select View to see the certificate that was generated.** It includes your hostname, information on when the certificate was issued and when it expires, and lots of other organization information.

4. **Close that window, and then select Confirm Security Exception to accept the connection.** You should now see your default web page using HTTPS protocol. From now on, your browser will accept HTTPS connections to the web server using that certificate and encrypt all communications between the server and browser.

Because you don't want your website to scare off users, the best thing to do is to get a valid certificate to use with your site. The next best thing to do is to create a self-signed certificate that at least includes better information about your site and organization. The following section describes how to do that.

Generating an SSL key and self-signed certificate

To begin setting up SSL, use the `openssl` command, which is part of the `openssl` package, to generate your public and private key. After that, you can generate your own self-signed certificate to test the site or to use internally.

1. **If the `openssl` package is not already installed, install it as follows:**

   ```
   # yum install openssl
   ```

2. **Generate a 1024-bit RSA private key and save it to a file:**

   ```
   # cd /etc/pki/tls/private
   # openssl genrsa -out server.key 1024
   # chmod 600 server.key
   ```

> **NOTE**
>
> You can use a filename other than `server.key` and should do so if you plan to have more than one SSL host on your machine (which requires more than one IP address). Just make sure you specify the correct filename in the Apache configuration later.

   Or, in higher-security environments, encrypting the key by adding the `-des3` argument after the `genrsa` argument on the `openssl` command line is a good idea. When prompted for a passphrase, press Enter:

   ```
   # openssl genrsa -des3 -out server.key 1024
   ```

3. **If you don't plan to have your certificate signed, or if you want to test your configuration, generate a self-signed certificate and save it in a file named `server.crt` in the `/etc/pki/tls/certs` directory:**

```
# cd /etc/pki/tls/certs
# openssl req -new -x509 -nodes -sha1 -days 365 \
   -key /etc/pki/tls/private/server.key \
   -out server.crt
Country Name (2 letter code) [AU]: US
State or Province Name (full name) [Some-State]: NJ
Locality Name (eg, city) [Default City]: Princeton
Organization Name (eg, company) [Default Company Ltd
Ltd]:TEST USE ONLY
Organizational Unit Name (eg, section) []:TEST USE ONLY
Common Name (eg, YOUR name) []:secure.example.org
Email Address []:dom@example.org
```

4. **Edit the /etc/httpd/conf.d/ssl.conf file to change the key and certificate locations to use the ones you just created.** For example:

   ```
   SSLCertificateFile /etc/pki/tls/certs/server.crt
   SSLCertificateKeyFile /etc/pki/tls/private/server.key
   ```

5. **Restart or reload the httpd server.**

6. **Open https://localhost from a local browser again, repeat the procedure to review, and accept the new certificate.**

For internal use or testing, a self-signed certificate might work for you. However, for public websites, you should use a certificate that is validated by a certificate authority (CA). The procedure for doing that is covered next.

Generating a certificate signing request

If you plan to have your certificate signed by a CA (including one that you run yourself), you can use your private key to generate a certificate signing request (CSR):

1. **Create a directory for storing your CSR.**

   ```
   # mkdir /etc/pki/tls/ssl.csr
   # cd /etc/pki/tls/ssl.csr/
   ```

2. **Use the openssl command to generate the CSR.** The result is a CSR file in the current directory named server.csr. When you enter the information, the Common Name should match the name that clients will use to access your server. Be sure to get the other details right so it can be validated by a third-party CA. Also, if you had entered a passphrase for your key, you are prompted to enter it here to use the key.

   ```
   # openssl req -new -key ../private/server.key -out server.csr

   Country Name (2 letter code) [AU]:US
   State or Province Name (full name) [Some-State]:Washington
   ```

```
Locality Name (eg, city) []:Bellingham
Organization Name (eg, company) [Internet Widgits Pty
Ltd]:Example Company, LTD.
Organizational Unit Name (eg, section) []:Network
 Operations
Common Name (eg, YOUR name) []:secure.example.org
Email Address []:dom@example.org

Please enter the following 'extra' attributes
to be sent with your certificate request
A challenge password []:
An optional company name []:
```

3. **Visit the website of the certificate signing authority you choose, and request a signed certificate.** At some point, the CA site will probably ask you to copy and paste the contents of your CSR (`server.csr` file in this example) into a form needed to make the request.

4. **When the CA sends you the certificate (probably via email), save it in the `/etc/pki/tls/certs/` directory using a name based on the site you are hosting — for example, `example.org.crt`.**

5. **Change the value of `SSLCertificateFile` in the `/etc/httpd/conf.d/ssl.conf` file to point to your new CRT file.** Or, if you have multiple SSL hosts, you might want to create a separate entry (possibly in a separate `.conf` file) that looks like the following:

```
Listen 192.168.0.56:443
<VirtualHost *:443>
    ServerName      secure.example.org
    ServerAlias     web.example.org
    DocumentRoot    /home/username/public_html/
    DirectoryIndex  index.php index.html index.htm
    SSLEngine       On
    SSLCertificateKeyFile /etc/pki/tls/private/server.key
    SSLCertificateFile /etc/pki/tls/certs/example.org.crt
</VirtualHost>
```

The IP address shown in the `Listen` directive should be replaced by the public IP address representing the SSL host you are serving. Remember that each SSL host should have its own IP address.

Troubleshooting Your Web Server

In any complex environment, you occasionally run into problems. This section includes tips for isolating and resolving the most common errors that you may encounter.

Checking for configuration errors

You may occasionally run into configuration errors or script problems that prevent Apache from starting or that prevent specific files from being accessible. Most of these problems can be isolated and resolved using two Apache-provided tools: the `apachectl` program and the system error log.

When encountering a problem, first use the `apachectl` program with the `configtest` parameter to test the configuration. In fact, it's a good idea to develop the habit of running this every time you make a configuration change:

```
# apachectl configtest
Syntax OK
# apachectl graceful
/usr/sbin/apachectl graceful: httpd gracefully restarted
```

In the event of a syntax error, `apachectl` indicates where the error occurs and also does its best to give a hint about the nature of the problem. You can then use the `graceful` restart option (`apachectl graceful`) to instruct Apache to reload its configuration without disconnecting any active clients.

> **NOTE**
>
> The `graceful` restart option in `apachectl` automatically tests the configuration before sending the reload signal to `apache`, but getting in the habit of running the manual configuration test after making any configuration changes is still a good idea.

Some configuration problems pass the syntax tests performed by `apachectl` but cause the HTTP daemon to exit immediately after reloading its configuration. If this happens, use the `tail` command to check Apache's error log for useful information. On Fedora and RHEL systems, the error log is in `/var/log/httpd/error.log`. On other systems, you can find the location by looking for the `ErrorLog` directive in your Apache configuration.

You might encounter an error message that looks something like this:

```
[crit] (98)Address already in use: make_sock: could not bind to
    port 80
```

This error often indicates that something else is bound to port 80 (not very common unless you have attempted to install another web server), that another Apache process is already running (`apachectl` usually catches this), or that you have told Apache to bind the same IP address and port combination in more than one place. My friend Richard said he has seen students who installed Skype on Linux in a way that causes Skype to use TCP port 80 when running in the background.

You can use the `netstat` command to view the list of programs (including Apache) with TCP ports in the LISTEN state:

```
# netstat -nltp
Active Internet connections (only servers)
Proto  Local Address  Foreign Address  State   PID/Program name
tcp6   :::80          :::*             LISTEN  2105/httpd
```

The output from `netstat` (which was shortened to fit here) indicates that an instance of the `httpd` process with a process ID of 2105 is listening (as indicated by the LISTEN state) for connections to any local IP address (indicated by :::80) on port 80 (the standard HTTP port). If a different program is listening to port 80, it is shown there. You can use the `kill` command to terminate the process, but if it is something other than `httpd`, you should also find out why it is running.

If you don't see any other processes listening on port 80, it could be that you have accidentally told Apache to listen on the same IP address and port combination in more than one place. Three configuration directives can be used for this: `BindAddress`, `Port`, and `Listen`:

- `BindAddress` enables you to specify a single IP address to listen on, or you can specify all IP addresses using the * wildcard. You should never have more than one `BindAddress` statement in your configuration file.

- `Port` specifies which TCP port to listen on but does not enable you to specify the IP address. `Port` is generally not used more than once in the configuration.

- `Listen` enables you to specify both an IP address and a port to bind to. The IP address can be in the form of a wildcard, and you can have multiple `Listen` statements in your configuration file.

To avoid confusion, it is generally a good idea to use only one of these directive types. Of the three, `Listen` is the most flexible, so it is probably the one you want to use the most. A common error when using `Listen` is to specify a port on all IP addresses (`*:80`) as well as that same port on a specific IP address (`1.2.3.4:80`), which results in the error from `make_sock`.

Configuration errors relating to SSL commonly result in Apache starting improperly. Make sure all key and certificate files exist and that they are in the proper format (use `openssl` to examine them).

For other error messages, try doing a web search to see whether somebody else has encountered the problem. In most cases, you can find a solution within the first few matches.

If you aren't getting enough information in the `ErrorLog`, you can configure it to log more information using the `LogLevel` directive. The options available for this directive, in increasing order of verbosity, are `emerg`, `alert`, `crit`, `error`, `warn`, `notice`, `info`, and `debug`. Select only one of these.

17

Any message that is at least as important as the `LogLevel` you select are stored in the `ErrorLog`. On a typical server, `LogLevel` is set to `warn`. You should not set it to any value lower than `crit` and should avoid leaving it set to `debug` because that can slow down the server and result in a very large `ErrorLog`.

As a last resort, you can also try running `httpd -X` manually to check for crashes or other error messages. The `-X` runs `httpd` so it displays debug and higher messages on the screen.

Accessing forbidden and server internal errors

The two common types of errors that you may encounter when attempting to view specific pages on your server are permission errors and server internal errors. Both types of errors can usually be isolated using the information in the error log. After making any of the changes described in the following list to attempt to solve one of these problems, try the request again and check the error log to see whether the message has changed (for example, to show that the operation completed successfully).

> **NOTE**
>
> "File not found' errors can be checked in the same way as "access forbidden" and "server internal errors." You may sometimes find that Apache is not looking where you think it is for a specific file. Generally, the entire path to the file shows up in the error log. Make sure you are accessing the correct virtual host, and check for any `Alias` settings that might be directing your location to a place you don't expect.

- **File permissions**—A "File permissions prevent access" error indicates that the `apache` process is running as a user that is unable to open the requested file. By default, `httpd` is run by the `apache` user and group. Make sure the account has execute permissions on the directory and every directory above it, as well as read permissions on the files themselves. Read permissions on a directory are also necessary if you want Apache to generate an index of files. See the manual page for `chmod` for more information about how to view and change permissions.

> **NOTE**
>
> Read permissions are not necessary for compiled binaries, such as those written in C or C++, but can be safely added unless a need exists to keep the contents of the program secret.

- **Access denied**—A "Client denied by server configuration" error indicates that Apache was configured to deny access to the object. Check the configuration files for `Location` and `Directory` sections that might affect the file you are trying to access. Remember that settings applied to a path are also applied to any paths below it. You can override these by changing the permissions only for the more specific path to which you want to allow access.

- **Index not found**—The "Directory index forbidden by rule" error indicates that Apache could not find an index file with a name specified in the `DirectoryIndex` directive and was configured to not create an index containing a list of files in a directory. Make sure your index page, if you have one, has one of the names specified in the relevant `DirectoryIndex` directive, or add an `Options Indexes` line to the appropriate `Directory` or `Location` section for that object.

- **Script crashed**—"Premature end of script headers" errors can indicate that a script is crashing before it finishes. On occasion, the errors that caused this also show up in the error log. When using `suexec` or `suPHP`, this error may also be caused by a file ownership or permissions error. These errors appear in log files in the `/var/log/httpd` directory.

- **SELinux errors**—If file permissions are open, but messages denying permission appear in log files, SELinux could be causing the problem. Set SELinux to Permissive mode temporarily (`setenforce 0`), and try to access the file again. If the file is now accessible, set SELinux to Enforcing mode again (`setenforce 1`) and check file contexts and Booleans. File contexts must be correct for `httpd` to be able to access a file. A Boolean might prevent a file being served from a remotely mounted directory or prevent a page from sending an e-mail or uploading a file. Type **man httpd_selinux** for details about SELinux configuration settings associated with the `httpd` services. (Install the `selinux-policy-devel` package to have that man page added to your system.)

Summary

The open source Apache project is the world's most popular web server. Although Apache offers tremendous flexibility, security, and complexity, a basic Apache web server can be configured in just a few minutes in Fedora, RHEL, and most other Linux distributions.

The chapter described the steps for installing, configuring, securing, and troubleshooting a basic Apache web server. You learned how to configure virtual hosting and secure SSL hosts. You also learned how to configure Apache to allow any user account on the system to publish content from his or her own `public_html` directory.

Continuing on the topic of server configuration, in Chapter 18, you learn how to set up an FTP server in Linux. The examples illustrate how to configure an FTP server using the `vsftpd` package.

Exercises

The exercises in this section cover topics related to installing and configuring an Apache web server. As usual, I recommend you use a spare Fedora or Red Hat Enterprise Linux system to do the exercises. Don't do these exercises on a production machine because these exercises modify the Apache configuration files and service and could damage services you have currently configured. Try to find a computer where it will do no harm to interrupt services on the system.

These exercises assume that you are starting with a Fedora or RHEL installation on which the Apache server (httpd package) is not yet installed.

If you are stuck, solutions to the tasks are shown in Appendix B. These show you one approach to each task, although Linux may offer multiple ways to complete a task.

1. From a Fedora system, install all the packages associated with the Web Server group.

2. Create a file called index.html in the directory assigned to DocumentRoot in the main Apache configuration file. The file should have the words "My Own Web Server" inside.

3. Start the Apache web server, and set it to start up automatically at boot time. Check that it is available from a web browser on your local host. (You should see the words "My Own Web Server" displayed if it is working properly.)

4. Use the netstat command to see which ports the httpd server is listening on.

5. Try to connect to your Apache web server from a web browser that is outside the local system. If it fails, correct any problems you encounter by investigating the firewall, SELinux, and other security features.

6. Using the openssl or similar command, create your own private RSA key and self-signed SSL certificate.

7. Configure your Apache web server to use your key and self-signed certificate to serve secure (HTTPS) content.

8. Use a web browser to create an HTTPS connection to your web server and view the contents of the certificate you created.

9. Create a file named /etc/httpd/conf.d/example.org.conf, which turns on name-based virtual hosting and creates a virtual host that does these things:

   - Listens on port 80 on all interfaces
   - Has a server administrator of joe@example.org
   - Has a server name of joe.example.org
   - Has a DocumentRoot of /var/www/html/example.org
   - Has a DirectoryIndex that includes at least index.html

   Create an index.html file in DocumentRoot that contains the words "Welcome to the House of Joe" inside.

10. Add the text **joe.example.org** to the end of the localhost entry in your /etc/hosts file on the machine that is running the web server. Then type **http://joe.example.org** into the location box of your web browser. You should see "Welcome to the House of Joe" when the page is displayed.

Configuring an FTP Server

The File Transfer Protocol (FTP) is one of the oldest protocols in existence for sharing files over networks. Although there are more secure protocols for network file sharing, FTP is still used quite often for making files freely available on the Internet.

Several FTP server projects are available with Linux today. However, the one often used with Fedora, Red Hat Enterprise Linux, Ubuntu, and other Linux distributions is the Very Secure FTP Daemon (vsftpd package). This chapter describes how to install, configure, use, and secure an FTP server using the vsftpd package.

Understanding FTP

FTP operates in a client/server model. An FTP server daemon listens for incoming requests (on TCP port 21) from FTP clients. The client presents a login and password. If the server accepts the login information, the client can interactively traverse the filesystem, list files and directories, and then download (and sometimes upload) files.

What makes FTP insecure is that everything sent between the FTP client and server is done in clear text. The FTP protocol was created at a time when most computer communication was done on private lines or over dial-up, where encryption was not thought to be critical. If you use FTP over a public network, someone sniffing the line anywhere between the client and server would be able to see not only the data being transferred, but also the authentication process (login and password information).

So FTP is not good for sharing files privately (use SSH commands such as sftp, scp, or rsync if you need private, encrypted file transfers). However, if you are sharing public documents, open source software repositories, or other openly available data, FTP is a good choice. Regardless of the operating system people use, they surely have an FTP file transfer application available to get files you offer from your FTP server.

When users authenticate to an FTP server in Linux, their usernames and passwords are authenticated against the standard Linux user accounts and passwords. There is also a special, non-authenticated account used by the FTP server called *anonymous*. The anonymous account can be accessed by anyone because it does not require a valid password. In fact, the term *anonymous FTP server* is often used to describe a public FTP server that does not require (or even allow) authentication of a legitimate user account.

> **NOTE**
>
> Although the ability to log in to the vsftpd server using a regular Linux user account is enabled by default in Fedora and Red Hat Enterprise Linux, if SELinux is set to Enforcing mode, it prevents the logins and file transfers from succeeding. If you want to keep SELinux in Enforcing mode, yet still allow Linux logins, you can change a Boolean (see the "Configuring SELinux for your FTP server" section) to allow regular user logins to succeed.

After the authentication phase (on the control port, TCP port 21), a second connection is made between the client and server. FTP supports both *active* and *passive* connection types. With an active FTP connection, the server sends data from its TCP port 20 to some random port the server chooses above port 1023 on the client. With passive FTP, the client requests the passive connection and requests a random port from the server.

Many browsers support passive FTP mode so that, if the client has a firewall, it doesn't block the data port the FTP server might use in active mode. Supporting passive mode requires some extra work on the server's firewall to allow random connections to ports above 1023 on the server. The section "Opening up your firewall for FTP" later in this chapter describes what you need to do to your Linux firewall to make both passive and active FTP connections work.

After the connection is established between the client and server, the client's current directory is established. For the anonymous user, the /var/ftp directory is that user's home directory. The anonymous user cannot go outside the /var/ftp directory structure. If a regular user, let's say joe, logs in to the FTP server, /home/joe is joe's current directory, but joe can change to any part of the filesystem for which joe has permission.

Command-oriented FTP clients (such as lftp and ftp commands) go into an interactive mode after connecting to the server. From the prompt you see, you can run many commands that are similar to those you would use from the shell. You could use pwd to see your current directory, ls to list directory contents, and cd to change directories. When you see a file you want, you use the get and put commands to download files from or upload them to the server, respectively.

With graphical tools for accessing FTP servers (such as a web browser), you type the URL of the site you want to visit (such as **ftp://docs.example.com**) into the location box of the browser. If you add no username or password, an anonymous connection is made and the contents of the home directory of the site are displayed. Click links to directories to change to those directories. Click links to files to display or download those files to your local system.

Armed with some understanding of how FTP works, you are now ready to install an FTP server (vsftpd package) on your Linux system.

Installing the vsftpd FTP Server

Setting up the Very Secure FTP server requires only one package in Fedora, RHEL, and other Linux distributions: vsftpd. Assuming you have a connection to your software repository, to install vsftpd, just type the following as root for Fedora or RHEL:

```
# yum install vsftpd
```

If you are using Ubuntu (or other Linux distribution based on Debian packaging), type the following to install vsftpd:

```
$ sudo apt-get install vsftpd
```

After the vsftpd package is installed, here are some commands you can run to familiarize yourself with the contents of that package. From Fedora or RHEL, run this command to get some general information about the package:

```
# rpm -qi vsftpd
...
Packager     : Fedora Project
Vendor       : Fedora Project
URL          : https://security.appspot.com/vsftpd.html
Summary      : Very Secure Ftp Daemon
Description : vsftpd is a Very Secure FTP daemon. It was written
               completely from scratch.
```

If you want to get more information about vsftpd, follow the URL listed to the related website (https://security.appspot.com/vsftpd.html). You can get additional documentation and information about the latest revisions of vsftpd.

You can view the full contents of the vsftpd package (rpm -ql vsftpd). Or you can view just the documentation (-qd) or configuration files (-qc). To see the documentation files in the vsftpd package, use the following:

```
# rpm -qd vsftpd
/usr/share/doc/vsftpd-3.0.2-6/EXAMPLE/INTERNET_SITE/README
...
/usr/share/doc/vsftpd-3.0.2-6/EXAMPLE/PER_IP_CONFIG/README
...
```

18

```
/usr/share/doc/vsftpd-3.0.2-6/EXAMPLE/VIRTUAL_HOSTS/README
/usr/share/doc/vsftpd-3.0.2-6/EXAMPLE/VIRTUAL_USERS/README
...
/usr/share/doc/vsftpd-3.0.2-6/FAQ
...
/usr/share/doc/vsftpd-3.0.2-6/vsftpd.xinetd
/usr/share/man/man5/vsftpd.conf.5.gz
/usr/share/man/man8/vsftpd.8.gz
```

In the `/usr/share/doc/vsftpd-*/EXAMPLE` directory structure, there are sample configuration files included to help you configure `vsftpd` in ways that are appropriate for an Internet site, multiple IP address site, and virtual hosts. The main `/usr/share/doc/vsftpd*` directory contains an FAQ (frequently asked questions), installation tips, and version information.

The man pages might have the most useful information when you set out to configure the `vsftpd` server. Type **man vsftpd.conf** to read about the configuration file and **man vsftpd** to read about the daemon process.

To list the configuration files, type the following:

```
# rpm -qc vsftpd
/etc/logrotate.d/vsftpd
/etc/pam.d/vsftpd
/etc/vsftpd/ftpusers
/etc/vsftpd/user_list
/etc/vsftpd/vsftpd.conf
```

The main configuration file is `/etc/vsftpd/vsftpd.conf`. The `ftpusers` and `user_list` files in the same directory store information about user accounts that are restricted from accessing the server. The `/etc/pam.d/vsftpd` file sets how authentication is done to the FTP server. The `/etc/logrotate.d/vsftpd` file configures how log files are rotated over time.

Now you have `vsftpd` installed and have taken a quick look at its contents. The next step is to start up and test the `vsftpd` service.

Starting the vsftpd Service

No configuration is required to launch the `vsftpd` service if you want to just use the default settings. If you start `vsftpd` as it is delivered with Fedora, this is what you get:

- The `vsftpd` service starts the `vsftpd` daemon, which runs in the background.
- The standard port on which the `vsftpd` daemon listens is TCP port 21. By default, data is transferred to the user, after the connection is made, on TCP port 20. TCP port 21 must be open in the firewall to allow new connections to access the service.

(See the section "Securing Your FTP Server" for details on opening ports, enabling connection tracking needed for passive FTP, and setting other firewall rules related to FTP.)

- The `vsftpd` daemon reads `vsftpd.conf` to determine what features the service allows.

- Linux user accounts (excluding administrative users) and the anonymous user account (no password required) can access the FTP server. (If SELinux is in Enforcing mode, you need to set a Boolean to allow regular users to log in to the FTP server. See the section "Securing Your FTP Server" for details.)

- The anonymous user has access only to the `/var/ftp` directory and its subdirectories. A regular user starts with his or her home directory as the current directory but can access any directory the user would be able to via a regular login or SSH session. Lists of users in the `/etc/vsftpd/user_list` and `/etc/vsftpd/ftpusers` files define some administrative and special users that do not have access to the FTP server (root, bin, daemon, and others).

- The anonymous user can download files from the server but not upload them, by default. A regular user can upload or download files, based on regular Linux permissions.

- Log messages detailing file uploads or downloads are written in the `/var/log/xferlogs` file. Those log messages are stored in a standard xferlog format.

If you are ready to start your server using the defaults just described, the following examples show you how to do that. If you want to change some settings first, go to the section "Configuring Your FTP Server," finalize your settings, and then come back here for instructions on how to enable and start your server.

Before you start the `vsftpd` service, you can check whether it is running already. In Fedora or Red Hat Enterprise Linux 7, you do the following:

```
# systemctl status vsftpd.service
vsftpd.service - Vsftpd ftp daemon
      Loaded: loaded (/lib/systemd/system/vsftpd.service; disabled)
      Active: inactive (dead)
```

In Red Hat Enterprise Linux 6, you need two commands to see the same information:

```
# service vsftpd status
vsftpd is stopped
# chkconfig --list vsftpd
vsftpd                   0:off    1:off    2:off    3:off    4:off
     5:off     6:off
```

In both the Fedora and RHEL examples above, the `service`, `chkconfig` and `systemctl` commands show the status as stopped. You can also see that it is disabled in Fedora and

18

RHEL 7 and off at every runlevel for RHEL 6. Disabled (off) means that the service will not turn on automatically when your start the system.

To start and enable vsftpd in Fedora or RHEL 7 (then check the status), type the following:

```
# systemctl start vsftpd.service
# systemctl enable vsftpd.service
ln -s '/lib/systemd/system/vsftpd.service'
   '/etc/systemd/system/multi-user.target.wants/vsftpd.service'
# systemctl status vsftpd.service
vsftpd.service - Vsftpd ftp daemon
        Loaded: loaded (/lib/systemd/system/vsftpd.service; enabled)
        Active: active (running) since Wed, 2014-08-27 00:09:54 EDT;
   22s ago
        Main PID: 4229 (vsftpd)
        CGroup: name=systemd:/system/vsftpd.service
                 └4229 /usr/sbin/vsftpd /etc/vsftpd/vsftpd.conf
```

In Red Hat Enterprise Linux 6, start and turn on (enable) vsftpd (then check the status), as follows:

```
# service vsftpd start
Starting vsftpd for vsftpd:                             [  OK  ]
# chkconfig vsftpd on ; chkconfig --list vsftpd
vsftpd              0:off    1:off    2:on    3:on    4:on    5:on
     6:off
```

Now, on either system, you could check that the service is running using the netstat command:

```
# netstat -tupln | grep vsftpd
tcp     0      0 0.0.0.0:21        0.0.0.0:*        LISTEN        4229/
     vsftpd
```

From the netstat output, you can see that the vsftpd process (process ID of 4229) is listening (LISTEN) on all IP addresses for incoming connections on port 21 (0.0.0.0:21) for the TCP (tcp) protocol. A quick way to check that vsftpd is working is to put a file in the /var/ftp directory and try to open it from your web browser on the local host:

```
# echo "Hello From Your New FTP Server" > /var/ftp/hello.txt
```

From a web browser on the local system, type the following into the location box of Firefox or other browser:

```
ftp://localhost/hello.txt
```

If the text `Hello From Your New FTP Server` appears in the web browser, the `vsftpd` server is working and accessible from your local system. Next, try again, replacing `localhost` with your host's IP address or fully qualified host name, from a web browser on another system. If that works, the `vsftpd` server is publicly accessible. If it doesn't, which it quite possibly may not, see the next section, "Securing Your FTP Server." That section tells you how to open firewalls and modify other security features to allow access and otherwise secure your FTP server.

Securing Your FTP Server

Even though it is easy to get a `vsftpd` FTP server started, that doesn't mean it is immediately fully accessible. If you have a firewall in place on your Linux system, it is probably blocking access to all services on your system except for those that you have explicitly allowed.

If you decide that the default `vsftpd` configuration works for you as described in the previous section, you can set to work allowing the appropriate access and providing security for your `vsftpd` service. So you can secure your vsftpd server, the next sections describe how to configure your firewall (`iptables`), TCP wrappers (`hosts.allow` and `hosts.deny`), and SELinux (Booleans and file contexts).

Opening up your firewall for FTP

If you have a firewall implemented on your system, you need to add firewall rules that allow incoming requests to your FTP site and allow packets to return to your system on established connections. Firewalls are implemented using `iptables` rules and managed with the `iptables` service or `firewalld` service (see Chapter 25, "Securing Linux on a Network," for details about firewall services).

In Fedora and Red Hat Enterprise Linux, firewall rules have traditionally been stored in the `/etc/sysconfig/iptables` file and the underlying service was `iptables` (RHEL) or `iptables.service` (Fedora). Modules are loaded into your firewall from the `/etc/sysconfig/iptables-config` file. In RHEL 7 and Fedora 21, the new `firewalld` service manages those rules and rules are stored in the `/etc/firewalld/zones` directory.

> **NOTE**
>
> It is best to work on your firewall directly from a system console, if possible, instead of over a remote login (such as `ssh`) because a small error can immediately lock you out of your server. After that, you must go over to the console to get back into the server and fix the problem.

You need to add a few things to your firewall to allow access to your FTP server without opening up access to other services. First, you need to allow your system to accept requests on TCP port 21; then you need to make sure the connection tracking module is loaded.

In RHEL 7 and Fedora 20, you can use the new Firewall configuration window to enable your firewall and open access to your FTP service. From the GNOME 3 desktop Activities screen, select the Firewall icon. Enter the root password when prompted. The Firewall Configuration window should appear, as shown in Figure 18.1.

FIGURE 18.1

Open access to your FTP service from the Firewall Configuration window.

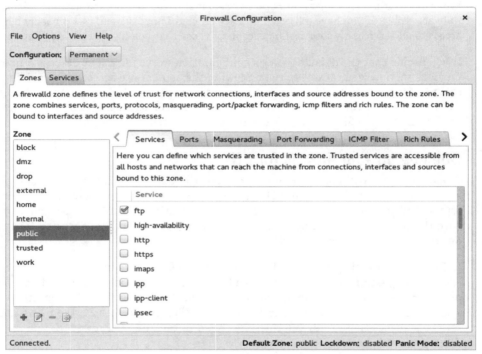

Next, to permanently open access to your FTP service, click the Configuration box and select Permanent. Then add a check box next to ftp under the Services tab. This automatically opens TCP port 21 (FTP) on your firewall and loads kernel modules needed to allow access to passive FTP service.

For RHEL 6 and earlier systems, you can add rules directly to the /etc/sysconfig/ iptables file. If you are using a default firewall, rules in the beginning open access to requests for any services coming from the local host and allow packets to come in that are associated with, or related to, established connections. In the middle are rules that open ports for service requests you have already allowed, such as the secure shell service (sshd on TCP port 22). At the end of the rules, a final rule usually DROPs or REJECTs any request that has not explicitly been allowed.

To allow public access to someone requesting your FTP server, you want to allow new requests to TCP port 21. You typically want to add the rule somewhere before the final DROP or REJECT rule. The following output shows partial contents of the /etc/sysconfig/iptables file with the rule allowing access to your FTP server in bold:

```
*filter
:INPUT ACCEPT [0:0]
:FORWARD ACCEPT [0:0]
:OUTPUT ACCEPT [0:0]
-A INPUT -m state --state ESTABLISHED,RELATED -j ACCEPT
-A INPUT -i lo -j ACCEPT
-A INPUT -m state --state NEW -m tcp -p tcp --dport 22 -j ACCEPT
-A INPUT -m state --state NEW -m tcp -p tcp --dport 21 -j ACCEPT
...
-A INPUT -j REJECT --reject-with icmp-host-prohibited
COMMIT
```

This example shows that, for the filter table, the firewall accepts packets from established connections, connections from local hosts, and any new requests on TCP port 22 (SSH service). The line we just added (--dport 21) allows any packets on new connections to TCP port 21 to be accepted.

18

NOTE

It is important to have the ESTABLISHED, RELATED line in your iptables firewall rules. Without that line, users would be able to connect to your SSH (port 22) and FTP (port 21) services, but would not be able to communicate after that. So, a user could get authenticated, but not be able to transfer data.

The next thing you must do on RHEL 6 and earlier systems is set up the FTP connection tracking module to be loaded each time the firewall starts up. Edit this line at the beginning of the /etc/sysconfig/iptables-config file to appear as follows:

```
IPTABLES_MODULES="nf_conntrack_ftp"
```

At this point, you can restart your firewall (keeping in mind that a mistake could lock you out if you are logged in remotely). Use one of the following two commands to restart your firewall, depending on whether your system is using the older iptables service or the newer firewalld service:

```
# service iptables restart
```
or

```
# systemctl restart firewalld.service
```

Try again to access your FTP server from a remote system (using a web browser or some other FTP client).

Allowing FTP access in TCP wrappers

The TCP wrappers feature in Linux lets you add information to the /etc/hosts.allow and /etc/hosts.deny files to indicate who can or cannot access selected services. Not all services implement TCP wrappers, but vsftpd does.

By default, the hosts.allow and hosts.deny files are empty, which places no restrictions on who can access services protected by TCP wrappers. However, if you are blocking access in the hosts.deny file to all services that have not been explicitly allowed (by adding an ALL:ALL line to hosts.deny), adding a line such as the following to the beginning of the /etc/hosts.allow file allows access to the vsftpd server:

```
vsftpd:    ALL :   ALLOW
```

For more information on how to use TCP wrappers, refer to Chapter 25, "Securing Linux on a Network," or the hosts.allow man page (type **man hosts.allow**).

Configuring SELinux for your FTP server

If SELinux is set to Permissive or Disabled, it does not block access to the vsftpd service in any way. However, if SELinux is in Enforcing mode, a few SELinux issues could cause your vsftpd server to not behave as you would like. Use the following commands to check the state of SELinux on your system:

```
# getenforce
Enforcing
# grep ^SELINUX= /etc/sysconfig/selinux
SELINUX=enforcing
```

The getenforce command shows how SELinux is currently set (here, it's in Enforcing mode). The SELINUX= variable in /etc/sysconfig/selinux shows how SELinux is set when the system comes up. If it is in Enforcing mode, as it is here, check the ftpd_selinux man page for information about SELinux settings that can impact the operation of your vsftpd service. Here are some examples of file contexts that must be set for SELinux to allow files and directories to be accessed by vsftpd:

- To share content so it can be downloaded to FTP clients, that content must be marked with a public_content_t file context. Files created in the /var/ftp directory or its subdirectories inherit public_content_t file context automatically. (Be sure to create new content or copy existing content to the /var/ftp directories. Moving the files there may not change the file context properly.)

- To allow files to be uploaded by anonymous users, the file context on the directory you upload to must be set to public_content_rw_t. (Other permissions, SELinux Booleans, and vsftpd.conf settings must be in place for this to work as well.)

If you have files in the `/var/ftp` directory structure that have the wrong file contexts (which can happen if you move files there from other directories instead of copying them), you can change or restore the file context on those files so they can be shared. For example, to recursively change the file context of the `/var/ftp/pub/stuff` directory so the content can be readable from the FTP server through SELinux, type the following:

```
# semanage fcontext -a -t public_content_t "/var/ftp/pub/stuff(/.*)?"
# restorecon -F -R -v /var/ftp/pub/stuff
```

If you want to allow users to also write to a directory as well as read from it, you need to assign the `public_content_rw_t` file context to the directory to which you want to allow uploads. This example tells SELinux to allow uploading of files to the `/var/ftp/pub/uploads` directory:

```
# semanage fcontext -a -t public_content_rw_t "/var/ftp/pub/uploads(/.*)?"
# restorecon -F -R -v /var/ftp/pub/uploads
```

FTP server features that are considered insecure by SELinux have Booleans that let you allow or disallow those features. Here are some examples:

- To allow regular users to be able to authenticate and read and write files and directories via the FTP server, the Boolean `ftp_home_dir` must be on. This is one of the most common FTP Booleans to turn on (it is off by default). To turn it on permanently, type this:

  ```
  # setsebool -P ftp_home_dir on
  ```

- For SELinux to allow anonymous users to read and write files and directories, you need to turn on the `allow_ftpd_anon_write` Boolean:

  ```
  # setsebool -P allow_ftpd_anon_write on
  ```

- To be able to mount remote NFS or CIFS (Windows) shared filesystems and share them from your `vsftpd` server, you need to turn on the following two Booleans, respectively:

  ```
  # setsebool -P allow_ftpd_use_nfs on
  # setsebool -P allow_ftpd_use_cifs on
  ```

If you ever find that you cannot access files or directories from your FTP server that you believe should be accessible, try turning off SELinux temporarily:

```
# setenforce 0
```

If you can access the files or directories with SELinux now in Permissive mode, put the system back in Enforcing mode (`setenforce 1`). Now, you know you have to go back through your SELinux settings and find out what is preventing access. (See Chapter 24, "Enhancing Linux Security with SELinux," for more information on SELinux.)

18

Relating Linux file permissions to vsftpd

The `vsftpd` server relies on standard Linux file permissions to allow or deny access to files and directories. As you would expect, for an anonymous user to view or download a file, at least read permission must be open for `other` (`------r--`). To access a directory, at least execute permission must be on for `other` (`--------x`).

For regular user accounts, the general rule is that if a user can access a file from the shell, that user can access the same file from an FTP server. So, typically, regular users should at least be able to get (download) and put (upload) files to and from their own home directories, respectively. After permissions and other security provisions are in place for your FTP server, you may want to consider other configuration settings for your FTP server.

Configuring Your FTP Server

Most of the configuration for the `vsftpd` service is done in the `/etc/vsftpd/vsftpd.conf` file. Examples of the `vsftpd.conf` for different types of sites are included in the `/usr/share/doc/vsftpd-*` directory. Depending on how you want to use your FTP site, the following sections discuss a few ways to configure your FTP server.

Remember to restart the `vsftpd` service after making any configuration changes.

Setting up user access

The `vsftpd` server comes with both the anonymous user and all local Linux users (those listed in the `/etc/passwd` file) configured to access the server. This is based on the following `vsftpd.conf` settings:

```
anonymous_enable=YES
local_enable=YES
```

As noted earlier, despite the `local_enable` setting, SELinux actually prevents `vsftpd` users from logging in and transferring data. Either changing SELinux out of Enforcing mode or setting the correct Boolean allows local accounts to log in and transfer data.

Some web server companies let users use FTP to upload the content that is used in the users' own web servers. In some cases, the users have FTP-only accounts, meaning that they cannot log in to a shell, but they can log in via FTP to manage their content. Creating a user account that has no default shell (actually, `/sbin/nologin`) is how you can keep a user from logging into a shell, but still allow FTP access. For example, the `/etc/passwd` entry for the FTP-only user account `bill` might look something like the following:

```
bill:x:1000:1000:Bill Jones:/home/bill:/sbin/nologin
```

With the user account set with `/sbin/nologin` as the default shell, any attempts to log in from a console or via `ssh` as the user `bill` are denied. However, as long as `bill` has a password and local account access to the FTP server is enabled, `bill` should be able to log in to the FTP server via an FTP client.

Not every user with an account on the Linux system has access to the FTP server. The setting `userlist_enable=YES` in `vsftpd.conf` says to deny access to the FTP server to all accounts listed in the `/etc/vsftpd/user_list` file. That list includes administrative users `root`, `bin`, `daemon`, `adm`, `lp`, and others. You can add other users to that list to whom you would like to deny access.

If you change `userlist_enable` to `NO`, the `user_list` file becomes a list of only those users who do have access to the server. In other words, setting `userlist_enable=NO`, removing all usernames from the `user_list` file, and adding the usernames `chris`, `joe`, and `mary` to that file cause the server to allow only those three users to log in to the server.

No matter how the value of `userlist_enable` is set, the `/etc/vsftpd/ftpusers` file always includes users who are denied access to the server. Like the `userlist_enable` file, the `ftpusers` file includes a list of administrative users. You can add more users to that file if you want them to be denied FTP access.

One way to limit access to users with regular user accounts on your system is to use `chroot` settings. Here are examples of some `chroot` settings:

```
chroot_local_user=YES
chroot_list_enable=YES
chroot_list_file=/etc/vsftpd/chroot_list
```

With the settings just shown uncommented, you could create a list of local users and add them to the `/etc/vsftpd/chroot_list` file. After one of those users logged in, that user would be prevented from going to places in the system that were outside that user's home directory structure.

If uploads to your FTP server are allowed, the directories a user tries to upload to must be writeable by that user. However, uploads can be stored under a username other than that of the user who uploaded the file. This is one of the features discussed next, in the "Allowing uploading" section.

Allowing uploading

To allow any form of writing to the `vsftpd` server, you must have `write_enable=YES` set in the `vsftpd.conf` file (which it is, by default). Because of that, if local accounts are enabled, users can log in and immediately begin uploading files to their own home directories. However, anonymous users are denied the ability to upload files by default.

To allow anonymous uploads with vsftpd, you must have the first option in the following code example and you may want the second line of code as well (both can be enabled by uncommenting them from the vsftpd.conf file). The first allows anonymous users to upload files; the second allows them to create directories:

```
anon_upload_enable=YES
anon_mkdir_write_enable=YES
```

The next step is to create a directory where anonymous users can write. Any directory under the /var/ftp directory that has write permissions for the user ftp, the ftp group, or other can be written to by an anonymous user. A common thing is to create an uploads directory with permission open for writing. The following are examples of commands to run on the server:

```
# mkdir /var/ftp/uploads
# chown ftp:ftp /var/ftp/uploads
# chmod 775 /var/ftp/uploads
```

As long as the firewall is open and SELinux Booleans are set properly, an anonymous user can cd to the uploads directory and put a file from the user's local system into the uploads directory. On the server, the file would be owned by the ftp user and ftp group. The permissions set on the directory (775) would allow you to see the files that were uploaded, but not change or overwrite them.

One reason for allowing anonymous FTP, and then enabling it for anonymous uploads, is to allow people you don't know to drop files in your uploads folder. Because anyone who can find the server can write to this directory, some form of security needs to be in place. You want to prevent an anonymous user from seeing files uploaded by other users, taking files, or deleting files uploaded by other anonymous FTP users. One form of security is the chown feature of FTP.

By setting the following two values, you can allow anonymous uploads. The result of these settings is that when an anonymous user uploads a file, that file is immediately assigned ownership of a different user. The following is an example of some chown settings you could put in your vsftpd.conf file to use with your anonymous upload directory:

```
chown_uploads=YES
chown_username=joe
```

If an anonymous user were to upload a file after vsftpd was restarted with these settings, the uploaded file would be owned by the user joe and the ftp group. Permissions would be read/write for the owner and nothing for anyone else (rw-------).

So far, you have seen configuration options for individual features on your vsftpd server. Some sets of vsftp.conf variables can work together in ways that are appropriate for certain kinds of FTP sites. The next section contains one of these examples, represented by a sample vsftpd.conf configuration file that come with the vsftpd package. That file can be copied from a directory of sample files to the /etc/vsftpd/vsftpd.conf file, to use for an FTP server that is available on the Internet.

Setting up vsftpd for the Internet

To safely share files from your FTP server to the Internet, you can lock down your server by limiting it to only allow downloads and only from anonymous users. To start with a configuration that is designed to have vsftpd share files safely over the Internet, back up your current /etc/vsftpd/vsftpd.conf file and copy this file to overwrite your vsftpd.conf:

/usr/share/doc/vsftpd-*/EXAMPLE/INTERNET_SITE/vsftpd.conf

The following paragraphs describe the contents of that vsftpd.conf. Settings in the first section set the access rights for the server:

```
# Access rights
anonymous_enable=YES
local_enable=NO
write_enable=NO
anon_upload_enable=NO
anon_mkdir_write_enable=NO
anon_other_write_enable=NO
```

Turning on anonymous_enable (YES) and turning off local_enable (NO) ensures that no one can log in to the FTP server using a regular Linux user account. Everyone must come in through the anonymous account. No one can upload files (write_enable=NO). Then, the anonymous user cannot upload files (anon_upload_enable=NO), create directories (anon_mkdir_write_enable=NO), or otherwise write to the server (anon_other_write_enable=NO). Here are the Security settings:

```
# Security
anon_world_readable_only=YES
connect_from_port_20=YES
hide_ids=YES
pasv_min_port=50000
pasv_max_port=60000
```

Because the vsftpd daemon can read files assigned to the ftp user and group, setting anon_world_readable_only=YES ensures that anonymous users can see files where the read permission bit is turned on for other (------r--), but not write files. The connect_from_port_20=YES setting gives the vsftpd daemon slightly more permission to send data the way a client might request by allowing PORT-style data communications.

Using hide_ids=YES hides the real permissions set on files so, to the user accessing the FTP site, everything appears to be owned by the ftp user. The two pasv settings restrict the range of ports that can be used with passive FTP (where the server picks a higher number port on which to send data) to between 50000 and 60000.

The next section contains features of the vsftpd server:

```
# Features
xferlog_enable=YES
ls_recurse_enable=NO
ascii_download_enable=NO
async_abor_enable=YES
```

With xferlog_enable=YES, all file transfers to and from the server are logged to the /var/log/xferlog file. Setting ls_recurse_enable=NO prevents users from recursively listing the contents of an FTP directory (in other words, it prevents the type of listing you could get with the ls -R command) because on a large site, that could drain resources. Disabling ASCII downloads forces all downloads to be in binary mode (preventing files from being translated in ASCII, which is inappropriate for binary files). The async_abor_enable=YES setting ensures that some FTP clients that might hang when aborting a transfer will not hang.

The following settings have an impact on performance:

```
# Performance
one_process_model=YES
idle_session_timeout=120
data_connection_timeout=300
accept_timeout=60
connect_timeout=60
anon_max_rate=50000
```

With one_process_model=YES set, performance can improve because vsftpd launches one process per connection. Reducing the idle_session_timeout from the default 300 seconds to 120 seconds causes FTP clients that are idle more than 2 minutes to be disconnected. So less time is spent managing FTP sessions that are no longer in use. If a data transfer stalls for more than data_connection_timeout seconds (300 seconds here), the connection to the client is dropped.

The accept_timeout setting of 60 seconds allows 1 minute for a PASV connection to be accepted by the remote client. The connect_timeout sets how long a remote client has to respond to a request to establish a PORT-style data connection. Limiting the transfer rate to 50000 (bytes per second) with anon_max_rate can improve overall performance of the server by limiting how much bandwidth each client can consume.

Using FTP Clients to Connect to Your Server

Many client programs come with Linux that you can use to connect to your FTP server. If you simply want to do an anonymous download of some files from an FTP server, your Firefox web browser provides an easy interface to do that. For more complex interactions between your FTP client and server, you can use command-line FTP clients. The following section describes some of these tools.

Accessing an FTP server from Firefox

The Firefox web browser provides a quick and easy way to test access to your FTP server or to access any public FTP server. On your own system, type **ftp://localhost** into the location box. If your server is accessible, you should see something similar to the example shown in Figure 18.2.

FIGURE 18.2

Accessing an FTP server from Firefox

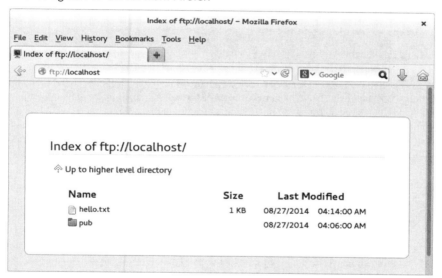

To log in to an FTP server as a particular user from Firefox, you can precede the host name with a username:password@ notation. For example:

```
ftp://chris:MypassWd5@localhost
```

If you provide the correct username and password, you should immediately see the contents of your home directory. Click a folder to open it. Click a file to download or view the file.

Accessing an FTP server with the lftp command

To test your FTP server from the command line, you can use the lftp command. To install the lftp command in Fedora or RHEL, type the following from the command line:

```
# yum install lftp
```

If you use the `lftp` command with just the name of the FTP server you are trying to access, the command tries to connect to the FTP server as the anonymous user. By adding the `-u` username, you can type the user's password when prompted and gain access to the FTP server as the user you logged in as.

After you have added your user and password information, you get an `lftp` prompt, ready for you to start typing commands. The connection is made to the server when you type your first command. You can use the commands to move around the FTP server, and then use the `get` and `put` commands to download and upload files.

The following example shows how to use commands as just described. It assumes that the FTP server (and associated security measures) has been configured to allow local users to connect and to read and write files:

```
# lftp -u chris localhost
Password:
********
lftp chris@localhost:~> pwd
ftp://chris@localhost/%2Fhome/chris
lftp chris@localhost:~> cd stuff/state/
lftp chris@localhost:~/stuff/state> ls
-rw-r--r--    1 13597      13597         1394 Oct 23  2014 enrolled-
   20141012
-rw-r--r--    1 13597      13597          514 Oct 23  2014 enrolled-
   20141013
lftp chris@localhost:~/stuff/state> !pwd
/root
lftp chris@localhost:~/stuff/state> get survey-20141023.txt
3108 bytes transferred
lftp chris@localhost:~/stuff/state> put /etc/hosts
201 bytes transferred
lftp chris@localhost:~/stuff/state> ls
-rw-r--r--    1 13597      13597         1394 Oct 23  2014 enrolled-
   20141012
-rw-r--r--    1 13597      13597          514 Oct 23  2014 enrolled-
   20141013
-rw-r--r--    1 0          0              201 May 03 20:22 hosts
lftp chris@localhost:~/stuff/state> !ls
anaconda-ks.cfg          bin              install.log
dog                      Pictures         sent
Downloads                Public           survey-20141023.txt
lftp chris@localhost:~/stuff/state> quit
```

After providing the username (`-u chris`), `lftp` prompts for chris's Linux user password. Typing `pwd` shows that chris is logged in to the local host and that `/home/chris` is the current directory. Just as you would from a regular Linux command line shell, you can use `cd` to change to another directory and `ls` to list that directory's contents.

To have the commands you run interpreted by the client system, you can simply put an exclamation mark (!) in front of a command. For example, running !pwd shows that the current directory on the system that initiated the lftp is /root. This is good to know because if you get a file from the server without specifying its destination, it goes to the client's current directory (in this case, /root). Other commands you might run so they are interpreted by the client system include !cd (to change directories) or !ls (to list files).

Assuming you have read permission of a file on the server and write permission from the current directory on the initiating system, you can use the get command to download a file from the server (get survey-20141023.txt). If you have write and upload permission on the current directory on the server, you can use put to copy a file to the server (put /etc/hosts).

Running an ls command shows that the /etc/hosts file was uploaded to the server. Running the !ls command lets you see that the survey-20141023.txt file was downloaded from the server to the initiating system.

Using the gFTP client

Many other FTP clients are available with Linux as well. Another FTP client you could try is gFTP. The gFTP client provides an interface that lets you see both the local and remote sides of your FTP session. To install gFTP in Fedora and Red Hat Enterprise Linux, run the following command to install the gftp package:

```
# yum install gftp
```

To start gFTP, launch it from the applications menu or run gftp & from the shell. To use it, type the URL of the FTP server you want to connect to, enter the username you want to use (such as anonymous), and press Enter. Figure 18.3 shows an example of gFTP being used to connect to a documentation directory at the site ftp://kernel.org.

To traverse the FTP site from gFTP, just double-click folders (just as you would from a file manager window). The full paths to the local directory (on the left) and remote directory (on the right) are shown above the listings of files and folders below.

To transfer a file from the remote side to the local side, select the file you want from the right and click the arrow in the middle of the screen pointing to the left. Watch the progress of the file transfer from messages on the bottom of the screen. When the transfer completes, the file appears in the left pane.

You can bookmark the address information you need to connect to an FTP site. That address is added to a set of bookmarks already stored under the Bookmarks menu. You can select sites from the list to try out the gFTP. Most of the sites are for Linux distributions and other open source software sites.

FIGURE 18.3

The gFTP FTP client lets you see both sides of an FTP session.

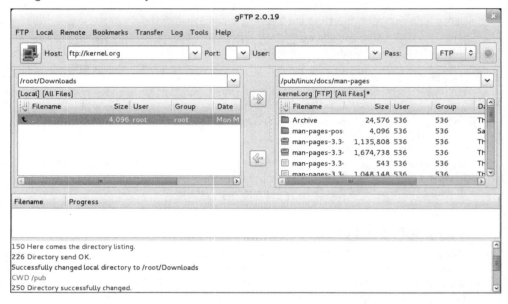

Summary

Setting up an FTP server is an easy way to share files over a TCP network. The Very Secure FTP Daemon (vsftpd package) is available for Fedora, Red Hat Enterprise Linux, Ubuntu, and other Linux systems.

A default vsftpd server allows anonymous users to download files from the server and regular Linux users to upload or download files (provided some security settings are changed). Moving around on an FTP server is similar to moving around a Linux filesystem. You move up and down the directory structure to find the content you want.

There are both graphical and text-based FTP clients. A popular text-based client for Linux is lftp. As for graphical FTP clients, you can use a regular web browser, such as Firefox, or dedicated FTP clients, such as gFTP.

FTP servers are not the only way to share files over a network from Linux. The Samba service provides a way to share files over a network so the shared Linux directory looks like a shared directory from a Windows system. Chapter 19 describes how to use Samba to offer Windows-style file sharing.

Exercises

The exercises in this section describe tasks related to setting up an FTP server in RHEL or Fedora and connecting to that server using an FTP client. You could do this procedure on an Ubuntu system, but it would require extra configuration because Ubuntu doesn't support anonymous FTP by default. If you are stuck, solutions to the tasks are shown in Appendix B. Keep in mind that the solutions shown in Appendix B are usually just one of multiple ways to complete a task.

Don't do these exercises on a Linux system running a public FTP server because they almost certainly interfere with that server.

1. Determine which package provides the Very Secure FTP Daemon service.

2. Install the Very Secure FTP Daemon package on your system, and search for the configuration files in that package.

3. Start the Very Secure FTP Daemon service, and set it to start when the system boots.

4. On the system running your FTP server, create a file named test in the anonymous FTP directory that contains the words "Welcome to your vsftpd server."

5. From a web browser on the system running your FTP server, open the test file from the anonymous FTP home directory. Be sure you can see that file's contents.

6. From a web browser outside the system that is running the FTP server, try to access the test file in the anonymous FTP home directory. If you cannot access the file, check that your firewall, SELinux, and TCP wrappers are configured to allow access to that file.

7. Configure your vsftpd server to allow file uploads by anonymous users to a directory named in.

8. Install the lftp FTP client (if you don't have a second Linux system, install lftp on the same host running the FTP server). If you cannot upload files to the in directory, check that your firewall, SELinux, and TCP wrappers are configured to allow access to that file.

9. Using any FTP client you choose, visit the /pub/linux/docs/man-pages directory on the ftp://kernel.org site and list the contents of that directory.

10. Using any FTP client you choose, download the man-pages-3.41.tar.gz file from the kernel.org directory you just visited to the /tmp directory on your local system.

18

Configuring a Windows File Sharing (Samba) Server

IN THIS CHAPTER

Getting and installing Samba

Using Samba security features

Editing the smb.conf configuration file

Accessing Samba from Linux and Windows clients

Using Samba in the enterprise

S amba is the project that implements open source versions of protocols used to share files and printers, as well as authenticate users and restrict hosts, among Windows systems. Samba offers a number of ways to share files among Windows, Linux, and Mac OS/X systems that are well known and readily available to users of those systems.

This chapter steps you through the process of installing and configuring a Samba server. It describes security features you need to know to share your file and printer resources and describes how to access those resources from Linux and Windows systems.

Understanding Samba

Samba (www.samba.org) is a suite of programs that allows Linux, UNIX, and other systems to interoperate with Microsoft Windows file and printer sharing protocols. Windows, DOS, OS/2, Mac OS/X, and other client systems can access Samba servers to share files and printers in the same ways they would from Windows file and print servers.

With Samba, you can use standard TCP/IP networking to communicate with clients. For name service, Samba supports regular TCP/IP hostnames, as well as NetBIOS names. For that reason, Samba doesn't require the NetBEUI (Microsoft Raw NetBIOS frame) protocol. File sharing is done using the Common Internet File System (CIFS), which is an open implementation of the Server Message Block (SMB) protocol.

The Samba project has gone to great lengths to make its software secure and robust. In fact, many people prefer using Samba servers over Windows file servers because of the added security that is inherent in running Windows-style file sharing services on Linux or other UNIX-like operating systems.

Beyond all the technical mumbo-jumbo, however, the end result is that Samba makes it easy to share files and printers between Linux servers and Windows desktop systems. For the server, only a few configuration files and tools are needed to manage Samba. For the clients, shared resources just show up under the Network selection in the window manager or in the Network Neighborhood on older Windows systems.

Interfaces for managing Samba on a Linux server include the Samba Server Configuration window (`system-config-samba`) and the Samba SWAT (Samba Web Administration Tool) web-based interface. As an alternative, you can directly edit Samba configuration files (particularly `smb.conf`) and run a few commands to configure Samba.

Working with Samba SWAT

I do not cover this topic in this chapter, but many people prefer the Samba SWAT interface to directly editing configuration files. On some Linux distributions, Samba SWAT may be the only point-and-click interface available. Others, such as Fedora, no longer include it.

Here's a quick guide to getting Samba SWAT working on your RHEL 6 system:

1. Install the `samba-swat` and `xinetd` packages.
2. Edit the `/etc/xinetd.d/swat` file, and change the disable line to read `disable = no`.
3. Restart `xinetd`: `service xinetd start` ; `chkconfig xinetd on`.
4. Open your local web browser to this address: `http://localhost:901`.

The Samba Web Administration Tool screen that opens in your browser (after entering the root username and password) provides a different interface for configuring your Samba server, shared directories, and printers that are described in the rest of this chapter. By clicking around, you should be able to find how to plug that information into the SWAT interface.

To begin using Samba on your Linux system, you need to install a few software packages, as described in the next section.

Installing Samba

In Red Hat Enterprise Linux and Fedora, to configure a Samba file and print server, the only required packages are the `samba` and `samba-common` packages. Among other components, the `samba` package includes the Samba service daemon (`/usr/sbin/smbd`) and NetBIOS name server daemon (/usr/sbin/nmbd). The samba-common package contains server configuration files (smb.conf, lmhosts, and others) and commands for adding passwords and testing configuration files, along with other Samba features.

Features from other packages are referenced in this chapter, so I describe how to install those packages as well. Those packages include the following:

- **samba-client package**—Contains command-line tools such as smbclient (for connecting to Samba or Windows shares), nmblookup (for looking up host addresses), and findsmb (to find SMB hosts on the network).

- **system-config-samba package**—Contains a graphical interface for managing Samba.

- **system-config-samba-docs package**—Contains documentation associated with the system-config-samba graphical interface.

- **samba-swat package**—Contains a web-based interface for configuring a Samba server. (No longer in Fedora.)

- **samba-winbind package**—Includes components that allow your Samba server in Linux to become a complete member of a Windows domain, including using Windows user and group accounts in Linux.

To install all the packages just mentioned (samba-common is installed as a dependency of samba, so it doesn't need to be noted specifically), type the following as root from the command line in Fedora:

```
# yum install samba samba-client samba-winbind \
    system-config-samba system-config-samba-docs
...
Dependencies Resolved
================================================================
 Package                  Arch     Version             Repository  Size
================================================================
Installing:
 samba                    x86_64   2:4.1.15-1.fc21     updates      555 k
 samba-client             x86_64   2:4.1.15-1.fc21     updates      513 k
 samba-winbind            x86_64   2:4.1.15-1.fc21     updates      445 k
 system-config-samba      noarch   1.2.100-3.fc21      fedora       282 k
 system-config-samba-docs noarch   1.0.9-7.fc21        fedora       274 k
Installing for dependencies:
 libsmbclient             x86_64   2:4.1.15-1.fc21     updates      112 k
 samba-common             x86_64   2:4.1.15-1.fc21     updates      685 k
 samba-libs               x86_64   2:4.1.15-1.fc21     updates      4.2 M
 samba-winbind-modules    x86_64   2:4.1.15-1.fc21     updates       93 k
Transaction Summary
================================================================
Install  5 Packages (+4 Dependent packages)
Total download size: 7.1 M
```

```
Installed size: 25 M
Is this ok [y/d/N]: y
```

After you have installed the Samba packages, look at the configuration files in the samba-common package:

```
# rpm -qc samba-common
/etc/logrotate.d/samba
/etc/sysconfig/samba
/etc/samba/lmhosts
/etc/samba/smb.conf
```

The /etc/logrotate.d/samba and /etc/sysconfig/samba files are usually not modified. The first sets how files in /var/log/samba log files are rotated (copied to other files and removed) over time. The second is a file where you could put options that are passed to the smbd, nmbd, or winbindd daemons, so you could turn off features such as debugging.

Most configuration files you would modify for Samba are in the /etc/samba directory. The smb.conf file is the primary configuration file, where you put global settings for the Samba server as well as individual file and printer share information (more on that later). The lmhosts file enables the Samba NetBIOS hostname to be mapped into IP addresses.

Although it doesn't exist by default, you can create a file named /etc/samba/smbusers to map Linux user names into Windows user names. As you configure your Samba server, you can refer to the smb.conf man page (man smb.conf). There are also man pages for Samba commands, such as smbpasswd (to change passwords), smbclient (to connect to a Samba server), and nmblookup (to look up NetBIOS information).

After you have installed Samba packages and completed a quick survey of what they contain, try starting up the Samba service and see what you get in a default configuration.

Starting and Stopping Samba

With samba and samba-common installed, you can start the server and investigate how it runs in the default configuration. Two main services are associated with a Samba server, each of which has its own service daemon. Those services include the following:

- **smb**—This service controls the smbd daemon process, which provides the file and print sharing services that can be accessed by Windows clients.

- **nmb**—This service controls the nmbd daemon. By providing NetBIOS name service name-to-address mapping, nmbd can map requests from Windows clients for NetBIOS names so they can be resolved into IP addresses.

To share files and printers with other Linux systems with Samba, only the smb service is required. The next section describes how to start and enable the smb service.

Starting the Samba (smb) service

The smb service is what starts the smbd server and makes files and printers available from your local system to other computers on the network. As usual, services are enabled and started differently on different Linux systems. For different Linux systems, you need to find the name of the service and the correct tool to start the smbd daemon.

In Fedora and RHEL 7, to enable Samba to start when the system boots and start Samba immediately, type the following from the command line as root:

```
# systemctl enable smb.service
# systemctl start smb.service
# systemctl status smb.service
smb.service - Samba SMB Daemon
  Loaded: loaded (/usr/lib/systemd/system/smb.service; enabled)
  Active: active (running) since Sun 2014-08-31 07:23:37 EDT; 6s ago
 Main PID: 4838 (smbd)
CGroup: /system.slice/smb.service
  ├ 4838 /usr/sbin/smbd
  └ 4840 /usr/sbin/smbd
```

The first systemctl command enables the service, the second starts it immediately, and the third shows the status. To investigate further, notice that the service file is located at /usr/lib/systemd/system/smb.service. Look at the contents of that file:

```
# cat /usr/lib/systemd/system/smb.service
[Unit]
Description=Samba SMB Daemon
After=syslog.target network.target nmb.service winbind.service
[Service]
Type=notify
NotifyAccess=all
PIDFile=/run/smbd.pid
LimitNOFILE=16384
EnvironmentFile=-/etc/sysconfig/samba
ExecStart=/usr/sbin/smbd $SMBDOPTIONS
ExecReload=/usr/bin/kill -HUP $MAINPID
[Install]
WantedBy=multi-user.target
```

The Samba daemon process (smbd) starts up after the syslog, network, nmb, and winbind services. The /etc/sysconfig/samba file contains variables that are passed as arguments to the /usr/sbin/smbd daemon when it starts. No options are set by default for the smbd daemon (none are set for nmbd or winbindd daemons either, which can also have options entered in that file). The WantedBy line indicates that smb.service should start when the system boots up into multi-user mode (multi-user.target), which it does by default.

In RHEL 6 and earlier, you can start the Samba service as follows:

```
# service smb start
Starting SMB services:          [  OK  ]
# chkconfig smb on
# service smb status
smbd (pid  28056) is running...
# chkconfig --list smb
smb                  0:off  1:off  2:on  3:on  4:on  5:on  6:off
```

Whether you are running your Samba server on RHEL, Fedora, or another Linux system, you can check access to the Samba server using the smbclient command (from the samba-client package). You can get basic information from a Samba server using the following command:

```
# smbclient -L localhost
Enter root's password: <ENTER>
Anonymous login successful
Domain=[MYGROUP] OS=[Unix] Server=[Samba 4.1.15]
    Sharename      Type      Comment
    ---------      ----      -------
    IPC$           IPC       IPC Service
                             (Samba Server Version 4.1.15)
    DeskJet        Printer   DeskJet
    Jeeves         Printer   HP Deskjet 3050 J610 series
    deskjet-5550   Printer   hp deskjet 5550
Anonymous login successful
Domain=[MYGROUP] OS=[Unix] Server=[Samba 4.1.15]
        Server               Comment
        ---------            -------

        Workgroup            Master
        ---------            -------
```

The smbclient output allows you to see what services are available from the server. By default, anonymous login is allowed when querying the server (so I just pressed Enter when prompted for a password).

You can discern a number of things about the default Samba server setup from this output:

- The default domain (this is a Windows domain and not a DNS domain) is set to MYGROUP.
- The default server name is set to the current version of Samba, in this case Samba 4.1.15.
- All printers that are shared via the CUPS server on your Linux system are, by default, also made available from the Samba server running on that same system.
- No directories are shared yet from the server.
- There is no NetBIOS name service running yet from the Samba server.

Next, you can decide whether you want to run the NetBIOS name service on your Samba server.

Starting the NetBIOS (nmbd) name server

If no Windows domain server is running on the network, as is the case here, you can start the nmb service on the Samba host to provide that service. To start the nmb service (nmbd daemon) in Fedora or RHEL 7, type the following:

```
# systemctl enable nmb.service
# systemctl start nmb.service
# systemctl status nmb.service
```

In RHEL 6 and earlier, you would type the following to start the nmb service:

```
# service nmb start
# service nmb status
# chkconfig nmb on
# chkconfig --list nmb
```

Regardless of how the NetBIOS service was started, the nmbd daemon should now be running and ready to serve NetBIOS name-to-address mapping. Run the smbclient -L command again, followed by the IP address of the server. This time, the last few lines of the output should show information obtained from the NetBIOS server now running on the server. In this case, the last few lines looked like this:

```
# smbclient -L localhost
   ...
   Server            Comment
   ---------         -------
   FEDORA21          Samba Server Version 4.1.15
   Workgroup         Master
   ---------         -------
   MYGROUP           FEDORA21
```

You can see that the new NetBIOS server's name is FEDORA21 and that it is the master server for the workgroup. To query the nmbd server for the IP address of FEDORA21, you would type the following:

```
# nmblookup -U localhost FEDORA21
querying FEDORA21 on 127.0.0.1
192.168.0.101 FEDORA21<00>
```

You should be able to see your Samba server running from the local system now. The hostname assigned to the system (in this case FEDORA21) is assigned by default.

However, if you have a firewall configured or SELinux enabled, you may not be able to fully access the Samba server from a remote system yet. The next section should help you open

19

Samba to systems outside the local system, as well as allow some Samba features that may be turned off by SELinux.

Stopping the Samba (smb) and NetBIOS (nmb) services

To stop the smb and nmb services in Fedora or RHEL 7, you can use the same systemctl command you used to start them. You can use the same command to disable the services as well, so they do not start up again when the system boots. Here are examples of how to immediately stop the smb and nmb services:

```
# systemctl stop smb.service
# systemctl stop nmb.service
```

In RHEL 6 and earlier, you would type the following to stop the smb and nmb services:

```
# service smb stop
# service nmb stop
```

To prevent the smb and nmb services from starting the next time the system reboots, type the following commands in Fedora or RHEL 7:

```
# systemctl disable smb.service
# systemctl disable nmb.service
```

In Red Hat Enterprise Linux 6, type the following commands to disable the smb and nmb services:

```
# chkconfig smb off
# chkconfig nmb off
```

Of course, you only want to stop or disable the smb and nmb services if you no longer want to use the Samba service. If you are ready to continue to configure your Samba service, you can continue on and begin to configure your Linux security features to allow the Samba service to become available to others on your network.

Securing Samba

If you cannot access your Samba server immediately after starting it, you probably have some security work to do. Because many default installations of Linux prevent, rather than allow, access to the system, dealing with security for a service such as Samba usually has more to do with making it available than making it secure.

Here are the security features you should be aware of when configuring your Samba system:

- **Firewalls**—The default firewall for Fedora, RHEL, and other Linux systems prevents any access to local services from outside systems. So, to allow users from other computers to access your Samba service, you must create firewall rules that open one or more ports for selected protocols (TCP in particular).

- **SELinux**—Many features of Samba are designated as potentially insecure by SELinux. Because the default SELinux Booleans (on/off switches for certain features) are set to provide the least access required, you need to turn Booleans on for features such as allowing users to access their own home directories with Samba. In other words, you can configure Samba to share user home directories, but SELinux prohibits someone trying to use that feature unless you explicitly configure SELinux to allow that feature.

- **Host and user restrictions**—Within the Samba configuration files themselves, you can indicate which hosts and users can have access to the Samba server as a whole or to particular shared directories.

The next sections describe how to set up the security features just mentioned for Samba.

Configuring firewalls for Samba

If an `iptables` or `firewalld` firewall is configured for your system when you first install it, the firewall typically allows any requests for services from local users, but none by outside users. That's why, at the end of the installation section of this chapter, you should have been able to test that Samba was working using the `smbclient` command from the local system. However, if the request originated from another system, it would have been rejected.

Configuring firewall rules for Samba consists mainly of opening up incoming ports that the `smbd` and `nmbd` daemons are listening on. These are the ports you should open to get a working Samba service on your Linux system:

- **TCP port 445**—This is the primary port the Samba `smbd` daemon listens on. Your firewall must support incoming packet requests on this port for Samba to work.

- **TCP port 139**—The `smbd` daemon also listens on TCP port 139, to handle sessions associated with NetBIOS hostnames. It is possible to use Samba over TCP without opening this port, but it is not recommended.

- **UDP ports 137 and 138**—The `nmbd` daemon uses these two ports for incoming NetBIOS requests. If you are using the `nmbd` daemon, these two ports must be open for new packet requests for NetBIOS name resolution.

For Fedora and RHEL 7, allowing incoming access to those four ports is easy. Simply open the Firewall Configuration window, and select the check boxes next to the `samba` and `samba-client` entries on the public zone, Services tab. Those ports become immediately accessible (no restart of the `firewalld` service is required).

For earlier Fedora and RHEL systems that use `iptables` directly instead of the `firewalld` service, opening the firewall is a more manual process. Consider a default firewall from Fedora that allows incoming packets from the local host, from established connections, and related to established connections, but denies all other incoming packets. The following

19

example represents a set of firewall rules in the /etc/sysconfig/iptables file, with four new rules (highlighted in the example that follows) added to open ports for Samba:

```
*filter
:INPUT ACCEPT [0:0]
:FORWARD ACCEPT [0:0]
:OUTPUT ACCEPT [0:0]
-A INPUT -m state --state ESTABLISHED,RELATED -j ACCEPT
-A INPUT -p icmp -j ACCEPT
-A INPUT -i lo -j ACCEPT
-I INPUT -m state --state NEW -m udp -p udp --dport 137 -j ACCEPT
-I INPUT -m state --state NEW -m udp -p udp --dport 138 -j ACCEPT
-I INPUT -m state --state NEW -m tcp -p tcp --dport 139 -j ACCEPT
-I INPUT -m state --state NEW -m tcp -p tcp --dport 445 -j ACCEPT
-A INPUT -j REJECT --reject-with icmp-host-prohibited
-A FORWARD -j REJECT --reject-with icmp-host-prohibited
COMMIT
```

Your firewall may include additional rules to allow incoming packet requests for other services, such as Secure Shell (sshd) or web (httpd) services. You can leave those in place. The main point is to have your Samba rules placed somewhere before the final REJECT rules.

If your iptables firewall is enabled, you can restart it to have the new rules take effect. To do that, type **systemctl restart iptables.service** (in older Fedora systems) or **service restart iptables** (in RHEL 6 or earlier). Try connecting to the Samba service by using the smbclient command again, or by using other techniques described in the section "Accessing Samba Shares" later in this chapter.

See Chapter 25, "Securing Linux on a Network," for more information on using iptables.

Configuring SELinux for Samba

There are both file context and Boolean considerations related to using Samba with SELinux in Enforcing mode. File contexts must be properly set on a directory that is shared by Samba. Booleans allow you to override the secure-by-default approach to certain Samba features.

You can find information on how SELinux confines Samba on the samba_selinux man page (man samba_selinux). You must install the selinux-policy-devel package to get that man page. For a deeper understanding of SELinux, refer to Chapter 24, "Enhancing Linux Security with SELinux."

Setting SELinux Booleans for Samba

There are several ways to see the Booleans associated with Samba. In Fedora and RHEL, you could install the policycore-utils-gui package and run the `system-config-selinux` command. On the SELinux Administration window that appears, select Booleans from the left column and look for Booleans listed with the samba module.

Another way to list Booleans for Samba is to use the `semanage` command, as follows:

```
# semanage boolean -l | egrep "smb|samba"
```

The following is a list of SELinux Booleans that apply to Samba and their descriptions. The first Boolean allows you to leave SELinux in Enforcing mode, but prevents SELinux from restricting scripts the Samba server can run. All others set which files and directories the Samba server can read and write on behalf of Samba users:

- **samba_run_unconfined**—Allows samba to run unconfined scripts.
- **smbd_anon_write**—Allows Samba to let anonymous users modify public files used for public file transfer services. Files and directories must be labeled `public_content_rw_t`.
- **samba_enable_home_dirs**—Allows Samba to share users' home directories.
- **samba_export_all_ro**—Allows Samba to share any file and directory read-only.
- **use_samba_home_dirs**—Allows a remote Samba server to access home directories on the local machine.
- **samba_create_home_dirs**—Allows Samba to create new home directories (for example, via PAM).
- **samba_export_all_rw**—Allows Samba to share any file or directory read/write.

The following Booleans affect Samba's ability to share directories that are themselves mounted from other remote services (such as NFS) or to act as a Windows domain controller:

- **samba_share_fusefs**—Allows Samba to export `ntfs/fusefs` volumes.
- **samba_share_nfs**—Allows Samba to export NFS volumes.
- **samba_domain_controller**—Allows Samba to act as the domain controller, add users and groups, and change passwords.

The `setsebool` command is used to turn the SELinux Booleans on or off. Used with the `-P` option, `setsebool` sets the Boolean you indicate permanently. For example, to allow Samba to share any file or directory with read-only permission from the server, you could type the following from a shell as root user:

```
# setsebool -P samba_export_all_ro on
# getsebool samba_export_all_ro
samba_export_all_ro --> on
```

The `setsebool` command sets the Boolean, in this case to on. The `getsebool` lets you see the value of the Boolean.

19

Setting SELinux file contexts for Samba

SELinux confines the files that the Samba service can access. Instead of allowing any file with the proper read and write permission to be shared by the Samba server, SELinux (when in Enforcing mode) requires that files and directories have the correct file contexts set on them before the Samba service can even see that the files exist.

In order for the Samba service to function with SELinux immediately, some files and directories come preset with the proper file contexts. For example, Samba configuration files (/etc/samba/*), log files (/var/log/samba/*), and libraries (/var/lib/samba/*) have rules assigned to ensure they get the proper file contexts. To find files and directories associated with the Samba service and smbd daemon that have file contexts preset, run the following:

```
# semanage fcontext -l | grep -i samba
# semanage fcontext -l | grep -i smb
```

The file context portion that you are interested in ends with _t: for example, samba_etc_t, samba_log_t, and smbd_var_t, for the /etc/samba, /var/log/samba, and /var/lib/samba directories, respectively.

You may find that you need to change file contexts—for example, when you put files in nonstandard locations (such as moving the smb.conf file to /root/smb.conf) or when you want to share a directory (other than home directories, which can be turned on by setting a Boolean). Unlike the vsftpd (FTP) and httpd (web) servers that come with Linux, Samba has no default shared content directories (those just mentioned used /var/ftp and /var/www/html).

You can change a file context permanently by creating a new file context rule and then applying that rule to the file or directory for which it is intended. You can do that with the semanage command (to make the rule) and restorecon command (to apply the rule). For example, if you wanted to share a directory, /mystuff, you would create that directory with the proper permissions and run the following command to make it available for read/write access from Samba:

```
# semanage fcontext -a -t samba_share_t "/mystuff(/.*)?"
# restorecon -v /mystuff
```

After those commands are run, the /mystuff directory, along with any files and directories below that point, have the file context of samba_share_t. It is then up to you to assign the correct Linux ownership and file permissions to allow access to the users you choose. The section "Configuring Samba" provides an example of creating a share and shows you how to add permissions and ownership to a shared directory using standard Linux commands.

Configuring Samba host/user permissions

Within the smb.conf file itself, you can allow or restrict access to the entire Samba server or to specific shares based on the hosts or user trying to gain access. You can also restrict access to the Samba server by providing the service only on particular interfaces.

For example, if you have one network interface card connected to the Internet and another connected to the local network, you can tell Samba to serve requests only on the local network interface. The next section describes how to configure Samba, including how to identify which hosts, users, or network interfaces can access your Samba server.

Configuring Samba

Most Samba configuration is done in the /etc/samba/smb.conf file. As you configure your Samba server, you can also add host information to the lmhosts file.

To configure smb.conf, you can use a plain-text editor. However, Fedora has a graphical interface for configuring Samba (system-config-samba). The next sections step through how to use the graphical interfaces to configure Samba. After that, you look at the resulting smb.conf file.

Using system-config-samba

On Fedora systems, you can install the system-config-samba package to use the Samba Server Configuration window to configure Samba. From that window, you can configure basic server settings, add shares, and set up user accounts so people can access those shares. If you have not already installed system-config-samba, type the following as root at the command line:

```
# yum install system-config-samba*
```

With system-config-samba and system-config-samba-docs packages installed, you can launch it from Fedora from the Applications page by double-clicking the Samba icon. Or you could just type the following from the shell:

```
# system-config-samba &
```

The Samba Server Configuration window should appear on your desktop. You can now configure your basic Samba server and begin adding shared directories.

Choosing Samba server settings

From the Samba Server Configuration window, you should first set your basic settings and the type of authentication you are using. Start by selecting Preferences ➪ Server Settings. The Server Settings pop-up window appears, as shown in Figure 19.1.

In this example, the name of the Workgroup is changed to datagroup and Sales Data is set as the Description. Next, select the Security tab. The default Authentication mode is User, which means that Samba (Windows) usernames are mapped into real user accounts on the Linux system. No outside systems are contacted to authenticate users.

FIGURE 19.1

Choose basic Samba server settings.

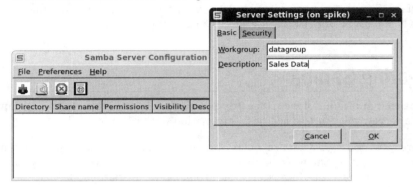

FIGURE 19.2

Choose Samba server security settings.

Encrypted passwords are used by default. Also by default, there is no guest account. If you would like to have an unauthenticated guest account that can access your Samba server, click the box that says No guest account, and choose which Linux user is assigned to the guest user. For example, if you assigned joe to the guest account, the user account joe would need to have access to a shared directory or file for a guest user to access it. Figure 19.2 shows an example of the Security settings.

Configuring Samba user accounts

If you are using the default User type of authentication, as I am here, you can configure user accounts to access your Fedora system by selecting Preferences ⇨ Samba Users. At first, there are no Samba users listed. To add a Samba user, select Add User from the Samba Users window.

From the Create New Samba User screen that pops up, select the local Linux user account (UNIX Username) from the drop-down box. You can use the same name or a different one for the Windows Username. Then fill in the Samba password for that user, and select OK. Figure 19.3 shows you how to create a new Samba user named chris that has the same permission the Linux user chris has to access the system.

FIGURE 19.3

Add user accounts to your Samba server.

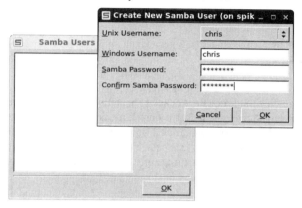

You can configure as many users as you like from your Linux user accounts to grant them access to files and directories via your Samba server. With the basic system and user settings in place, you can start creating shared directories.

Creating a Samba shared folder

Before you can create a shared folder, that folder (directory) must exist and have the proper permissions set. In this example, the /var/salesdata directory is shared. You want the data to be writable by the user named chris but visible to anyone on your network. To create that directory and set the proper permissions and SELinux file contexts, type the following as root user:

```
# mkdir /var/salesdata
# chmod 775 /var/salesdata
# chown chris:chris /var/salesdata
# semanage fcontext -a -t samba_share_t /var/salesdata
# restorecon -v /var/salesdata
```

Next, from the Samba Server Configuration window, select File ⇨ Add Share. The Create Samba Share window appears. Start by filling in the folder name (select Choose to browse for it), a name to represent the share, and a description. Then you want to choose whether you want to let anyone write to it and whether you want the existence of the share to be visible to anyone. Figure 19.4 shows an example of this window.

19

FIGURE 19.4

Choose the folder and name of the new share.

After filling in the Basic information, select the Access tab. Any Samba user you have created to this point appears in the Access tab. Put a check mark next to any user you want to allow to access this shared directory. Because I assigned ownership to chris and left read/write permissions open to chris, the user chris can read from and write to that directory via Samba. Figure 19.5 shows an example of the Access settings for the share.

FIGURE 19.5

Set access to the new share.

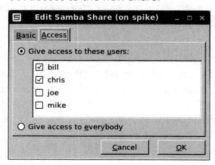

Select OK when you are finished configuring the share. Next you want to test that the share is available.

Checking the Samba share

For the changes to your Samba configuration to take effect, you need to restart the smb service. After that is done, check that the Samba share you created is available and that any user you assigned to the share can access it. To do those things, type the following as root user from a shell on the Samba server:

```
# systemctl restart smb.service
# smbclient -L localhost
Enter root's password: <ENTER>
Anonymous login successful
Domain=[DATAGROUP] OS=[Unix] Server=[Samba 4.1.15]
        Sharename    Type   Comment
        ---------    ----   -------
        salesdata    Disk   Sales data for current year
        IPC$         IPC    IPC Service (Samba Server Version 4.1.15))
Anonymous login successful
Domain=[DATAGROUP] OS=[Unix] Server=[Samba 4.1.15]
...
```

Here you can see the share name (salesdata), the Domain set to the workgroup name DATAGROUP, and the description entered earlier (Sales data for current year). Next, a quick way to test access to the share is to use the smbclient command. You can use the hostname or IP address with smbclient to access the share. Because I am on the local system in this example, I just use the name localhost and the user I added (chris):

```
# smbclient -U chris //localhost/salesdata
Enter chris's password: ********
Domain=[DATAGROUP] OS=[Unix] Server=[Samba 4.1.15]
smb: \> lcd /etc
smb: \> put hosts
putting file hosts as \hosts (43.5 kb/s) (average 43.5 kb/s)
smb: \> ls
  .                             D      0  Sun Oct 23 09:52:51 2014
  ..                            D      0  Sun Oct 23 09:11:50 2014
  hosts                         A     89  Sun Oct 23 09:52:51 2014
            39941 blocks of size 524288. 28197 blocks available
smb: \> quit
```

A Samba share is in the form //*host*/*share* or *host**share*. However, when you identify a Samba share from a Linux shell in the latter case, backslashes need to be escaped. So, as an argument, the first example of the share would have to appear as \\\\localhost\\ salesdata. So the first form is easier to use.

NOTE

Escaping a character that you type from the shell is done by putting a backslash (\) in front of that character. It tells the shell to use the character following the backslash literally, instead of giving the character a special meaning to the shell. (The * and ? characters are examples of characters with special meaning.) Because the backslash itself has special meaning to the shell, if you want to literally use a backslash, you need to precede it with a backslash. That is why, when you want to type a Samba address that includes two backslashes, you have to actually enter four backslashes.

19

When prompted, enter the Samba password for that user (it may be different from the Linux user's password). You see the smb: \> prompt after that.

At this point, you have a session open to the Samba host that is similar to an lftp session for traversing an FTP server. The lcd /etc command makes /etc the current directory on the local system. The put hosts command uploads the hosts file from the local system to the shared directory. Typing ls shows that the file exists on the server. The quit command ends the session.

Instead of configuring the server, users, and shares with the system-config-samba window, in some Linux systems you could use the samba-swat web-based interface or edit the smb.conf file directly. The next section shows you how to use the smb.conf file directly to configure Samba.

Configuring Samba in the smb.conf file

Inside the /etc/samba/smb.conf file are settings for configuring your Samba server, defining shared printers, configuring how authentication is done, and creating shared directories. The file consists of the following predefined sections:

- **[global]**—Settings that apply to the Samba server as a whole are placed in this section. This is where you set the server's description, its workgroup (domain), the location of log files, the default type of security, and other settings.

- **[homes]**—This section determines whether users with accounts on the Samba server can see their home directories (browseable) or write to them (writable).

- **[printers]**—In this section, settings tell Samba whether to make printers available through Samba that are configured for Linux printing (CUPS).

Inside the smb.conf file, many sections are commented out by the lines beginning with semicolons (;). Removing the semicolons enables you to quickly set up different kinds of shared information. The other information illustrated in the smb.conf file in the next sections reflects the same Samba configuration I added during the system-config-samba procedure.

Keep in mind that you don't have to use any graphical interface at all when configuring Samba. You can simply edit the smb.conf file directly, using the techniques described in this section. Editing smb.conf directly is the most common way to configure Samba on a Red Hat Enterprise Linux server that has no graphical desktop interface installed.

Configuring the [global] section

If you look at the [global] section of the smb.conf file, you can see that some settings were modified and others are commented out, ready for you to modify as you like:

```
[global]
        workgroup = datagroup
        server string = Sales Data
```

```
;          netbios name = MYSERVER
;          interfaces = lo eth0 192.168.12.2/24 192.168.13.2/24
;          hosts allow = 127. 192.168.12. 192.168.13.
           log file = /var/log/samba/log.%m
           max log size = 50
           security = user
           cups options = raw
```

The workgroup (also used as the domain name) is set to datagroup in this example. When a client communicates with the Samba server, this name tells the client which workgroup the Samba server is in. Any value set for the server string is used later to fill in comment values presented next to IPC lines and in the printer comment box when that information is presented to client applications.

By default, your server's DNS hostname (type hostname to see what it is) is used as your Samba server's NetBIOS name as well. You can override that and set a separate NetBIOS name by uncommenting the netbios name line and adding the server name you want. For example: netbios name = myownhost. localhost is used as your NetBIOS name if it has not been otherwise set.

As the log file value is set, logs associated with Samba activity are written to /var/log/samba/log.%m, where %m represents the name or IP address of the system contacting the Samba server. This makes it easy to debug problems associated with requests from a particular system because each client is assigned its own log file.

The max log size limits the size of each log file to a set number of kilobytes (50KB by default). After that size is exceeded, Samba copies the file to a log file of the same name with a .old appended to it. The default security type is set to user (Samba usernames and passwords), and cups options lets you pass any options you like to the CUPS printers served by your Samba server. By default, only raw is set, which allows Windows clients to use their own print drivers. Printers on your Samba server print the pages they are presented in raw form.

Several options are commented out that you can consider setting. Setting the netbios name causes the name you set to be used as the hostname for the Samba service. If this is not set, the host portion of the system's fully qualified domain name is used as the hostname.

If you want to restrict access to the Samba server so it only responds on certain interfaces, you can uncomment the interfaces line and add either the IP address or name (lo, eth0, eth1, and so on) of the network interfaces you want.

You can restrict access to the Samba server to specific hosts as well. Uncomment the hosts allow line (remove the semicolon), and insert the IP addresses of the hosts you want to allow. To enter a range of addresses, simply end the subnetwork portion of the address, followed by a dot. For example, 127. is associated with IP addresses that point to the local host. The 192.168.12. entry matches all IP addresses from 192.168.12.1 to 192.168.12.254.

19

Configuring the [homes] section

The [homes] section is configured, by default, to allow any Samba user account to be able to access its own home directory via the Samba server. The browseable = no setting prevents the Samba server from displaying the availability of the shared home directories. Users who can provide their own Samba usernames and passwords can read and write in their own home directories (writable = yes). Here is what the default homes entry looks like:

```
[homes]
        comment = Home Directories
        browseable = no
        writable = yes
;       valid users = %S
;       valid users = MYDOMAIN\%S
```

Notice that two examples of valid users entries are commented out. With this value not set (as it is by default), any valid users can log in to Samba. Setting it to %S substitutes the current service name, which allows any valid users of the service. You can also limit user access by indicating that only a particular workgroup (domain) name can be used to match users requesting this service.

If, after starting the smb service, you cannot log in using a valid user account, you may need to change some security features on your system. On Fedora and RHEL systems, in particular, SELinux features need to be changed to allow users to access their home directories if you are in SELinux Enforcing mode.

For example, if you tried to use smbclient to log in to your home directory, the login would succeed, but when you tried to list the contents of the home directory, you might see the following message:

```
NT_STATUS_ACCESS_DENIED listing \*
```

To tell SELinux to allow Samba users to access their home directories as Samba shares, turn on the samba_enable_home_dirs Boolean by typing the following as root from a shell:

```
# setsebool -P samba_enable_home_dirs on
```

The setsebool command turns on the capability of Samba to share home directories (which is off by default). The form for using the smbclient command to check access to the user's home directory, again for the user chris, would be the following (replacing the IP address with the name or address of your Samba server):

```
$ smbclient -U chris //192.168.0.119/chris
Enter chris's password:
Domain=[DATAGROUP] OS=[Unix] Server=[Samba 4.1.15]
smb: \> ls file.txt
  file.txt                  149946368  Sun Dec  7 09:28:53 2014
          39941 blocks of size 524288. 28191 blocks available
```

The main point to remember is that, even though the share is not browseable, you can request it by giving the Samba server's hostname or IP address, followed by the user's name (here, chris), to access the user's home directory.

Configuring the [printers] section

Any printer that you configure for CUPS printing on your Linux system is automatically shared to others over Samba, based on the [printers] section that is added by default. The global cups options = raw setting makes all printers raw printers (meaning that the Windows client needs to provide the proper printer driver for each shared printer).

Here's what the default printers section looks like in the smb.conf file:

```
[printers]
        comment = All Printers
        path = /var/spool/samba
        browseable = no
;       guest ok = no
;       writable = No
        printable = yes
```

The printable = yes line causes all your CUPS printers on the local system to be shared by Samba. Printers are writable and allow guest printing by default. You can uncomment the guest ok = no line and the writable = No line, respectively, to change those settings.

To see that those printers are available, you could run the smbclient -L command from a Linux system, as shown earlier. On a Windows system, you can select Network from the Windows Explorer file manager window and select the icon representing your Samba server. All shared printers and folders appear in that window. (See the section "Accessing Samba Shares" later in this chapter for details on viewing and using shared printers.)

Creating custom shared directories

With the basic configuration of your Samba server in place, you can begin creating custom sections to share specific printers and folders and secure them as you choose. For the first example, here is what the share created in the system-config-samba demonstration earlier in this chapter (called salesdata) looks like in the smb.conf file:

```
[salesdata]
        comment = Sales data for current year
        path = /var/salesdata
        read only = no
;       browseable = yes
        valid users = chris
```

Before creating this share, the /var/salesdata directory was created, with chris assigned as the user and group, and the directory was set to be readable and writable by chris. (The SELinux file context must also be set, if SELinux is in Enforcing mode.)

The Samba username chris must be presented along with the associated password to access the share. After chris is connected to the share, chris has read and write access to it (read only = no).

Now that you have seen default settings for Samba and an example of a simple shared directory (folder), read the next few sections to see how to further configure shares. In particular, the examples demonstrate how to make shares available to particular users, hosts, and network interfaces.

Restricting Samba access by network interface

To restrict access to all your shares, you can set the global interfaces setting in the smb.conf file. Samba is designed more for local file sharing than sharing over wide area networks. If your computer has a network interface connected to a local network and one connected to the Internet, consider allowing access only to the local network.

To set which interfaces Samba listens on, uncomment the interfaces line in the [global] section of the smb.conf file. Then add the interface names or IP address ranges of those computers you want to allow access to your computer. Here is an example:

```
interfaces = lo 192.168.22.15/24
```

This interfaces entry allows access to the Samba service to all users on the local system (lo). It also allows access to any systems on the 192.168.22 network. See the smb.conf man page's description of different ways of identifying hosts and network interfaces.

Restricting Samba access by host

Host access to the Samba server can be set for the entire service or for single shares. The syntax used is similar to that of the hosts.allow and hosts.deny files in the TCP wrappers feature. Here, however, hosts allow and hosts deny entries are added directly to the smb.conf file.

Here are some examples of hosts allow and hosts deny entries:

```
hosts allow = 192.168.22. EXCEPT 192.168.22.99
hosts allow = 192.168.5.0/255.255.255.0
hosts allow = .example.com market.example.net
hosts deny = evil.example.org 192.168.99.
```

These entries can be put in the [global] section or in any shared directory section. The first example allows access to any host in the 192.168.22. network, except for 192.168.22.99, which is denied. Note that a dot is required at the end of the network number. The 192.168.5.0/255.255.255.0 example uses netmask notation to identify 192.168.5 as the set of addresses that are allowed.

In the third line of the sample code, any host from the .example.com network is allowed, as is the individual host market.example.net. The hosts deny example shows that you can use the same form to identify names and IP addresses to prevent access from certain hosts.

Restricting Samba access by user

Particular Samba users and groups can be allowed access to specific Samba shares by identifying those users and groups within a share in the smb.conf file. Aside from guest users, which you may or may not allow, the default user authentication for Samba requires you to add a Samba (Windows) user account that maps into a local Linux user account.

To allow a user to access the Samba server, you need to create a password for the user. Here is an example of how to add a Samba password for the user jim:

```
# smbpasswd -a jim
New SMB password: *******
Retype new SMB password: *******
```

After running that smbpasswd command, jim can use that username and password to access the Samba server. The /var/lib/samba/private/passdb.tdb file holds the password just entered for jim. After that, the user jim can change the password by simply typing smbpasswd when he is logged in. The root user can change the password by rerunning the command shown in the example, but dropping the -a option.

If you wanted to give jim access to a share, you could add a valid users line to that shared block in the smb.conf file. For example, to provide both chris and jim access to a share, you could add the following line:

```
valid users = jim, chris
```

If the read only option is set to no for the share, both users could potentially write files to the share (depending on file permissions). If read only is set to yes, you could still allow access to jim and chris to write files by adding a write list line as follows:

```
write list = jim, chris
```

The write list can contain groups (that is, Linux groups contained in the /etc/group file) to allow write permission to any Linux user that belongs to a particular Linux group. You can add write permission for a group by putting a plus (+) character in front of a name. For example, the following adds write access for the market group to the share with which this line is associated:

```
write list = jim, chris, +market
```

There are many ways to change and extend the features of your shared Samba resources. For further information on configuring Samba, be sure to examine the smb.conf file itself (which includes many useful comments) and the smb.conf man page.

Accessing Samba Shares

After you have created some shared directories in Samba, many client tools are available in both Linux and Windows for accessing those shares. Command-line tools in Linux include

19

the `smbclient` command, demonstrated earlier in this chapter. For graphical means of accessing shares, you can use the file managers available in both Windows (Windows Explorer) and Linux (Nautilus, with the GNOME desktop).

Accessing Samba shares in Linux

Opening a file manager in Linux can provide you access to the shared directories from Linux (Samba) and Windows (SMB). How you access the file manager is different on different Linux desktops. In GNOME 3, you can click the Files icon. In other desktops, open the Home folder.

With the Nautilus window manager displayed, look for a Connect to Server selection in the left pane or (in some versions of Nautilus) select File ➪ Connect to Server. In Fedora 21, the Connect to Server window should appear as shown in Figure 19.6.

Fill in the address of a Samba share you want to access and click Connect. In the example, the `salesdata` share was chosen. If required, you are prompted for a username, domain, and password. Enter that information and click Connect.

FIGURE 19.6

Identify a Samba share from the Nautilus Connect to Server window.

If the user and password are accepted, you should see the contents of the remote directory. If you have write access to the share, you can open another Nautilus window and drag and drop files between the two systems. Figure 19.7 shows an example of the Nautilus window after I have connected to the `salesdata` share.

FIGURE 19.7

Opening Samba shares from Connect to Server in Nautilus.

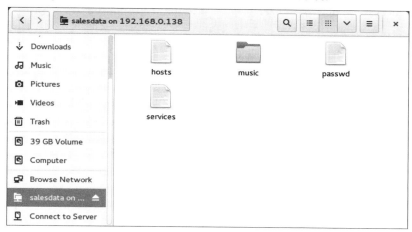

Because a Samba shared directory can be viewed as a remote filesystem, you can use common Linux tools to connect a Samba share (temporarily or permanently) to your Linux system. Using the standard mount command, you can mount a remote Samba share as a CIFS filesystem in Linux. This example mounts the salesdata share from the host at IP address 192.168.0.119 on the local directory /mnt/sales:

```
# mkdir /mnt/sales
# mount -t cifs -o user=chris,password=mypass \
     //192.168.0.119/salesdata /mnt/sales
Password: *******
# ls /mnt/sales
hosts    services
```

When prompted, enter the Samba password for chris. Given that the user chris in this example has read-write permission to the shared directory, users on your system should be able to read and write to the mounted directory. Regardless of who saves files on the shared directory, on the server those files are owned by the user chris. This mount lasts until the system is rebooted or you run the umount command on the directory. If you want the share to be mounted permanently (that is, every time the system boots up) in the same location, you can do some additional configuration. First, open the /etc/fstab file and add an entry similar to the following:

```
//192.168.0.119/salesdata /mnt/sales cifs credentials=/root/
     cif.txt 0 0
```

19

Next, create a credentials file (in this example, /root/cif.txt). In that file, put the name of the user and the user's password you want to present when the system tries to mount the filesystem. Here is an example of the contents of that file:

```
user=chris
pass=mypass
```

Before you reboot to check that the entry is correct, try mounting it from the command line. A mount -a command tries to mount any filesystem listed in the /etc/fstab file that is not already mounted. The df command shows information about disk space for the mounted directory. For example:

```
# mount -a
# df -h /mnt/sales
Filesystem                  Size  Used  Avail  Ues%  Mounted on
//192.168.0.119/salesdata   20G   5.7G    14G   30%  /mnt/sales
```

You should now be able to use the shared Samba directory as you do any directory on the local system.

Accessing Samba shares in Windows

As with Linux, you can access Samba shares from the file manager window, in this case Windows Explorer. To do this, open any folder in Windows, and select Network from the left panel. An icon representing the Samba server should appear on the screen. Click that icon, and enter a password if prompted for one. You should see all shared printers and folders from that server (see Figure 19.8).

FIGURE 19.8

Accessing Samba shares from Windows.

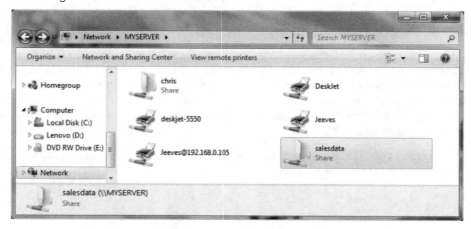

In Figure 19.8, you can see that there are two shared folders (directories): chris and salesdata. There are also several shared printers. To use the folders, double-click them and enter the required authentication information. Because printers are set up to use raw drivers by default, you need to obtain Windows drivers to use any of the Samba printers.

Using Samba in the Enterprise

Although beyond the scope of this book, Windows file and printer sharing via Samba servers is a very popular application in large enterprises. Despite the fact that Linux has made huge inroads in the enterprise-quality server market, Microsoft Windows systems are still the predominant systems used on the desktop.

The major features needed to integrate Samba servers into a large enterprise with many Microsoft Windows desktops are related to authentication. Most large enterprises use Microsoft Active Directory Services (ADS) servers for authentication. On the Linux side, that means configuring Kerberos on the Linux system and using ADS (instead of user) for the type of security in the smb.conf file.

The advantage of central authentication is that users have to remember only one set of credentials throughout the enterprise, and system administrators need to manage fewer user accounts and passwords. If you are interested in investigating this subject further, I recommend you read the Samba & Active Directory page on the wiki at Samba.org:

    http://wiki.samba.org/index.php/Samba_&_Active_Directory

Summary

Because of the popularity of Windows desktops, Samba servers have become popular for sharing files and printers among Windows and Linux systems. Samba provides a way to interoperate with Windows systems by implementing the Server Message Block (SMB) or Common Internet File (CIFS) protocol for sharing resources over a network.

This chapter stepped through the process of installing, starting, securing, configuring, and accessing Samba servers on a Linux system. Both graphical and command-line tools can be used to both set up a Samba server and get to it from Linux and Windows systems.

The next chapter describes the Network File System (NFS) facility. NFS is the native Linux facility for sharing and mounting filesystems over networks with other Linux and UNIX systems.

19

Exercises

The exercises in this section describe tasks related to setting up a Samba server in Linux and accessing that server using a Samba client. As usual, there are often several ways to accomplish some of the tasks here. So don't worry if you don't go about the exercises in exactly the same way as shown in the answers, as long as you get the same results. See Appendix B for suggested solutions.

Don't do these exercises on a Linux system running a Samba server because they will almost certainly interfere with that server. These exercises were tested on a Fedora system. Some of the steps might be slightly different on another Linux system.

1. Install the samba and samba-client packages.

2. Start and enable the smb and nmb services.

3. Set the Samba server's workgroup to TESTGROUP, the netbios name to MYTEST, and the server string to Samba Test System.

4. Add a Linux user named phil to your system, and add a Linux password and Samba password for phil.

5. Set the [homes] section so that home directories are browseable (yes) and writable (yes), and phil is the only valid user.

6. Set any SELinux Boolean that is necessary to make it so phil can access his home directory via a Samba client.

7. From the local system, use the smbclient command to list that the homes share is available.

8. From a Nautilus (file manager) window on the local system, connect to the homes share for the user phil on the local Samba server in a way that allows you to drag and drop files to that folder.

9. Open up the firewall so anyone who has access to the server can access the Samba service (smbd and nmbd daemons).

10. From another system on your network (Windows or Linux), try to open the homes share again as the user phil and again make sure you can drag and drop files to it.

Configuring an NFS File Server

Instead of representing storage devices as drive letters (A, B, C, and so on), as they are in Microsoft operating systems, Linux systems invisibly connect filesystems from multiple hard disks, floppy disks, CD-ROMs, and other local devices to form a single Linux filesystem. The Network File System (NFS) facility enables you to extend your Linux filesystem to connect filesystems on other computers to your local directory structure.

An NFS file server provides an easy way to share large amounts of data among the users and computers in an organization. An administrator of a Linux system that is configured to share its filesystems using NFS has to perform the following tasks to set up NFS:

1. **Set up the network**. NFS is typically used on private LANs as opposed to public networks, such as the Internet.

2. **Start the NFS service**. Several service daemons need to start up and run to have a fully operational NFS service. In Fedora, you can start up the `nfs-server` service; in Red Hat Enterprise Linux, you start the `nfs` service.

3. **Choose what to share from the server**. Decide which filesystems on your Linux NFS server to make available to other computers. You can choose any point in the filesystem and make all files and directories below that point accessible to other computers.

4. **Set up security on the server**. You can use several different security features to apply the level of security with which you are comfortable. Mount-level security enables you to restrict the computers that can mount a resource and, for those allowed to mount it,

enables you to specify whether it can be mounted read/write or read-only. In NFS, user-level security is implemented by mapping users from the client systems to users on the NFS server (based on UID and not username) so they can rely on standard Linux read/write/execute permissions, file ownership, and group permissions to access and protect files.

5. **Mount the filesystem on the client**. Each client computer that is allowed access to the server's NFS shared filesystem can mount it anywhere the client chooses. For example, you may mount a filesystem from a computer called maple on the /mnt/maple directory in your local filesystem. After it is mounted, you can view the contents of that directory by typing ls /mnt/maple. Then you can use the cd command below the /mnt/maple mount point to see the files and directories it contains.

Figure 20.1 illustrates a Linux file server using NFS to share (export) a filesystem and a client computer mounting the filesystem to make it available to its local users.

FIGURE 20.1

NFS can make selected filesystems available to other computers.

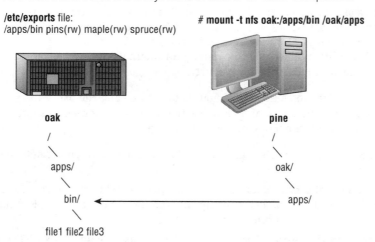

In this example, a computer named oak makes its /apps/bin directory available to clients on the network (pine, maple, and spruce) by adding an entry to the /etc/exports file. The client computer (pine) sees that the resource is available and mounts the resource on its local filesystem at the mount point /oak/apps, after which any files, directories, or subdirectories from /apps/bin on oak are available to users on pine (given proper permissions).

Although it is often used as a file server (or other type of server), Linux is a general-purpose operating system, so any Linux system can share filesystems (export) as a server or use another computer's filesystems (mount) as a client.

> **NOTE**
>
> A filesystem is usually a structure of files and directories that exists on a single device (such as a hard disk partition or CD-ROM). The term *Linux filesystem* refers to the entire directory structure (which may include filesystems from several disk partitions, NFS, or a variety of network resources), beginning from root (/) on a single computer. A shared directory in NFS may represent all or part of a computer's filesystem, which can be attached (from the shared directory down the directory tree) to another computer's filesystem.

Installing an NFS Server

To run an NFS server, you need a set of kernel modules (which are delivered with the kernel itself) plus some user-level tools to configure the service, run daemon processes, and query the service in various ways. For Fedora and RHEL, the components you need that are not already in the kernel can be added by installing the nfs-utils package:

```
# yum install nfs-utils
```

Besides a few documents in the /usr/share/doc/nfs-utils* directory, most documentation in the nfs-utils package includes man pages for its various components. To see the list of documentation, type the following:

```
# rpm -qd nfs-utils | less
```

There are tools and man pages for both the NFS server side (for sharing a directory with others) and the client side (for mounting a remote NFS directory locally). To configure a server, you can refer to the exports man page (to set up the /etc/exports file to share your directories). The man page for the exportfs command describes how to share and view the list of directories you share from the /etc/exports file. The nfsd man page describes options you can pass to the rpc.nfsd server daemon, which lets you do such things as run the server in debugging mode.

Man pages on the client side include the mount.nfs man page (to see what mount options you can use when mounting remote NFS directories on your local system). There is also an nfsmount.conf man page, which describes how to use the /etc/nfsmount.conf file to configure how your system behaves when you mount remote resources locally. The showmount man page describes how to use the showmount command to see what shared directories are available from NFS servers.

20

To find out more about the nfs-utils package, you can run the following commands to see information about the package, configuration files, and commands, respectively:

```
# rpm -qi nfs-utils
# rpm -qc nfs-utils
# rpm -ql nfs-utils | grep bin
```

Starting the NFS service

Starting the NFS server involves launching several service daemons. The service is started in different ways for different Linux distributions. The basic NFS service in Fedora and RHEL 7 is called nfs-server. To start that service, enable it (so it starts each time your system boots) and check the status by running the following three commands:

```
# systemctl start nfs-server.service
# systemctl enable nfs-server.service
# systemctl status nfs-server.service
nfs-server.service - NFS Server
     Loaded: loaded (/lib/systemd/system/nfs-server.service; enabled)
     Active: active (exited) since Mon 2014-9-01 15:15:11 EDT; 24s
        ago
   Main PID: 7767 (code=exited, status=0/SUCCESS)
     CGroup: /system.slice/nfs-server.service
```

You can see from the status that the nfs-server service is enabled and active. The NFS service also requires that the RPC service be running (rpcbind). The nfs-server service automatically starts the rpcbind service, if it is not already running.

In Red Hat Enterprise Linux 6, you need the service and chkconfig commands to check, start, and enable the NFS service (nfs). The following commands show the nfs service not running currently and disabled:

```
# service nfs status
rpc.svcgssd is stopped
rpc.mountd is stopped
nfsd is stopped
# chkconfig --list nfs
nfs  0:off  1:off  2:off  3:off  4:off  5:off  6:off
```

As mentioned earlier, the rpcbind service must be running for NFS to work. You could use the following commands to start and permanently enable both the rpcbind and nfs services.

```
# service rcpbind start
Starting rpcbind:                       [  OK  ]
# service nfs start
Starting NFS services:                  [  OK  ]
Starting NFS quotas:                    [  OK  ]
Starting NFS daemon:                    [  OK  ]
Starting NFS mountd:                    [  OK  ]
# chkconfig rpcbind on
# chkconfig nfs on
```

After the service is running, the commands (mount, exportfs, and so on) and files (/etc/exports, /etc/fstab, and so on) for actually configuring NFS are basically the same on every Linux system. So after you have NFS installed and running, just follow the instructions in this chapter to start using NFS.

Sharing NFS Filesystems

To share an NFS filesystem from your Linux system, you need to export it from the server system. Exporting is done in Linux by adding entries into the /etc/exports file. Each entry identifies a directory in your local filesystem that you want to share with other computers. The entry also identifies the other computers that can share the resource (or opens it to all computers) and includes other options that reflect permissions associated with the directory.

Remember that when you share a directory, you are sharing all files and subdirectories below that directory as well (by default). You need to be sure that you want to share everything in that directory structure. You can still restrict access within that directory structure in many ways; those are discussed later in this chapter.

> **NOTE**
>
> In Fedora, there is an NFS Server Configuration window you can install by typing `yum install system-config-nfs`; the command to launch the window is the same name as the package. Although this window can help you configure shares in the /etc/exports file, it can also help you do trickier things, such as lock down a service to specific ports and configure user access.
>
> Although I describe how to configure NFS by directly editing the configuration file, it is quite reasonable to use this graphical tool instead. Figure 20.2 shows an example of the NFS Server Configuration window.

20

FIGURE 20.2

The NFS Server Configuration window (`system-config-nfs`) provides a graphical way of configuring NFS services.

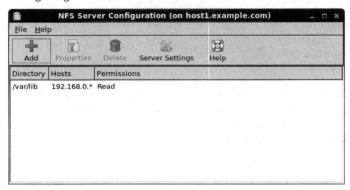

Configuring the /etc/exports file

To make a directory from your Linux system available to other systems, you need to export that directory. Exporting is done on a permanent basis by adding information about an exported directory to the `/etc/exports` file.

Here's the format of the `/etc/exports` file:

```
Directory    Host(Options...)   Host(Options...)   # Comments
```

In this example, `Directory` is the `Host` indicates the client computer to which the sharing of this directory is restricted. `Options` can include a variety of options to define the security measures attached to the shared directory for the host. (You can repeat Host/ Option pairs.) `Comments` are any optional comments you want to add (following the # sign).

The `exports` man page (`man exports`) contains details about the syntax of the `/etc/ exports` file. In particular, you can see the options you can use to limit access and secure each shared directory.

As root user, you can use any text editor to configure `/etc/exports` to modify shared directory entries or add new ones. Here's an example of an `/etc/exports` file:

```
/cal     *.linuxtoys.net(rw)            # Company events
/pub     *(ro,insecure,all_squash)      # Public dir
/home    maple(rw,root_squash) spruce(rw,root_squash)
```

The `/cal` entry represents a directory that contains information about events related to the company. Any computer in the company's domain (`*.linuxtoys.net`) can mount that NFS share. Users can write files to the directory as well as read them (indicated by the rw option). The comment (# Company events) simply serves to remind you of what the directory contains.

The /pub entry represents a public directory. It allows any computer and user to read files from the directory (indicated by the ro option) but not to write files. The insecure option enables any computer, even one that doesn't use a secure NFS port, to access the directory. The all_squash option causes all users (UIDs) and groups (GIDs) to be mapped to the user ID 65534 (which is the nfsnobody user in Fedora or RHEL and the nobody user in Ubuntu), giving them minimal permission to files and directories.

The /home entry enables a set of users to have the same /home directory on different computers. Suppose, for example, that you are sharing /home from a computer named oak. The computers named maple and spruce could each mount that directory on their own /home directories. If you gave all users the same username/UID on all machines, you could have the same /home/user directory available for each user, regardless of which computer he or she is logged into. The root_squash is used to exclude the root user from another computer from having root privilege to the shared directory.

These are just examples; you can share any directories that you choose, including the entire filesystem (/). Of course, there are security implications of sharing the whole filesystem or sensitive parts of it (such as /etc). Security options that you can add to your /etc/exports file are described throughout the sections that follow.

Hostnames in /etc/exports

You can indicate in the /etc/exports file which host computers can have access to your shared directory. If you want to associate multiple hostnames or IP addresses with a particular shared directory, be sure to have a space before each hostname. However, add no spaces between a hostname and its options. For example:

```
/usr/local maple(rw) spruce(ro,root_squash)
```

Notice that there is a space after (rw) but none after maple. You can identify hosts in several ways:

- **Individual host**—Enter one or more TCP/IP hostnames or IP addresses. If the host is in your local domain, you can simply indicate the hostname. Otherwise, use the full host.domain format. These are valid ways to indicate individual host computers:

```
maple
maple.handsonhistory.com
10.0.0.11
```

- **IP network**—Allow access to all hosts from a particular network address by indicating a network number and its netmask, separated by a slash (/). Here are valid ways to designate network numbers:

```
10.0.0.0/255.0.0.0 172.16.0.0/255.255.0.0
192.168.18.0/255.255.255.0
192.168.18.0/24
```

20

- **TCP/IP domain**—Using wildcards, you can include all or some host computers from a particular domain level. Here are some valid uses of the asterisk and question mark wildcards:

```
*.handsonhistory.com
*craft.handsonhistory.com
???.handsonhistory.com
```

The first example matches all hosts in the `handsonhistory.com` domain. The second example matches `woodcraft`, `basketcraft`, or any other hostnames ending in `craft` in the `handsonhistory.com` domain. The final example matches any three-letter hostnames in the domain.

- **NIS groups**—You can allow access to hosts contained in an NIS group. To indicate an NIS group, precede the group name with an at (@) sign (for example, `@group`).

Access options in /etc/exports

You don't have to just give away your files and directories when you export a directory with NFS. In the options part of each entry in `/etc/exports`, you can add options that allow or limit access by setting read/write permission. These options, which are passed to NFS, are as follows:

- `ro`—Client can mount this exported filesystem read-only. The default is to mount the filesystem read/write.

- `rw`—Explicitly asks that a shared directory be shared with read/write permissions. (If the client chooses, it can still mount the directory as read-only.)

User mapping options in /etc/exports

In addition to options that define how permissions are handled generally, you can use options to set the permissions that specific users have to NFS shared filesystems.

One method that simplifies this process is to have each user with multiple user accounts have the same username and UID on each machine. This makes it easier to map users so they have the same permissions on a mounted filesystem as they do on files stored on their local hard disks. If that method is not convenient, user IDs can be mapped in many other ways. Here are some methods of setting user permissions and the `/etc/exports` option that you use for each method:

- **root user**—The client's root user is mapped by default into the `nfsnobody` username (UID 65534). This prevents a client computer's root user from being able to change all files and directories in the shared filesystem. If you want the client's root user to have root permission on the server, use the `no_root_squash` option.

> **TIP**
>
> Keep in mind that even though root is squashed, the root user from the client can still become any other user account and access files for those user accounts on the server. So be sure that you trust root with all your user data before you share it read/write with a client.

- **nfsnobody or nobody user/group**—By using the 65534 user ID and group ID, you essentially create a user/group with permissions that do not allow access to files that belong to any real users on the server, unless those users open permission to everyone. However, files created by the 65534 user or group are available to anyone assigned as the 65534 user or group. To set all remote users to the 65534 user/group, use the all_squash option.

  The 65534 UIDs and GIDs are used to prevent the ID from running into a valid user or group ID. Using anonuid or anongid options, you can change the 65534 user or group, respectively. For example, anonuid=175 sets all anonymous users to UID 175, and anongid=300 sets the GID to 300. (Only the number is displayed when you list file permission unless you add entries with names to /etc/password and /etc/group for the new UIDs and GIDs.)

- **User mapping**—If a user has login accounts for a set of computers (and has the same ID), NFS, by default, maps that ID. This means that if the user named mike (UID 110) on maple has an account on pine (mike, UID 110), he can use his own remotely mounted files on either computer from either computer.

  If a client user who is not set up on the server creates a file on the mounted NFS directory, the file is assigned to the remote client's UID and GID. (An ls -l on the server shows the UID of the owner.) Use the map_static option to identify a file that contains user mappings.

Exporting the shared filesystems

After you have added entries to your /etc/exports file, run the exportfs command to have those directories exported (made available to other computers on the network). Reboot your computer or restart the NFS service, and the exportfs command runs automatically to export your directories. If you want to export them immediately, run exportfs from the command line (as root).

TIP

Running the exportfs command after you change the exports file is a good idea. If any errors are in the file, exportfs identifies them for you.

Here's an example of the exportfs command:

```
# /usr/sbin/exportfs -a -r -v
exporting maple:/pub
exporting spruce:/pub
exporting maple:/home
exporting spruce:/home
exporting *:/mnt/win
```

The -a option indicates that all directories listed in /etc/exports should be exported. The -r resyncs all exports with the current /etc/exports file (disabling those exports

20

no longer listed in the file). The -v option says to print verbose output. In this example, the /pub and /home directories from the local server are immediately available for mounting by those client computers that are named (maple and spruce). The /mnt/win directory is available to all client computers.

Securing Your NFS Server

The NFS facility was created at a time when encryption and other security measures were not routinely built into network services (such as remote login, file sharing, and remote execution). Therefore, NFS (even up through version 3) suffers from some rather glaring security issues.

NFS security issues made it an inappropriate facility to use over public networks and even made it difficult to use securely within an organization. These are some of the issues:

- **Remote root users**—Even with the default root_squash (which prevents root users from having root access to remote shares), the root user on any machine to which you share NFS directories can gain access to any other user account. Therefore, if you are doing something like sharing home directories with read/write permission, the root user on any box you are sharing to has complete access to the contents of those home directories.

- **Unencrypted communications**—Because NFS traffic is unencrypted, anyone sniffing your network can see the data that is being transferred.

- **User mapping**—Default permissions to NFS shares are mapped by user ID. So, for example, a user with UID 500 on an NFS client has access to files owned by UID 500 on the NFS server. This is regardless of the usernames used.

- **Filesystem structure exposed**—Up to NFSv3, if you shared a directory over NFS, you exposed the location of that directory on the server's filesystem. (In other words, if you shared the /var/stuff directory, clients would know that /var/stuff was its exact location on your server).

That's the bad news. The good news is that most of these issues are addressed in NFSv4 but require some extra configuration. By integrating Kerberos support, NFSv4 lets you configure user access based on each user obtaining a Kerberos ticket. For you, the extra work is configuring a Kerberos server. As for exposing NFS share locations, with NFSv4 you can bind shared directories to an /exports directory, so when they are shared, the exact location of those directories is not exposed.

Visit https://help.ubuntu.com/community/NFSv4Howto for details on NFSv4 features in Ubuntu.

As for standard Linux security features associated with NFS, iptables firewalls, TCP wrappers, and SELinux can all play a role in securing and providing access to your NFS server from remote clients. In particular, getting `iptables` firewall features working with NFS can be particularly challenging. These security features are described in the sections that follow.

Opening up your firewall for NFS

The NFS service relies on several different service daemons for normal operation, with most of these daemons listening on different ports for access. For the default NFSv4 used in Fedora, TCP and UDP ports 2049 (`nfs`) and 111 (`rpcbind`) must be open for an NFS server to perform properly. The server must also open TCP and UDP ports 20048 for the `showmount` command to be able to query available NFS shared directories from the server.

For RHEL 7, Fedora 21, and other systems that use the firewalld service, you can use the Firewall Configuration window (`yum install firewall-config`) to open the firewall for your NFS service. Type `firewall-config`, then make sure that nfs and rpc-bind are checked in the window to open the appropriate ports to allow access to your NFS service. Figure 20.3 shows an example of this window:

FIGURE 20.3

Open your firewall to allow access to the NFS service using the Firewall Configuration window

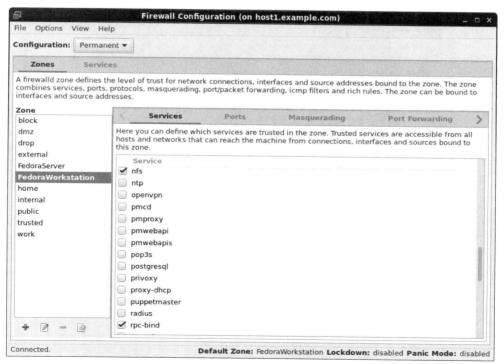

For RHEL 6 and other systems that use iptables service directly (prior to firewalld being added), to open ports on the NFS server's firewall, make sure `iptables` is enabled and started with firewall rules similar to the following added to the `/etc/sysconfig/iptables` file :

```
-A INPUT -m state --state NEW -m tcp -p tcp --dport 111 -j ACCEPT
-A INPUT -m state --state NEW -m udp -p udp --dport 111 -j ACCEPT
-A INPUT -m state --state NEW -m tcp -p tcp --dport 2049 -j ACCEPT
-A INPUT -m state --state NEW -m udp -p udp --dport 2049 -j ACCEPT
-A INPUT -m state --state NEW -m tcp -p tcp --dport 20048 -j ACCEPT
-A INPUT -m state --state NEW -m udp -p udp --dport 20048 -j ACCEPT
```

In Red Hat Enterprise Linux 6.x and earlier, the firewall issue is a bit more complex. The problem, as it relates to firewalls, is that several different services are associated with NFS that listen on different ports, and those ports are assigned randomly. To get around that problem, you need to lock down the port numbers those services use and open the firewall so those ports are accessible.

To make locking down NFS server ports easier, entries in the `/etc/sysconfig/nfs` file can be added to assign specific port numbers to services. The following are examples of options in the `/etc/sysconfig/nfs` file with static port numbers set:

```
RQUOTAD_PORT=49001
LOCKD_TCPPORT=49002
LOCKD_UDPPORT=49003
MOUNTD_PORT=49004
STATD_PORT=49005
STATD_OUTGOING_PORT=49006
RDMA_PORT=49007
```

With those ports set, I restarted the `nfs` service (`service nfs restart`). Using the `netstat` command, you can see the resulting processes that are listening on those assigned ports:

```
tcp  0  0 0.0.0.0:49001   0.0.0.0:*   LISTEN   4682/rpc.rquotad
tcp  0  0 0.0.0.0:49002   0.0.0.0:*   LISTEN   -
tcp  0  0 0.0.0.0:49004   0.0.0.0:*   LISTEN   4698/rpc.mountd
tcp  0  0 :::49002        :::*        LISTEN   -
tcp  0  0 :::49004        :::*        LISTEN   4698/rpc.mountd
udp  0  0 0.0.0.0:49001   0.0.0.0:*            4682/rpc.rquotad
udp  0  0 0.0.0.0:49003   0.0.0.0:*            -
udp  0  0 0.0.0.0:49004   0.0.0.0:*            4698/rpc.mountd
udp  0  0 :::49003        :::*                 -
udp  0  0 :::49004        :::*                 4698/rpc.mountd
```

With those port numbers set and being used by the various services, you can now add `iptables` rules, as you did with ports 2049 and 111 for the basic NFS service.

Allowing NFS access in TCP wrappers

For services such as vsftpd and sshd, TCP wrappers in Linux enable you to add information to /etc/hosts.allow and /etc/hosts.deny files to indicate which hosts can or cannot access the service. Although the nfsd server daemon itself is not enabled for TCP wrappers, the rpcbind service is.

For NFSv3 and earlier versions, simply adding a line such as the following to the /etc/hosts.deny file would deny access to the rpcbind service, but would also deny access to your NFS service:

```
rpcbind: ALL
```

For servers running NFSv4 by default, however, the rpcbind: ALL line just shown prevents outside hosts from getting information about RPC services (such as NFS) using commands like showmount. However, it does not prevent you from mounting an NFS shared directory.

Configuring SELinux for your NFS server

With SELinux set to Permissive or Disabled, it does not block access to the NFS service. In Enforcing mode, however, you should understand a few SELinux Booleans. To check the state of SELinux on your system, type the following:

```
# getenforce
Enforcing
# grep ^SELINUX= /etc/sysconfig/selinux
SELINUX=enforcing
```

If your system is in Enforcing mode, as it is here, check the nfs_selinux man page for information about SELinux settings that can impact the operation of your vsftpd service. Here are a few SELinux file contexts associated with NFS that you might need to know about:

- nfs_export_all_ro—With this Boolean set to on, SELinux allows you to share files with read-only permission using NFS. NFS read-only file sharing is allowed with this on, regardless of the SELinux file context set on the shared files and directories.

- nfs_export_all_rw—With this Boolean set to on, SELinux allows you to share files with read/write permission using NFS. As with the previous Boolean, this works regardless of the file context set on the shared files and directories.

- use_nfs_home_dirs — To allow the NFS server to share your home directories via NFS, set this Boolean to on.

20

Of the Booleans just described, the first two are on by default. The use_nfs_home_dirs Boolean is off. To turn on the use_nfs_home_dirs directory, you could type the following:

```
# setsebool -P use_nfs_home_dirs on
```

You can ignore all the Booleans related to NFS file sharing, however, by changing the file contexts on the files and directories you want to share via NFS. The public_content_t and public_content_rw_t file contexts can be set on any directory you want to share via NFS (or other file share protocols, such as HTTP, FTP, and others, for that matter). For example, to set the rule to allow the /whatever directory and its subdirectories to be shared read/write via NFS, and then apply that rule, type the following:

```
# semanage fcontext -a -t public_content_rw_t "/whatever(/.*)?"
# restorecon -F -R -v /whatever
```

If you wanted to allow users to just be able to read files from a directory, but not write to it, you could assign the public_content_t file context to the directory instead.

Using NFS Filesystems

After a server exports a directory over the network using NFS, a client computer connects that directory to its own filesystem using the mount command. That's the same command used to mount filesystems from local hard disks, CDs, and USB drives, but with slightly different options.

The mount command enables a client to automatically mount NFS directories added to the /etc/fstab file, just as it does with local disks. NFS directories can also be added to the /etc/fstab file in such a way that they are not automatically mounted (so you can mount them manually when you choose). With a noauto option, an NFS directory listed in /etc/fstab is inactive until the mount command is used, after the system is up and running, to mount the filesystem.

In addition to the /etc/fstab file, you can also set mount options using the /etc/nfsmount.conf file. Within that file, you can set mount options that apply to any NFS directory you mount or only those associated with specific mount points or NFS servers.

Before you set about mounting NFS shared directories, however, you probably want to check out what shared directories are available via NFS using the showmount command.

Viewing NFS shares

From a client Linux system, you can use the showmount command to see what shared directories are available from a selected computer. For example:

```
$ /usr/sbin/showmount -e server.example.com
/export/myshare client.example.com
/mnt/public      *
```

The `showmount` output shows that the shared directory named `/export/myshare` is available only to the host `client.example.com`. The `/mnt/public` shared directory, however, is available to anyone.

Manually mounting an NFS filesystem

After you know that the directory from a computer on your network has been exported (that is, made available for mounting), you can mount that directory manually using the `mount` command. This is a good way to make sure it is available and working before you set it up to mount permanently. The following is an example of mounting the `/stuff` directory from a computer named maple on your local computer:

```
# mkdir /mnt/maple
# mount maple:/stuff /mnt/maple
```

The first command (`mkdir`) creates the mount point directory. (`/mnt` is a common place to put temporarily mounted disks and NFS filesystems.) The `mount` command identifies the remote computer and shared filesystem, separated by a colon (`maple:/stuff`), and the local mount point directory (`/mnt/maple`) follows.

> **NOTE**
>
> If the mount fails, make sure the NFS service is running on the server and that the server's firewall rules don't deny access to the service. From the server, type `ps ax | grep nfsd` to see a list of `nfsd` server processes. If you don't see the list, try to start your NFS daemons as described earlier in this chapter. To view your firewall rules, type `iptables -vnL`. By default, the `nfsd` daemon listens for NFS requests on port number 2049. Your firewall must accept `udp` requests on ports 2049 (`nfs`) and 111 (`rpc`). In Red Hat Enterprise Linux 6 and earlier versions of Fedora, you may need to set static ports for related services, and then open ports for those services in the firewall. Refer to the section "Securing Your NFS Server" to review how to overcome these security issues.

To ensure that the NFS mount occurred, type **mount -t nfs**. This command lists all mounted NFS filesystems. Here is an example of the `mount` command and its output (with filesystems not pertinent to this discussion edited out):

```
# mount -t nfs
maple:/stuff on /mnt/maple type nfs (rw,relatime,vers=3,rsize=65536,
    wsize=65536,namlen=255,hard,proto=tcp,timeo=600,retrans=2,sec=sys,
    mountaddr=192.168.0.122,mountvers=3,mountport=892,mountproto=udp,
    local_lock=none,addr=192.168.0.122)
```

The output from the `mount -t nfs` command shows only those filesystems mounted from NFS file servers. The just-mounted NFS filesystem is the `/stuff` directory from

20

maple (maple:/stuff). It is mounted on /mnt/maple, and its mount type is nfs. The filesystem was mounted read/write (rw), and the IP address of maple is 192.168.0.122 (addr=192.168.0.122). Many other settings related to the mount are shown as well, such as the read and write sizes of packets and the NFS version number.

The mount operation just shown temporarily mounts an NFS filesystem on the local system. The next section describes how to make the mount more permanent (using the /etc/fstab file) and how to select various options for NFS mounts.

Mounting an NFS filesystem at boot time

To set up an NFS filesystem to mount automatically on a specified mount point each time you start your Linux system, you need to add an entry for that NFS filesystem to the /etc/fstab file. That file contains information about all different kinds of mounted (and available to be mounted) filesystems for your system.

Here's the format for adding an NFS filesystem to your local system:

```
host:directory      mountpoint      nfs      options      0      0
```

The first item (host:directory) identifies the NFS server computer and shared directory. mountpoint is the local mount point on which the NFS directory is mounted. It is followed by the filesystem type (nfs). Any options related to the mount appear next in a comma-separated list. (The last two zeros configure the system to not dump the contents of the filesystem and to not run fsck on the filesystem.)

The following are examples of NFS entries in /etc/fstab:

```
maple:/stuff    /mnt/maple nfs    bg,rsize=8192,wsize=8192  0 0
oak:/apps       /oak/apps  nfs    noauto,ro                 0 0
```

In the first example, the remote directory /stuff from the computer named maple (maple:/stuff) is mounted on the local directory /mnt/maple (the local directory must already exist). If the mount fails because the share is unavailable, the bg causes the mount attempt to go into the background and retry again later.

The filesystem type is nfs, and read (rsize) and write (wsize) buffer sizes (discussed in the section "Using mount options" later in this chapter) are set at 8192 to speed data transfer associated with this connection. In the second example, the remote directory is /apps on the computer named oak. It is set up as an NFS filesystem (nfs) that can be mounted on the /oak/apps directory locally. This filesystem is not mounted automatically (noauto), however, and can be mounted only as read-only (ro) using the mount command after the system is already running.

Mounting noauto filesystems

Your /etc/fstab file may also contain devices for other filesystems that are not mounted automatically. For example, you might have multiple disk partitions on your hard disk or an NFS shared filesystem that you want to mount only occasionally. A noauto filesystem can be mounted manually. The advantage is that when you type the mount command, you can type less information and have the rest filled in by the contents of the /etc/fstab file. So, for example, you could type:

```
# mount /oak/apps
```

With this command, mount knows to check the /etc/fstab file to get the filesystem to mount (oak:/apps), the filesystem type (nfs), and the options to use with the mount (in this case ro, for read-only). Instead of typing the local mount point (/oak/apps), you could have typed the remote filesystem name (oak:/apps) and had other information filled in.

Using mount options

You can add several mount options to the /etc/fstab file (or to a mount command line itself) to influence how the filesystem is mounted. When you add options to /etc/fstab, they must be separated by commas. For example, here, the noauto, ro, and hard options are used when oak:/apps is mounted:

```
oak:/apps     /oak/apps   nfs    noauto,ro,hard    0 0
```

The following are some options that are valuable for mounting NFS filesystems. You can read about these and other NFS mount options you can put in the /etc/fstab file from the nfs man page (man 5 nfs):

- hard—If this option is used and the NFS server disconnects or goes down while a process is waiting to access it, the process hangs until the server comes back up.

20

This is helpful if it is critical that the data you are working with stay in sync with the programs that are accessing it. (This is the default behavior.)

- soft—If the NFS server disconnects or goes down, a process trying to access data from the server times out after a set period when this option is on. An input/output error is delivered to the process trying to access the NFS server.

- rsize—This is the size of the blocks of data (in bytes) that the NFS client will request be used when it is reading data from an NFS server. The default is 1024. Using a larger number (such as 8192) gets you better performance on a network that is fast (such as a LAN) and is relatively error-free (that is, one that doesn't have lots of noise or collisions).

- wsize—This is the size of the blocks of data (in bytes) that the NFS client will request be used when it is writing data to an NFS server. The default is 1024. Performance issues are the same as with the rsize option.

- timeo=#—This sets the time after an RPC timeout occurs that a second transmission is made, where # represents a number in tenths of a second. The default value is seven-tenths of a second. Each successive timeout causes the timeout value to be doubled (up to 60 seconds maximum). Increase this value if you believe that timeouts are occurring because of slow response from the server or a slow network.

- retrans=#— This sets the number of minor timeouts and retransmissions that need to happen before a major timeout occurs.

- retry=#—This sets how many minutes to continue to retry failed mount requests, where # is replaced by the number of minutes to retry. The default is 10,000 minutes (which is about one week).

- bg—If the first mount attempt times out, try all subsequent mounts in the background. This option is very valuable if you are mounting a slow or sporadically available NFS filesystem. By placing mount requests in the background, your system can continue to mount other filesystems instead of waiting for the current one to complete.

> **NOTE**
>
> If a nested mount point is missing, a timeout to allow for the needed mount point to be added occurs. For example, if you mount /usr/trip and /usr/trip/extra as NFS filesystems and /usr/trip is not yet mounted when /usr/trip/extra tries to mount, /usr/trip/extra times out. If you're lucky, /usr/trip comes up and /usr/trip/extra mounts on the next retry.

- fg—If the first mount attempt times out, try subsequent mounts in the foreground. This is the default behavior. Use this option if it is imperative that the mount be successful before continuing (for example, if you were mounting /usr).

Not all NFS mount options need to go into the /etc/fstab file. On the client side, the /etc/nfsmount.conf file can be configured for Mount, Server, and Global sections. In the

Mount section, you can indicate which mount options are used when an NFS filesystem is mounted to a particular mount point. The Server section lets you add options to any NFS filesystem mounted from a particular NFS server. Global options apply to all NFS mounts from this client.

The following entry in the /etc/nfsmount.conf file sets a 32KB read and write block size for any NFS directories mounted from the system named thunder.example.com:

```
[ Server "thunder.example.com" ]
   rsize=32k
   wsize=32k
```

To set default options for all NFS mounts for your systems, you can uncomment the NFSMount_Global_Options block. In that block, you can set such things as protocols and NFS versions, as well as transmission rates and retry settings. Here is an example of an NFSMount_Global_Options block:

```
[ NFSMount_Global_Options ]
# This sets the default version to NFS 4
Defaultvers=4
# Sets the number of times a request will be retried before
# generating a timeout
Retrans=2
# Sets the number of minutes before retrying a failed
# mount to 2 minutes
# Retry=2
```

In the example just shown, the default NFS version is 4. Data is retransmitted twice (2) before generating a timeout. The wait time is 2 minutes before retrying a failed transmission. You can override any of these default values by adding mount options to the /etc/fstab or to the mount command line when the NFS directory is mounted.

Using autofs to mount NFS filesystems on demand

Recent improvements to auto-detecting and mounting removable devices have meant that you can simply insert or plug in those devices to have them detected, mounted, and displayed. However, to make the process of detecting and mounting remote NFS filesystems more automatic, you still need to use a facility such as autofs (short for automatically mounted filesystems).

The autofs facility mounts network filesystems on demand when someone tries to use the filesystems. With the autofs facility configured and turned on, you can cause any available NFS shared directories to mount on demand. To use the autofs facility, you need to have the autofs package installed. (For Fedora and RHEL, you can type **yum install autofs** or for Ubuntu or Debian **apt-get install autofs** to install the package from the network.)

20

Automounting to the /net directory

With `autofs` enabled, if you know the hostname and directory being shared by another host computer, simply change (cd) to the `autofs` mount directory (/net or /var/autofs by default). This causes the shared resource to be automatically mounted and made accessible to you.

The following steps explain how to turn on the `autofs` facility in Fedora or RHEL:

1. **In Fedora or RHEL, as root user from a Terminal window, open the** /etc/auto. master **file and look for the following line:**

   ```
   /net    -hosts
   ```

   This causes the /net directory to act as the mount point for the NFS shared directories you want to access on the network. (If there is a comment character at the beginning of that line, remove it.)

2. **To start the** `autofs` **service in Fedora or RHEL 7, type the following as root user:**

   ```
   # systemctl start autofs.service
   ```

3. **On a Fedora or RHEL 7 system, set up the** `autofs` **service to restart every time you boot your system:**

   ```
   # systemctl enable autofs
   ```

Believe it or not, that's all you have to do. If you have a network connection to the NFS servers from which you want to share directories, try to access a shared NFS directory. For example, if you know that the /usr/local/share directory is being shared from the computer on your network named shuttle, you can do the following:

```
$ cd /net/shuttle/
```

If that computer has any shared directories that are available to you, you can successfully change to that directory.

You also can type the following:

```
$ ls
usr
```

You should be able to see that the usr directory is part of the path to a shared directory. If there were shared directories from other top-level directories (such as /var or /tmp), you would see those as well. Of course, seeing any of those directories depends on how security is set up on the server.

Try going straight to the shared directory as well. For example:

```
$ cd /net/shuttle/usr/local/share
$ ls
info man music television
```

At this point, the ls should reveal the contents of the /usr/local/share directory on the computer named shuttle. What you can do with that content depends on how it was configured for sharing by the server.

This can be a bit disconcerting because you don't see any files or directories until you actually try to use them, such as changing to a network-mounted directory. The ls command, for example, doesn't show anything under a network-mounted directory until the directory is mounted, which may lead to a sometimes-it's-there-and-sometimes-it's-not impression. Just change to a network-mounted directory, or access a file on such a directory, and autofs takes care of the rest.

In the example shown, the hostname shuttle is used. However, you can use any name or IP address that identifies the location of the NFS server computer. For example, instead of shuttle, you might have used shuttle.example.com or an IP address such as 192.168.0.122.

Automounting home directories

Instead of just mounting an NFS filesystem under the /net directory, you might want to configure autofs to mount a specific NFS directory in a specific location. For example, you could configure a user's home directory from a centralized server that could be automounted from a different machine when a user logs in. Likewise, you could use a central authentication mechanism, such as LDAP (as described in Chapter 11, "Managing User Accounts"), to offer centralized user accounts as well.

The following procedure illustrates how to set up a user account on an NFS server and share the home directory of a user named joe from that server so it can be automounted when joe logs into a different computer. In this example, instead of using a central authentication server, matching accounts are created on each system.

1. **On the NFS server (mynfs.example.com) that provides a centralized user home directory for the user named joe, create a user account for joe with a home directory of /home/shared/joe as its name.** Also find joe's user ID number from the /etc/passwd file (third field) so you can match it when you set up a user account for joe on another system.

   ```
   # mkdir /home/shared
   # useradd -c "Joe Smith" -d /home/shared/joe joe
   # grep joe /etc/passwd
   joe:x:507:507:Joe Smith:/home/shared/joe:/bin/bash
   ```

2. **On the NFS server, export the /home/shared/ directory to any system on your local network (I use 192.168.0.* here), so you can share the home directory for joe and any other users you create, by adding this line to the /etc/exports file:**

   ```
   # /etc/exports file to share directories under /home/shared
   # only to other systems on the 192.168.0.0/24 network:
   /home/shared 192.168.0.*(rw,insecure)
   ```

20

> **NOTE**
>
> In the exports file example above, the insecure option allows clients to use ports above port 1024 to make mount requests. Some NFS clients require this, because they do not have access to NFS-reserved ports.

3. **On the NFS server, restart the `nfs-server` service or, if it is already running, you can simply export the shared directory as follows:**

   ```
   # exportfs -a -r -v
   ```

4. **On the NFS server, make sure the appropriate ports are open on the firewall.** See the section "Securing Your NFS Server" for details.

5. **On the NFS client system, add an entry to the `/etc/auto.master` file that identifies the mount point where you want the remote NFS directory to be mounted and a file (of your choosing) where you will identify the location of the remote NFS directory.** I added this entry to the `auto.master` file:

   ```
   /home/remote /etc/auto.joe
   ```

6. **On the NFS client system, add an entry to the file you just noted (`/etc/auto.joe` is what we used) that contains an entry like the following:**

   ```
   joe        -rw      mynfs.example.com:/home/shared/joe
   ```

7. **On the NFS client system, restart the autofs service:**

   ```
   # systemctl restart autofs.service
   ```

8. **On the NFS client system, create a user named `joe` using the `useradd` command.** For that command line, you need to get the UID for `joe` on the server (507 in this example), so that `joe` on the client system owns the files from `joe`'s NFS home directory. When you run the following command, the `joe` user account is created, but you see an error message stating that the home directory already exists (which is correct):

   ```
   # useradd -u 507 -c "Joe Smith" -d /home/remote/joe joe
   # passwd joe
   Changing password for user joe.
   New password: ********
   Retype new password: ********
   ```

9. **On the NFS client system, log in as `joe`.** If everything is working properly, when `joe` logs in and tries to access his home directory (`/home/remote/joe`), the directory `/home/share/joe` should be mounted from the `mynfs.example.com` server. The NFS directory was both shared and mounted as read/write with ownership to UID 507 (`joe` on both systems), so the user `joe` on the local system should be able to add, delete, change, and view files in that directory.

After `joe` logs off (actually, when he stops accessing the directory) for a timeout period (10 minutes, by default), the directory is unmounted.

Unmounting NFS filesystems

After an NFS filesystem is mounted, unmounting it is simple. You use the `umount` command with either the local mount point or the remote filesystem name. For example, here are two ways you could unmount `maple:/stuff` from the local directory `/mnt/maple`:

```
# umount maple:/stuff
# umount /mnt/maple
```

Either form works. If `maple:/stuff` is mounted automatically (from a listing in `/etc/fstab`), the directory is remounted the next time you boot Linux. If it was a temporary mount (or listed as `noauto` in `/etc/fstab`), it isn't remounted at boot time.

> **TIP**
>
> The command is `umount`, not unmount. This is easy to get wrong.

If you get the message `device is busy` when you try to unmount a filesystem, it means the unmount failed because the filesystem is being accessed. Most likely, one of the directories in the NFS filesystem is the current directory for your shell (or the shell of someone else on your system). The other possibility is that a command is holding a file open in the NFS filesystem (such as a text editor). Check your Terminal windows and other shells, and then `cd` out of the directory if you are in it, or just close the Terminal windows.

If an NFS filesystem doesn't unmount, you can force it (`umount -f /mnt/maple`) or unmount and clean up later (`umount -l /mnt/maple`). The `-l` option is usually the better choice because a forced unmount can disrupt a file modification that is in progress. Another alternative is to run `fuser -v` *mountpoint* to see what users are holding your mounted NFS share open, and then `fuser -k` *mountpoint* to kill all those processes.

Summary

Network File System (NFS) is one of the oldest computer file sharing products in existence today. It is still the most popular for sharing directories of files between UNIX and Linux systems. NFS allows servers to designate specific directories to make available to designated hosts and then allows client systems to connect to those directories by mounting them locally.

NFS can be secured using firewall (`iptables`) rules, TCP wrappers (to allow and deny host access), and SELinux (to confine how file sharing protocols can share NFS resources). Although NFS was inherently insecure when it was created (data is shared unencrypted and user access is fairly open), new features in NFS version 4 have helped improve the overall security of NFS.

20

This NFS chapter is the last of the book's server chapters. Chapter 21 covers a wide range of desktop and server topics as it helps you understand techniques for troubleshooting your Linux system.

Exercises

Exercises in this section take you through tasks related to configuring and using an NFS server in Linux. If possible, have two Linux systems available that are connected on a local network. One of those Linux systems will act as an NFS server while the other will be an NFS client.

To get the most from these exercises, I recommend that you don't use a Linux server that has NFS already up and running. You can't do all the exercises here without disrupting an NFS service that is already running and sharing resources.

See Appendix B for suggested solutions.

1. On the Linux system you want to use as an NFS server, install the packages needed to configure an NFS service.
2. On the NFS server, list the documentation files that come in the package that provides the NFS server software.
3. On the NFS server, determine the name of the NFS service and start it.
4. On the NFS server, check the status of the NFS service you just started.
5. On the NFS server, create the /var/mystuff directory and share it from your NFS server with the following attributes: available to everyone, read-only, and the root user on the client has root access to the share.
6. On the NFS server, make sure the share you created is accessible to all hosts by opening TCP wrappers, iptables, and SELinux.
7. On a second Linux system (NFS client), view the shares available from the NFS server. (If you don't have a second system, you can do this from the same system.) If you do not see the shared NFS directory, go back to the previous question and try again.
8. On the NFS client, create a directory called /var/remote and temporarily mount the /var/mystuff directory from the NFS server on that mount point.
9. On the NFS client, unmount /var/remote, add an entry so that the same mount is done automatically when you reboot (with a bg mount option), and test that the entry you created is working properly.
10. From the NFS server, copy some files to the /var/mystuff directory. From the NFS client, make sure you can see the files just added to that directory and make sure you can't write files to that directory from the client.

Troubleshooting Linux

I n any complex operating system, lots of things can go wrong. You can fail to save a file because you are out of disk space. An application can crash because the system is out of memory. The system can fail to boot up properly for, well, lots of different reasons.

In Linux, the dedication to openness and the focus on making the software run with maximum efficiency has led to an amazing number of tools you can use to troubleshoot every imaginable problem. In fact, if software isn't working as you would like, you even have the ultimate opportunity to rewrite the code yourself (although we don't cover how to do that here).

This chapter takes on some of the most common problems you can run into on a Linux system and describes the tools and procedures you can use to overcome those problems. Topics are broken down by areas of troubleshooting, such as the boot process, software packages, networking, memory issues, and rescue mode.

Boot-Up Troubleshooting

Before you can begin troubleshooting a running Linux system itself, that system needs to boot up. For a Linux system to boot up, a series of things has to happen. A Linux system installed directly on a PC architecture computer goes through the following steps to boot up:

- Turning on the power
- Starting the hardware (from BIOS or UEFI firmware)

- Finding the location of the boot loader and starting it
- Choosing an operating system from the boot loader
- Starting the kernel and initial RAM disk for the selected operating system
- Starting the initialization process (init or systemd)
- Starting all the services associated with the selected level of activity (runlevel or default target)

The exact activities that occur at each of these points have undergone a transformation in recent years. Boot loaders are changing to accommodate new kinds of hardware. The initialization process is changing so services can start more efficiently, based on dependencies and in reaction to the state of the system (such as what hardware is plugged in or what files exist) rather than a static boot order.

Troubleshooting the Linux boot process begins when you turn on your computer and ends when all the services are up and running. At that point, typically a graphical or text-based login prompt is available from the console, ready for you to log in.

After reading the short descriptions of startup methods, go to "Starting from the firmware" to understand what happens at each stage of the boot process and where you might need to troubleshoot. Because the general structure of the Linux boot process is the same for the three Linux systems featured here (Fedora, RHEL, and Ubuntu), I go through the boot process only once, but I describe the differences between them as I go.

Understanding Startup Methods

It's up to the individual Linux distribution how the services associated with the running Linux system are started. After the boot loader starts the kernel, how the rest of the activities (mounting filesystems, setting kernel options, running services, and so on) are done is all managed by the initialization process.

As I describe the boot process, I focus on two different types of initialization: System V init and systemd. I also briefly mention a third type called Upstart, which has been deployed until recently on Debian and Ubuntu distribution, but is now being replaced with systemd. (Ubuntu 14.04, LTS used in this book still uses Upstart by default.)

Starting with System V init scripts

The System V init facility consists of the init process (the first process to run after the kernel itself), an /etc/inittab file that directs all start-up activities, and a set of shell scripts that starts each of the individual services. The first Fedora releases and up to RHEL 5 used the System V init process. RHEL 6 contains a sort of hybrid of System V init, with the init process itself replaced by the Upstart init process.

System V init was developed for UNIX System V at AT&T in the mid-1980s when UNIX systems first incorporated the start-up of network interfaces and the services connected to them.

It has been supplanted only over the past few years by Upstart and systemd to better suit the demands of modern operating systems.

In System V init, sets of services are assigned to what is referred to as *runlevels*. For example, the multi-user runlevel can start basic system services, network interfaces, and network services. Single-user mode just starts enough of the basic Linux system so someone can log in from the system console, without starting network interfaces or services. After a System V init system is up and running, you can use commands such as reboot, shutdown, and init to change runlevels. You can use commands such as service and chkconfig to start/stop individual services or enable/disable services, respectively.

The System V init scripts are set to run in a specific order, with each script having to complete before the next can start. If a service fails, there is no provision for that service to restart automatically. In contrast, systemd and Upstart were designed to address these and other System V init shortcomings.

Starting with systemd

The systemd facility is quickly becoming the present and future of the initialization process for many Linux systems. It was adopted in Fedora 15, in RHEL 7, and is scheduled to replace Upstart in Debian and Ubuntu 15.04. Although systemd is more complicated than System V init, it also offers many more features, such as these:

- **Targets**—Instead of runlevels, systemd focuses on targets. A target can start a set of services, as well as create or start other types of units (such as directory mounts, sockets, swap areas, and timers).

- **System V compatibility**—There are targets that align with System V runlevels, if you are used to dealing with runlevels. For example, graphical.target aligns with runlevel 5 while multi-user.target is essentially runlevel 3. However, there are many more targets than runlevels, giving you the opportunity to more finely manage sets of units. Likewise, systemd supports System V init scripts and commands such as chkconfig and service for manipulating those services.

- **Dependency-based start-up**—When the system starts up, any service in the default target (graphical.target for desktops and multi-user.target for most servers) that has had its dependencies met can start. This feature can speed up the boot process, by ensuring that a single stalled service doesn't stall other services from starting if they don't need the stalled service.

- **Resource usage**—With systemd, you can use cgroups to limit how much of your system's resources is consumed by a service. For example, you can limit the amount of memory, CPU, or other resources an entire service can consume, so a runaway process or a service that spins off an unreasonable number of child processes cannot consume more than the entire service is allowed.

When a systemd-enabled Linux system starts up, the first running process (PID 1) is the systemd daemon (instead of the init daemon). Later, the primary command for managing systemd services is the systemctl command. Managing systemd journal (log) messages is done with the journalctl command. You also have the ability to use old-style System V init commands, such as init, poweroff, reboot, runlevel, and shutdown to manage services.

Starting with Upstart

As noted earlier, the Debian and Ubuntu Linux distributions used the Upstart project for a while to replace the older System V init facility. Although those distributions plan to move soon to systemd, if you are using a recent Debian or Ubuntu (pre-14.10) system, chances are that Upstart is controlling the startup of your system services.

Like systemd, Upstart allowed services to start in parallel, after their particular dependencies were met. Another of Upstart's major improvements over System V init is that it can start services by reacting when certain events occur (such as when a piece of hardware is connected).

If you are using a Linux system the employs Upstart, you should know a few things about it. The first process that starts on an Upstart system is still called the init process, but it is actually an Upstart daemon. After it is running, services in an Upstart system register events with the Upstart daemon. When an event occurs, Upstart can start, stop, or change a process to react to that event.

Because Upstart is being phased out of the Linux distributions covered in this book (Fedora, RHEL, Debian, and Ubuntu), our discussion of understanding and troubleshooting the boot process is focused on the traditional System V init process and the newer systemd facility.

Starting from the firmware (BIOS or UEFI)

When you physically turn on a computer, firmware is loaded to initialize the hardware and find an operating system to boot. On PC architectures, that firmware has traditionally been referred to as BIOS (Basic Input Output System). In recent years, a new type of firmware has become available (to replace BIOS on some computers), called UEFI (Unified Extensible Firmware Interface). The two are mutually exclusive.

UEFI was designed to allow a secure boot feature, which can be used to ensure that only operating systems whose components have been signed can be used during the boot process. UEFI can still be used with nonsigned operating systems by disabling the secure boot feature.

For Ubuntu, Secure boot was first supported in 12.04.2. RHEL 7 also officially supports secure boot. The main job of BIOS and UEFI firmware is to initialize the hardware and then hand off control of the boot process to a boot loader. The boot loader then finds and starts the operating system. After an operating system is installed, typically you should let the firmware do its work and not interrupt it.

There are, however, occasions when you want to interrupt the firmware. For this discussion, we focus on how BIOS generally works. Right after you turn on the power, you should see a BIOS screen that usually includes a few words noting how to go into Setup mode and change the boot order. If you press the function key noted (often F1, F2, or F12) to choose one of those two items, here's what you can do:

- **Setup utility**—The setup utility lets you change settings in the BIOS. These settings can be used to enable or disable certain hardware components or turn on or off selected hardware features.

- **Boot order**—Computers are capable of starting an operating system, or more specifically, a boot loader that can start an operating system, from several different devices attached to the computer. Those devices can include a CD drive, DVD drive, hard disk, USB driver, or network interface card. The boot order defines the order in which those devices are checked. By modifying the boot order, you can tell the computer to temporarily ignore the default boot order and try to boot from the device you select.

For my Dell workstation, after I see the BIOS screen, I immediately press the F2 function key to go to into Setup or F12 to temporarily change the boot order. The next sections explore what you can troubleshoot from the Setup and Boot Order screens.

Troubleshooting BIOS setup

As I already noted, you can usually let the BIOS start without interruption and have the system boot up to the default boot device (probably the hard drive). However, here are some instances when you may want to go into Setup mode and change something in the BIOS:

- **To see an overview of your hardware**—If your troubleshooting problem is hardware-related, the BIOS setup is a great place to start examining your system. The Setup screen tells you the type of system, its BIOS version, its processors, its memory slots and types, whether it is 32-bit or 64-bit, which devices are in each slot, and many details about the types of devices attached to the system.

  If you can't get an operating system booted at all, the BIOS Setup screen may be the only way to determine the system model, processor type, and other information you need to search for help or call for support.

- **To disable/enable a device**—Most devices connected to your computer are enabled and made available for use by the operating system. To troubleshoot a problem, you may need to disable a device.

  For example, let's say your computer has two network interface cards (NICs). You want to use the second NIC to install Linux over a network, but the installer keeps trying to use the first NIC to connect to the network. You can disable the first NIC so the installer doesn't even see the NIC when it tries to connect to the network. Or, you can keep the NIC visible to the computer, but simply disable the NIC's ability to PXE boot.

Maybe you have an audio card and you want to disable the integrated audio on the motherboard. That can be done in the BIOS as well.

Conversely, sometimes you want to enable a device that has been disabled. Perhaps you were given a computer that had a device disabled in the BIOS. From the operating system, for example, it may look like you don't have a parallel (LPT) port or CD drive. Looking at the BIOS tells you whether those devices are not available simply because they have been disabled in the BIOS.

- **To change a device setting**—Sometimes, the default settings that come in your BIOS don't work for your situation. You might want to change the following settings in the BIOS:

  - **NIC PXE boot settings**—Most modern NICs are capable of booting from servers found on the network. If you need to do that, and you find that the NIC doesn't come up as a bootable device on your Boot Order screen, you may have to enable that feature in the BIOS.

  - **Virtualization settings**—If you want to run a RHEL system as a virtual host, the computer's CPU must include Intel Virtual Technology or AMD Secure Virtual Machine (SVM) support. It is possible, however, that even if your CPU comes with that support, it may not be enabled in the BIOS. To enable it, go to the BIOS Setup screen and look for a Virtualization selection (possibly under the Performance category). Make sure it is set to On.

Troubleshooting boot order

Depending on the hardware attached to your computer, a typical boot order might boot a CD/DVD drive first, then the hard drive, then a USB device, and finally the network interface card. The BIOS would go to each device, looking for a boot loader in the master boot record for that device. If the BIOS finds a boot loader, it starts it. If no boot loader is located, the BIOS moves on to the next device, until all are tried. If no boot loader is found, the computer fails to boot.

One problem that could occur with the boot order is that the device you want to boot may not appear in the boot order at all. In that case, going to the Setup screen, as described in the previous section, to either enable the device or change a setting to make it bootable, may be the thing to do.

If the device you want to boot from does appear in the boot order, typically you just have to move the arrow key to highlight the device you want and press Enter. The following are reasons for selecting your own device to boot:

- **Rescue mode**—If Linux does not boot from the hard disk, selecting the CD drive or a USB drive allows you to boot to a rescue mode (described later in this chapter) that can help you repair the hard disk on an unbootable system. See the section "Troubleshooting in Rescue Mode" later in this chapter for further information.

- **Fresh install**—Sometimes, the boot order has the hard disk listed first. If you decide you need to do a fresh install of the operating system, you need to select the boot device that is holding your installation medium (CD, DVD, USB drive, or NIC).

Assuming you get past any problems you have with the BIOS, the next step is for the BIOS to start the boot loader.

Troubleshooting the GRUB boot loader

Typically, the BIOS finds the master boot record on the first hard disk and begins loading that boot loader in stages. Chapter 9, "Installing Linux," describes the GRUB boot loader that is used with most modern Linux systems, including RHEL, Fedora, and Ubuntu. The GRUB boot loader in RHEL 6, described here, is an earlier version than the GRUB 2 boot loader included with RHEL 7, Fedora, and Ubuntu. (Later, I introduce you to the GRUB 2 boot loader as well.)

In this discussion, I am interested in the boot loader from the perspective of what to do if the boot loader fails or what ways you might want to interrupt the boot loader to change the behavior of the boot process.

Here are a few ways in which the boot loader might fail in RHEL 6 and some ways you can overcome those failures:

- **Could not locate active partition**—When a boot loader is installed on a storage medium, the partition is usually marked as bootable. If you see this message, it means that no bootable partition was found. If you feel sure the boot loader is on the disk, try using the `fdisk` command (probably from rescue media) to make the partition bootable and try again. See the section "Partitioning Hard Disks" of Chapter 12, "Managing Disks and Filesystems," for more information on the `fdisk` command.

- **Selected boot device not available**—You might see a message like this when the master boot record has been deleted from the hard drive. Or it may just be that the contents of the hard disk expect to be loaded from another boot loader, such as a boot CD. First, try seeing if the system will boot from other media. If it turns out that the master boot record was erased, you can try booting rescue media to attempt to recover the contents of the disk. However, if the master boot record is lost, it is possible that other data on the disk is either also erased or would require disk forensics to find. If the master boot record was simply overwritten (which could happen if you installed another operating system on a different disk partition), it could be possible to reinstall the master boot record from rescue mode (described in the section "Troubleshooting in Rescue Mode" later in this chapter).

- **Text-based GRUB prompt appears**—It is possible for the BIOS to start GRUB and go straight to a GRUB prompt, with no operating system selections available.

This probably means that the master boot record portion of GRUB was found, but when GRUB looked on the hard drive to find the next stage of the boot process and a menu of operating systems to load, it could not find them. Sometimes this happens when the BIOS detects the disks in the wrong order and looks for the grub.conf file on the wrong partition.

One workaround to this problem, assuming grub.conf is on the first partition of the first disk, is to list the contents of this file and enter the root, kernel, and initrd lines manually. To list the file, type cat (hd0,0)/grub/grub.conf. If that doesn't work, try hd0,1 to access the next partition on that disk (and so on) or hd1,0 to try the first partition of the next disk (and so on). When you find the lines representing the grub.conf file, manually type the root, kernel, and initrd lines for the entry you want (replacing the location of the hard drive you found on the root line). Then type **boot**. The system should start up, and you can go and manually fix your boot loader files. See Chapter 9 for more information on the GRUB boot loader.

If the BIOS finds the boot loader in the master boot record of the disk and that boot loader finds the GRUB configuration files on the disk, the boot loader starts a countdown of about three to five seconds. During that countdown, you can interrupt the boot loader (before it boots the default operating system) by pressing any key.

When you interrupt the boot loader, you should see a menu of available entries to boot. Those entries can represent different available kernels to boot. But they may also represent totally different operating systems (such as Windows, BSD, or Ubuntu).

Here are some reasons to interrupt the boot process from the boot menu to troubleshoot Linux:

- **To start in a different runlevel**—RHEL 6 systems typically start in runlevel 3 (boot to text prompt) or 5 (boot to graphical interface). You can override the default runlevel by putting a different runlevel number at the end of the kernel line from the boot menu. To do this, highlight the operating system entry you want, type **e**, highlight the kernel, type **e**, and add the new runlevel to the end of the line (for example, add a space and the number 1 to go into single-user mode). Then press Enter, and type **b** to boot the new entry.

  Why would you boot to different runlevels for troubleshooting? Runlevel 1 bypasses authentication, so you boot directly to a root prompt. This is good if you have forgotten the root password and need to change it (type **passwd** to do that). Runlevel 3 bypasses the start of your desktop interface. Go to runlevel 3 if you are having problems with your video driver and want to try to debug it without it trying to automatically start up the graphical interface.

- **To select a different kernel**—When RHEL installs a new kernel via yum, it always keeps at least one older kernel around. If the new kernel fails, you can always boot the previous, presumably working, older kernel. To boot a different kernel from the

GRUB menu, just use the arrow key to highlight the one you want, and press Enter to boot it.

- **To select a different operating system**—If you happen to have another operating system installed on your hard drive, you can select to boot that one instead of RHEL. For example, if you have Fedora and RHEL on the same computer, and RHEL isn't working, you can boot to Fedora, mount the RHEL filesystems you need, and try to fix the problem.

- **To change boot options**—On the kernel line, notice that there are lots of options being passed to the kernel. At the very least, those options must contain the name of the kernel (such as vmlinuz-2.6.32.el6.x86_64) and the partition containing the root filesystem (such as /dev/mapper/abc-root). If you want, you can add other options to the kernel line.

  You may want to add kernel options to add features to the kernel or temporarily disable hardware support for a particular component. For example, adding init=/bin/bash causes the system to bypass the init process and go straight to a shell (similar to running init 1). In RHEL 7, adding 1 as a kernel option is not supported, so init=/bin/bash is the best way to get into a sort of single-user mode. Adding nousb would temporarily disable the USB ports (presumably to make sure anything connected to those ports would be disabled as well).

Assuming you have selected the kernel you want, the boot loader tries to run the kernel, including the content of the initial RAM disk (which contains drivers and other software needed to boot your particular hardware).

Starting the kernel

After the kernel starts, there isn't much to do except watch for potential problems. For RHEL, you see a Red Hat Enterprise Linux screen with a slow-spinning icon. If you want to watch messages detailing the boot process scroll by, press the Esc key.

At this point, the kernel tries to load the drivers and modules needed to use the hardware on the computer. The main things to look for at this point (although they may scroll by quickly) are hardware failures that may prevent some feature from working properly. Although much more rare than it used to be, there may be no driver available for a piece of hardware, or the wrong driver may get loaded and cause errors.

In addition to scrolling past on the screen, messages produced when the kernel boots are copied to the *kernel ring buffer*. As its name implies, the kernel ring buffer stores kernel messages in a buffer, throwing out older messages after that buffer is full. After the computer boots up completely, you can log into the system and type the following command to capture these kernel messages in a file (then view them with the less command):

```
# dmesg > /tmp/kernel_msg.txt
# less /tmp/kernel_msg.txt
```

I like to direct the kernel messages into a file (choose any name you like) so the messages can be examined later or sent to someone who can help debug any problems. The messages appear as components are detected, such as your CPU, memory, network cards, hard drives, and so on.

In Linux systems that support systemd, kernel messages are stored in the systemd journal. So instead of using the dmesg command, you can run journalctl to see kernel messages from boot time to the present. For example, here are kernel messages output from a RHEL 7 system:

```
# journalctl -k
Sep 07 12:03:07 host kernel: CPU0 microcode updated early to revision
    0xbc
Sep 07 12:03:07 host kernel: Initializing cgroup subsys cpuset
Sep 07 12:03:07 host kernel: Initializing cgroup subsys cpu
Sep 07 12:03:07 host kernel: Initializing cgroup subsys cpuacct
Sep 07 12:03:07 host kernel: Linux version 3.10.0-123.6.3.el7.x86_64
Sep 07 12:03:07 host kernel: Command line:
    BOOT_IMAGE=/vmlinuz-3.10.0-123.6.3.el7.x86_64 root=/dev/mapper/vg
Sep 07 12:03:07 host kernel: e820: BIOS-provided physical RAM map:
    . . .
```

Look for drivers that fail to load or messages that show that certain features of the hardware failed to be enabled. For example, I once had a TV tuner card (for watching television on my computer screen) that set the wrong tuner type for the card that was detected. Using information about the TV card's model number and the type of failure, I found that passing an option to the card's driver allowed me to try different settings until I found the one that matched my tuner card.

In describing how to view kernel startup messages, I have gotten ahead of myself a bit. Before you can log in and see the kernel messages, the kernel needs to finish bringing up the system. As soon as the kernel is done initially detecting hardware and loading drivers, it passes off control of everything else that needs to be done to boot the system to the initialization system.

Troubleshooting the initialization system

The first process to run on a system where the kernel has just started depends on the initialization facility that system is using. For System V init, the first process to run is the init process. For systemd, the first process is systemd. Depending on which you see running on your system (type ps -ef | head to check), follow either the System V or systemd descriptions below. RHEL 6, which contains a hybrid of Upstart and System V init, is used in the example of System V initialization.

Troubleshooting System V initialization

Most Linux systems up to a few years ago used System V init to initialize the services on the Linux system. In RHEL 6, when the kernel hands off control of the boot process to the init process, the init process checks the /etc/inittab file for directions on how to boot the system.

The inittab file tells the init process what the default runlevel is and then points to files in the /etc/init directory to do such things as remap some keystrokes (such as Ctrl+Alt+Delete to reboot the system), start virtual consoles, and identify the location of the script for initializing basic services on the system: /etc/rc.sysinit.

When you're troubleshooting Linux problems that occur after the init process takes over, two likely culprits are the processing by the rc.sysinit file and the runlevel scripts.

Troubleshooting rc.sysinit

As the name implies, the /etc/rc.sysinit script initializes many basic features on the system. When that file is run by init, rc.sysinit sets the system's hostname, sets up the /proc and /sys filesystems, sets up SELinux, sets kernel parameters, and performs dozens of other actions.

One of the most critical functions of rc.sysinit is to get the storage set up on the system. In fact, if the boot process fails during processing of rc.sysinit, in all likelihood, the script was unable to find, mount, or decrypt the local or remote storage devices needed for the system to run.

The following is a list of some common failures that can occur from tasks run from the rc.sysinit file and ways of dealing with those failures.

- **Local mounts fail**—If an entry in the /etc/fstab fails to mount, the boot process ends before runlevel services start. This typically happens when you add an entry to the /etc/fstab that has a mistake in it, but you neglected to test it before you rebooted. When the fstab file fails, you are dropped to a shell for the root user with the root filesystem mounted read-only. To fix the problem, you need to remount the root filesystem, correct the fstab file, mount the filesystem entry to make sure it now works, and reboot. Here's what that sequence of commands looks like:

```
# mount -o remount,rw /
# vim /etc/fstab
# mount -a
# reboot
```

> **NOTE**
>
> The vim command is used particularly when editing the /etc/fstab file because it knows the format of that file. When you use vim, the columns are in color and some error checking is done. For example, entries in the Mount Options field turn green when they are valid and black when they are not.

- **Hostname not set**—If your hostname is not set properly, you can check through the processing of `rc.sysinit` to see what might have gone wrong. To set the system's hostname, `rc.sysinit` uses the value of the `HOSTNAME=` in the `/etc/sysconfig/network` file. If that is not set, the name localhost is used instead. The hostname value can also be acquired from the DHCP server.

- **Cannot decrypt filesystem**—The `rc.sysinit` script looks in the `/etc/crypttab` file for information needed to decrypt encrypted filesystems. If that file becomes corrupted, you may need to find a backup of the file to be able to decrypt your filesystem. If you are prompted for a password and you don't know what that is, you might be out of luck.

Other features are set up by the `rc.sysinit` file as well. The `rc.sysinit` script sets the SELinux mode and loads hardware modules. The script constructs software RAID arrays and sets up Logical Volume Management volume groups and volumes. Troubles occurring in any of these areas are reflected in error messages that appear on the screen after the kernel boots and before runlevel processes start up.

Troubleshooting runlevel processes

In Red Hat Enterprise Linux 6.*x* and earlier, when the system first comes up, services are started based on the default runlevel. There are seven different runlevels, from 0 to 6. The default runlevel is typically 3 (for a server) or 5 (for a desktop). Here are descriptions of the runlevels in Linux systems up to RHEL 6:

- **0**—Shutdown runlevel. All processes are stopped and the computer is powered down.

- **1**—Single-user runlevel. Only those processes that are needed to boot the computer (including mounting all filesystems) and have the system available from the console are run. Networking and network services are not started. This runlevel bypasses normal authentication and boots up to a root user prompt (called `sulogin`). If you boot up to this mode, you can use it to immediately become root user to change a forgotten root password. (You could also use the word `single` instead of 1 to get to single-user runlevel. The difference between `single` and 1 is that `single` does not start scripts in the `/etc/rc1.d` directory.)

- **2**—Multiuser runlevel. This runlevel is rarely used today. The original meaning of this runlevel has been lost. Early UNIX systems used this runlevel to start `tty` processes for systems where there were multiple dumb terminals connected to the system for people to use. This allowed many people to access a system simultaneously from character-based terminals (lots of people working from a shell with no graphical interface). Network interfaces were not started, usually because always-up network interfaces were not common. These days, runlevel 2 usually starts network interfaces, although not all network services are started.

- **3**—Multiuser plus networking runlevel. This runlevel is typically used on Linux servers that do not boot up to a graphical interface, but rather just a plain text prompt at the console. The network is started, as are all network services. A graphical desktop environment may or may not be installed (typically not) on machines that boot to runlevel 3, but the graphical environments must be started after boot time to be used.

- **4**—Undefined. This runlevel tends to start the same services as runlevel 3. It can be used if you want to have different services available from runlevels 3 and 4. This runlevel is typically not used. Instead, runlevel 3 or 5 is used to boot to, with an administrator simply turning services on or off as required for the running system.

- **5**—Multiuser, networking, plus graphical interface runlevel. This is the runlevel typically used with desktop Linux systems. It typically starts networking and all networked services; plus, it launches a graphical login prompt at the console. When the users log in, they see a graphical desktop environment.

- **6**—Reboot runlevel. This is like runlevel 0 in that it brings down all services and stops all processes. However, runlevel 6 then starts the system back up again.

Runlevels are meant to set the level of activity on a Linux system. A default runlevel is set in the `/etc/inittab` file, but you can change the runlevel any time you like using the `init` command. For example, as root, you might type **init** 0 to shutdown, **init** 3 if you want to kill the graphical interface (from runlevel 5) but leave all other services up, or **init** 6 to reboot.

Normal default runlevels (in other words, the runlevel you boot to) are 3 (for a server) and 5 (for a desktop). Often, servers don't have desktops installed, so they boot to runlevel 3 so they don't incur the processing overhead or the added security risks for having a desktop running on their web servers or file servers.

You can go either up or down with runlevels. For example, an administrator doing maintenance on a system may boot to runlevel 1 and then type **init** 3 to boot up to the full services needed on a server. Someone debugging a desktop may boot to runlevel 5 and then go down to runlevel 3 to try to fix the desktop (such as install a new driver or change screen resolution) before typing **init** 5 to return to the desktop.

The level of services at each runlevel is determined by the runlevel scripts that are set to start. There are rc directories for each runlevel: /etc/rc0.d/, /etc/rc1.d/, /etc/rc2.d/, /etc/rc3.d/, and so on. When an application has a startup script associated with it, that script is placed in the /etc/init.d/ directory and then symbolically linked to a file in each /etc/rc?.d/ directory.

Scripts linked to each /etc/rc?.d directory begin with either the letter K or S, followed by two numbers and the service name. A script beginning with K indicates that the service should be stopped, while one beginning with an S indicates it should be started. The two numbers that follow indicate the order in which the service is started. Here are a few files you might find in the /etc/rc3.d/ directory, which are set to start up (with a description of each to the right):

- S01sysstat—Start gathering system statistics.
- S08iptables—Start iptables firewall.
- S10network—Start network interfaces.
- S12rsyslog—Start system logging.
- S28autofs—Start automounter.
- S50bluetooth—Start Bluetooth service.
- S55sshd—Start the secure shell service.
- S58ntpd—Start NTP time synchronization service.
- S85httpd—Start the Apache web service.
- S90crond—Start the crond service.
- S91smb—Start the samba service.
- S97rhnsd—Start the Red Hat Network service.
- S99local—Start user-defined local commands.

This example of a few services started from the /etc/rc3.d directory should give you a sense of the order in which processes boot up when you enter runlevel 3. Notice that the sysstat service (which gathers system statistics) and the iptables service (which creates the system's firewall) are both started before the networking interfaces are started. Those are followed by rsyslog (system logging service) and then the various networked services.

By the time the runlevel scripts start, you should already have a system that is basically up and running. Unlike some other Linux systems that start all the scripts for runlevel 1, then 2, then 3, and so on, RHEL goes right to the directory that represents the runlevel, first stopping all services that begin with K and starting all those that begin with S in that directory.

As each S script runs, you should see a message saying whether the service started. Here are some things that might go wrong during this phase of system startup:

- **A service can fail.** A service may require access to network interfaces to start properly or access to a disk partition that is not mounted. Most services time out, fail, and allow the next script to run. After you are able to log in, you can debug the service. Some techniques for debugging services include adding a debug option to the daemon process so it spews more data into a log file or running the daemon process manually so error messages come straight to your screen. See Chapter 15 for further information on starting services manually.

- **A service can hang.** Some services that don't get what they need to start can hang indefinitely, keeping you from logging in to debug the problem. Some processes take longer to come up the first time after a fresh install, so you might want to wait for a few minutes to see if the script is still working and not just spinning forever.

If you cannot get past a hanging service, you can reboot into an *interactive startup mode*, where you are prompted before starting each service. To enter interactive startup mode in RHEL, reboot and interrupt the boot loader (press any key when you see the 5 second countdown). Highlight the entry you want to boot, and type **e**. Highlight the kernel line, and type **e**. Then add the word `confirm` to the end of the kernel line, press Enter, and type **b** to boot the new kernel.

Figure 21.1 shows an example of the messages that appear when RHEL boots up in interactive startup mode.

FIGURE 21.1

Confirm each service in RHEL interactive startup mode.

```
                    Welcome to Red Hat Enterprise Linux Server
  Starting udev:                                              [  OK  ]
  Setting hostname triumph.example.com:                       [  OK  ]
  Setting up Logical Volume Management:    2 logical volume(s) in volume group "vg_
  triumph" now active
                                                              [  OK  ]
  Checking filesystems
  /dev/mapper/vg_triumph-lv_root: clean, 88953/363600 files, 656405/1452032 blocks
  /dev/sda1: clean, 38/128016 files, 49037/512000 blocks
                                                              [  OK  ]
  Remounting root filesystem in read-write mode:              [  OK  ]
  Mounting local filesystems:                                 [  OK  ]
  Enabling local filesystem quotas:                           [  OK  ]
  Enabling /etc/fstab swaps:                                  [  OK  ]
  Entering interactive startup
  Start service sysstat (Y)es/(N)o/(C)ontinue? [Y]
```

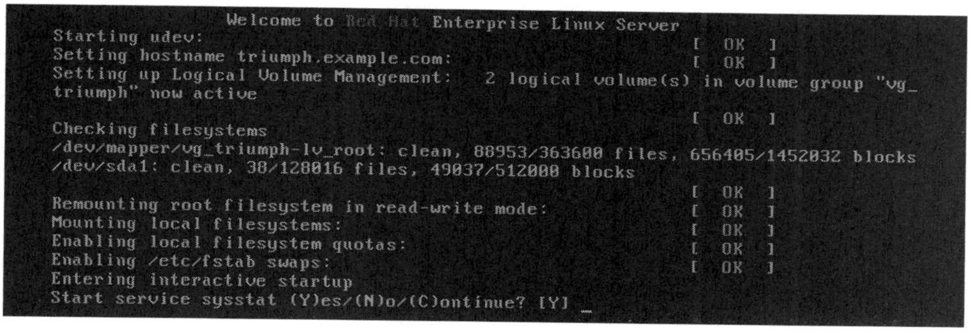

Most messages shown in Figure 21.1 are generated from `rc.sysinit`.

After the Welcome message, `udev` starts (to watch for new hardware that is attached to the system and load drivers as needed). The hostname is set, Logical Volume Management (LVM) volumes are activated, all filesystems are checked (with the added LVM volumes), any filesystems not yet mounted are mounted, the root filesystem is remounted read-write, and any LVM swaps are enabled. Refer to Chapter 12 for further information on LVM and other partition and filesystem types.

The last "Entering interactive startup" message tells you that `rc.sysinit` is finished and the services for the selected runlevel are ready to start. Because the system is in interactive mode, a message appears asking if you want to start the first service (`sysstat`). Type **Y** to start that service and go to the next one.

After you see the broken service requesting to start, type **N** to keep that service from starting. If, at some point, you feel the rest of the services are safe to start, type **C** to continue starting the rest of the services. After your system comes up, with the broken services not started, you can go back and try to debug those individual services.

One last comment about startup scripts: The /etc/rc.local file is one of the last services to run at each runlevel. As an example, in runlevel 5, it is linked to /etc/rc5.d/ S99local. Any command you want to run every time your system starts up can be put in the rc.local file.

You might use rc.local to send an e-mail message or run a quick iptables firewall rule when the system starts. In general, it's better to use an existing startup script or create a new one yourself (so you can manage the command or commands as a service). Know that the rc.local file is a quick and easy way to get some commands to run each time the system boots.

Troubleshooting systemd initialization

The latest versions of Fedora, RHEL, and soon Ubuntu use systemd instead of System V init as their initialization system. When the systemd daemon (/usr/lib/systemd/ systemd) is started after the kernel starts up, it sets in motion all the other services that are set to start up. In particular, it keys off the contents of the /etc/systemd/system/ default.target file. For example:

```
# cat /etc/systemd/system/default.target
...
[Unit]
Description=Graphical Interface
Documentation=man:systemd.special(7)
Requires=multi-user.target
After=multi-user.target
Conflicts=rescue.target
Wants=display-manager.service
AllowIsolate=yes

[Install]
Alias=default.target
```

The default.target file is actually a symbolic link to a file in the /lib/systemd/system directory. For a server, it may be linked to the multi-user.target file; for a desktop, it is linked to the graphical.target file (as is shown here).

Unlike with the System V init facility, which just runs service scripts in alphanumeric order, the systemd service needs to work backward from the default.target to determine which services and other targets are run. In this example, default.target is a symbolic link to the graphical.target file. When you list the contents of that file, you can see the following:

- The multi-user.target is required to start first.
- The display-manager.service is started after that.

By continuing to discover what those two units require, you can find what else is required. For example, `multi-user.target` requires the `basic.target` (which starts a variety of basic services) and `display-manager.service` (which starts up the display manager, gdm) to launch a graphical login screen.

To see services the `multi-user.target` starts, list contents of the `/etc/systemd/system/multi-user.target.wants` directory. For example:

```
# ls /etc/systemd/system/multi-user.target.wants/
abrt-ccpp.service        chronyd.service        nfs.target
abrtd.service            crond.service          nmb.service
abrt-oops.service        cups.path              remote-fs.target
abrt-vmcore.service      httpd.service          rngd.service
abrt-xorg.service        irqbalance.service     smb.service
atd.service              mcelog.service         sshd.service
auditd.service           mdmonitor.service      vmtoolsd.service
autofs.service           ModemManager.service   vsftpd.service
avahi-daemon.service     NetworkManager.service
```

These files are symbolic links to files that define what starts for each of those services. On your system, these may include remote shell (sshd), printing (cups), auditing (auditd), networking (NetworkManager), and others. Those links were added to that directory either when the package for a service is installed or when the service is enabled from a `systemctl enable` command.

Keep in mind that, unlike System V init, systemd can start, stop, and otherwise manage unit files that represent more than just services. It can manage devices, automounts, paths, sockets, and other things. After systemd has started everything, you can log into the system to investigate and troubleshoot any potential problems.

After you log in, running the `systemctl` command lets you see every unit file that systemd tried to start up. Here is an example:

```
# systemctl
UNIT                                             LOAD    ACTIVE SUB
      DESCRIPTION
proc-sys-fs-binfmt_misc.automount                loaded active waiting
      Arbitrary Executable File Formats File System
sys-devices-pc...:00:1b.0-sound-card0.device loaded active plugged
      631xESB/632xESB High Definition Audio Control
sys-devices-pc...:00:1d.2-usb4-4\x2d2.device loaded active plugged
      DeskJet 5550
...
-.mount                                          loaded active mounted
   /
boot.mount                                       loaded active mounted
   /boot
```

```
...
autofs.service                                loaded active running
     Automounts filesystems on demand
cups.service                                  loaded active running
     CUPS Printing Service
httpd.service                                 loaded failed failed
     The Apache HTTP Server
```

From the `systemctl` output, you can see whether any unit file failed. In this case, you can see that the `httpd.service` (your Web server) failed to start. To further investigate, you can run `journalctl -u` for that service to see whether any error messages were reported:

```
# journalctl -u httpd.service
...
Sep 07 18:40:52 host systemd[1]: Starting The Apache HTTP Server...
Sep 07 18:40:53 host httpd[16365]: httpd: Syntax error on line 361 of
     /etc/httpd/conf/httpd.conf: Expected </Director> but saw
   </Directory>
Sep 07 18:40:53 host systemd[1]: httpd.service:
     main process exited, code=exited, status=1/FAILURE
Sep 07 18:40:53 host systemd[1]: Failed to start The Apache HTTP
     Server.
Sep 07 18:40:53 host systemd[1]: Unit httpd.service entered failed
     state.
```

From the output, you can see that there was a mismatch of the directives in the `httpd.conf` file (I had Director instead of Directory). After that was corrected, I could start the service (`systemctl start httpd`). If more unit files appear as failed, you can run the `journalctl -u` command again, using those unit filenames as arguments.

The next section describes how to troubleshoot issues that can arise with your software packages.

Troubleshooting Software Packages

Software packaging facilities (such as `yum` for RPM and `apt-get` for DEB packages) are designed to make it easier for you to manage your system software. (See Chapter 10, "Getting and Managing Software," for the basics on how to manage software packages.) Despite efforts to make it all work, however, sometimes software packaging can break.

The following sections describe some common problems you can encounter with RPM packages on a RHEL or Fedora system and how you can overcome those problems.

Sometimes, when you try to install or upgrade a package using the `yum` command, error messages tell you that the dependent packages you need to do the installation you want are not available. This can happen on a small scale (when you try to install one package) or a grand scale (where you are trying to update or upgrade your entire system).

Because of the short release cycles and larger repositories of Fedora and Ubuntu, inconsistencies in package dependencies are more likely to occur than they are in smaller, more stable repositories (such as those offered by Red Hat Enterprise Linux). To avoid dependency failures, here are a few good practices you can follow:

- **Use recent, well-tested repositories.** There are thousands of software packages in Fedora. If you use the main Fedora repositories to install software from the current release, it is rare to have dependency problems.

  When packages are added to the repository, as long as the repository maintainers run the right commands to set up the repository (and you don't use outside repositories), everything you need to install a selected package should be available. However, when you start using third-party repositories, those repositories may have dependencies on repositories that they can't control. For example, if a repository creates a new version of its own software that requires later versions of basic software (such as libraries), the versions they need might not be available from the Fedora repository.

- **Consistently update your system.** Running `yum update` every night makes it less likely that you will encounter major dependency problems than if you update your system only every few months. In Fedora, there is a `yum-updatesd` package that lets you do nightly checks for updates and then send e-mail to a user of your choice if updates are available. In RHEL, you could build a `cron` job to check for or run nightly updates. See the sidebar "Using cron for Software Updates" for details on how to do that.

- **Occasionally upgrade your system.** Fedora and Ubuntu have new releases every six months. Fedora stops supplying updated packages for each version 13 months after it is released. So, although you don't have to upgrade to the new release every six months, you should upgrade once per year or face possible dependency and security problems when Fedora stops supplying updates. If you are looking for a stable system, Red Hat Enterprise Linux is a better bet because it provides updates for each major release for seven years or more.

> **NOTE**
>
> If you use the `apt-get` command in Ubuntu to update your packages, keep in mind that there are different meanings to the `update` and `upgrade` options in Ubuntu with `apt-get` than with the `yum` command (Fedora and RHEL).
>
> In Ubuntu, `apt-get update` causes the latest packaging metadata (package names, version numbers, and so on) to be downloaded to the local system. Running `apt-get upgrade` causes the system to upgrade any installed packages that have new versions available, based on the latest downloaded metadata.
>
> In contrast, every time you run a `yum` command in Fedora or RHEL, the latest metadata about new packages is downloaded. When you then run `yum update`, you get the latest packages available for the current release of Fedora or RHEL. When you run `yum upgrade`, the system actually attempts to upgrade to a whole new version of those distributions (such as Fedora 20 to Fedora 21).

When you encounter a dependency problem, here are a few things you can do to try to resolve the problem:

- **Use stable repositories.** For recent releases of well-known distributions (RHEL, Fedora, or Ubuntu, for example), dependency problems are rare and often fixed quickly. However, if you are relying on repositories for older releases or development-oriented repositories (such as Fedora's Rawhide repository), expect to find more dependency problems. Reinstalling or upgrading can often fix dependency problems.

- **Only use third-party apps and repositories when necessary.** The further you are from the core of a Linux distribution, the more likely you are to someday have dependency problems. Always look in the main repositories for your distribution before you look elsewhere for a package or try to build one yourself.

  Even if it works when you first install it, a package someone just handed to you might not have a way to be upgraded. A package from a third-party repository may break if the creators don't provide a new version when dependent packages change.

- **Solve kernel-related dependencies.** If you get third-party RPM packages for such things as video cards or wireless network cards that contain kernel drivers and you install a later kernel, those drivers no longer work. The result might be that the graphical login screen doesn't start when the system boots or your network card fails to load, so you have no wireless networking.

  Because most Linux systems keep the two most recent kernels, you can reboot, interrupt GRUB, and select the previous (still working) kernel to boot from. That gets your system up and running, with the old kernel and working drivers, while you look for a more permanent fix.

  The longer-term solution is to get a new driver that has been rebuilt for your current kernel. Sites such as rpmfusion.org build third-party, non–open source driver packages and upgrade those drivers when a new kernel is available. With the rpmfusion.org repository enabled, your system should pick up the new drivers when the new kernel is added.

  As an alternative to sites such as rpmfusion.org, you can go straight to the website for the manufacturer and try to download their Linux drivers (Nvidia offers Linux drivers for its video cards), or if source code is available for the driver, you can try to build it yourself.

- **Exclude some packages from update.** If you are updating lots of packages at once, you can exclude the packages that fail to get the others to work as you pursue the problem with the broken ones. Here's how to update all packages needing upgrade, except for a package named *somepackage* (replace *somepackage* with the name of the package you want to exclude):

```
# yum -y --exclude=somepackage update
```

- **Try preupgrade for upgrades.** If you are upgrading Fedora from one version to another (for example, Fedora 20 to Fedora 21), you can use the `preupgrade` tool instead of just typing `yum upgrade`. The advantage of running `preupgrade` first is that it checks dependencies and downloads all needed packages before committing your system to the upgrade so you don't end up with a half upgraded system. You can also keep using your system during this process.

  If you do have dependency problems during `preupgrade`, you can work them out before the upgrade actually takes place. Removing packages that have dependency problems is one way to deal with the problem (*yum remove somepackage*). After the upgrade is done, you can often add the package back in, using a version of the package that may be more consistent with the new repositories you are using.

Using cron for Software Updates

The cron facility provides a means of running commands at predetermined times and intervals. You can set the exact minute, hour, day, or month that a command runs. You can configure a command to run every five minutes, every third hour, or at a particular time on Friday afternoon.

If you want to use `cron` to set up nightly software updates, you can do that as the root user by running the `crontab -e` command. That opens a file using your default editor (`vi` command by default) that you can configure as a crontab file. Here's an example of what the `crontab` file you create might look like:

```
#  min  hour  day/month  month  day/week  command
   59   23    *          *      *         yum -y update | mail root@localhost
```

A crontab file consists of five fields, designating day and time, and a sixth field, containing the command line to run. I added the comment line to indicate the fields. Here, the `yum -y update` command is run, with its output mailed to the user root@localhost. The command is run at 59 minutes after hour 23 (11:59 p.m.). The asterisks (*) are required as placeholders, instructing `cron` to run the command on every day of the month, month, and day of the week.

When you create a `cron` entry, make sure you either direct the output to a file or pipe the output to a command that can deal with the output. If you don't, any output is sent to the user that ran the `crontab -e` command (in this case, root).

In a `crontab` file, you can have a range of numbers, a list of numbers, or skip numbers. For example, 1, 5, or 17 in the first field causes the command to be run 1, 5, and 17 minutes after the hour. An `*/3` in the second field causes the command to run every three hours (midnight, 3 a.m., 6 a.m., and so on). A 1-3 in the fourth field tells `cron` to run the command in January, February, and March. Days of the week and months can be entered as numbers or words.

For more information on the format of a `crontab` file, type **man 5 crontab**. To read about the `crontab` command, type **man 1 crontab**.

Fixing RPM databases and cache

Information about all the RPM packages on your system is stored in your local RPM database. Although it happens much less often than it did with earlier releases of Fedora and RHEL, it is possible for the RPM database to become corrupted. This stops you from installing, removing, or listing RPM packages.

If you find that your rpm and yum commands are hanging or failing and returning an *rpmdb open fails* message, you can try rebuilding the RPM database. To verify that there is a problem in your RPM database, you can run the yum check command. Here is an example of what the output of that command looks like with a corrupted database:

```
# yum check
error: db4 error(11) from dbenv->open: Resource temporarily
    unavailable
error: cannot open Packages index using db4 - Resource temporarily
    unavailable (11)
error cannot open Packages database in /var/lib/rpm
CRITICAL:yum.main:
Error: rpmdb open fails
```

The RPM database and other information about your installed RPM packages are stored in the /var/lib/rpm directory. You can remove the database files that begin with __db* and rebuild them from the metadata stored in other files in that directory.

Before you start, it's a good idea to back up the /var/lib/rpm directory. Then you need to remove the old __db* files and rebuild them. Type the following commands to do that:

```
# cp -r /var/lib/rpm /tmp
# cd /var/lib/rpm
# rm __db*
# rpm --rebuilddb
```

New __db* files should appear after a few seconds in that directory. Try a simple rpm or yum command to make sure the databases are now in order.

Just as RPM has databases of locally installed packages, the Yum facility stores information associated with Yum repositories in the local /var/cache/yum directory. Cached data includes metadata, headers, packages, and yum plug-in data.

If there is ever a problem with the data cached by yum, you can clean it out. The next time you run a yum command, necessary data is downloaded again. Here are some reasons for cleaning out your yum cache:

- **Metadata is obsolete.** The first time you connect to a Yum repository (by downloading a package or querying the repository), metadata is downloaded to your system. The metadata consists of information on all the available packages from the repository.

As packages are added and removed from the repository, the metadata has to be updated, or your system will be working from old packaging information. By default, if you run a yum command, yum checks for new metadata if the old metadata is more than 90 minutes old (or by however many minutes metadata_expire= is set to in the /etc/yum.conf file).

If you suspect the metadata is obsolete but the expire time has not been reached, you can run yum clean metadata to remove all metadata, forcing new metadata to be uploaded with the next upload. Alternatively, you could run yum makecache to get metadata from all repositories up to date.

- **You are running out of disk space.** Normally, yum might cache as much as a few hundred megabytes of data in /var/cache/yum directories. However, depending on the settings in your /etc/yum.conf file (such as keepcache=1, which keeps all downloaded RPMs, even after they are installed), the cache directories can contain multiple gigabytes of data.

  To clean out all packages, metadata, headers, and other data stored in the /var/cache/yum directory, type the following:

  ```
  # yum clean all
  ```

At this point, your system gets up-to-date information from repositories the next time a yum command is run.

The next section covers information about network troubleshooting.

Troubleshooting Networking

With more and more of the information, images, video, and other content we use every day now available outside our local computers, a working network connection is required on almost every computer system. So, if you drop your network connection or can't reach the systems you want to communicate with, it's good to know that there are many tools in Linux for looking at the problem.

For client computers (laptops, desktops, and handheld devices), you want to connect to the network to reach other computer systems. On a server, you want your clients to be able to reach you. The following sections describe different tools for troubleshooting network connectivity for Linux client and server systems.

Troubleshooting outgoing connections

You open your web browser, but are unable to get to any website. You suspect that you are not connected to the network. Maybe the problem is with name resolution, but it may be with the connection outside your local network.

To check whether your outgoing network connections are working, you can use many of the commands described in Chapter 14, "Administering Networking." You can test connectivity using a simple ping command. To see if name-to-address resolution is working, use host and dig.

The following sections cover problems you can encounter with network connectivity for outgoing connections and what tools to use to uncover the problems.

View network interfaces

To see the status of your network interfaces, use the ip command. The following output shows that the loopback interface (lo) is up (so you can run network commands on your local system), but eth0 (your first wired network card) is down (state DOWN). If the interface had been up, an inet line would show the IP address of the interface. Here, only the loopback interface has an inet address (127.0.0.1).

```
# ip addr show
1: lo: <LOOPBACK,UP,LOWER_UP> mtu 16436 qdisc noqueue state UNKNOWN
     link/loopback 00:00:00:00:00:00 brd 00:00:00:00:00:00
     inet 127.0.0.1/8 scope host lo
     inet6 ::1/128 scope host
        valid_lft forever preferred_lft forever
2: eth0: <NO-CARRIER,BROADCAST,MULTICAST,UP> mtu 1500 state DOWN
        qlen 1000
     link/ether f0:de:f1:28:46:d9 brd ff:ff:ff:ff:ff:ff
```

In RHEL 7 and Fedora, by default, network interfaces are now named based on how they are connected to the physical hardware. For example, in RHEL 7, you might see a network interface of enp11s0. That would indicate that the NIC is a wired Ethernet card (en) on PCI board 11 (p11) and slot 0 (s0). A wireless card would start with wl instead of en. The intention is to make the NIC names more predictable, because when the system is rebooted, it is not guaranteed which interfaces would be named eth0, eth1, and so on by the operating system.

Check physical connections

For a wired connection, make sure your computer is plugged into the port on your network switch. If you have multiple NICs, make sure the cable is plugged into the correct one. If you know the name of a network interface (eth0, p4p1, or other), to find which NIC is associated with the interface, type ethtool -p eth0 from the command line and look behind your computer to see which NIC is blinking (Ctrl+C stops the blinking). Plug the cable into the correct port.

If, instead of seeing an interface that is down, the ip command shows no interface at all, check that the hardware isn't disabled. For a wired NIC, the card may not be fully seated in its slot or the NIC may have been disabled in the BIOS.

On a wireless connection, you may click the NetworkManager icon and not see an available wireless interface. Again, it could be disabled in the BIOS. However, on a laptop, check to see if there is a tiny switch that disables the NIC. I've seen several people shred their networking configurations only to find that this tiny switch on the front or side of their laptops had been switched to the off position.

Check routes

If your network interface is up, but you still can't reach the host you want to reach, try checking the route to that host. Start by checking your default route. Then try to reach the local network's gateway device to the next network. Finally, try to ping a system somewhere on the Internet:

```
# route
route
Kernel IP routing table
Destination  Gateway       Genmask        Flags Metric  Ref   Use Iface
192.168.0.0  *             255.255.255.0  U     2       0       0 eth0
default      192.168.0.1   0.0.0.0        UG    0               0 eth0
```

The default line shows that the default gateway (UG) is at address 192.168.0.1 and that the address can be reached over the eth0 card. Because there is only the eth0 interface here and only a route to the 192.168.0.0 network is shown, all communication not addressed to a host on the 192.168.0.0/24 network is sent through the default gateway (192.168.0.1). The default gateway is more properly referred to as a router.

To make sure you can reach your router, try to ping it. For example:

```
# ping -c 2 192.168.0.1
PING 192.168.0.1 (192.168.0.1) 56(84) bytes of data.
From 192.168.0.105 icmp_seq=1 Destination Host Unreachable
From 192.168.0.105 icmp_seq=2 Destination Host Unreachable
--- 192.168.0.1 ping statistics ---

2 packets transmitted, 0 received, +2 errors, 100% packet loss
```

The "Destination Host Unreachable" message tells you that the router is either turned off or not physically connected to you (maybe the router isn't connected to the switch you share). If the ping succeeds and you can reach the router, the next step is to try an address beyond your router.

Try to ping a widely accessible IP address. For example, the IP address for the Google public DNS server is 8.8.8.8. Try to ping that (ping -c2 8.8.8.8). If that ping succeeds, your network is probably fine, and it is most likely your hostname-to-address resolution that is not working properly.

If you can reach a remote system, but the connection is very slow, you can use the traceroute command to follow the route to the remote host. For example, this command shows each hop taken en route to http://www.google.com:

```
# traceroute www.google.com
```

The output shows the time taken to make each hop along the way to the Google site. Instead of `traceroute`, you can use the `mtr` command (`yum install mtr`) to watch the route taken to a host. With `mtr`, the route is queried continuously, so you can watch the performance of each leg of the journey over time.

Check hostname resolution

If you cannot reach remote hosts by name, but you can reach them by pinging IP addresses, your system is having a problem with hostname resolution. Systems connected to the Internet do name-to-address resolution by communicating to a domain name system (DNS) server that can provide them with the IP addresses of the requested hosts.

The DNS server your system uses can be entered manually or picked up automatically from a DHCP server when you start your network interfaces. In either case, the names and IP addresses of one or more DNS servers end up in your `/etc/resolv.conf` file. Here is an example of that file:

```
search example.com
nameserver 192.168.0.254
nameserver 192.168.0.253
```

When you ask to connect to a hostname in Fedora or Red Hat Enterprise Linux, the `/etc/hosts` file is searched; then the first name server entry in `resolv.conf` is queried; then each subsequent name server is queried. If a hostname you ask for is not found, all those locations are checked before you get some sort of "Host Not Found" message. Here are some ways of debugging name-to-address resolution:

- **Check if DNS server can be reached.** Knowing the name server addresses, you can try to ping each name server's IP address to see if it is accessible. For example: `ping -c 2 192.168.0.254`. If the IP address can be reached, it could be that either you were assigned the wrong address for the DNS server or it is currently down.

- **Check if DNS server is working.** You specifically try to use each DNS server with the `host` or `dig` command. For example, either of these two commands can be used to see if the DNS server at `192.168.0.254` can resolve the hostname `www.google.com` into an IP address. Repeat this for each name server's IP address until you find which ones work:

  ```
  # host www.google.com 192.168.0.254
  # dig @192.168.0.254 www.google.com
  ```

- **Correct your DNS servers.** If you determine that you have the wrong IP addresses set for your DNS servers, changing them can be a bit tricky. Search `/var/log/messages` for your DNS servers' IP addresses. If NetworkManager is used to start your networking and connect to a DHCP server, you should see name server lines with the IP addresses being assigned. If the addresses are wrong, you can override them.

With NetworkManager enabled, you can't just add name server entries to the `/etc/resolv.conf` file because NetworkManager overwrites that file with its own name server entries. Instead, add a `PEERDNS=no` line to the `ifcfg` file for the network interface (for example, `ifcfg-eth0` in the `/etc/sysconfig/network-scripts` directory). Then set `DNS1=192.168.0.254` (or whatever your DNS server's IP address is). The new address is used the next time you restart your networking.

If you are using the network service, instead of NetworkManager, you can still use `PEERDNS=no` to prevent the DHCP server from overwriting your DNS addresses. However, in that case, you can edit the `resolv.conf` file directly to set your DNS server addresses.

The procedures just described for checking your outgoing network connectivity apply to any type of system, whether it is a laptop, desktop, or server. For the most part, incoming connections are not an issue with laptops or desktops because most requests are simply denied. However, for servers, the next section describes ways of making your server accessible if clients are having trouble reaching the services you provide from that server.

Troubleshooting incoming connections

If you are troubleshooting network interfaces on a server, there are different considerations than on a desktop system. Because most Linux systems are configured as servers, you should know how to troubleshoot problems encountered by those who are trying to reach your Linux servers.

I'll start with the idea of having an Apache web server (`httpd`) running on your Linux system, but no web clients can reach it. The following sections describe things you can try to see where the problem is.

Check if the client can reach your system at all

To be a public server, your system's hostname should be resolvable so any client on the Internet can reach it. That means locking down your system to a particular, public IP address and registering that address with a public DNS server. You can use a domain registrar (such as `http://www.networksolutions.com`) to do that.

When clients cannot reach your website by name from their web browsers, if the client is a Linux system, you can go through `ping`, `host`, `traceroute`, and other commands described in the previous section to track down the connectivity problem. Windows systems have their own version of `ping` that you can use from those systems.

If the name-to-address resolution is working to reach your system and you can `ping` your server from the outside, the next thing to try is the availability of the service.

Check if the service is available to the client

From a Linux client, you can check if the service you are looking for (in this case httpd) is available from the server. One way to do that is using the nmap command.

The nmap command is a favorite tool for system administrators checking for various kinds of information on networks. However, it is a favorite cracker tool as well because it can scan servers, looking for potential vulnerabilities. So it is fine to use nmap to scan your own systems to check for problems. But know that using nmap on another system is like checking the doors and windows on someone's house to see if you can get in. You look like an intruder.

Checking your own system to see what ports to your server are open to the outside world (essentially, checking what services are running) is perfectly legitimate and easy to do. After nmap is installed (yum install nmap), use your system hostname or IP address to use nmap to scan your system to see what is running on common ports:

```
# nmap 192.168.0.119
Starting Nmap 5.21 ( http://nmap.org ) at 2012-06-16 08:27 EDT
Nmap scan report for spike (192.168.0.119)
Host is up (0.0037s latency).
Not shown: 995 filtered ports
PORT     STATE  SERVICE
21/tcp   open   ftp
22/tcp   open   ssh
80/tcp   open   http
443/tcp  open   https
631/tcp  open   ipp
MAC Address: 00:1B:21:0A:E8:5E (Intel Corporate)
Nmap done: 1 IP address (1 host up) scanned in 4.77 seconds
```

The preceding output shows that TCP ports are open to the regular (http) and secure (https) web services. When you see that the state is open, it indicates that a service is listening on the port as well. If you get to this point, it means your network connection is fine and you should direct your troubleshooting efforts to how the service itself is configured (for example, you might look in /etc/httpd/conf/httpd.conf to see if specific hosts are allowed or denied access).

If TCP ports 80 and/or 443 are not shown, it means they are being filtered. You need to check whether your firewall is *blocking* (not accepting packets to) those ports. If the port is not filtered, but the state is closed, it means that the httpd service either isn't running or isn't listening on those ports. The next step is to log into the server and check those issues.

Check the firewall on the server

From your server, you can use the iptables command to list the filter table rules that are in place. Here is an example:

```
# iptables -vnL
Chain INPUT (policy ACCEPT 0 packets, 0 bytes)
pkts bytes target prot opt in out source      destination
...
    0     0 ACCEPT tcp  --  *  *   0.0.0.0/0 0.0.0.0/0   state NEW
      tcp dpt:80
    0     0 ACCEPT tcp  --  *  *   0.0.0.0/0 0.0.0.0/0   state NEW
      tcp dpt:443
...
```

For the RHEL 7 and Fedora 20 systems where the firewalld service is enabled, you can use the Firewall configuration window to open the ports needed. With the public Zone and Services tab selected, click the check boxes for http and https to immediately open those ports for all incoming traffic.

If your system is using the basic iptables service, there should be firewall rules like the two shown in the preceding code among your other rules. If there aren't, add those rules to the /etc/sysconfig/iptables file. Here are examples of what those rules might look like:

```
-A INPUT -m state --state NEW -m tcp -p tcp --dport 80 -j ACCEPT
-A INPUT -m state --state NEW -m tcp -p tcp --dport 443 -j ACCEPT
```

With the rules added to the file, clear out all your firewall rules (systemctl stop iptables.service or service iptables stop), and then start them again (systemctl start iptables.service or service iptables start).

If the firewall is still blocking client access to the web server ports, here are a few things to check in your firewall:

- **Check rules order.** Look at rules in /etc/sysconfig/iptables, and see if a DROP or REJECT rule comes before the rules opening ports 80 and/or 443. Moving the rules to open those ports before any final DROP or REJECT lines can solve the problem.

- **Look for denied hosts.** Check whether any rules drop or reject packets from particular hosts or networks. Look for rules that include -s or --source, followed by an IP address or address range and then a -j DROP or ACCEPT. Modify the rule or add a rule prior to your rules to make an exception for the host you want to allow to access your service.

If the port is now open, but the service itself is closed, check that the service itself is running and listening on the appropriate interfaces.

Check the service on the server

If there seems to be nothing blocking client access to your server through the actual ports providing the service you want to share, it is time to check the service itself. Assuming the service is running (depending on your system, type **service httpd status** or `systemctl status httpd` to check), the next thing to check is that it is listening on the proper ports and network interfaces.

The `netstat` command is a great general-purpose tool for checking network services. The following command lists the names and process IDs (p) for all processes that are listening (l) for TCP (t) and UDP (u) services, along with the port number (n) they are listening on. The following command line filters out all lines except those associated with the `httpd` process:

```
# netstat -tupln | grep httpd
tcp    0   0 :::80          :::*         LISTEN      2567/httpd
tcp    0   0 :::443         :::*         LISTEN      2567/httpd
```

The previous example shows that the `httpd` process is listening on port 80 and 443 for all interfaces. It is possible that the `httpd` process might be listening on selected interfaces. For example, if the `httpd` process were only listening on the local interface (127.0.0.1) for HTTP requests (port 80) the entry would look as follows:

```
tcp    0   0 127.0.0.1:80 :::*          LISTEN      2567/httpd
```

For `httpd`, as well as for other network services that listen for requests on network interfaces, you can edit the service's main configuration file (in this case, /etc/httpd/conf/httpd.conf) to tell it to listen on port 80 for all addresses (`Listen 80`) or a specific address (`Listen 192.168.0.100:80`).

Troubleshooting Memory

Troubleshooting performance problems on your computer is one of the most important, although often elusive, tasks you need to complete. Maybe you have a system that was working fine, but begins to slow down to a point where it is practically unusable. Maybe applications begin to just crash for no apparent reason. Finding and fixing the problem may take some detective work.

Linux comes with many tools for watching activities on your system and figuring out what is happening. Using a variety of Linux utilities, you can do such things as find out which processes are consuming large amounts of memory or placing high demands on your processors, disks, or network bandwidth. Solutions can include:

- **Adding capacity**—Your computer may be trying to do what you ask of it, but failures might occur because you don't have enough memory, processing power, disk space, or network capacity to get reasonable performance. Even nearing the boundaries of resource exhaustion can cause performance problems. Improving your computer hardware capacity is often the easiest way of solving performance problems.
- **Tuning the system**—Linux comes with default settings that define how it internally saves data, moves data around, and protects data. System tunable parameters

can be changed if the default settings don't work well for the types of applications you have on your system.

- **Uncovering problem applications or users**—Sometimes, a system performs poorly because a user or an application is doing something wrong. Misconfigured or broken applications can hang or gobble up all the resources they can get. An inexperienced user might mistakenly start multiple instances of a program that drain system resources. As a system administrator, you want to know how to find and fix these problems.

To troubleshoot performance problems in Linux, you use some of the basic tools for watching and manipulating processes running on your system. Refer to Chapter 6, "Managing Running Processes," if you need details on commands such as `ps`, `top`, `kill`, and `killall`. In this section, I add commands such as `memstat` to dig a little deeper into what processes are doing and where things are going wrong.

The most complex area of troubleshooting in Linux relates to managing virtual memory. The next sections describe how to view and manage virtual memory.

Uncovering memory issues

Computers have ways of storing data permanently (hard disks) and temporarily (*random access memory*, or *RAM*, and *swap space*). Think of yourself as a CPU, working at a desk trying to get your work finished. You would put data that you want to keep permanently in a filing cabinet across the room (that's like hard disk storage). You would put information that you are currently using on your desk (that's like RAM memory on a computer).

Swap space is a way of extending RAM. It is really just a place to put temporary data that doesn't fit in RAM but is expected to be needed by the CPU at some point. Although swap space is on the hard disk, it is not a regular Linux filesystem in which data is stored permanently.

Compared to disk storage, random access memory has the following attributes:

- **Nearer the processor**—Like the desk being near you as you work, memory is physically near the CPU on the computer's motherboard. So any data the CPU needs, it can just grab immediately if the data is in RAM.

- **Faster**—Its proximity to the CPU and the way it is accessed (solid state versus optical) makes it much faster for the CPU to get information from RAM than it can from a hard disk. It's quicker to look at a piece of paper on your desk (a small, close space) than to walk to a row of file cabinets and start searching for what you want.

- **Less capacity**—A new computer might have a 1TB hard drive but 8GB or 16GB of RAM. Although it would make the computer run faster to put every file and every piece of data the processor may need into RAM, in most cases there just wouldn't be the room. Also, both the physical memory slots on the computer and the computer system itself (64-bit computers can address more RAM than 32-bit computers) can limit how much RAM a computer is capable of having.

- **More expensive**—Although RAM is tremendously more affordable than it was a decade or two ago, it is still much more expensive (per GB) than hard disks.

- **Temporary**—RAM holds data and metadata that the CPU is using now for the work it is doing (plus some content the Linux kernel is keeping around because it suspects a process will need it before long). When you turn off the computer, however, everything in RAM is erased. When the CPU is done with data, that data is discarded if it is no longer needed, left in RAM for possible later use, or marked to be written to disk for permanent storage if it needs to be saved.

It is important to understand the difference between temporary (RAM) and permanent (hard disk) storage, but that doesn't tell the whole story. If the demand for memory exceeds the supply of RAM, the kernel can temporarily move data out of RAM to an area called swap space.

If we revisit the desk analogy, this would be like saying, "There is no room left on my desk, yet I have to add more papers to it for the projects I'm currently working on. Instead of storing papers I'll need soon in a permanent file cabinet, I'll have one special file cabinet (like a desk drawer) to hold those papers I'm still working with, but that I'm not ready to store permanently or throw away."

Refer to Chapter 12, "Managing Disks and Filesystems," for more information on swap files and partitions and how to create them. For the moment, however, there are a few things you should know about these kinds of swap areas and when they are used:

- When data is swapped from RAM to a swap area (swapped out), you get a performance hit. Remember, writing to disk is much slower than writing to RAM.

- When data is returned from swap to RAM because it is needed again (swapped in), you get another performance hit.

- When Linux runs out of space in RAM, swapping is like being wounded in battle. It's not something you aspire to, but it's better than being killed. In other words, all your processes stay active and they don't lose any data or fail completely, but the system performance can significantly slow down.

- If both RAM and swap are full, and no data can be discarded or written to disk, your system can reach an *out-of-memory* (*OOM*) condition. When that happens, the kernel OOM killer kicks in and begins killing off processes, one by one, to regain as much memory as the kernel needs to begin functioning properly again.

The general rule has always been that swapping is bad and should be avoided. However, some would argue that, in certain cases, more aggressive swapping can actually improve performance.

Think of the case where you open a document in a text editor and then minimize it on your desktop for several days as you work on different tasks. If data from that document were swapped out to disk, more RAM would be available for more active applications that could put that space to better use. The performance hit would come the next time you needed to access the data from the edited document and the data was swapped in from disk to RAM. The settings that relate to how aggressively a system swaps are referred to as *swappiness*.

As much as possible, Linux wants to make everything that an open application needs immediately available. So, using the desk analogy, if I am working on nine active projects and there is space on the desk to hold the information I need for all nine projects, why not leave them all within reach on the desk? Following that same way of thinking, the kernel sometimes keeps libraries and other content in RAM that it thinks you might eventually need, even if a process is not looking for it immediately.

The fact that the kernel is inclined to store information in RAM that it expects may be needed soon (even if it is not needed now) can cause an inexperienced system administrator to think that the system is almost out of RAM and that processes are about to start failing. That is why it is important to know the different kinds of information being held in memory—so you can tell when real out-of-memory situations can occur. The problem is not just running out of RAM; it is running out of RAM when only nonswappable data is left.

Keep this general overview of *virtual memory* (RAM and swap) in mind, as the next section describes ways to go about troubleshooting issues related to virtual memory.

Checking for memory problems

Let's say that you are logged into a Linux desktop, with lots of applications running, and everything begins to slow down. To find out if the performance problems have occurred because you have run out of memory, you can try commands such as top and ps to begin looking for memory consumption on your system.

To run the top command to watch for memory consumption, type **top** and then type a capital **M**. Here is an example:

```
# top
top - 22:48:24 up  3:59,  2 users,  load average: 1.51, 1.37, 1.15
Tasks: 281 total,   2 running, 279 sleeping,   0 stopped,   0 zombie
Cpu(s): 16.6%us,  3.0%sy,  0.0%ni, 80.3%id,  0.0%wa,  0.0%hi,
    0.2%si,  0.0%st
Mem:   3716196k total,  2684924k used,  1031272k free,   146172k
    buffers
Swap:  4194296k total,        0k used,  4194296k free,   784176k
    cached
  PID USER      PR  NI  VIRT  RES  SHR S %CPU %MEM   TIME+  COMMAND
 6679 cnegus    20   0 1665m 937m  32m S  7.0 25.8  1:07.95 firefox
 6794 cnegus    20   0  743m 181m  30m R 64.8  5.0  1:22.82
    npviewer.bin
```

```
3327 cnegus    20   0 1145m 116m  66m S  0.0  3.2  0:39.25
     soffice.bin
6939 cnegus    20   0  145m  71m  23m S  0.0  2.0  0:00.97 acroread
2440 root      20   0  183m  37m  26m S  1.3  1.0  1:04.81 Xorg
2795 cnegus    20   0 1056m  22m  14m S  0.0  0.6  0:01.55 nautilus
```

There are two lines (Mem and Swap) and four columns of information (VIRT, RES, SHR, and %MEM) relating to memory in the top output. In this example, you can see that RAM is not exhausted from the Mem line (only 268492k of 3716196k is used) and that nothing is being swapped to disk from the Swap line (0k used).

However, adding up just these first six lines of output in the VIRT column, you would see that 4937MB of memory has been allocated for those applications, which exceeds the 3629MB of total RAM (3716196k) that is available. That's because the VIRT column shows only the amount of memory that has been promised to the application. The RES line shows the amount of nonswappable memory that is actually being used, which totals only 1364MB.

Notice that, when you ask to sort by memory usage by typing a capital **M**, top knows to sort on that RES column. The SHR column shows memory that could potentially be shared by other applications (such as libraries), and %MEM shows the percentage of total memory consumed by each application.

If you think that the system is reaching an out-of-memory state, here are a few things to look for:

- The free space shown on the Mem line would be at or near zero.

- The used space shown on the Swap line would be nonzero and would continue to grow. That should be accompanied with a slowdown of system performance.

- As the top screen redraws every few seconds, if there is a process with a memory leak (continuously asking for and using more memory, but not giving any memory back), the amount of VIRT memory grows, but more important, the RES memory continues to grow for that process.

- If the Swap space actually runs out, the kernel starts to kill off processes to deal with this out-of-memory condition.

Dealing with memory problems

In the short term, you can do several things to deal with this out-of-memory condition:

- **Kill a process.** If the memory problem is due to one errant process, you can simply kill that process. Assuming you are logged in as root or as the user who owns the runaway process, type **k** from the top window, and then enter the PID of the process you want to kill and choose 15 or 9 as the signal to send.

- **Drop page caches.** If you just want to clear up some memory right now, as you otherwise deal with the problem, you can tell the system to drop inactive page caches. When you do this, some memory pages are written to disk; others are just discarded (because they are stored permanently and can be gotten again from disk when they are needed).

  This action is the equivalent of cleaning your desk and putting all but the most critical information into the trash or into a file cabinet. You may need to retrieve information again shortly from a file cabinet, but you almost surely don't need it all immediately. Keep top running in one Terminal window to see the Mem line change as you type the following (as root) into another Terminal window:

  ```
  # echo 3 > /proc/sys/vm/drop_caches
  ```

- **Kill an out-of-memory process.** Sometimes, memory exhaustion has made the system so unusable that you may not be able to get a response from a shell or GUI. In those cases, you might be able to use Alt+SysRq keystrokes to kill an out-of-memory process. The reason you can use Alt+SysRq keystrokes on an otherwise unresponsive system is that the kernel processes Alt+SysRq requests ahead of other requests.

  To enable Alt+SysRq keystrokes, the system must have already set /proc/sys/kernel/sysrq to 1. An easy way to do this is to add kernel.sysrq = 1 to the /etc/sysctl.conf file. Also, you must run the Alt+SysRq keystrokes from a text-based interface (such as the virtual console you see when you press Ctrl+Alt+F2).

  With kernel.sysrq set to 1, you can kill the process on your system with the highest OOM score by pressing Alt+SysRq+f from a text-based interface. A listing of all processes running on your system appears on the screen, with the name of the process that was killed listed at the end. You can repeat those keystrokes until you have killed enough processes to be able to access the system normally from the shell again.

> **NOTE**
> There are many other Alt+SysRq keystrokes you can use to deal with an unresponsive system. For example, Alt+SysRq+e terminates all processes except for the init process. Alt+SysRq+t dumps a list of all current tasks and information about those tasks to the console. To reboot the system, press Alt+SysRq+b. See the sysrq.txt file in the /usr/share/doc/kernel-doc*/Documentation directory for more information about Alt+SysRq keystrokes.

Troubleshooting in Rescue Mode

If your Linux system becomes unbootable, your best option for fixing it is probably to go into *rescue mode*. To go into rescue mode, you bypass the Linux system installed on your hard disk and boot some rescue medium (such as a bootable USB key or boot CD). After the rescue medium boots, it tries to mount any filesystems it can find from your Linux system so you can repair any problems.

For many Linux distributions, the installation CD or DVD can serve as boot media for going into rescue mode. Here's an example of how to use a Fedora installation DVD to go into rescue mode to fix a broken Linux system:

1. Get the installation CD or DVD image you want to use, and burn it to the appropriate medium (CD or DVD). See Appendix A, "Media," for information on burning CDs and DVDs. (For my example, I used a Red Hat Enterprise Linux 7 Server installation DVD.)

2. Insert the CD or DVD into the drive on the computer that has the broken Linux system installed, and reboot.

3. The moment you see the BIOS screen, press the function key noted on that screen for selecting the boot device (possibly the F12 or F2 function key).

4. Choose the drive (CD or DVD) from the list of bootable devices, and press Enter.

5. When the RHEL 7 boot menu appears, use the arrow keys to highlight the word *Troubleshooting* and press Enter. In other Linux boot media, the selection could say *Rescue Mode* or something similar. On the next screen that appears, select Rescue a Red Hat Enterprise Linux system and press Enter.

6. After a few moments, the Linux system on the rescue medium boots up. When prompted, select your language and keyboard. You are asked if you want to start network interfaces on the system.

7. If you think you might need to get something from another system on your network (such as RPM packages or debugging tools), select Yes and try to configure your network interfaces. You are then asked if you want to try to mount filesystems from your installed Linux system under /mnt/sysimage.

8. Select Continue to have your filesystems mounted (if possible) under the /mnt/sysimage directory. If this is successful, a Rescue message appears, telling you your filesystems have been mounted under /mnt/sysimage.

9. Select OK to continue. You should see a shell prompt for the root user (#). You are ready to begin troubleshooting from rescue mode. After you are in rescue mode, the portion of your filesystem that is not damaged is mounted under the /mnt/sysimage directory. Type **ls /mnt/sysimage** to check that the files and directories from the hard disk are there.

Right now, the root of the filesystem (/) is from the filesystem that comes on the rescue medium. To troubleshoot your installed Linux system, however, you can type the following command:

```
# chroot /mnt/sysimage
```

Now the `/mnt/sysimage` directory becomes the root of your filesystem (`/`) so it looks like the filesystem installed on your hard disk. Here are some things you can do to repair your system while you are in rescue mode:

- **Fix /etc/fstab.** If your filesystems couldn't mount because of an error in your `/etc/fstab` file, you could try to correct any entries that might have problems (such as wrong device names or a mount point directory that doesn't exist). Type `mount -a` to make sure all the filesystems mount.

- **Reinstall missing components.** It might be that the filesystems are fine, but the system failed to boot because some critical command or configuration file is missing. You might be able to fix the problem by reinstalling the package with the missing components. For example, if someone had deleted `/bin/mount` by mistake, the system would have no command to mount filesystems. Reinstalling the `util-linux` package would replace the missing `mount` command.

- **Check the filesystems.** If your booting problems stem from corrupt filesystems, you can try running the `fsck` command (filesystem check) to see if there is any corruption on the disk partition. If there is, `fsck` attempts to correct problems it encounters.

When you are finished fixing your system, type **exit** to exit the `chroot` environment and return to the filesystem layout that the live medium sees. If you are completely finished, type **reboot** to restart your system. Be sure to pop out the medium before the system restarts.

Summary

Troubleshooting problems in Linux can start from the moment you turn on your computer. Problems can occur with your computer BIOS, boot loader, or other parts of the boot process that you can correct by intercepting them at different stages of the boot process.

After the system has started, you can troubleshoot problems with software packages, network interfaces, or memory exhaustion. Linux comes with many tools for finding and correcting any part of the Linux system that might break down and need fixing.

The next chapter covers the topic of Linux security. Using the tools described in that chapter, you can provide access to those services you and your users need, while blocking access to system resources that you want to protect from harm.

Exercises

The exercises in this section enable you to try out useful troubleshooting techniques in Linux. Because some of the techniques described here can potentially damage your system,

I recommend you do not use a production system that you cannot risk damaging. See Appendix B for suggested solutions.

These exercises relate to troubleshooting topics in Linux. They assume you are booting a PC with standard BIOS. To do these exercises, you need to be able to reboot your computer and interrupt any work it may be doing.

1. Boot your computer, and as soon as you see the BIOS screen, go into Setup mode as instructed on the BIOS screen.

2. From the BIOS Setup screen, determine if your computer is 32-bit or 64-bit, if it includes virtualization support, and if your network interface card is capable of PXE booting.

3. Reboot and just after the BIOS screen disappears, when you see the countdown to booting the Linux system, press any key to get to the GRUB boot loader.

4. From the GRUB boot loader, add an option to boot up to runlevel 1, so you can do some system maintenance.

5. Reboot a computer with Red Hat Enterprise Linux 6 installed and, from the GRUB boot loader, add an option that causes system services to prompt you to confirm as each service is started.

6. After the system boots up, look at the messages that were produced in the kernel ring buffer that show the activity of the kernel as it booted up.

7. In Fedora or RHEL, run a trial `yum update` and exclude any kernel package that is available.

8. Check to see what processes are listening for incoming connections on your system.

9. Check to see what ports are open on your external network interface.

10. Run the `top` command in a Terminal window. Open a second Terminal window, clear your page cache, and notice on the `top` screen if more RES memory is now available.

Part V

Learning Linux Security Techniques

IN THIS PART

Understanding Basic Linux Security

IN THIS CHAPTER

Implementing basic security

Monitoring security

Auditing and reviewing security

U nderstanding security is a crucial part of Linux system administration. No longer are a username and simple password sufficient for protecting your server. The number and variety of computer attacks escalate every day, and the need to improve computer security continues to grow with them.

Your first step is to gather knowledge of basic security procedures and principles. With this information, you can begin the process of locking down and securing your Linux servers. Also, you can learn how to stay informed of daily new threats and the new ways to continue protecting your organization's valuable information assets.

Understanding Security Basics

Securing your Linux systems must be done in several layers. It begins by physically securing the computers Linux runs on and proceeds through using good basic techniques for properly defining and securing user accounts. These and other techniques are the first lines of defense in securing your Linux systems.

Implementing physical security

A lock on the computer server room door is a first line of defense. Although a very simple concept, it is often ignored. Access to the physical server means access to all the data it contains. No security software can fully protect your systems if someone with malicious intent has physical access to the Linux server.

Basic server room physical security includes items such as these:

- A lock or security alarm on the server room door
- Access controls that allow only authorized access and identify who accessed the room and when the access occurred, such as a card key entry system
- A sign stating "no unauthorized access allowed" on the door
- Policies on who can access the room and when access may occur, for groups such as the cleaning crew, server administrators, and others

Physical security includes environmental controls. Appropriate fire suppression systems and proper ventilation for your server room must be implemented.

In addition to basic physical security of a server room, attention should be given to what is physically at each worker's desk. Desktops and laptops may need to be locked. Fingerprints are often left on computer tablets, which can reveal PINs and passwords. Therefore, a tablet screen wiping policy may need to be implemented.

A *Clean Desk Policy* (CDP) mandates either that only the papers being currently worked on are on a desk or that all papers must be locked away at the end of the day. A CDP protects classified information from being gleaned by nosy and unauthorized personnel. And, finally, a "no written passwords" policy is mandatory.

Implementing disaster recovery

Disasters do happen, and they can expose your organization's data to insecure situations. Therefore, part of computer security includes preparing for a disaster. Disaster recovery includes creating disaster recovery plans, testing the plans, and conducting plan reviews. Plans must be tested and updated to maintain their reliability in true disaster situations.

Disaster recovery plans should include these things:

- What data is to be included in backups
- Where backups are to be stored
- How long backups are maintained
- How backup media is rotated through storage

Backup data, media, and software should be included in your Access Control Matrix checklist.

CAUTION

It is important to determine how many backup copies of each object should be maintained. Whereas you may need only three backup copies of one particular object, another may have enough importance for you to maintain more copies.

Backup utilities on a Linux system include the following:

- amanda (Advanced Maryland Automatic Network Disk Archiver)
- cpio
- dump/restore
- tar

The cpio, dump/restore, and tar utilities are typically pre-installed on a Linux distribution. Only amanda is not installed by default. However, amanda is extremely popular because it comes with a great deal of flexibility and can even back up a Windows system. If you need more information on the amanda backup utility, see www.amanda.org. The utility you ultimately pick should meet your organization's particular security needs for backup.

With luck, disasters occur only rarely. However, every day, users log in to your Linux system. User accounts and passwords have basic security settings that should be reviewed and implemented as needed.

Securing user accounts

User accounts are part of the authentication process allowing users into the Linux system. Proper user account management enhances a system's security. Setting up user accounts was covered in Chapter 11. However, a few additional rules are necessary to increase security through user account management:

- One user per user account.
- Limit access to the root user account.
- Set expiration dates on temporary accounts.
- Remove unused user accounts.

One user per user account

Accounts should enforce accountability. Thus, multiple people should not be logging in to one account. When multiple people share an account, there is no way to prove a particular individual completed a particular action. Their actions are deniable, which is called *repudiation* in the security world. Accounts should be set up for *nonrepudiation*. In other words, there should be one person per user account, so actions cannot be denied.

> **TIP**
>
> You always want to set up your computer security for nonrepudiation. But that term can be confusing. To help you remember the terms, think of them this way:
>
> *repudiation*—The user can deny actions or refuse accountability.
>
> *nonrepudiation*—The user cannot deny actions or refuse accountability.

Limit access to the root user account

If multiple people can log in to the root account, you have another repudiation situation. You cannot track individual use of the root account. To allow tracking of root account use by individuals, a policy for using sudo (see Chapter 8) instead of logging into root should be instituted.

Instead of giving multiple people root permission on a Linux system, you can grant root access on a per-command basis with the sudo command. Using sudo provides the following security benefits:

- The root password does not have to be given out.
- You can fine-tune command access.
- All sudo use (who, what, when) is recorded in /var/log/secure.

All failed sudo access attempts are logged.

After you grant someone sudo permission, you can try to restrict root access to certain commands in the /etc/sudoers file (with the visudo command). However, after you grant root permission to a user, even in a limited way, it is difficult to be sure that a determined user can't find ways to gain full root access to your system and do what he or she wants to it.

One way to keep a misbehaving administrator in check is to have security messages intended for the /var/log/secure file sent to a remote log server that none of the local administrators have access to. In that way, any misuse of root privilege is attached to a particular user and is logged in a way that the user can't cover his or her tracks.

Setting expiration dates on temporary accounts

If you have consultants, interns, or temporary employees who need access to your Linux systems, it is important to set up their user accounts with expiration dates. The expiration date is a safeguard, in case you forget to remove their accounts when they no longer need access to your organization's systems.

To set a user account with an expiration date, use the usermod command. The format is usermod -e *yyyy-mm-dd user _name*. In the following code, the account tim has been set to expire on January 1, 2017.

```
# usermod -e 2017-01-01 tim
```

To verify that the account has been properly set to expire, double-check yourself by using the chage command. The chage command is primarily used to view and change a user account's password aging information. However, it also contains account expiration information. The -l option allows you to list the various information chage has access to. To keep it simple, pipe the output from the chage command into grep and search for the word "Account." This produces only the user account's expiration date.

```
# chage -l tim | grep Account
Account expires                         :  Jan  01,  2017
```

The account expiration date was successfully changed for tim to January 1, 2017.

> **TIP**
>
> If you do not use the `/etc/shadow` file for storing your account passwords, the `chage` utility doesn't work. In most cases, this is not a problem because the `/etc/shadow` file is configured to store password information by default on most Linux systems..

Set account expiration dates for all transitory employees. In addition, consider reviewing all user account expiration dates as part of your security monitoring activities. These activities help to eliminate any potential backdoors to your Linux system.

Removing unused user accounts

Keeping old expired accounts around is asking for trouble. After a user has left an organization, it is best to perform a series of steps to remove his or her account along with data:

1. Find files on the system owned by the account, using the following command:
   find / -user *username*
2. Expire or disable the account.
3. Back up the files.
4. Remove the files or reassign them to a new owner.
5. Delete the account from the system.

Problems occur when Step 5 is forgotten, and expired or disabled accounts are still on the system. A malicious user gaining access to your system could renew the account and then masquerade as a legitimate user.

To find these accounts, search through the `/etc/shadow` file. The account's expiration date is in the eighth field of each record. It would be convenient if a date format were used. Instead, this field shows the account's expiration date as the number of days since January 1, 1970.

You can use a two-step process to find expired accounts in the `/etc/shadow` file automatically. First, set up a shell variable (see Chapter 7) with today's date in "days since January 1, 1970" format. Then, using the `gawk` command, you can obtain and format the information needed from the `/etc/shadow` file.

Setting up a shell variable with the current date converted to the number of days since January 1, 1970 is not particularly difficult. The `date` command can produce the number of seconds since January 1, 1970. To get what you need, divide the result from the `date` command by the number of seconds in a day: 86,400. The following demonstrates how to set up the shell variable TODAY.

```
# TODAY=$(echo $(($(date --utc --date "$1" +%s)/86400)))
# echo $TODAY
16373
```

Next, the accounts and their expiration dates are pulled from the /etc/shadow file using gawk. The gawk command is the GNU version of the awk program used in UNIX. The command's output is shown in the code that follows. As you would expect, many of the accounts do not have an expiration date. However, two accounts, Consultant and Intern, show an expiration date in the "days since January 1, 1970" format. Note that you can skip this step. It is just for demonstration purposes.

```
# gawk -F: '{print $1,$8}' /etc/shadow
. . .
chrony
tcpdump
johndoe
Consultant 13819
Intern 13911
```

The $1 and $8 in the gawk command represent the username and expiration date fields in the /etc/shadow file records. To check those accounts' expiration dates and see if they are expired, a more refined version of the gawk command is needed.

```
# gawk -F: '{if (($8 > 0) && ($TODAY > $8)) print $1}' /etc/shadow
Consultant
Intern
```

Only accounts with an expiration date are collected by the ($8 > 0) portion of the gawk command. To make sure these expiration dates are past the current date, the TODAY variable is compared with the expiration date field, $8. If TODAY is greater than the account's expiration date, the account is listed. As you can see in the preceding example, two expired accounts still exist on the system and need to be removed.

That is all you need to do. Set up your TODAY variable, and execute the gawk command. All the expired accounts in the /etc/shadow file are listed for you. To remove these accounts, use the userdel command.

User accounts are only a portion of the authentication process, allowing users into the Linux system. User account passwords also play an important role in the process.

Securing passwords

Passwords are the most basic security tool of any modern operating system and, consequently, the most commonly attacked security feature. It is natural for users to want to choose a password that is easy to remember, but often this means they choose a password that is also easy to guess.

Brute force methods are commonly employed to gain access to a computer system. Trying the popular passwords often yields results. Some of the most common passwords are:

- 123456
- Password

- princess
- rockyou
- abc123

Just use your favorite Internet search engine and look for "common passwords." If you can find these lists, then malicious attackers can, too. Obviously, choosing good passwords is critical to having a secure system.

Choosing good passwords

In general, a password must not be easy to guess, be common or popular, or be linked to you in any way. Here are some rules to follow when choosing a password:

- Do not use any variation of your login name or your full name.
- Do not use a dictionary word.
- Do not use proper names of any kind.
- Do not use your phone number, address, family, or pet names.
- Do not use website names.
- Do not use any contiguous line of letters or numbers on the keyboard (such as "qwerty" or "asdfg").
- Do not use any of the above with added numbers or punctuation to the front or end, or typed backward.

So now that you know what not to do, look at the two primary items that make a strong password:

- A password should be at least 15 to 25 characters in length.
- A password should contain all of the following:
    - Lowercase letters
    - Uppercase letters
    - Numbers
    - Special characters, such as : ! $ % * ( ) - + = , < > : : " '

Twenty-five characters is a long password. However, the longer the password, the more secure it is. What your organization chooses as the minimum password length is dependent upon its security needs.

TIP

Gibson Research Center has some excellent material on strong passwords, including an article called "How big is your haystack...and how well hidden is your needle?" at `www.grc.com/haystack.htm`.

Choosing a good password can be difficult. It has to be hard enough not to be guessed and easy enough for you to remember. A good way to choose a strong password is to take the first letter from each word of an easily remembered sentence. Be sure to add numbers, special characters, and varied case. The sentence you choose should have meaning only to you, and should not be publicly available. Table 22.1 lists examples of strong passwords and the tricks used to remember them.

TABLE 22.1 **Ideas for Good Passwords**

Password	How to Remember It
Mrci7yo!	My rusty car is 7 years old!
2emBp1ib	2 elephants make BAD pets, 1 is better
ItMc?Gib	Is that MY coat? Give it back

The passwords look like nonsense but are rather easy to remember. Of course, be sure not to use the passwords listed here. Now that they are public, they will be added to malicious attackers' dictionaries.

Setting and changing passwords

You set your own password using the passwd command. Type the passwd command, and it enables you to change your password. First, it prompts you to enter your old password. To protect against someone shoulder surfing and learning your password, the password is not displayed as you type.

Assuming you type your old password correctly, the passwd command prompts you for the new password. When you type your new password, it is checked using a utility called cracklib to determine whether it is a good or bad password. Nonroot users are required to try a different password if the one they have chosen is not a good password.

The root user is the only user who is permitted to assign bad passwords. After the password has been accepted by cracklib, the passwd command asks you to enter the new password a second time to make sure there are no typos (which are hard to detect when you can't see what you are typing).

When running as root, changing a user's password is possible by supplying that user's login name as a parameter to the passwd command. For example:

```
# passwd joe
Changing password for user joe.
New UNIX password: ********
Retype new UNIX password: ********
passwd: all authentication tokens updated successfully.
```

Here, the passwd command prompts you twice to enter a new password for joe. It does not prompt for his old password in this case.

Enforcing best password practices

Now, you know what a good password looks like and how to change a password, but how do you enforce it on your Linux system? To get a good start on enforcing best password practices, educate system users. Educated users are better users. Here are some ideas for education:

- Add an article on best password practices to your organization's monthly newsletter.
- Post tip sheets in the break rooms, such as "The Top Ten Worst Passwords."
- Send out regular employee computer security e-mails containing password tips.
- Provide new employees training on passwords.

Employees who understand password security often strive to create good passwords at work as well as at home. One of the "hooks" to gain user attention is to let employees know that these passwords work well also when creating personal passwords, such as for their online banking accounts.

Still, you always have a few users who refuse to implement good password practices. Plus, company security policies often require that a password be changed every so many days. It can become tiresome to come up with new, strong passwords every 30 days! That is why some enforcing techniques are often necessary.

TIP

If users are having a difficult time creating secure and unique passwords, consider installing the pwgen utility on your Linux system. This open source password generating utility creates passwords that are made to be pronounceable and memorable. You can use these generated words as a starting point for creating account passwords.

Default values in the /etc/login.defs file for new accounts were covered in Chapter 11. Within the login.defs file are some settings affecting password aging and length:

```
PASS_MAX_DAYS    30
PASS_MIN_DAYS    5
PASS_MIN_LEN     16
PASS_WARN_AGE    7
```

In this example, the maximum number of days, PASS_MAX_DAYS, until the password must be changed is 30. The number you set here is dependent upon your particular account setup. For organizations that practice one person to one account, this number can be much larger than 30. If you have shared accounts or multiple people know the root password, it is imperative that you change the password often. This practice effectively refreshes the list of those who know the password.

To keep users from changing their password to a new password and then immediately changing it back, you need to set the PASS_MIN_DAYS to a number larger than 0. In the preceding example, the soonest a user could change his password again is 5 days.

The PASS_WARN_AGE setting is the number of days a user is warned before being forced to change his password. People tend to need lots of warnings and prodding, so the preceding example sets the warning time to 7 days.

Earlier in the chapter, I mentioned that a strong password is between 15 and 25 characters long. With the PASS_MIN_LEN setting, you can force users to use a certain minimum number of characters in their passwords. The setting you choose should be based upon your organization's security life cycle plans.

> **NOTE**
>
> Ubuntu does not have the PASS_MIN_LEN setting in its login.defs file. Instead, this setting is handled by the PAM utility. PAM is covered in Chapter 23.

For accounts that have already been created, you need to control password aging via the chage command. The options needed to control password aging with chage are listed in Table 22.2. Notice that there is not a password length setting in the chage utility.

TABLE 22.2 chage Options

Option	Description
-M	Sets the maximum number of days before a password needs to be changed. Equivalent to PASS_MAX_DAYS in /etc/login.defs
-m	Sets the minimum number of days before a password can be changed again. Equivalent to PASS_MIN_DAYS in /etc/login.defs
-W	Sets the number of days a user is warned before being forced to change the account password. Equivalent to PASS_WARN_AGE in /etc/login.defs

The example that follows uses the chage command to set password aging parameters for the tim account. All three options are used at once.

```
# chage -l tim | grep days
Minimum number of days between password change        : 0
Maximum number of days between password change        : 99999
Number of days of warning before password expires     : 7
```

```
# chage -M 30 -m 5 -W 7 tim
# chage -l tim | grep days
Minimum number of days between password change      : 5
Maximum number of days between password change      : 30
Number of days of warning before password expires   : 7
```

You can also use the chage command as another method of account expiration, which is based upon the account's password expiring. Earlier, the usermod utility was used for account expiration. Use the chage command with the -M and the -I options to lock the account. In the code that follows, the tim account is viewed using chage -l. Only the information for tim's account passwords is extracted.

```
# chage -l tim | grep Password
Password expires           : never
Password inactive          : never
```

You can see that there are no settings for password expiration (Password expires) or password inactivity (Password inactive). In the following code, the account is set to be locked 5 days after tim's password expires, by using only the -I option.

```
# chage -I 5 tim
# chage -l tim | grep Password
Password expires           : never
Password inactive          : never
```

Notice that no settings changed! Without a password expiration set, the -I option has no effect. Thus, using the -M option, the maximum number of days is set before the password expires and the setting for the password inactivity time should take hold.

```
# chage -M 30 -I 5 tim
# chage -l tim | grep Password
Password expires           : Mar 03, 2017
Password inactive          : Mar 08, 2017
```

Now, tim's account will be locked 5 days after his password expires. This is helpful in situations where an employee has left the company, but his user account has not yet been removed. Depending upon your organization's security needs, consider setting all accounts to lock a certain number of days after passwords have expired.

Understanding the password files and password hashes

Early Linux systems stored their passwords in the /etc/passwd file. The passwords were *hashed*. A hashed password is created using a one-way mathematical process. After you create the hash, you cannot re-create the original characters from the hash. Here's how it works.

When a user enters the account password, the Linux system rehashes the password and then compares the hash result to the original hash in /etc/passwd. If they match, the user is authenticated and allowed into the system.

The problem with storing these password hashes in the `/etc/passwd` file has to do with the filesystem security settings (see Chapter 4). The filesystem security settings for the `/etc/passwd` file are listed here:

```
# ls -l /etc/passwd
-rw-r--r--. 1 root root 1644 Feb  2 02:30 /etc/passwd
```

As you can see, everyone can read the password file. You might think that this is not a problem because the passwords are all hashed. However, individuals with malicious intent have created files called *rainbow tables*. A rainbow table is simply a dictionary of potential passwords that have been hashed. For instance, the rainbow table would contain the hash for the popular password "Password," which is:

```
$6$dhN5ZMUj$CNghjYIteau5xl8yX.f6PTOpendJwTOcXjlTDQUQZhhy
V8hKzQ6Hxx6Egj8P3VsHJ8Qrkv.VSR5dxcK3QhyMc.
```

Because of the ease of access to the password hashes in the `/etc/passwd` file, it is only a matter of time before a hashed password is matched in a rainbow table and the plaintext password uncovered.

> **NOTE**
>
> Security experts will tell you that the passwords are not just hashed, but they are also salted. Salting a hash means that a randomly generated value is added to the original password before it is hashed. This makes it even more difficult for the hashed password to be matched to its original password. However, in Linux, the hash salt is also stored with the hashed passwords. Thus, read access to the `/etc/passwd` file means you have the hash value and its salt.

Thus, the hashed passwords were moved to a new configuration file, `/etc/shadow`, many years ago. This file has the following security settings:

```
# ls -l /etc/shadow
----------. 1 root root 1049 Feb  2 09:45 /etc/shadow
```

Despite having no permissions open, `root`, but no other user, can view this file. Thus, the hashed passwords are protected. Here is the tail end of a `/etc/shadow` file. You can see that there are long, nonsensical character strings in each user's record. Those are the hashed passwords.

```
# tail -2 /etc/shadow
johndoe:$6$jJjdRN9/qELmb8xWM1LgOYGhEIxc/:15364:0:99999:7:::
Tim:$6$z760AJ42$QXdhFyndpbVPVM5oVtNHs4B/:15372:5:30:7:16436::
```

> **CAUTION**
>
> You may inherit a Linux system that still uses the old method of keeping the hashed passwords in the `/etc/passwd` file. It is easy to fix. Just use the `pwconv` command, and the `/etc/shadow` file is created and hashed passwords moved to it.

The following are also stored in the `/etc/shadow` file, in addition to the account name and hashed password:

- Number of days (since January 1, 1970) since the password was changed
- Number of days before password can be changed
- Number of days before a password must be changed
- Number of days to warn a user before a password must be changed
- Number of days after password expires that an account is disabled
- Number of days (since January 1, 1970) that an account has been disabled

These should sound familiar because they are the settings for password aging covered earlier in the chapter. Remember that the `chage` command does not work if you do not have a `/etc/shadow` file set up, nor is the `/etc/login.defs` file available.

Obviously, filesystem security settings are very important for keeping your Linux system secure. This is especially true with all Linux systems' configuration files and others.

Securing the filesystem

Another important part of securing your Linux system is setting proper filesystem security. The basics for security settings were covered in Chapter 4 and Access Control Lists (ACL) in Chapter 11. However, there are a few additional points that need to be added to your knowledge base.

Managing dangerous filesystem permissions

If you gave full `rwxrwxrwx` (777) access to every file on the Linux system, you can imagine the chaos that would follow. In many ways, similar chaos can occur by not closely managing the SetUID (`SUID`) and the SetGID (`SGID`) permissions (see Chapters 4 and 11).

Files with the `SUID` permission in the `Owner` category and execute permission in the `Other` category allow anyone to temporarily become the file's owner while the file is being executed in memory. The riskiest case is if the file's owner is root.

Similarly, files with the `SGID` permission in the `Owner` category and execute permission in the `Other` category allow anyone to temporarily become a group member of the file's group while the file is being executed in memory. `SGID` can also be set on directories. This sets the group ID of any files created in the directory to the group ID of the directory.

Executable files with `SUID` or `SGID` are favorites of malicious users. Thus, it is best to use them sparingly. However, some files do need to keep these settings. Two examples are the `passwd` and the `sudo` commands, which follow. Each of these files should maintain their `SUID` permissions.

```
$ ls -l /usr/bin/passwd
-rwsr-xr-x. 1 root root 28804 Aug 17 20:50 /usr/bin/passwd
```

```
$ ls -l /usr/bin/sudo
---s--x--x. 2 root root 77364 Nov 3 08:10 /usr/bin/sudo
```

Commands such as `passwd` and `sudo` are designed to be used as SUID programs. Even though those commands run as root user, as a regular user you can only change your own password with `passwd` and can only escalate to root permission with `sudo` if you were given permission in the `/etc/sudoers` file. A more dangerous situation would be if a hacker created a SUID bash command; anyone running that command could effectively change everything on the system that had root access.

Using the `find` command, you can search your system to see if there are any hidden or otherwise inappropriate SUID and SGID commands on your system. Here is an example:

```
# find / -perm /6000 -ls
4597316 52 -rwxr-sr-x 1 root games 51952 Dec 21 2013 /usr/bin/atc
4589119 20 -rwxr-sr-x 1 root tty   19552 Nov 18 2013 /usr/bin/write
4587931 60 -rwsr-xr-x 1 root root  57888 Aug  2 2013 /usr/bin/at
4588045 60 -rwsr-xr-x 1 root root  57536 Sep 25 2013 /usr/bin/crontab
4588961 32 -rwsr-xr-x 1 root root  32024 Nov 18 2013 /usr/bin/su
. . .
5767487 85 -rwsrwsr-x 1 root  root 68928 Sep 13 11:52 /var/.bin/myvi
. . .
```

Notice that `find` uncovers SetUID and SetGID commands that regular users can run to escalate their permission for particular reasons. In this example, there is also a file that a user tried to hide (`myvi`). This is a copy of the `vi` command that, because of permission and ownership, can change files owned by root. This is obviously a user doing something he should not be doing.

Securing the password files

The `/etc/passwd` file is the file the Linux system uses to check user account information and was covered earlier in the chapter. The `/etc/passwd` file should have the following permission settings:

- Owner: root
- Group: root
- Permissions: (644) Owner: rw- Group: r-- Other: r--

The example that follows shows that the `/etc/passwd` file has the appropriate settings.

```
# ls -l /etc/passwd
-rw-r--r--. 1 root root 1644 Feb  2 02:30 /etc/passwd
```

These settings are needed so users can log in to the system and see usernames associated with user ID and group ID numbers. However, users should not be able to modify the `/etc/passwd` directly. For example, a malicious user could add a new account to the file if write access were granted to Other.

The next file is the /etc/shadow file. Of course, it is closely related to the /etc/passwd file because it is also used during the login authentication process. This /etc/shadow file should have the following permissions settings:

- Owner: root
- Group: root
- Permissions: (000) Owner: --- Group: --- Other: ---

The code that follows shows that the /etc/shadow file has the appropriate settings.

```
# ls -l /etc/shadow
----------. 1 root root 1049 Feb  2 09:45 /etc/shadow
```

The /etc/passwd file has read access for the owner, group, and other. Notice how much more the /etc/shadow file is restricted than the /etc/passwd file. For the /etc/shadow file, there is no access permission on, although the root user can still access the file. So if only root can view this file, how can a user change his or her password because it is stored in /etc/shadow? The passwd utility, /usr/bin/passwd, uses the special permission SUID. This permission setting is shown here:

```
# ls -l /usr/bin/passwd
-rwsr-xr-x. 1 root root 28804 Aug 17 20:50 /usr/bin/passwd
```

Thus, the user running the passwd command temporarily becomes root while the command is executing in memory and can then write to the /etc/shadow file, but only to change the user's own password-related information.

> **NOTE**
>
> root does not have write access to the /etc/shadow permissions, so how does root write to the /etc/shadow file? The root user is all-powerful and has complete access to all files, whether the permissions are listed or not.

The /etc/group file (see Chapter 11) contains all the groups on the Linux system. Its file permissions should be set exactly as the /etc/passwd file:

- Owner: root
- Group: root
- Permissions: (644) Owner: rw- Group: r-- Other: r--

Also, the group password file, /etc/gshadow, needs to be properly secured. As you would expect, the file permission should be set exactly as the /etc/shadow file:

- Owner: root
- Group: root
- Permissions: (000) Owner: --- Group: --- Other: ---

Locking down the filesystem

The filesystem table (see Chapter 12), /etc/fstab, needs some special attention, too. The /etc/fstab file is used at boot time to mount storage devices on filesystems. It is also used by the mount command, the dump command, and the fsck command. The /etc/fstab file should have the following permission settings:

- Owner: root
- Group: root
- Permissions: (664) Owner: rw- Group: rw- Other: r--

Within the filesystem table, there are some important security settings that need to be reviewed. Besides your root, boot, and swap partitions, filesystem options are fairly secure by default. However, you may want to also consider the following:

- Typically, you put the /home subdirectory, where user directories are located, on its own partition and when you add mount options, you can do the following:
  - You can set the nosuid option to prevent SUID and SGID permission-enabled executable programs running from there. Programs that need SUID and SGID permissions should not be stored in /home and are most likely malicious.
  - You can set the nodev option so no device file located there will be recognized. Device files should be stored in /dev and not in /home.
  - You can set the noexec option so no executable programs, which are stored in /home, can be run.
- You can put the /tmp subdirectory, where temporary files are located, on its own partition and use the same options settings as for /home:
  - nosuid
  - nodev
  - noexec
- You can put the /usr subdirectory, where user programs and data are located, on its own partition and set the nodev option so no device file located there is recognized. After software is installed, the /usr directory often has little or no change (sometimes, it is even mounted read-only for security reasons).
- If the system is configured as a server, you probably want to put the /var subdirectory on its own partition. The /var directory is meant to grow, as log messages and content for web, FTP, and other servers are added. You can use the same mount options with the /var partition as you do for /home:
  - nosuid
  - nodev
  - noexec

Putting the preceding into your `/etc/fstab` would look similar to the following:

```
/dev/sdb1    /home    ext4    nodev,noexec,nosuid    1 2
/dev/sdc1    /tmp     ext4    nodev,noexec,nosuid    1 1
/dev/sdb2    /usr     ext4    nodev                  1 2
/dev/sdb3    /var     ext4    nodev,noexec,nosuid    1 2
```

These mount options will help to further lock down your filesystem and add another layer of protection from those with malicious intent.

Again, managing the various file permissions and fstab options should be part of your security policy. The items you choose to implement must be determined by your organization's security needs.

Managing software and services

22

Often, the administrator's focus is on making sure the needed software and services are on a Linux system. From a security standpoint, you need to take the opposite viewpoint and make sure the unneeded software and services are not on a Linux system.

Updating software packages

In addition to removing unnecessary services and software, keeping current software up to date is critical for security. The latest bug fixes and security patches are obtained via software updates. Software package updates were covered in Chapters 9 and 10.

Software updates need to be done on a regular basis. How often and when you do it, of course, depends upon your organization's security needs.

You can easily automate software updates, but like removing services and software, it would be wise to test the updates in a test environment first. When updated software shows no problems, you can then update the software on your production Linux systems.

Keeping up with security advisories

As security flaws are found in Linux software, the Common Vulnerabilities and Exposures (CVE) project tracks them and helps to quickly get fixes for those flaws worked on by the Linux community. Companies such as Red Hat provide updated packages to fix the security flaws and deliver them in what is referred to as *errata*. Errata may consist of a single updated package or multiple updated packages. If you are running Red Hat Enterprise Linux, you search for, identify, and install the packages associated with a particular CVE and delivered in errata.

For more on how security updates are handled in Red Hat Enterprise Linux, refer to the Security Updates page on the Red Hat customer portal (`https://access.redhat.com/security/updates/`). The site contains a wealth of knowledge related to security vulnerabilities and how they are being dealt with. Being able to get timely security updates is one of the primary reasons companies subscribe critical systems to Red Hat Enterprise Linux.

Advanced implementation

You should be aware of several other important security topics as you are planning your deployments. They include cryptography, Pluggable Authentication Modules (PAM), and SELinux. These advanced and detailed topics are in separate chapters, Chapter 23 and Chapter 24.

Monitoring Your Systems

If you do a good job of planning and implementing your system's security, most malicious attacks will be stopped. However, if an attack should occur, you need to be able to recognize it. Monitoring must go on continuously.

Monitoring your system includes watching over log files, user accounts, and the filesystem itself. In addition, you need some tools to help you detect intrusions and other types of malware.

Monitoring log files

Understanding how message logging is done is critical to maintaining and troubleshooting a Linux system. Before the `systemd` facility was used to gather messages in what is referred to as the `systemd` journal, messages generated by the kernel and system services were directed to file in the `/var/log` directory. While that is still true to a great extent with `systemd`, you can now also view log messages directly from the `systemd` journal using the `journalctl` command.

The log files for your Linux system are primarily located in the `/var/log` directory. Most of the files in the `/var/log` directory are directed there from the `systemd` journal through the `rsyslogd` service (see Chapter 13). Table 22.3 contains a list of `/var/log` files and a brief description of each.

TABLE 22.3 Log Files in the /var/log Directory

System Log Name	Filename	Description
Apache Access Log	`/var/log/httpd/access_log`	Logs requests for information from your Apache Web server.
Apache Error Log	`/var/log/httpd/error_log`	Logs errors encountered from clients trying to access data on your Apache Web server.
Bad Logins Log	`btmp`	Logs bad login attempts.

System Log Name	Filename	Description
Boot Log	boot.log	Contains messages indicating which system services have started and shut down successfully and which (if any) have failed to start or stop. The most recent bootup messages are listed near the end of the file.
Kernel Log	dmesg	Records messages printed by the kernel when the system boots.
Cron Log	cron	Contains status messages from the crond daemon.
dpkg Log	dpkg.log	Contains information concerning installed Debian packages.
FTP Log	vsftpd.log	Contains messages relating to transfers made using the vsFTPd daemon (FTP server).
FTP Transfer Log	xferlog	Contains information about files transferred using the FTP service.
GNOME Display Manager Log	/var/log/gdm/:0.log	Holds messages related to the login screen (GNOME display manager). Yes, there really is a colon in the filename.
LastLog	lastlog	Records the last time an account logs in to the system.
Login/out Log	wtmp	Contains a history of logins and logouts on the system.
Mail Log	maillog	Contains information about addresses to which and from which email was sent. Useful for detecting spamming.
MySQL Server Log	mysqld.log	Includes information related to activities of the MySQL database server (mysqld).
News Log	spooler	Provides a directory containing logs of messages from the Usenet News server if you are running one.
Samba Log	/var/log/samba/log.smbd	Shows messages from the Samba SMB file service daemon.
Security Log	secure	Records the date, time, and duration of login attempts and sessions.
Sendmail Log	sendmail	Shows error messages recorded by the sendmail daemon.
Squid Log	/var/log/squid/access.log	Contains messages related to the squid proxy/caching server.

Continues

22

TABLE 22.3 *(continued)*

System Log Name	Filename	Description
System Log	`messages`	Provides a general-purpose log file where many programs record messages.
UUCP Log	`uucp`	Shows status messages from the UNIX to UNIX Copy Protocol daemon.
YUM Log	`yum.log`	Shows messages related to RPM software packages.
X.Org X11 Log	`Xorg.0.log`	Includes messages output by the X.Org X server.

The log files that are in your system's /var/log directory depend upon what services you are running. Also, some log files are distribution-dependent. For example, if you use Fedora Linux, you would not have the dpkg log file.

Most of the log files are displayed using the commands cat, head, tail, more, or less. However, a few of them have special commands for viewing (see Table 22.4).

TABLE 22.4 Viewing Log Files That Need Special Commands

Filename	View Command
`btmp`	`dump-utmp btmp`
`dmesg`	`dmesg`
`lastlog`	`lastlog`
`wtmp`	`dump-utmp wtmp`

With the change in Fedora, RHEL, Ubuntu, and other Linux distributions to systemd (which manages the boot process and services), as noted earlier, the mechanism for gathering and displaying log messages associated with the kernel and system services has changed as well. Those messages are directed to the systemd journal and can be displayed with the journalctl command.

You can view journal messages directly from the systemd journal instead of simply listing the contents of /var/log files. In fact, the /var/log/messages file, which many services direct log messages to by default, does not even exist in the latest Fedora release. Instead, you can use the journalctl command to display log messages in various ways.

To page through kernel messages, type the following command:

```
# journalctl -k
-- Logs begin at Sun 2014-08-17 15:33:30 EDT,
```

```
       end at Sat 2014-09-13 22:29:00 EDT. --
Aug 29 23:14:38 fedora20 kernel: Initializing cgroup subsys cpuset
Aug 29 23:14:38 fedora20 kernel: Initializing cgroup subsys cpu
Aug 29 23:14:38 fedora20 kernel: Initializing cgroup subsys cpuacct
Aug 29 23:14:38 fedora20 kernel: Linux version
  3.11.10-301.fc20.x86_64 (mockbuild@bkernel01.fedoraproject.org)
    (gcc version 4.8.2 201
Aug 29 23:14:38 fedora20.example.com kernel: Command line:
    BOOT_IMAGE=/vmlinuz-3.11.10-301.fc20.x86_64
     root=/dev/mapper/fedora_fedora20-root ro rd.lvm
Aug 29 23:14:38 fedora20.example.com kernel: e820:
    BIOS-provided physical RAM map:

   . . .
```

To view messages associated with a particular service, use the -u option followed by the service name. For example:

```
# journalctl -u NetworkManager.service
# journalctl -u httpd.service
# journalctl -u avahi-daemon.service
```

If you think a security breach is in progress, you can watch all or selected messages as they come in by following messages. For example, to follow kernel messages or httpd messages as they come in, add the -f option (press Ctrl+C when you are finished):

```
# journalctl -k -f
# journalctl -f -u NetworkManager.service
```

To check only boot messages, you can list the boot IDs for all system boots and then boot the particular boot instance that interests you. The following examples display boot IDs and then show boot messages for a selected boot ID:

```
# journalctl --list-boots
-2 eb3d5cbdda8f4f8da7bdbc71fb94e61e
    Sun 2014-08-17 15:33:30 EDT—Wed 2014-08-20 06:43:29 EDT
-1 534713a5a65c41c1b5b3d056487a16db
    Wed 2014-08-20 06:45:15 EDT—Fri 2014-08-29 12:01:01 EDT
 0 64147da7154b4499a312a88a696c19bd
    Fri 2014-08-29 23:14:38 EDT—Sun 2014-09-14 07:15:26 EDT
# journalctl -b 534713a5a65c41c1b5b3d056487a16dbb
-- Logs begin at Sun 2014-08-17 15:33:30 EDT, end at
    Sun 2014-09-14 07:23:09 EDT. --
Aug 20 06:45:15 fedora20.example.com systemd-journal[81]:
    Runtime journal is using 8.0M (m
   . . .
```

Many other options are available with the journalctl command. For information on those options, see the journalctl man page (man journalctl). For more information about the systemd journal itself, type man systemd-journald.service.

Monitoring user accounts

User accounts are often used in malicious attacks on a system by gaining unauthorized access to a current account, creating new bogus accounts, or leaving an account behind to access later. To avoid such security issues, watching over user accounts is an important activity.

Detecting counterfeit new accounts and privileges

Accounts created without going through the appropriate authorization should be considered counterfeit. Also, modifying an account in any way that gives it a different unauthorized User Identification (UID) number or adds unauthorized group memberships is a form of rights escalation. Keeping an eye on the /etc/passwd and /etc/group files will monitor these potential breaches.

To help you monitor the /etc/passwd and /etc/group files, you can use the audit daemon. The audit daemon is an extremely powerful auditing tool that allows you to select system events to track and record them, and provides reporting capabilities.

To begin auditing the /etc/passwd and /etc/group files, you need to use the auditctl command. Two options at a minimum are required to start this process:

- **-w** *filename*—Place a watch on *filename*. The audit daemon tracks the file by its inode number. An *inode number* is a data structure that contains information concerning a file, including its location.

- **-p** *trigger(s)*—If one of these access types occurs (r=read, w=write, x=execute, a=attribute change) to *filename*, then trigger an audit record.

In the following example, a watch has been placed on the /etc/passwd file using the auditctl command. The audit daemon will monitor access, which consists of any reads, writes, or file attribute changes:

```
# auditctl -w /etc/passwd -p rwa
```

> **NOTE**
>
> After you have started a file audit, you may want to turn it off at some point. To turn off an audit, use the command auditctl -W *filename* -p *trigger(s)*.
>
> To see a list of current audited files and their watch settings, type auditctl -l at the command line.

To review the audit logs, use the audit daemon's ausearch command. The only option needed here is the -f option, which specifies which records you want to view from the audit log. The following is an example of the /etc/passwd audit information:

```
# ausearch -f /etc/passwd
time->Fri Feb  7 04:27:01 2014
type=PATH msg=audit(1328261221.365:572):
```

```
item=0 name="/etc/passwd" inode=170549
dev=fd:01 mode=0100644 ouid=0 ogid=0
rdev=00:00 obj=system_u:object_r:etc_t:s0
type=CWD msg=audit(1328261221.365:572):  cwd="/"
...
time->Fri Feb  7 04:27:14 2014
type=PATH msg=audit(1328261234.558:574):
item=0 name="/etc/passwd" inode=170549
dev=fd:01 mode=0100644 ouid=0 ogid=0
rdev=00:00 obj=system_u:object_r:etc_t:s0
type=CWD msg=audit(1328261234.558:574):
cwd="/home/johndoe"
type=SYSCALL msg=audit(1328261234.558:574):
arch=40000003 syscall=5 success=yes exit=3
a0=3b22d9 a1=80000 a2=1b6 a3=0 items=1 ppid=3891
pid=21696 auid=1000 uid=1000 gid=1000 euid=1000
suid=1000 fsuid=1000 egid=1000 sgid=1000 fsgid=1000
tty=pts1 ses=2 comm="vi" exe="/bin/vi"
 subj=unconfined_u:unconfined_r:unconfined_t:s0-s0:c0.c1023"
----
```

This is lots of information to review. A few items will help you see what audit event happened to trigger the bottom record.

- `time`—The time stamp of the activity
- `name`—The filename, /etc/passwd, being watched
- `inode`—The /etc/passwd's inode number on this filesystem
- `uid`—The user ID, 1000, of the user running the program
- `exe`—The program, /bin/vi, used on the /etc/passwd file

To determine what user account is assigned the UID of 1000, look at the /etc/password file. In this case, the UID of 1000 belongs to the user johndoe. Thus, from the audit event record displayed above, you can determine that account johndoe has attempted to use the vi editor on the /etc/passwd file. It is doubtful that this was an innocent action and it requires more investigation.

NOTE
The ausearch command returns nothing if no watch events on a file have been triggered.

The `audit` daemon and its associated tools are extremely rich. To learn more about it, look at the man pages for the following audit daemon utilities and configuration files:

- **auditd**—The audit daemon
- **auditd.conf**—The audit daemon configuration file

- **autditctl**—Controls the auditing system
- **audit.rules**—Configuration rules loaded at boot
- **ausearch**—Searches the audit logs for specified items
- **aureport**—Report creator for the audit logs
- **audispd**—Sends audit information to other programs

The audit daemon is one way to keep an eye on important files. You should review your account and group files on a regular basis also with a "human eye" to see if anything looks irregular.

Important files, such as /etc/passwd, do need to be monitored for unauthorized account creation. However, just as bad as a new unauthorized user account is an authorized user account with a bad password.

Detecting bad account passwords

Even with all your good efforts, bad passwords will slip in. Therefore, you do need to monitor user account passwords to ensure they are strong enough to withstand an attack.

One password strength monitoring tool you can use is the same one malicious users use to crack accounts, John the Ripper. John the Ripper is a free and open source tool that you can use at the Linux command line. It's not installed by default. For a Fedora distribution, you need to issue the command yum install john to install it.

> **TIP**
>
> To install John the Ripper on Ubuntu, use the command sudo apt-get install john.

In order to use John the Ripper to test user passwords, you must first extract account names and passwords using the unshadow command. This information needs to be redirected into a file for use by john, as shown here:

> # **unshadow /etc/passwd /etc/shadow > password.file**

Now, edit the password.file using your favorite text editor to remove any accounts without passwords. Because it is wise to limit John the Ripper to testing a few accounts at a time, remove any account names you do not wish to test presently.

> **CAUTION**
>
> The john utilities are extremely CPU-intensive. It does set its nice value to 19 in order to lower its priority. However, it would be wise to run it on a nonproduction system or during off-peak hours and for only a few accounts at a time.

Now, use the `john` command to attempt password cracks. To run `john` against the created password file, issue the command *john filename*. In the following code snippet, you can see the output from running `john` against the sample `password.file`. For demonstration purposes, only one account was left in the sample file. And the account, `Samantha`, was given the bad password of `password`. You can see how little time it took for John the Ripper to crack the password.

```
# john password.file
Loaded 1 password hash (generic crypt(3) [?/32])
password          (Samantha)
guesses: 1  time: 0:00:00:44 100% (2)   c/s: 20.87
 trying: 12345 - missy
Use the "--show" option to display all of the
 cracked passwords reliably
```

To demonstrate how strong passwords are vital, consider what happens when the `Samantha` account's password is changed from `password` to `Password1234`. Even though `Password1234` is still a weak password, it takes longer than 7 days of CPU time to crack it. In the code that follows, `john` was finally aborted to end the cracking attempt.

```
# passwd Samantha
Changing password for user Samantha.
...
# john password.file
Loaded 1 password hash (generic crypt(3) [?/32])
...
time: 0:07:21:55 (3)  c/s: 119  trying: tth675 - tth787
Session aborted
```

As soon as password cracking attempts have been completed, the `password.file` should be removed from the system. To learn more about John the Ripper, visit `www.openwall.com/john`.

Monitoring the filesystem

Malicious programs often modify files. They also can try to cover their tracks by posing as ordinary files and programs. However, there are ways to uncover them through various monitoring tactics covered in this section.

Verifying software packages

Typically, if you install a software package from a standard repository or download a reputable site's package, you won't have any problems. But it is always good to double-check your installed software packages to see if they have been compromised. The command to accomplish this is *rpm -V package_name*.

When you verify the software, information from the installed package files is compared against the package metadata (see Chapter 10) in the rpm database. If no problems are found, the rpm -V command returns nothing. However, if there are discrepancies, you get a coded listing. Table 22.5 shows the codes used and a description of the discrepancy.

TABLE 22.5 Package Verification Discrepancies

Code	Discrepancy
S	File size
M	File permissions and type
5	MD5 check sum
D	Device file's major and minor numbers
L	Symbolic links
U	User ownership
G	Group ownership
T	File modified times (mtime)
P	Other installed packages this package is dependent upon (aka capabilities)

In the partial list that follows, all the installed packages are given a verification check. You can see that the codes 5, S, and T were returned, indicating some potential problems.

```
# rpm -qaV
5S.T.....  c /etc/hba.conf
...
...T.....    /lib/modules/3.2.1-3.fc16.i686/modules.devname
...T.....    /lib/modules/3.2.1-3.fc16.i686/modules.softdep
```

You do not have to verify all your packages at once. You can verify just one package at a time. For example, if you want to verify your nmap package, you simply enter **rpm -V nmap.**

NOTE

To verify packages on Ubuntu, you need the debsums utility. It is not installed by default. To install debsums, use the command sudo apt-get install debsums. To check all installed packages, use the debsums -a command. To check one package, type **debsums packagename.**

Scanning the filesystem

Unless you have recently updated your system, binary files should not have been modified for any reason. To check for binary file modification, you can use the files' modify time, or mtime. The file mtime is the time when the contents of a file were last modified. Also, you can monitor the file's create/change time or ctime.

If you suspect malicious activity, you can quickly scan your filesystem to see if any binaries were modified or changed today (or yesterday, depending upon when you think the intrusion took place). To do this scan, use the find command.

In the example that follows, a scan is made of the /sbin directory. To see if any binary files were modified less than 24 hours ago, the command find /sbin -mtime -1 is used. In the example, several files display, showing they were modified recently. This indicates that malicious activity is taking place on the system. To investigate further, review each individual file's times, using the stat *filename* command, as shown here:

```
# find /sbin -mtime -1
/sbin
/sbin/init
/sbin/reboot
/sbin/halt
# stat /sbin/init
  File: '/sbin/init' -> '../bin/systemd'
  Size: 14      Blocks: 0      IO Block: 4096    symbolic link
Device: fd01h/64769d      Inode: 9551        Links: 1
Access: (0777/lrwxrwxrwx)
Uid: (    0/    root)  Gid: (    0/    root)
Context: system_u:object_r:bin_t:s0
Access: 2016-02-03 03:34:57.276589176 -0500
Modify: 2016-02-02 23:40:39.139872288 -0500
Change: 2016-02-02 23:40:39.140872415 -0500
 Birth: -
```

You could create a database of all the binary's original mtimes and ctimes and then run a script to find current mtimes and ctimes, compare them against the database, and note any discrepancies. However, this type of program has already been created and works well. It's called an Intrusion Detection System and is covered later in this chapter.

You need to perform several other filesystem scans on a regular basis. Favorite files or file settings of malicious attackers are listed in Table 22.6. The table also lists the commands to perform the scans and why the file or file setting is potentially problematic.

TABLE 22.6 Additional Filesystem Scans

File or Setting	Scan Command	Problem with File or Setting
SetUID permission	find / -perm -4000	Allows anyone to temporarily become the file's owner while the file is being executed in memory.
SetGID permission	find / -perm -2000	Allows anyone to temporarily become a group member of the file's group while the file is being executed in memory.

Continues

TABLE 22.6   *(continued)*

File or Setting	Scan Command	Problem with File or Setting
rhost files	`find /home -name .rhosts`	Allows a system to fully trust another system. Should not be in /home directories.
Ownerless files	`find / -nouser`	Indicates files that are not associated with any user name.
Groupless files	`find / -nogroup`	Indicates files that are not associated with any group name.

These filesystem scans help monitor what is going on in your system and help detect malicious attacks. However, other types of attacks can occur to your files, including viruses and rootkits.

Detecting viruses and rootkits

Two popular malicious attack tools are viruses and rootkits because they stay hidden while performing their malicious activities. Linux systems need to be monitored for both such tools.

Monitoring for viruses

A *computer virus* is malicious software that can attach itself to already installed system software and has the ability to spread through media or networks. It is a misconception that there are no Linux viruses. The malicious creators of viruses do often focus on the more popular desktop operating systems, such as Windows. However, that does not mean viruses are not created for the Linux systems.

Even more important, Linux systems are often used to handle services, such as mail servers, for Windows desktop systems. Therefore, Linux systems used for such purposes need to be scanned for Windows viruses as well.

Antivirus software scans files using virus signatures. A *virus signature* is a hash created from a virus's binary code. The hash will positively identify that virus. Antivirus programs have a virus signature database that is used to compare against files to see if there is a signature match. Depending upon the number of new threats, a virus signature database can be updated often to provide protection from these new threats.

A good antivirus software for your Linux system, which is open source and free, is ClamAV. To install ClamAV on a Fedora or RHEL system, type the command `yum install clamav`. You can find out more about ClamAV at `http://www.clamav.net/index.html`, where there is documentation on how to set up and run the antivirus software.

TIP

You can review the packages available for Ubuntu installation by entering the command `apt-cache search clamav`. A couple of different packages are available for Ubuntu, so review the ClamAV website information before you choose a package.

Monitoring for rootkits

A rootkit is a little more insidious than a virus. A *rootkit* is a malicious program that:

- Hides itself, often by replacing system commands or programs
- Maintains high-level access to a system
- Can circumvent software created to locate it

The purpose of a rootkit is to get and maintain root-level access to a system. The term was created by putting together "root," which means that it has to have administrator access, and "kit," which means it is usually several programs that operate in concert.

A rootkit detector that can be used on a Linux system is chkrootkit. To install chkrootkit on a Fedora or RHEL system, issue the command yum install chkrootkit. To install chkrookit on an Ubuntu system, use the command sudo apt-get install chkrootkit.

> **TIP**
>
> It is best to use a Live CD or flash drive to run chkrootkit so the results are not circumvented by a rootkit. The Fedora Security Spin has chkrootkit on its Live CD. You can get this distribution at http://spins .fedoraproject.org/security.

Finding a rootkit with chkrootkit is simple. After installing the package or booting up the Live CD, type in **chkrootkit** at the command line. It searches the entire file structure, denoting any infected files.

The code that follows shows a run of chkrootkit on an infected system. The grep command was used to search for the key word INFECTED. Notice that many of the files listed as "infected" are bash shell command files. This is typical of a rootkit.

```
# chkrootkit | grep INFECTED
Checking 'du'... INFECTED
Checking 'find'... INFECTED
Checking 'ls'... INFECTED
Checking 'lsof'... INFECTED
Checking 'pstree'... INFECTED
Searching for Suckit rootkit... Warning: /sbin/init INFECTED
```

In the last line of the preceding chkrootkit code is an indication that the system has been infected with the Suckit rootkit. It actually is not infected with this rootkit. When running utilities, such as antivirus and rootkit-detecting software, you often get a number of false positives. A *false positive* is an indication of a virus, rootkit, or other malicious activity that does not really exist. In this particular case, this false positive is caused by a known bug.

The chkrootkit utility should have regularly scheduled runs and, of course, should be run whenever a rootkit infection is suspected. To find more information on chkrootkit, go to http://chkrootkit.org.

Detecting an intrusion

Intrusion Detection System (IDS) software—a software package that monitors a system's activities (or its network) for potential malicious activities and reports these activities— can help you monitor your system for potential intrusions. Closely related to Intrusion Detection System software is a software package that prevents an intrusion, called Intrusion Prevention software. Some of these packages are bundled together to provide Intrusion Detection and Prevention.

Several Intrusion Detection System software packages are available for a Linux system. A few of the more popular utilities are listed in Table 22.7. You should know that tripwire is no longer open source. However, the original tripwire code is still available. See the tripwire website listed in Table 22.8 for more details.

TABLE 22.7 **Popular Linux Intrusion Detection Systems**

IDS Name	Installation	Website
aide	yum install aide apt-get install aide	http://aide.sourceforge.net
Snort	rpm or tarball packages from website	http://snort.org
tripwire	yum install tripwire apt-get install tripwire	http://tripwire.org

The Advanced Intrusion Detection Environment (aide) IDS uses a method of comparison to detect intrusions. When you were a child, you may have played the game of comparing two pictures and finding what was different between them. The aide utility uses a similar method. A "first picture" database is created. At some time later, another database "second picture" is created, and aide compares the two databases and reports what is different.

To begin, you need to take that "first picture." The best time to create this picture is when the system has been freshly installed. The command to create the initial database is aide -i and takes a long time to run. Some of its output follows. Notice that aide tells you where it is creating its initial "first picture" database.

```
# aide -i
AIDE, version 0.15.1

### AIDE database at /var/lib/aide/aide.db.new.gz initialized.
```

The next step is to move the initial "first picture" database to a new location. This protects the original database from being overwritten. Plus, the comparison does not work unless the database is moved. The command to move the database to its new location and give it a new name is as follows:

```
# cp /var/lib/aide/aide.db.new.gz /var/lib/aide/aide.db.gz
```

When you are ready to check whether your files have been tampered with, you need to create a new database, the "second picture," and compare it to the original database, the "first picture." The check option on the aide command, -c, creates a new database and runs a comparison against the old database. The output shown next illustrates this comparison being done and the aide command reporting on some problems.

```
# aide -C
...
--------------------------------------------------
Detailed information about changes:
--------------------------------------------------
File: /bin/find
Size : 189736 , 4620
Ctime : 2015-02-10 13:00:44 , 2015-02-11 03:05:52
MD5 : <NONE> , rUJj8NtNa1v4nmV5zfoOjg==
RMD160 : <NONE> , 0CwkiYhqNnfwPUPM12HdKuUSFUE=
SHA256 : <NONE> , jg60Soawj4S/UZXm5h4aEGJ+xZgGwCmN

File: /bin/ls
Size : 112704 , 6122
Ctime : 2015-02-10 13:04:57 , 2015-02-11 03:05:52
MD5 : POeOop46MvRx9qfEoYTXOQ== , IShMBpbSOY8axhw1Kj8Wdw==
RMD160 : N3V3Joe5Vo+cOSSnedf9PCDXYkI= ,
 e0ZneB7CrWHV42hAEgT2lwrVfP4=
SHA256 : vuOFe6FUgoAyNgIxYghOo6+SxR/zxS1s ,
 Z6nEMMBQyYm8486yFSIbKBuMUi/+jrUi


File: /bin/ps
Size : 76684 , 4828
Ctime : 2015-02-10 13:05:45 , 2015-02-11 03:05:52
MD5 : 1pCVAWbpeXINiBQWSUEJfQ== , 4ElJhyWkyMtm24vNLya6CA==
RMD160 : xwICWNtQH242jHsH2E8rV5kgSkU= ,
 AZlI2QNlKrWH45i3/V54H+1QQZk=
SHA256 : ffUDesbfxx3YsLDhD0bLTW0c6nykc3m0 ,
 wlqXvGWPFzFir5yxN+n6t3eOWw1TtNC/
...
File: /usr/bin/du
Size : 104224 , 4619
```

```
Ctime : 2015-02-10 13:04:58 , 2015-02-11 03:05:53
MD5 : 5DUMKWj6LodWj4C0xfPBIw== , nzn7vrwfBawAeL8nkayICg==
RMD160 : Zlbm0f/bUWRLgi1B5nVjhanuX9Q= ,
 2e5S00lBWqLq4Tnac4b6QIXRCwY=
SHA256 : P/jVAKr/SO0epBBxvGP900nLXrRY9tnw ,
 HhTqWgDyIkUDxA1X232ijmQ/OMA/kRgl

File: /usr/bin/pstree
Size : 20296 , 7030
Ctime : 2015-02-10 13:02:18 , 2015-02-11 03:05:53
MD5 : <NONE> , ry/MUZ7XvU4L2QfWJ4GXxg==
RMD160 : <NONE> , tFZer6As9EoOi58K7/LgmeiExjU=
SHA256 : <NONE> , iAsMkqNShagD4qe7dL/EwcgKTRzvKRSe
...
```

The files listed by the aide check in this example are infected. However, aide can also display many false positives.

Where aide databases are created, what comparisons are made, and several other configuration settings are handled in the /etc/aide.conf file. The following is a partial display of the file. You can see the names of the database file and the log file directories set here:

```
# cat /etc/aide.conf
# Example configuration file for AIDE.

@@define DBDIR /var/lib/aide
@@define LOGDIR /var/log/aide

# The location of the database to be read.
database=file:@@{DBDIR}/aide.db.gz

# The location of the database to be written.
#database_out=sql:host:port:database:login_name:passwd:table
#database_out=file:aide.db.new
database_out=file:@@{DBDIR}/aide.db.new.gz
...
```

An Intrusion Detection System can be a big help in monitoring the system. When potential intrusions are detected, comparing the output to information from other commands (such as rpm -V) and log files can help you better understand and correct any attacks on your system.

Auditing and Reviewing Linux

You must understand two important terms when you are auditing the health of your Linux system. A *compliance review* is an audit of the overall computer system environment to ensure that policies and procedures you have set for the system are being carried out correctly. A *security review* is an audit of current policies and procedures to ensure that they follow accepted best security practices.

Conducting compliance reviews

Similar to audits in other fields, such as accounting, audits can be conducted internally or by external personnel. These reviews can be as simple as someone sitting down and comparing implemented security to your company's stated policies. However, a more popular method is conducting audits using penetration testing.

Penetration testing is an evaluation method used to test a computer system's security by simulating malicious attacks. It is also called pen testing and ethical hacking. No longer do you have to gather tools and the local neighborhood hacker to help you conduct these tests. The following are Linux distributions you can use to conduct very thorough penetration tests:

- BackTrack (www.backtrack-linux.org)
  - Linux distribution created specifically for penetration testing
  - Can be used from a live DVD or a flash drive
  - Training on use of BackTrack offered by www.offensive-security.com
- Fedora Security Spin (http://spins.fedoraproject.org/security)
  - Also called Fedora Security Lab
  - Spin of the Fedora Linux distribution
  - Provides a test environment to work on security auditing
  - Can be used from a flash drive

While penetration testing is lots of fun, for a thorough compliance review, a little more is needed. You should also use checklists from industry security sites.

Conducting security reviews

Conducting a security review requires that you know current best security practices. There are several ways to stay informed about best security practices. The following is a brief list of organizations that can help you.

- United States Computer Emergency Readiness Team (CERT)
  - URL: www.us-cert.gov
  - Offers the National Cyber Alert System
  - Offers RSS feeds on the latest security threats

- The SANS Institute
  - URL: www.sans.org/security-resources
  - Offers Computer Security Research newsletters
  - Offers RSS feeds on the latest security threats
- Gibson Research Corporation
  - URL: www.grc.com
  - Offers the Security Now! security netcast

Information from these sites will assist you in creating stronger policies and procedures. Given how fast the best security practices change, it would be wise to conduct security reviews often, depending upon your organization's security needs.

Now you understand a lot more about basic Linux security. The hard part is actually putting all these concepts into practice.

Summary

Basic Linux security practices such as managing user accounts, securing passwords, and managing software and services form the foundation for all other security on your Linux system. With that foundation in place, ongoing monitoring of your system includes watching over system log files, checking for malicious intrusions, and monitoring the filesystem.

Reviews of your security policies are also important to keep up on a regular basis. Audits assist in ensuring that your Linux system is secured and the proper security policies and practices are in place.

You have completed your first step of gathering basic security procedures and principles knowledge. It is not enough to just know the basics. You need to add advanced Linux security tools to your security toolbox. In the next chapter, advanced security topics of cryptography and authentication modules are covered.

Exercises

Refer to the material in this chapter to complete the tasks that follow. If you are stuck, solutions to the tasks are shown in Appendix B (although in Linux, there are often multiple ways to complete a task). Try each of the exercises before referring to the answers. These tasks assume you are running a Fedora or Red Hat Enterprise Linux system (although some tasks will work on other Linux systems as well).

1. Check log messages from the `systemd` journal for the following services: `NetworkManager.service`, `sshd.service`, and `auditd.service`.

2. List the permissions of the file containing your system's user passwords, and determine if they are appropriate.

3. Determine your account's password aging and if it will expire using a single command.

4. Start auditing writes to the `/etc/shadow` with the `auditd` daemon, and then check your audit settings.

5. Create a report from the `auditd` daemon on the `/etc/shadow` file, and then turn off auditing on that file.

6. Install the lemon package, damage the `/usr/bin/lemon` file (perhaps copy `/etc/services` there), verify that the file has been tampered with, and remove the lemon package.

7. You suspect you have had a malicious attack on your system today and important binary files have been modified. What command should you use to find these modified files?

8. Install and run `chkrootkit` to see if the malicious attack from Exercise 7 installed a rootkit.

9. Find files with the `SetUID` or `SetGID` permission set.

10. Install the `aide` package, run the `aide` command to initialize the aide database, copy the database to the correct location, and run the `aide` command to check if any important files on your system have been modified.

22

Understanding Advanced Linux Security

D ue to ever changing and growing threats, implementing basic computer security is no longer enough. As malicious users gain access to and knowledge of advanced tools, so must a Linux systems administrator. Understanding advanced computer security topics and tools must be part of your preparation.

In this chapter, you learn about cryptography basics, such as ciphers and encryption. You also learn how the authentication module utility can simplify your administrative duties, even though it is an advanced security topic.

Implementing Linux Security with Cryptography

Using cryptography enhances the security of your Linux system and its network communications. *Cryptography* is the science of concealing information. It has a long and rich history that goes back far before computers were around. Because of its heavy use of mathematical algorithms, cryptography has easily transitioned to computers. Linux comes with many cryptographic tools ready for you to use.

To understand cryptographic concepts and the various Linux tools, you should know a few cryptography terms:

- **Plaintext**—Text that a human or machine can read and comprehend
- **Cipher text**—Text that a human or machine cannot read and comprehend

- **Encryption**—The process of converting plaintext into cipher text using an algorithm
- **Decryption**—The process of converting cipher text into plaintext using an algorithm
- **Cipher**—The algorithm used to encrypt plaintext into cipher text and decrypt cipher text into plaintext
- **Block cipher**—A cipher that breaks data into blocks before encrypting
- **Stream cipher**—A cipher that encrypts the data without breaking it up
- **Key**—A piece of data required by the cipher to successfully encrypt or decrypt data

Parents often use a form of cryptography. They spell words instead of speaking them. A parent may take the plaintext word "candy" and turn it into cipher text by saying to the other parent "C-A-N-D-Y." The other parent decrypts the word by using the same spelling cipher, and recognizes the word is "candy." Unfortunately, it does not take children long to learn how to decrypt via the spelling cipher.

You may have noticed that hashing was not included in the preceding cryptography definition list. Hashing needs some special attention because it is often confused with encryption.

Understanding hashing

Hashing is not encryption, but it is a form of cryptography. Remember from Chapter 22 that *hashing* is a one-way mathematical process used to create cipher text. However, unlike encryption, after you create a hash, you cannot de-hash it back to its original plaintext.

In order for a hashing algorithm to be used in computer security, it needs to be *collision-free*, which means that the hashing algorithm does not output the same hash for two totally different inputs. Each input must have a unique hashed output. Thus, *cryptographic hashing* is a one-way mathematical process that is collision-free.

By default, cryptography is already in use on a Linux system. For example, the /etc/shadow file contains hashed passwords. Hashing is used on Linux systems for:

- Passwords (Chapter 22)
- Verifying files
- Digital signatures
- Virus signatures (Chapter 22)

A hash is also called a message digest, checksum, fingerprint, or signature. One Linux utility that produces message digests is the md5sum utility. In Chapter 10, "Getting and Managing Software," you learned about getting software for your Linux system. When you download a software file, you can make sure the file was not corrupted on download.

Figure 23.1 shows the website for downloading the Linux Mint distribution software (stored as a file in the form that is referred to as an *ISO image*). The web page contains a Message

Digest 5 (MD5) number you can use to ensure that the ISO image you download was not corrupted during the download.

FIGURE 23.1

The Linux Mint ISO download web page provides an MD5 number.

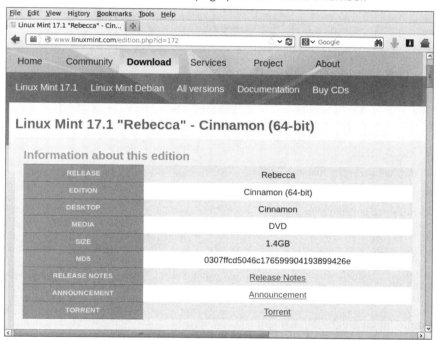

A hash is made of a software file at its original location, using the MD5 hash algorithm. The hash results can be posted in public, as was done in Figure 23.1. To ensure the integrity of your downloaded software file, you create an MD5 hash of the software file at your location. You then compare the results of your hash to the posted hash results. If they match, the software file was not corrupted upon download.

To create your hash, run the hashing algorithm on the ISO image after you download it, using md5sum. The md5sum hash results for the downloaded software file are shown in the code that follows:

```
$ md5sum linuxmint-17.1-cinnamon-64bit.iso
0307ffcd5046c176599904193899426e  linuxmint-17.1-cinnamon-64bit.iso
```

The resulting hash *does* match the one posted on the website in Figure 23.1. This means the downloaded ISO file has not been corrupted and is ready for use.

> **CAUTION**
>
> While MD5 hashing is fine for ensuring that a downloaded software file has not been corrupted, the algorithm is not collision-free. Therefore, it is no longer considered a true cryptographic hash. For true cryptographic hashing, you need to use one of the SHA cryptographic hashes discussed later in this chapter.

You can implement even more cryptography besides hashing on your Linux system. The Linux utilities to do so are very easy to use. However, first you need to understand a few more underlying cryptography concepts.

Understanding encryption/decryption

The primary use of cryptography on a Linux system is to encode data to hide it (encryption) from unauthorized eyes and then decode the data (decryption) for authorized eyes. On a Linux system, you can encrypt the following:

- Individual files
- Partitions and volumes
- Web page connections
- Network connections
- Backups
- Zip files

These encryption/decryption processes use special math algorithms to accomplish their task. The algorithms are called *cryptographic ciphers*.

Understanding cryptographic ciphers

One of the original ciphers, called the Caesar Cipher, was created and used by Julius Caesar. However, it was terribly easy to crack. Today, many more secure ciphers are available. Understanding how each cipher works is important because the strength of the cipher you choose should directly relate to the security needs of your data. Table 23.1 lists a few modern ciphers.

TABLE 23.1 **Cryptography Ciphers**

Method	Description
AES (Advanced Encryption Standard) also called Rijndael	Symmetric cryptography.
	Block cipher, encrypting data in 128-, 192-, or 256-bit blocks using a 128-, 192-, or 256-bit key for encrypting/decrypting.
Blowfish	Symmetric cryptography.
	Block cipher, encrypting data in 64-bit blocks using the same 32-bit to 448-bit keys for encrypting/decrypting.

Method	Description
CAST5	Symmetric cryptography.
	Block cipher, encrypting data in 64-bit blocks using the same up to 128-bit key for encrypting/decrypting.
DES (Data Encryption Standard)	No longer considered secure.
	Symmetric cryptography.
	Block cipher, encrypting data in 64-bit blocks using the same 56-bit key for encrypting/decrypting.
3DES	Improved DES cipher.
	Symmetric cryptography.
	Data is encrypted up to 48 times with 3 different 56-bit keys before the encryption process is completed.
El Gamal	Asymmetric cryptography.
	Uses two keys derived from a logarithm algorithm.
Elliptic Curve Cryptosystems	Asymmetric cryptography.
	Uses two keys derived from an algorithm containing two randomly chosen points on an elliptic curve.
IDEA	Symmetric cryptography.
	Block cipher, encrypting data in 64-bit blocks using the same 128-bit key for encrypting/decrypting.
RC4 also called ArcFour or ARC4	Stream cipher, encrypting data in 64-bit blocks using a variable key size for encrypting/decrypting.
RC5	Symmetric cryptography.
	Block cipher, encrypting data in 32-, 64-, or 128-bit blocks using the same up to 2,048-bit keys for encrypting/decrypting.
RC6	Symmetric cryptography.
	Same as RC5, but slightly faster.
Rijndael also called AES	Symmetric cryptography.
	Block cipher, encrypting data in 128-, 192-, or 256-bit blocks using a 128-, 192-, or 256-bit key for encrypting/decrypting.
RSA	Most popular asymmetric cryptography.
	Uses two keys derived from an algorithm containing a multiple of two randomly generated prime numbers.

Understanding cryptographic cipher keys

Cryptographic ciphers require a piece of data, called a key, to complete their mathematical process of encryption/decryption. The key can be either a single key or a pair of keys.

Notice the different cipher key sizes listed in Table 23.1. The key size is directly related to how easily the cipher is cracked. The bigger the key size, the less the chance of cracking the cipher. For example, DES is no longer considered secure because of its small 56-bit key size. However, a cipher with a key size of 256 bits or 512 bits is considered secure because it would take trillions of years to brute-force crack such a keyed cipher.

Symmetric key cryptography

Symmetric cryptography, also called *secret key* or *private key* cryptography, encrypts plaintext using a single keyed cipher. The same key is needed in order to decrypt the data. The advantage of symmetric key cryptography is speed. The disadvantage is the need to share the single key if the encrypted data is to be decrypted by another person.

An example of symmetric key cryptography on a Linux system is accomplished using the OpenPGP utility, GNU Privacy Guard, gpg2. The gnupg2 package is installed by default in Fedora and RHEL. For Ubuntu, you need to install the gnupg2 package to get the gpg2 command.

The example that follows shows the tar command used to create a compressed tar archive (backup.tar.gz) and the gpg2 utility used to encrypt the file. With the -c option, gpg2 encrypts the file with a symmetric key. The original file is kept and a new encrypted file, backup.tar.gz.gpg, is created.

```
# tar -cvzf /tmp/backup.tar.gz /etc
# gpg2 -c --force-mdc -o tmp/backup.tar.gz.gpg /tmp/backup.tar.gz
Enter passphrase: ******
Repeat passphrase: ******
# cd /tmp ; file backup*
backup.tar.gz: gzip compressed data, last modified: ...
backup.tar.gz.gpg: GPG symmetrically encrypted data (CAST5 cipher)
```

The single key used to encrypt the file is protected by a passphrase. This passphrase is simply a password or phrase chosen by the user at the time of encryption.

To decrypt the file, use the gpg2 utility again. For example, if you were to hand the file to another user, that user could run gpg2 with the -d option and provide the passphrase for the secret key.

```
$ gpg2 -d --force-mdc /tmp/backup.tar.gz.gpg > /tmp/backup.tar.gz
<A pop-up window asks for your passphrase>
gpg: CAST5 encrypted data
gpg: encrypted with 1 passphrase
This is my secret message.
. . .
```

The result is that the original tar file is decrypted and copied to /tmp/backup.tar.gz. If the gpg-agent daemon is running on the system, that passphrase is cached, so that file could be decrypted again without entering the passphrase again.

Symmetric key cryptography is rather simple and easy to understand. Asymmetric cryptography is much more complicated and often is a point of confusion in cryptography.

Asymmetric key cryptography

Asymmetric cryptography, also called private/public key cryptography, uses two keys, called a *key pair*. A key pair consists of a public key and a private key. The public key is just that—public. There is no need to keep it secret. The private key needs to be kept secret.

The general idea of asymmetric key cryptography is shown in Figure 23.2. A plaintext file is encrypted using a public key of a key pair. The encrypted file then can be securely transmitted to another person. To decrypt the file, the private key is used. This private key must be from the public/private key pair. Thus, data that has been encrypted with the public key can only be decrypted with its private key. The advantage of asymmetric cryptography is heightened security. The disadvantages are speed and key management.

FIGURE 23.2

Basic asymmetric key cryptography

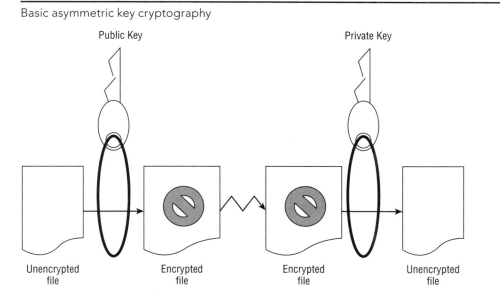

Public Key			Private Key
Unencrypted file	Encrypted file	Encrypted file	Unencrypted file

You can perform asymmetric encryption on your Linux system using gpg2. It is a very versatile cryptographic utility. Before you can encrypt a file, you must first create your key pair and a "key ring." In the example that follows, the gpg2 --gen-key command was used. This command creates a public/private key pair for the user johndoe, according to his desired specifications. It also generates a key ring to store his keys.

```
$ gpg2 --gen-key
gpg (GnuPG) 2.0.22; Copyright (C)
 2013 Free Software Foundation, Inc.
 ...
Please select what kind of key you want:
    (1) RSA and RSA (default)
    (2) DSA and Elgamal
    (3) DSA (sign only)
    (4) RSA (sign only)
Your selection? 1
RSA keys may be between 1024 and 4096 bits long.
What keysize do you want? (2048) 2048
Requested keysize is 2048 bits
Please specify how long the key should be valid.
        0 = key does not expire
      <n>  = key expires in n days
      <n>w = key expires in n weeks
      <n>m = key expires in n months
      <n>y = key expires in n years
Key is valid for? (0) 7
Key expires at Mon 05 Dec 2016 03:55:29 AM EST
Is this correct? (y/N) y

You need a user ID to identify your key.

Real name: John Doe
Email address: jdoe@example.com
Comment: The User
You selected this USER-ID:
    "John Doe (The User) <jdoe@gmail.com>"

Change (N)ame, (C)omment, (E)mail or (O)kay/(Q)uit? O
You need a Passphrase to protect your secret key.
Enter passphrase: **********
Repeat passphrase: **********
...
gpg: /home/johndoe/.gnupg/trustdb.gpg: trustdb created
gpg: key 3B2E46D5 marked as ultimately trusted
public and secret key created and signed.
...
pub   2048R/3B2E46D5 2015-12-08 [expires: 2015-12-15]
      Key fingerprint = E202 8E43 3784 69EF 118B
  275C BA45 7DBF 3B2E 46D5
uid                 John Doe (The User) <jdoe@example.com>
sub   2048R/0F0E0672 2015-12-087 [expires: 2016-12-15]
```

In the preceding example, the gpg2 utility asks for several specifications to generate the desired private/public keys:

- **Cryptography cipher**—RSA was chosen in the example.
- **Bit size**—A longer key size provides higher security.
- **Validity period**—Seven days was chosen in the example.
- **User ID**—This identifies the public key portion of the public/private key pair.
- **Passphrase**—This is used to identify and protect the private key portion of the public/private key pair.

> **CAUTION**
>
> It is difficult, if not mathematically impossible, to derive the private key from the public key. However, a potential vulnerability has been discovered. A key pair set is generated using two prime random numbers. The idea is that no two key pairs would be identical. Security researchers have discovered that the random numbers generated are not that random. Thus, there is the potential to have the same key pair as someone else on the Internet. If you share the same key pair, you have the ability to decrypt their public key encrypted messages with your private key. Therefore, you should, at a minimum, use the 2,048-bit key size to reduce the chance of this potential situation.

The user johndoe can check his key ring by using the gpg2 --list-keys command, as shown in the code that follows. Notice the User ID (UID) of the public key is displayed just as it was created, containing johndoe's real name, comment, and e-mail address.

```
$ gpg2 --list-keys
/home/johndoe/.gnupg/pubring.gpg
--------------------------------
pub   2048R/3B2E46D5 2015-12-08 [expires: 2016-12-15]
uid                  John Doe (The User) <jdoe@example.com>
sub   2048R/0F0E0672 2015-12-08 [expires: 2016-12-15]
```

After the key pair and key ring are generated, files can be encrypted and decrypted. First, the public key must be extracted from the key ring so it can be shared. In the example that follows, the gpg2 utility is used to extract the public key from johndoe's key ring. The extracted key is put into a file to be shared. The filename can be any name you wish it to be. In this case, the user johndoe chose the filename JohnDoe.pub.

```
$ gpg2 --export John Doe > JohnDoe.pub
$ ls *.pub
JohnDoe.pub
```

The file containing the public key can be shared any number of ways. It can be sent as an attachment via email or even posted on a web page. The public key is considered public, so there is no need to hide it. In the example that follows, johndoe has given the file containing his public key to the user jill. She adds johndoe's public key to her key ring, using the gpg2 --import command. The user jill verifies that johndoe's public key is added using the gpg2 --list-keys command to view her key ring.

```
$ ls *.pub
JohnDoe.pub
$ gpg2 --import JohnDoe.pub
gpg: directory '/home/jill/.gnupg' created
...
gpg: key 3B2E46D5:
 public key "John Doe (The User) <jdoe@example.com>" imported
gpg: Total number processed: 1
gpg:                   imported: 1   (RSA: 1)
$ gpg2 --list-keys
/home/jill/.gnupg/pubring.gpg
-----------------------------------
pub   2048R/3B2E46D5 2016-12-08 [expires: 2016-12-15]
uid                  John Doe (The User) <jdoe@example.com>
sub   2048R/0F0E0672 2016-12-08 [expires: 2016-12-15]
```

After the key is added to the key ring, that public key can be used to encrypt data for the public key's original owner. In the example code that follows, note the following:

- jill has created a text file, MessageForJohn.txt, for user johndoe.
- She encrypts the file using *his* public key.
- The encrypted file, MessageForJohn, is created by the --out option.
- The option --recipient identifies johndoe's public key using only the real name portion of his public key's UID in quotation marks, "John Doe".

```
$ gpg2 --out MessageForJohn --recipient "John Doe" \
  --encrypt MessageForJohn.txt
...
$ ls
JohnDoe.pub  MessageForJohn  MessageForJohn.txt
```

The encrypted message file, MessageForJohn, created from the plaintext file, MessageForJohn.txt, can be securely sent to the user johndoe. In order to decrypt this message, johndoe uses *his* private key, identified and protected by the secret passphrase used to originally create the key. After johndoe provides the proper passphrase, gpg2 decrypts the message file and puts it into the file, JillsMessage, designated by the --out option. Once decrypted, he can read the plaintext message.

```
$ ls MessageForJohn
MessageForJohn
$ gpg2 --out JillsMessage --decrypt MessageForJohn

You need a passphrase to unlock the secret key for
user: "John Doe (The User) <jdoe@gmail.com>"
2048-bit RSA key, ID 0F0E0672, created 2016-12-08
 (main key ID 3B2E46D5)

gpg: encrypted with 2048-bit RSA key, ID 0F0E0672,
 created 2016-02-27
```

```
        "John Doe (The User) <jdoe@example.com>"
$ cat JillsMessage
I know you are not the real John Doe.
```

To review, the steps needed for encryption/decryption of files using asymmetric keys include the following:

1. Generate the key pair and the key ring.
2. Export a copy of your public key to a file.
3. Share the public key file.
4. Individuals who want to send you encrypted files add your public key to their key ring.
5. A file is encrypted using *your* public key.
6. The encrypted file is sent to you.
7. You decrypt the file using *your* private key.

You can see why asymmetric keys can cause confusion! Remember that in asymmetric cryptography, each public and private key is a paired set that works together.

Understanding digital signatures

A *digital signature* is an electronic originator used for authentication and data verification. A digital signature is not a scan of your physical signature. Instead, it is a cryptographic token sent with a file, so the file's receiver can be assured that the file came from you and has not been modified in any way.

When you create a digital signature, the following steps occur:

1. You create a file or message.
2. Using the gpg2 utility, you create a hash or message-digest of the file.
3. The gpg2 utility then encrypts the hash and the file, using an asymmetric key cipher. For the encryption, the private key of the public/private key pair is used. This is now a digitally signed encrypted file.
4. You send the encrypted hash (a.k.a. digital signature) and file to the receiver.
5. The receiver recreates the hash or message digest of the received encrypted file.
6. Using the gpg2 utility, the receiver decrypts the received digital signature using the public key, to obtain the original hash or message digest.
7. The gpg2 utility compares the original hash to the recreated hash to see if they match. If they match, the receiver is told the digital signature is good.
8. The receiver can now read the decrypted file.

Notice in Step 3 that the private key is used first. In the description of asymmetric key cryptography, the public key was used first. Asymmetric key cryptography is flexible enough to allow you to use your private key to encrypt and the receiver to use your public key to decrypt.

As you can see, a digital signature contains both cryptographic hashing and asymmetric key cryptography. This complicated process is often handled by an application that has been configured to do so, instead of being directly handled by Linux system users. However, you can manually add your own digital signatures to documents.

Let's say that user `johndoe` is going to send a message to the user `christineb`, along with his digital signature. He has created a file containing the plaintext message to send. He uses the `gpg2` utility to create the signature file and encrypt the message file. The `--sign` option tells the `gpg2` utility that `MessageForChristine.txt` is the file to encrypt and use to create the digital signature. In response, the `gpg2` utility:

- Creates a message digest (a.k.a. hash) of the message file
- Encrypts the message digest, which creates the digital signature
- Encrypts the message file
- Places the encrypted contents into the file specified by the `--output` option, `JohnDoe.DS`

The file `JohnDoe.DS` now contains an encrypted and digitally signed message. The following code demonstrates this process:

```
$ gpg2 --output JohnDoe.DS --sign MessageForJill.txt

You need a passphrase to unlock the secret key for
user: "John Doe (The User) <jdoe@example.com>"
2048-bit RSA key, ID 3B2E46D5, created 2016-12-08
```

After the user `jill` receives the signed and encrypted file, she can use the `gpg2` utility to check the digital signature and decrypt the file in one step. In the code that follows, the `--decrypt` option is used along with the name of the digitally signed file, `JohnDoe.DS`. The file's message is decrypted and shown. The digital signature of the file is checked and found to be valid.

```
$ gpg2 --decrypt JohnDoe.DS
I am the real John Doe!
gpg: Signature made Mon 27 Feb 2016 09:42:36 AM EST
 using RSA key ID 3B2E46D5
gpg: Good signature from "John Doe (The User) <jdoe@example.com>"
 ...
```

Without johndoe's public key on her key ring, jill would not be able to decrypt this message and check the digital signature.

> **TIP**
>
> The previous example of digitally signing a document allows anyone with the public key the ability to decrypt the document. In order to keep it truly private, use the public key of the recipient to encrypt with the gpg2 options: --sign and --encrypt. The recipient can decrypt with his or her private key.

Understanding a few cryptography basics will help you get started on securing your Linux system with encryption. Keep in mind that we've covered just the basics in this chapter. There are many more cryptography topics, such as digital certificates and public key infrastructure, that would be worth your time to learn.

Implementing Linux cryptography

Many cryptography tools are available on your Linux system. Which ones you choose to use depend upon your organization's security requirements. The following is a brief review of some of the Linux cryptography tools available.

Ensuring file integrity

Earlier in this chapter, an ISO's file integrity was checked using the message digest utility md5sum. The other most popular message digest tool is one that uses the SHA-1 hash, sha1sum. It works identically at the command line to the md5sum utility, as shown in the code that follows. If an ISO file has an SHA-1 hash listed, instead of an MD5 checksum, you can use the following to check the hash.

```
$ sha1sum Fedora-Live-Desktop-x86_64-20-1.iso
a4cec536ed5bd0c0754eb8840d5af475  Fedora-Live-Desktop-x86_64-20-1.iso
```

Unfortunately, as of 2005, the SHA-1 hash standard was no longer considered to be a cryptographic hash due to some "mathematical weaknesses." However, as with the MD5, that has not diminished its popularity for checking file integrity.

If your particular organization requires a true cryptographic hash utility, you must use one of the SHA-2 cryptographic hash tools. On Linux, these include:

- sha224sum
- sha256sum
- sha384sum
- sha512sum

These tools work just like the sha1sum command, except, of course, they use the SHA-2 cryptographic hash standard. The only difference between the various SHA-2 tools is the key length they use. The sha224sum command uses a key length of 224 bits, the sha256sum command uses a key length of 256 bits, and so on. Remember that the longer the key length, the less the chance of cracking the cipher.

The SHA-2 cryptographic hash standard was created by the National Security Agency (NSA). They have another cryptographic hash standard to be released soon, SHA-3.

Encrypting a Linux filesystem

You may need to encrypt an entire filesystem on your Linux server. This can be done in a number of different ways, including using a Free and Open Source Software (FOSS) third-party tool such as TrueCrypt (www.truecrypt.org) or Linux Unified Key Setup (LUKS) (https://code.google.com/p/cryptsetup/).

One of your options in Linux is to encrypt your root partition upon installation (see Chapter 9, "Installing Linux"). Many Linux distributions include an encryption option during their installation process. Figure 23.3 shows the encryption option during a Fedora installation.

FIGURE 23.3

Linux Fedora installation encryption option

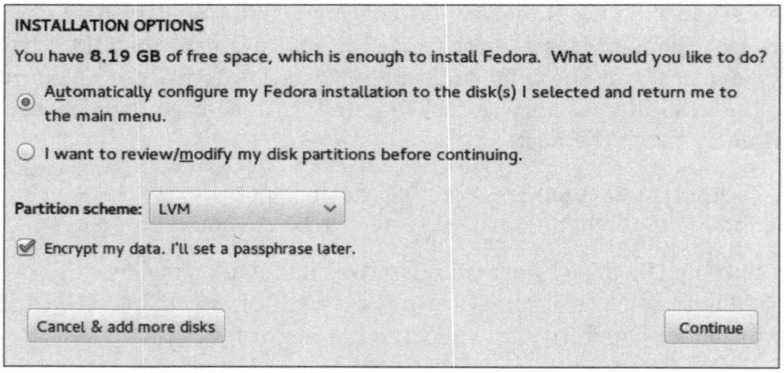

After you select this option during installation, you are asked for a password. This is symmetric key cryptography with a password protecting the single key. Figure 23.4 shows the installation asking for the key's password. The password must be at least eight characters long.

If you select this encryption option, whenever you boot the system, you are asked for the symmetric key password. Figure 23.5 shows what this looks like. This protects the root partition, should the disk it resides on be stolen.

FIGURE 23.4

Linux Fedora encryption symmetric key password

DISK ENCRYPTION PASSPHRASE

You have chosen to encrypt some of your data. You will need to create a passphrase that you will use to access your data when you start your computer.

Passphrase: ●●●●●●●●●●●●●●

⌨ ie   Strong ▮▮▮▮

Confirm: ●●●●●●●●●●●●●●

⚠ Warning: You won't be able to switch between keyboard layouts (from the default one) when you decrypt your disks after install.

Cancel   Save Passphrase

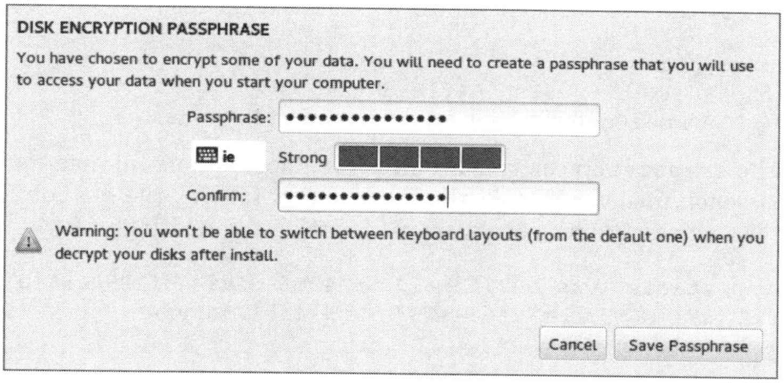

FIGURE 23.5

Asking for the encryption symmetric key password at boot

If you inherit a system with an encrypted disk, using root privileges, you can use the `lvs` and `cryptsetup` commands and the `/etc/crypttab` file to help. In the following, the `lvs` command shows all the logical volumes current on the system and their underlying device names. See Chapter 12, "Managing Disks and Filesystems," for a review of the `lvs` command.

```
# lvs -o devices
Devices
/dev/mapper/luks-b099fbbe-0e56-425f-91a6-44f129db9f4b(56)
/dev/mapper/luks-b099fbbe-0e56-425f-91a6-44f129db9f4b(0)
```

On this system, notice that the underlying device names start with `luks`. This indicates that the Linux Unified Key Setup (LUKS) standard for hard disk encryption has been used.

NOTE

Ubuntu does not have the `lvs` command installed by default. To install it, type `sudo apt-get install lvm2` at the command line.

The encrypted logical volumes are mounted at boot time using the information from the /etc/crypttab file, as shown in the following code. Notice that the luks names are the same as those listed by the lvs command in the previous example.

```
# cat /etc/crypttab
luks-b099fbbe-0e56-425f-91a6-44f129db9f4b
      UUID=b099fbbe-0e56-425f-91a6-44f129db9f4b none
```

You can also use the cryptsetup command to help you uncover more information about your Linux system's encrypted volumes. In the example that follows, the status option is used along with the luks device name to determine further information.

```
# cryptsetup status luks-b099fbbe-0e56-425f-91a6-44f129db9f4b
/dev/mapper/luks-b099fbbe-0e56-425f-91a6-44f129db9f4b
 is active and is in use.
  type:    LUKS1
  cipher:  aes-xts-plain64
  keysize: 512 bits
  device:  /dev/sda3
  offset:  4096 sectors
  size:    493819904 sectors
  mode:    read/write
```

Encrypting a Linux directory

You can also use the ecryptfs utility to encrypt on a Linux system. The ecryptfs utility is not a filesystem type as the name would imply. Instead, it is a POSIX-compliant utility that allows you to create an encryption layer on top of any filesystem.

The ecryptfs utility is not installed by default on Fedora and RHEL. To install that utility, you must use the command yum install ecryptfs-utils. If it is not installed on a Debian system, use the command sudo apt-get install ecrypt-utils.

> **TIP**
>
> Because the ecryptfs utility is used for encryption, it is a common mistake to put the letter n after the letter e in the syntax ecryptfs. If you get an error while using the ecryptfs utilities, make sure you did not use the syntax encryptfs by mistake.

In the example that follows, the user johndoe will have a subdirectory encrypted using the ecryptfs utility. First, there should be no files currently residing in the directory before it is encrypted. If there are files located there, move them to a safe place until after the encryption has been completed. If you do not move them, you cannot access them while the directory is encrypted.

Now, to encrypt the directory /home/johndoe/Secret, use the mount command. Look at the mount command used in the example that follows. It is somewhat similar to the regular mount command, except the partition type used is ecryptfs. The item to mount and its mount point are the same directory! You are literally encrypting the directory and mounting it upon itself. The other unusual item about this mount command is that it kicks off the ecryptfs utility, which asks a few interactive questions.

```
# mount -t ecryptfs /home/johndoe/Secret /home/johndoe/Secret
Select key type to use for newly created files:
 1) tspi
 2) passphrase
 3) pkcs11-helper
 4) openssl
Selection: 2
Passphrase: **********
Select cipher:
 1) aes: blocksize = 16;
 min keysize = 16; max keysize = 32 (loaded)
 2) blowfish: blocksize = 16;
 min keysize = 16; max keysize = 56 (not loaded)
 3) des3_ede: blocksize = 8;
 min keysize = 24; max keysize = 24 (not loaded)
 4) twofish: blocksize = 16;
 min keysize = 16; max keysize = 32 (not loaded)
 5) cast6: blocksize = 16;
 min keysize = 16; max keysize = 32 (not loaded)
 6) cast5: blocksize = 8;
 min keysize = 5; max keysize = 16 (not loaded)
Selection [aes]: 1
Select key bytes:
 1) 16
 2) 32
 3) 24
Selection [16]: 16
Enable plaintext passthrough (y/n) [n]: n
Enable filename encryption (y/n) [n]: n
Attempting to mount with the following options:
  ecryptfs_unlink_sigs
  ecryptfs_key_bytes=16
  ecryptfs_cipher=aes
  ecryptfs_sig=70993b8d49610e67
WARNING: Based on the contents of [/root/.ecryptfs/sig-cache.txt]
it looks like you have never mounted with this key
before. This could mean that you have typed your
passphrase wrong.

Would you like to proceed with the mount (yes/no)? : yes
Would you like to append sig [70993b8d49610e67] to
[/root/.ecryptfs/sig-cache.txt]
in order to avoid this warning in the future (yes/no)? : yes
Successfully appended new sig to user sig cache file
Mounted eCryptfs
```

The `ecryptfs` utility allows you to choose the following:

- Key type
- Passphrase
- Cipher
- Key size (in bytes)
- To enable or disable plaintext to pass through
- To enable or disable filename encryption

It also warns you when you are first mounting this encrypted directory because the key has not been used before. The utility allows you to apply a digital signature to the mounted directory so that if you mount it again, it just mounts the directory and does not require a passphrase.

> **TIP**
> Write down the selections you make when you mount an `ecryptfs` folder for the first time. You need the exact selections you chose the next time you remount the folder.

To verify that the encrypted directory is now mounted, you can use the `mount` command again. In the example that follows, the `mount` command is used and then piped into `grep` to search for the `/home/johndoe/Secret` directory. The directory is mounted with an `ecryptfs` type.

```
# mount | grep /home/johndoe/Secret
/home/johndoe/Secret on /home/johndoe/Secret type ecryptfs
(rw,relatime,ecryptfs_sig=70993b8d49610e67,ecryptfs_cipher=aes,
ecryptfs_key_bytes=16,ecryptfs_unlink_sigs)
```

So far, you have not seen the effects of this mounted and encrypted directory. In the text that follows, the file `my_secret_file` is copied to the encrypted directory. User `johndoe` can still use the `cat` command to display the file in plaintext. The file is automatically decrypted by the `ecryptfs` layer.

```
$ cp my_secret_file Secret
$ cat /home/johndoe/Secret/my_secret_file
Shh... It's a secret.
```

The root user also can use the `cat` command to display the file in plaintext.

```
# cat /home/johndoe/Secret/my_secret_file
Shh... It's a secret.
```

However, after the encrypted directory is unmounted using the `umount` command, the files are no longer automatically decrypted. The file `my_secret_file` is now gibberish and cannot be read, even by the root user.

```
# umount /home/johndoe/Secret
```

Thus, the `ecryptfs` utility allows you to create a location on the file system to quickly encrypt and decrypt files. However, after that directory is no longer mounted as an `ecryptfs` type, the files are secure and cannot be decrypted.

Encrypting a Linux file

The most popular tool for file encryption on a Linux system is the OpenPGP utility GNU Privacy Guard, `gpg`. Its flexibility and variety of options, along with the fact that it is installed by default on most Linux distributions, add to its appeal.

> **CAUTION**
>
> If your organization uses a third-party cloud storage company, you need to know that some of these companies, such as Dropbox, do not encrypt the files until they are received. This means that the company has the keys needed to decrypt your files and can leave your organization's data vulnerable. Encrypting files on your Linux system before they are sent to the cloud adds the extra layer of protection needed.

However, you can use several other cryptography tools on a Linux system to encrypt files. And just like `gpg`, many of these tools allow you to do much more than just file encryption. The following are some of the popular Linux cryptography tools you can use to encrypt files:

- `aescrypt`—It uses the symmetric key cipher Rijndael, also called AES. This third-party FOSS tool is available for download from `www.aescript.com`.

- `bcrypt`—This tool uses the symmetric key cipher blowfish. It is not installed by default. After `bcrypt` is installed, man pages are available.
  - For Fedora and RHEL: `yum install bcrypt`.
  - For Ubuntu: `sudo apt-get install bcrypt`.

- `ccrypt`—This tool uses the symmetric key cipher Rijndael, also called AES. It was created to replace the standard Unix `crypt` utility and is not installed by default. After `ccrypt` is installed, man pages are available.
  - For Fedora and RHEL: `yum install ccrypt`.
  - For Ubuntu: `sudo apt-get install ccrypt`.

- `gpg`—This utility can use either asymmetric key pairs or a symmetric key. It is installed by default and is the cryptography tool of choice for Linux servers. The default cipher to use is set in the `gpg.conf` file. There are man pages available as well as `info gnupg`.

Keep in mind that this list just covers the more popular tools. Also, remember that many of these file cryptography tools can be used for more than just file cryptography.

Encrypting Linux with miscellaneous tools

You can apply cryptology to just about everything in Linux. Besides filesystems, directories, and files, you can also encrypt backups, Zip files, network connections, and more.

Table 23.2 lists some of the miscellaneous Linux cryptology tools and what they do. If you want to see a full list of installed cryptography tools on your current Linux distribution, type `man -k crypt` at the command line.

TABLE 23.2 Linux Miscellaneous Cryptography Tools

Tool	Description
Duplicity	Encrypts backups. Installed by default on Fedora and RHEL. To install on Ubuntu, type **sudo apt-get install duplicity** at the command line.
gpg-zip	Uses GNU Privacy Guard to encrypt or sign files into an archive. Installed by default.
Openssl	A toolkit that implements Secure Socket Layer (SSL) and Transport Layer Security (TLS) protocols. These protocols require encryption. Installed by default.
Seahorse	A GNU Privacy Guard encryption key manager. Installed by default on Ubuntu. To install on Fedora and RHEL, type **yum install seahorse** at the command line.
Ssh	Encrypts remote access across a network. Installed by default.
Zipcloak	Encrypts entries in a Zip file. Installed by default.

Like many other items on a Linux system, the cryptography tools available are rich and plentiful. This gives you the flexibility and variety you need in order to implement the cryptology standards your particular organization requires.

Using Encryption from the Desktop

The Passwords and Keys window provides a means of viewing and managing keys and passwords from the GNOME desktop. This window can be launched by selecting the Passwords and Keys icon from the Activities screen or by running the seahorse command. With the window that appears, you can work with the following:

- **Passwords**—When you access a website and enter a username and password (and you select to save that password), it is stored on your system for the next time you visit that site. Select the Login entry under the Passwords heading to see each of these saved usernames and passwords.

- **Certificates**—You can view certificates associated with the Gnome2 Key Storage, User Key Storage, System Trust, and Default Trust.

- **PGP keys**—You can view the GPG keys you create by selecting the GnuPG keys entry. Figure 23.6 shows the results of selecting the entry for John Doe created earlier in this chapter to see details about that user's private key.

- **Secure shell**—You can create public and private OpenSSH keys that let you log in to remote systems using those keys instead of passwords for authentication with ssh, scp, rsync, sftp, and related commands. Select OpenSSH keys to view any keys you have created for this purpose. (See the "Using key-based passwordless authentication" section of Chapter 13 for information on creating these types of keys.)

FIGURE 23.6

View private keys on your system from the Passwords and Keys window (seahorse).

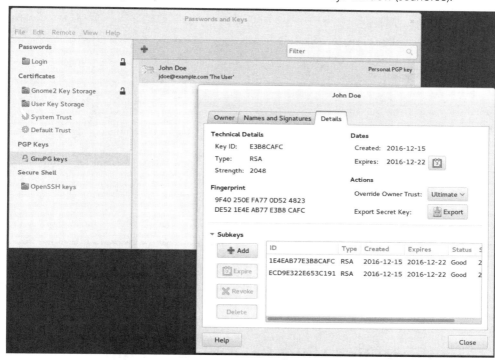

For Figure 23.6, I selected the Details tab for the private keys created earlier for John Doe. From that tab, you can see information such as when the key was made and when it expires, the type of key and its fingerprint, and subkeys to the key that can be expired or revoked.

Encrypting Files with Pyrite

If you like working with file encryption from a graphical window, I recommend trying the Pyrite tool (https://github.com/ryran/pyrite) created by Ryan Sawhill Aroha. Follow the instructions from the Pyrite page to download and install it. With Pyrite, you can encrypt and decrypt files using passwords or keys and a variety of ciphers (AES256, Twofish, CAST5, and so on).

To try Pyrite, type some text in the Message Input/Output box, encrypt it, and copy the output to a file to send to another person who could decrypt it (given the proper credentials). Likewise, you can select the box below "Input File For Direct Operation" to find an encrypted file in your filesystem to decrypt. The figure shows an example of the Pyrite window.

Continues

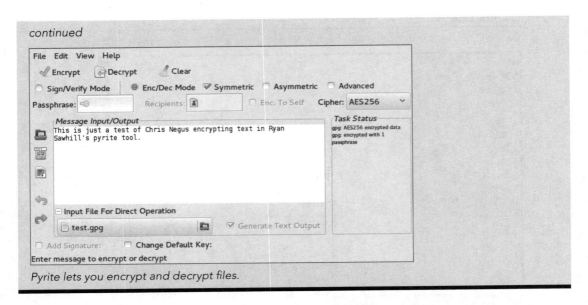

continued

Pyrite lets you encrypt and decrypt files.

Another extremely powerful security tool available on Linux is PAM. The next section in this chapter covers basic PAM concepts and how you can use this tool to even further enhance your Linux system's security.

Implementing Linux Security with PAM

Pluggable Authentication Modules (PAM) was invented by Sun Microsystems and originally implemented in the Solaris operating system. The Linux-PAM project began in 1997. Today, most Linux distributions use PAM.

PAM simplifies the authentication management process. Remember that *authentication* (see Chapter 22, "Understanding Basic Linux Security") is the process of determining that a subject (a.k.a. user or process) is who he says he is. This process is sometimes called "identification and authentication." PAM is a centralized method of providing authentication for the Linux system and applications.

Applications can be written to use PAM and are called "PAM-aware." A PAM-aware application does not have to be rewritten and recompiled to have its authentication settings changed. Any needed changes are made within a PAM configuration file for the PAM-aware applications. Thus, authentication management for these applications is centralized and simplified.

You can see whether a particular Linux application or utility is PAM-aware. Check whether it is compiled with the PAM library, `libpam.so`. In the example that follows, the `crontab` application is being checked for PAM awareness. The `ldd` command checks a file's shared library dependencies. To keep it simple, `grep` is used to search for the PAM library. As you can see, `crontab` on this particular Linux system is PAM-aware.

```
# ldd /usr/bin/crontab | grep pam
libpam.so.0 => /lib/libpam.so.0 (0x44d12000)
```

The benefits of using PAM on your Linux system include the following:

- Simplified and centralized authentication management from the administrator viewpoint
- Simplified application development, because developers can write applications using the documented PAM library, instead of writing their own authentication routines
- Flexibility in authentication:
  - Allow or deny access to resources based on traditional criteria, such as identification
  - Allow or deny access based on additional criteria, such as time of day restrictions
  - Set subject limitations, such as resource usage

Although the benefits of PAM simplify authentication management, the way PAM actually works is not so simple.

Understanding the PAM authentication process

When a subject (user or process) requests access to a PAM-aware application or utility, two primary components are used to complete the subject authentication process:

- The PAM-aware application's configuration file
- The PAM modules the configuration file uses

Each PAM-aware application configuration file is at the center of the process. The PAM configuration files call upon particular PAM modules to perform the needed authentication. PAM modules authenticate subjects from system authorization data, such as a centralized user account using LDAP (see Chapter 11, "Managing User Accounts").

Linux comes with many applications that are PAM-aware, their needed configuration files and PAM modules already installed. If you have any special authentication needs, you can most likely find a PAM module that has already been written for that need. However, before you start tweaking PAM, you need to understand more about how PAM operates.

A series of steps is taken by PAM using the modules and configuration files to ensure that proper application authentication occurs:

1. A subject (user or process) requests access to an application.
2. The application's PAM configuration file, which contains an access policy, is open and read.

The access policy is set via a list of all the PAM modules to be used in the authentication process. This PAM module(s) list is called a *stack*.

3. Each PAM module in the stack is invoked in the order it is listed.

4. Each PAM module returns either a success or failure status.

5. The stack continues to be read in order and is not necessarily stopped by a single returned failure status.

6. The status results of all the PAM modules are combined into a single overall result of authentication success or failure.

Typically, if a single PAM module returns a failure status, access to the application is denied. However, this is dependent upon the configuration file settings.

Most PAM configuration files are located in /etc/pam.d. The general format of a PAM configuration file is:

```
context    control flag    PAM module   [module options]
```

The following shows the PAM configuration file for the poweroff command. Notice that the file starts with a comment line. Every line starting with a # character is ignored.

```
$ cat /etc/pam.d/poweroff
#%PAM-1.0
auth       sufficient    pam_rootok.so
auth       required      pam_console.so
#auth       include      system-auth
account    required      pam_permit.so
```

Remember that all the PAM modules listed in the configuration file's stack are called, in order, and asked to return a status. In the preceding PAM configuration file, three statuses are returned to determine whether the subject may access the poweroff command. To better understand how these configuration files are used, you need to review each piece of the general format.

Tip

On Ubuntu, PAM configuration files can include other PAM configuration files for authentication. The configuration file to be included is listed with an "@" in front of its name.

Understanding PAM contexts

PAM modules have standard functions that provide different authentication services. These standard functions within a PAM module can be divided into function types, called *contexts*. Contexts can also be called *module interfaces* or *types*. In Table 23.3, the different PAM contexts are listed along with what type of authentication service they provide.

TABLE 23.3   **PAM Contexts**

Context	Service Description
auth	Provides authentication management services, such as verifying account passwords
account	Provides account validation services, such as time of day access restrictions
password	Manages account passwords, such as password length restrictions
session	Manages the beginning and end of an authenticated session, such as sending information to security logs

In the poweroff configuration file, shown again here, only two PAM contexts are used, auth and account. Thus, there is no need for this application to have PAM password or session management services. Notice that one of the auth contexts is ignored because its line starts with a # character:

```
$ cat /etc/pam.d/poweroff
#%PAM-1.0
auth       sufficient    pam_rootok.so
auth       required      pam_console.so
#auth       include      system-auth
account    required      pam_permit.so
```

The auth context is listed twice in the configuration file shown in the preceding code. However, for each auth context, a different control flag and PAM module are used. Each control flag has a special meaning and function.

Understanding PAM control flags

In a PAM configuration file, control flags are used to determine the overall status, which are returned to the application. A control flag is either of the following:

- **Simple keyword**—The only concern here is if the corresponding PAM module returns a response of either "failed" or "success." See Table 23.4 for how these statuses are handled.

- **Series of actions**—The returned module status is handled through the series of actions listed in the file.

Table 23.4 shows the various keyword control flags and their responses to the returned module status. Notice that a few of the control flags need to be carefully placed within the configuration file's stack. Some control flags cause the authentication process to stop immediately and the rest of the PAM modules are not called. The control flags simply control how the PAM module status results are combined into a single overall result. Table 23.4 demonstrates how the status results are combined.

TABLE 23.4 PAM Configuration Control Flags and Response Handling

Control Flag	Response Handling Description
required	If failed, returns a failure status to the application, after the rest of the contexts have been run in the stack.
	For example, a requisite control might cause a login to fail if someone types in an invalid user. But the user might not be told of the failure until after entering a password, hiding the fact that the bad username caused the failure.
requisite	If failed, returns a failure status to the application immediately without running the rest of the stack. (Be careful where you place this control in the stack.)
	For example, a requisite control might require key-based authentication and fail immediately when a valid key is not provided. In that case, it could fail before even prompting for a username/password.
sufficient	If failed, the module status is ignored. If success, then a success status is immediately returned to the application without running the rest of the stack. (Be careful where you place this control in the stack.)
optional	This control flag is important only for the final overall return status of success or failure. Think of it as a tie-breaker. When the other modules in the configuration file stack return statuses that are not clear-cut failure or success statuses, this optional module's status is used to determine the final status or break the tie. In cases where the other modules in the stack are returning a clear-cut path of failure or success, this status is ignored.
include	Get all the return statuses from this particular PAM configuration file's stack to include in this stack's overall return status. It's as if the entire stack from the named configuration file is now in this configuration file.
substack	Similar to the include control flag, except for how certain errors and evaluations affect the main stack. This forces the included configuration file stack to act as a substack to the main stack. Thus, certain errors and evaluations affect only the substack and not the main stack.

You should know that the PAM modules return many more status result codes than just "success" or "failure." For example, a module may return the status code of PAM_ACCT_ EXPIRED, which means the user account has expired. This would be deemed a "failure."

Understanding PAM modules

A PAM module is actually a suite of shared library modules (DLL files) stored in /lib/ security. You can see a list of the various installed PAM modules on your system by typing **ls /lib/security/pam*.so** at the command line.

> **NOTE**
> On Ubuntu, to find your PAM modules, type the command sudo find / -name pam*.so at the command line.

Your Linux system comes with many of the PAM modules needed already installed. You cannot write any PAM modules yourself. If you do need a module not already installed, most likely someone else has already written it. Check out sources such as:

- http://www.openwall.com/pam/
- http://puszcza.gnu.org.ua/software/pam-modules/download.html

Understanding PAM system event configuration files

So far, the focus has been on PAM-aware applications and their configuration files. However, other system events, such as logging into the Linux system, also use PAM. Thus, these events also have configuration files.

The following is a partial directory listing of the PAM configuration file directory. Notice that there are PAM-aware application configuration files, such as cond, and system event configuration files, such as postlogin-ac.

```
# ls -l /etc/pam.d
total 204
-rw-r--r--. 1 root root  272 Nov 15 10:06 atd
...
-rw-r--r--. 1 root root  232 Jan 31 12:35 config-util
-rw-r--r--. 1 root root  293 Oct 26 23:10 crond
...
-rw-r--r--. 1 root root  109 Feb 28 01:33 postlogin-ac
-rw-r--r--. 1 root root  147 Oct  3 11:51 poweroff
...
-rw-r--r--. 1 root root  981 Feb 28 01:33 system-auth-ac
...
```

You can modify these system event configuration files to implement your organization's specific security needs. For example, the system-auth-ac file can be modified to force certain password restrictions.

> **CAUTION**
>
> Modifying or deleting PAM system event configuration files incorrectly can lock you out of your own system. Make sure you test any changes in a virtual or test environment before modifying your production Linux servers.

These PAM system event configuration files operate in exactly the same way as the PAM-aware application configuration files. They have the same format, use the same syntax, and call upon PAM modules. However, many of these files are symbolically linked (see Chapter 4, "Moving around the Filesystem"). Therefore, these configuration files require a few extra steps when changes are made to them. The "how-to's" are covered later in this chapter.

Even though Linux comes with many PAM-aware applications, various configuration files, and PAM modules already installed, you cannot just hope PAM will take care of herself. Certain administrative steps are needed to manage PAM.

Administering PAM on your Linux system

The task of administering PAM on your Linux system is rather minimal. You need to verify that PAM is properly implemented and make adjustments to meet your particular organization's security needs.

Also, PAM does a little more than just the application authentication steps described previously. PAM can also limit resources, restrict access times, enforce good password selection, and so on.

Managing PAM-aware application configuration files

You should review PAM configuration files for your PAM-aware applications and utilities to ensure that their authentication process matches your organization's desired authentication process. Your Access Control Matrix (see Chapter 22, "Understanding Basic Linux Security") and the information on understanding PAM provided in this chapter should help you conduct an audit of the PAM configuration files.

Each PAM-aware application should have its very own PAM configuration file. Each configuration file defines what particular PAM modules are used for that application. If no configuration file exists, a security hole may be created for that application. This hole could be used for malicious intent. As a safety precaution, PAM comes with the "other" configuration file. If a PAM-aware application does not have a PAM configuration file, it defaults to using the "other" PAM configuration file.

You can verify whether your Linux system has the /etc/pam.d/other configuration file by using the ls command. The example that follows shows that the /etc/pam.d/other PAM configuration file does exist on this system.

```
$ ls /etc/pam.d/other
/etc/pam.d/other
```

The PAM /etc/pam.d/other configuration file should deny all access, which in terms of security is referred to as Implicit Deny. In computer security access control, *Implicit Deny* means that if certain criteria are not clearly met, access must be denied. In this case, if no configuration file exists for a PAM-aware application, all access to it is denied. The following shows a /etc/pam.d/other file's contents:

```
$ cat /etc/pam.d/other
#%PAM-1.0
auth     required     pam_deny.so
account  required     pam_deny.so
password required     pam_deny.so
session  required     pam_deny.so
```

Notice that all four PAM contexts—auth, account, password, and session—are listed. Each context uses the required control flag and the pam_deny.so module. The pam_deny.so PAM module is used to deny access.

Even with the "other" configuration file in place, if a PAM configuration file for a PAM-aware application is not there, it must be created. Add this item to your PAM audit checklist. You should also review your PAM "other" configuration file on your Linux system to ensure that it enforces Implicit Deny.

Managing PAM system event configuration files

Similar to PAM-aware application and utility configuration files, your PAM system event configuration files need to be audited with your organization's Access Control Matrix. However, for any needed modifications to these files, there are extra steps that must be taken.

In the material that follows, you learn how to set up special security requirements via PAM on your Linux system, such as account login time restrictions. Many of the special requirements require you to make a change to PAM system event configuration files, such as /etc/pam.d/system-auth-ac.

The problem with making changes to some of these PAM system event configuration files is that the utility authconfig can rewrite these files and remove any locally made changes. Fortunately, each PAM configuration file that runs this risk has it documented in a comment line within. Using grep, you can quickly find which PAM configuration files have this potential problem.

```
# grep "authconfig" /etc/pam.d/*
/etc/pam.d/fingerprint-auth:# User changes will be destroyed
   the next time authconfig is run.
/etc/pam.d/fingerprint-auth-ac:# User changes will be destroyed
   the next time authconfig is run.
...
/etc/pam.d/system-auth:# User changes will be destroyed
   the next time authconfig is run.
/etc/pam.d/system-auth-ac:# User changes will be destroyed
   the next time authconfig is run.
...
```

These PAM system event configuration files use symbolic links (see Chapter 4, "Moving around the Filesystem"). For example, you can see that the file `system-auth` is actually a symbolic link pointing to the file `system-auth-ac`. The first character in the file's security is an `l`. This indicates that the file is linked. The `->` symbol shows that the file is symbolically linked.

```
# ls -l system-auth
lrwxrwxrwx. 1 root root 14 Feb 28 01:36
 system-auth -> system-auth-ac
```

> **NOTE**
>
> Not every Linux distribution, such as Ubuntu, has the `authconfig` utility, which overwrites PAM configuration files. To check whether your distribution has the `authconfig` utility, type **`which authconfig`** at the command line. If nothing is returned, your Linux distribution does not have that utility.
>
> On some Linux distributions, the utility `pam-auth-config` is similar to the `authconfig` utility in its ability to overwrite configuration files. This can happen if the command `pam-auth-config --force` is entered at the command line. Read the `man pam-auth-config` man page to learn more about this utility if it is installed on your system.

The `authconfig` utility does not use the symbolic links, nor does it modify them. Thus, you can create a new local PAM system event configuration file and point the symbolic link to it. This allows your system to have the needed security modifications implemented and enables you to avoid having the configuration files overwritten by the `authconfig` utility. The basic steps are as follows, including an example of performing these steps for the `system-auth-ac` file:

1. Copy the current PAM system event configuration file to a new file, adding a new filename ending, such as "local."

   ```
   # cp system-auth-ac system-auth-local
   ```

2. Make the needed changes to the new configuration file.

   ```
   # vi system-auth-local
   ```

3. Remove the old symbolic link file.

   ```
   # ls -l system-auth
   lrwxrwxrwx. 1 root root 14 Feb 28 01:36
    system-auth -> system-auth-ac
   # rm -i system-auth
   rm: remove symbolic link 'system-auth'? y
   ```

4. Create a new symbolic link pointing to the new configuration file.

   ```
   # ln -s system-auth-local system-auth
   # ls -l system-auth
   lrwxrwxrwx. 1 root root 17 Feb 28 01:37
    system-auth -> system-auth-local
   ```

After these changes have been made, you can make any needed changes to the "local" PAM system event configuration files without worrying about the authconfig utility overwriting the files.

Implementing resource limits with PAM

Managing resources is not just a system administrative task. It is also a security administrative task. Setting resource limitations helps you avoid many adverse problems on your Linux system. Problems such as fork bombs can be averted by limiting the number of processes a single user can create. A *fork bomb* occurs when a process spawns one process after another in a recursive manner until system resources are consumed. Fork bombs can be malicious or just accidental—such as those created by poor program code development.

The PAM module pam-limits uses a special configuration file to set these resource limits: /etc/security/limits.conf. By default, this file has no resource limits set within it. Therefore, you need to review the file and set resource limits to match your organization's security needs.

> **NOTE**
> PAM configuration files are in the /etc/pam.d directory and the /etc/security directory.

The following snippet shows the /etc/security/limits.conf file. The file is well documented. You should read through the contents of that file for thorough format descriptions and examples of limits that can be set.

```
$ cat /etc/security/limits.conf
# /etc/security/limits.conf
#Each line describes a limit for a user in the form:
#<domain>        <type>  <item>  <value>
#Where:
...
#*              soft    core        0
#*              hard    rss         10000
#@student       hard    nproc       20
#@faculty       soft    nproc       20
#@faculty       hard    nproc       50
#ftp            hard    nproc       0
#@student       -       maxlogins   4
# End of file
```

23

The format items *domain* and *type* need some further explanation than what is documented in the configuration file:

- domain—The limit applies to the listed user or group. If the domain is "*", it applies to *all* users.

- type—A hard limit cannot be exceeded. A soft limit can be exceeded, but only temporarily.

Look at the limits.conf file setting example that follows. The group faculty is listed, but notice nproc. The nproc limit sets the maximum number of processes a user can start. This setting is what prevents a fork bomb. Notice that the type select is hard; thus, the limit of 50 processes cannot be exceeded. Of course, this limit is not enforced because the line is commented out with a # symbol.

```
#@faculty          hard     nproc              50
```

Limit settings are set per login and only last for the duration of the login session. A malicious user could log in several times to create a fork bomb. Thus, setting the maximum number of logins for these user accounts is a good idea, too.

Limiting the maximum number of logins may have to be done on a per-user basis. For example, johndoe needs to log in to the Linux system only once. To prevent others from using johndoe's account, set his account's maxlogins to 1.

```
johndoe          hard     maxlogins          1
```

The final step in limiting this resource is to ensure that the PAM module using limits.conf is included in one of the PAM system event configuration files. The PAM module using limits.conf is pam_limits. In the partial listing that follows, grep is used to verify that the PAM module is used within the system event configuration files.

```
# grep "pam_limits" /etc/pam.d/*
...
system-auth:session          required     pam_limits.so
system-auth-ac:session       required     pam_limits.so
system-auth-local:session    required     pam_limits.so
```

Time limits for access to services and accounts are not handled by the PAM /etc/security/limits.conf configuration file. Instead, they are handled by the time.conf file.

Implementing time restrictions with PAM

PAM can make your entire Linux system operate on "PAM time." Time restrictions such as access to particular applications during certain times of the day or allowing logins only during specified days of the week are all handled by PAM.

The PAM configuration file that handles these restrictions is located in the /etc/ security directory. The following code shows the well-documented /etc/security/ time.conf PAM configuration file.

```
$ cat /etc/security/time.conf
# this is an example configuration file for the pam_time module
...
# the syntax of the lines is as follows:
#
#          services;ttys;users;times
...
```

I recommend you read through the contents of the time.conf file. Note that the format for each valid entry follows this syntax: *services;ttys;users;times*. Fields are separated by semicolons. The valid field values are documented in the time.conf configuration file.

While time.conf is well-documented, an example is always helpful. For instance, you have decided that regular users should be allowed to log in on terminals on weekdays only (Monday through Friday). They can log in from 7 a.m. to 7 p.m. on these weekdays. The following list describes what elements need to be set:

- *services*—Login
- *ttys*—* (Designating that all terminals are to be included)
- *users*—Everyone but root (!root)
- *times*—Allowed on weekdays (Wd) from 7 a.m. (0700) to 7 p.m. (1900)

The entry in time.conf would look like the following:

```
login; * ; !root ; Wd0700-1900
```

The final step in implementing this example time restriction is to ensure that the PAM module using time.conf is included in one of the PAM system event configuration files. The PAM module using time.conf is pam_time. In the partial listing that follows, grep shows the PAM module; pam_time is not used within any of the system event configuration files.

```
# grep "pam_time" /etc/pam.d/*
config-util:auth                   sufficient    pam_timestamp.so
config-util:session                optional      pam_timestamp.so
selinux-polgengui:auth             sufficient    pam_timestamp.so
selinux-polgengui:session          optional      pam_timestamp.so
system-config-selinux:auth         sufficient    pam_timestamp.so
system-config-selinux:session optional           pam_timestamp.so
```

Because pam_time is not listed, you must modify the /etc/pam.d/system-auth file in order for PAM to enforce it the time restrictions. The PAM configuration file system-auth is used by PAM at system login and during password modifications. This configuration file checks many items, such as time restrictions.

Add the following near the top of the "account" section of the configuration file. Now the pam_time module checks login restrictions you set within the /etc/security/time.conf file.

```
account      required     pam_time.so
```

> **NOTE**
>
> On Ubuntu, you need to modify the /etc/pam.d/common-auth file instead of the system-auth configuration file.

Remember that system-auth is a symbolically linked file. If you modify this file, you must take extra steps to preserve the modifications from the authconfig utility. Review the section "Managing PAM system event configuration files" earlier in this chapter.

You can employ additional PAM modules and configuration files to set even more restrictions on subjects. One important security module is pam_cracklib.

Enforcing good passwords with PAM

When a password is modified, the PAM module pam_cracklib is involved in the process. The module prompts the user for a password and checks its strength against a system dictionary and a set of rules for identifying poor choices.

> **NOTE**
>
> The pam_cracklib module is installed by default on Fedora and RHEL. For Ubuntu Linux systems, it is not installed by default. Therefore, to get access to the pam_cracklib module on Ubuntu, issue the command sudo apt-get install libpam-cracklib.

Using pam_cracklib, you can check a newly chosen password for the following:

- Is it a dictionary word?
- Is it a palindrome?
- Is it the old password with the case changed?
- Is it too much like the old password?
- Is it too short?
- Is it a rotated version of the old password?
- Does it use the same consecutive characters?
- Does it contain the username in some form?

You can change the rules pam_cracklib uses for checking new passwords by making modifications to the /etc/pam.d/system-auth file. You may think that the changes should be made in the PAM-aware passwd configuration file. However, the /etc/pam.d/ passwd includes the system-auth file in its stack.

```
# cat /etc/pam.d/passwd
#%PAM-1.0
auth        include     system-auth
account     include     system-auth
password    substack    system-auth
-password   optional    pam_gnome_keyring.so use_authtok
password    substack    postlogin
```

NOTE

On Ubuntu, you need to modify the /etc/pam.d/common-password file, instead of the system-auth configuration file.

The current settings of the system-auth file are shown here. Currently, one entry calls the pam_cracklib PAM module.

```
# cat /etc/pam.d/system-auth
#%PAM-1.0
# This file is auto-generated.
# User changes will be destroyed the next time authconfig is run.
auth        required     pam_env.so
auth        sufficient   pam_fprintd.so
auth        sufficient   pam_unix.so nullok try_first_pass
auth        requisite    pam_succeed_if.so uid >= 1000 quiet
auth        required     pam_deny.so

account     required     pam_unix.so
account     sufficient   pam_localuser.so
account     sufficient   pam_succeed_if.so uid < 1000 quiet
account     required     pam_permit.so

password    requisite    pam_cracklib.so try_first_pass retry=3
...
```

The pam_cracklib entry in the preceding listing uses the keyword retry. The following keywords are available for cracklib:

- **retry=N**
  - Default = 1
  - Prompt user at most N times before returning with an error.

- `difok=N`

  - Default = 5

  - The number of characters in the new password that must not be present in the old password.

  - Exception 1: If half of the characters in the new password are different, then the new password is accepted.

  - Exception 2: See `difignore`.

- `difignore=N`

  - Default = 23

  - The number of characters the password has before the `difok` setting is ignored.

- `minlen=N`

  - Default = 9

  - The minimum acceptable size for the new password.

  - See `dcredit`, `ucredit`, `lcredit`, and `ocredit` for how their settings affect `minlen`.

- `dcredit=N`

  - Default =1

  - If (N >= 0): The maximum credit for having digits in the new password. If you have less than or N digits, each digit counts +1 toward meeting the current `minlen` value.

  - If (N < 0): The minimum number of digits that must be met for a new password.

- `ucredit=N`

  - Default = 1

  - If (N >= 0): The maximum credit for having uppercase letters in the new password. If you have less than or N uppercase letters, each letter counts +1 toward meeting the current `minlen` value.

  - If (N < 0): The minimum number of uppercase letters that must be met for a new password.

- `lcredit=N`

  - Default = 1

  - If (N >= 0): The maximum credit for having lowercase letters in the new password. If you have less than or N lowercase letters, each letter counts +1 toward meeting the current `minlen` value.

  - If (N < 0): The minimum number of lowercase letters that must be met for a new password.

- `ocredit=N`

  - Default = 1

  - If (N >= 0): The maximum credit for having other characters in the new password. If you have less than or N other characters, each character counts +1 toward meeting the current `minlen` value.

  - If (N < 0): The minimum number of other characters that must be met for a new password.

- `minclass=N`

  - Default = 0

  - N out of four character classes is required for the new password. The four classes are digits, uppercase letters, lowercase letters, and other characters.

- `maxrepeat=N`

  - Default = 0

  - Reject passwords that contain more than N same consecutive characters.

- `reject_username`

  Check whether the name of the user in straight or reversed form is contained in the new password. If it is found, the new password is rejected.

- `try_first_pass`

  Try to get the password from a previous PAM module. If that does not work, prompt the user for the password.

- `use_authtok`

  This argument is used to *force* the module to not prompt the user for a new password. Instead, the new password is provided by the previously stacked *password* module.

- `dictpath=/path`

  Path to the `cracklib` dictionaries.

For example, if your organization requires passwords to be ten characters long and they must contain two digits, you would add a line similar to the following to the /etc/pam.d/ system-auth file:

```
password required pam_cracklib.so minlen=10 dcredit=-2
```

The keywords used in this example with `pam_cracklib` are:

- `minlen=10`—The new password must be at least ten characters.

- `dcredit=-2`—The new password must contain two numbers.

Encouraging sudo use with PAM

To allow tracking of root-account use by individuals and avoid a repudiation situation (see Chapter 22, "Understanding Basic Linux Security"), you should restrict the use of the su command and encourage the use of sudo. If your organization has such a policy, you can accomplish this with PAM in just a few steps.

The su command is PAM-aware, which greatly simplifies things. It uses the PAM module pam_wheel to check for users in the wheel group. The /etc/pam.d/su configuration file is shown here:

```
# cat /etc/pam.d/su
#%PAM-1.0
auth            sufficient      pam_rootok.so
# Uncomment the following line to implicitly trust users
# in the "wheel" group.
#auth           sufficient  pam_wheel.so trust use_uid
# Uncomment the following line to require a user to be
# in the "wheel" group.
#auth           required     pam_wheel.so use_uid
auth            include      system-auth
auth            include      postlogin
account         sufficient   pam_succeed_if.so uid = 0 use_uid quiet
account         include      system-auth
password        include      system-auth
session         include      system-auth
session         include      postlogin
session         optional     pam_xauth.so
```

First, to restrict the use of su, if you are using the wheel group as your administrative group, you need to reassign your administrative group to a new group (see Chapter 11, "Managing User Accounts"). If you are not using the wheel group, just be sure not to assign anyone in the future to this group.

Next, you need to edit the /etc/pam.d/su configuration file. Remove the comment mark, #, from the following line:

```
#auth           required     pam_wheel.so use_uid
```

With these modifications, PAM disables the use of the su command. Administrative users now must use sudo, which the system tracks and which provides a desired nonrepudiation environment (see Chapter 22, "Understanding Basic Linux Security").

Locking accounts with PAM

Your organization's specific security requirements may call for locking a user account after a certain number of failed login attempts. The typical standard is to lock an account after three failed attempts. This is to thwart a brute-force password attack against an account.

The PAM module used to manage login attempts is pam_tally2. The PAM configuration file to edit is /etc/pam.d/system-auth.

NOTE

Older Linux distributions may use the PAM module pam_tally instead of pam_tally2.

Again, you should make these changes to your local system-auth-local file instead of system-auth-ac because authconfig overwrites your modifications the next time it is run. The tally2 lines you need to add to system-auth-local are highlighted in the sample file that follows. Their placement in this file is extremely important.

```
# cat system-auth-local
#%PAM-1.0
# Local system-auth file.
# Changes will not be destroyed by authconfig
auth          required        pam_tally2.so deny=3 quiet
auth          required        pam_env.so
auth          sufficient      pam_fprintd.so
auth          sufficient      pam_unix.so nullok try_first_pass
auth          requisite       pam_succeed_if.so uid >= 1000 quiet
auth          required        pam_deny.so

account       required        pam_tally2.so
account       required        pam_unix.so
account       sufficient      pam_localuser.so
account       sufficient      pam_succeed_if.so uid < 1000 quiet
account       required        pam_permit.so
...
```

CAUTION

Make a backup copy of system-auth-local, and test your changes in a test environment before you make changes to your production Linux system. An incorrect modification could lock everyone out of your system, including the root user.

On the first auth context line involving pam_tally.so in the preceding code, notice that two options have been added, deny=3 and quiet. The deny=3 option allows a user only three failed attempts to log in before the account is locked.

The `quiet` option does not tell the user the account is locked if it becomes locked. It keeps giving "incorrect password" messages to the user. Keeping a user ignorant of what has happened to an account is helpful if you are being attacked maliciously. The malicious attacker does not know the account has been locked and thinks he has just entered another incorrect password. This can allow you time to track down what is happening.

Using the `quiet` option can, however, cause lots of problems for your users. For example, a user may not realize that he or she has entered the wrong password enough times to lock the account. This may cause a delay in seeking help. You can remove the `quiet` option from the configuration file setting so that when a user has had too many failed attempts to log in, he or she receives a message such as "Account locked due to 4 failed logins."

> **NOTE**
>
> On Ubuntu, instead of the `system-auth` configuration file, you need to add the `auth` context information to the `/etc/pam.d/common-auth` file and add the `account` context information to the `/etc/pam.d/common-account` file.

The `pam_tally2` module also includes a command line interface that you can use to monitor login failure attempts. If the `pam_tally2` module is included in one of your PAM system event configuration files, it keeps a tally of how many failed login attempts have occurred on your system. To see these failures, you enter the `pam_tally2` command, as shown in the following code:

```
# pam_tally2
Login           Failures Latest failure      From
Samantha            2     03/10/15 06:24:01  pts/1
```

The username, number of failures, and latest attempt are listed along with the terminal where the latest failure occurred. You can also use the `pam_tally2` command to unlock a user account after it has been locked by the PAM `pam_tally2` module.

When an account is locked by PAM, it is not listed as locked in the `/etc/shadow` file, and you cannot unlock it by using the `usermod -U` *username* command. To unlock it, you need to use the `pam_tally2` command.

In the example that follows, the user account `Samantha` has had too many failed login attempts. However, the account is not listed as locked in the `/etc/shadow` file, shown by the `passwd` command. Locking the account using the `usermod -L` command causes the account to be locked via the `/etc/shadow` file, not via PAM.

```
# pam_tally2
Login           Failures Latest failure      From
Samantha            5     03/10/16 06:32:24  pts/1
```

```
# passwd -S Samantha
Samantha PS 2016-03-09 0 99999 7 -1 (Password set, SHA512 crypt.)
# usermod -L Samantha
# passwd -S Samantha
Samantha LK 2016-03-09 0 99999 7 -1 (Password locked.)
# usermod -U Samantha
# passwd -S Samantha
Samantha PS 2016-03-09 0 99999 7 -1 (Password set, SHA512 crypt.)
```

In the code that follows, the command pam_tally2 -r -u Samantha is issued to unlock the user account Samantha. Notice that the pam_tally2 command again lists the number of failed login attempts as it removes the "lock." When the pam_tally2 command is issued again, the user Samantha's failed attempt records have been removed because the lock was removed.

```
# pam_tally2 -r -u Samantha
Login              Failures Latest failure     From
Samantha                  5   03/10/15 06:34:09  pts/1
# pam_tally2
```

You can use many more options with pam_tally2. To explore this PAM module further, issue the command man pam_tally2 at the command line.

Obtaining more information on PAM

PAM is another rich and versatile security tool available to you on the Linux system. In your own Linux system's man pages, you can read about managing the PAM configuration files and about the modules in your /lib/security directory.

- To get more information on PAM configuration files, use the command man pam.conf.

- You can see all the PAM modules available on your system by typing ls /lib/security/pam*.so at the command line. To get more information on each PAM module, type man pam_*module_name*. Be sure to leave off the file extension of "so" for the *pam_module_name*. For example, type man pam_lastlog to learn more about the pam_lastlog.so module.

Several websites can provide additional information on PAM:

- The Official Linux-PAM website: http://linux-pam.org

- The Linux-PAM System Administrator's Guide: http://linux-pam.org/Linux-PAM-html/Linux-PAM_SAG.html

- PAM Module reference: http://linux-pam.org/Linux-PAM-html/sag-module-reference.html

Summary

Cryptography tools offer ways of protecting and verifying the validity of the data you use on your Linux system. The PAM facility provides a means of creating policies to secure the tools that are used to authenticate users on your system.

Both the cryptography tools and PAM should be handled with care as you learn about Linux. Be sure to test any modifications you make on a test Linux system or a virtualized Linux system before you implement them on a production machine.

The next chapter covers SELinux. While cryptography and PAM are tools you can use on your Linux system, SELinux is an entire security enhancement layer.

Exercises

Use these exercises to test your knowledge of using cryptography tools and PAM. These tasks assume you are running a Fedora or Red Hat Enterprise Linux system (although some tasks work on other Linux systems as well). If you are stuck, solutions to the tasks are shown in Appendix B (although in Linux, there are often multiple ways to complete a task).

1. Encrypt a file using the gpg2 utility and a symmetric key.

2. Generate a public key ring using the gpg2 utility.

3. List out the key ring you generated.

4. Encrypt a file, and add your digital signature using the gpg2 utility.

5. Go to the Linux Mint home page at www.linuxmint.com. From the Download page, select one of the Linux Mint distributions to download. When the download is complete, use the appropriate message digest utility to ensure that the downloaded file was not corrupted.

6. Using the command which su, determine the su command's full filename. Next, determine whether the su command on your Linux system is PAM-aware.

7. Does the su command have a PAM configuration file? If so, display the configuration file on the screen and list what PAM contexts it uses.

8. List out the various PAM modules on your system to your screen.

9. Find the PAM "other" configuration file on your system. Does it exist? Does it enforce Implicit Deny?

10. Find the PAM limits configuration file. Does it have a setting to keep a fork bomb from occurring on your system?

Enhancing Linux Security with SELinux

S ecurity Enhanced Linux (SELinux) was developed by the National Security Agency (NSA) along with other security research organizations, such as Secure Computing Corporation (SCC). SELinux was released to the open source community in 2000 and became popular when Red Hat included SELinux in its Linux distributions. Now, SELinux is used by many organizations and is widely available.

Understanding SELinux Benefits

SELinux is a security enhancement module deployed on top of Linux. It provides additional security measures, is included by default, and is set to be in Enforcing mode in RHEL and Fedora.

SELinux provides improved security on the Linux system via Role Based Access Controls (RBAC) on subjects and objects (aka processes and resources). "Traditional" Linux security uses Discretionary Access Controls (DAC).

SELinux is not a replacement for DAC. Instead, it is an additional security layer.

- DAC rules are still used when using SELinux.
- DAC rules are checked first, and if access is allowed, then SELinux policies are checked.
- If DAC rules deny access, SELinux policies are not reviewed.

If a user tries to execute a file that he does not have execute access to (rw-), the "traditional" Linux DAC controls deny access. Thus, the SELinux policies are not even checked.

> **NOTE**
>
> SELinux is the default security enhancement of Red Hat distributions, whereas AppArmor is the default security enhancement for Ubuntu. You can still install SELinux on Ubuntu by using the command `sudo apt-get install selinux` and then reboot. If you want to learn more about AppArmor, go to `https://help.ubuntu.com/community/AppArmor`.

Even though "traditional" Linux security controls still work, there are several benefits to using SELinux. These are a few of SELinux's benefits:

- **It implements the RBAC access control model.** This is considered the strongest access control model.

- **It uses least privilege access for subjects (for example, users and processes).** The term *least privilege* means that every subject is given a limited set of privileges that are only enough to allow the subject to be functional in its tasks. With least privilege implemented, a user or process is limited on the accidental (or on-purpose) damage to objects they can cause.

- **It allows process sandboxing.** The term *process sandboxing* means that each process runs in its own area (sandbox). It cannot access other processes or their files unless special permissions are granted. These areas where processes run are called "domains."

- **It allows a test of its functionality before implementation.** SELinux has a Permissive mode, which allows you to see the effect of enforcing SELinux on your system. In Permissive mode, SELinux still logs what it considers security breaches (called AVC denials), but it doesn't prevent them.

Another way to look at SELinux benefits is to examine what can happen if SELinux is not running on your Linux system. For example, your web server daemon (httpd) is listening on a port for something to happen. A simple request from a web browser comes in to view a home page. Going through its normal routine, the httpd daemon hears the request and only "traditional" Linux security is applied. Being unconstrained by SELinux, httpd can do these things:

- Access *any* file or directory, based on read/write/execute permissions for the associated owner and group.

- Perform potentially insecure activities, such as allowing a file upload or changing system limits.

- Listen on any port it likes for incoming requests.

On a system constrained by SELinux, the httpd daemon is much more tightly controlled. Using the preceding example, httpd can only listen on the port SELinux allows it to listen on. SELinux prevents httpd from accessing any file that doesn't have the proper security context set and denies insecure activities that are not explicitly enabled in SELinux. In essence, SELinux severely limits malicious code and activity on your Linux system.

Understanding How SELinux Works

SELinux could be compared to a guard at a door: In this comparison, the subject (the user) wants to access the object (the file) inside the room. To gain access to this object:

1. The subject must present an ID badge to the guard.

2. The guard reviews the ID badge and access rules kept in a large manual.

   - If the access rules allow this particular ID badge inside the door, the subject may enter the room to access the object.

   - If the access rules do not allow this particular ID badge access to the object, then the guard refuses entry.

SELinux provides a combination of Role Based Access Control (RBAC) and either *Type Enforcement (TE)* or *Multi-Level Security (MLS)*. In Role Based Access Control, access to an object is based on a subject's assigned role in the organization. Therefore, it is not based on the subject's username or process ID. Each role is granted access rights.

Understanding type enforcement

Type Enforcement (TE) is necessary to implement the RBAC model. *Type Enforcement* secures a system through these methods:

- Labeling objects as certain security types

- Assigning subjects to particular domains and roles

- Providing rules allowing certain domains and roles to access certain object types

The example that follows uses the ls -l command to show the DAC controls on the file my_stuff. The file has owner and group listed as well as its assignments for read, write, and execute. If you need a review of file permissions, see Chapter 4, "Moving around the Filesystem."

```
$ ls -l my_stuff
-rw-rw-r--. 1 johndoe johndoe 0 Feb 12 06:57 my_stuff
```

The example that follows includes ls -Z and the same file, my_stuff, but instead of just the DAC controls, the -Z option displays the SELinux security RBAC controls, too.

```
$ ls -Z my_stuff
-rw-rw-r--. johndoe johndoe
unconfined_u:object_r:user_home_t:s0 my_stuff
```

The `ls -Z` example displays four items associated with the file that are specific to SELinux:

- A user (`unconfined_u`)
- A role (`object_r`)
- A type (`user_home_t`)
- A level (`s0`)

These four RBAC items (user, role, type, and level) are used in the SELinux access control to determine appropriate access levels. Together, the items are called the SELinux *security context*. A security context (ID badge) is sometimes called a "security label."

These security context assignments are given to subjects (processes and users). Each security context has a specific name. The name given depends upon what object or subject it has been assigned: Files have a file context, users have a user context, and processes have a process context, also called a "domain."

The rules allowing access are called "allow rules" or "policy rules." A *policy rule* is the process SELinux follows to grant or deny access to a particular system security type. Returning to the comparison of SELinux with the guard, SELinux serves as the guard who must see the subject's security context (ID badge) and review the policy rules (access rules manual) before allowing or denying access to an object. Thus, Type Enforcement ensures that only certain "types" of subjects can access certain "types" of objects.

Understanding multi-level security

With SELinux, the default policy type is called *targeted*, which primarily controls how network services (such as web servers and file servers) can access on a Linux system. The targeted policy places fewer restrictions on what valid user accounts can do on the system. For a more restricted policy, you can choose Multi-Level Security (MLS). MLS uses Type Enforcement along with the additional feature of security clearances. It also offers Multi-Category Security, which gives classification levels to objects.

> **TIP**
>
> The Multi-Level Security (MLS) names can cause confusion. Multi-Category Security (MCS) is sometimes called Multi-Clearance Security. Because MLS offers MCS, it is sometimes called MLS/MCS.

Multi-Level Security enforces the Bell-LaPadula Mandatory Access security model. The Bell-LaPadula model was developed by the U.S. government to impose information confidentiality. Enforcing this model is accomplished by granting object access based on the role's security clearance and the object's classification level.

Security clearance is an attribute granted to roles allowing access to classified objects. *Classification level* is an attribute granted to an object, providing protection from subjects who have a security clearance attribute that is too low. You most likely have heard the classification level "Top Secret." The fictional book and movie character James Bond had a top-secret security clearance, which granted him access to top-secret classified information. This is a classic example of the Bell-LaPadula model.

The combination of RBAC along with either Type Enforcement (TE) or Multi-Level Security (MLS) enables SELinux to provide such a strong security enhancement. SELinux also offers different Operational Modes for its use.

Implementing SELinux security models

The Role Based Access Control model, Type Enforcement, Multi-Level Security, and Bell-LaPadula models are all interesting topics. SELinux implements these models through a combination of four primary SELinux pieces:

- Operational Modes
- Security contexts
- Policy types
- Policy rule packages

Although I've touched on some of these design elements, the following gives you an in-depth understanding of them. This understanding is needed before you begin configuring SELinux on your system.

Understanding SELinux operational modes

SELinux comes with three Operational Modes: Disabled, Permissive, and Enforcing. Each of these modes offers different benefits for Linux system security.

Using the Disabled mode

In the Disabled mode, SELinux is turned off. The default method of access control, Discretionary Access Control (DAC), is used instead. This mode is useful for circumstances in which enhanced security is not required.

If at all possible, Red Hat recommends setting SELinux to Permissive mode rather than disabling it. However, sometimes disabling SELinux is appropriate.

If you are running applications that are working properly (from your perspective), but generating massive amounts of SELinux AVC denial messages (even in Permissive mode), you may end up filling up log files to the point of making your systems unusable.

The better approach is to set the proper security context on the files you want applications to access. But disabling SELinux is the quicker fix.

Before you disable SELinux, however, think about whether you may ever want to enable it on that system again. If you decide to set it to Enforcing or Permissive later, the next time you reboot your system, your system goes through an automatic SELinux file relabel before it comes up.

TIP

If all you care about is turning SELinux off, you have found the answer. Just edit the configuration file `/etc/selinux/config` and change the text `SELINUX=` to the following: `SELINUX=disabled`. SELinux will be disabled after a system reboot. You can now skip the rest of this chapter.

Using the Permissive mode

In Permissive mode, SELinux is turned on, but the security policy rules are not enforced. When a security policy rule should deny admission, access is still allowed. However, a message is sent to a log file denoting that access should have been denied.

SELinux Permissive mode is used for the following:

- Auditing the current SELinux policy rules
- Testing new applications to see what effect SELinux policy rules will have on them
- Testing new SELinux policy rules to see what effect the new rules will have on current services and applications
- Troubleshooting why a particular service or application is no longer working properly under SELinux

In some cases, you can use the `audit2allow` command to read the SELinux audit logs and generate new SELinux rules to selectively allow the denied actions. This can be a quick way to get your applications working on your Linux system without disabling SELinux.

Using the Enforcing mode

The name says it all. In Enforcing mode, SELinux is turned on and all the security policy rules are enforced.

Understanding SELinux security contexts

As mentioned earlier, an SELinux security context is the method used to classify objects (such as files) and subjects (such as users and programs). The defined security context allows SELinux to enforce policy rules for subjects accessing objects. A security context consists of four attributes: `user`, `role`, `type`, and `level`.

- `user`—The `user` attribute is a mapping of a Linux username to an SELinux name. This is not the same as a user's login name and is referred to specifically as the

SELinux user. The SELinux username ends with a *u*, making it easier to identify in the output. Regular unconfined users have an `unconfined_u` user attribute in the default targeted policy.

- `role`—A designated role in the company is mapped to an SELinux role name. The `role` attribute is then assigned to various subjects and objects. Each role is granted access to other subjects and objects based on the role's security clearance and the object's classification level. More specifically, for SELinux, users are assigned a role and roles are authorized for particular types or domains. Using roles can force accounts, such as root, into a less privileged position. The SELinux role name has an "r" at the end. On a targeted SELinux system, processes run by the root user have a `system_r` role, while regular users run under the `unconfined_r` role.

- `type`—This attribute defines a domain type for processes, a user type for users, and a file type for files. This attribute is also called "security type." Most policy rules are concerned with the security type of a process and what files, ports, devices, and other elements of the system that process has access to (based on their security types). The SELinux type name ends with a `t`.

- `level`—The `level` is an attribute of Multi-Level Security (MLS) and enforces the Bell-LaPadula model. It is optional in TE, but required if you are using MLS.

  The MLS level is a combination of the sensitivity and category values that together form the security level. A level is written as `sensitivity : category`.

  - `sensitivity`

    - Represents the security or sensitivity level of an object, such as confidential or top secret.

    - Is hierarchical with `s0` (unclassified) typically being the lowest.

    - Is listed as a pair of sensitivity levels (*lowlevel-highlevel*) if the levels differ.

    - Is listed as a single sensitivity level (`s0`) if there are no low and high levels. Yet in some cases, even if there are no low and high levels, the range is still shown (`s0-s0`).

  - `category`

    - Represents the category of an object, such as No Clearance, Top Clearance, and so on.

    - Traditionally, the values are between `c0` and `c255`.

    - Is listed as a pair of category levels (*lowlevel:highlevel*) if the levels differ.

    - Is listed as a single category level (*level*) if there are no low and high levels.

Users have security contexts

To see your SELinux user context, enter the id command at the shell prompt. The following is an example of the security context for user johndoe:

```
$ id
uid=1000(johndoe) gid=1000(johndoe) groups=1000(johndoe)
 context=unconfined_u:unconfined_r:unconfined_t:s0-s0:c0.c1023
```

The user's security context list shows the following:

- user—The Linux user, johndoe, is mapped to the SELinux unconfined_u user.
- role—The SELinux user, unconfined_u, is mapped to the role of the unconfined_r.
- type—The user has been given the type of unconfined_t.
- level—
    - sensitivity—The user has only one sensitivity level, and it is the lowest level of s0.
    - categories—The user has access to c0.c1023, which is all categories (c0 through to c1023).

Files have security contexts

A file also has a security context. To see an individual file's context, use the -Z option on the ls command. The following is a security context for the file my_stuff:

```
$ ls -Z my_stuff
-rw-rw-r--. johndoe johndoe
 unconfined_u:object_r:user_home_t:s0 my_stuff
```

The file context list shows the following:

- user—The file is mapped to the SELinux unconfined_u user.
- role—The file is mapped to the role of object_r.
- type—The file is considered to be part of the user_home_t domain.
- level—
    - sensitivity—The user has only one sensitivity level, and it is the lowest level of s0.
    - categories—MCS is not set for this file.

Processes have security contexts

A process's security context has the same four attributes as a user and a file's context. To see process information on a Linux system, you typically use a variant of the ps command. In the following code, the ps -el command was used.

```
# ps -el | grep bash
0 S  1000  1589  1583  0  80   0 -  1653 n_tty_ pts/0  00:00:00 bash
```

```
0 S  1000  5289  1583  0  80   0 -  1653 wait   pts/1  00:00:00 bash
4 S     0  5350  5342  0  80   0 -  1684 wait   pts/1  00:00:00 bash
```

To see a process's security context, you need to use the -Z option on the ps command. In the example that follows, the ps -eZ command was used and then piped into grep to search for only processes running the bash shell.

```
# ps -eZ | grep bash
unconfined_u:unconfined_r:unconfined_t:s0-s0:c0.c1023 1589 pts/
    0 00:00:00 bash
unconfined_u:unconfined_r:unconfined_t:s0-s0:c0.c1023 5289 pts/
    1 00:00:00 bash
unconfined_u:unconfined_r:unconfined_t:s0-s0:c0.c1023 5350 pts/
    1 00:00:00 bash
```

The process context list shows the following:

- user—Process is mapped to the SELinux unconfined_u user.
- role—Process is running as the unconfined_r role.
- type—Process is running in the unconfined_t domain.
- level—
  - sensitivity—Process has only level s0.
  - categories—Process has access to c0.c1023, which is all categories (c0 through to c1023).

These security contexts can be changed to meet your organization's particular security needs. However, before you learn how to change the settings of these security contexts, you need to understand another piece of the SELinux puzzle, SELinux policy types.

Understanding SELinux policy types

The policy type chosen directly determines what sets of policy rules are used to dictate what an object can access. The policy type also determines what specific security context attributes are needed. This is where you start to see the fine level of access control that can be implemented via SELinux.

> **NOTE**
>
> The policy types available on your distribution may not match the ones listed here. For example, on older Linux distributions, the strict policy is still available. On newer distributions, the strict policy has been merged into the Targeted policy, with Targeted used by default.

SELinux has different policies you can choose among:

- Targeted
- MLS
- Minimum

Each policy implements different access control to match your organization's needs. It is critical to understand these policy types in order to select the correct one for your particular security requirements.

Targeted policy

The Targeted policy's primary purpose is to restrict "targeted" daemons. However, it can also restrict other processes and users. Targeted daemons are sandboxed. A *sandbox* is an environment where programs can run, but their access to other objects is tightly controlled.

A process running in such an environment is said to be "sandboxed." Thus, a targeted daemon is restricted so that no malicious attacks launched through it can affect other services or the Linux system as a whole. Targeted daemons make it safer for you to share your print server, file server, web server, or other services, while limiting the risks that access to those services poses to other assets on your system.

All subjects and objects not targeted are run in the unconfined_t domain. The unconfined_t domain has no SELinux policy restrictions and thus only uses the "traditional" Linux security.

SELinux comes with the Targeted policy set as the default. Thus, by default, SELinux targets only a few daemons.

MLS (Multi-Level Security) policy

The MLS policy's primary purpose is to enforce the Bell-LaPadula model. It grants access to other subjects and objects based upon a role's *security clearance* and the object's *classification level*.

In the MLS policy, a security context's MLS attribute is critical. Otherwise, the policy rules will not know how to enforce access restrictions.

Minimum policy

This policy is just as it sounds—minimal. It was originally created for low-memory machines or devices such as smart phones.

The Minimum policy is essentially the same as the Targeted policy, but only the base policy rule package is used. This "bare bones" policy can be used to test out the effects of SELinux on a single designated daemon. For low-memory devices, the Minimum policy allows SELinux to run without consuming a great deal of resources.

Understanding SELinux policy rule packages

Policy rules, also called *allow rules*, are the rules used by SELinux to determine if a subject has access to an object. Policy rules are installed with SELinux and are grouped into packages, also called *modules*. Each particular policy package file ends with a * . pp.

The /etc/selinux/*policy_type*/modules/active/modules directory contains a number of policy package (*.pp) files. The example that follows shows the policy rule packages for a Linux system with the Targeted policy implemented:

```
# ls /etc/selinux/targeted/modules/active/modules/*.pp
/etc/selinux/targeted/modules/active/modules/abrt.pp
/etc/selinux/targeted/modules/active/modules/accountsd.pp
/etc/selinux/targeted/modules/active/modules/acct.pp
/etc/selinux/targeted/modules/active/modules/ada.pp
/etc/selinux/targeted/modules/active/modules/afs.pp
...
/etc/selinux/targeted/modules/active/modules/xserver.pp
/etc/selinux/targeted/modules/active/modules/zabbix.pp
/etc/selinux/targeted/modules/active/modules/zarafa.pp
/etc/selinux/targeted/modules/active/modules/zebra.pp
/etc/selinux/targeted/modules/active/modules/zosremote.pp
```

On your Linux system, there is user documentation on these various policy modules, in the form of HTML files. To view this documentation on Fedora or RHEL, open your system's browser and type in the following URL: file:///usr/share/doc/selinux-policy-selinuxversion#/html/index.html. For Ubuntu, the URL is file:///usr/share/doc/selinux-policy-doc/html/index.html. If you do not have the policy documentation on your system, you can install it on a Fedora or RHEL system, by typing **yum install selinux-policy-doc** at the command line. On Ubuntu, type **sudo apt-get install selinux-policy-doc** at the command line.

You can review this policy documentation to see how policy rules are created and packaged.

The policy rule packages, along with the SELinux operation mode, policy type, and various security contexts, work together to secure your Linux system via SELinux. The following section covers how to begin configuring SELinux to meet your particular organization's security needs.

Configuring SELinux

SELinux comes preconfigured. You can use the SELinux features without any configuration work. However, rarely do the preconfigured settings meet all your Linux system's security needs.

SELinux configurations can only be set and modified by the root user. Configuration and policy files are located in the /etc/selinux directory. The primary configuration file is the /etc/selinux/config file and it appears as follows:

```
# cat /etc/selinux/config
# This file controls the state of SELinux on the system.
```

```
# SELINUX= can take one of these three values:
#       enforcing - SELinux security policy is enforced.
#       permissive - SELinux prints warnings instead of enforcing.
#       disabled - SELinux is fully disabled.
SELINUX=enforcing
# SELINUXTYPE= type of policy in use. Possible values are:
#       targeted - Only targeted network daemons are protected.
#       strict - Full SELinux protection.
SELINUXTYPE=targeted
```

This main SELinux configuration file allows you to set the mode and the policy type.

Setting the SELinux mode

To see SELinux's current mode on your system, use the getenforce command. To see both the current mode and the mode set in the configuration file, use the sestatus command. Both commands are shown in the code that follows:

```
# getenforce
Enforcing
# sestatus
SELinux status:                 enabled
SELinuxfs mount:                /sys/fs/selinux
SELinux root directory:         /etc/selinux
Loaded policy name:             targeted
Current mode:                   enforcing
Mode from config file:          enforcing
Policy MLS status:              enabled
Policy deny_unknown status:     allowed
Max kernel policy version:      28
```

To change the mode setting, you can use the setenforce *newsetting*, where *newsetting* is either:

- enforcing or 1
- permissive or 0

Notice that you cannot use the setenforce command to change SELinux to disabled mode.

The example that follows shows the SELinux mode being changed immediately to permissive mode via the setenforce command. The sestatus command shows the current Operational Mode and the mode in the configuration file, which has not been modified. When the system is rebooted, it determines the SELinux Operational Mode from the configuration file. Thus, the permissive mode set in the example that follows is temporary because the enforcing mode is set via the configuration file when the system is rebooted.

```
# setenforce 0
# getenforce
```

```
Permissive
# sestatus
SELinux status:              enabled
SELinuxfs mount:             /sys/fs/selinux
Loaded policy name:          targeted
Current mode:                permissive
Mode from config file:       enforcing
...
```

CAUTION

It is best to switch from the disabled to the enforcing mode by modifying the configuration file and rebooting. Switching from disabled to enforcing via the setenforce command may hang your system as a result of incorrect file labels. Keep in mind that, when rebooting after changing from disabled mode, there could be a long wait for your filesystem to be relabeled after the system comes back up in permissive or enforcing mode.

To disable SELinux, you must edit the SELinux configuration file. Rebooting the system always changes the mode back to what is set in that configuration file. The preferred method of changing the SELinux mode is to modify the configuration file and then reboot the system.

When switching from disabled to either enforcing or permissive mode, SELinux automatically relabels the filesystem after a reboot. This means SELinux checks and changes the security contexts of any files with incorrect security contexts (for example, mislabeled files) that can cause problems in the new mode. Also, any files not labeled are labeled with contexts. This relabeling process can take a long time because each file's context is checked. The following is the message you receive when a system is going through a relabeling process after a reboot:

```
*** Warning -- SELinux targeted policy relabel is required.
*** Relabeling could take a very long time, depending on file
*** system size and speed of hard drives.
```

To modify the mode in the /etc/selinux/config file, change the line SELINUX= to one of the following:

- disabled
- enforcing
- permissive

The SELinux configuration file example that follows shows that the mode has been set to permissive. Now, when a system reboot occurs, the mode is changed.

```
# cat /etc/selinux/config
# This file controls the state of SELinux on the system.
# SELINUX= can take one of these three values:
#       enforcing - SELinux security policy is enforced.
```

24

```
#        permissive - SELinux prints warnings instead of enforcing.
#        disabled - SELinux is fully disabled.
SELINUX=permissive
...
```

The primary SELinux configuration file does not just contain the mode setting. It also specifies the policy type, which will be enforced.

Setting the SELinux policy type

The policy type you choose determines whether SELinux enforces TE, MLS, or a base package. This type setting directly determines the sets of policy rules used to dictate what an object can access.

By default, the policy type is set to targeted. To change the default policy type, edit the /etc/selinux/config file. Change the line SELINUXTYPE= to one of the following:

- targeted
- mls
- minimum

If you set the SELinux type to mls or minimum, you need to make sure you have their policy package installed first. Check by typing the following command: **yum list selinux-policy-mls** or **yum list selinux-policy-minimum**.

> **NOTE**
>
> To check the SELinux policy packages on Ubuntu, use the command sudo apt-cache policy *package_name*.

The example of the SELinux configuration file that follows shows that the type has been set to mls. Now, when a system reboot occurs, the policy type is changed.

```
# cat /etc/selinux/config
# This file controls the state of SELinux on the system.
...
# SELINUXTYPE= type of policy in use. Possible values are:
#        targeted - Only targeted network daemons are protected.
#        strict - Full SELinux protection.
SELINUXTYPE=mls
```

> **CAUTION**
>
> Do not be fooled by the out-of-date comments in the SELinux configuration file. You cannot set SELINUXTYPE to strict in newer Linux distributions. If you do, the system hangs on the next reboot and you must use grub commands to fix the problem. The strict policy type is now a part of the targeted policy type.

Managing SELinux security contexts

SELinux security contexts allow SELinux to enforce policy rules for subjects accessing objects. Your Linux system comes with security contexts already assigned.

To view current SELinux file and process security contexts, use the secon command. Table 24.1 lists options available on the secon command.

TABLE 24.1 secon Command Options

Option	Description
-u	Use this option to show the user of the security context.
-r	Use this option to show the role of the security context.
-t	Use this option to show the type of the security context.
-s	Use this option to show the sensitivity level of the security context.
-c	Use this option to show the clearance level of the security context.
-m	Use this option to show the sensitivity and clearance level of the security context as an MLS range.

If you use the secon command with no designation, it shows you the current process's security context. To see another process's security context, use the -p option. The example that follows shows you how to use secon to view the current and the systemd process's security context.

```
# secon -urt
user: unconfined_u
role: unconfined_r
type: unconfined_t
# secon -urt -p 1
user: system_u
role: system_r
type: init_t
```

To view a file's security context, you use the -f option, as shown here:

```
# secon -urt -f /etc/passwd
user: system_u
role: object_r
type: etc_t
```

A user's security context is not viewed using the secon command. To see a user's security context, the id command must be used. To see a user's security context besides your own, the command syntax is id -Z username.

Managing the user security context

Remember that every system user login ID is mapped to a particular SELinux user ID. To see a mapping list on your system, enter the **semanage login -1** command. The semanage command and its output are shown in the code that follows. If a user login ID is not listed, then it uses the "default" login mapping, which is the Login Name of _default_. Notice that the associated MLS/MCS settings for each SELinux user are shown as well.

```
# semanage login -1
Login Name              SELinux User        MLS/MCS Range       Service
__default__             unconfined_u        s0-s0:c0.c1023      *
root                    unconfined_u        s0-s0:c0.c1023      *
system_u                system_u            s0-s0:c0.c1023      *
```

To see a current display of the SELinux users and their associated roles, use the command semanage user -1. The partial display that follows shows roles mapped to SELinux usernames:

```
# semanage user -1
                Labeling MLS/     MLS/
SELinux User    Prefix   MCS Level MCS Range          SELinux Roles
guest_u         user     s0        s0                 guest_r
...
user_u          user     s0        s0                 user_r
xguest_u        user     s0        s0                 xguest_r
```

If you need to add a new SELinux username, the semanage utility is used again. This time, the command is semanage user -a *selinux_username*. To map a login ID to the newly added SELinux username, the command is semanage login -a -s *selinux_username loginID*. The semanage utility is a powerful tool in managing your SELinux configuration. For more information on the semanage utility, see the man pages.

Managing the file security context

Labeling files is critical to maintaining proper access control to each file's data. SELinux does set file security labels upon installation and upon system reboot when the SELinux mode is switched from disabled. To see a file's current label (aka security context), use the ls -Z command, as shown here:

```
# ls -Z /etc/passwd
-rw-r--r--. root root system_u:object_r:etc_t:s0 /etc/passwd
```

You can use several commands to manage file security context labels, as shown in Table 24.2.

TABLE 24.2 File Security Context Label Management Commands

Utility	Description
chcat	Use this to change a file's security context label's category.
chcon	Use this to change a file's security context label.
fixfiles	This calls the restorecon/setfiles utility.
restorecon	This does the exact same thing as setfiles utility, but it has a different interface than setfiles.
setfiles	Use this to verify and/or correct security context labels. It can be run for file label verification and/or relabeling files when adding a new policy module to the system. Does exactly the same thing as the restorecon utility, but has a different interface than restorecon.

The chcat and chcon commands, shown in Table 24.2, allow you to change a file's security context. In the example below, the chcon command is used to change the SELinux user associated with file.txt from undefined_u to system_u.

```
# ls -Z file.txt
-rw-rw-r--. johndoe johndoe
 unconfined_u:object_r:user_home_t:s0 file.txt
# chcon -u system_u file.txt
# ls -Z file.txt
-rw-rw-r--. johndoe johndoe
 system_u:object_r:user_home_t:s0 file.txt
```

Notice in Table 24.2 that fixfiles, restorecon, and setfiles are essentially the same utility. However, restorecon is the popular choice to use when fixing files' labels. The command restorecon -R *filename* changes a file back to its default security context.

Managing the process security context

The definition of a process is a running program. When you run programs or start services on a Linux system, each one is given a process ID (see Chapter 6). On a system with SELinux, a process is also given a security context.

How a process gets its security context depends upon which process started it. Remember that systemd (previously init) is the "mother" of all processes (see Chapter 15). Thus, many daemons and processes are started by systemd. The processes systemd starts are given new security contexts. For instance, when the apache daemon is started by systemd, it is assigned the type (aka domain) httpd_t. The context assigned is handled

24

by the SELinux policy written specifically for that daemon. If no policy exists for a process, then it is assigned a default type, unconfined_t.

For a program or application run by a user (parent process), the new process (child process) inherits the user's security context. Of course, this occurs only if the user is allowed to run the program. A process can also run a program. The child process in this case also inherits its parent process's security context. Thus, the child process runs in the same domain.

So a process's security context is set before the program is run and depends upon who started it. You can use a couple of commands to change the security contexts under which a program is run:

- runcon—Run the program using options to determine the user, role, and type (aka domain).
- sandbox—Run the program within a tightly controlled domain (aka sandbox).

You can cause several problems by using runcon, so use it with caution. However, sandbox offers a great deal of protection. It allows flexibility in testing out new programs on your Linux system.

Managing SELinux policy rule packages

Policy rules are the rules used by SELinux to determine whether a subject has access to an object. They are grouped into packages, also called modules, and are installed with SELinux. An easy way to view the modules on your system is to use the semodule -l command. It lists all the policy modules along with their current version number. An example of the semodule -l command is shown here:

```
# semodule -l
abrt          1.2.0
accountsd     1.0.6
acct          1.5.1
...
xserver       3.8.4
zabbix        1.5.3
zarafa        1.1.0
zebra         1.12.0
zoneminder    1.1.1
zosremote     1.1.1
```

Several tools can help you to manage and even create your own policy modules. Table 24.3 shows the various Policy rule package tools available on a Fedora system.

TABLE 24.3   SELinux Policy Package Tools

Policy Tool	Description
audit2allow	Generates policy allow/dontaudit rules from logs of denied operations
audit2why	Generates a description of why the access was denied from logs of denied operations
checkmodule	Compiles policy modules
checkpolicy	Compiles SELinux policies
load_policy	Loads new policies into the kernel
semodule	Manages policy modules
semodule_deps	Lists dependencies between policy packages
semodule_expand	Expands a policy module package
semodule_link	Links policy module packages together
semodule_package	Creates a policy module package

The following is an example policy typically used as a framework to create local policy rules. The example policy is rather long, so only a portion of it is shown.

```
# cat /usr/share/selinux/devel/example.te
policy_module(myapp,1.0.0)
########################################
#
# Declarations
#

type myapp_t;
type myapp_exec_t;
domain_type(myapp_t)
domain_entry_file(myapp_t, myapp_exec_t)

type myapp_log_t;
logging_log_file(myapp_log_t)

type myapp_tmp_t;
files_tmp_file(myapp_tmp_t)
...
```

24

```
allow myapp_t myapp_tmp_t:file manage_file_perms;
files_tmp_filetrans(myapp_t,myapp_tmp_t,file)
```

The preceding example code shows that a special syntax is used in policy code. To create and modify policy rules, you need to learn this policy rule language syntax, learn how to use the SELinux policy compilers, and learn how to link policy rule files together to form modules; you probably need to take a couple of day-long classes. You may be tempted to give up on SELinux at this point. However, it is much easier to use Booleans to modify policies.

Managing SELinux via booleans

SELinux policy rule writing and module creation is a rather complicated and time-consuming activity. Creating incorrect policy rules could potentially compromise your Linux system's security. Thankfully, SELinux provides Booleans.

A Boolean is a toggle switch that toggles a setting on or off. A Boolean switch allows you to change parts of SELinux policy rules, without any knowledge of policy writing. These policy changes can be done without a system reboot, too!

To see a list of all the current Booleans used in SELinux, use the getsebool -a command. The following is an example of the SELinux policy rules with Booleans on a Fedora Linux system:

```
# getsebool -a
abrt_anon_write --> off
abrt_handle_event --> off
. . .
xserver_object_manager --> off
zabbix_can_network --> off
```

To see a specific policy that can be modified by a Boolean, the getsebool command is used again. This time, the policy name is passed to it, as shown in the following example:

```
# getsebool httpd_can_connect_ftp
httpd_can_connect_ftp --> off
```

To toggle a policy, you can use either the setsebool command or the togglebool command. Both of these commands change the policy rule temporarily. When the system is rebooted, the Boolean returns to its original setting. If you need this setting to be permanent, you can use only the setsebool with the -P option.

The togglebool command just toggles the current Boolean setting of the policy you specify between on and off. For instance, if you issued the command togglebool httpd_can_connect_ftp, you would change the policy setting status from its previous setting of "off" to "on."

The `setsebool` command has six settings: three for turning a policy on (on, 1, or true), and three for turning a policy off (off, 0, or false).

For an example using `setsebool`, in some situations, it is not good security to allow users to execute programs from their /home directory. To prevent this from happening, the `allow_user_exec_content` policy rule needs to be turned off. The example that follows shows the `setsebool` command being used to do just that. Notice that the -P option is used to make this setting permanent.

```
# setsebool -P allow_user_exec_content off
```

The `getsebool` command verifies that the Boolean setting has been correctly made:

```
# getsebool allow_user_exec_content
allow_user_exec_content --> off
```

Booleans make modifying current SELinux policy rules much easier. Overall, the SELinux command line configuration utilities, such as `getsebool`, are easy to use. However, if you want a GUI configuration tool, SELinux has one. It is installed via the command `yum install policycoreutils-gui`. On Ubuntu, use the command `sudo apt-get install policycoreutils`. To use this configuration tool, simply type in the command `system-config-selinux` and a GUI interface appears.

Monitoring and Troubleshooting SELinux

SELinux is another tool for monitoring your system. It logs all access denials, which can help you determine whether an attack is being attempted. These same SELinux log files are also useful in troubleshooting SELinux problems.

Understanding SELinux logging

SELinux uses a cache called the Access Vector Cache (AVC) when reviewing policy rules for particular security contexts. When access is denied, called an AVC denial, a denial message is put into a log file.

These logged denial messages can help you diagnose and address routine SELinux policy violations. Where these denial messages are logged depends upon the status of the `auditd` and `rsyslogd` daemons:

- If the `auditd` daemon is running, the denial messages are logged to /var/log/audit/audit.log.

- If `auditd` is not running, but the `rsyslogd` daemon is running, the denial messages are logged to /var/log/messages.

24

NOTE

If both `auditd` and `rsyslogd` are running, and you have the `setroubleshootd` daemon on your system, denial messages are sent to both the `audit.log` and `messages` log files. However, denial information in the `messages` log file is put into a more understandable format by the `setroubleshootd` daemon.

Reviewing SELinux messages in the audit log

If you have the `auditd` daemon running, you can quickly see if any AVC denials have been logged by using the `aureport` command. The example that follows shows the use of `aureport` and `grep` to search for AVC denials. At least one denial has been logged to `/var/log/audit/audit.log`:

```
# aureport | grep AVC
Number of AVC's: 1
```

After you discover that an AVC denial has been logged in `audit.log`, you can use `ausearch` to review the denial message(s). The example that follows shows the `ausearch` command being used to review the logged AVC denial message.

```
# ausearch -m avc
type=AVC msg=audit(1411184014.986:69860): avc: denied { create } for
  pid=21875 comm="vsftpd" name="services"
  scontext=system_u:system_r:ftpd_t:s0-s0:c0.c1023
  tcontext=system_u:object_r:user_home_t:s0 tclass=file
```

The display provides information on who was attempting access, along with his security context when attempting it. Look for these key words in an AVC denial message:

- `type=AVC`
- `avc: denied`
- `pid=`
- `exe=`
- `subj=`

This can give you enough data to either begin fixing a problem or track down malicious activity.

Reviewing SELinux messages in the messages log

If you have the `rsyslogd` running, you can find AVC denial messages by searching through the `/var/log/messages` file using `grep`. For RHEL 7, Fedora 21, or any Linux using `systemd`, you can run the `journalctl` command to check for AVC denial log messages. In each log message is an `sealert` command line that you can run to get information about each AVC denial. For example:

```
# journalctl | grep sealert
Sep 18 23:58:03 fedora20.example.com setroubleshoot[13449]:
  SELinux is preventing /usr/sbin/vsftpd from getattr access on the
```

```
directory /home/chris/Music. For complete SELinux messages.
run sealert -l 8f52dd56-8025-4208-af41-7d296bdaa46b
```

From the example, you can see that a Linux user attempted to log into an FTP service (vsftpd) as a particular user. Because FTP uses clear text passwords, that action is considered insecure and is, therefore, denied by SELinux. Notice that the AVC denial message tells you that you can run the `sealert -l` command to get more information.

The `sealert` utility allows you to get more information on a particular AVC denial message. The information format `sealert` provides can help you diagnose your problems. The example that follows shows the information `sealert` provides concerning the AVC denial, which was shown in the previous example. Notice the command used is exactly the same command suggested from the preceding message log file. The long number used in the `sealert` command is the AVC denial message's ID number.

```
# sealert -l 8f52dd56-8025-4208-af41-7d296bdaa46b

SELinux is preventing /usr/sbin/vsftpd from getattr access
    on the directory /home/chris/Music.
*****  Plugin catchall_boolean (47.5 confidence) suggests   ********
    **********
If you want to determine whether ftpd can read and write files in
user home directories.
Then you must tell SELinux about this by enabling the 'ftp_home_dir'
    boolean.
You can read 'None' man page for more details.
Do setsebool -P ftp_home_dir 1

*****  Plugin catchall_boolean (47.5 confidence) suggests   ********
    **********
If you want to determine whether ftpd can login to local users and
    can read and write all files on the system, governed by DAC.
Then you must tell SELinux about this by enabling the
    'ftpd_full_access' boolean.
You can read 'ftpd_selinux' man page for more details.

Do setsebool -P ftpd_full_access 1
. . .
```

The `sealert` output provides a great deal of helpful information. In this case, it gives the proper diagnosis that if you want to allow a user to log into an existing user account from an FTP service, you must turn on the `ftp_home_dir` boolean (`setsebool -P ftp_home_dir=on`). If you have SELinux enforced on your system, it would be wise to have the `setroubleshootd` daemon running as well.

Troubleshooting SELinux logging

Obviously, the log files are extremely important for diagnosing and addressing SELinux policy violations. The log files or directly querying the `systemd` journal (`journalctl` command) are your first steps in troubleshooting SELinux. Thus, it is important to make sure your Linux system is logging messages in the first place.

A quick way to determine if the logging is taking place is to check if the proper daemons are running: `auditd`, `rsyslogd`, and/or `setroubleshootd`. Use an appropriate command, such as `systemctl status auditd.service`. Of course, the command you use depends on your Linux distribution and its version. See Chapter 15 for more details. If the daemon is not running, start it so that logging may begin to occur.

> **CAUTION**
>
> Sometimes AVC denials are not logged because of `dontaudit` policy rules. Although the `dontaudit` rules help reduce false positives in the logs, they can cause you problems when you're troubleshooting. To fix this, temporarily disable all `dontaudit` policy rules using the command `semodule -DB`.

Troubleshooting common SELinux problems

When you begin working with SELinux, it is easy to overlook the obvious. Whenever access is denied, you should first check the "traditional" Linux DAC permissions. For example, use the `ls -l` command and double-check that a file's owner, group, and read, write, and execute assignments are correct.

With SELinux, several regular items can cause problems:

- Using a nonstandard directory for a service
- Using a nonstandard port for a service
- Moving files that result in losing their security context labels
- Having Booleans set incorrectly

Each one of these problems can be solved fairly quickly.

Using a nonstandard directory for a service

For various reasons, you may decide to store a service's files in a nonstandard directory. When you do this, SELinux needs to know that this nonstandard behavior has occurred. Otherwise, it denies access to legitimate service access requests.

For example, you decided to keep your HTML files in a different location from the standard /var/www/html. You put the files in /abc/www/html. You must let SELinux know you want the `http` service to be able to access the files within /abc/www/html.

The commands to accomplish this are `semanage` and `restorecon`. In the following, the commands are used to add the proper security context type on the /abc/www/html directory and all it contains:

```
# semanage fcontext -a -t httpd_sys_content_t  "/abc/www/html(/.*)?"
```

To actually set the new security context type to the files within the directory, you need to use the `restorecon -R` command. This is accomplished in the following:

```
# restorecon -R -v /srv/www/html
```

Now the `httpd` daemon has permission to access your HTML files in their nonstandard directory location.

Using a nonstandard port for a service

Similar to the problem just described, you may decide to have a service listening on a non-standard port. When you make this port change, the service often fails to start.

For example, you decide for security purposes to move `sshd` from port 22 to a nonstandard port, 47347. SELinux does not know about this port, and the service fails to start. To fix this problem, you must first find the security context type for `sshd`. This is accomplished using the code that follows by issuing the `semanage port -l` command and piping the results into `grep` to search for `ssh`.

```
# semanage port -l | grep ssh
ssh_port_t                      tcp                 22
```

In the preceding example, the context type needed is `ssh_port_t`. Now, using the `semanage` command again, add that type to port 47347, as shown here:

```
# semanage port -a -t ssh_port_t -p tcp 47347
```

Next, edit the /etc/ssh/sshd_config file to add a `Port 47347` line to the file. Then restart the `sshd` service so the service listens on the nonstandard port 47347.

Moving files and losing security context labels

You used the `cp` command to move a file from /etc temporarily to the /tmp directory. Then you used the `mv` command to put it back. Now, the file has the security context of the temporary directory instead of its original security context, and your system is getting AVC denial messages when the service using that file tries to start up.

This is an easy fix, thanks to the `restorecon -R` command. Simply type **restorecon -R** *file*, and the file has its original security context restored.

24

Booleans set incorrectly

Another common problem is setting a Boolean incorrectly. This can give you several AVC denials.

For example, if your system's scripts are no longer able to connect to the network and you are getting AVC denials in your logs, you need to check the httpd Booleans. Use the getsebool -a command, and pipe it into grep to search for any Booleans that affect httpd. The example here shows these commands being used:

```
# getsebool -a | grep http
...
httpd_can_network_connect --> off
...
```

The getsebool command shows the Boolean httpd_can_network_connect is set to off. To change this Boolean, use the following command: setsebool -P httpd_can_network_connect on. Notice the -P option was used to make the setting permanent. Now, your scripts should be able to connect out to the network.

As you encounter various problems with SELinux, your troubleshooting skills will improve. Meanwhile, here is another excellent resource to help you with troubleshooting: http://docs.redhat.com. The Red Hat document "Red Hat Enterprise Linux" has an entire chapter (Chapter 8) dedicated to troubleshooting SELinux.

Putting It All Together

Obviously, SELinux is a rather complicated and rich tool. You now have a good, solid foundation on the SELinux basics. Here are some recommendations as you get started implementing SELinux on your system.

You can use the default targeted SELinux mode to secure most basic network services (httpd, vsftpd, Samba, and so on) without needing to assign special user roles or otherwise lock down your system. In this case, the main things you need to do are put files in standard locations (or run commands to assign the proper file contexts to nonstandard locations), make sure Booleans are turned on for less secure features you want on anyway, and watch AVC denials for problems.

- Start with the permissive operational mode. This allows requests that SELinux sees as insecure to succeed.

- Run your current system for a significant amount of time in Permissive mode. Review the logs and see what problems may occur with the default SELinux settings. You can then change Booleans or file contexts so features improperly denied can be allowed. After the problems are worked out, turn on enforcing mode.

- Overall, implement SELinux configuration changes one at a time, in a test environment or using Permissive mode. See what kind of effect each configuration change has before moving on to the next one. You can then use the `audit2allow` command to selectively allow actions that cause AVC denials to be added to the policy of what is allowed for a service.

Obtaining More Information on SELinux

Several additional sources of information can help you with SELinux on your Linux system:

- **Your system's man pages**—Issue the command `man -k selinux` to find all the various man pages you can review for the SELinux utilities currently installed on your system. If you are debugging SELinux problems for a well-known service (such as `httpd`, `vsftpd`, Samba, and so on), there is probably a man page associated with how to specifically fix SELinux problems with that service.

- **The Red Hat Enterprise Linux manuals**—Located at `http://docs.redhat.com`, this site contains an entire manual on SELinux.

- **The Fedora Project SELinux Guide**—Located at `http://docs.fedoraproject.org`, this site has a Security-Enhanced Linux Guide. However, the guide is not updated for every Fedora version, so you may need to look in older versions to find it. Also, the SELinux Guide is not located within the Security manual, but the Security manual is a good manual to review as well.

- **SELinux on Ubuntu**—Because there are subtle differences between SELinux on RHEL/Fedora and Ubuntu, the site `https://wiki.ubuntu.com/SELinux` provides you with the additional help you need.

- **SELinux Project Wiki**—This is the official SELinux project page. Several resources are available at this site, which is located at `http://selinuxproject.org`.

- **SELinux News**—Just as it sounds, there is current news on SELinux at `http://selinuxnews.org`.

Summary

SELinux provides a security enhancement to Linux and is installed by default on many Linux distributions. In this chapter, you learned the benefits of SELinux, how it works, how to set it up, how to fix various problems with SELinux, and how to get more information about this important security enhancement.

SELinux at first glance appears rather complicated. However, after it's broken down into its various components—Operational Modes, Security contexts, Policy types, and policy packages—you can see how the various pieces work together. Each component has an important role for enforcing and testing the chosen security requirements for your organization.

You learned the various steps to configure SELinux. Even though SELinux comes preconfigured, you may need to make some modifications to meet your organization's security needs.

24

Each component has its own configuration steps and settings to choose. Though policy rule creation was not covered, you did learn how to modify the supplied policies via Booleans.

SELinux provides another tool for monitoring your Linux system's security. Because SELinux logs all access denials, it can help you determine if an attack has been or is being attempted. Even the best made plans can go badly. Therefore, in this chapter, you learned how to fix common SELinux configuration problems.

In the next chapter, you'll learn how to protect your Linux system on a network. You'll learn about controlling access, managing firewalls, and securing remote access.

Exercises

Use these exercises to test your knowledge of using SELinux. These tasks assume you are running a Fedora or Red Hat Enterprise Linux system (although some tasks work on other Linux systems as well). If you are stuck, solutions to the tasks are shown in Appendix B (although in Linux, there are often multiple ways to complete a task).

1. Making no changes to the SELinux primary configuration file, write down the command to set your system into the Permissive Operating Mode for SELinux.

2. Making no changes to the SELinux primary configuration file, write down the command to set your system into the Enforcing mode for SELinux.

3. What current and permanent SELinux policy types are set on your system, and how did you find them?

4. List the security context for the /etc/hosts file, and identify its different security context attributes.

5. Create a file called test.html in your home directory, and assign its type to httpd_sys_content_t. (This is something you might do to make content available to be shared by your web server outside the common /var/www/html directory.)

6. List the security context for the running crond process, and identify its security context attributes.

7. Create a file called /etc/test.txt, change its file context to user_tmp_t, restore it to its proper content (the default context for the /etc directory), and remove the file. Use the ls -Z /etc/test.txt command to check the file at each point in the process.

8. You have an FTP server on your private network, and you want to allow users to log into that server with their regular user accounts (while SELinux is in enforcing mode). Determine what Boolean allows users to access their home directories via FTP, and turn that Boolean on.

9. What command would list out all the SELinux policy modules on your system, along with their version number?

10. Prepare your system to run a vsftpd FTP server that is protected by SELinux (I did this on a Fedora system). Then log in as a regular, and try to copy a file (which should cause an AVC denial) as follows:

```
# getenforce
Enforcing
# yum install vsftpd lftp rsyslog setroubleshoot-server
# systemctl start syslog
# systemctl start vsftpd
# semodule -DB
# getsebool ftp_home_dir
ftp_home_dir --> off
# lftp -u chris localhost
Password: ********
lftp chris@localhost:~> put /etc/services
put: Access failed: 553 Could not create file. (services)
lftp chris@localhost:~> quit
```

Your assignment is to list the AVC denial from your system's log messages. View information about the denial, and change the Boolean to allow FTP access, as the AVC denial's description suggests.

24

Securing Linux on a Network

Setting up your Linux system on a network, especially a public network, creates a whole new set of challenges when it comes to security. The best way to secure your Linux system is to keep it off all networks. However, that is rarely a feasible option.

Entire books have been filled with information on how to secure a computer system on a network. Many organizations hire full-time computer security administrators to watch over their network-attached Linux systems. Therefore, think of this chapter as a brief introduction to securing Linux on a network.

Auditing Network Services

Most Linux systems used for large enterprises are configured as servers that, as the name implies, offer services to remote clients over a network. A *network service* is any task that the computer performs requiring it to send and receive information over the network using some predefined set of rules. Routing email is a network service, as is serving web pages.

A Linux server has the potential to provide thousands of services. Many of them are listed in the /etc/services file. Consider the following sections from the /etc/services file:

```
$ cat /etc/services
# /etc/services:
# $Id: services,v 1.55 2013/04/14 ovasik Exp $
#
# Network services, Internet style
# IANA services version: last updated 2013-04-10
#
```

```
# Note that it is presently the policy of IANA to assign ...
# Each line describes one service, and is of the form:
#
# service-name  port/protocol  [aliases ...]    [# comment]
...
echo            7/tcp
echo            7/udp
discard         9/tcp          sink null
discard         9/udp          sink null
systat          11/tcp         users
systat          11/udp         users
daytime         13/tcp
daytime         13/udp
qotd            17/tcp         quote
qotd            17/udp         quote
...
chargen         19/tcp         ttytst source
chargen         19/udp         ttytst source
ftp-data        20/tcp
ftp-data        20/udp
# 21 is registered to ftp, but also used by fsp
ftp             21/tcp
...
http            80/tcp         www www-http   # WorldWideWeb HTTP
http            80/udp         www www-http   # HyperText Transfer
                                                 Protocol
http            80/sctp                       # HyperText Transfer
                                                 Protocol
kerberos        88/tcp         kerberos5 krb5 # Kerberos v5
kerberos        88/udp         kerberos5 krb5 # Kerberos v5
...
blp5            48129/udp         # Bloomberg locator
com-bardac-dw   48556/tcp         # com-bardac-dw
com-bardac-dw   48556/udp         # com-bardac-dw
iqobject        48619/tcp           # iqobject
iqobject        48619/udp           # iqobject
```

After the comment lines, notice three columns of information. The left column contains the name of each service. The middle column defines the port number and protocol type used for that service. The right column contains an optional alias or list of aliases for the service.

Many Linux distributions come with unneeded network services running. An unnecessary service exposes your Linux system to malicious attacks. For example, if your Linux server is a print server, then it should only be offering printing services. It should not also offer Apache web services. This would only unnecessarily expose your print server to any malicious attacks that take advantage of web service vulnerabilities.

Evaluating access to network services with nmap

A wonderful tool to help you review your network services from a network standpoint is the nmap security scanner. The nmap utility is available in most Linux distribution repositories and has a web page full of information at http://nmap.org.

To install nmap on a Fedora or RHEL distribution, use the yum command (using root privileges), as shown in the example that follows.

```
# yum install nmap -y
Loaded plugins: langpacks, product-id, subscription-manager
...
Resolving Dependencies
--> Running transaction check
---> Package nmap.x86_64 2:6.40-4.el7 will be installed
--> Finished Dependency Resolution

Dependencies Resolved
...Installing:
 nmap       x86_64    2:6.47-1.fc21y    rhel-7-server-rpms    4.0 M
 ...
Installed:  nmap-6.47-1.fc21

Complete!
```

To install the nmap utility on an Ubuntu distribution, type **sudo apt-get install nmap** at the command line.

The nmap utility's full name is Network Mapper. It has a variety of uses for security audits and network exploration. Using nmap to do various port scans allows you to see what services are running on all the servers on your local network and whether they are advertising their availability.

> **NOTE**
>
> What is a port? Ports or, more correctly, *network ports*, are numeric values used by the TCP and UDP network protocols as access points to services on a system. Standard port numbers are assigned to services so a service knows to listen on a particular port number and a client knows to request the service on that port number.
>
> For example, port 80 is the standard network port for unencrypted (HTTP) traffic to the Apache web service. So, if you ask for www.example.com from your Web browser, the browser assumes you mean to use TCP port 80 on the server that offers that Web content. Think of a network port as a door to your Linux server. Each door is numbered. And behind every door is a particular service waiting to help whoever knocks on that door.

To audit your server's ports, the nmap utility offers several useful scan types. The nmap site has an entire manual on all the port scanning techniques you can use at

25

`http://nmap.org/book/man-port-scanning-techniques.html`. Here are two basic port scans to get you started on your service auditing:

- **TCP Connect port scan**—For this scan, nmap attempts to connect to ports using the Transmission Control Protocol (TCP) on the server. If a port is listening, the connect attempt succeeds.

  TCP is a network protocol used in the TCP/IP network protocol suite. TCP is a connection-oriented protocol. Its primary purpose is to negotiate and initiate a connection using what is called a "three-way handshake." TCP sends a synchronize packet (SYN) to a remote server, specifying a specific port number in the packet. The remote server receives the SYN and replies with an acknowledgment packet (SYN-ACK) to the originating computer. The original server then acknowledges (ACK) the response, and a TCP connection is officially established. This three-way handshake is often called a SYN-SYN-ACK or SYN, SYN-ACK, ACK.

  If you select a TCP Connect port scan, the nmap utility uses this three-way handshake to do a little investigative activity on a remote server. Any services that use the TCP protocol will respond to the scan.

- **UDP port scan**—For this scan, nmap sends a UDP packet to every port on the system being scanned. UDP is another popular protocol in the TCP/IP network protocol suite. Unlike TCP, however, UDP is a connectionless protocol. If the port is listening and has a service that uses the UDP protocol, it responds to the scan.

> **TIP**
>
> Keep in mind that Free and Open Source Software (FOSS) utilities are also available to those with malicious intent. While you are doing these nmap scans, realize that the remote scan results you see for your Linux server are the same scan results others will see. This will help you evaluate your system's security settings in terms of how much information is being given out to port scans. Keep in mind that you should use tools like nmap only on your own systems, because scanning ports on other people's computers can give the impression that you are trying to break in.

When you run the nmap utility, it provides a handy little report with information on the system you are scanning and the ports it sees. The ports are given a "state" status. nmap reports six possible port states:

- open—This is the most dangerous state an nmap scan can report for a port. An open port indicates that a server has a service handling requests on this port. Think of it as a sign on the door, "Come on in! We are here to help you." Of course, if you are offering a public service, you want the port to be open.

- closed—A closed port is accessible, but there is no service waiting on the other side of this door. However, the scan status still indicates that there is a Linux server at this particular IP address.

- filtered—This is the best state to secure a port that you don't want anyone to access. It cannot be determined if a Linux server is actually at the scanned

IP address. It is possible that a service could be listening on a particular port, but the firewall is blocking access to that port, effectively preventing any access to the service through the particular network interface.

- unfiltered—The nmap scan sees the port but cannot determine if the port is open or closed.

- open|filtered—The nmap scan sees the port but cannot determine if the port is open or filtered.

- closed|filtered—The nmap scan sees the port but cannot determine if the port is closed or filtered.

To help you better understand how to use the nmap utility, review the following example. For the purposes of building a network services list, the example nmap scans are conducted on a Fedora system. The first scan is a TCP Connect scan from the command line, using the loop back address, 127.0.0.1.

```
# nmap -sT 127.0.0.1
Starting Nmap 5.51 ( http://nmap.org ) at 2016-03-22 10:33 EDT
Nmap scan report for localhost.localdomain (127.0.0.1)

Host is up (0.016s latency).
Not shown: 998 closed ports

PORT      STATE SERVICE
25/tcp    open  smtp
631/tcp   open  ipp

Nmap done: 1 IP address (1 host up) scanned in 1.34 seconds
```

The TCP Connect nmap scan reports that two TCP ports are open and have services listening on the localhost (127.0.0.1) for requests to these ports:

- Simple Mail Transfer Protocol (SMTP) is listening at TCP port 25.

- Internet Printing Protocol (IPP) is listening at TCP port 631.

The next nmap scan is an UDP scan on the Fedora system's loopback address.

```
# nmap -sU 127.0.0.1

Starting Nmap 5.51 ( http://nmap.org ) at 2016-03-22 10:36 EDT
Nmap scan report for localhost.localdomain (127.0.0.1)
Host is up (0.00048s latency).
Not shown: 997 closed ports

PORT      STATE          SERVICE
68/udp    open|filtered  dhcpc
```

25

```
631/udp  open|filtered ipp

Nmap done: 1 IP address (1 host up) scanned in 2.24 seconds
```

The UDP nmap scan reports that two UDP ports are open and have services listening on those ports:

- Dynamic Host Control Protocol client (dhcpc) is listening at port 68.
- Internet Printing Protocol (ipp) is listening at port 631.

Notice that port 631's IPP is listed under both nmap's TCP Connect scan and the UDP scan because the IPP protocol used both the TCP and the UDP protocol and thus is listed in both scans.

Using these two simple nmap scans, TCP Connect and UDP, on your loopback address, you can build a list of the network services offered by your Linux server.

Keep in mind that port numbers are associated with a particular protocol (TCP or UDP) and a particular network interface. For example, if you have one network interface card (NIC) on a computer that faces the Internet and another that faces a private network, you may want to offer a private service (like the CUPS service for printing) to the NIC on your private network. But you may want to filter that port (631) on the NIC that faces the Internet.

Using nmap to audit your network services advertisements

You probably want lots of people to visit your Web site (httpd service). You probably don't want everyone on the Internet able to access your SMB file shares (smb service). To make sure you are properly separating access to those two types of services, you want to be able to check what a malicious scanner can see of the services available on your public-facing network interfaces.

The idea here is to compare what your Linux server looks like from the inside versus what it looks like from the outside. If you determine that some network services are accessible that you intended to keep private, you can take steps to block access to them from external interfaces.

> **TIP**
>
> You may be tempted to skip the scans from inside your organization's internal network. Don't. Malicious activity often occurs from a company's own employees or by someone who has already penetrated external defenses.

Again, the nmap utility is a great help here. To get a proper view of how your Linux server's ports are seen, you need to conduct scans from several locations. For example, a simple audit would set up scans in these places:

- On the Linux server itself
- From another server on the organization's same network
- From outside the organization's network

In the following examples, part of a simple audit is conducted. The nmap utility is run on a Fedora system, designated as "Host-A." Host-A is the Linux server whose network services are to be protected. Host-B is a Linux server, using the Linux Mint distribution, and is on the same network as Host-A.

> **TIP**
>
> Security settings on various network components, such as the server's firewall and the company's routers, should all be considered when conducting audit scans.

For this audit example, a scan is run from Host-A, using not the loopback address, but the actual IP address. First, the IP address for Host-A is determined using the ifconfig command. The IP address is 10.140.67.23.

```
# ifconfig

lo   Link encap:Local Loopback
     inet addr:127.0.0.1  Mask:255.0.0.0
     inet6 addr: ::1/128 Scope:Host
     UP LOOPBACK RUNNING  MTU:16436  Metric:1
     RX packets:4 errors:0 dropped:0 overruns:0 frame:0
     TX packets:4 errors:0 dropped:0 overruns:0 carrier:0
     collisions:0 txqueuelen:0
     RX bytes:240 (240.0 b)  TX bytes:240 (240.0 b)

p2p1 Link encap:Ethernet  HWaddr 08:00:27:E5:89:5A
     inet addr:10.140.67.23
   Bcast:10.140.67.255  Mask:255.255.255.0
     inet6 addr: fe80::a00:27ff:fee5:895a/64 Scope:Link
     UP BROADCAST RUNNING MULTICAST  MTU:1500  Metric:1
     RX packets:81 errors:0 dropped:0 overruns:0 frame:0
     TX packets:102 errors:0 dropped:0 overruns:0 carrier:0
     collisions:0 txqueuelen:1000
     RX bytes:50015 (48.8 KiB)  TX bytes:14721 (14.3 KiB)
```

Now, using the Host-A IP address, an nmap TCP Connect scan is issued from Host-A. The nmap scan goes out to the network to conduct the scan. All ports are reported as having a status of closed.

```
# nmap -sT 10.140.67.23
Starting Nmap 5.51 ( http://nmap.org ) at 2016-03-22 10:33 EDT
Nmap scan report for 10.140.67.23
```

25

```
Host is up (0.010s latency).
All 1000 scanned ports on 10.140.67.23 are closed

Nmap done: 1 IP address (1 host up) scanned in 1.48 seconds
```

The nmap scan is moved from originating at Host-A to originating on Host-B. Now the TCP Connect scan is attempted on Host-A's ports from Host-B's command line.

```
$ nmap -sT 10.140.67.23
Starting Nmap 5.21 ( http://nmap.org ) at 2015-03-22 05:34 HADT

Note: Host seems down. If it is really up,
  but blocking our ping probes, try -PN

Nmap done: 1 IP address (0 hosts up) scanned in 0.11 seconds
```

Here, nmap gives a helpful hint. Host-A appears to be down, or it could just be blocking the probes. So another nmap scan is attempted from Host-B, using nmap's advice of disabling the scan's ping probes via the -PN option.

```
$ nmap -sT -PN 10.140.67.23
Starting Nmap 5.21 ( http://nmap.org ) at 2016-03-22 05:55 HADT

Nmap scan report for 10.140.67.23

Host is up (0.0015s latency).
All 1000 scanned ports on 10.140.67.23 are filtered

Nmap done: 1 IP address (1 host up) scanned in 5.54 seconds
```

You can see that Host-A (10.140.67.23) is up and running and all its ports have a status of filtered. This means there is a firewall in place on Host-A. These scans from Host-B give you a better idea of what a malicious scanner may see when scanning your Linux server. In this example, the malicious scanner would not see much.

> **NOTE**
>
> If you are familiar with nmap, you know that the TCP SYN scan is the default scan nmap uses. The TCP SYN scan does an excellent job of probing a remote system in a stealthy manner. Because you are probing your own system for security auditing purposes, it makes sense to use the more "heavy-duty" nmap utility scans. If you still want to use the TCP SYN scan, the command is nmap -sS ip_address.

The services currently running on Host-A are not that "juicy." In the example that follows, another service, ssh, is started on Host-A using the systemctl command (see Chapter 15). This should give the nmap utility a more interesting target to look for.

```
# systemctl start sshd.service
# systemctl status sshd.service
sshd.service - OpenSSH server daemon
  Loaded: loaded (/lib/systemd/system/sshd.service; disabled)
  Active: active (running) since
 Thu, 22 Mar 2016 10:57:24 -0400; 12s ago
Main PID: 1750 (sshd)
  CGroup: name=systemd:/system/sshd.service
     └1750 /usr/sbin/sshd -D
```

Also, because Host-A's firewall is blocking the nmap scans from Host-B, it would be interesting to see what an nmap scan can report when the firewall is down. The example that follows shows the firewall being disabled on Host-A for a Fedora 21 or RHEL 7 system (for other systems, you probably need to disable the iptables service):

```
# systemctl stop firewalld.service
# systemctl status firewalld.service
```

With a new service running and Host-A's firewall lowered, the nmap scans should find something. In the following, nmap scans are run again from Host-B. This time the nmap utility shows the ssh service running on open port 22. Notice with the firewall down on Host-A, both nmap scans pick up much more information. This really demonstrates the importance of your Linux server's firewall.

```
# nmap -sT 10.140.67.23
Starting Nmap 5.21 ( http://nmap.org ) at 2012-03-22 06:22 HADT
Nmap scan report for 10.140.67.23
Host is up (0.016s latency).
Not shown: 999 closed ports

PORT    STATE SERVICE
22/tcp open  ssh

Nmap done: 1 IP address (1 host up) scanned in 0.40 seconds

# nmap -sU 10.140.67.23
[sudo] password for johndoe: ***************
Starting Nmap 5.21 ( http://nmap.org ) at 2012-03-22 06:22 HADT
Nmap scan report for 10.140.67.23
Host is up (0.00072s latency).
Not shown: 997 closed ports

PORT      STATE          SERVICE
68/udp    open|filtered  dhcpc
631/udp   open|filtered  ipp
...
Nmap done: 1 IP address (1 host up) scanned in 1081.83 seconds
```

25

In order to conduct a thorough audit, be sure to include the UDP scan. Also, there are additional nmap scans that may be beneficial to your organization. Look at the nmap utility's website for additional suggestions.

You still need to implement controls for those services your Linux server should offer. One way to accomplish this is via TCP wrappers.

Controlling access to network services

Completely disabling an unused service is fine, but for needed network services, you must set up access control. This needed access control can be accomplished, via the /etc/hosts.allow and /etc/hosts.deny files, for selected services on Linux systems that incorporate TCP Wrapper support.

If it has TCP Wrapper support, a network service uses libwrap. To check for libwrap, you can run the ldd command on the network service daemon. The following example shows that the ssh daemon uses TCP Wrappers. If your Linux system's sshd does not use TCP Wrappers, then no output is shown.

```
$ ldd /usr/sbin/sshd | grep libwrap
libwrap.so.0 => /lib/libwrap.so.0 (0x0012f000)
```

When a network service that incorporates TCP Wrapper support is requested, the hosts.allow and hosts.deny files are scanned and checked for an entry that matches the address of the remote system making the request. The following steps occur when a remote system requests access to a TCP Wrapper–supported service:

1. **The hosts.allow file is checked.**
   - If the remote system's address is listed:
     - Access is allowed.
     - No further TCP Wrapper checks are made.
   - If the remote system's address is *not* listed, the TCP Wrapper check process continues on to the hosts.deny file.

2. **The hosts.deny file is checked.**
   - If the remote system's address is listed, access is denied.
   - If the remote system's address is *not* listed, access is allowed.

The order in which the hosts files are evaluated is important. For example, you cannot deny access to a host in the hosts.deny file that has already been given access in the hosts.allow file.

Listing every single address that may try to connect to your computer is not necessary. The hosts.allow and hosts.deny files enable you to specify entire subnets and groups of addresses. You can even use the keyword ALL to specify all possible IP addresses. Also, you can restrict specific entries in these files so they apply only to specific network services. Consider the following example of a typical pair of hosts.allow and hosts.deny files.

```
# cat /etc/hosts.allow
# hosts.allow This file describes the names of the hosts that are
#            allowed to use the local INET services, as decided
#            by the '/usr/sbin/tcpd' server.
#
sshd: 199.170.177.
vsftpd: ALL
#
# cat /etc/hosts.deny
# hosts.deny This file describes names of the hosts which are
#            *not* allowed to use the local INET services, as
#            decided by the '/usr/sbin/tcpd' server.
#
ALL: ALL
```

In the hosts files, lines beginning with a # character are comments and are ignored. Other lines consist of a comma-separated list of service names followed by a colon (:) character and then a comma-separated list of client addresses to check. In this context, a client is any computer that attempts to access a network service on your system.

The preceding example is a rather restrictive configuration. The line:

```
sshd: 199.170.177.
```

in the hosts.allow file allows connections to the sshd services from certain remote systems. The line:

```
vsftpd: ALL
```

allows all remote systems to connect to the FTP service, vsftpd. However, if the remote system is not requesting a connection to the sshd or vsftpd, it is denied access by the line in the hosts.deny file:

```
ALL: ALL
```

A client entry can be a numeric IP address (such as 199.170.177.25) or a hostname (such as jukebox.linuxtoys.net). Often, a wildcard variation is used that specifies an entire range of addresses. Notice in the example host.allow file, the sshd entry's allowed IP address is 199.170.177. This matches any IP address that begins with that string, such as

25

199.170.177.25. The ALL wildcard used in the hosts.deny file specifies that *all* remote systems reaching this file, requesting *any* TCP Wrapper–supported network services, are denied.

A good general rule is to make your hosts.deny file as restrictive as possible and then explicitly enable only those services that you really need.

Along with TCP Wrappers, firewalls control access to your Linux system's ports as well. In fact, firewalls do much more than just protect network services.

Working with Firewalls

A firewall in a building is a fireproof wall that prevents the spread of fire through the building. A *firewall* for a computer blocks the transmission of malicious or unwanted data into and out of a computer system or network. For example, a firewall can block malicious scans from your Linux server ports. A firewall can also allow desired software upgrades to download to the same server.

Understanding firewalls

Although you may tend to think of a firewall as a complete barrier, a firewall is really just a filter that checks each network packet or application request coming into or out of a computer system or network.

Firewalls can be placed into different categories, depending upon their function. Each category has an important place in securing your server and network.

- **A firewall is either network-based or host-based.** A network-based firewall is one that is protecting the entire network or subnet. An example of a network firewall is in your workplace, where the network should be protected by a screening router's firewall.

  A host-based firewall is one that is running on and protecting an individual host or server. You most likely have a firewall on your PC at home. This is a host-based firewall. Another example of a host-based firewall is the `firestarter` application. You can learn more about `firestarter` at `http://www.fs-security.com`.

- **A firewall is either a hardware or a software firewall.** Firewalls can be located on network devices, such as routers. Their filters are configured in the router's firmware. In your home, your Internet service provider (ISP) may provide a DSL or cable modem to gain access to the Internet. The modem contains firewall firmware and is considered a hardware firewall.

  Firewalls can be located on a computer system as an application. The application allows filtering rules to be set, which filter the incoming traffic. This is an example of a software firewall. A software firewall is also called a rule-based firewall.

- **A firewall is either a network-layer filter or application-layer filter.** A firewall that examines individual network packets is also called a *packet filter*. A network-layer firewall allows only certain packets into and out of the system. It operates on the lower layers of the OSI reference model.

  An application-layer firewall filters at the higher layers of the OSI reference model. This firewall allows only certain applications access to/from the system.

You can see how these firewall categories overlap. The best firewall setup is a combination of all the categories. As with many security practices, the more layers you have, the harder it is for malicious activity to penetrate.

Implementing firewalls

On a Linux system, the firewall is a host-based, network-layer, software firewall managed by the `iptables` utility. With `iptables`, you can create a series of rules for every network packet coming through your Linux server. You can fine-tune the rules to allow network traffic from one location but not from another. These rules essentially make up a network access control list for your Linux server.

Fedora, RHEL, and other Linux distributions have added the `firewalld` service on top of iptables, to provide a more dynamic way of managing firewall rules. The Firewall Configuration window (`firewall-config` command) provides an easy way to open ports on your firewall and do masquerading (routing private addresses to a public network) or port forwarding. The `firewalld` service can react to changes in conditions, which the static iptables service can't do as well on its own. By enabling access to a service, `firewalld` can also do things like load modules needed to allow access to a service.

25

> **TIP**
> The `iptables` utility manages the Linux firewall, called `netfilter`. Thus, you will often see the Linux firewall referred to as `netfilter/iptables`.

Starting with firewalld

The `firewalld` service may already be installed on your Linux system. If it's not, you can install the service and the associated graphical user interface, and then start the `firewalld` service as follows:

```
# yum install firewalld firewall-config
# systemctl start firewalld.service
# systemctl enable firewalld.service
```

To manage the `firewalld` service, you can start the Firewall Configuration window. Do this by typing:

```
# firewall-config &
```

Figure 25.1 shows an example of the Firewall Configuration window.

FIGURE 25.1

Firewall Configuration

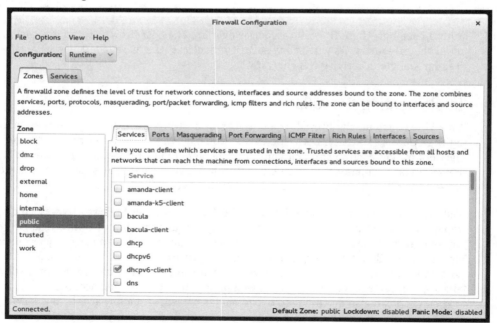

If all you need to do is open some firewall ports to allow access to selected services, that's very easy to do from the Firewall Configuration window. With the public zone selected, just click the services you want to open. The port allowing access to that service is opened immediately (when you select the Runtime configuration) and opened permanently (when you select the Permanent configuration).

One nice feature of the Firewall Configuration window is that, when you select to allow access to a service, you do more than just open a port. For example, enabling the FTP service also causes connection tracking modules to be loaded that allow nonstandard ports to be accessed through the firewall when needed.

As mentioned earlier, underlying the `firewalld` service is the iptables facility. If you have a Linux system without the `firewalld` service (or with `firewalld` disabled), you can still use the `iptables` service. The next section describes how you can set `iptables` firewall rules manually and use the `iptables` service directly, without the `firewalld` service.

Understanding the iptables utility

Before you start changing the firewall rules via the `iptables` utility, you need to understand `netfilter/iptables` basics, which include the following:

- Tables
- Chains
- Policies
- Rules

Each of these basics is critical to setting up and managing your Linux server firewall properly.

netfilter/iptables tables

The `iptables` firewall has the ability to do more than just low-level packet filtering. It defines what type of firewall functionality is taking place. There are four tables in the `iptables` utility, with an additional table added by SELinux. The tables offer the following functionalities:

- `filter`—The `filter` table is the packet filtering feature of the firewall. In this table, access control decisions are made for packets traveling to, from, and through your Linux system.
- `nat`—The `nat` table is used for Network Address Translation (NAT). Firewalls can be set up for NAT, which is a different security feature than packet filtering.
- `mangle`—As you suspect, packets are mangled (modified) according to the rules in the `mangle` table. Mangling packets is used in Network Address Translation.

- raw—The `raw` table is used to exempt certain network packets from something called "connection tracking." This feature is important when you are using Network Address Translation and Virtualization on your Linux server.

- security—This table is available only on Linux distributions that have SELinux (see Chapter 24, "Enhancing Linux Security with SELinux"). The `security` table is used to filter network packets using MAC rules (see Chapter 22). This table is used with the `filter` table. The `security` table rules are applied only after the rules in the `filter` table are applied. This way the MAC rules are applied only after the DAC rules (see Chapter 22) are applied, which is consistent with SELinux implementation.

Of all the tables listed, three focus on Network Address Translation. Therefore, the `filter` table is the primary table to focus on for basic firewall packet filtering.

netfilter/iptables chains

The `netfilter/iptables` firewall categorizes network packets into categories, called chains. There are five chains (categories) that a network packet can be designated as, as follows:

- INPUT—Network packets coming *into* the Linux server
- FORWARD—Network packets coming into the Linux server that are to be *routed* elsewhere
- OUTPUT—Network packets coming *out* of the Linux server
- PREROUTING—Used by NAT, for modifying network packets when they come into the Linux server
- POSTROUTING—Used by NAT, for modifying network packets before they come out of the Linux server

Which `netfilter/iptables` table you choose to work with determine what chains are available for categorizing network packets. Table 25.1 shows what chains are available for each table.

TABLE 25.1 Chains Available for Each netfilter/iptables Table

Table	Chains Available
filter	INPUT, FORWARD, OUTPUT
nat	PREROUTING, OUTPUT, POSTROUTING
mangle	INPUT, FORWARD, PREROUTING, OUTPUT, POSTROUTING
raw	PREROUTING, OUTPUT
security	INPUT, FORWARD, OUTPUT

After a network packet is categorized into a specific chain, `iptables` can determine what policies or rules apply to that particular packet.

netfilter/iptables rules, policies, and targets

For each network packet, a rule can be set up defining what to do with that individual packet. Network packets can be identified many ways by the `netfilter/iptables` firewall. These are a few of the ways:

- Source IP address
- Destination IP address
- Network protocol
- Inbound port
- Outbound port
- Network state

If no rule exists for a particular packet, then the overall policy is used. Each packet category or chain has a default policy. After a network packet matches a particular rule or falls to the default policy, action on the packet can occur. The action taken depends upon what `iptable` target is set. Here are a couple of actions (targets) that can be taken:

- `ACCEPT`—Network packet is accepted into the server.
- `REJECT`—Network packet is dropped and not allowed into the server. A rejection message is sent.
- `DROP`—Network packet is dropped and not allowed into the server. No rejection message is sent.

While `REJECT` gives a rejection message, `DROP` is quiet. You may consider using `REJECT` for internal employees, who should be told that you are rejecting their outbound network traffic and why. Consider using `DROP` for inbound traffic so that any malicious personnel are unaware that their traffic is being blocked.

> **TIP**
>
> There are a couple of additional more sophisticated targets for `iptables`, such as `QUEUE`. You can find out more about these targets via the `man iptables` command.

The `iptables` utility implements a software firewall using the `filter` table via policies and rules. Now that you have a general understanding of the software firewall implementation, you can begin to dig deeper into the specific commands for implementing the firewall via the `iptables` utility.

25

Using the iptables utility

Your Linux server should come with the firewall up and running. However, it's a good idea to check and see if it really is enabled. Before you check, you first must understand that the netfilter/iptables firewall services are slightly different depending upon the Linux distribution:

- **RHEL 6 or earlier netfilter/iptables firewall**—The firewall interface service running on this distribution is iptables. To see if this firewall service is running, type **service iptables status** at the command line.

  - To enable the firewall, type **service iptables start** at the command line.
  - To disable the firewall, type **service iptables stop** at the command line.

- **RHEL 7 and recent Fedora systems netfilter/iptables firewall**—The firewall interface service running on these distributions is firewalld. The iptables service is not run directly by default on these systems. To see if this firewall service is running, type **systemctl status firewalld.service** at the command line.

  - To enable the firewall, type **systemctl start firewalld.service** at the command line.
  - To disable the firewall, type **systemctl stop firewalld.service** at the command line.

- **Ubuntu netfilter/iptables firewall**—The firewall interface service running on this distribution is ufw. To see if the firewall service is running, type **sudo ufw status** at the command line. The ufw service is an interface to the iptables utility that does not run as a service on Ubuntu. You can use ufw commands to manipulate firewall rules. However, all the iptables utility commands are still valid for Ubuntu:

  - To enable the firewall, type **sudo ufw enable** at the command line.
  - To disable the firewall, type **sudo ufw disable** at the command line.

Thankfully, after you have checked the status and enabled or disabled the netfilter/iptables firewall, the differences between the distributions end.

To see what policies and rules are currently in place for the filter table, type **iptables -t filter -vnL** at the command line. In the example that follows, this command is entered on a Linux Mint system.

```
# iptables -t filter -vnL
Chain INPUT (policy ACCEPT 0 packets, 0 bytes)...
```

Note that on systems with firewalld enabled, there are many more iptables chains and rules listed by default than you might be used to on a system using iptables directly. This is done to offer more flexibility in building your firewalls by allowing your rules to be split into zones for different types of interfaces.

Only the first line of the iptables output is shown in the preceding example. That line shows that the INPUT chain's default policy is applied to all the network packets that don't match another rule. Currently, all the default INPUT, FORWARD and OUTPUT policies are set to ACCEPT. All network packets are allowed in, through, and out. A firewall in this state is essentially disabled until specific REJECT or DROP rules are added.

> **TIP**
>
> If your Linux server is dealing with IP v6 network packets, you can use the `ip6tables` utility to manage your firewall for IPv6 addresses. The `ip6tables` utility is nearly identical to the `iptables` utility. For more information, type `man ip6tables` at the command line.

Modifying iptables policies and rules

Before you begin to modify the `netfilter/iptables` firewall, it is helpful to understand a few command options. Below are a few options for modifying the firewall:

- `-t table`

  The `iptables` command listed along with this switch is applied to the `table`. By default, the `filter` table is used. Example:

  ```
  # iptables -t filter -P OUTPUT DROP
  ```

- `-P chain target`

  Sets the overall policy for a particular `chain`. The rules in the `chain` are checked for matches. If no match occurs, then the `chain`'s listed `target` is used. Example:

  ```
  # iptables -P INPUT ACCEPT
  ```

- `-A chain`

  Sets a rule, called an "appended rule," which is an exception to the overall policy for the `chain` designated. Example:

  ```
  # iptables -A OUTPUT -d 10.140.67.25 -j REJECT
  ```

- `-I rule# chain`

  Inserts an appended rule into a specific location, designated by the `rule#`, in the appended rule list for the `chain` designated. Example:

  ```
  # iptables -I 5 INPUT -s 10.140.67.23 -j DROP
  ```

- `-D chain rule#`

  Deletes a particular rule, designated by the `rule#`, from the `chain` designated. Example:

  ```
  # iptables -D INPUT 5
  ```

- `-j target`

25

If the criteria in the rule are met, the firewall should jump to this designated *target* for processing. Example:

```
# iptables -A INPUT -s 10.140.67.25 -j DROP
```

- -d *IP address*

  Assigns the rule listed to apply to the designated destination *IP address*. Example:

  ```
  # iptables -A OUTPUT -d 10.140.67.25 -j REJECT
  ```

- -s *IP address*

  Assigns the rule listed to apply to the designated source *IP address*. Example:

  ```
  # iptables -A INPUT -s 10.140.67.24 -j ACCEPT
  ```

- -p *protocol*

  Assigns the rule listed to apply to the *protocol* designated. Example:

  ```
  # iptables -A INPUT -p icmp -j DROP
  ```

- --dport *port#*

  Assigns the rule listed to apply to certain protocol packets coming into the designated *port#*. Example:

  ```
  # iptables -A INPUT -p tcp --dport 22 -j DROP
  ```

- --sport *port#*

  Assigns the rule listed to apply to certain protocol packets going out of the designated *port#*. Example:

  ```
  # iptables -A OUTPUT -p tcp --sport 22 -j ACCEPT
  ```

- -m *state* --state *network state*

  Assigns the rule listed to apply to the designated *network state*(s). Example:

  ```
  # iptables -A INPUT -m state --state RELATED,ESTABLISH -j ACCEPT
  ```

To see how the iptables options work, consider the following example. You have a Linux server (Host-A) at IP address 10.140.67.23. There are two other Linux servers on your network. One is Host-B at IP address 10.140.67.22 and the other is Host-C at IP address 10.140.67.25. Your goal is to accomplish the following:

- Allow Host-C full access to Host-A.
- Block remote login connections using ssh from Host-B to Host-A.

Setting a policy of Drop. The following code shows the default policies of Host-A's firewall. In this example, the firewall is wide open with no restrictions implemented. No rules are set, and the policies are all set to ACCEPT.

```
# iptables -vnL
Chain INPUT (policy ACCEPT)
target      prot opt source            destination
Chain FORWARD (policy ACCEPT)
target      prot opt source            destination
Chain OUTPUT (policy ACCEPT)
target      prot opt source            destination
```

First, what would happen if the INPUT policy was changed from ACCEPT to DROP? Would that reach the goal? Look at what happens when this is tried. Remember that if no rules are listed for an incoming packet, then the chain's policy is followed. This change is made to Host-A's firewall in the example that follows.

```
# iptables -P INPUT DROP
# iptables -vnL
Chain INPUT (policy DROP)
target      prot opt source            destination
Chain FORWARD (policy ACCEPT)
target      prot opt source            destination
Chain OUTPUT (policy ACCEPT)
target      prot opt source            destination
```

> **TIP**
>
> For policies, you cannot set the target to REJECT. It fails, and you receive the message "iptables: Bad policy name." Use DROP as your policy instead.

Host-B attempts to ping Host-A and then attempts an ssh connection as shown in the example that follows. As you can see, both attempts fail. Because ping commands are blocked, this does not meet the objective to block only remote login connections using ssh from Host-B.

```
$ ping -c 2 10.140.67.23
PING 10.140.67.23 (10.140.67.23) 56(84) bytes of data.

--- 10.140.67.23 ping statistics ---
2 packets transmitted, 0 received, 100% packet loss, time 1007ms
$ ssh root@10.140.67.23

ssh: connect to host 10.140.67.23 port 22: Connection timed out
```

25

When Host-C attempts to ping Host-A and make an ssh connection, both attempts fail. Thus, it is confirmed that the firewall setting, INPUT policy equals DROP, is not what is needed to reach the goal.

```
$ ping -c 2 10.140.67.23
PING 10.140.67.23 (10.140.67.23) 56(84) bytes of data.

--- 10.140.67.23 ping statistics ---
2 packets transmitted, 0 received, 100% packet loss, time 1008ms
$ ssh root@10.140.67.23

ssh: connect to host 10.140.67.23 port 22: Connection timed out
```

Blocking a source IP address. What if instead only Host-B's IP address were blocked? That would allow Host-C to reach Host-A. Would this setting reach the desired goal?

In the example that follows, the policy of DROP must first be changed to ALLOW in Host-A's iptables. After that, a specific rule must be appended to block network packets from Host-B's IP address, 10.140.67.22, alone.

```
# iptables -P INPUT ACCEPT
# iptables -A INPUT -s 10.140.67.22 -j DROP
# iptables -vnL
Chain INPUT (policy ACCEPT)
target     prot opt source              destination
DROP       all  --  10.140.67.22              anywhere
Chain FORWARD (policy ACCEPT)
target     prot opt source              destination
Chain OUTPUT (policy ACCEPT)
target     prot opt source              destination
```

Host-C can now successfully ping and ssh into Host-A, meeting one of the set goals.

```
$ ping -c 2 10.140.67.23
PING 10.140.67.23 (10.140.67.23) 56(84) bytes of data.
64 bytes from 10.140.67.23: icmp_req=1 ttl=64 time=11.7 ms
64 bytes from 10.140.67.23: icmp_req=2 ttl=64 time=0.000 ms

--- 10.140.67.23 ping statistics ---
2 packets transmitted, 2 received, 0% packet loss, time 1008ms
rtt min/avg/max/mdev = 0.000/5.824/11.648/5.824 ms
$ ssh root@10.140.67.23
root@10.140.67.23's password:
```

However, Host-B can neither `ping` nor `ssh` into Host-A. Thus, the appended rule is not quite what is needed to reach the entire goal.

```
$ ping -c 2 10.140.67.23
PING 10.140.67.23 (10.140.67.23) 56(84) bytes of data.
--- 10.140.67.23 ping statistics ---
2 packets transmitted, 0 received, 100% packet loss, time 1007ms
$ ssh root@10.140.67.23
ssh: connect to host 10.140.67.23 port 22: Connection timed out
```

Blocking a protocol and port. What if, instead of blocking Host-B's IP address entirely, only connections to the `ssh` port (port 22) from Host-B's IP address were blocked? Would that reach the goal of allowing Host-C full access to Host-A, and only blocking `ssh` connections from Host-B?

In the example that follows, the `iptables` rules for Host-A are modified to try blocking Host-B's IP address from port 22. Note that the `--dport` option must accompany a particular protocol, for example, `-p tcp`. Before the new rule is added, the rule from the previous example must be deleted using the `-D` option. Otherwise, the rule from the previous example would be used by the `netfilter/iptables` firewall for packets from 10.140.67.22 (Host-B).

```
# iptables -D INPUT 1
# iptables -A INPUT -s 10.140.67.22 -p tcp --dport 22 -j DROP
# iptables -vnL
Chain INPUT (policy ACCEPT)
target     prot opt source       destination
DROP       tcp  --  10.140.67.22    anywhere     tcp dpt:ssh
Chain FORWARD (policy ACCEPT)
target     prot opt source       destination
Chain OUTPUT (policy ACCEPT)
target     prot opt source       destination
```

First, the new `iptables` rule is tested from Host-C to ensure both `ping` attempts and `ssh` connections remain unaffected. It works successfully.

```
$ ping -c 2 10.140.67.23
PING 10.140.67.23 (10.140.67.23) 56(84) bytes of data.
64 bytes from 10.140.67.23: icmp_req=1 ttl=64 time=1.04 ms
64 bytes from 10.140.67.23: icmp_req=2 ttl=64 time=0.740 ms
```

25

```
--- 10.140.67.23 ping statistics ---
2 packets transmitted, 2 received, 0% packet loss, time 1000ms
rtt min/avg/max/mdev = 0.740/0.892/1.045/0.155 ms

$ ssh root@10.140.67.23
root@10.140.67.23's password:
```

Next, the new iptables rule is tested from Host-B to ensure that ping works and ssh connections are blocked. It also works successfully!

```
$ ping -c 2 10.140.67.23
PING 10.140.67.23 (10.140.67.23) 56(84) bytes of data.
64 bytes from 10.140.67.23: icmp_req=1 ttl=64 time=1.10 ms
64 bytes from 10.140.67.23: icmp_req=2 ttl=64 time=0.781 ms
--- 10.140.67.23 ping statistics ---
2 packets transmitted, 2 received, 0% packet loss, time 1001ms
rtt min/avg/max/mdev = 0.781/0.942/1.104/0.164 ms
$ ssh root@10.140.67.23
ssh: connect to host 10.140.67.23 port 22: Connection timed out
```

Again, your organization's Access Control Matrix (see Chapter 22) helps you in creating the necessary rules for the netfilter/iptables firewall on your Linux server. And each modification should be tested in a test or virtual environment before implementing it in your production Linux system's firewall.

Saving an iptables configuration

After you have done all the hard work of creating your Linux server's firewall configuration policies and rules, you will want to save them. All modifications must be saved to the iptables configuration file, /etc/sysconfig/iptables, because this is the file used at system boot to load the firewall.

In the example that follows, the modifications made earlier are still in the firewall. Before they are saved to the configuration file, a backup copy of the original file is made. This is always a good idea. The modifications are then saved using the iptables-save command. Notice that the output is directed into the /etc/sysconfig/iptables file using a redirection symbol, > (see the last line of code in the example).

```
# iptables -vnL
Chain INPUT (policy ACCEPT)
target     prot opt source       destination
DROP       tcp  --  10.140.67.22  anywhere   tcp dpt:ssh
Chain FORWARD (policy ACCEPT)
target     prot opt source       destination
Chain OUTPUT (policy ACCEPT)
target     prot opt source       destination
# cp /etc/sysconfig/iptables/etc/sysconfig/iptables.bck
# iptables-save > /etc/sysconfig/iptables
```

You can also remove all the modifications for the current `netfilter/iptables` firewall by using the flush option, `iptables -F`. After this is completed, all the rules (but not the policies) are removed, as shown in the code that follows. This is useful for testing out individual policies and rules.

```
# iptables -F
# iptables -vnL
Chain INPUT (policy ACCEPT)
target     prot opt source        destination
Chain FORWARD (policy ACCEPT)
target     prot opt source        destination
Chain OUTPUT (policy ACCEPT)
target     prot opt source        destination
```

A flush of the rules does not affect the `iptables` configuration file. To restore the firewall to its original condition, use the `iptables-restore` command. In the example that follows, the `iptables` configuration file is redirected into the `restore` command and the original DROP rule for `10.140.67.22` is restored.

```
# iptables-restore < /etc/sysconfig/iptables
# iptables -vnL
Chain INPUT (policy ACCEPT)
target     prot opt source        destination
DROP       tcp  --  10.140.67.22  anywhere    tcp dpt:ssh
Chain FORWARD (policy ACCEPT)
target     prot opt source        destination
Chain OUTPUT (policy ACCEPT)
target     prot opt source        destination
```

> **NOTE**
>
> For an Ubuntu system, saving and restoring your `netfilter/iptables` modifications are very similar. You can still use the `iptables-save` command to create an `iptables` configuration file from the current `iptables` setting and use `iptables-restore` to restore it. However, having a saved `iptables` configuration load on boot is a little more complicated. There is no `/etc/sysconfig/iptables` file. There are several options for loading a configuration file on system boot. See the Ubuntu community website at `https://help.ubuntu.com/community/IptablesHowTo` for the various options.

You can also save your `netfilter/iptables` firewall rules to create an audit report. Reviewing these rules periodically should be part of your organization's System Life Cycle Audit/Review phase.

25

Summary

Securing your Linux server is critical on a network. Inherently, a majority of the malicious attacks originate from a network, especially the Internet. This chapter covered some of the basics, such as the OSI model, that you need in order to get started on this process.

Protecting your network services can be simplified after you determine and remove any unneeded network services. The nmap utility helps you here. Also, you can use nmap to audit your Linux server's advertising of network services. These audits assist in determining what firewall modifications are needed.

For needed network services, access control must be implemented. TCP wrappers can assist in this activity. On a per-service basis, access can be allowed or denied, fine-tuning access to each network service.

Recent versions of Fedora and RHEL have added the firewalld service as a front-end to the iptables firewall facility that is built into the Linux kernel. Using the firewalld-config window, you can easily open ports in your firewall to allow access to selected services. The netfilter/iptables firewall facility is a host-based, network-layer, software firewall. It is managed by the iptables and ip6tables utilities. With these utilities, a series of policies and rules can be created for every network packet coming through your Linux server. These policies and rules essentially make up an access control list for your Linux server network.

At this point in the book, you should have a good grasp of what goes into setting up and securing Linux desktop and server systems. In the next two chapters, I'm going to help you extend that knowledge into cloud computing and virtualization.

Exercises

Refer to the material in this chapter to complete the tasks that follow. If you are stuck, solutions to the tasks are shown in Appendix B (although in Linux, you can often complete a task in multiple ways). Try each of the exercises before referring to the answers. These tasks assume you are running a Fedora or Red Hat Enterprise Linux system (although some tasks work on other Linux systems as well).

Please don't use a production system to try out the iptables commands in these exercises. Although the commands shown here do not permanently change your firewall (the old rules will return when the firewall service restarts), improperly modifying your firewall can result in unwanted access.

1. Install the Network Mapper utility on your local Linux system.
2. Run a TCP Connect scan on your local loopback address. What ports have a service running on them?
3. Run a UDP Connect scan on your Linux system from a remote system.

4. Check to see if the ssh daemon on your Linux system uses TCP Wrapper support.

5. Using the TCP Wrapper files, allow access to the ssh tools on your Linux system from a designated remote system. Deny all other access.

6. Determine your Linux system's current netfilter/iptables firewall policies and rules.

7. Flush your Linux system's current firewall rules, and then restore them.

8. For your Linux system's firewall, set a filter table policy for the input chain to reject.

9. Change your Linux system firewall's filter table policy back to accept for the input chain, and then add a rule to drop all network packets from the IP address 10.140.67.23.

10. Without flushing or restoring your Linux system firewall's rules, remove the rule you added above.

25

Part VI

Extending Linux into the Cloud

IN THIS PART

Using Linux for Cloud Computing

IN THIS CHAPTER

How Linux is used in clouds

Trying basic cloud technology

To cloud users, cloud computing means being able to request some computing service from their local computer to some server on a network, without necessarily knowing how the request is fulfilled. What makes it a cloud is how those delivering the services set up their computer infrastructures to fulfill the requests.

Cloud technology today makes it possible to view datacenters as large, fluid pools of host computers *(hypervisors)*, controllers, storage nodes, network configurations, and many other components. You may wonder what Linux has to do with cloud computing. Well, Linux just happens to be at the heart of many of today's public and private cloud technologies.

This chapter introduces you to concepts of cloud computing, in general, and cloud technologies associated with Linux, in particular. After introducing cloud concepts, this chapter has you set up some of the basic building blocks of cloud technology: hypervisors, virtual machines, and shared storage.

After you have tried some of those basic cloud technologies, the chapter describes how enterprise-quality clouds extend those basic concepts so they can scale up to meet the needs of modern datacenters.

Overview of Linux and Cloud Computing

Cloud moves us into an arena where everything you learned in this book is being abstracted and automated. For cloud, when you install a system, you are probably not booting from a physical DVD, erasing the local hard drive, and installing Linux directly on a computer sitting in front of you. You are not logging in using an entry in the /etc/passwd file or drawing on the processing power of a single machine.

Instead, you are installing to a virtual machine or container that is running on some host system in the cloud. The network interfaces you see may not be represented by a physical switch, but may be virtual networks that exist on a single computer or span multiple hypervisors.

Today, every software aspect of cloud computing can be fulfilled using open source technology running on Linux systems. My goal here is not to describe how to use every aspect of a Linux-based cloud environment. Instead, I want to tell you how emerging technologies are expanding everything we have covered in this book to work efficiently in a cloud environment. Then I give you a chance to configure some basic cloud technologies to get a feel for how it all works.

Cloud hypervisors (a.k.a. compute nodes)

In cloud computing, the operating systems serving cloud users are not running directly on computer hardware. Instead, hypervisors are configured to run many operating systems as what are referred to as *virtual machines*.

Depending on your cloud environment, you may hear a hypervisor referred to as a *compute node* or simply as a *host*. Because hypervisors tend to be commodity items (dozens or hundreds of hypervisors may be set up for a location), Linux is the logical choice as the operating system running as hypervisors directly on hardware.

Kernel-based Virtual Machine (KVM) is the basic virtualization technology implemented to make a Linux system into a hypervisor. KVM is supported on Ubuntu, Red Hat Enterprise Linux, Fedora, and many other Linux systems.

The other major technology that can be used instead of KVM to make a Linux system into a hypervisor is Xen (www.xenproject.org). Xen has been around longer than KVM and is supported in products from Citrix Systems and Oracle.

Later in this chapter, I describe how to check to see if a computer has the hardware features to be used as a hypervisor and how to configure it to be used with KVM.

Cloud controllers

Because a cloud configuration can include multiple hypervisors, pools of storage, multiple virtual networks, and many virtual machines, you need centralized tools to manage and monitor those features. You can use both graphical and command-based tools for controlling cloud environments.

Although not considered a full cloud controller, the Virtual Machine Manager (virt-manager) GUI and virsh command can be used to manage a small cloud-like environment. Using virt-manager, you can get a feel for managing multiple virtual machines across several hypervisors, and you can learn how to deal with virtual networks and shared storage pools.

Full-blown cloud platforms have their own controllers for offering much more complex interactions between cloud components. For the OpenStack cloud platform, the OpenStack Dashboard (Horizon project) provides a web-based interface to OpenStack components. For Red Hat Enterprise Virtualization (RHEV), the RHEV Manager provides the same features.

Later in this chapter, I describe how to use `virt-manager` to manage your first mini-cloud-like environment.

Cloud storage

New demands on data storage arise when you move your operating systems and applications into a cloud environment. For a virtual machine to be able to move to run on another hypervisor, its storage must be available from that new hypervisor. Storage needs for clouds include needing places to store the back-end storage for your VMs, images for launching VMs, and databases for storing information about the cloud itself.

Shared storage between hypervisors can be done as simply as creating an NFS share (see Chapter 20) and mounting it on the same mount point between multiple hypervisors. NFS is one of the easiest ways to implement shared storage.

More robust shared storage that can handle disk failures and provide better performance works better for clouds providing critical services. Shared block storage, where you mount a whole disk or disk partition, can be accomplished using technologies such as iSCSI or Fibre Channel.

Ceph (`http://ceph.com`) is an open source project for managing both block and object storage that is popular for managing storage in cloud environments. GlusterFS (`www.gluster.org`) is a scale-out filesystem that is often used in cloud environments.

For the simple mini-cloud example in this chapter, I use NFS to provide shared storage between the hypervisors.

Cloud authentication

To be able to limit how much cloud resources a user can consume, and possibly track and change for that use, you need authentication mechanisms. Authentication is necessary for those who are using cloud features as well as for those who are allowed to administer cloud features.

Cloud platform projects sometimes let you connect centralized authentication mechanisms to validate and authorize cloud users. These can include Kerberos, Microsoft Active Directory, and others. In Linux, Identity, Policy, and Audit (IPA) software (see `www.freeipa.org`) offers a full set of authentication features that can be used across an enterprise cloud platform.

Cloud deployment and configuration

If you are managing a large cloud infrastructure, you don't want to have to walk over to each machine and click through a graphical installation every time you want to add a hypervisor or other node on your network. Today, many tools can deploy and configure Linux systems as simply as rebooting the computer and having it boot up to a preconfigured installer.

In Chapter 9, I talk about how to use a PXE server (to automatically boot a Linux installer over the network from your network interface card) and kickstart files (to identify all the answers you need to complete an installation). With that setup in place, you can simply boot a computer from a network interface and come back a short time later to find a fully installed Linux system.

After a computer is deployed, systems can be configured and possibly monitored and updated, using tools such as Puppet (http://puppetlabs.com) and Chef (www.chef .io). Whole work environments can be deployed in virtual machines using Vagrant (www.vagrantup.com). Ansible (www.ansible.com) is another tool for automating IT infrastructures and the applications that run on it.

Cloud platforms

If you want to implement your own, private cloud within your organization, the open source OpenStack project is probably the most popular choice. It offers a huge amount of flexibility and power in how you configure and use it.

Red Hat Enterprise Virtualization (RHEV) is another popular cloud platform. RHEV makes it easy to start with a simple RHEV Manager and one or two hypervisors and grow by adding more hypervisors, storage pools, and other features.

If you want to use public clouds that are based on open source technology to run the operating systems you need, you can use any of several different cloud providers. Public cloud providers that you can use to run Linux VMs include Amazon Web Services (www.amazon .com/aws), Google Cloud Platform (https://cloud.google.com), and Rackspace (www .rackspace.com). Chapter 27 covers how to deploy Linux to some of these cloud providers.

Now that you have heard about many of the technologies that make up Linux cloud computing, you can get your first small taste of some of the foundational technologies of Linux clouds by setting up your own mini-cloud in the next section.

Trying Basic Cloud Technology

To help you understand cloud technology from the ground up, this section illustrates some of the basic building blocks of a modern cloud infrastructure. Using three computers, I'll help you create a setup that includes:

- **Hypervisors**—A hypervisor is a computer system that allows you run other computer systems on it. Those other systems are referred to as *virtual machines*. A cloud infrastructure may have dozens or hundreds of hypervisors running, possibly running thousands of virtual machines.

- **Virtual machines**—The virtual machines you run on a Linux hypervisor can be the same type of Linux system, a different Linux system, a Windows system, or any other type of system that is compatible with the hardware on which the hypervisor runs. So the virtual machines that run on the hypervisors we build here could include Fedora, Ubuntu, RHEL, CentOS, Microsoft Windows, and others.

- **Shared storage**—To offer the greatest flexibility, the storage that hypervisors make available to virtual machines is often shared among a pool of hypervisors. This allows a set of hypervisors to share a set of images they use to install or start virtual machines. It also lets the same set of virtual machines run on any hypervisor in that group and even move to a different hypervisor without shutting down the VM. Moving running VMs can be useful if a hypervisor becomes overloaded or needs to shut down for maintenance.

The setup we build during this procedure allows you to work with virtual machines in the following ways:

- Install a new virtual machine on a hypervisor
- Set features on your virtual machines
- Log in to and use a virtual machine running on a hypervisor
- Migrate a running virtual machine to another hypervisor

The technologies we explore here include:

- **Kernel Virtualization Module (KVM)**—KVM is the basic kernel technology that allows virtual machines to interact with the Linux Kernel.

- **QEMU Processor Emulator**—One qemu process runs for each active virtual machine on the system. QEMU provides features that make it appear to each virtual machine as though it is running on physical hardware.

- **Libvirt Service Daemon (libvirtd)**—A single libvirtd service runs on each hypervisor. The libvirtd daemon listens for requests to start, stop, pause, and otherwise manage virtual machines on a hypervisor. Those requests can come from an application designed to manage virtual machines (such as virt-manager or OpenStack Dashboard) or from an application you create to talk directly to the libvirt application programming interface.

- **Virtual Machine Manager**—The Virtual Machine Manager (virt-manager command) is a GUI tool for managing virtual machines. Besides letting you request to start and stop virtual machines, virt-manager lets you install, configure, and manage VMs in different ways. You can use the virsh command to pass options to the command line to work with virtual machines, instead of clicking in a GUI window.

- **Virtualization Viewer**—The `virt-viewer` command launches a virtual machine console window on your desktop. The window that appears allows you to work from a console window to a Desktop or command line interface to the selected virtual machine (depending on what that VM has to offer).

After this small cloud-like infrastructure is built, you have the basis for what is sometimes referred to as a Platform-as-a-Service (or PaaS) cloud. This means that someone consuming your PaaS could bundle together their own operating system, application, configuration files, and data and deploy them. They would rely on your PaaS to provide the compute power, storage, memory, network interfaces, and management features needed to run the virtual machines containing their applications.

Examples of a PaaS include OpenStack and Red Hat Enterprise Virtualization (RHEV). Those projects provide a much more refined way of accessing PaaS resources. Our mini-PaaS, however, gets similar results.

Setting Up a Small Cloud

With three physical machines connected together on a network, you can illustrate some of the basic concepts you need to understand to build your own cloud. The three computers running Fedora 21 and the network connecting them are configured as follows:

- **Networking**—A high-speed, wired network was set up to connect the three computers. Fast network connections are critical to successful VM migration. In this example, each hypervisor also has a network bridge configured so each virtual machine can pick up an IP address directly from a DHCP service on the network.

- **Hypervisors**—Two of the computers are configured as hypervisors. A hypervisor (sometimes referred to as a host or a computer node) allows you to run virtual machines. In Fedora 21, the basic hypervisor technology is called Kernel-based Virtual Machine (KVM) while the actual virtual machines are managed by the `libvirtd` service.

- **Storage**—One computer is configured to offer shared storage between the two hypervisors. For simplicity, NFS is used to create the shared storage, although in a production environment, iSCSI or Fibre Channel would be better solutions.

> **NOTE**
>
> For test purposes, you could use one of the two hypervisors to provide the shared storage. However, one of the main purposes of configuring two hypervisors and separate shared storage is that you want to be able to shut down any hypervisor and still have all your virtual machines operate normally. If you have shared storage available from one of the hypervisors, you could never bring that hypervisor down without shutting down all the VMs using that storage.

Configuring hypervisors

In this procedure, I installed Fedora 21 on two physical computers and configured them as KVM hosts running the `libvirtd` service. Follow these steps to accomplish this for yourself.

Step 1: Get Linux software

Go to the Get Fedora page (https://getfedora.org) and download Fedora 21. I chose to download the Fedora 21 64-bit Workstation edition DVD ISO. If a later version of Fedora is available, you could likely use that instead.

Use any available DVD burning application to burn the image to DVD or otherwise make the image available to install (such as by PXE booting).

Step 2: Check your computers

The computers you use as hypervisors in Fedora 21 need to meet a few requirements. You should check these things on your computer before you start installing:

- **Support virtualization**—You can check for virtualization support by looking at the flags set in the CPU.
- **Memory**—The computer must have enough RAM not only to run the host operating system, but for each virtual machine that you expect to run on the system.
- **Processing power**—Keep in mind that each virtual machine consumes processing power for itself and any application running inside the virtual machine.

Storage is another consideration. But because we intend to configure storage from a separate node on the network, we address that issue later.

To check that the available features of your computers meet the requirements, boot a Linux live CD or DVD, open a Terminal window, and type the following commands:

```
# cat /proc/cpuinfo | grep --color -E "vmx|svm|lm"
flags   : fpu vme de pse tsc msr pae mce cx8 apic sep mtrr pge mca
    cmov pat pse36 clflush dts acpi mmx fxsr sse sse2 ss ht tm pbe
    syscall nx pdpe1gb rdtscp lm constant_tsc arch_perfmon pebs bts
    rep_good xtopology nonstop_tsc aperfmperf pni pclmulqdq dtes64
    monitor ds_cpl vmx smx es...
    ...
```

The previous command shows that this computer is a 64-bit computer (lm) and that an Intel chip supports virtualization features (vmx). If the CPU were an AMD chip, instead of vmx, you would see svm highlighted (if the AMD chip supported virtualization). Those settings show that this computer can be used as a hypervisor.

When you start running VMs on a host, memory is often the bottleneck. For memory requirements, you must add what is needed by the host to whatever you need for each VM.

You can lower memory requirements by not having Desktop software installed, as most hypervisors do. In this case, however, I did a Fedora Workstation install, which comes with a Desktop. To check the memory and swap on the computer, I typed the following:

```
# free -m
          total     used     free   shared  buff/cache   available
Mem:       7867     3433     2835      298        1598        3860
Swap:     12287        0    12287
```

This system has about 8GB of RAM and 12GB of swap. I estimate that 4GB is good for a desktop system. If I allow 1GB or 2GB for each VM, this system should be able to run two to four VMs along with the desktop. Check the memory requirements for the operating systems and applications you plan to run to better determine your memory needs.

To check the number and types of processors on your computer, type the following:

```
# grep processor /proc/cpuinfo
processor : 0
...
processor : 6
processor : 7
# head /proc/cpuinfo
processor   : 0
vendor_id   : GenuineIntel
cpu family  : 6
model       : 60
model name  : Intel(R) Core(TM) i7-4800MQ CPU @ 2.70GHz
stepping    : 3
cpu MHz     : 2701.000
cache size  : 6144 KB
...
```

The first command in the preceding code shows that there are eight (0 through 7) processors on the computer. With the second command, for the first processor, you can see that it is GenuineIntel, the model, model name, the CPU speed, and other information.

To do live VM migration between the two hypervisors, the CPUs must be in the same family. If they don't have compatible CPUs, you could migrate a VM by shutting it down on one hypervisor and starting it up from shared storage on the other.

After you have sized up the two hypervisor computers, start installing Fedora on them.

Step 3: Install Linux on hypervisors

Using the Fedora 21 Workstation installation media, begin installing the two hypervisors. Follow descriptions in Chapter 9 for installing Fedora. You should know these things that are specific to the installation for this procedure:

- **Name the hypervisors**—I set the hostnames on the hypervisors to host1.example.com and host2.example.com.

- **Partitioning**—When partitioning, I erased the entire hard disk. Then I created a 500MB /boot partition and a 12GB swap partition, and I assigned the rest of the disk space to the root partition (/). The /var/lib/libvirt/images directory holds most of the data on this system, but that is a shared directory, available from another system on the network and shared between the two hypervisors. (More on that later.)

- **Networking**—If given the option, turn on wired network interfaces for each hypervisor. The hypervisors and storage should all be on the same local network, because the speed of your network connection between those machines is critical to getting good performance.

- **Software packages**—During installation, I install only the default Fedora Workstation packages. After installation is complete and the system is rebooted, I install more of the software that's needed for each hypervisor.

Reboot the computer when installation is finished (ejecting the DVD and starting up on the hard disk). After the system is rebooted, update the Fedora software, add new packages, and reboot the system again, as follows:

```
# yum update -y
# yum install virt-manager libvirt-daemon-config-network
# reboot
```

The virt-manager package contains the GUI tool for managing your virtual machines. The libvirt-daemon-config-network package creates the default network interface that lets the virtual machines access external networks (through the host) using Network Address Translation (NAT). The default address range assigned to the virtual machines is 192.168.122.2 through 192.168.122.254.

Other packages you need should already be included with the Fedora Workstation install. If you did a different install type, make sure you have the following packages also added: libvirt-client (for the virsh command) and libvirt-daemon (to get the libvirtd service).

Step 4: Start services on the hypervisors

You need to make sure that the libvirtd service is running on both hypervisors. Start the sshd service as well. They may already be running, but just to make sure do the following as root on both hypervisors:

```
# systemctl start sshd.service
# systemctl enable sshd.service
# systemctl start libvirtd.service
# systemctl enable libvirtd.service
```

The sshd service allows you to log into the hypervisors over the network, if necessary. The libvirtd service is the one you might not be as familiar with. It is listening for requests to manage your virtual machines on each host.

Step 5: Edit /etc/hosts or set up DNS

To make it convenient to communicate between the hypervisors and storage system, you should assign host names to each system and map those names to IP addresses. Setting up a DNS server that all the systems point to is probably the best way to do that. However, for our simple example, you can just edit the /etc/hosts file on each system and add entries for each host.

Here is an example of what additional entries to your /etc/hosts file might look like for the three systems used in this procedure:

```
192.168.0.138  host1.example.com host1
192.168.0.139  host2.example.com host2
192.168.0.1    storage.example.com storage
```

Next you need to configure the storage.

Configuring storage

You can provide networked storage to the hypervisors for this procedure in many ways. I chose to set up a separate Fedora system on the same local network as the hypervisors and use NFS to attach the shared storage to both hypervisors.

NFS is not the most efficient method of sharing storage among hypervisors, but it is one of the easiest and most common to set up. In this procedure, I use the Virtualization Manager window (virt-manager) to configure the NFS storage pool.

For consistency's sake, the NFS share set up from the storage system is the /var/lib/ libvirt/images directory. It is mounted in the same place on each of the hypervisors. (For testing, if you only have two machines available, you can configure storage from one of the hypervisors. Keep in mind, however, that this means you can't turn off that hypervisor without shutting down all your VMs.)

Step 1: Install Linux software

To set up your storage on an NFS server, you can use pretty much any Linux system that has an NFS service available. Consider these things when you install Linux:

- **Disk space**—Make sure you have enough storage space available on the partition that contains the shared directory. For this example, /var/lib/libvirt/images is the shared directory.

- **Performance**—For best performance, you want to have a disk that has fast access times and data transfer rates.

For Fedora and RHEL, NFS server software is available from the `nfs-utils` package. For Ubuntu, you need the `nfs-kernel-server` package.

After initial installation is finished, check that the NFS server software is installed. If it isn't, you can install it on Fedora or RHEL with this command:

```
# yum install nfs-utils
```

For Ubuntu and similar systems, type this:

```
# apt-get install nfs-kernel-server
```

Step 2: Configure NFS share

To create an NFS share, you need to identify the directory to share and add information about it to the `/etc/exports` file. Follow these steps:

a. **Create a directory.** You can share any directory containing the space you want to share. Consider making a new directory and mounting a whole disk or partition on it. For this example, I create a directory named `/var/storage`:

```
# mkdir -p /var/storage
```

b. **Allow exporting.** On your storage system, create an entry in the `/etc/exports` file to share the directory with selected systems (by name or IP address). For this example, I allowed read-write access (`rw`) to all systems on the 192.168.0 subnetwork:

```
/var/storage 192.168.0.*(no_root_squash,rw,sync)
```

Step 3: Start the NFS service

Start the NFS service and open the firewall on the storage system to allow access to that service. Here's how:

a. **Start and enable NFS.** On the latest Fedora and RHEL systems, type the following to start the NFS server:

```
# systemctl start nfs-server.service
# systemctl enable nfs-server.service
```

On RHEL 6, older Fedora and some Ubuntu systems, use these commands to start and enable the NFS service:

```
# service nfs start
# chkconfig nfs on
```

b. **Open the firewall.** To open the firewall ports so those outside the local system can use your NFS share, do the following on Fedora 21:

```
# firewall-cmd --permanent --add-service=rpc-bind
# firewall-cmd --permanent --add-service=nfs
# systemctl restart firewalld
```

For systems using `iptables` directly, see Chapter 20 for information on how to open your firewall for the NFS service.

Step 4: Mount the NFS share on the hypervisors

Log in to each hypervisor and follow these steps to make the share available locally. Note that the location of the mount point directory on each hypervisor must be the same. Here's how:

a. **Check the NFS share availability.** From each of the two hypervisors, make sure that you can see the available share by typing the following:

```
# showmount -e storage.example.com
Export list for storage.example.com:

/var/storage 192.168.0.*
```

b. **Mount the NFS share.** Add information about the share to the /etc/fstab file. For our example, to allow the directory from the 192.168.0.1 system to be mounted on the same directory locally each time the system boots, the entry in the /etc/fstab file could look like this:

```
storage.example.com:/storage /var/lib/libvirt/images nfs defaults 0 0
```

c. **Test the NFS mount.** To check that you got the mount entry correct, run the following command to mount all entries in the /etc/fstab file that have not already been mounted and check that the NFS share was mounted:

```
# mount -a
# mount | grep libvirt
storage.example.com:/var/storage on /var/lib/libvirt/images type
nfs4
(rw,relatime,vers=4.0,rsize=1048576,wsize=1048576,namlen=255,hard,
proto=tcp,port=0,timeo=600,retrans=2,sec=sys,
clientaddr=192.168.0.1,local_lock=none,addr=192.168.0.138)
```

With your hypervisors and storage now in place, you can now begin creating your virtual machines.

Creating virtual machines

The Virtual Machine Manager (virt-manager) is a good tool to use to create your first virtual machines. It steps you through the installation and setup of virtual machines and provides a way to view and change the status of your existing virtual machines.

Later, when you understand the kinds of features that go into creating virtual machines, you can use the virt-install command to create virtual machines instead. The advantage of virt-install is that you can script or easily copy and paste a command line to create a virtual machine, instead of having to click through a GUI window.

You downloaded the Fedora 21 Workstation ISO image earlier in this chapter, so I'll use that in the example for creating a virtual machine. However, if you prefer, you can install many different versions of Linux or Windows as your virtual machine.

Step 1: Get images to make virtual machines

You can create a virtual machine in many ways. In general, you start with either a pre-built image (basically a copy of a working virtual machine) or just install from an installation ISO image into a fresh storage area. Here, we are going to do the latter and create a VM from the Fedora 21 Workstation installation ISO image.

Assuming you are logged in to one of the hypervisors as root and the ISO image is in the current directory, copy the ISO to the default directory used by virt-manager for storage (/var/lib/libvirt/images):

```
# cp Fedora-Live-Workstation-x86_64-21-5.iso /var/lib/libvirt/images/
```

Because that directory is shared by both hypervisors, you can go to either hypervisor to use that image.

Step 2: Check the network bridge

On each hypervisor, there should be a default network bridge name virbr0. All hypervisors will be added to this network interface and automatically assigned an IP address. By default, the hypervisor uses the address range of 192.168.122.2 through 192.168.122.254 to assign to the virtual machines. Using Network Address Translation (NAT), the host can route packets from the virtual machines using these private addresses to external network interfaces.

Do the following on each hypervisor to check the bridge for each:

```
# brctl show virbr0
bridge name    bridge id              STP enabled   interfaces
virbr0         8000.001aa0d7483e      yes           vnet0
# ip addr show virbr0
5: virbr0: <BROADCAST,MULTICAST,UP,LOWER_UP> mtu 1500 qdisc noqueue
        state UP group default
    link/ether fe:54:00:57:71:67 brd ff:ff:ff:ff:ff:ff
    inet 192.168.122.1 brd 192.168.122.255 scope global dynamic virbr0
```

Step 3: Start Virtual Machine Manager (virt-manager)

From the desktop on either hypervisor, do the following to open Virtual Machine Manager and connect it to the hypervisor:

a. **Start virt-manager.** Go to the Activities screen, type **Virtual Machine Manager** into the search box and press Enter, or type **virt-manager** from the shell. Type the root password when prompted. You should see the Virtual Machine Manager window.

b. **Check the connection to the hypervisor.** From the Add Connection pop-up, the hypervisor (QEMU/KVM) should already be set and the Autoconnect check box should be checked. Click Connect to connect to the local hypervisor if it has not already been done.

Step 4: Check connection details

After connecting to the hypervisor, set up some connection details. To do that from the Virtual Machine Manager window, do the following:

a. **View the connection details.** Select Edit ⇨ Connection Details to see the Connection Details window. Select the Overview, Virtual Networks, Storage, and Network Interfaces tabs to familiarize yourself with the connection information for your hypervisor. For example, the Storage tab appears in Figure 26.1, showing that there are 438.40GB of free space in the location used by default for storage by this hypervisor (/var/lib/libvirt/images directory).

FIGURE 26.1

Start Virtual Machine Manager and check connection details.

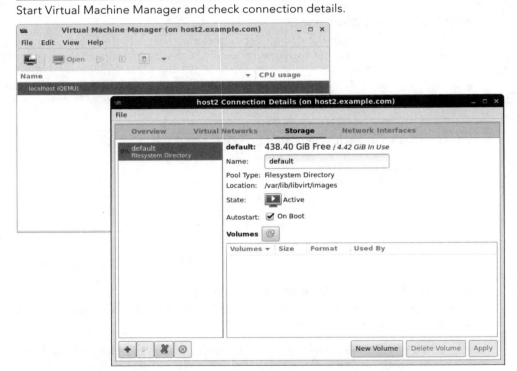

b. **Check that the network bridge is available.** Select the Network Interfaces tab and make sure the bridge we just created (bridge0) is in the list of available network interfaces.

Step 5: Create a new virtual machine

To create a new virtual machine from the Virtual Machine Manager window, do the following:

a. **Start the wizard.** To start the Create a New Virtual Machine wizard, select File ⇨ New Virtual Machine. The Create a New Virtual Machine window appears.

b. **Choose the installation method.** Four ways of creating the virtual machine are presented. The first three are ways to identify the location of installation media. The fourth lets you import an existing disk image. For our example, choose the first selection (Local install media) and click Forward.

c. **Choose the ISO.** Select the Use ISO Image button and choose Browse. In the window that appears, select or browse to the Fedora 21 Workstation ISO, select Choose Volume, and click Forward to continue.

d. **Choose the memory and CPU.** Choose the amount of RAM and number of processors available to the VM, and click Forward. I suggest at least 1024MB of RAM and at least one processor. Using 2048MB of RAM, if it is available, is better.

e. **Enable storage.** Choose the amount of disk space you want the VM to consume. I suggest at least 10GB for a Fedora Workstation, but you could probably get by with less. The qcow2 image that is created grows to the size you actually consume (up to the amount allocated), so overallocating space causes no problem until you actually try to use that space. Click Forward.

f. **Review the settings before the installation starts.** Choose the name for the virtual machine, and review the other setting for your installation. Click Advanced Options, and make sure the "bridge0" entry is selected. Select Customize Configuration Before Install to further review settings. Leave other settings at the default for now, and click Finish.

g. **Review the hardware settings.** If you selected "Customize" on the previous screen, you can review the settings in more detail. When you are satisfied, select Begin Installation.

h. **Install the virtual machine.** You are prompted to install the system just as you would be if you were installing directly to hardware. Complete the installation, and reboot the virtual machine. If the VM window isn't open, double-click the VM entry (in this case, fedora21) in the virt-manager window and log in. Figure 26.2 shows an example of the virt-manager window with the Fedora 21 Workstation virtual machine displayed.

FIGURE 26.2

Open the virtual machine and begin using it.

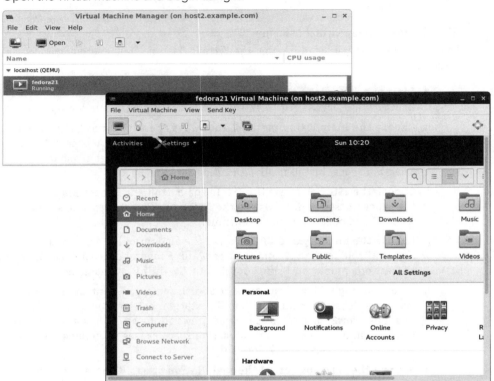

Managing virtual machines

After you have one or more virtual machines installed on a hypervisor, you can manage each VM in much the same ways you manage a computer system installed directly on hardware. You can do these things:

- **View the system from a console.** Double-click a running VM in the virt-manager window. A console window opens to the VM, allowing you to use the VM just as you would from a physical console to access an operating system installed directly on the hardware.

- **Shut down the VM.** Right-click the VM entry, and select Shut down. Then select either Shut down (to shut down properly) or Force off (effectively pulling the plug). Or you can select Reboot.

- **Start the VM.** If the VM is currently shut down, right-click the entry and select Run to start the VM running.
- **Delete the VM.** If you are totally finished using the VM, select Delete. You are asked if you want to delete the storage as well. Uncheck the box if you want to keep the storage associated with the VM.

Now that you are comfortable using your virtual machines, you can try migrating a VM to another hypervisor.

Migrating virtual machines

Being able to migrate your virtual machines between different hypervisors gives you tremendous flexibility in managing your computer workloads. Here are some of the advantages:

- **Improve performance** by moving VMs from hypervisors that are overloaded to ones that have more available memory and CPU capacity.
- **Do routine maintenance** on a hypervisor while keeping your VMs running.
- **Move VMs off underutilized hypervisors** so you can shut them off to save energy until they are needed again.
- **Move VMs off site** if you are expecting to shut down a datacenter or expecting a hurricane or other catastrophe to hit your datacenter.

Live migration, in particular, is valuable if you need work to continue on the VMs without interruption. The key to getting live VM migration to work is setting up your environment properly. Make sure the following are in place:

- Shared networked storage among the hypervisors
- The same network interfaces configured on each hypervisor
- Compatible CPUs between hypervisors (Often, a set of hypervisors have the exact same hardware.)
- A fast network connection between the hypervisors and storage
- The same or similar versions of virtualization software on the hypervisors (In our case, we used Fedora 21 on both and installed them similarly.)

With all that in place, live migration requires only a few steps to get going.

Step 1: Identify other hypervisors

Assuming that the Virtual Machine Manager window is still up and running on one of your hypervisors, go to that window and do the following to connect to the other hypervisor:

a. **Connect to the hypervisor.** Select File ⇨ Add Connection. The Add Connection window should appear.

b. **Add the connection.** Select the Connect to Remote Host check box, choose SSH as the Method, use the user name `root`, and type the hostname of the other hypervisor (for example, `host1.example.com`). When you click Connect, you may be prompted to enter a password for the remote hypervisor's root user and enter other information.

An entry for the new hypervisor should appear on the Virtual Machine Manager window.

Step 2: Migrate running VM to another hypervisor

Right-click any VM that is currently running, and select Migrate. The Migrate the Virtual Machine window appears, as shown in Figure 26.3.

FIGURE 26.3

Choose which hypervisor to migrate the VM to.

Select the new host. In my example, the VM is currently running on host2, so I want to select host1 as the new host. After a bit of time for the memory image of the VM to copy over to the other host, the VM should appear as running on that host.

If, for some reason, your migration fails (incompatible CPUs or other problems), you can always shut down the VM on one host and start it again on the other host. Doing that only requires that your shared storage is in place. On the second host, simply run the Create a new virtual machine wizard, but select to run an existing image instead of an installation ISO.

The hypervisor configuration I just showed you might suit you well for your home workstation or even a small business. Although it is beyond the scope of this book to help you develop an entire cloud computing platform, it is within our charter to help you use different cloud platforms to run your Linux systems. The next chapter helps you do that.

Summary

Linux is in the foundation on which most of today's emerging cloud technologies are being built. This chapter describes many of the basic components that go into building a cloud based on Linux and other open source technology. It then helps you learn about some of those basic technologies by setting up a couple of hypervisors and launching virtual machines.

Exercises

The exercises in this section describe tasks related to setting up a hypervisor (KVM host computer) and using it to run virtual machines. If you are stuck, solutions to the tasks are shown in Appendix B. Keep in mind that the solutions shown in Appendix B are usually just one of multiple ways to complete a task.

Although the example shown in this chapter for setting up hypervisors uses three physical machines, these exercises can be done on a single physical machine.

1. Check your computer to see if it can support KVM virtualization.
2. Install a Linux system along with the packages needed to use it as a KVM host and to run the Virtual Machine Manager application.
3. Make sure that the `sshd` and `libvirtd` services are running on the system.
4. Get a Linux installation ISO image that is compatible with your hypervisor, and copy it to the default directory used by Virtual Machine Manager to store images.

5. Check that the default network bridge (virbr0) is currently active.

6. Install a virtual machine using the ISO image you copied earlier.

7. Make sure you can log into and use the virtual machine.

8. Check that your virtual machine can connect to the Internet or other network outside the hypervisor.

9. Stop the virtual machine so it is no longer running.

10. Start the virtual machine again so it is running and available.

Deploying Linux to the Cloud

IN THIS CHAPTER

Creating Linux cloud images

Deploying a cloud image to virt-manager (libvirtd)

Deploying a cloud image to OpenStack

Deploying a cloud image to Amazon EC2

To get a new Linux system to use, instead of just running a standard installation program from a physical DVD, you can get a Linux image and deploy it to a cloud. One way to do that is to take a generic Linux image (one that is bootable but unconfigured) and provide information to configure that image to your needs. Another way is to go to a cloud provider, choose an image, click through selections to configure it, and launch it.

The point is that cloud computing is offering new ways to start up and use Linux systems. In Chapter 26, I had you do a standard Linux installation to create a virtual machine that runs on a Linux hypervisor. In this chapter, I show you how to use cloud images to start up a fresh Linux system.

First, I describe how to use cloud-init to manually combine a Linux cloud image with configuration information, to allow it to run in a variety of environments. Next, I tell how a similar process is done on an OpenStack Cloud or an Amazon Elastic Compute Cloud (EC2), by clicking through easy-to-use cloud controllers to choose images and settings to run the Linux cloud instance you want.

Getting Linux to Run in a Cloud

Cloud platforms are great for spinning up new virtual machines quickly and efficiently. They can do so because a fresh install is not required each time you want a new instance of an operating system.

Public clouds, such as Amazon EC2 (http://aws.amazon.com/ec2), offer instances of different Linux distributions for you to start and use. You choose a Linux instance, such as Ubuntu, Red Hat Enterprise Linux (RHEL), or SUSE Linux Enterprise Server (SLES), that is tuned for specific purposes. For example, there are instances that are optimized for high-performance processing or memory-intensive applications.

The content of a cloud instance tends to be generic in nature. It is expected that more information is attached to the image by the cloud user or the cloud provider using a service such as `cloud-init`. This information falls into two general categories: meta-data and user-data:

- **meta-data**—Included with meta-data is information that is needed before the image boots. This is data that is outside the contents of the image and is typically managed by the cloud provider. Some of this data comes from the fact that things such as storage, memory, and processing power are drawn from a pool of resources, rather than from the physical machine you are installing on. So the meta-data tells the cloud provider how much of those resources, and possibly others, to allocate early in the process of starting up the instance.

- **user-data**—The user-data information is inserted into the operating system that exists on the image. This is data that the person using the virtual machine provides. This might include a user account and password, configuration files, commands to run on first boot, the identities of software repositories, or anything else you might want to run or change within the operating system itself.

When you go to run a Linux instance in a cloud environment, you typically enter the meta-data and user-data information by clicking check boxes and filling in forms from a Web-based cloud controller (such as the OpenStack Dashboard or Red Hat Enterprise Virtualization Manager). The information may not be identified as meta-data and user-data when you configure the instance through the cloud controller.

The cloud you use to run your Linux virtual machines may be a public cloud, a private cloud, or a hybrid cloud. The type of cloud you choose may depend on your needs and your budget:

- **Public cloud**—Amazon EC2 and Google Compute Engine are examples of cloud platforms that let you launch and use Linux virtual machines from a web-based interface. You pay for the time that the instance is running. The amount of memory, storage, and virtual CPUs you use to run the service are also figured into the costs. The advantage of public clouds is that you don't have to purchase and maintain your own cloud infrastructure.

- **Private cloud**—With a private cloud, you put your own computing infrastructure in place (hypervisors, controllers, storage, network configuration, and so on). Setting up your own private cloud means taking on more up-front costs to own and maintain infrastructure. But it gives you added security and control of your computing resources. Because you control the infrastructure, you can create the images users have access to in your OpenStack infrastructure and account for user usage of that infrastructure in your own way.

■ **Hybrid cloud**—Many companies are looking toward hybrid cloud solutions. A hybrid cloud can allow multiple cloud platforms to be managed by a central facility. For example, Red Hat Cloudforms can deploy and manage virtual machines on OpenStack, VMware vSphere, and Red Hat Enterprise Virtualization platforms, provisioning different types of workloads to appropriate environments. At times of peak demand, Cloudforms can also direct virtual machines to run on Amazon EC2 clouds.

These cloud environments have different ways of provisioning and configuring virtual machines. However, the features that clouds need to provide to virtual machine management are similar. Having an understanding of those features can help you when you configure a Linux system to run in a cloud.

To get a better feel for configuring Linux cloud instances, the next section describes how `cloud-init` works to configure Linux cloud instances. It then helps you create your own meta-data and user-data files and apply them to your cloud instance so the information can be used when the cloud image boots.

Creating Linux Images for Clouds

Think about what you did when you installed a Linux system in Chapter 9. During a manual installation process, you set a root password, created a regular user account and password, possibly defined your network interfaces, and did other tasks. The information you entered became a permanent part of the operating system that remained each time you booted the system.

When you start with a prebuilt cloud image as your Linux system, you can use `cloud-init` to get a Linux system ready to run. The `cloud-init` facility (`http://launchpad.net/cloud-init`) sets up a generic virtual machine instance to run in the way you want it to run without going through an install process. The next section describes some ways of using `cloud-init`.

Configuring and running a cloud-init cloud instance

In the next procedure, I show you how to manually create data that can be combined with a bootable Linux cloud image, so when that image boots, it is configured based on your data. Combining data with the image at runtime allows you to change the data each time before the image is run, instead of installing it permanently in the image.

I suggest that you run this procedure on one of the hypervisors you configured in Chapter 26. This not only allows you to create the customized data for your Linux cloud image, but also lets you run that image as a virtual machine on that hypervisor.

27

To add data and run an existing cloud image, this procedure requires you to obtain a cloud image, create data files, and generate a new image that combines those elements. This procedure is meant to be very simple to get a cloud image booted. Later, I tell you how to add more features to these data files. To configure and run a cloud image, follow these steps:

1. **Create a `cloud-init` meta-data file.** Create a file named `meta-data` to hold data that identifies information about the cloud instance from the outside. For example, you can add a name to identify the instance (`instance-id`), a hostname (`local-hostname`), and other information. To keep it simple for the first try, I assign only two fields (set them to any names you like):

   ```
   instance-id: FedoraWS01
   local-hostname: fedora01
   ```

2. **Create a `cloud-init` user-data file.** Create a file named `user-data` to hold data that configures inside the operating system on the image itself. For this simple case, I just set a password for the default user (fedora) to `cloudpass` and `cloud-init` not to expire the password:

   ```
   #cloud-config
   password: cloudpass
   chpasswd: {expire: False}
   ```

3. **Combine the data into a separate image.** With the `meta-data` and `user-data` files in the current directory, create an ISO image that contains that data. Later, we present this image as a CD-ROM to the Linux image, so `cloud-init` knows how to configure the Linux image. (Install the `genisoimage` package first, if you haven't already.)

   ```
   # yum install genisoimage
   # genisoimage -output fedora21-data.iso -volid cidata \
           -joliet -rock user-data meta-data
   ```

4. **Get a base cloud image.** Cloud images for Ubuntu, Fedora, and RHEL are configured for use with `cloud-init`. Get an official Fedora cloud image (images for other distributions are described later), and do the following:

   - **Go to getfedora.org.** Open a web browser, and go to `https://getfedora.org/en/cloud/download/`.
   - **Click OpenStack.** Click the "Are you an OpenStack user" link under General Purpose and select the "Download" button that appears to get a `qcow2` image that can be used in an OpenStack environment. The image name is something like: `Fedora-Cloud-Base-20141203-21.x86_64.qcow2`.

5. **Snapshot the image.** You probably need to run this procedure a few times before you get the exact image you want. So, instead of using the downloaded image directly, make a snapshot of it. To keep track of my versions, I added `01` to the new snapshot name:

```
# qemu-img create -f qcow2 \
  -o backing_file=Fedora-Cloud-Base-20141203-21.x86_64.qcow2 \
  Fedora-Cloud-Base-01.qcow2
```

6. **Copy the files to the images directory.** It's good practice to copy images to the
   /var/lib/libvirt/images/ directory when you are using them on a hypervisor
   (libvirtd service). For example, to copy the cloud image and data image to that
   directory, type the following:

```
# cp Fedora-Cloud-Base-20141203-21.x86_64.qcow2 \
  Fedora-Cloud-Base-01.qcow2 \
  fedora21-data.iso           \
  /var/lib/libvirt/images/
```

7. **Start the cloud instance.** With the files in place, run the following commands to
   start an instance of your cloud image:

```
# cd /var/lib/libvirt/images
# virt-install --import --name fedora21-01 --ram 4096 --vcpus 2 \
  --disk path=Fedora-Cloud-Base-01.qcow2,format=qcow2,bus=virtio \
  --disk path=fedora21-data.iso,device=cdrom \
  --network bridge=virbr0 &
```

The previous virt-install example shows that the virtual machine is assigned to consume
4GB of RAM (--ram 4096) and two virtual CPUs (--vcpus 2). The RAM and VCPU values on
your system may be different, depending on the resources your computer has.

At this point, a virtual machine named fedora21-01 is running on your hypervisor. As
the virtual machine boots up, a console window should open allowing you to log into the
new cloud virtual machine.

Investigating the cloud instance

To investigate the cloud image we created you can open up the running instance and look
inside. One way to do that, if it is not already open, is to open the virtual machine with
virt-viewer:

```
# virt-viewer fedora21-01
```

From the console window that appears, use the data we added to the image to log in.
Use fedora as the user and cloudpass as the password to log in. The fedora user has
sudo privilege, so you can use that account to investigate the instance by typing some
commands:

Here, you see where the user-data was copied into the instance:

```
$ sudo cat /var/lib/cloud/instances/FedoraWS01/user-data.txt
#cloud-config
password: cloudpass
chpasswd: {expire: False}
```

The basic cloud configuration is done in the `/etc/cloud/cloud.cfg` file. You can see here that the root user account is disabled by default. At the bottom of the file, you can see that the user named `fedora` is the default user and has `sudo` privilege without requiring a password.

```
$ sudo cat /etc/cloud/cloud.cfg
users:
 - default
disable_root: 1
...
system_info:
  default_user:
    name: fedora0
    lock_paswd: true
    gecos: Fedora Cloud User
    groups: [wheel, adm, systemd-journal]
    sudo: ["ALL=(ALL) NOPASSWD:ALL"]
    shell: /bin/bash
  distro: fedora
  paths:
    cloud_dir: /var/lib/cloud
    templates_dir: /etc/cloud/templates
  ssh_svcname: sshd

# vim:syntax=yaml
```

You can see other things in the `cloud.cfg` file as well. You can see which `cloud_init_modules` run during initialization (such as those that set the hostname or start `rsyslog` logging). You can see `cloud_config_modules` that set the locale, set the time zone, and run further configuration tools (such as chef and puppet).

Because `yum` repositories are enabled, provided you have an available network connection (DHCP should have assigned addresses to the virtual machine by default), you can install any packages available from the Fedora repositories.

Cloning the cloud instance

If you decide you like the cloud instance you created, you can save a copy of it to run later by making a clone of the two images (cloud and data image) that make up the cloud instance. To create a clone of the running cloud instance, using `virt-manager`, do the following:

1. **Launch `virt-manager`.** On the host system running the virtual machine, run the `virt-manager` command or start Virtual Machine Manager from the Activities screen on your desktop.

2. **Pause the virtual machine.** Right-click the virtual machine instance entry in the `virt-manager` window, and select Pause. This makes the virtual machine inactive for the moment.

3. **Clone the virtual machine.** Right-click the virtual machine instance entry again, and select Clone. The Clone Virtual Machine window appears, as shown in Figure 27.1.

FIGURE 27.1

Cloning lets you save a permanent copy of a cloud instance.

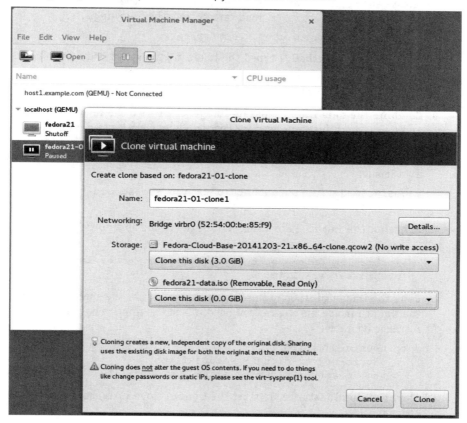

4. **Choose the clone settings.** For the cloud base image and the data image, you can choose to either make new copies or share them with the existing virtual machine. After you do, select clone.

The cloned cloud instance is now available to start, stop, and otherwise manage as you like from the Virtual Machine Manager window or the `virsh` command.

Trying an Ubuntu cloud image

Any Linux image that is enabled for `cloud-init` can be configured in much the same way as has just been shown for Fedora. Here is an example of how to get Ubuntu cloud image running without a cloud provider on your local Linux hypervisor:

1. **Download the Ubuntu cloud tarball.** Go to the Ubuntu site, and select the release and specific images you want. I downloaded the `ubuntu-14.10-server-cloudimg-amd64.tar.gz` cloud tarball from the following site:

   `http://cloud-images.ubuntu.com/releases/`

2. **Untar the cloud tarball.** I typed the following to extract the files from the tarball:

   ```
   # tar xvf ubuntu-14.10-server-cloudimg-amd64.tar.gz
   ```

3. **Combine the data into a separate image.** Start with the same `meta-data` and `user-data` files you used for Fedora. Change the meta-data names to ubuntu instead of `fedora`. The default user is different (ubuntu), but you can assign a password in the same way. Run this command to create the data image:

   ```
   # genisoimage -output ubuntu-data.iso -volid cidata \
         -joliet -rock user-data meta-data
   ```

4. **Snapshot the image.** Take a snapshot of the image as follows:

   ```
   # qemu-img create -f qcow2 \
     -o backing_file=utopic-server-cloudimg-amd64.img \
     utopic-server-01.img
   ```

5. **Copy the image files.** Copy the Ubuntu image files to the appropriate directory. For the Ubuntu image file to run, you need to add the floppy image to make the cloud instance bootable:

   ```
   # cp ubuntu-data.iso          \
        utopic-server-cloudimg-amd64-floppy \
        utopic-server-cloudimg-amd64.img /var/lib/libvirt/images/
   ```

6. **Start the cloud instance.** To start the Ubuntu cloud instance, run the following command:

   ```
   # cd /var/lib/libvirt/images
   # virt-install --import --name ubuntu1410-01 --ram 4096 --vcpus 2 \
     --disk path=utopic-server-cloudimg-amd64-floppy,device=floppy \
     --disk path=utopic-server-cloudimg-amd64.img,format=raw,bus=virtio \
     --disk path=ubuntu-data.iso,device=cdrom --network bridge=virbr0 &
   ```

At this point, you have a bare-bones Ubuntu cloud instance running. Log in as the user ubuntu and the password defined in the user-data file.

Expanding your cloud-init configuration

You can add much more information to your meta-data and user-data files to configure your cloud instances. Examples of `cloud-init` settings can be found on the Cloud-Init Config Examples page (`http://cloudinit.readthedocs.org/en/latest/topics/examples.html`). The following sections show examples of settings you can add to your user-data files.

> **NOTE**
> The user-data and meta-data files are in yaml format. The yaml format uses indents and well-known delimiters. Items in a list are preceded by a hyphen and a space. Keys and values are separated by a colon and a space. If you are not familiar with yaml, I recommend digging around the Yaml Project site (`https://github.com/yaml`).

Adding ssh keys with cloud-init

Instead of using passwords to log into your cloud instances, you can use key-based authentication along with the `ssh` command to log in over the network. This is commonly used by cloud providers to allow user access to cloud images.

If you have already generated public and private `ssh` keys for the user account you plan to use to `ssh` into the cloud instance, you can use that public key for this procedure. If you had generated an RSA keypair, the public key is located in the `id_rsa.pub` file by default:

```
# cat $HOME/.ssh/id_rsa.pub
ssh-rsa AAAAB3NzaC1yc2EAAAADAQABAAABAQDMzdq6hqDUhueWzl7rIUwjxB/rrJY4o
ZpoWINzeGVf6m8wXlHmmqd9C7LtnZg2P24/ZBb3S1j7vK2WymOcwEoWekhbZHBAyYeqXK
YQQjUB2E2Mr6qMkmrjQBx6ypxbz+VwADNCwegY5RCUoNjrN43GVu6nSOxhFf7hv6dtCjv
osOvtt0979YS3UcEyrobpNzreGSJ8FMPMRFMWWg68Jz5hOMCIE1IldhpODvQVbTNsn/ST
xO7ZwSYV6kfDj0szvdoDDCyh8mPNC1kIDhf/qu/Zn1kxQ9xfecQ+SUi+2IwN69o1fNpex
JPFr+Bwjkwcrk58C6uowG5eNSgnuu7GMUkT root@host2.example.com
```

The public key from that file is typically copied to the `$HOME/.ssh/authorized_keys` file for the user on the remote system you want to log in to. We can have the key added to that file on our cloud instance using entries in the user-data file that looks like this:

```
users:
  - default
  - name: wsmith
    gecos: William B. Smith
    primary-group: wsmith
    sudo: ALL=(ALL) NOPASSWD:ALL
    lock-passwd: true
    ssh-authorized-keys:
```

```
         - ssh-rsa AAAAB3NzaC1yc2EAAAADAQABAAABAQDMzdq6hqDUhueWzl7rIUwjx
B/rrJY4oZpoWINzeGVf6m8wXlHmmqd9C7LtnZg2P24/ZBb3S1j7vK2WymOcwEoWekhbZH
BAyYeqXKYQQjUB2E2Mr6qMkmrjQBx6ypxbz+VwADNCwegY5RCUoNjrN43GVu6nSOxhFf7
hv6dtCjvosOvtt0979YS3UcEyrobpNzreGSJ8FMPMRFMWWg68Jz5hOMCIE1IldhpODvQV
bTNsn/STxO7ZwSYV6kfDj0szvdoDDCyh8mPNC1kIDhf/qu/Zn1kxQ9xfecQ+SUi+2IwN6
9o1fNpexJPFr+Bwjkwcrk58C6uowG5eNSgnuu7GMUkT root@host2.example.com
```

From the previous information, you can see that wsmith is the default user. The gecos
entry is typically the user's full name, used in the fifth field of the /etc/passwd file.
The password is locked for this user. However, because the ssh-rsa entry from my root
account on host2.example.com is provided here under ssh-authorized-keys for the
user, I can log into the cloud instance as wsmith over ssh without typing a password (provided my private key is associated with that public key).

Adding network interfaces with cloud-init

If you want network interfaces to be configured on your cloud instances early in the boot
process, you can add network-interfaces entries to your meta-data file for those cloud
instances. Here is an example:

```
network-interfaces: |
    iface eth0 inet static
    address 192.168.100.50
    network 192.168.100.0
    netmask 255.255.255.0
    broadcast 192.168.1.255
    gateway 192.168.100.1
bootcmd:
    - ifdown eth0
    - ifup eth0
```

The network-interfaces values shown here identify the eth0 interface within the
cloud instance as containing static addresses (in other words, not from DHCP). The IP
address for the interface is set to 192.168.100.50, while the gateway that routes packets
out to the world is set to 192.168.100.1. To bring that interface up on the new address,
the bootcmd is set to bring the interface down (ifdown eth0) and then back up
(ifup eth0).

Adding software with cloud-init

You aren't limited to the software already on your cloud image. Inside your user-data
file, you can define yum repositories (in Fedora and RHEL) or apt repositories (in Ubuntu
or Debian), and then identify any packages you want to have installed when the cloud
instance starts.

The following example shows what entries in a user-data file might look like to add a yum
repository (for Fedora or RHEL) to your cloud instance and then install packages from that
repository or any other enabled repository:

```
myownrepo:
    baseurl: http://myrepo.example.com/pub/myrepo/
    enabled: true
    gpgcheck: true
    gpgkey: file:///etc/pki/rpm-gpg/RPM-GPG-KEY-MYREPO
    name: My personal software repository
packages:
 - nmap
 - mycoolcmd
 - [libmystuff, 3.10.1-2.fc21.noarch]
```

In the example just shown, a new yum repository is created in the file /etc/yum.
repos.d/myownrepo.repo. A gpgkey is provided to check the validity of installed packages, and GPG checking is turned on. After that, the nmap package is installed (that's in
the standard Fedora yum repository), the mycoolcmd package is installed (from my private
repository), and a specific version of the libmystuff package is installed.

Configuring apt software repositories for Ubuntu is done a bit differently. Failsafe primary
and security apt package mirrors are configured by default (in the cloud.cfg file in the
image), along with settings to cause the instance, if run in an Amazon EC2 cloud, to search
the closest region for packages. To add more repositories, entries in your user-data file
could look as follows:

```
apt_mirror: http://us.archive.ubuntu.com/ubuntu/
apt_mirror_search:
 - http://myownmirror.example.com
 - http://archive.ubuntu.com
packages:
 - nmap
 - mycoolcmd
 - [libmystuff, 3.16.0-25]
```

The myownmirror.example.com entry tells apt to use your own private apt repository
to search for packages. Note that packages you want to install can be entered in basically
the same format as you did with Fedora, although specific version information (if entered)
might look different in some cases.

You can add many other settings to your user-data and meta-data files. Again, refer to the
Cloud-Init Cloud Config Examples page (http://cloudinit.readthedocs.org/en/
latest/topics/examples.html) for details.

Using cloud-init in enterprise computing

So far, the cloud-init examples in this chapter have focused on taking a cloud image,
manually adding configuration data, and running it as a virtual machine temporarily on
your local hypervisor. This approach is useful if you want to understand how cloud-init
works and the opportunities you have for tuning cloud images to your specifications. But
this approach doesn't scale well if you are managing large enterprises of virtual machines.

`Cloud-init` supports the concept of *datasources*. By placing user-data and meta-data in a datasource, you don't have to manually inject that information into a cloud instance, as we did earlier in this chapter. Instead, when the `cloud-init` service starts running on the instance, it knows to look not only on the local system for data sources, but also outside it.

For Amazon EC2 clouds, `cloud-init` queries a particular IP address (`http://169.254.169.254/`) for data. For example, it may check `http://169.254.169.254/2009-04-04/meta-data/` for meta-data and `http://169.254.169.254/2009-04-04/user-data/` for user-data. This allows the configuration data to be stored and accessed from a central location.

As for what might be inside the meta-data and user-data, far more complex configuration schemes can be developed for deployment of your cloud instances. `Cloud-init` supports configuration tools, such as Puppet (`http://puppetlabs.com/puppet/puppet-open-source`) and Chef (`https://www.chef.io/chef/`). These tools let you apply scripts of configuration information to your cloud instances, even doing such things as replace components or restart services as needed to return the system to a desired state.

At this point, however, my job is not to make you into a full-blown cloud administrator (a few hundred pages ago, you could have been a Linux novice). Instead, I want you to understand what you will be dealing with if you eventually land in a cloud data center ... because many people believe that most data centers will be managed as cloud infrastructures in the not-too-distant future.

So far in this chapter, you have looked at the inside of configuring Linux for cloud computing. Next, let's step back and look at how you can use two of the most popular Linux-based cloud platforms to run your own Linux-based virtual machines: OpenStack and Amazon EC2.

Using OpenStack to Deploy Cloud Images

By most accounts, OpenStack is the hottest open source project today. With OpenStack, you get a continually evolving platform for managing your physical cloud computing infrastructure, as well as the virtual systems that run on it. OpenStack lets you deploy your own private cloud or offer it up to the world as a public cloud.

Rather than have you set up your own OpenStack cloud, I'm going to show how you can use OpenStack to deploy virtual machines from an OpenStack Dashboard. If you want to try it yourself, OpenStack is available in the following ways:

- **Linux distributions**—Fedora, Ubuntu, and CentOS have free versions of OpenStack that you can deploy yourself. Red Hat Enterprise Linux offers a version of OpenStack that is available by subscription. It's tricky to set up. Some all-in-one setups for OpenStack can run on a single machine, but I think you will have a better experience if you start with three physical machines: one controller node and two hypervisors.

- **Public OpenStack clouds**—You can try out public OpenStack clouds for varying costs. A list of public OpenStack clouds is available from the OpenStack project site (`http://www.openstack.org/marketplace/public-clouds/`).

My first point is to help you run a Linux system in a cloud, when you don't have the capacity to do what you want on your own computers. However, my other point is to show you how a cloud provider's web-based interface (like OpenStack Dashboard) can greatly simplify the cloud configuration we did manually with `cloud-init` earlier in this chapter.

Starting from the OpenStack Dashboard

I'm going to start with an OpenStack setup that is already in place. The OpenStack environment's administrator has created a project for me called `cnegus-test-project` and a user account (`cnegus`) that lets me access that project. Here's what I plan to do:

- **Configure networking**—Just as I would set up a router and physically plug my computers into that router, I'm going to set up a virtual network. That virtual network will include a set of addresses that are distributed to my virtual machines via DHCP.

- **Configure virtual machines**—I'll step through the process of choosing, configuring, and deploying a couple of virtual machines.

The version of OpenStack used for this demonstration is Red Hat Enterprise Linux OpenStack Platform (RHEL-OSP). However, the experience would be similar on any OpenStack environment. The next section shows you how to start configuring your network.

Configuring your OpenStack virtual network

1. **Log in to OpenStack.** Using the username and password assigned to you by the OpenStack administrator, log in to the OpenStack Dashboard from your web browser. You should see an Overview screen, similar to the one shown in Figure 27.2.

2. **Create a network.** To create a network, from the left column on the Overviews page, select Networks. From the Networks screen that appears, create a new network as follows (the examples I used are in parentheses):

   a. **Select the Create Network button.**

   b. **On the Network tab, type a Network Name** (`mynet`).

   c. **On the Subnet tab, type a Subnet name** (`mysub01`), **Network Address** (`192.168.100.0/24`), **IP Version** (`IPv4`), **and Gateway IP** (`192.168.100.1`), **and leave Disable Gateway unchecked.**

FIGURE 27.2

Log in to the OpenStack Dashboard.

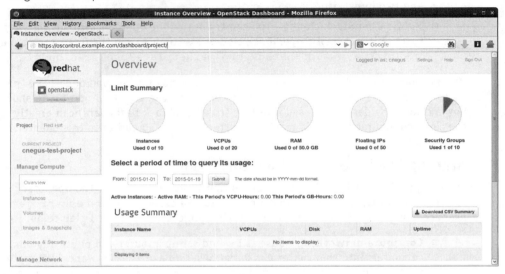

d. **On the Subnet Detail tab, type a comma-separated range of IP addresses in the Allocation Pool box.** For my example, I chose `192.168.100.10,192.168.100.50` to hand out a range of IP addresses to clients from 192.168.100.10 to 192.168.100.50. Get a name server suggestion from the administrator of your OpenStack cloud or use a public DNS server (such as Google's 8.8.8.8 or 8.8.4.4).

e. **Select Create to create the new network.** The new network appears on the Networks screen.

3. **Create a router.** For your virtual machines to be able to access the Internet, you need to identify a router that is attached to your private network on one interface and a network that can reach the public Internet on the other. Here's how to do that:

a. **From the left column, select Routers.**

b. **Click the Create Router button.**

c. **Type a Router Name (`myrouter01`), and click Create router.**

d. **Select the Set Gateway button.**

e. **From the Set Gateway screen, click the External Network box and choose from the available external networks.** Leave the Router Name and Router ID as they are. Click Set Gateway. The new router appears on the Routers screen.

4. **Connect your network to the external router.** From the Routers screen (you should still be on that screen), select the name of the router you just created (myrouter1):

    a.   **From the Router Details screen, select the Add Interface button.**

    b.   **From the Add Interface screen, click the Subnet box and choose the subnet you created earlier (**mynet: 192.168.100.0/24 mysub01**).** You shouldn't have to change Router Name or Router ID.

    c.   **Click Add Interface.**

5. **View the network topology.** Click Network Topology from the left column. Then hover your mouse pointer over the router name (myroute01). Figure 27.3 shows an example of what your network configuration might look like.

27

FIGURE 27.3

View your Network Topology from the OpenStack Dashboard.

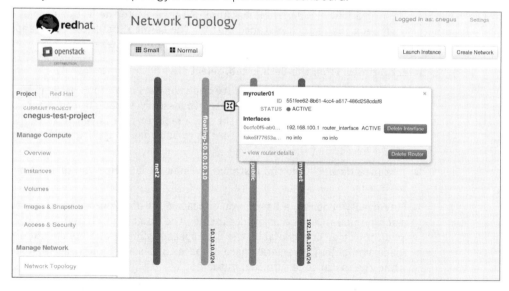

With your networking in place, you can create keys to use to access your virtual machines in OpenStack.

Configuring keys for remote access

The normal way to configure access to your virtual machines in a cloud environment is to create a public/private keypair that provides secure access to your virtual machines using ssh and related tools from your desktop system. The private key is stored in your desktop user's home directory, and the public key is injected into the virtual machine so you can log in remotely (via `ssh`) to the virtual machine without typing a password. Here's how to set up your keys:

1. **Select Access & Security.** From the left column, select Access & Security.

2. **Create a keypair.** If you already have a keypair, you can skip to the next step. If not, select the Keypairs tab and click the Create Keypair button. When the Create Keypair window appears, do this:

   a. **Type a Keypair Name (**`mycloudkey`**), and click the Create Keypair button.** A pop-up window asks if you want to open or save the `*.pem` file.

   b. **Select Save File, and click OK.** When prompted where to save it, save it to the `.ssh` directory in your home directory.

You are ready to deploy an OpenStack instance (cloud-based virtual machine).

Launching a virtual machine in OpenStack

To begin launching a new cloud virtual machine instance, go to the left column and select Instances. Then click the Launch instance button. The Launch Instance screen appears. To fill in the information you need to launch the instance, follow these steps:

1. **Select Details.** From the Details tab, select the following items:

   ■ **Availability Zone**—An availability zone consists of a group of compute hosts. Separate zones are sometimes created to identify a group of computers that are physically together (such as on the same rack) or that have the same hardware features (so they could be used for the same types of applications). Choose one of the zones from the list.

   ■ **Instance Name**—Give the instance any name that helps you remember what it is.

   ■ **Flavor**—By choosing a flavor, you allocate a set of resources to your virtual machine instance. The resources include the number of virtual CPU cores, the amount of memory available, the disk space assigned, and ephemeral disk space available. (Ephemeral space is space that is available from the local disk while the instance is running, but is not saved when the instance shuts down.) Default flavors include `m1.tiny`, `m1.small`, `m1.medium`, `m1.large`, and `m1.xlarge`. Other flavors can be added by your cloud administrator.

   ■ **Instance Count**—By default, this is set to 1, to start one instance. Change the number to start more instances if you like.

   ■ **Instance Boot Source**—The instance can be booted from an image, a snapshot, a volume, an image that includes a new volume, or a volume snapshot that includes a new volume.

   ■ **Image Name**—Select the image you want to start. The names typically include the names of the operating systems you are booting.

■ **Device size and Device Name (optional)**—If, when you selected your Instance Boot Source, you selected to include a new volume, you set the size (in GB) and device name for the volume in these fields. For the Device Name, if you choose vda as the device name (for the first disk on a virtual machine), the device representing that device would be /dev/vda.

2. **Select Access & Security.** Select the Access & Security tab, and choose the keypair you created earlier.

3. **Select Networking.** Select the Networking tab. From the list of available networks, grab the one you want with your mouse and drag it into the Selected Networks box.

4. **Add Post-Creation settings.** You can add commands and scripts that configure the system further after it is booted. This is where you can add the kinds of information you added in the user-data files described in the sections on cloud-init earlier in this chapter.

Select Launch to start up the virtual machine. With the virtual machine running, you can log in to that system by selecting the instance and clicking the Console tab. The virtual machine's console window should present you with a login prompt. If you want to be able to gain access to the virtual machine using ssh over the network, go on to the next section.

Accessing the virtual machine via ssh

With your public key injected into your running virtual machine, it is ready for you to log in using ssh. However, before you can do that, you must take these steps:

1. **Add a floating IP address.** From the OpenStack Dashboard, select Instances from the left column, click More on the entry containing the instance, and click Associate Floating IP. Select the plus sign (+) next to the IP Address box, select a Pool that has floating IPs available, and click Allocate IP. The allocated address should appear in the IP Address field. Select the Port to be associated, and click Associate.

2. **Use ssh to access the instance.** From a Linux system that has access to the network on which the floating address was assigned, run the ssh command to log in. Assuming your key's .pem file was called mycloud.pem, the default user on the instance is cloud-user, and the IP address is 10.10.10.100, you could type the following to log in:

```
# ssh -i mycloud.pem cloud-user@10.10.10.100
```

You should be able to log in now without a password. To do administration on the system, you can use the sudo command as the default user.

Using Amazon EC2 to Deploy Cloud Images

Amazon Elastic Computer Cloud (Amazon EC2) is a cloud platform that is particularly suited for pay-as-you-go cloud computing. Like OpenStack, it lets you choose from preconfigured virtual machine images and configure them as you need.

To start using Amazon EC2 to launch virtual machines, go to the Getting Started with Amazon Web Services page and follow links to create a new account (http://aws .amazon.com/getting-started/). After you log in, the full range of AWS services is displayed. Select EC2, and you see the EC2 Management Console, as shown in Figure 27.4.

FIGURE 27.4

Launch cloud instances using the Amazon EC2 Management Console.

To start your first instance, select the Launch Instance button. You are then given a choice of Linux (Red Hat Enterprise Linux, SUSE Linux, Ubuntu, and so on) and Windows images to start up. The wizard takes you through the selection of different instance types (general purpose or optimized) and lets you configure instance details, add storage, tag the instance, and configure security.

After the virtual machine is configured, you can work with the virtual machine directly from a console window or log in over the network using ssh and public/private keypairs. At any point, you can go back to the EC2 Management Console to keep track of the resources you are consuming and watch over the health of your virtual machines.

Summary

Understanding how cloud computing differs from simply installing an operating system directly on computer hardware will help you adapt as more and more data centers move toward cloud computing. In the beginning of this chapter, I encouraged you to get your hands on some cloud images, combine them with data, and launch them on a local Linux hypervisor to understand how cloud images work.

After that, I demonstrated how you can launch your own virtual images in an OpenStack cloud platform. That included configuring network interfaces, choosing how the virtual instance would run, and launching the virtual image. I also quickly introduced the Amazon Elastic Compute Cloud service, where you can pay to use cloud storage and processing time if you don't have enough computing resources of your own.

This chapter has no exercises because I meant it to be a stretch beyond the scope of this book. I hope you find this material useful after you have locked down your basic Linux skills and are ready to extend those skills into the clouds.

27

Part VII

Appendixes

Media

IN THIS APPENDIX

Getting Linux distributions

Creating a bootable CD or DVD

U nless you bought a computer with Linux preinstalled or had someone install it for you, you need to find a way to get a Linux distribution and then either install or run it live on your computer. Fortunately, Linux distributions are widely available and come in a variety of forms.

In this appendix, you learn how to:

- Get a few different Linux distributions
- Create a bootable disk to install your distribution
- Boot Linux from a USB drive

To use this book effectively, you should have a Linux distribution in front of you to work on. It's important to be able to experience Linux as you read. So try the examples and do the exercises.

Linux distributions are most commonly available from the websites of the organizations that produce them. The following sections describe websites associated with Linux distributions that offer ISO images you can download.

> **NOTE**
>
> An ISO is a disk image that is formatted in the ISO 9660 file system format, a format that is commonly used with CD and DVD images. Because this is a well-known format, it is readable by Windows, Mac, and Linux systems.
>
> An ISO image can be burned to a CD or DVD medium, depending on the size of the image. An ISO image in your file system can be mounted on a Linux system in loopback mode, so you can view or copy its contents.
>
> When an ISO image contains a Linux Live CD or installation image, the images are bootable. This means that instead of starting up an operating system, such as Windows or Linux, from the computer's hard disk, you can tell your computer to boot from the CD or DVD instead. This enables you to run a totally different operating system than is installed on your hard disk without changing or damaging the data on that disk.

Getting Fedora

You can download Fedora from the `https://getfedora.org` site. That page contains links to download images for installing Fedora Workstation, Server, and Cloud flavors.

> **NOTE**
>
> I recommend downloading the Fedora Workstation Live Image to work along with this book because most of the book works with that distribution. You can run it live without committing to overwriting your computer's hard disk until you feel comfortable enough to install it permanently.

To test the examples in this book, I used Fedora 21, 32-bit or the 64-bit Fedora Workstation Image. If you have a 64-bit ISO, you must use a 64-bit machine. If you have a 32-bit ISO, it works on 32-bit or 64-bit machines.

Later versions of Fedora that come with a GNOME desktop should work as well. Here's a link to the exact ISO used for the Fedora 21 Workstation: `http://download.fedoraproject .org/pub/fedora/linux/releases/21/Workstation/x86_64/iso/Fedora-Live- Workstation-x86_64-21-5.iso`. Keep in mind that the latest Fedora Workstation ISO image does not fit on a CD, so you must burn it to DVD. See the descriptions of CD/DVD burning tools available for Windows, Mac OS X, and Linux later in this appendix.

Figure A.1 shows an example of the Get Fedora page.

Today, the default download is an ISO image of a 64-bit PC-type Fedora Workstation (GNOME) Live DVD. You can boot this image on your computer, and if you choose, you can permanently install it to your computer's hard disk. To download this image, do the following:

1. Select Workstation, Server, or Cloud. I recommend Workstation to follow along with this book.

2. Select the Download Now button, and click the Download button. A pop-up should appear, asking what you want to do with the ISO.

3. Select to save the ISO. Depending on your settings, either you are asked where you want to download it or it simply begins downloading to a default folder (in Linux, it is probably a Downloads folder).

4. If you are prompted for where to put the ISO, select a folder that has enough space to hold it. Remember where this folder is because you need to locate the ISO when you go to burn it later.

If you need more information about what to do with the downloaded image, there are links to help you on the Fedora page that appears. At the time of this writing, there are links to "burn the image to a blank DVD disc," "write the image to a USB flash drive," "find common tips" for booting the media, and read the "complete Installation Guide."

FIGURE A.1

Download Fedora ISO images from the Get Fedora page.

You have other choices for downloading ISOs from Fedora. From the bottom of the Get Fedora page, you can download specially configured Fedora ISO images called *spins* (https://spins.fedoraproject.org). Here are some special types of Fedora spins that might interest you:

- **Desktop spins**—People who prefer the KDE desktop to the GNOME desktop can download the KDE spin. If you are trying Linux on a computer with less memory or processing power, consider Xfce and LXDE spins (representing lightweight desktops of the same name). The MATE-Compiz spin offers more of the other extreme, with desktop effects like wobbly windows and desktops that rotate on a cube.
- **Security spins**—One of the early uses of live Linux media was to provide bootable, removable media containing security tools. If you have an unbootable or otherwise

broken computer, the Security spin can be booted up to repair file systems, debug network problems, or do hundreds of other tasks to check and fix the computer (even if the installed operating system is Windows or some other Linux version).

- **Design-suite**—The Design-suite spin contains a consolidation of software for creative endeavors. This includes tools for working with documents, images, video, audio, and other media.
- **Games**—Try the wide array of open source and free software games available today in the Fedora Games spin.

These special spins can be fun, but to work along with most of the book I recommend the standard Workstation ISO image. After you have downloaded the ISO image, proceed to the description later in this chapter of how to burn that image to CD or DVD.

Getting Red Hat Enterprise Linux

Many large corporations, government agencies, and universities use Red Hat Enterprise Linux to run their mission-critical applications. While most of the procedures in this book will run well on Fedora, there are many references to how things are done differently in Red Hat Enterprise Linux because, when you go to get a job as a Linux system administrator, you will, in most cases, be working with Red Hat Enterprise Linux systems.

Although the source code for Red Hat Enterprise Linux is freely available, the ISOs containing the packages you install (often referred to as the binaries) are available only to those who have accounts on the Red Hat customer portal (https://access.redhat.com) or through evaluation copies.

If you don't have an account, you can try signing up for a 30-day trial. If either you or your company has an account with Red Hat, you can download the ISOs you need. Go to the following site and follow the instructions to download a Red Hat Enterprise Linux server ISO or sign up to get an evaluation copy:

https://access.redhat.com/downloads

Red Hat does not offer live versions of Red Hat Enterprise Linux. Instead, you can download installation DVDs that you can install as described in Chapter 9 of this book.

> **NOTE**
>
> If you are unable to obtain a Red Hat Enterprise Linux installation DVD, you can get a similar experience using the CentOS installation DVD. CentOS is not exactly the same as RHEL. However, if you download the CentOS installation DVD for CentOS 7 from links on the CentOS site (http://www.centos.org/download/), the installation procedure is similar to the one described for Red Hat Enterprise Linux in Chapter 9.

Getting Ubuntu

Many people new to Linux begin by downloading and installing Ubuntu. Ubuntu has a huge fan base and many active contributors. If you have problems with Ubuntu, there are large, active forums where many people are willing to help you overcome problems.

If you already have an Ubuntu system installed, you can follow along with most of this book. You can get Ubuntu with a GNOME desktop, and its default dash shell is similar to bash (or you can switch to bash in Ubuntu to match the shell examples in this book). Although most of the examples of this book focus on Fedora and RHEL, I have added many more references to Ubuntu through out the book in this edition.

To get Ubuntu, you can download a Live ISO image or installation medium from the Download Ubuntu page: `http://www.ubuntu.com/download/ubuntu/downloaddesktop`.

Figure A.2 shows an example of the Download Ubuntu Desktop page.

FIGURE A.2

Download Ubuntu Live CD ISO images, or choose an alternative download.

As with Fedora, the easiest way to download Ubuntu is to select the 64-bit Ubuntu Live CD, download it, and burn it. Here's how to do that from the Download Ubuntu page:

1. Click the Download button. By default, this downloads the most recent 64-bit Ubuntu desktop Live ISO image.

2. Either you are asked where you want to download the ISO image or it simply begins downloading to a default folder.

A

3. If you are asked where to put the ISO, select a folder that has enough space to hold the ISO. Remember where this folder is because you need to locate the ISO when you go to burn it later.

After the download is complete, burn the ISO image to a DVD using procedures described in the "Creating Linux CDs and DVDs" section.

Other types of Ubuntu installation media are also available. To find other Ubuntu media, go to the Alternative Downloads page (`http://www.ubuntu.com/download/alternative-downloads`). From this site, you can get media that contains a variety of desktop and server installs.

Creating Linux CDs and DVDs

After you have downloaded a Linux CD or DVD image, you can use several tools to create bootable CDs or DVDs for either installing or just running Linux live from those media. Before you begin, you must have the following:

- **DVD or CD ISO images**—Download the ISO images to your computer that represent the physical DVD or CD you will ultimately burn. Today, many Linux ISO images are too big to fit on a DVD (including those for RHEL, Fedora, and Ubuntu).
- **Blank DVDs/CDs**—You need blank DVDs or CDs to burn the images to. CDs hold up to about 700MB; DVDs hold up to about 4.7GB (single layer).
- **CD/DVD burner**—You need a drive that is capable of burning CDs or DVDs, depending on which you are burning. Not all CD/DVD drives can burn DVDs (especially older ones). So you may need to find a computer with a drive that has that capability.

The following sections describe how to burn bootable CDs and DVDs from Windows, Mac OS X, and Linux systems.

Burning CDs/DVDs in Windows

If you have downloaded your Linux ISO image to a Windows system, you can burn that image to CD or DVD in different ways. Here are some examples:

- **Windows**—In the latest Windows releases, the function of burning ISO images to CD or DVD is built into Windows. After an ISO image is downloaded, simply insert the appropriate CD or DVD into your computer's drive (assuming the drive is writeable), right-click the ISO image icon from the folder you downloaded it to, and select Burn disc image. When the Windows Disc Image Burner window appears, select Burn to burn the image.

- **Roxio Creator**—This third-party Windows application contains many features for ripping and burning CDs and DVDs. You can read about the product here: http://www.roxio.com/enu/products/creator/.

- **Nero CD/DVD Burning ROM**—Nero is another popular CD/DVD burning software product for Windows systems. You can find out more about Nero here: http://www.nero.com.

Burning CDs/DVDs on a Mac OS X system

Like Windows, Mac OS X has CD/DVD burning software built into the operating system. To burn an ISO image to disk on a Mac OS X system, follow these steps:

1. Download the ISO image you want on your Mac OS X system. An icon representing the ISO should appear on your desktop.

2. Insert a blank CD or DVD into your CD/DVD burner, as appropriate for the size of the image.

3. Right-click the icon representing the Linux ISO you just downloaded, and select Burn "Linux" to Disk. A pop-up window appears, asking if you are sure you want to burn the image.

4. Fill in the name you want to give the ISO and the write speed. Then select Burn. The image begins burning to disk.

5. After the image has been burned, eject the disk; you are ready to boot the CD or DVD on an appropriate computer.

Burning CDs/DVDs in Linux

Linux has both graphical and command-line tools for burning CD and DVD images to physical media. Examples in this section show how to use K3b from the desktop or cdrecord (or wodim) to burn ISO images to CD or DVD. If they are not installed, you can install either one as follows:

```
# yum install k3b
# yum install wodim
```

Burning CDs from a Linux desktop

Here's how to create bootable Linux CDs from a running Linux system (such as Fedora) using K3b. K3b comes with the KDE desktop but runs on the GNOME desktop as well.

1. Download the ISO images you want to your computer's hard drive. (A CD image is under about 700MB in size. Single-layer DVD images are under 4.7GB.)

2. Open a CD/DVD burning application. For this procedure, I recommend K3b CD and DVD Kreator (http://www.k3b.org). In Fedora, select Activities and type **K3b**

A

(or type **k3b** from a Terminal window). The "K3b – The CD and DVD Kreator" window appears.

3. From the K3b window, select Tools ⇨ Burn Image to burn a CD or DVD ISO Image. You are asked to choose an image file.

4. Browse to the image you just downloaded or copied to hard disk, and select it. After you select the image you want, the Burn Image window appears, as does a checksum on the image. (Often, you can compare the checksum number that appears against the number in an md5 file from the download directory where you got the image, to make sure the image was not corrupted.) Figure A.3 shows the Burn CD Image window ready to burn an image of Fedora.

FIGURE A.3

Use K3b to burn your Linux CDs or DVDs.

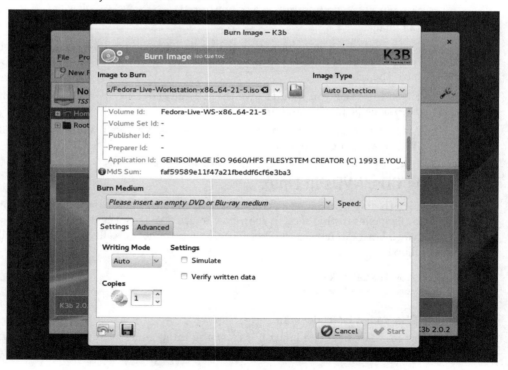

5. Insert a blank CD or DVD into the CD/DVD drive, which may be a combination CD/DVD drive. (If a CD/DVD Creator window pops up, you can close it.)

6. Check the settings in the Burn CD Image window (often, the defaults are fine, but you may want to slow down the speed if you get some bad burns). You can also select the Simulate check box to test the burn before actually writing to the CD/DVD. Click Start to continue.

7. When the CD is finished burning, eject it (or it may eject automatically) and mark it appropriately (information such as the distribution name, version number, date, and name of the ISO image).

Now you're ready to begin installing (or booting) the Linux distribution you just burned.

Burning CDs from a Linux command line

If you have no GUI, or you don't mind working from the shell, you can use the `cdrecord` command to burn the ISOs. With a blank CD inserted and the ISO image you want to burn in the current directory, you can use the following simple command line for burning a CD image to CD using `cdrecord`:

```
# cdrecord -v whatever.iso
```

See the `cdrecord` man page (`man cdrecord`) for other options available with the `cdrecord` command.

Booting Linux from a USB Drive

Instead of burning ISO images to a CD or DVD, you can put your Linux system on a USB drive. USB drives offer the advantage of being writable as well as readable, so you can save your content between sessions. Most modern computers can boot from a USB drive, although you may have to interrupt the boot process to tell the BIOS to boot from USB instead of hard drive or CD/DVD drive.

You can find procedures for putting Fedora and Ubuntu on a USB drive in the following locations:

- **Fedora on USB drive**—Using a tool called Live USB Creator (`https://fedorahosted .org/liveusb-creator/`), you can install a Fedora ISO image to a USB drive in either Windows or Linux. To run Fedora from that drive, insert it into a USB port on your computer, reboot the computer, interrupt the BIOS as it is booting (possibly F12), and select to boot from a USB drive. The procedure for using Live USB creator is located at `https://fedoraproject.org/wiki/ How_to_create_and_use_Live_USB`.

- **Ubuntu on USB drive**—Ubuntu has procedures for creating a bootable USB drive with Ubuntu on it that work from Windows, Mac OS X, or Linux. To find out how to do this, go to the Ubuntu Download page and under "Easy ways to switch to

A

Ubuntu," look for the appropriate "How to create a bootable USB stick..." procedure for Ubuntu, Windows, or Mac OS X: `http://www.ubuntu.com/download/ubuntu/downloaddesktop`.

Visit the *Linux Bible* website

To find links to various Linux distributions and other useful content related to Linux, go to the *Linux Bible*, Ninth Edition website: `http://www.wiley.com/go/linuxbible9`.

Exercise Answers

This appendix provides answers to each of the chapter exercises. There are many ways to accomplish tasks in Linux. The answers provided here are suggestions.

Some of the exercises require that you modify system files that could change the basic functioning of your system, or even make it unbootable. Therefore, I recommend that you do the exercises on a Linux system that you are free to modify and erase if something should go wrong.

Chapter 2: Creating the Perfect Linux Desktop

The following section details some ways these tasks can be completed on both the GNOME 2 and GNOME 3 desktops.

1. To get started, you need a Linux system in front of you to do the procedures in this book. An installed system is preferable so you don't lose your changes when you reboot. To start out, you can use a Fedora Live CD (or installed system), an Ubuntu installed system, or a Red Hat Enterprise Linux installed system. Here are your choices:

    - **Fedora Live CD (GNOME 3)**—Get a Fedora Live CD as described in Appendix A. Run it live, as described in the "Starting with the Fedora GNOME Desktop Live CD" section of Chapter 2, or install it and run it from hard disk as described in Chapter 9, "Installing Linux."

    - **Ubuntu (GNOME 3)**—Install Ubuntu, and install the GNOME Shell software as described in the beginning of Chapter 2.

    - **Red Hat Enterprise Linux 7 (GNOME 3)**—Install Red Hat Enterprise Linux 7 as described in Chapter 9.

    - **Red Hat Enterprise Linux 6 or earlier (GNOME 2)**—Install Red Hat Enterprise Linux 6 as described in Chapter 9.

2. To launch the Firefox web browser and go to the GNOME home page (http://gnome.org), there are some easy steps to take. If your networking is not working, refer to Chapter 14, "Administering Networking," for help connecting to wired and wireless networks.

    - For GNOME 3, you can press the Windows key to get to the Overview screen. Then type **Firefox** to highlight just the Firefox Web Browser icon. Press Enter to launch it. Type **http://gnome.org** in the location box, and press Enter.

    - For GNOME 2, select the Firefox icon from the top menu bar. Type **http://gnome.org** in the location box, and press Enter.

3. To pick a background you like from the GNOME art site (`http://gnome-look. org`), download it to your Pictures folder, and select it as your current background on both GNOME 2 and GNOME 3 systems, do the following:

    a. Type `http://gnome-look.org/` in the Firefox location box, and press Enter.

    b. Find a background you like and select it, and then click zoom to display it.

    c. Right-click the image, and select Set as Desktop Background.

    d. From the pop-up that appears, select the position and color of the background image.

    e. Select the Set Desktop Background button. The image is used as your desktop background, and the image is copied to the file `Firefox_wallpaper.png` in your home directory.

4. To start a Nautilus File Manager window and move it to the second workspace on your desktop, do the following:

    - For GNOME 3:

    a. Press the Windows key.

    b. Grab the Files icon from the Dash (left side) and drag it onto an unused workspace on the right side. A new instance of Nautilus starts in that workspace.

    - For GNOME 2:

    a. Open the Home folder from the GNOME 2 desktop (double-click).

    b. Right-click in the Nautilus title bar that appears, and select either Move to Workspace Right or Move to Another Workspace (you can select which workspace you want from the list).

5. To find the image you downloaded to use as your desktop background and open it in any image viewer, first go to your Home folder.

    The image should appear in that folder when you open Nautilus. Simply double-click the `Firefox_wallpaper.png` icon to open the image in the default image viewer. If you have multiple image viewers on your system, right-click the icon and select the application you want to use to open it.

6. Moving back and forth between the workspace with Firefox on it and the one with the Nautilus file manager is fairly straightforward.

    If you did the previous exercises properly, Nautilus and Firefox should be in different workspaces. Here's how you can move between those workspaces in GNOME 3 and GNOME 2:

    - In GNOME 3, press the Windows key, and double-click the workspace you want in the right column. As an alternative, you can go directly to the application you want by pressing Alt+Tab and pressing Tab again to highlight the application you want to open.

- In GNOME 2, select the workspace you want with your mouse by clicking the small representation of the workspace in the right side of the lower panel. If you happen to have Desktop Effects enabled (System ⇨ Preferences Desktop Effects ⇨ Compiz), try pressing Ctrl+Alt+right arrow (or left arrow) to spin to the next workspace.

7. To open a list of applications installed on your system and select an image viewer to open from that list using as few clicks or keystrokes as possible, do the following:

   - In GNOME 3, move the mouse to the upper-left corner of the screen to get to the Overview screen. Select Applications, select Graphics from the right column, and then select Image Viewer.

   - In GNOME 2, select Applications ⇨ Graphics ⇨ Image Viewer to open an image viewer window on the desktop.

8. To change the view of the windows on your current workspace to smaller views of those windows you can step through, do the following:

   - In GNOME 3, with multiple windows open on multiple workspaces, press and hold the Alt+Tab keys. While continuing to hold the Alt key, press Tab until you highlight the application you want. Release the Alt key to select it. (Notice that applications that are not on the current workspace are to the right of a line dividing the icons.)

   - In GNOME 2, with multiple windows open on multiple workspaces, press and hold the Ctrl+Alt+Tab keys. While continuing to hold the Ctrl+Alt keys, press Tab until you have highlighted the application you want. Release the Ctrl and Alt keys to select it.

9. To launch a music player from your desktop using only the keyboard, do the following:

   - In GNOME 3:

   a. Press the Windows key to go to the Overview screen.

   b. Type **Rhyth** (until the icon appears and is highlighted), and press Enter. (In Ubuntu, if you don't have Rhythmbox installed, type **Bansh** to open the Banshee Media Player.)

   - In GNOME 2:

   Press Alt+F2. From the Run Application box that appears, type **rhythmbox** and press Enter.

10. To take a picture of your desktop using only keystrokes, press the Print Screen key to take a screenshot of your entire desktop in both GNOME 3 and GNOME 2. Press Alt+Print Screen to take a screenshot of just the current window. In both cases, the images are saved to the Pictures folder in your home folder.

B

Chapter 3: Using the Shell

1. To switch virtual consoles and return to the desktop:

   a. Hold Ctrl+Alt and press F2 (Ctrl+Alt+F2). A text-based console should appear.

   b. Type your username (press Enter) and password (press Enter).

   c. Type a few commands, such as **id**, **pwd**, and **ls**.

   d. Type **exit** to exit the shell and return to the login prompt.

   e. Press Ctrl+Alt+F1 to return to the virtual console that holds your desktop. (On different Linux systems, the desktop may be on different virtual consoles. Ctrl+Alt+F7 is another common place to find it.)

2. For your Terminal window, to make the font red and the background yellow:

   a. From the GNOME desktop, select Applications⇨System Tools⇨Terminal to open a Terminal window.

   b. From the Terminal window, select Edit⇨Profiles.

   c. With Default highlighted from the Profiles window, select Edit.

   d. Select the Colors Tab and deselect the Use colors from system theme box.

   e. Select the box next to Text Color, click the color red you want from the color wheel, and click OK.

   f. Select the box next to Background Color, click the color yellow you want from the color wheel, and click OK.

   g. Click Close on each window to go back to the Terminal window with the new colors.

   h. Go back and reselect the Use colors from system theme box to go back to the default Terminal colors.

3. To find the mount command and tracepath man page:

   - Run type mount to see that the mount command's location is /bin/mount.

   - Run locate tracepath to see that the tracepath man page is at /usr/share/man/man8/tracepath.8.gz.

4. To run, recall, and change these commands as described:

   ```
   $ cat /etc/passwd
   $ ls $HOME
   $ date
   ```

   a. Press the up arrow until you see the cat /etc/passwd command. If your cursor is not already at the end of the line, press Ctrl+E to get there. Backspace over the word passwd, type the word **group**, and press Enter.

   b. Type **man ls** and find the option to list by time (-t). Press the up arrow until you see the ls $HOME command. Use the left arrow key or Alt+B to position your cursor to the left of $HOME. Type **-t**, so the line appears as ls -t $HOME. Press Enter to run the command.

c. Type **man date** to view the date man page. Use the up arrow to recall the date command and add the format indicator you found. A single %D format indicator gets the results you need:

```
$ date +%D
12/08/11
```

5. Use tab completion to type **basename /usr/share/doc/**. Type **basen<Tab> /u<Tab>sh<Tab>do<Tab>** to get basename /usr/share/doc/.

6. Pipe /etc/services to the less command: $ **cat /etc/services | less**.

7. Make output from the date command appear in this format: Today is Thursday, December 10, 2015.

```
$ echo "Today is $(date +'%A, %B %d, %Y')"
```

8. View variables to find your current hostname, username, shell, and home directories.

```
$ echo $HOSTNAME
$ echo $USERNAME
$ echo $SHELL
$ echo $HOME
```

9. To add a permanent mypass alias that displays the contents of the /etc/passwd file:

a. Type **nano $HOME/.bashrc**.

b. Move the cursor to an open line at the bottom of the page (press Enter to open a new line if needed).

c. On its own line, type **alias m="cat /etc/passwd"**.

d. Type Ctrl+O to save and Ctrl+X to exit the file.

d. Type **source $HOME/.bashrc**.

e. Type **alias m** to make sure the alias was set properly: alias m='cat /etc/ passwd'.

f. Type **m** (the /etc/passwd file displays on the screen).

10. To display the man page for the mount system call, use the man -k command to find man pages that include the word mount (using the ^ ensures that only commands beginning with the word mount are displayed). Then use the mount command with the correct section number (2) to get the proper mount man page:

```
$ man -k ^mount
mount              (2)  - mount file system
mount              (8)  - mount a filesystem
mountpoint         (1)  - see if a directory is a mountpoint
mountstats         (8)  - Displays NFS client per-mount statistics
```

B

785

```
$ man 2 mount
MOUNT(2)          Linux Programmer's Manual                MOUNT(2)
NAME
       mount - mount file system
SYNOPSIS
       #include <sys/mount.h>
       .
       .
       .
```

Chapter 4: Moving around the Filesystem

1. Create the projects directory, create nine empty files (house1 to house9), and list just those files.

   ```
   $ mkdir $HOME/projects/
   $ touch $HOME/projects/house{1..9}
   $ ls $HOME/projects/house{1..9}
   ```

2. Make the $HOME/projects/houses/doors/ directory path, and create some empty files in that path.

   ```
   $ cd
   $ mkdir projects/houses
   $ touch $HOME/projects/houses/bungalow.txt
   $ mkdir $HOME/projects/houses/doors/
   $ touch $HOME/projects/houses/doors/bifold.txt
   $ mkdir -p $HOME/projects/outdoors/vegetation/
   $ touch projects/outdoors/vegetation/landscape.txt
   ```

3. Copy the files house1 and house5 to the $HOME/projects/houses/ directory.

   ```
   $ cp $HOME/projects/house[15]  $HOME/projects/houses
   ```

4. Recursively copy the /usr/share/doc/initscripts* directory to the $HOME/ projects/ directory.

   ```
   $ cp -ra /usr/share/doc/initscripts*/ $HOME/projects/
   ```

5. Recursively list the contents of the $HOME/projects/ directory. Pipe the output to the less command so you can page through the output.

   ```
   $ ls -lR $HOME/projects/ | less
   ```

6. Remove the files house6, house7, and house8 without being prompted.

   ```
   $ rm -f $HOME/projects/house[678]
   ```

7. Move house3 and house4 to the $HOME/projects/houses/doors directory.

   ```
   $ mv projects/house{3,4} projects/houses/doors/
   ```

8. Remove the $HOME/projects/houses/doors directory and its contents.

   ```
   $ rm -rf projects/houses/doors/
   ```

9. Change the permissions on the $HOME/projects/house2 file so it can be read and written to by the user who owns the file, only read by the group, and have no permission for others.

```
$ chmod 640 $HOME/projects/house2
```

10. Recursively change the permissions of the $HOME/projects/ directory so that nobody has write permission to any files or directory beneath that point in the file system.

```
$ chmod -R a-w $HOME/projects/
$ ls -lR /home/joe/projects/
/home/joe/projects/:
total 12
-r--r--r--. 1 joe joe    0 Jan 16 06:49 house1
-r--r-----. 1 joe joe    0 Jan 16 06:49 house2
-r--r--r--. 1 joe joe    0 Jan 16 06:49 house5
-r--r--r--. 1 joe joe    0 Jan 16 06:49 house9
dr-xr-xr-x. 2 joe joe 4096 Jan 16 06:57 houses
dr-xr-xr-x. 2 joe joe 4096 Jul  1  2014 initscripts-9.03.40
dr-xr-xr-x. 3 joe joe 4096 Jan 16 06:53 outdoors
```

Chapter 5: Working with Text Files

1. Follow these steps to create the /tmp/services file, and then edit it so that "WorldWideWeb" appears as "World Wide Web".

```
$ cp /etc/services /tmp
$ vi /tmp/services
/WorldWideWeb<Enter>
cwWorld Wide Web<Esc>
```

The next two lines show the before and after.

```
http            80/tcp        www www-http    # WorldWideWeb HTTP
http            80/tcp        www www-http    # World Wide Web HTTP
```

2. One way to move the paragraph in your /tmp/services file is to search for the first line of the paragraph, delete five lines (5dd), go to the end of the file (G), and put in the text (p):

```
$ vi /tmp/services
/Note that it is<Enter>
5dd
G
p
```

3. To use ex mode to search for every occurrence of the term tcp (case sensitive) in your /tmp/services file and change it to WHATEVER, you can type the following:

```
$ vi /tmp/services
:g/tcp/s//WHATEVER/g<Enter>
```

B

4. To search the /etc directory for every file named passwd and redirect errors from your search to /dev/null, you can type the following:

```
$ find /etc -name passwd 2> /dev/null
```

5. Create a directory in your home directory called TEST. Create files in that directory named one, two, and three that have full read/write/execute permissions on for everyone (user, group, and other). Construct a find command that would find those files and any other files that have write permission open to "others" from your home directory and below.

```
$ mkdir $HOME/TEST
$ touch $HOME/TEST/{one,two,three}
$ chmod 777 $HOME/TEST/{one,two,three}
$ find $HOME -perm -002 -type f -ls
148120 0 -rwxrwxrwx 1 chris chris 0 Jan 1 08:56 /home/chris/TEST/two
148918 0 -rwxrwxrwx 1 chris chris 0 Jan 1 08:56 home/chris/TEST/three
147306 0 -rwxrwxrwx 1 chris chris 0 Jan 1 08:56 /home/chris/TEST/one
```

6. Find files under the /usr/share/doc directory that have not been modified in more than 300 days.

```
$ find /usr/share/doc -mtime +300
```

7. Create a /tmp/FILES directory. Find all files under the /usr/share directory that are more than 5MB and less than 10MB and copy them to the /tmp/FILES directory.

```
$ mkdir /tmp/FILES
$ find /usr/share -size +5M -size -10M -exec cp {} /tmp/FILES \;
$ du -sh /tmp/FILES/*
7.0M    /tmp/FILES/cangjie5.db
5.4M    /tmp/FILES/cangjie-big.db
8.3M    /tmp/FILES/icon-theme.cache
```

8. Find every file in the /tmp/FILES directory and make a backup copy of each file in the same directory. Use each file's existing name and just append .mybackup to create each backup file.

```
$ find /tmp/FILES/ -type f -exec cp {} {}.mybackup \;
```

9. Install the kernel-doc package in Fedora or Red Hat Enterprise Linux. Using grep, search inside the files contained in the /usr/share/doc/kernel-doc* directory for the term e1000 (case insensitive) and list the names of the files that contain that term.

NOTE: The kernel-doc package was dropped for Fedora 21. To complete this exercise for Fedora 21, install kernel-core and use the /usr/share/kcbench-data/ linux-*/Documentation directory instead of /usr/share/doc/kernel-doc*.

```
# yum install kernel-doc
$ cd /usr/share/doc/kernel-doc*
$ grep -rli e1000 .
./Documentation/powerpc/booting-without-of.txt
./Documentation/networking/e100.txt
. . .
```

10. Search for the `e1000` term again in the same location, but this time list every line that contains the term and highlight the term in color.

```
$ cd /usr/share/doc/kernel-doc-*
$ grep -ri --color e1000 .
```

Chapter 6: Managing Running Processes

1. To list all processes running on your system with a full set of columns, while piping the output to `less`, type the following:

```
$ ps -ef | less
```

2. To list all processes running on the system and sort those processes by the name of the user running each process, type the following:

```
$ ps -ef --sort=user | less
```

3. To list all processes running on the system with the column names process ID, user name, group name, nice value, virtual memory size, resident memory size, and command, type the following:

```
$ ps -eo 'pid,user,group,nice,vsz,rss,comm' | less
PID USER       GROUP     NI    VSZ    RSS COMMAND
  1 root       root       0  19324  1236 init
  2 root       root       0      0     0 kthreadd
  3 root       root       -      0     0 migration/0
  4 root       root       0      0     0 ksoftirqd/0
```

4. To run the `top` command and then go back and forth between sorting by CPU usage and memory consumption, type the following:

```
$ top
P
M
P
M
```

5. To start the `gedit` process from your desktop and use the System Monitor window to kill that process, type the following:

```
$ gedit &
```

Next, in GNOME 2 select Applications ⇨ System Tools ⇨ System Monitor, or in GNOME 3 type System Monitor from the Activities screen and press Enter. Find the `gedit` process on the Processes tab (you can sort alphabetically to make it easier by clicking the Process Name heading). Right-click the `gedit` command, and then select either End Process or Kill Process; the `gedit` window on your screen should disappear.

B

6. To run the `gedit` process and use the `kill` command to send a signal to pause (stop) that process, type the following:

```
$ gedit &
[1] 21532
$ kill -SIGSTOP 21578
```

7. To use the `killall` command to tell the `gedit` command (paused in the previous exercise) to continue working, do the following:

```
$ killall -SIGCONT gedit
```

Make sure the text you typed after `gedit` was paused now appears in the window.

8. To install the `xeyes` command, run it about 20 times in the background, and run `killall` to kill all 20 `xeyes` processes at once, type the following:

```
# yum install xorg-x11-apps
$ xeyes &
$ xeyes &
. . .
$ killall xeyes
```

Remember, you need to be the root user to install the package. After that, remember to repeat the `xeyes` command 20 times. Spread the windows around on your screen, and move the mouse for fun to watch the eyes move. All the `xeyes` windows should disappear at once when you type `killall xeyes`.

9. As a regular user, run the `gedit` command so it starts with a nice value of 5.

```
$ nice -n 5 gedit &
[1] 21578
```

10. To use the `renice` command to change the nice value of the `gedit` command you just started to 7, type the following:

```
$ renice -n 7 21578
21578: old priority 0, new priority 7
```

Use any command you like to verify that the current nice value for the `gedit` command is now set to 7. For example, you could type this:

```
$ ps -eo 'pid,user,nice,comm' | grep gedit
21578 chris        7 gedit
```

Chapter 7: Writing Simple Shell Scripts

1. Here's an example of how to create a script in your $HOME/bin directory called myownscript. When the script runs, it should output information that looks as follows:

```
Today is Sat Dec 10 15:45:04 EDT 2016.
You are in /home/joe and your host is abc.example.com.
```

The following steps show one way to create the script named `myownscript`:

a. If it doesn't already exist, create a bin directory:

```
$ mkdir $HOME/bin
```

b. Using any text editor, create a script called $HOME/bin/myownscript that contains the following:

```
#!/bin/bash
# myownscript
# List some information about your current system
echo "Today is $(date)."
echo "You are in $(pwd) and your host is $(hostname)."
```

c. Make the script executable:

```
$ chmod 755 $HOME/bin/myownscript
```

2. To create a script that reads in three positional parameters from the command line, assigns those parameters to variables named ONE, TWO, and THREE, respectively, and then outputs that information in the specified format, do the following:

a. Replace X with the number of parameters and Y with all parameters entered. Then replace A with the contents of variable ONE, B with variable TWO, and C with variable THREE.

Here is an example of what that script could contain:

```
#!/bin/bash
# myposition
ONE=$1
TWO=$2
THREE=$3
echo "There are $# parameters that include: $@"
echo "The first is $ONE, the second is $TWO, the third is
$THREE."
```

b. To create a script called $HOME/bin/myposition and make the script executable, type this:

```
$ chmod 755 $HOME/bin/myposition
```

c. To test it, run it with some command-line arguments, as in the following:

```
$ myposition Where Is My Hat Buddy?
There are 5 parameters that include: Where Is My Hat Buddy?
The first is Where, the second is Is, the third is My.
```

3. To create the script described, do the following:

a. To create a file called $HOME/bin/myhome and make it executable, type this:

```
$ touch $HOME/bin/myhome
$ chmod 755 $HOME/bin/myhome
```

B

b. Here's what the script `myhome` might look like:

```
#!/bin/bash
# myhome
read -p "What street did you grow up on? " mystreet
read -p "What town did you grow up in? " mytown
echo "The street I grew up on was $mystreet and the town was
$mytown."
```

c. Run the script to check that it works. The following example shows what input and output for the script could look like:

```
$ myhome
What street did you grow up on? Harrison
What town did you grow up in? Princeton
The street I grew up on was Harrison and the town was Princeton.
```

4. To create the required script, do the following:

a. Using any text editor, create a script called $HOME/bin/myos and make the script executable:

```
$ touch $HOME/bin/myos
$ chmod 755 $HOME/bin/myos
```

b. The script could contain the following:

```
#!/bin/bash
# myos
read -p "What is your favorite operating system, Mac, Windows or
    Linux? " opsys
if [ $opsys = Mac ] ; then
  echo "Mac is nice, but not tough enough for me."
elif [ $opsys = Windows ] ; then
  echo "I used Windows once. What is that blue screen for?"
elif [ $opsys = Linux ] ; then
  echo "Great Choice!"
else
  echo "Is $opsys an operating system?"
fi
```

5. To create a script named $HOME/bin/animals that runs the words moose, cow, goose, and sow through a for loop and have each of those words appended to the end of the line, "I have a...," do the following:

a. Make the script executable:

```
$ touch $HOME/bin/animals
$ chmod 755 $HOME/bin/animals
```

b. The script could contain the following:

```
#!/bin/bash
# animals
```

```
for ANIMALS in moose cow goose sow ; do
  echo "I have a $ANIMALS"
done
```

c. When you run the script, the output should look as follows:

```
$ animals
I have a moose
I have a cow
I have a goose
I have a sow
```

Chapter 8: Learning System Administration

1. You can open the Date & Time window from a GNOME desktop in RHEL or Fedora by doing one of the following:

   - If it isn't already installed, install the system-config-date package (`yum install system-config-date`).

   - Open a Terminal window and type **system-config-date**. If you do that as a regular user, you are prompted for the root password.

   - From a GNOME 2.X desktop, select System Administration Date & Time.

   - From a GNOME 3 desktop, select Activities and type System-Config-Date. When the Date & Time window opens, select the Time Zone tab to check your time zone.

2. To use System Monitor to sort all processes running on your system by username, type System Monitor from the Activities screen and press Enter. Click the settings button (icon with three lines), click All Processes, and click the User column. This sorts the processes by user name. Scroll down to see the processes.

3. To find all files under the `/var/spool` directory that are owned by users other than root and do a long listing of them, type the following (I recommend becoming root to find files that might be closed off to other users):

```
$ su -
Password: *********
# find /var/spool -not -user root -ls | less
```

4. To become root user and create an empty or plain text file named `/mnt/test.txt`, type the following:

```
$ su -
Password: *********
# touch /mnt/test.txt
# ls -l /mnt/test.txt
-rw-r--r--. 1 root root 0 Jan  9 21:51 /mnt/test.txt
```

B

5. To become root and edit the /etc/sudoers file to allow your regular user account (for example, bill) to have full root privilege via the sudo command, do the following:

```
$ su -
Password: *********
# visudo
o
bill      ALL=(ALL)      ALL
Esc ZZ
```

Because visudo opens the /etc/sudoers file in vi, the example types o to open a line, and then types in the line to allow bill to have full root privilege. After the line is typed, press ESC to return to command mode and type ZZ to write and quit.

6. To use the sudo command to create a file called /mnt/test2.txt and verify that the file is there and owned by the root user, type the following:

```
[bill]$ sudo touch /mnt/test2.txt
We trust you have received the usual lecture from the local System
Administrator. It usually boils down to these three things:
    #1) Respect the privacy of others.
    #2) Think before you type.
    #3) With great power comes great responsibility.
[sudo] password for bill:
*********
[bill]$ ls -l /mnt/text2.txt
-rw-r--r--. 1 root root 0 Jan  9 23:37 /mnt/text2.txt
```

7. Do the following to mount and unmount a USB drive and watch the system journal during this process:

   a. Run the journalctl -f command as root in a Terminal window and watch the output from here for the next few steps.

```
# journalctl -f
Jan 25 16:07:59 host2 kernel: usb 1-1.1: new high-speed USB device
    number 16 using ehci-pci
Jan 25 16:07:59 host2 kernel: usb 1-1.1: New USB device found,
    idVendor=0ea0, idProduct=2168
Jan 25 16:07:59 host2 kernel: usb 1-1.1: New USB device strings:
    Mfr=1, Product=2, SerialNumber=3
Jan 25 16:07:59 host2 kernel: usb 1-1.1: Product: Flash Disk
Jan 25 16:07:59 host2 kernel: usb 1-1.1: Manufacturer: USB
...
Jan 25 16:08:01 host2 kernel: sd 18:0:0:0: [sdb] Write Protect is off
Jan 25 16:08:01 host2 kernel: sd 18:0:0:0: [sdb]
    Assuming drive cache: write through
Jan 25 16:08:01 host2 kernel:  sdb: sdb1
Jan 25 16:08:01 host2 kernel: sd 18:0:0:0: [sdb]
    Attached SCSI removable disk
```

b. Plug in a USB storage drive, which should mount a filesystem from that drive automatically. If it does not, run the following commands in a second terminal (as root) to create a mount point directory and mount the device:

```
# mkdir /mnt/test
# mount /dev/sdb1 /mnt/test
```

c. Unmount the device and unplug the USB drive:

```
# umount /dev/sdb1
```

8. To see what USB devices are connected to your computer, type the following:

```
$ lsusb
```

9. To load the bttv module, list the modules that were loaded, and unload it, type the following:

```
# modprobe -a bttv
# lsmod | grep bttv
bttv                   124516  0
v4l2_common             10572  1 bttv
videobuf_dma_sg          9814  1 bttv
videobuf_core           20076  2 bttv,videobuf_dma_sg
btcx_risc                4416  1 bttv
rc_core                 19686  7 ir_lirc_codec,ir_sony_decoder,
     ir_jvc_decoder,ir_rc6_decoder
tveeprom                14042  1 bttv
videodev                76244  3 bttv,v4l2_common,uvcvideo
i2c_algo_bit             5728  2 bttv,i915
i2c_core                31274  9 bttv,v4l2_common,tveeprom,videodev,
     i2c_i801,i915,drm_kms_helper
```

Notice that other modules (v4l2_common, videodev, and others) were loaded when you loaded bttv with modprobe -a.

10. Type the following to remove the bttv module along with any other modules that were loaded with it. Notice that they were all gone after running modprobe -r.

```
# modprobe -r bttv
# lsmod | grep bttv
```

Chapter 9: Installing Linux

1. To install a Fedora system from Fedora live media, follow the instructions in the "Installing Fedora from Live Media" section. In general, those steps include:

a. Booting the Live media.

b. Selecting to install to hard drive when the system boots up.

c. Adding information from the summary page about your language, storage, hostname, time zone, root password, and other items needed to initially configure your system.

    d. Rebooting your computer, removing the Live medium, so the newly installed system boots from hard disk.

2. To update the packages, after the Fedora Live media installation is complete, do the following:

    a. Reboot the computer and fill in the first boot questions as prompted.

    b. Using a wired or wireless connection, make sure you have a connection to the Internet. Refer to Chapter 14, "Administering Networking," if you have trouble getting your networking connection to work properly. Open a shell as the root user and type `yum update`.

    c. When prompted, type `y` to accept the list of packages displayed. The system begins downloading and installing the packages.

3. To run the RHEL installation in text mode, do the following:

    a. Boot the RHEL DVD.

    b. When you see the boot menu, highlight one of the installation boot entries and press Tab. Move the cursor right to the end of the kernel line and type the literal option `text` at the end of that line. Press Enter to start the installer.

    c. Try out the rest of the installation in text mode.

4. To set the disk partitioning as described in Question 4 for a Red Hat Enterprise Linux DVD installation, do the following:

> **CAUTION**
>
> This procedure ultimately deletes all content on your hard disk. If you want to just use this exercise to practice partitioning, you can reboot your computer before clicking Next at the very end of this procedure without harming your hard disk. After you go forward and partition your disk, assume that all data has been deleted.

    a. On a computer you can erase with at least 10GB of disk space, insert a RHEL installation DVD, reboot, and begin stepping through the installation screens.

    b. When you get to the Installation Summary screen, select Installation Destination.

    c. From the Installation Destination screen, select the device to use for the installation (probably `sda` if you have a single hard disk that you can completely erase or `vda` for a virtual install).

    d. Select the "I will configure partitioning" button.

    e. Select Done to get to the Manual Partitioning screen.

    f. If the existing disk space is already consumed, you need to delete the partitions before proceeding.

    g. Click the plus (+) button at the bottom of the screen. Then add each of the following mount points:

```
/boot - 400M
/ - 3G
/var - 2G
/home -2G
```

h. Select Done. You should see a summary of changes.

i. If the changes look acceptable, select Accept Changes. If you are just practicing and don't actually want to change your partitions, select Cancel & Return to Custom Partitioning. Then simply exit the installer.

Chapter 10: Getting and Managing Software

1. To search the YUM repository for the package that provides the mogrify command, type the following:

   ```
   # yum provides mogrify
   ```

2. To display information about the package that provides the mogrify command and determine what that package's home page (URL) is, type the following:

   ```
   # yum info ImageMagick
   ```

   You will see that the URL to the home page for ImageMagick is http://www
   .imagemagick.org.

3. To install the package containing the mogrify command, type the following:

   ```
   # yum install ImageMagick
   ```

4. To list all the documentation files contained in the package that provides the mogrify command, type the following:

   ```
   # rpm -qd ImageMagick
   ...
   /usr/share/doc/ImageMagick/README.txt
   ...
   /usr/share/man/man1/identify.1.gz
   /usr/share/man/man1/import.1.gz
   /usr/share/man/man1/mogrify.1.gz
   ```

5. To look through the change log of the package that provides the mogrify command, type the following:

   ```
   # rpm -q --changelog ImageMagick | less
   ```

6. To delete the mogrify command from your system and verify its package against the RPM database to see that the command is indeed missing, type the following:

   ```
   # type mogrify
   mogrify is /usr/bin/mogrify
   # rm /usr/bin/mogrify
   ```

B

```
rm remove regular file '/usr/bin/mogrify'? y
# rpm -V ImageMagick
missing   /usr/bin/mogrify
```

7. To reinstall the package that provides the mogrify command and make sure the entire package is intact again, type the following:

```
# yum reinstall ImageMagick
# rpm -V ImageMagick
```

8. To download the package that provides the mogrify command to your current directory, type the following:

```
# yumdownloader ImageMagick
ImageMagick-6.8.8.10-5.fc21.x86_64.rpm
```

9. To display general information about the package you just downloaded by querying the package's RPM file in the current directory, type the following:

```
# rpm -qip ImageMagick-6.8.8.10-5.fc21.x86_64.rpm
Name        : ImageMagick
Version     : 6.8.8.10
Release     : 5.fc21
Architecture: x86_64
...
```

10. To remove the package containing the mogrify command from your system, type the following:

```
# yum remove ImageMagick
```

Chapter 11: Managing User Accounts

For questions that involve adding and removing user accounts, you can use the Users window, the User Manager window, or command-line tools such as useradd and usermod. The point is to make sure that you get the correct results shown in the answers that follow, not necessarily do it exactly the same way I did. There are multiple ways you can achieve the same results. The answers here show how to complete the exercises from the command line. (Become root user when you see a # prompt.)

1. To add a local user account to your Linux system that has a username of jbaxter and a full name of John Baxter, that uses /bin/sh as its default shell, and that is the next available UID (yours may differ from the one shown here), type the following. You can use the grep command to check the new user account. Then set the password for jbaxter to: My1N1teOut!

```
# useradd -c "John Baxter" -s /bin/sh jbaxter
# grep jbaxter /etc/passwd
jbaxter:x:1001:1001:John Baxter:/home/jbaxter:/bin/sh
# passwd jbaxter
```

```
Changing password for user jbaxter
New password: My1N1te0ut!
Retype new password: My1N1te0ut!
passwd: all authentication tokens updated successfully
```

2. To create a group account named testing that uses group ID 315, type the following:

```
# groupadd -g 315 testing
# grep testing /etc/group
testing:x:315:
```

3. To add jbaxter to the testing group and the bin group, type the following:

```
# usermod -aG testing,bin jbaxter
# grep jbaxter /etc/group
bin:x:1:bin,daemon,jbaxter
jbaxter:x:1001:
testing:x:315:jbaxter
```

4. To become jbaxter and temporarily have the testing group be jbaxter's default group, run touch /home/jbaxter/file.txt—so the testing group is assigned as the file's group—and do the following:

```
$ su - jbaxter
Password: My1N1te0ut!
sh-4.2$ newgrp testing
sh-4.2$ touch /home/jbaxter/file.txt
sh-4.2$ ls -l /home/baxter/file.txt
-rw-rw-r--. 1 jbaxter testing 0 Jan 25 06:42 /home/jbaxter/file.txt
sh-4.2$ exit ; exit
```

5. Note what user ID has been assigned to jbaxter, and then delete the user account without deleting the home directory assigned to jbaxter.

```
$ userdel jbaxter
```

6. Use the following command to find any files in the /home directory (and any subdirectories) that are assigned to the user ID that recently belonged to the user named jbaxter (when I did it, the UID/GID were both 1001; yours may differ). Notice that the username jbaxter is no longer assigned on the system, so any files that user created are listed as belonging to UID 1001 and GID 1001, except for a couple of files that were assigned to the testing group, because of the newgrp command run earlier:

```
# find /home -uid 1001 -ls
262184   4 drwx------ 4 1001   1001   4096 Jan 25 08:00 /home/jbaxter
262193   4 -rw-r--r-- 1 1001   1001    176 Jan 27  2011 /home/jbaxter/
    .bash_profile
262196   4 -rw------- 1 13602 testing 93 Jan 25 08:00 /home/jbaxter/
    .bash_history
262194   0 -rw-rw-r-- 1 13602 testing  0 Jan 25 07:59 /home/jbaxter/
    file.txt
...
```

B

7. Run these commands to copy the `/etc/services` file to the `/etc/skel/` directory; then add a new user to the system named `mjones`, with a full name of Mary Jones and a home directory of `/home/maryjones`. List her home directory to make sure the services file is there.

```
# cp /etc/services /etc/skel/
# useradd -d /home/maryjones -c "Mary Jones" mjones
# ls -l /home/maryjones
total 628
-rw-r--r--. 1 mjones mjones 640999 Jan 25 06:27 services
```

8. Run the following command to find all files under the `/home` directory that belong to `mjones`. If you did the exercises in order, notice that after you deleted the user with the highest user ID and group ID, those numbers were assigned to `mjones`. As a result, any files left on the system by `jbaxter` now belong to `mjones`. (For this reason, you should remove or change ownership of files left behind when you delete a user.)

```
# find /home -user mjones -ls
262184 4 drwx------ 4 mjones mjones 4096 Jan 25 08:00 /home/jbaxter
262193 4 -rw-r--r-- 1 mjones mjones 176 Jan 27 2011 /home/jbaxter/
        .bash_profile
262189 4 -rw-r--r-- 1 mjones mjones 18 Jan 27 2011 /home/jbaxter/
        .bash_logout
262194 0 -rw-rw-r-- 1 mjones testing 0 Jan 25 07:59 /home/jbaxter/
        file.txt
262188 4 -rw-r--r-- 1 mjones mjones 124 Jan 27 2011 /home/jbaxter/
        .bashrc
262197 4 drwx------ 4 mjones  mjones 4096 Jan 25 08:27 /home/
        maryjones
262207 4 -rw-r--r-- 1 mjones mjones 176 Jan 27 2011 /home/
maryjones/
        .bash_profile
262202 4 -rw-r--r-- 1 mjones mjones 18 Jan 27 2011 /home/maryjones/
        .bash_logout
262206 628 -rw-r--r-- 1 mjones mjones 640999 Jan 25 08:27 /home/
        maryjones/services
262201 4 -rw-r--r-- 1 mjones mjones 124 Jan 27 2011 /home/
        maryjones/.bashrc
```

9. As the user `mjones`, you can use the following to create a file called `/tmp/maryfile.txt` and use ACLs to assign the bin user read/write permission and the lp group read/write permission to that file.

```
[mjones]$ touch /tmp/maryfile.txt
[mjones]$ setfacl -m u:bin:rw /tmp/maryfile.txt
[mjones]$ setfacl -m g:lp:rw /tmp/maryfile.txt
[mjones]$ getfacl /tmp/maryfile.txt
# file: tmp/maryfile.txt
# owner: mjones
```

```
# group: mjones
user::rw-
user:bin:rw-
group::rw-
group:lp:rw-
mask::rw-
other::r—
```

10. Run this set of commands (as mjones) to create a directory named /tmp/mydir and use ACLs to assign default permissions to it so that the adm user has read/write/execute permission to that directory and any files or directories created in it. Test that it worked by creating the /tmp/mydir/testing/ directory and /tmp/mydir/newfile.txt.

```
[mary]$ mkdir /tmp/mydir
[mary]$ setfacl -m d:u:adm:rwx /tmp/mydir
[mjones]$ getfacl /tmp/mydir
# file: tmp/mydir
# owner: mjones
# group: mjones
user::rwx
group::rwx
other::r-x
default:user::rwx
default:user:adm:rwx
default:group::rwx
default:mask::rwx
default:other::r-x
[mjones]$ mkdir /tmp/mydir/testing
[mjones]$ touch /tmp/mydir/newfile.txt
[mjones]$ getfacl /tmp/mydir/testing/
# file: tmp/mydir/testing/
# owner: mjones
# group: mjones
user::rwx
user:adm:rwx
group::rwx
mask::rwx
other::r-x
default:user::rwx
default:user:adm:rwx
default:group::rwx
default:mask::rwx
default:other::r-x
[mjones]$ getfacl /tmp/mydir/newfile.txt
# file: tmp/mydir/newfile.txt
# owner: mjones
# group: mjones
user::rw-
```

```
user:adm:rwx        #effective:rw-
group::rwx          #effective:rw-
mask::rw-
other::r--
```

Notice that the adm user effectively has only rw- permission. To remedy that, you need to expand the permissions of the mask. One way to do that is with the chmod command, as follows:

```
[mjones]$ chmod 775 /tmp/mydir/newfile.txt
[mjones]$ getfacl /tmp/mydir/newfile.txt
# file: tmp/mydir/newfile.txt
# owner: mjones
# group: mjones
user::rwx
user:adm:rwx
group::rwx
mask::rwx
other::r-x
```

Chapter 12: Managing Disks and Filesystems

1. To determine the device name of a USB flash drive that you want to insert into your computer, type the following and insert the USB flash drive (press Ctrl+C after you have seen the appropriate messages).

```
# tail -f /var/log/messages
kernel: [sdb] 15667200 512-byte logical blocks:
     (8.02 GB/7.47 GiB)
Feb 11 21:55:59 cnegus kernel: sd 7:0:0:0:
     [sdb] Write Protect is off
Feb 11 21:55:59 cnegus kernel: [sdb] Assuming
     drive cache: write through
Feb 11 21:55:59 cnegus kernel: [sdb] Assuming
     drive cache: write through
```

2. To list partitions on the USB flash drive on a RHEL 6 system, type the following:

```
# fdisk -c -u -l /dev/sdb
```

To list partitions on a RHEL 7 or Fedora system, type the following:

```
# fdisk -l /dev/sdb
```

3. To delete partitions on the USB flash drive, assuming device /dev/sdb, do the following:

```
# fdisk /dev/sdb
Command (m for help): d
Partition number (1-6): 6
Command (m for help): d
```

```
Partition number (1-5): 5
Command (m for help): d
Partition number (1-5): 4
Command (m for help): d
Partition number (1-4): 3
Command (m for help): d
Partition number (1-4): 2
Command (m for help): d
Selected partition 1
Command (m for help): w
# partprobe /dev/sdb
```

4. To add a 100MB Linux partition, 200MB swap partition, and 500MB LVM partition to the USB flash drive, type the following:

```
# fdisk /dev/sdb

Command (m for help): n
Command action
   e   extended
   p   primary partition (1-4)
p
Partition number (1-4): 1
First sector (2048-15667199, default 2048):  <ENTER>
Last sector, +sectors or +size{K,M,G} (default 15667199): +100M
Command (m for help): n
Command action
   e   extended
   p   primary partition (1-4)
p
Partition number (1-4): 2
First sector (616448-8342527, default 616448):  <ENTER>
Last sector, +sectors or +size{K,M,G} (default 15667199): +200M
Command (m for help): n
Command action
   e   extended
   p   primary partition (1-4)
p
Partition number (1-4): 3
First sector (616448-15667199, default 616448):  <ENTER>
Using default value 616448
Last sector, +sectors or +size{K,M,G} (default 15667199): +500M
Command (m for help): t
Partition number (1-4): 2
Hex code (type L to list codes): 82
Changed system type of partition 2 to 82 (Linux swap / Solaris)
Command (m for help): t
Partition number (1-4): 3
Hex code (type L to list codes): 8e
```

B

```
Changed system type of partition 3 to 8e (Linux LVM)
Command (m for help): w
# partprobe /dev/sdb
# grep sdb /proc/partitions
   8       16     7833600 sdb
   8       17      102400 sdb1
   8       18      204800 sdb2
   8       19      512000 sdb3
```

5. To put an ext3 filesystem on the Linux partition, type the following:

```
# mkfs -t ext3 /dev/sdb1
```

6. To create a mount point called /mnt/mypart and mount the Linux partition on it temporarily, do the following:

```
# mkdir /mnt/mypart
# mount -t ext3 /dev/sdb1 /mnt/mypart
```

7. To enable the swap partition and turn it on so additional swap space is immediately available, type the following:

```
# mkswap /dev/sdb2
# swapon /dev/sdb2
```

8. To create a volume group called abc from the LVM partition, create a 200MB logical volume from that group called data, create a VFAT filesystem on it, temporarily mount the logical volume on a new directory named /mnt/test, and then check that it was successfully mounted, type the following:

```
# pvcreate /dev/sdb3
# vgcreate abc /dev/sdb3
# lvcreate -n data -L 200M abc
# mkfs -t vfat /dev/mapper/abc-data
# mkdir /mnt/test
# mount /dev/mapper/abc-data /mnt/test
```

9. To grow the logical volume from 200MB to 300MB, type the following:

```
# lvextend -L +100M /dev/mapper/abc-data
# resize2fs -p /dev/mapper/abc-data
```

10. To safely remove the USB flash drive from the computer, do the following:

```
# umount /dev/sdb1
# swapoff /dev/sdb2
# umount /mnt/test
# lvremove /dev/mapper/abc-data
# vgremove abc
# pvremove /dev/sdb3
```

You can now safely remove the USB flash drive from the computer.

Chapter 13: Understanding Server Administration

1. To log in to any account on another computer using the ssh command, type the following, and then enter the password when prompted:

```
$ ssh joe@localhost
joe@localhost's password:
*********
[joe]$
```

2. To display the contents of a remote /etc/system-release file and have its contents displayed on the local system using remote execution with the ssh command, do the following:

```
$ ssh joe@localhost "cat /etc/system-release"
joe@localhost's password: *********
Fedora release 21 (Twenty One)
```

3. To use X11 forwarding to display a gedit window on your local system and then save a file on the remote home directory, do the following:

```
$ ssh -X joe@localhost "gedit newfile"
joe@localhost's password: ********
$ ssh joe@localhost "cat newfile"
joe@localhost's password: ********
This is text from the file I saved in joe's remote home directory
```

4. To recursively copy all the files from the /usr/share/selinux directory on a remote system to the /tmp directory on your local system in such a way that all the modification times on the files are updated to the time on the local system when they are copied, do the following:

```
$ scp -r joe@localhost:/usr/share/selinux /tmp
joe@localhost's password: ********
irc.pp.bz2                                   100% 9673      9.5KB/s   00:00
dcc.pp.bz2                                   100%  15KB  15.2KB/s   00:01
$ ls -l /tmp/selinux | head
total 20
drwxr-xr-x. 3 root root  4096 Apr 18 05:52 devel
drwxr-xr-x. 2 root root  4096 Apr 18 05:52 packages
drwxr-xr-x. 2 root root 12288 Apr 18 05:52 targeted
```

5. To recursively copy all the files from the /usr/share/logwatch directory on a remote system to the /tmp directory on your local system in such a way that all the modification times on the files from the remote system are maintained on the local system, try this:

```
$ rsync -av joe@localhost:/usr/share/logwatch /tmp
joe@localhost's password: ********
receiving incremental file list
```

B

```
logwatch/
logwatch/default.conf/
logwatch/default.conf/logwatch.conf
$ ls -l /tmp/logwatch | head
total 16
drwxr-xr-x. 5 root root 4096 Apr 19  2011 default.conf
drwxr-xr-x. 4 root root 4096 Feb 28  2011 dist.conf
drwxr-xr-x. 2 root root 4096 Apr 19  2011 lib
```

6. To create a public/private key pair to use for SSH communications (no passphrase on the key), copy the public key file to a remote user's account with ssh-copy-id, and use key-based authentication to log in to that user account without having to enter a password, use the following code:

```
$ ssh-keygen
Generating public/private rsa key pair.
Enter file in which to save the key (/home/joe/.ssh/id_rsa): ENTER
/home/joe/.ssh/id_rsa already exists.
Enter passphrase (empty for no passphrase): ENTER
Enter same passphrase again: ENTER
Your identification has been saved in /home/joe/.ssh/id_rsa.
Your public key has been saved in /home/joe/.ssh/id_rsa.pub.
The key fingerprint is:
58:ab:c1:95:b6:10:7a:aa:7c:c5:ab:bd:f3:4f:89:1e joe@cnegus.csb
The key's randomart image is:
$ ssh-copy-id -i ~/.ssh/id_rsa.pub joe@localhost
joe@localhost's password: ********
Now try logging into the machine, with "ssh 'joe@localhost'",
and check in:
.ssh/authorized_keys
to make sure we haven't added extra keys that you weren't expecting.
$ ssh joe@localhost
$ cat .ssh/authorized_keys
ssh-rsa AAAAB3NzaC1yc2EAAAABIwAAAQEAyN2Psp5/LRUC9E8BDCx53yPUa0qoOPd
v6H4sF3vmn04V6E7D1iXpzwPzdo4rpvmR1ZiinHR2xGAEr2uZag7feKgLnww2KPcQ6S
iR7lzrOhQjV+SGb/a1dxrIeZqKMq1Tk07G4EvboIrq//9J47vI4l7iNu0xRmjI3TTxa
DdCTbpG6J3uSJm1BKzdUtwb413x35W2bRgMI75aIdeBsDgQBBiOdu+zuTMrXJj2viCA
XeJ7gIwRvBaMQdOSvSdlkX353tmIjmJheWdgCccM/1jKdoELpaevg9anCe/yUP3so31
tTo4I+qTfzAQD5+66oqW0LgMkWVvfZI7dUz3WUPmcMw== chris@abc.example.com
```

7. To create an entry in /etc/rsyslog.conf that stores all authentication messages at the info level and higher into a file named /var/log/myauth, do the following. Watch from one terminal as the data comes in.

```
# vim /etc/rsyslog.conf
authpriv.info                              /var/log/myauth
# service rsyslog restart
    or
# systemctl restart rsyslog.service
<Terminal 1>                       <Terminal 2>
```

```
# tail -f /var/log/myauth            $ ssh joe@localhost
Apr 18 06:19:34 abc unix_chkpwd[30631]    joe@localhost's password:
Apr 18 06:19:34 abc sshd[30631]       Permission denied,try again
 :pam_unix(sshd:auth):
 authentication failure;logname= uid=501
 euid=501 tty=ssh ruser= rhost=localhost
 user=joe
Apr 18 06:19:34 abc sshd[30631]:
 Failed password for joe from
 127.0.0.1 port 5564 ssh2
```

8. To determine the largest directory structures under /usr/share, sort them from largest to smallest, and list the top 10 of those directories in terms of size using the du command, type the following:

```
$ du -s /usr/share/* | sort -rn | head

527800 /usr/share/locale
277108 /usr/share/fonts
265772 /usr/share/icons
253844 /usr/share/doc
. . .
```

9. To show the space that is used and available from all the filesystems currently attached to the local system, but exclude any tmpfs or devtmpfs filesystems by using the df command, type the following:

```
$ df -h -x tmpfs -x devtmpfs
Filesystem       Size  Used Avail Use% Mounted on
/deev/sda4       20G   4.2G 16G    22% /
```

10. To find any files in the /usr directory that are more than 10MB in size, do the following:

```
$ find /usr -size +10M
/usr/lib/jvm/java-1.6.0-openjdk-1.6.0.0/jre/lib/rt.jar
/usr/lib/jvm/java-1.7.0-openjdk-1.7.0.3/jre/lib/rt.jar
/usr/lib/llvm/libLLVM-2.9.so
/usr/lib/flash-plugin/libflashplayer.so
```

Chapter 14: Administering Networking

1. To use the desktop to check that NetworkManager has successfully started your network interface (wired or wireless), do the following:

Left-click the NetworkManager icon in your top panel. Any active wired or wireless network connections should be highlighted in bold.

B

If it has not connected to the network, select from the list of wired or wireless networks available, and then enter the username and password, if prompted, to start an active connection.

2. To run a command to check the active network interfaces available on your computer, type:

```
$ ifconfig
```

or

```
$ ip addr show
```

3. Try to contact google.com from the command line in a way that ensures that DNS is working properly:

```
$ ping google.com
Ctrl-C
```

4. To run a command to check the routes being used to communicate outside your local network, type:

```
$ route
```

5. To trace the route being taken to connect to google.com, use the traceroute command:

```
$ traceroute google.com
```

6. To turn off and disable NetworkManager and start the network service, do the following:

From an RHEL 6 system, type:

```
# service NetworkManager stop
# service network restart
# chkconfig NetworkManager off
# chkconfig network on
```

For RHEL 7 or newer Fedora systems, type:

```
# systemctl stop NetworkManager.service
# systemctl disable NetworkManager.service
# service network restart
# chkconfig network on
```

7. To create a host entry that allows you to communicate with your local host system using the name myownhost, do the following:

Edit the /etc/hosts file (vi /etc/hosts) and add myownhost to the end of the localhost entry so it appears as follows (then ping myownhost to see if it worked):

```
127.0.0.1              localhost.localdomain localhost myownhost
# ping myownhost
Ctrl+C
```

8. To add the public Google DNS server (IP address 8.8.8.8) as the last in your list of DNS servers, take the following action:

Make a copy of your `resolv.conf` file before proceeding (then copy it back after the procedure is done):

```
# cp /etc/resolv.conf $HOME
```

If you are using the NetworkManager service, left-click the NetworkManager icon and select Network Settings. Select the IPv4 Settings. Then select the Method box and choose Automatic (DHCP) addresses only and fill in 8.8.8.8 in the DNS servers box (along with any other DNS servers you need). If that doesn't work, try one of the DNS servers listed in the `resolv.conf` file you just copied to your home directory.

Or, if you are using the network service, edit the `/etc/resolv.conf` file directly, so the file includes at least the following line:

```
nameserver 8.8.8.8
```

In either case, use the `dig` command to check that the DNS server was able to resolve an address:

```
# dig google.com
. . .
google.com.      91941   IN      NS      ns3.google.com.
;; Query time: 0 msec
;; SERVER: 8.8.8.8#53(8.8.8.8)
;; WHEN: Mon Apr 30 13:57:44 2012
;; MSG SIZE  rcvd: 276
```

9. To create a custom route that directs traffic destined for the 192.168.99.0/255.255.255.0 network to some IP address on your local network, such as 192.168.0.5 (first ensuring that the 10.0.99 network is not being used at your location), do the following:

Determine the name of your network interface. For RHEL, your first network interface is probably eth0. In that case, as root run the following commands:

```
# cd /etc/sysconfig/network-scripts
# vi route-eth0
```

Add the following lines to that file:

```
ADDRESS0=192.168.99.0
NETMASK0=255.255.255.0
GATEWAY0=192.168.0.5
```

Restart networking and run `route` to see that the route is active:

```
# service network restart
# route
Destination  Gateway      Genmask         Flags Metric Ref Use Iface
default      192.168.0.1  0.0.0.0          UG    0      0    0 eth0
```

B

```
192.168.0.0   *           255.255.255.0  U    1       0       0 eth0
192.168.99.0  192.168.0.5  255.255.255.0  UG   0       0       0 eth0
```

To check to see if your system has been configured to allow IPv4 packets to be routed between network interfaces on your system, type the following:

```
# cat /proc/sys/net/ipv4/ip_forward
0
```

A 0 shows that IPv4 packet forwarding is disabled; a 1 shows it is enabled.

Chapter 15: Starting and Stopping Services

1. To determine which initialization daemon your server is currently using, consider the following:

   - You have Upstart if your Linux server runs one of the following distributions: RHEL version 6, Fedora versions 9 through 14, Ubuntu versions 6–14.10, or open-SUSE versions 11.3–12.1, and the strings command shows the Upstart init process in use as demonstrated in the following example:

   ```
   $ strings /sbin/init | grep -i upstart
   upstart-devel@lists.ubuntu.com
   UPSTART_CONFDIR
   UPSTART_NO_SESSIONS
   ...
   ```

   - You have the systemd daemon if your Linux server runs Fedora version 15 or greater, RHEL 7, Ubuntu 15.04 or OpenSUSE 12.02 or greater. In some cases, PID 1 is the systemd process. In earlier cases, PID 1 is the init daemon. To tell if it is a systemd init daemon, you can run the following strings command to show systemd in use:

   ```
   # strings /sbin/init | grep -i systemd
   systemd.unit=
   systemd.log_target=
   systemd.log_level=
   ...
   ```

   - Most likely, you have the SysVinit or BSD init daemon if your init daemon is not the Upstart init daemon or systemd. But double-check at http://wikipedia.org/wiki/Init.

2. The tools you use to manage services depend primarily on which initialization system is in use. Try to run the initctl, systemctl, and service commands to determine the type of initialization script in use for the ssh service on your system:

   - A positive result, shown here, means the sshd has been converted to Upstart:

   ```
   # initctl status ssh
   ssh start/running, process 2390
   ```

- For `systemd`, a positive result, shown here, means the `sshd` has been converted to `systemd`:

```
# systemctl status sshd.service
sshd.service - OpenSSH server daemon
  Loaded: loaded (/lib/systemd/system/sshd.service; enabled)
  Active: active (running) since Mon, 30 Apr 2015 12:35:20...
```

- If you don't see positive results for the preceding tests, try the following command for the SysVinit `init` daemon. A positive result here, along with negative results for the preceding tests, means `sshd` is still using the `SysVinit` daemon.

```
# service ssh status
sshd (pid 2390) is running...
```

3. To determine your server's previous and current runlevel, use the `runlevel` command. It still works on all `init` daemons:

```
$ runlevel
N 3
```

4. To change the default runlevel or target unit on your Linux server, you can do one of the following (depending upon your server's `init` daemon):

- For SysVinit, edit the file `/etc/inittab` and change the `#` in the line `id:#:initdefault:` to either 2, 3, 4, or 5.

- For Upstart daemon, edit the file `/etc/inittab` and change the `#` in the line `id:#:initdefault:` to either 2, 3, 4, or 5.

- For `systemd`, change the `default.target` symbolic link to the desired `runlevel#.target`, where `#` is either 2, 3, 4, or 5. The following shows you how to change the symbolic link for the target unit to `runlevel3.target`.

```
# ln -sf /lib/systemd/system/runlevel3.target \
         /etc/systemd/system/default.target
/lib/systemd/system/runlevel3.target
```

5. To list out services running (or active) on your server, you need to use different commands, depending upon the initialization daemon you are using.

- For SysVinit, use the `service` command as shown in this example:

```
# service --status-all | grep running... | sort
anacron (pid 2162) is running...
atd (pid 2172) is running...
...
```

- For Upstart, use the `initctl` command. However, also be sure to use the `service` command, because not all services may have been ported to Upstart:

```
# initctl list | grep start/running
tty (/dev/tty3) start/running, process 1163
...
```

B

```
# service --status-all | grep running
abrtd (pid  1118) is running...
...
```

- For systemd, use the systemctl command, as follows:

```
# systemctl list-unit-files --type=service | grep -v disabled
UNIT FILE                                    STATE
abrt-ccpp.service                            enabled
abrt-oops.service                            enabled
...
```

6. To list out the running (or active) services on your Linux server, use the appropriate command(s) determined in Answer 5 for the initialization daemon your server is using.

7. For each initialization daemon, the following command(s) show a particular service's current status:

   - For SysVinit, the service *service_name* status command is used.

   - For Upstart, the initctl status *service_name* command is used.

   - For systemd, the systemctl status *service_name* command is used.

8. To show the status of the cups daemon on your Linux server, use the following:

   - For SysVinit:

   ```
   # service cups status
   cupsd (pid 8236) is running...
   ```

   - For Upstart:

   ```
   # initctl status cups
   cups start/running, process 2390
   ```

   - Remember that if a service has not yet been ported to Upstart, you need to use the service command instead of initctl.

   - For systemd:

   ```
   # systemctl status cups.service
   cups.service - CUPS Printing Service
        Loaded: loaded (/lib/systemd/system/cups.service; enabled)
        Active: active (running) since Tue, 01 May 2015 04:43:5...
     Main PID: 17003 (cupsd)
        CGroup: name=systemd:/system/cups.service
                17003 /usr/sbin/cupsd -f
   ```

9. To attempt to restart the cups daemon on your Linux server, use the following:

   - For SysVinit:

   ```
   # service cups restart
   Stopping cups:             [  OK  ]
   Starting cups:             [  OK  ]
   ```

- For Upstart:

```
# initctl restart cups
cups start/running, process 2490
```

- Remember that if a service has not yet been ported to Upstart, you need to use the `service` command instead of `initctl`.

- For `systemd`:

```
# systemctl restart cups.service
```

10. To attempt to reload the `cups` daemon on your Linux server, use the following:

- For SysVinit:

```
# service cups reload
Reloading cups:              [  OK  ]
```

- For Upstart:

```
# initctl reload cups
```

Remember that if a service has not yet been ported to Upstart, you need to use the `service` command instead of `initctl`.

- For `systemd`, this is a trick question. You cannot reload the `cups` daemon on a `systemd` Linux server!

```
# systemctl reload cups.service
Failed to issue method call: Job type reload is
  not applicable for unit cups.service.
```

Chapter 16: Configuring a Print Server

1. To use the Print Settings window to add a new printer called `myprinter` to your system (generic PostScript printer, connected to a port), do the following from Fedora 21:

   a. Install the system-config-printer package:

   ```
   # yum install system-config-printer
   ```

   b. From the GNOME 3 desktop, select Print Settings from the Activities screen.

   c. Unlock the interface and enter the root password.

   d. Select the Add button.

   e. Select an LPT or other port as the device and click Forward.

   f. For the driver, choose Generic and click Forward; then choose PostScript and click Forward.

   g. Click Forward to skip any installable options, if needed.

B

h. For the printer name, call it `myprinter`, give it any Description and Location you like, and click Apply.

i. Click Cancel to not print a test page. The printer should appear in the Print Settings window.

2. To use the `lpc` command to see the status of all your printers, type the following:

```
# lpc status
myprinter:
  queuing is enabled
  printing is enabled
  no entries
  daemon present
```

3. To use the `lpr` command to print the `/etc/hosts` file, type the following:

```
$ lpr /etc/hosts -P myprinter
```

4. To check the print queue for that printer, type the following:

```
# lpq -P myprinter
myprinter is not ready
Rank    Owner    Job    File(s)          Total Size
1st     root     655    hosts            1024 bytes
```

5. To remove the print job from the queue (cancel it), type the following.

```
# lprm -P myprinter
```

6. To use the printing window to set the basic server setting that publishes your printers so other systems on your local network can print to your printers, do the following:

a. On a GNOME 3 desktop, from the Activities screen, type **Print Settings** and press Enter.

b. Select Server⇨Settings and type the root password if prompted.

c. Click the check box next to Publish shared printers connected to this system, and click OK.

7. To allow remote administration of your system from a web browser, follow these steps:

a. On a GNOME 3 desktop, from the Activities screen, type **Print Settings** and press Enter.

b. Select Server⇨Settings and type the root password if prompted.

c. Click the check box next to Allow remote administration, and click OK.

8. To demonstrate that you can do remote administration of your system from a web browser on another system, do the following:

a. In the location box from a browser window from another computer on your network, type the following replacing **hostname** with the name or IP address of the system running your print service: **http://hostname:631**.

b. Type root as the user and the root password, when prompted. The CUPS home page should appear from that system.

9. To use the netstat command to see which addresses the cupsd daemon is listening on, type the following:

```
# netstat -tupln | grep 631
tcp    0    0 0.0.0.0:631      0.0.0.0:*       LISTEN      6492/cupsd
```

10. To delete the myprinter printer entry from your system, do the following:

a. Click the Unlock button and type the root password when prompted.

b. From the Print Settings window, right-click the myprinter icon and select Delete.

c. When prompted, select Delete again.

Chapter 17: Configuring a Web Server

1. To install all the packages associated with the Web Server group on a Fedora system, do the following:

```
# yum groupinstall "Web Server"
```

2. To create a file called index.html in the directory assigned to DocumentRoot in the main Apache configuration file (with the words My Own Web Server inside), do the following:

a. Determine the location of DocumentRoot:

```
# grep ^DocumentRoot /etc/httpd/conf/httpd.conf
DocumentRoot "/var/www/html"
```

b. Echo the words "My Own Web Server" into the index.html file located in DocumentRoot:

```
# echo "My Own Web Server" > /var/www/html/index.html
```

3. To start the Apache web server and set it to start up automatically at boot time, then check that it is available from a web browser on your local host, do the following (you should see the words "My Own Web Server" displayed if it is working properly):

The httpd service is started and enabled differently on different Linux systems. In recent Fedora or RHEL 7 or later, type the following:

```
# systemctl start httpd.service
# systemctl enable httpd.service
```

B

In RHEL 6 or earlier, type:

```
# service httpd start
# chkconfig httpd on
```

4. To use the netstat command to see which ports the httpd server is listening on, type the following:

```
# netstat -tupln | grep httpd
tcp6    0   0 :::80       :::*      LISTEN    2496/httpd
tcp6    0   0 :::443      :::*      LISTEN    2496/httpd
```

5. Try to connect to your Apache web server from a web browser that is outside the local system. If it fails, correct any problems you encounter by investigating the firewall, SELinux, and other security features.

   If you don't have DNS set up yet, use the IP address of the server to view your Apache server from a remote web browser, such as http://192.168.0.1. If you are not able to connect, retry connecting to the server from your browser after performing each of the following steps on the system running the Apache server:

```
# iptables -F
# setenforce 0
# chmod 644 /var/www/html/index.html
```

   The iptables -F command flushes the firewall rules temporarily. If connecting to the web server succeeds after that, you need to add new firewall rules to open tcp ports 80 and 443 on the server. On a system using the firewalld service, do this by clicking the check box next to those ports on the Firewall window. For systems running the iptables service, add the following rules before the last DROP or REJECT rule.

```
-A INPUT -m state --state NEW -m tcp -p tcp --dport 80 -j ACCEPT
-A INPUT -m state --state NEW -m tcp -p tcp --dport 443 -j ACCEPT
```

   The setenforce 0 command puts SELinux in permissive mode temporarily. If connecting to the web server succeeds after that, you need to correct SELinux file context and/or Boolean issues (probably file context in this case). The following should work:

```
# chcon --reference=/var/www/html /var/www/html/index.html
```

   If the chmod command works, it means that the apache user and group did not have read permission to the file. You should be able to leave the new permissions as they are.

6. To use the openssl or similar command to create your own private RSA key and self-signed SSL certificate, do the following:

```
# yum install openssl
# cd /etc/pki/tls/private
# openssl genrsa -out server.key 1024
# chmod 600 server.key
```

```
# cd /etc/pki/tls/certs
# openssl req -new -x509 -nodes -sha1 -days 365 \
  -key /etc/pki/tls/private/server.key \
  -out server.crt
Country Name (2 letter code) [AU]: US
State or Province Name (full name) [Some-State]: NJ
Locality Name (eg, city) []: Princeton
Organization Name (eg, company) [Internet Widgits Pty
Ltd]:TEST USE ONLY
Organizational Unit Name (eg, section) []:TEST USE ONLY
Common Name (eg, YOUR name) []:secure.example.org
Email Address []:dom@example.org
```

You should now have a /etc/pki/tls/private/server.key key file and a
/etc/pki/tls/certs/server.crt certificate file.

7. To configure your Apache web server to use your key and self-signed certificate to
   serve secure (HTTPS) content, do the following:

   a. Edit the /etc/httpd/conf.d/ssl.conf file to change the key and certifi-
      cate locations to use the ones you just created:

      ```
      SSLCertificateFile /etc/pki/tls/certs/server.crt
      SSLCertificateKeyFile /etc/pki/tls/private/server.key
      ```

   b. Restart the httpd service:

      ```
      # systemctl restart httpd.service
      ```

8. To use a web browser to create an HTTPS connection to your web server and view
   the contents of the certificate you created, do the following:

   From the system running the Apache server, type **https://localhost** in the
   browser's location box. You should see a message that reads, "This Connection is
   Untrusted." To complete the connection, do the following:

   a. Click I Understand the Risks.

   b. Click Add Exception.

   c. Click Get Certificate.

   d. Click Confirm Security Exception.

9. To create a file named /etc/httpd/conf.d/example.org.conf, which turns
   on name-based virtual hosting and creates a virtual host that 1) listens on port
   80 on all interfaces, 2) has a server administrator of joe@example.org, 3) has a
   server name of joe.example.org, 4) has a DocumentRoot of /var/www/html/
   joe.example.org, and 5) has a DirectoryIndex that includes at least index.
   html, and create an index.html file in DocumentRoot that contains the words
   "Welcome to the House of Joe" inside, do the following:

B

Create an `example.org.conf` file that looks like the following:

```
NameVirtualHost *:80
<VirtualHost *:80>
    ServerAdmin       joe@
example.org
    ServerName        joe.
example.org
    ServerAlias       web.example.org
    DocumentRoot      /var/www/html/joe.example.org/
    DirectoryIndex    index.html
</VirtualHost>
```

This is how you could create the text to go into the `index.html` file:

```
# echo "Welcome to the House of Joe" > /var/www/html/joe.example
    .org/index.html
```

10. To add the text **joe.example.org** to the end of the localhost entry in your `/etc/hosts` file on the machine that is running the web server, and check it by typing **http://joe.example.org** into the location box of your web browser to see "Welcome to the House of Joe" when the page is displayed, do the following:

   a. Reload the `httpd.conf` file modified in the previous exercise:

   ```
   # apachectl graceful
   ```

   b. Edit the `/etc/hosts` file with any text editor so the local host line appears as follows:

   ```
   127.0.0.1        localhost.localdomain localhost joe.example.org
   ```

   c. From a browser on the local system where `httpd` is running, you should be able to type `http://joe.example.org` into the location box to access the Apache web server using name-based authentication.

Chapter 18: Configuring an FTP Server

> **CAUTION**
> Don't do the tasks described here on a working, public FTP server, because these tasks will interfere with its operations. (You could, however, use these tasks to set up a new FTP server.)

1. To determine which package provides the Very Secure FTP Daemon service, type the following as root:

```
# yum search "Very Secure FTP"
...
================== N/S Matched: Very Secure FTP ==================
vsftpd.i686 : Very Secure Ftp Daemon
```

The search found the `vsftpd` package.

2. To install the Very Secure FTP Daemon package on your system and search for the configuration files in that package, type the following:

```
# yum install vsftpd
# rpm -qc vsftpd | less
```

3. To start the Very Secure FTP Daemon service and set it to start when the system boots, type the following on a Fedora or Red Hat Enterprise Linux 7 system:

```
# systemctl start vsftpd.service
# systemctl enable vsftpd.service
```

On a Red Hat Enterprise Linux 6 system, type the following:

```
# service vsftpd start
# chkconfig vsftpd on
```

4. On the system running your FTP server, type the following to create a file named `test` in the anonymous FTP directory that contains the words "Welcome to your vsftpd server":

```
# echo "Welcome to your vsftpd server" > /var/ftp/test
```

5. To open the `test` file from the anonymous FTP home directory, using a web browser on the system running your FTP server, do the following:

Start the Firefox web browser, type the following in the location box, and press Enter:

```
ftp://localhost/test
```

The text "Welcome to your Very Secure FTP Daemon server" should appear in the Firefox window.

6. To access the `test` file in the anonymous FTP home directory, do the following. (If you cannot access the file, check that your firewall, SELinux, and TCP wrappers are configured to allow access to that file, as described here.)

   a. Type the following into the location box of a browser on a system on your network that can reach the FTP server (replace *host* with your system's fully qualified hostname or IP address):

   ```
   ftp://host/test
   ```

   If you cannot see the welcome message in your browser window, check what may be preventing access. To temporarily turn off your firewall (flush your `iptables` rules), type the following command as the root user from a shell on your FTP server system and then try to access the site again:

   ```
   # iptables -F
   ```

   b. To temporarily disable SELinux, type the following, and then try to access the site again:

   ```
   # setenforce 0
   ```

B

c. To temporarily disable TCP wrappers, add the following to the beginning of the /etc/hosts.allow file (be sure to remove this line again when the test is done):

```
ALL: ALL
```

After you have determined what is causing the file on your FTP server to be unavailable, go back to the "Securing Your FTP Server" section and go through the steps to determine what might be blocking access to your file. These are likely possibilities:

- For iptables, make sure there is a rule opening TCP port 21 on the server.
- For SELinux, make sure the file context is set to public_content_t.
- For TCP wrappers, make sure that there is a vsftpd: ALL or similar line in the /etc/hosts.allow file. An entry such as this should be needed only if there is a line in the /etc/hosts.deny file that denies access to services that are not explicitly allowed.

7. To configure your Very Secure FTP Daemon server to allow file uploads by anonymous users to a directory named in, do the following as root on your FTP server:

   a. Create the in directory as follows:

   ```
   # mkdir /var/ftp/in
   # chown ftp:ftp /var/ftp/in
   # chmod 770 /var/ftp/in
   ```

   b. Inside the /etc/vsftpd/vsftpd.conf file, make sure that the following variables are set:

   ```
   anonymous_enable=YES
   write_enable=YES
   anon_upload_enable=YES
   ```

   c. For Fedora 20 or RHEL 7, open the Firewall Configuration window and check the FTP box under services to open access to your FTP service. For earlier RHEL and Fedora systems, configure your iptables firewall to allow new requests on TCP port 21 by adding the following rule at some point before a final DROP or REJECT rule in your /etc/sysconfig/iptables file:

   ```
   -A INPUT -m state --state NEW -m tcp -p tcp --dport 21 -j ACCEPT
   ```

   d. Configure your iptables firewall to do connection tracking by loading the appropriate module to the /etc/sysconfig/iptables-config file:

   ```
   IPTABLES_MODULES="nf_conntrack_ftp"
   ```

   e. For SELinux to allow uploading to the directory, first set file contexts properly:

   ```
   # semanage fcontext -a -t public_content_rw_t "/var/ftp/in(/.*)?"
   # restorecon -F -R -v /var/ftp/in
   ```

   f. Next, set the SELinux Boolean to allow uploading:

   ```
   # setsebool -P allow_ftpd_anon_write on
   ```

g. Restart the vsftpd service (service vsftpd restart or systemctl restart vsftpd.service).

8. To install the lftp FTP client (if you don't have a second Linux system, install lftp on the same host running the FTP server) and try to upload the /etc/hosts file to the incoming directory on the server, run the following commands as the root user:

```
# yum install lftp
# lftp localhost
lftp localhost:/> cd in
lftp localhost:/in> put /etc/hosts
89 bytes transferred
lftp localhost:/in> quit
```

You won't be able to see that you copied the hosts file to the incoming directory. However, type the following from a shell on the host running the FTP server to make sure the hosts file is there:

```
# ls /var/ftp/in hosts
```

If you cannot upload the file, troubleshoot the problem as described in Exercise 7, recheck your vsftpd.conf settings, and review the ownership and permissions on the /var/ftp/in directory.

9. Using any FTP client you choose, visit the /pub/linux/docs/man-pages directory on the ftp://kernel.org site and list the contents of that directory. Here's how to do that with the lftp client:

```
# lftp ftp://kernel.org/pub/linux/docs/man-pages
cd ok, cwd=/pub/linux/docs/man-pages
lftp kernel.org:/pub/linux/docs/man-pages> ls
drwxrwsr-x 2 536   536    24576 May 10 20:29 Archive
-rw-rw-r-- 1 536   536  1135808 Feb 09 23:23 man-pages-3.34.tar.bz2
-rw-rw-r-- 1 536   536  1674738 Feb 09 23:23 man-pages-3.34.tar.gz
-rw-rw-r-- 1 536   536      543 Feb 09 23:23 man-pages-3.34.tar.sign
...
```

10. Using any FTP client you choose, download the man-pages-3.78.tar.gz file from the kernel.org directory you just visited to the /tmp directory on your local system.

```
# lftp ftp://kernel.org/pub/linux/docs/man-pages
cd ok, cwd=/pub/linux/docs/man-pages
lftp kernel.org:man-pages> get man-pages-3.78.tar.gz
1739208 bytes transferred in 4 seconds (481.0K/s)
lftp kernel.org:man-pages> quit
```

B

Chapter 19: Configuring a Windows File Sharing (Samba) Server

1. To install the samba and samba-client packages, type the following as root from a shell on the local system:

```
# yum install samba samba-client
```

2. To start and enable the smb and nmb services, type the following as root from a shell on the local system:

```
# systemctl enable smb.service
# systemctl start smb.service
# systemctl enable nmb.service
# systemctl start nmb.service
```

or

```
# chkconfig smb on
# service smb start
# chkconfig nmb on
# service nmb start
```

3. To set the Samba server's workgroup to TESTGROUP, the netbios name to MYTEST, and the server string to Samba Test System, as root user in a text editor, open the /etc/samba/smb.conf file and change three lines so they appear as follows:

```
workgroup = TESTGROUP
netbios name = MYTEST
server string = Samba Test System
```

4. To add a Linux user named phil to your system and add a Linux password and Samba password for phil, type the following as root user from a shell (be sure to remember the passwords you set):

```
# useradd phil
# passwd phil
New password: *******
Retype new password: *******
# smbpasswd -a phil
New SMB password: *******
Retype new SMB password: *******
Added user phil.
```

5. To set the [homes] section so that home directories are browseable (yes) and writable (yes), and that phil is the only valid user, open the /etc/samba/smb.conf file as root and change the [homes] section so it appears as follows:

```
[homes]
        comment = Home Directories
```

```
        browseable = yes
        writable = yes
        valid users = phil
```

6. To set SELinux Booleans that are necessary to make it so phil can access his home directory via a Samba client, type the following as root from a shell:

```
# setsebool -P samba_enable_home_dirs on
```

7. From the local system, use the smbclient command to list that the homes share is available.

```
# smbclient -L localhost
Enter root's password:
<ENTER>
Anonymous login successful
Domain=[DATAGROUP] OS=[Unix] Server=[Samba 4.1.15]
    Sharename       Type        Comment
    ---------       ----        -------
    homes           Disk        Home Directories
  ...
```

8. To connect to the homes share from a Nautilus (file manager) window on the Samba server' local system for the user phil in a way that allows you to drag and drop files to that folder, do the following:

   a. Open the Nautilus window (select the files icon).

   b. Under the Network heading in the left pane, select Connect to Server.

   c. Type the Server address. For example, smb://localhost/phil/.

   d. When prompted, type **phil** as the username and enter phil's password.

   e. Open another Nautilus window and drop a file to phil's homes folder.

9. To open up the firewall so anyone who has access to the server can access the Samba service (smbd and nmbd daemons), you can simply open the Firewall Configuration window and check the samba and samba-client check boxes. If your system is running basic iptables (and not the firewalld service), change the /etc/sysconfig/iptables file so the firewall appears like the following (the rules you add being those in bold):

```
*filter
:INPUT ACCEPT [0:0]
:FORWARD ACCEPT [0:0]
:OUTPUT ACCEPT [0:0]
-A INPUT -m state --state ESTABLISHED,RELATED -j ACCEPT
-A INPUT -p icmp -j ACCEPT
-A INPUT -i lo -j ACCEPT
-I INPUT -m state --state NEW -m udp -p udp --dport 137 -j ACCEPT
-I INPUT -m state --state NEW -m udp -p udp --dport 138 -j ACCEPT
-I INPUT -m state --state NEW -m tcp -p tcp --dport 139 -j ACCEPT
-I INPUT -m state --state NEW -m tcp -p tcp --dport 445 -j ACCEPT
```

B

```
-A INPUT -j REJECT --reject-with icmp-host-prohibited
-A FORWARD -j REJECT --reject-with icmp-host-prohibited
COMMIT
```

Then type the following for the firewall rules to be reloaded:

```
# service iptables restart
```

10. To open the homes share again as the user phil from another system on your network (Windows or Linux), and make sure you can drag and drop files to it, do the following:

    This step is really just repeating the Nautilus example described previously or accessing a Windows Explorer window and opening the share (by selecting Network, then the Samba server). The trick is to make sure the service has been made available through the Linux server security features.

    If you cannot access the Samba share, try disabling your firewall and then disabling SELinux. If the share is accessible when you turn off either of those services, go back and debug the problems with the service that is not working:

    ```
    # setenforce 0
    # service iptables stop
    ```

    When you have fixed the problem, set SELinux back to Enforcing mode and restart iptables:

    ```
    # setenforce 1
    # service iptables start
    ```

Chapter 20: Configuring an NFS File Server

1. To install the packages needed to configure the NFS service on the Linux system you choose, type the following as root user at a shell (Fedora or RHEL):

   ```
   # yum install nfs-utils
   ```

2. To list the documentation files that come in the package that provides the NFS server software, type the following:

   ```
   # rpm -qd nfs-utils
   /usr/share/doc/nfs-utils-1.2.5/ChangeLog
   ...
   /usr/share/man/man5/exports.5.gz
   /usr/share/man/man5/nfs.5.gz
   /usr/share/man/man5/nfsmount.conf.5.gz
   /usr/share/man/man7/nfsd.7.gz
   /usr/share/man/man8/blkmapd.8.gz
   /usr/share/man/man8/exportfs.8.gz
   ...
   ```

3. To start and enable the NFS service, type the following as root user on the NFS server:

```
# systemctl start nfs-server.service
# systemctl enable nfs-server.service
```

4. To check the status of the NFS service you just started on the NFS server, type the following as root user:

```
# systemctl status nfs-server.service
```

5. To share a directory /var/mystuff from your NFS server as available to everyone, read-only, and with the root user on the client having root access to the share, first create the mount directory as follows:

```
# mkdir /var/mystuff
```

Then create an entry in the /etc/exports file that is similar to the following:

```
/var/mystuff    *(ro,no_root_squash,insecure)
```

To make the share available, type the following:

```
# exportfs -v -a
exporting *:/var/mystuff
```

6. To make sure the share you created is accessible to all hosts, first check that rpcbind is not blocked by TCP wrappers by adding the following entry to the beginning of the /etc/hosts.allow file:

```
rpcbind: ALL
```

To open the firewall in systems that use firewalld (RHEL 7 and recent Fedora systems), install the firewall-config package. Then run firewall-config and from the Firewall Configuration window that appears, make sure that nfs and rpc-bind are checked on for the Permanent firewall settings.

To open the ports needed to allow clients to reach NFS through the iptables firewall (RHEL 6 and earlier Fedora systems without firewalld), you need to open at least TCP and UDP ports 111 (rpcbind), 20048 (mountd), and 2049 (nfs) by adding the following rules to the /etc/sysconfig/iptables file and starting the iptables service:

```
-A INPUT -m state --state NEW -m tcp -p tcp --dport 111 -j ACCEPT
-A INPUT -m state --state NEW -m udp -p udp --dport 111 -j ACCEPT
-A INPUT -m state --state NEW -m tcp -p tcp --dport 2049 -j ACCEPT
-A INPUT -m state --state NEW -m udp -p udp --dport 2049 -j ACCEPT
-A INPUT -m state --state NEW -m tcp -p tcp --dport 20048 -j ACCEPT
-A INPUT -m state --state NEW -m udp -p udp --dport 20048 -j ACCEPT
```

SELinux should be able to share NFS filesystems while in Enforcing mode without any changes to file contexts or Booleans. To make sure the share you created can be shared read-only, run the following command as root user on the NFS server:

```
# setsebool -P nfs_export_all_ro on
```

B

7. To view the shares available from the NFS server, assuming the NFS server is named nfsserver, type the following from the NFS client:

```
# showmount -e nfsserver
Export list for nfsserver:
/var/mystuff   *
```

8. To create a directory called /var/remote and temporarily mount the /var/mystuff directory from the NFS server (named nfsserver in this example) on that mount point, type the following as root user from the NFS client:

```
# mkdir /var/remote
# mount -t nfs nfsserver:/var/mystuff /var/remote
```

9. To add an entry so that the same mount is done automatically when you reboot, first unmount /var/remote as follows:

```
# umount /var/remote
```

Then add an entry like the following to the /etc/fstab on the client system:

```
/var/remote    nfsserver:/var/mystuff   nfs bg,ro 0 0
```

To test that the share is configured properly, type the following on the NFS client as the root user:

```
# mount -a
# mount -t nfs
nfsserver:/var/mystuff on /var/remote type nfs4
 (ro,vers=4,rsize=524288...
```

10. To copy some files to the /var/mystuff directory, type the following on the NFS server:

```
# cp /etc/hosts /etc/services /var/mystuff
```

From the NFS client, to make sure you can see the files just added to that directory and to make sure you can't write files to that directory from the client, type the following:

```
# ls /var/remote
hosts     services
# touch /var/remote/file1
touch: cannot touch '/var/remote/file1': Read-only file system
```

Chapter 21: Troubleshooting Linux

1. To go into Setup mode from the BIOS screen on your computer, do the following:

   a. Reboot your computer.

   b. Within a few seconds, you should see the BIOS screen, with an indication of which function key to press to go into Setup mode. (On my Dell workstation, it's the F2 function key.)

    c. The BIOS screen should appear. (If the system starts booting Linux, you didn't press the function key fast enough.)

2. From the BIOS setup screen, do the following to determine whether your computer is 32-bit or 64-bit, whether it includes virtualization support, and whether your network interface card is capable of PXE booting.

   Your experience may be a bit different from mine, depending on your computer and Linux system. The BIOS setup screen is different for different computers. In general, however, you can use arrow keys and tab keys to move between different columns and press Enter to select an entry.

   - On my Dell workstation, under the System heading, I highlight Processor Info to see that mine is a 64-bit Technology computer. Look in the Processor Info, or similar, section on your computer to see the type of processor you have.

   - On my Dell workstation, under the Onboard Devices heading, I highlight Integrated NIC and press Enter. The Integrated NIC screen that appears to the right lets me choose to enable or disable the NIC (On or Off) or enable with PXE or RPL (if I intend to boot the computer over the network).

3. To interrupt the boot process to get to the GRUB boot loader, do the following:

   a. Reboot the computer.

   b. Just after the BIOS screen disappears, when you see the countdown to booting the Linux system, press any key (perhaps the spacebar).

   c. The GRUB boot loader menu should appear, ready to allow you to select which operating system kernel to boot.

4. To boot up your computer to runlevel 1 so you can do some system maintenance, get to the GRUB boot screen (as described in the previous exercise), and then do the following:

   a. Use the arrow keys to highlight the operating system and kernel you want to boot.

   b. Type **e** to see the entries needed to boot the operating system.

   c. Move your cursor to the line that included the kernel. (It should include the word vmlinuz somewhere on the line.)

   d. Move the cursor to the end of that line, add a space, and then type the number 1 or **init=/bin/bash**.

   e. Follow the instructions to boot the new entry. You will probably either press Ctrl+X or press Enter; then when you see the next screen, type **b**.

      If it worked, your system should bypass the login prompt and boot up directly to a root user shell, where you can do administrative tasks without providing a password.

5. To start up Red Hat Enterprise Linux (through RHEL 6.x) so you can confirm each service as it is started, do the following:

B

    a. Follow the previous two exercises, but instead of putting a 1 at the end of a kernel line, put the word `confirm`.

    b. When the boot process gets to the point where it is starting runlevel services, you are prompted to confirm (Y) or deny (N) each service, or continue (C) to simply start all the rest of the services.

    Note that this option is not available with the latest Fedora and Ubuntu releases.

6. To look at the messages that were produced in the kernel ring buffer (which shows the activity of the kernel as it booted up), type the following from the shell after the system finishes booting:

```
# dmesg | less
```

Or on a system using `systemd`, type the following:

```
# journalctl -k
```

7. To run a trial `yum update` from Fedora or RHEL and exclude any kernel package that is available, type the following (when prompted, type **N** to not actually go through with the update, if updates are available):

```
# yum update --exclude='kernel*'
```

8. To check to see what processes are listening for incoming connections on your system, type the following:

```
# netstat -tupln | less
```

9. To check to see what ports are open on your external network interface, do the following:

If possible, run the `nmap` command from another Linux system on your network, replacing `yourhost` with the hostname or IP address of your system:

```
# nmap yourhost
```

10. To clear your system's page cache and watch the effect it has on your memory usage, do the following:

    a. Select Terminal from an application menu on your desktop (it is located on different menus for different systems).

    b. Run the `top` command (to watch processes currently running on your system), and then type a capital **M** to sort processes by those consuming the most memory.

    c. From the Terminal window, select File and Open Terminal to open a second Terminal window.

    d. From the second Terminal window, become root user (`su -`).

    e. While watching the Mem line (used column) in the first Terminal window, type the following from the second Terminal window:

```
# echo 3 > /proc/sys/vm/drop_caches
```

f. The used RES memory should go down significantly on the Mem line. The numbers in the RES column for each process should go down as well.

Chapter 22: Understanding Basic Linux Security

1. To check log messages from the systemd journal for the NetworkManager.service, sshd.service, and auditd.service services, type the following:

```
# journalctl -u NetworkManager.service
...
# journalctl -u sshd.service
...
# journalctl -u auditd.service
...
```

2. User passwords are stored in the /etc/shadow file. To see its permissions, type ls -l /etc/shadow at the command line. (If no shadow file exits, then you need to run pwconv.)

The following are the appropriate settings:

```
# ls -l /etc/shadow
----------. 1 root root 1049 Feb  10 09:45 /etc/shadow
```

3. To determine your account's password aging and whether it will expire using a single command, type chage -l user_name . For example:

```
# chage -l chris
```

4. To start auditing writes to the /etc/shadow with the auditd daemon, type the following at the command line:

```
# auditctl -w /etc/shadow -p w
```

To check your audit settings, type in auditctl -l at the command line.

5. To create a report from the auditd daemon on the /etc/shadow file, type ausearch -f /etc/shadow at the command line. To turn off the auditing on that file, type auditctl -W /etc/shadow -p w at the command line.

6. To install the lemon package, damage the /usr/bin/lemon file, verify that the file has been tampered with, and remove the lemon package, type the following:

```
# yum install -y lemon
# cp /etc/services /usr/bin/lemon
# rpm -V lemon
S.5....T.   /usr/bin/lemon
# yum erase lemon
```

From the original lemon file, the file size (S), the md4sum (5), and the modification times (T) all differ. For Ubuntu, install the package with apt-get install lemon and type debsums lemon to check it.

7. If you suspect you have had a malicious attack on your system today and important binary files have been modified, you can find these modified files by typing the following at the command line: find *directory* -mtime -1 for the directories, /bin, /sbin, /usr/bin, and /usr/sbin.

8. To install and run chkrootkit to see if the malicious attack from the exercise above installed a rootkit, choose your distribution and do the following:

   a. To install on a Fedora or RHEL distribution, type yum install chkrootkit at the command line.

   b. To install on a Ubuntu or debian-based distribution, type sudo apt-get install chkrootkit at the command line.

   c. To run the check, type chkrootkit at the command line and review the results.

9. To find files anywhere in the system with the SetUID or SetGID permission set, type find / -perm /6000 at the command line.

10. Install the aide package, run the aide command to initialize the aide database, copy the database to the correct location, and run the aide command to check whether any important files on your system have been modified.

```
# yum install aide
# aide -i
# cp /var/lib/aide/aide.db.new.gz /var/lib/aide/aide.db.gz
# aide -C
```

To make the output more interesting, you could install the lemon package (described in an earlier exercise) before you run aide -i and modify it before running aide -C to see how a modified binary looks from aide.

Chapter 23: Understanding Advanced Linux Security

To do the first few exercises, you must have the gnupg2 package installed. This is not installed by default in Ubuntu, although it is for recent Fedora and RHEL releases.

1. To encrypt a file using the gpg2 utility and a symmetric key, type the following command (the gpg2 utility asks for a passphrase to protect the symmetric key):

   ```
   $ gpg2 -c filename
   ```

2. To generate a keypair using the gpg2 utility, type the following:

   ```
   $ gpg2 --gen-key
   ```

You must provide the following information:

   a. What kind of asymmetric key you want:

   - RSA and RSA (default)
   - DSA and Elgamal

- DSA (sign only)
- RSA (sign only)

b. What key size (in number of bits) you want

c. How many days, weeks, months, years the key should be valid. (You can also request that the key be valid permanently.)

d. Your real name, e-mail address, and a comment to create the User ID for the public key

e. A passphrase for the private key

3. To list out the keys you generated, type:

```
$ gpg2 --list-keys
```

4. To encrypt a file and add your digital signature using the gpg2 utility, do the following:

a. You must have first generated a key ring (Exercise 2).

b. After you have generated the key ring, type:

```
$ gpg2 --output EncryptedSignedFile --sign FiletoEncryptSign
```

5. To use the appropriate message digest utility to ensure that the downloaded file is not corrupted, you must do the following. (Remember that a message digest is also called a checksum.)

a. Review the download website for the MD5 or SHA-1 file or number.

- If it is a checksum number, you need to go to the next step.
- If it is a checksum file, you need to download that file too and then use the cat command to display the checksum file's contents to your screen.

b. If it is an MD5, type the following at the command line and compare the numbers to the MD5 checksum file or number on the website:

```
$ md5sum FirstDownloadedFile
```

c. If it is an SHA-1 hash, type the following at the command line and compare the numbers to the SHA-1 checksum file or number on the website:

```
$ sha1sum FirstDownloadedFile
```

6. To determine if the su command on your Linux system is PAM-aware, type:

```
$ ldd $(which su) | grep pam
  libpam.so.0 => /lib64/libpam.so.0 (0x00007fac89d48000)
  libpam_misc.so.0 => /lib64/libpam_misc.so.0 (0x00007fac89b44000)
```

If the su command on your Linux system is PAM-aware, you see a PAM library name listed when you issue the ldd command.

7. To determine if the su command has a PAM configuration file, type:

```
$ ls /etc/pam.d/su
```

B

If the file exists, type at the command line to display its contents. The PAM contexts it uses is any of the following: auth, account, password, session.

```
$ cat /etc/pam.d/su
```

8. To list out the various PAM modules on your Fedora or RHEL system, type:

```
$ ls /lib/security/pam*.so
```

To list out the various PAM modules on your Ubuntu Linux system, type:

```
$ sudo find / -name pam*.so.
```

9. To find the PAM "other" configuration file on your system, type ls /etc/pam.d/ other at the command line. An "other" configuration file that enforces Implicit Deny should look similar to the following code:

```
$ cat /etc/pam.d/other
#%PAM-1.0
auth       required      pam_deny.so
account    required      pam_deny.so
password   required      pam_deny.so
session    required      pam_deny.so
```

10. To find the PAM limits configuration file, type:

```
$ ls /etc/security/limits.conf
```

Display the file's contents by typing the following:

```
$ cat /etc/security/limits.conf
```

Settings in this file to prevent a fork bomb look like the following:

```
@staff        hard    nproc          50
@staff        hard    maxlogins       1
```

Chapter 24: Enhancing Linux Security with SELinux

1. To set your system into the permissive mode for SELinux, type **setenforce permissive** at the command line. It would also be acceptable to type **setenforce 0** at the command line.

2. To set your system into the enforcing Operating mode for SELinux without changing the SELinux primary configuration file, use caution. It is best not to run this command on your system for an exercise until you are ready for the SELinux to be enforced. Use the following command: **setenforce enforcing** at the command line. It would also be acceptable to type **setenforce 1** at the command line.

3. To find and view the permanent SELinux policy type (set at boot time), go to the main SELinux configuration file, /etc/selinux/config. To view it, type **cat /etc/selinux/config | grep SELINUX=** at the command line. To be sure how it is currently set, type the getenforce command.

4. To list the /etc/hosts file security context and identify the different security context attributes, type **ls -Z /etc/hosts** at the command line:

```
$ ls -Z /etc/hosts
-rw-r--r--. root root system_u:object_r:net_conf_t:s0  /etc/hosts
```

   a. The file's user context is system_u, indicating a system file.

   b. The file's role is object_r, indicating an object in the file system (a text file, in this case).

   c. The file's type is net_conf_t, because the file is a network configuration file.

   d. The file's sensitivity level is s0, indicating the lowest security level. (This number may be listed in a range of numbers from s0-s3.)

   e. The file's category level starts with a c and ends with a number. It may be listed in a range of numbers, such as c0-c102. This is not required except in highly secure environments and is not set here.

5. To create a file called test.html and assign its type as httpd_sys_content_t, type the following:

```
$ touch test.html
$ chcon -t httpd_sys_content_t test.html
$ ls -Z test.html
-rw-rw-r--. chris chris unconfined_u:object_r:httpd_sys_content_t:s0
    test.html
```

6. To list a current process's security context and identify the different security context attributes, type this at the command line:

```
$ ps -efZ | grep crond
system_u:system_r:crond_t:s0-s0:c0.c1023 root 665  1  0
    Sep18 ?   00:00:00 /usr/sbin/crond -n
```

   a. The process's user context is system_u, indicating a system process.

   b. The process's role is system_r, indicating a system role.

   c. The process's type or domain is crond_t.

   d. The process's sensitivity level starts s0-s0, indicating that it is not highly sensitive. (It is secure by normal Linux standards, however, because the process is run as the root user.)

   e. The process's category level is c0.c1023, with the c0 indicating that the category is also not highly secure from an SELinux standpoint.

7. To create an /etc/test.txt file, change its file context to user_tmp_t, restore it to its proper content (the default context for the /etc directory), and remove the file, type the following:

```
# touch /etc/test.txt
# ls -Z /etc/test.txt
-rw-r--r--. root root unconfined_u:object_r:etc_t:s0   /etc/test.txt
```

B

```
# chcon -t user_tmp_t /etc/test.txt
# ls -Z /etc/test.txt
-rw-r--r--. root root unconfined_u:object_r:user_tmp_t:s0 /etc/
    test.txt
# restorecon /etc/test.txt
# ls -Z /etc/test.txt
-rw-r--r--. root root unconfined_u:object_r:etc_t:s0   /etc/test.txt
# rm /etc/test.txt
rm: remove regular empty file '/etc/test.txt'? y
```

8. To determine what Boolean allows users to access their home directories via FTP and turn that Boolean on permanently, type the following commands:

```
# getsebool -a | grep ftp
ftp_home_dir --> off
ftpd_anon_write --> off
...
# setsebool -P ftp_home_dir=on
# getsebool ftp_home_dir
ftp_home_dir --> on
```

9. To list all SELinux policy modules on your system, along with their version numbers, type **semodule -l**.

> **NOTE**
>
> If you chose `ls /etc/selinux/targeted/modules/active/modules/*.pp` as your answer to Question 9, that is okay, but this command doesn't give you the version numbers of the policy modules. Only `semodule -l` gives the version numbers.

10. To prepare your system to run a `vsftpd` FTP server that is protected by SELinux, log in as a regular (we use `chris` in this example) and try to copy a file (which should cause an AVC denial), type the following:

```
# getenforce
Enforcing
# yum install vsftpd lftp rsyslog setroubleshoot-server
# systemctl start syslog
# systemctl start vsftpd
# semodule -DB
# getsebool ftp_home_dir
ftp_home_dir --> off
# lftp -u chris localhost
Password: *******
lftp chris@localhost:~> put /etc/services
put: Access failed: 553 Could not create file. (services)
lftp chris@localhost:~> quit
```

To view information about the denial, and change the Boolean to allow FTP access, do the following:

```
# ausearch -m avc
type=AVC msg=audit(1411217594.188:70555): avc: denied { create } for
    pid=25470 comm="vsftpd" name="services"
    scontext=system_u:system_r:ftpd_t:s0-s0:c0.c1023
    tcontext=system_u:object_r:user_home_t:s0 tclass=file
# journalctl | grep "SELinux is preventing"
Sep 20 08:53:18 fedora20 setroubleshoot: SELinux is preventing /usr/
    sbin/vsftpd from create access on the file services. For
    complete SELinux messages. run
    sealert -l 2ad99cba-13d8-4bb1-8d74-bbfc31b68f8b
# sealert -l 2ad99cba-13d8-4bb1-8d74-bbfc31b68f8b
SELinux is preventing /usr/sbin/vsftpd from create access on the file
    gshadow.
    *** Plugin catchall_boolean (47.5 confidence) suggests *********
    If you want to determine whether ftpd can read and write files
    in user home directories.
    Then you must tell SELinux about this by enabling
    the 'ftp_home_dir' boolean.
    You can read 'user_selinux' man page for more details.
    Do  setsebool -P ftp_home_dir 1
```

Chapter 25: Securing Linux on a Network

1. To install the Network Mapper (aka nmap) utility on your local Linux system:

   a. On Fedora or RHEL, type **yum install nmap** at the command line.

   b. On Ubuntu, nmap may come pre-installed. If not, type **sudo apt-get install nmap** at the command line.

2. To run a TCP Connect scan on your local loopback address, type **nmap -sT 127.0.0.1** at the command line. The ports you have running on your Linux server will vary. However, they may look similar to the following:

```
# nmap -sT 127.0.0.1
...
PORT     STATE SERVICE
25/tcp  open  smtp
631/tcp open  ipp
```

3. To run a UDP Connect scan on your Linux system from a remote system:

   a. Determine your Linux server's IP address by typing **ifconfig** at the command line. The output will look similar to the following and your system's IP address follows "inet addr:" in the ifconfig command's output.

B

```
# ifconfig
...
p2p1   Link encap:Ethernet   HWaddr 08:00:27:E5:89:5A
       inet addr:10.140.67.23
```

    b. From a remote Linux system, type the command **nmap -sU** *IP address* at the command line, using the *IP address* you obtained from above. For example:

```
# nmap -sU 10.140.67.23
```

4. To check whether the ssh daemon on your Linux system uses TCP Wrapper support, type **ldd /usr/sbin/sshd | grep libwrap** at the command line. The output will look similar to the following if it does use TCP Wrapper support. If it does not, there will be no output.

```
$ ldd /usr/sbin/sshd | grep libwrap
libwrap.so.0 => /lib/libwrap.so.0 (0x0012f000)
```

5. To allow access to the ssh tools on your Linux system from a designated remote system and deny all other access using TCP Wrappers, you need to modify both the /etc/hosts.allow file and the /etc/hosts.deny file. The modifications will look similar to the following:

```
# cat /etc/hosts.allow
...
sshd: 10.140.67.32
#
# cat /etc/hosts.deny
#...
ALL: ALL
```

6. To determine your Linux system's current netfilter/iptables firewall policies and rules, type **iptables -vnL** at the command line.

7. To flush your Linux system's current firewall rules, type **iptables -F** at the command line. To restore the firewall's rules on older Fedora systems or RHEL 6 systems, type **iptables-restore < /etc/sysconfig/iptables**. On a RHEL 7 or recent Fedora system, type **systemctl restart firewalld.service** to reinstate your system's permanent firewall rules.

8. This is a trick question! You cannot set a Linux system's firewall policy to reject. You can set it to drop, but not reject. To set your Linux system's firewall filter table for the input chain to a policy of DROP, type **iptables -P INPUT DROP** at the command line.

9. To change your Linux system firewall's filter table policy back to accept for the input chain, type **iptables -P INPUT ACCEPT** at the command line. To add a rule to drop all network packets from the IP address, 10.140.67.23, type **iptables -A INPUT -s 10.140.67.23 -j DROP** at the command line.

10. To remove the rule you added above, without flushing or restoring your Linux system's firewall's rules, type **iptables -D INPUT 1** at the command line. This is assuming that the rule you added above is rule 1. If not, change the 1 to the appropriate rule number in your iptables command.

Chapter 26: Using Linux for Cloud Computing

1. To check your computer to see if it can support KVM virtualization, type the following:

```
# cat /proc/cpuinfo | grep --color -E "vmx|svm|lm"
flags   : fpu vme de pse tsc msr pae mce cx8 apic sep mtrr pge mca
cmov pat pse36 clflush dts acpi mmx fxsr sse sse2 ss ht tm pbe
syscall
nx pdpe1gb rdtscp lm constant_tsc arch_perfmon pebs bts rep_good
xtopology nonstop_tsc aperfmperf pni pclmulqdq dtes64 monitor
ds_cpl vmx smx es...
...
```

The CPU must support either vmx or svm. The lm indicates that it is a 64-bit computer.

2. To install a Linux system along with the packages needed to use it as a KVM host and to run the Virtual Machine Manager application, do the following:

a. Get a live or installation image from a Linux site (such as getfedora.org), and burn it to a DVD (or otherwise make it available to install).

b. Boot the installation image, and select to install it to a hard disk.

c. For a Fedora Workstation, after the install is complete and you have rebooted, install the following package (for different Linux distributions, you might need to install a package that provides libvirtd as well):

```
# yum install virt-manager libvirt-daemon-config-network
```

3. To make sure that the sshd and libvirtd services are running on the system, type the following:

```
# systemctl start sshd.service
# systemctl enable sshd.service
# systemctl start libvirtd.service
# systemctl enable libvirtd.service
```

4. Get a Linux installation ISO image that is compatible with your hypervisor, and copy it to the default directory used by Virtual Machine Manager to store images. For example, if the Fedora Workstation DVD is in the current directory, you can type the following:

```
# cp Fedora-Live-Workstation-x86_64-21-5.iso /var/lib/libvirt/images/
```

B

5. To check the settings on the default network bridge (virbr0), type the following:

```
# brctl show
bridge name  bridge id  STP enabled  interfacesvirbr0
8000.000000000000  yes
# ip addr show virbr0
4: virbr0: <NO-CARRIER,BROADCAST,MULTICAST,UP> mtu 1500 qdisc
    noqueue state UP group default
  link/ether de:21:23:0e:2b:c1 brd ff:ff:ff:ff:ff:ff
   inet 192.168.122.1/24 brd 192.168.122.255 scope global virbr0
     valid_lft forever preferred_lft forever
```

6. To install a virtual machine using the ISO image you copied earlier, do the following.

   a. Type this command:

   ```
   # virt-manager &
   ```

   b. Select File, and then select New Virtual Machine.

   c. Select Local install media, and click Forward.

   d. Select Browse, choose the live or install ISO, click Choose Volume, and click Forward.

   e. Select memory and CPUs, and click Forward.

   f. Select the size of disk you want to use, and click Forward.

   g. Select "Virtual network default: NAT" (it may already be selected).

   h. If it all looks okay, click Finish.

   i. Follow the installation process indicated by the installation ISO.

7. To make sure you can log in to and use the virtual machine, do the following:

   a. Double-click the entry for the new virtual machine.

   b. When the viewer window appears, log in as you would normally.

8. To check that your virtual machine can connect to the Internet or other network outside the hypervisor, do one of the following:

   - Open a web browser and try to connect to a website on the Internet.

   - Open a Terminal window, type ping redhat.com, and then press Ctrl+C to exit.

9. Stop the virtual machine so it is no longer running.

   a. Right-click the entry for the VM in the virt-manager window.

   b. Select Shut Down, and then select Shut down again.

   c. If the VM doesn't shut down immediately, you can select Force Off instead, but that is like pulling the plug out and risks data loss.

10. Start the virtual machine again so it is running and available.

    Right-click the virtual machine entry, and select Run.

Index

E

Index

M

N

GNU General Public License

Version 3, 29 June 2007

Copyright © 2007 Free Software Foundation, Inc. http://fsf.org/

Everyone is permitted to copy and distribute verbatim copies of this license document, but changing it is not allowed.

Preamble

The GNU General Public License is a free, copyleft license for software and other kinds of works.

The licenses for most software and other practical works are designed to take away your freedom to share and change the works. By contrast, the GNU General Public License is intended to guarantee your freedom to share and change all versions of a program—to make sure it remains free software for all its users. We, the Free Software Foundation, use the GNU General Public License for most of our software; it applies also to any other work released this way by its authors. You can apply it to your programs, too.

When we speak of free software, we are referring to freedom, not price. Our General Public Licenses are designed to make sure that you have the freedom to distribute copies of free software (and charge for them if you wish), that you receive source code or can get it if you want it, that you can change the software or use pieces of it in new free programs, and that you know you can do these things.

To protect your rights, we need to prevent others from denying you these rights or asking you to surrender the rights. Therefore, you have certain responsibilities if you distribute copies of the software, or if you modify it: responsibilities to respect the freedom of others.

For example, if you distribute copies of such a program, whether gratis or for a fee, you must pass on to the recipients the same freedoms that you received. You must make sure that they, too, receive or can get the source code. And you must show them these terms so they know their rights.

Developers that use the GNU GPL protect your rights with two steps: (1) assert copyright on the software, and (2) offer you this License giving you legal permission to copy, distribute and/or modify it.

For the developers' and authors' protection, the GPL clearly explains that there is no warranty for this free software. For both users' and authors' sake, the GPL requires that modified versions be marked as changed, so that their problems will not be attributed erroneously to authors of previous versions.

Some devices are designed to deny users access to install or run modified versions of the software inside them, although the manufacturer can do so. This is fundamentally incompatible with the aim of protecting users' freedom to change the software. The systematic pattern of such abuse occurs in the area of products for individuals to use, which is precisely where it is most unacceptable. Therefore, we have designed this version of the GPL to prohibit the practice for those products. If such problems arise substantially in other domains, we stand ready to extend this provision to those domains in future versions of the GPL, as needed to protect the freedom of users.

Finally, every program is threatened constantly by software patents. States should not allow patents to restrict development and use of software on general-purpose computers, but in those that do, we wish to avoid the special danger that patents applied to a free program could make it effectively proprietary. To prevent this, the GPL assures that patents cannot be used to render the program non-free.

The precise terms and conditions for copying, distribution and modification follow.

Terms and Conditions

0. Definitions.

"This License" refers to version 3 of the GNU General Public License.

"Copyright" also means copyright-like laws that apply to other kinds of works, such as semiconductor masks.

"The Program" refers to any copyrightable work licensed under this License. Each licensee is addressed as "you". "Licensees" and "recipients" may be individuals or organizations.

To "modify" a work means to copy from or adapt all or part of the work in a fashion requiring copyright permission, other than the making of an exact copy. The resulting work is called a "modified version" of the earlier work or a work "based on" the earlier work.

A "covered work" means either the unmodified Program or a work based on the Program.

To "propagate" a work means to do anything with it that, without permission, would make you directly or secondarily liable for infringement under applicable copyright law, except executing it on a computer or modifying a private copy. Propagation includes copying, distribution (with or without modification), making available to the public, and in some countries other activities as well.

To "convey" a work means any kind of propagation that enables other parties to make or receive copies. Mere interaction with a user through a computer network, with no transfer of a copy, is not conveying.

An interactive user interface displays "Appropriate Legal Notices" to the extent that it includes a convenient and prominently visible feature that (1) displays an appropriate copyright notice, and (2) tells the user that there is no warranty for the work (except to the extent that warranties are provided), that licensees may convey the work under this License, and how to view a copy of this License. If the interface presents a list of user commands or options, such as a menu, a prominent item in the list meets this criterion.

1. Source Code.

The "source code" for a work means the preferred form of the work for making modifications to it. "Object code" means any non-source form of a work. A "Standard Interface" means an interface that either is an official standard defined by a recognized standards body, or, in the case of interfaces specified for a particular programming language, one that is widely used among developers working in that language. The "System Libraries" of an executable work include anything, other than the work as a whole, that (a) is included in the normal form of packaging a Major Component, but which is not part of that Major Component, and (b) serves only to enable use of the work with that Major Component, or to implement a Standard Interface for which an implementation is available to the public in source code form. A "Major Component", in this context, means a major essential component (kernel, window system, and so on) of the specific operating system (if any) on which the executable work runs, or a compiler used to produce the work, or an object code interpreter used to run it. The "Corresponding Source" for a work in object code form means all the source code needed to generate, install, and (for an executable work) run the object code and to modify the work, including scripts to control those activities. However, it does not include the work's System Libraries, or general-purpose tools or generally available free programs which are used unmodified in performing those activities but which are not part of the work. For example, Corresponding Source includes interface definition files associated with source files for the work, and the source code for shared libraries and dynamically linked subprograms that the work is specifically designed to require, such as by intimate data communication or control flow between those subprograms and other parts of the work. The Corresponding Source need not include anything that users can regenerate automatically from other parts of the Corresponding Source.

The Corresponding Source for a work in source code form is that same work.

2. Basic Permissions.

All rights granted under this License are granted for the term of copyright on the Program, and are irrevocable provided the stated conditions are met. This License explicitly affirms your unlimited permission to run the unmodified Program. The output from running a covered work is covered by this License only if the output, given its content, constitutes a covered work. This License acknowledges your rights of fair use or other equivalent, as provided by copyright law.

You may make, run and propagate covered works that you do not convey, without conditions so long as your license otherwise remains in force. You may convey covered works to others for the sole purpose of having them make modifications exclusively for you, or provide you with facilities for running those works, provided that you comply with the terms of this License in conveying all material for which you do not control copyright. Those thus making or running the covered works for you must do so exclusively on your behalf, under your direction and control, on terms that prohibit them from making any copies of your copyrighted material outside their relationship with you.

Conveying under any other circumstances is permitted solely under the conditions stated below. Sublicensing is not allowed; section 10 makes it unnecessary.

3. Protecting Users' Legal Rights From Anti-Circumvention Law.

No covered work shall be deemed part of an effective technological measure under any applicable law fulfilling obligations under article 11 of the WIPO copyright treaty adopted on 20 December 1996, or similar laws prohibiting or restricting circumvention of such measures.

When you convey a covered work, you waive any legal power to forbid circumvention of technological measures to the extent such circumvention is effected by exercising rights under this License with respect to the covered work, and you disclaim any intention to limit operation or modification of the work as a means of enforcing, against the work's users, your or third parties' legal rights to forbid circumvention of technological measures.

4. Conveying Verbatim Copies.

You may convey verbatim copies of the Program's source code as you receive it, in any medium, provided that you conspicuously and appropriately publish on each copy an appropriate copyright notice; keep intact all notices stating that this License and any non-permissive terms added in accord with section 7 apply to the code; keep intact all notices of the absence of any warranty; and give all recipients a copy of this License along with the Program.

You may charge any price or no price for each copy that you convey, and you may offer support or warranty protection for a fee.

5. Conveying Modified Source Versions.

You may convey a work based on the Program, or the modifications to produce it from the Program, in the form of source code under the terms of section 4, provided that you also meet all of these conditions:

a) The work must carry prominent notices stating that you modified it, and giving a relevant date.

b) The work must carry prominent notices stating that it is released under this License and any conditions added under section 7. This requirement modifies the requirement in section 4 to "keep intact all notices".

c) You must license the entire work, as a whole, under this License to anyone who comes into possession of a copy. This License will therefore apply, along with any applicable section 7 additional terms, to the whole of the work, and all its parts, regardless of how they are packaged. This License gives no permission to license the work in any other way, but it does not invalidate such permission if you have separately received it.

d) If the work has interactive user interfaces, each must display Appropriate Legal Notices; however, if the Program has interactive interfaces that do not display Appropriate Legal Notices, your work need not make them do so.

A compilation of a covered work with other separate and independent works, which are not by their nature extensions of the covered work, and which are not combined with it such as to form a larger program, in or on a volume of a storage or distribution medium, is called an "aggregate" if the compilation and its resulting copyright are not used to limit the access or legal rights of the compilation's users beyond what the individual works permit. Inclusion of a covered work in an aggregate does not cause this License to apply to the other parts of the aggregate.

6. Conveying Non-Source Forms.

You may convey a covered work in object code form under the terms of sections 4 and 5, provided that you also convey the machine-readable Corresponding Source under the terms of this License, in one of these ways:

a) Convey the object code in, or embodied in, a physical product (including a physical distribution medium), accompanied by the Corresponding Source fixed on a durable physical medium customarily used for software interchange.

b) Convey the object code in, or embodied in, a physical product (including a physical distribution medium), accompanied by a written offer, valid for at least three years and valid for as long as you offer spare parts or customer support for that product model, to give anyone who possesses the object code either (1) a copy of the Corresponding Source for all the software in the product that is covered by this License, on a durable physical medium customarily used for software interchange, for a price no more than your reasonable cost of physically performing this conveying of source, or (2) access to copy the Corresponding Source from a network server at no charge.

c) Convey individual copies of the object code with a copy of the written offer to provide the Corresponding Source. This alternative is allowed only occasionally and noncommercially, and only if you received the object code with such an offer, in accord with subsection 6b.

d) Convey the object code by offering access from a designated place (gratis or for a charge), and offer equivalent access to the Corresponding Source in the same way through the same place at no further charge. You need not require recipients to copy the Corresponding Source along with the object code. If the place to copy the object code is a network server, the Corresponding Source may be on a different server (operated by you or a third party) that supports equivalent copying facilities, provided you maintain clear directions next to the object code saying where to find the Corresponding Source. Regardless of what server hosts the Corresponding Source, you remain obligated to ensure that it is available for as long as needed to satisfy these requirements.

e) Convey the object code using peer-to-peer transmission, provided you inform other peers where the object code and Corresponding Source of the work are being offered to the general public at no charge under subsection 6d.

A separable portion of the object code, whose source code is excluded from the Corresponding Source as a System Library, need not be included in conveying the object code work.

A "User Product" is either (1) a "consumer product", which means any tangible personal property which is normally used for personal, family, or household purposes, or (2) anything designed or sold for incorporation into a dwelling. In determining whether a product is a consumer product, doubtful cases shall be resolved in favor of coverage. For a particular product received by a particular user, "normally used" refers to a typical or common use of that class of product, regardless of the status of the particular user or of the way in which the particular user actually uses, or expects or is expected to use, the product. A product is a consumer product regardless of whether the product has substantial commercial, industrial or non-consumer uses, unless such uses represent the only significant mode of use of the product.

"Installation Information" for a User Product means any methods, procedures, authorization keys, or other information required to install and execute modified versions of a covered work in that User Product from a modified version of its Corresponding Source. The information must suffice to ensure that the continued functioning of the modified object code is in no case prevented or interfered with solely because modification has been made.

If you convey an object code work under this section in, or with, or specifically for use in, a User Product, and the conveying occurs as part of a transaction in which the right of possession and use of the User Product is transferred to the recipient in perpetuity or for a fixed term (regardless of how the transaction is characterized), the Corresponding Source conveyed under this section must be accompanied by the Installation Information. But this requirement does not apply if neither you nor any third party retains the ability to install modified object code on the User Product (for example, the work has been installed in ROM).

The requirement to provide Installation Information does not include a requirement to continue to provide support service, warranty, or updates for a work that has been modified or installed by the recipient, or for the User Product in which it has been modified or installed. Access to a network may be denied when the modification itself materially and adversely affects the operation of the network or violates the rules and protocols for communication across the network.

Corresponding Source conveyed, and Installation Information provided, in accord with this section must be in a format that is publicly documented (and with an implementation available to the public in source code form), and must require no special password or key for unpacking, reading or copying.

7. Additional Terms.

"Additional permissions" are terms that supplement the terms of this License by making exceptions from one or more of its conditions. Additional permissions that are applicable to the entire Program shall be treated as though they were included in this License, to the extent that they are valid under applicable law. If additional permissions apply only to part of the Program, that part may be used separately under those permissions, but the entire Program remains governed by this License without regard to the additional permissions.

When you convey a copy of a covered work, you may at your option remove any additional permissions from that copy, or from any part of it. (Additional permissions may be written to require their own removal in certain cases when you modify the work.) You may place additional permissions on material, added by you to a covered work, for which you have or can give appropriate copyright permission.

Notwithstanding any other provision of this License, for material you add to a covered work, you may (if authorized by the copyright holders of that material) supplement the terms of this License with terms:

a) Disclaiming warranty or limiting liability differently from the terms of sections 15 and 16 of this License; or

b) Requiring preservation of specified reasonable legal notices or author attributions in that material or in the Appropriate Legal Notices displayed by works containing it; or

c) Prohibiting misrepresentation of the origin of that material, or requiring that modified versions of such material be marked in reasonable ways as different from the original version; or

d) Limiting the use for publicity purposes of names of licensors or authors of the material; or

e) Declining to grant rights under trademark law for use of some trade names, trademarks, or service marks; or

f) Requiring indemnification of licensors and authors of that material by anyone who conveys the material (or modified versions of it) with contractual assumptions of liability to the recipient, for any liability that these contractual assumptions directly impose on those licensors and authors.

All other non-permissive additional terms are considered "further restrictions" within the meaning of section 10. If the Program as you received it, or any part of it, contains a notice stating that it is governed by this License along with a term that is a further restriction, you may remove that term. If a license document contains a further restriction but permits relicensing or conveying under this License, you may add to a covered work material governed by the terms of that license document, provided that the further restriction does not survive such relicensing or conveying.

If you add terms to a covered work in accord with this section, you must place, in the relevant source files, a statement of the additional terms that apply to those files, or a notice indicating where to find the applicable terms.

Additional terms, permissive or non-permissive, may be stated in the form of a separately written license, or stated as exceptions; the above requirements apply either way.

8. Termination.

You may not propagate or modify a covered work except as expressly provided under this License. Any attempt otherwise to propagate or modify it is void, and will automatically terminate your rights under this License (including any patent licenses granted under the third paragraph of section 11).

However, if you cease all violation of this License, then your license from a particular copyright holder is reinstated (a) provisionally, unless and until the copyright holder explicitly and finally terminates your license, and (b) permanently, if the copyright holder fails to notify you of the violation by some reasonable means prior to 60 days after the cessation.

Moreover, your license from a particular copyright holder is reinstated permanently if the copyright holder notifies you of the violation by some reasonable means, this is the first time you have received notice of violation of this License (for any work) from that copyright holder, and you cure the violation prior to 30 days after your receipt of the notice.

Termination of your rights under this section does not terminate the licenses of parties who have received copies or rights from you under this License. If your rights have been terminated and not permanently reinstated, you do not qualify to receive new licenses for the same material under section 10.

9. Acceptance Not Required for Having Copies.

You are not required to accept this License in order to receive or run a copy of the Program. Ancillary propagation of a covered work occurring solely as a consequence of using peer-to-peer transmission to receive a copy likewise does not require acceptance. However, nothing other than this License grants you permission to propagate or modify any covered work. These actions infringe copyright if you do not accept this License. Therefore, by modifying or propagating a covered work, you indicate your acceptance of this License to do so.

10. Automatic Licensing of Downstream Recipients.

Each time you convey a covered work, the recipient automatically receives a license from the original licensors, to run, modify and propagate that work, subject to this License. You are not responsible for enforcing compliance by third parties with this License.

An "entity transaction" is a transaction transferring control of an organization, or substantially all assets of one, or subdividing an organization, or merging organizations. If propagation of a covered work results from an entity transaction, each party to that transaction who receives a copy of the work also receives whatever licenses to the work the party's predecessor in interest had or could give under the previous paragraph, plus a right to possession of the Corresponding Source of the work from the predecessor in interest, if the predecessor has it or can get it with reasonable efforts.

You may not impose any further restrictions on the exercise of the rights granted or affirmed under this License. For example, you may not impose a license fee, royalty, or other charge for exercise of rights granted under this License, and you may not initiate litigation (including a cross-claim or counterclaim in a lawsuit) alleging that any patent claim is infringed by making, using, selling, offering for sale, or importing the Program or any portion of it.

11. Patents.

A "contributor" is a copyright holder who authorizes use under this License of the Program or a work on which the Program is based. The work thus licensed is called the contributor's "contributor version".

A contributor's "essential patent claims" are all patent claims owned or controlled by the contributor, whether already acquired or hereafter acquired, that would be infringed by some manner, permitted by this License, of making, using, or selling its contributor version, but do not include claims that would be infringed only as a consequence of further modification of the contributor version. For purposes of this definition, "control" includes the right to grant patent sublicenses in a manner consistent with the requirements of this License.

Each contributor grants you a non-exclusive, worldwide, royalty-free patent license under the contributor's essential patent claims, to make, use, sell, offer for sale, import and otherwise run, modify and propagate the contents of its contributor version.

In the following three paragraphs, a "patent license" is any express agreement or commitment, however denominated, not to enforce a patent (such as an express permission to practice a patent or covenant not to sue for patent infringement). To "grant" such a patent license to a party means to make such an agreement or commitment not to enforce a patent against the party.

If you convey a covered work, knowingly relying on a patent license, and the Corresponding Source of the work is not available for anyone to copy, free of charge and under the terms of this License, through a publicly available network server or other readily accessible means, then you must either (1) cause the Corresponding Source to be so available, or (2) arrange to deprive yourself of the benefit of the patent license for this particular work, or (3) arrange, in a manner consistent with the requirements of this License, to extend the patent license to downstream recipients. "Knowingly relying" means you have actual knowledge that, but for the patent license, your conveying the covered work in a country, or your recipient's use of the covered work in a country, would infringe one or more identifiable patents in that country that you have reason to believe are valid.

If, pursuant to or in connection with a single transaction or arrangement, you convey, or propagate by procuring conveyance of, a covered work, and grant a patent license to some of the parties receiving the covered work authorizing them to use, propagate, modify or convey a specific copy of the covered work, then the patent license you grant is automatically extended to all recipients of the covered work and works based on it.

A patent license is "discriminatory" if it does not include within the scope of its coverage, prohibits the exercise of, or is conditioned on the non-exercise of one or more of the rights that are specifically granted under this License. You may not convey a covered work if you are a party to an arrangement with a third party that is in the business of distributing software, under which you make payment to the third party based on the extent of your activity of conveying the work, and under which the third party grants, to any of the parties who would receive the covered work from you, a discriminatory patent license (a) in connection with copies of the covered work conveyed by you (or copies made from those copies), or (b) primarily for and in connection with specific products or compilations that contain the covered work, unless you entered into that arrangement, or that patent license was granted, prior to 28 March 2007.

Nothing in this License shall be construed as excluding or limiting any implied license or other defenses to infringement that may otherwise be available to you under applicable patent law.

12. No Surrender of Others' Freedom.

If conditions are imposed on you (whether by court order, agreement or otherwise) that contradict the conditions of this License, they do not excuse you from the conditions of this License. If you cannot convey a covered work so as to satisfy simultaneously your obligations under this License and any other pertinent obligations, then as a consequence you may not convey it at all. For example, if you agree to terms that obligate you to collect a royalty for further conveying from those to whom you convey the Program, the only way you could satisfy both those terms and this License would be to refrain entirely from conveying the Program.

13. Use with the GNU Affero General Public License.

Notwithstanding any other provision of this License, you have permission to link or combine any covered work with a work licensed under version 3 of the GNU Affero General Public License into a single combined work, and to convey the resulting work. The terms of this License will continue to apply to the part which is the covered work, but the special requirements of the GNU Affero General Public License, section 13, concerning interaction through a network will apply to the combination as such.

14. Revised Versions of this License.

The Free Software Foundation may publish revised and/or new versions of the GNU General Public License from time to time. Such new versions will be similar in spirit to the present version, but may differ in detail to address new problems or concerns.

Each version is given a distinguishing version number. If the Program specifies that a certain numbered version of the GNU General Public License "or any later version" applies to it, you have the option of following the terms and conditions either of that numbered version or of any later version published by the Free Software Foundation. If the Program does not specify a version number of the GNU General Public License, you may choose any version ever published by the Free Software Foundation.

If the Program specifies that a proxy can decide which future versions of the GNU General Public License can be used, that proxy's public statement of acceptance of a version permanently authorizes you to choose that version for the Program.

Later license versions may give you additional or different permissions. However, no additional obligations are imposed on any author or copyright holder as a result of your choosing to follow a later version.

15. Disclaimer of Warranty.

THERE IS NO WARRANTY FOR THE PROGRAM, TO THE EXTENT PERMITTED BY APPLICABLE LAW. EXCEPT WHEN OTHERWISE STATED IN WRITING THE COPYRIGHT HOLDERS AND/OR OTHER PARTIES PROVIDE THE PROGRAM "AS IS" WITHOUT WARRANTY OF ANY KIND, EITHER EXPRESSED OR IMPLIED, INCLUDING, BUT NOT LIMITED TO, THE IMPLIED WARRANTIES OF MERCHANTABILITY AND FITNESS FOR A PARTICULAR PURPOSE. THE ENTIRE RISK AS TO THE QUALITY AND PERFORMANCE OF THE PROGRAM IS WITH YOU. SHOULD THE PROGRAM PROVE DEFECTIVE, YOU ASSUME THE COST OF ALL NECESSARY SERVICING, REPAIR OR CORRECTION.

16. Limitation of Liability.

IN NO EVENT UNLESS REQUIRED BY APPLICABLE LAW OR AGREED TO IN WRITING WILL ANY COPYRIGHT HOLDER, OR ANY OTHER PARTY WHO MODIFIES AND/OR CONVEYS THE PROGRAM AS PERMITTED ABOVE, BE LIABLE TO YOU FOR DAMAGES, INCLUDING ANY GENERAL, SPECIAL, INCIDENTAL OR CONSEQUENTIAL DAMAGES ARISING OUT OF THE USE OR INABILITY TO USE THE PROGRAM (INCLUDING BUT NOT LIMITED TO LOSS OF DATA OR DATA BEING RENDERED INACCURATE OR LOSSES SUSTAINED BY YOU OR THIRD PARTIES OR A FAILURE OF

THE PROGRAM TO OPERATE WITH ANY OTHER PROGRAMS), EVEN IF SUCH HOLDER OR OTHER PARTY HAS BEEN ADVISED OF THE POSSIBILITY OF SUCH DAMAGES.

17. Interpretation of Sections 15 and 16.

If the disclaimer of warranty and limitation of liability provided above cannot be given local legal effect according to their terms, reviewing courts shall apply local law that most closely approximates an absolute waiver of all civil liability in connection with the Program, unless a warranty or assumption of liability accompanies a copy of the Program in return for a fee.

END OF TERMS AND CONDITIONS

How to Apply These Terms to Your New Programs

If you develop a new program, and you want it to be of the greatest possible use to the public, the best way to achieve this is to make it free software which everyone can redistribute and change under these terms.

To do so, attach the following notices to the program. It is safest to attach them to the start of each source file to most effectively state the exclusion of warranty; and each file should have at least the "copyright" line and a pointer to where the full notice is found.

> <one line to give the program's name and a brief idea of what it does.>
>
> Copyright (C) <year> <name of author>
>
> This program is free software: you can redistribute it and/or modify it under the terms of the GNU General Public License as published by the Free Software Foundation, either version 3 of the License, or (at your option) any later version.
>
> This program is distributed in the hope that it will be useful, but WITHOUT ANY WARRANTY; without even the implied warranty of MERCHANTABILITY or FITNESS FOR A PARTICULAR PURPOSE. See the GNU General Public License for more details.
>
> You should have received a copy of the GNU General Public License along with this program. If not, see http://www.gnu.org/licenses/.

Also add information on how to contact you by electronic and paper mail.

If the program does terminal interaction, make it output a short notice like this when it starts in an interactive mode:

> <program> Copyright (C) <year> <name of author>
>
> This program comes with ABSOLUTELY NO WARRANTY; for details type 'show w'.
>
> This is free software, and you are welcome to redistribute it under certain conditions; type 'show c' for details.

The hypothetical commands 'show w' and 'show c' should show the appropriate parts of the General Public License. Of course, your program's commands might be different; for a GUI interface, you would use an "about box".

You should also get your employer (if you work as a programmer) or school, if any, to sign a "copyright disclaimer" for the program, if necessary.

For more information on this, and how to apply and follow the GNU GPL, see http://www .gnu.org/licenses/.

The GNU General Public License does not permit incorporating your program into proprietary programs. If your program is a subroutine library, you may consider it more useful to permit linking proprietary applications with the library. If this is what you want to do, use the GNU Lesser General Public License instead of this License. But first, please read http://www.gnu.org/philosophy/why-not-lgpl.html.